W9-BIQ-445

WHO'S WHO IN TWENTIETH CENTURY LITERATURE

WHO'S WHO IN TWENTIETH CENTURY LITERATURE

Martin Seymour-Smith

HOLT, RINEHART AND WINSTON NEW YORK

Printed in the United States of America

To Kenneth and Joan Pearce

CONTENTS

LIST OF ABBREVIATIONS

ad.	adapted
c.	circa
ed.	edited
ps.	pseudonym of
pt.	part
rev.	revised
sel.	selected
tr.	translated

INTRODUCTION

My chief wish for this book is that it should act not only as a reference but also as an indication of how many excellent and interesting authors remain unread. I was asked by the publisher to provide a text of 200,000 words; in the event I handed in over 350,000. Cutting was a painful affair; there are many authors who deserve entries and whom I should have wished to (indeed, did) discuss. The resultant selection is therefore necessarily biased towards British and American authors; but major foreign authors are included—and so are some less well known writers whom I feel have been undeservedly neglected. I had to be guided, too, by the availability of English translations. Writers known primarily as authors of children's books are excluded; so are most detective story writers. The length of an entry is not, for many reasons, all obvious, any guide to my own view of its subject's merit. My *Guide to Modern World Literature* (not consulted in the preparation of this volume) provides a comprehensive picture in somewhat the same style. Those who know that book will note a few changes of mind on my part: I am glad to acknowledge them.

There is a short index listing the names of movements, e.g. expressionism, and of authors who have not been given a separate entry but who are mentioned under other authors. The fact that a movement has been discussed in a certain entry is a matter of convenience—not necessarily of appropriateness. When I have cited studies of or monographs on particular authors, their titles are those of the author concerned—unless otherwise indicated. Any titles of books in translation that are the same as their originals have not been repeated.

I am grateful to Solly Jacobson for many stimulating discussions about books, authors, drink, neurosis, madness and other subjects pertinent to literature. Others who helped include Ronald Bottrall and Istvan Siklos. I have appreciated the patience and forbearance of Ann

Wilson and John Curtis. My wife provided her usual invaluable aid. My debt to those to whom I have dedicated the volume can know no bounds.

Martin Seymour-Smith
Modane, 14 August 1975

WHO'S WHO IN TWENTIETH CENTURY LITERATURE

Achebe, Chinua (1930) Nigerian novelist writing in English. Achebe is a major writer who has succeeded in drawing upon the British fictional tradition without in any way sacrificing his Nigerian identity; indeed, his novels give the most comprehensive, objective and imaginative picture of Nigeria available in any form. His themes, though localized, are the necessity to man of an inner spiritual strength and the difficulties of attaining this. In addition he has inherited from Conrad (q.v.) a certain vein of anguished mysticism. *Things Fall Apart* (1958), set in the latter half of the last century, presents entirely without bias both the nature of the Ibo tribal life and the impact upon it of the white man. It is a book of remarkable courage and strength; its ironies arise from its detachment. *No Longer at Ease* (1960) moves into modern times, its hero the grandson of that of the first book; as a whole this is not as good, but contains brilliantly revealing–and more overtly satirical–passages about modern Lagos. *Arrow of God* (1964) is a triumphant return to top form; it examines the precarious balance between Ibo tradition and 'civilization', upon which subject Achebe is invaluably fair. *A Man of the People* (1966), about political corruption, is even more satirical, but Achebe's motivation remains compassionate. He has written many good short stories (e.g. *Girls at War*, 1971), excellent essays, and poems. The Biafran war made a serious hole in Achebe's creative life but there is no reason to doubt that he will recover himself to produce more novels of high quality.

Achterberg, Gerrit (1905–62) The most influential Dutch poet of this century. He emerged into fame in his country after the war when the modernist critic and poet Paul Rodenko (1920) hailed him and Vestdijk (q.v.) as the exemplary members of an older generation. A poet of 'earth'–in Bachelard's (q.v.) sense–his persistent theme is his own version of the Orpheus myth, but his Eurydice is both mother and beloved and he desires to join her in death which is for him a transformation into 'being' (in the existentialist sense). His poetry, incantatory and characterized by its search for the pristine meanings of words (cf. Ungaretti, q.v.), has been called surrealistic. But this is misleading: he was a manic-depressive who had yielded to murderous impulses and his admittedly recondite work, which became increasingly traditional in form—and used an impassive, 'scientific' vocabulary—is in fact a form of therapeutic prayer (he was consistently religious, but ambivalent towards Christianity, which he seemed alternately to accept and then reject); it is tormentedly Oedipal but seeks to transcend this state. His poetry is difficult but haunting, fervently sincere and profoundly original. Few European poets of our time convey so intense a feeling of suffering. The poems were collected in the year following his death. Some are translated by James Brockway in *Odyssey* (1, 1961); *Matière* (1952) is a more substantial selection in French; the short selection *Breve Antologia* (1968) contains some excellent Spanish versions by Franco Carrasquer.

Adams, Henry (1838–1918) American thinker, historian, novelist. Adams is still widely regarded in the USA, but neglected elsewhere. He was famous as a historian but his more important writings are *Mont Saint-Michel and Chartres* (1904; 1913), *The Education of Henry Adams* (1906; 1918), *The Degradation of the Democratic Dogma* (1919) and the *Letters* (1938). He wrote two novels (*Democracy*, 1880; *Esther*, 1884), interesting only inasmuch as they provide clues to the central tragedy of his life: the character and subsequent suicide (1885) of his wife, whom he had married in 1872. He never wrote about this, but it was none the less the driving force behind his vital books; had he done so he might have become a major novelist: his sensibility was as acute as Henry James's (q.v.). His view of the thirteenth century was historically incorrect; but his postulation of 'the Virgin and the Dynamo' as opposed forces in modern life was both acute and prophetic. *A Henry Adams Reader* (1956) should send readers eagerly to its sources.

Ady, Endre (1877–1919) Hungarian poet, critic, story writer, journalist. The undisputed pioneer of early Hungarian modernism. Ady, an always controversial, perpetually convulsed, tender, ferocious, ambivalent man, was in some ways intellectually superficial; but his later poetry, an inimitable mixture of the archaic and the colloquial, is of great power. The mixture may not always be integrated but the sense of tragic beauty is seldom absent. (Poems dealing with his inhibited revolutionary fervour, and with his opposition to the war, are much less successful.) Son of Calvinist decaying gentry, Ady reacted against their puritanism but could not, doctrinally, completely separate himself from their conservatism. He went to Paris in 1904 (in the wake of a wealthy mistress), thought he had absorbed Baudelaire and the principles of symbolism, and burst on the Hungarian scene as an excited, exciting, radical poet and critic. *Új versek* (1906), *New Poems,* sealed his reputation and he became the leading light of *Nyugat* (1908–41; *West*), which throughout its long career resisted narrow nationalism and concerned itself with European movements. Ady undoubtedly fertilized Hungarian literature, but it remained for later figures (e.g. his friend Babits, q.v.) to reassess and give precision to his relatively crude critical apprehensions; Hungarians today are grateful to him but do not take his influence so seriously. Ady married in 1915 (his wife confessed to being happy 'by day'); travelled, relentlessly womanized, inveighed against the war, agonized between his decadent egocentricity and his ill-formulated wishes for his persecuted people; finally his aorta ruptured, diseased by syphilis (caught in 1900), alcohol and, his doctor said, 'passions, sufferings, angers and joys'. *Poems* (tr. 1969).

Agee, James (1909–55) American novelist, poet, prose writer, film critic, scriptwriter (Forrester's *The African Queen;* Crane's *The Bride Comes to Yellow Sky*). Agee began with a promising, confused book of poetry, *Permit Me Voyage* (1934), with a dedication (to God, his friends, Chaplin, Joyce, q.v. and others) eight pages long. He might have been a major novelist but his energies were mostly diverted into money-making activities. *Let Us Now Praise Famous Men* (1941), with photographs by Walker Evans, was his first important book. It describes the lives of poor white sharecroppers in Alabama, covering the same territory as Caldwell (q.v.) does in Georgia, but with a greater intellectual sharpness. Trilling (q.v.) called it 'the most important moral effort of our American generation'. *The Morning Watch* (1951), a novella, is autobiographical: a twelve-year-old boy tries but fails to attain true contrition in church on a Good Friday (Agee's religious problems are well stated in the posthumously collected *Letters to Father Flye,* 1962). *A Death in the Family* (1957) was unfinished when Agee died and was edited by his widow and publisher. This is, again, autobiographical and even though unfinished is Agee's chief book: a man is misled into believing that his father is dying; on his return from his abortive mission the son is killed in a car crash; Agee, whose own father died in an accident, traces the impact of this on the family with rare sensitivity, insight and tact. Agee was a serious loss to American letters. *Collected Poems* (1968); *Collected Short Prose* (1968); *Agee on Film* (1958–60), the second volume of which prints the film scripts.

Aiken, Conrad (1889–1973) American poet, fiction writer, critic, autobiographer. Although widely known, Aiken has never had his due: his most famous work, 'Silent Snow, Secret Snow' (a perfectly executed brief account of a child's descent into schizophrenia), is taken for granted, his poetry remains largely unread, and he is frequently dismissed as though he consisted of a catalogue of influences. But though Aiken certainly was influenced by Swinburne, Poe, Freud (q.v.), music, Bergson (q.v.), French symbolism and impressionism, William James (q.v.), Havelock Ellis (the bare catalogue becomes monotonous as one goes from reference book to reference book), he is more original and more modern than he is usually represented to be. His versatility is remarkable. If he had written only novels he would have been known as a major writer (*Collected Novels*, 1964). It is arguable that as a short-story writer he is in the first half-a-dozen English-language practitioners of the century. He possessed, a critic wrote in 1963, 'that cosmic sense which is perhaps the surest mark of the true poet; a sense in which Aiken . . . outsoars Pound and Eliot'. When Aiken was ten his physician father killed his wife and then himself; the importance of this event in his development can hardly be exaggerated, though it has led to the neglect of other factors. Aiken was later at Harvard with, among others, Eliot (q.v.) and Cummings (q.v.), and in *Ushant* (1952), 'an interior monologue autobiography of a literary man', he writes penetratingly of Eliot (the 'Tsetse'), of Monro (Aiken lived in England for much of the inter-war period), Lowry (q.v.) and of many others he knew, as well as of his childhood tragedy. Aiken is the modern master in English of the stream-of-consciousness (or interior monologue) method—more so even than Joyce (q.v.), who admired him, or Virginia Woolf (q.v.). He also understood psychoanalysis and, far from slavishly following Freud, he anticipated by almost half a century both phenomenological and 'existential' psychiatry. All his five novels have magnificent passages, but only the penultimate *A Heart for the Gods of Mexico* (1939) is wholly successful; the others are overloaded with a quite extraordinarily complex symbolism. The short-story form (*Collected Stories*, 1960) was more immediately useful to him and his stories are his most concrete work, for in his poetry he is always exploring himself, letting the words do the work. Aiken was from the beginning determined to use poetry as self-exploration; but to call his subjective method 'narcissitic' is seriously to mislead. As the retrospective collection *Reviewer's ABC* (1958) demonstrates, he possessed an acute critical intelligence. He knew that all art is in one sense subjective and he made no effort to pretend to objectivity. But in order to attain a measure of universality, to avoid a self-indulgent narcissism, he needed a method. He went to Robinson (q.v.), possibly to the Italian crepuscular poets (*see* Gozzano) and to his contemporaries, Eliot and Pound (q.v.), for his introspective characters out of tune with their times. He refused—and this was very unusual—to give up the *fin de siècle* mode which appealed to him; he chose instead to transform it into the kind of instrument he needed. Correctly finding coherence a necessity, but also committed to a more or less free-associative approach, he settled for an 'old-fashioned' diction to which, however, he applied an elaborate musical theory. Even his lyrics are prosodically extremely elaborate. The famous 'Discordants' is very carefully constructed. The longer pieces, collectively entitled *The Divine Pilgrim*, he called 'symphonies': *The Jig of Forslin* (1916), *The Charnel Rose, Senlin* (1918), *The Pilgrimage of Festus* (1923). *Senlin* is clearly influenced by Eliot's *Prufrock* (which was finished by 1911), but has its own rhythms and is less frighteningly empty. In *Preludes for Memnon* (1931; with *Time and the Rock* as *Preludes*, 1966) and *Brownstone Eclogues* (1942), meditative sequences, Aiken subdued his romanticism in favour of a more consciously philosophical style. As he wrote, 'the preludes were planned to be . . . the formulation of a new *Weltanschauung*'; what he said about these poems, however, is of less interest than the poems themselves, which are his best work. Some find them too 'gushing' but Aiken chose the only means available. Like Bottrall (q.v.), a poet with whom he has certain affinities, he risked embarrassing himself and the risk proved justified. The status of his 'lyric-epics', *John Deth* (1930) and *The Kid* (1947) is less certain, for they share some of the faults of his novels, but they are more complex and encompass more experience than the similar works by Crane (q.v.) and

Williams (q.v.). As Reuel Denney has written, there 'can be little doubt that Aiken's independence of the neoclassicism brought in by such men as Hulme and Eliot and his equal independence of the automatic Marxisms of the 1930s were costly to his vogue'. He is one of the few significant writers who maintained a persistently romantic stance, but this necessitated more restraint than his detractors have wanted to recognize. *Collected Poems* (1953); *Selected Poems* (1961); *The Morning Song of Lord Zero* (1963).

Akhmadulina, Bella (1937) Russian poet. She is the best of all the Soviet poets to emerge since the death of Stalin: non-publicist, independent, starkly original. She need make no effort to avoid 'masculinity'. She has described her compulsion to make poetry in her subtle erotic poem 'Fever'; and she shares with Pasternak (q.v.) a fascination with the poem-making process. Her poetry is that of a (famously) beautiful woman, in the tradition of Akhmatova (q.v.) and Marina Tsvetaeva (1892–1941)–she has written a memorable elegy to the latter–but different from either of these. She is lucid, ironic, buoyant and magnificently penetrative in her appraisals of men. *Fever* (1970) is a selection in English.

Akhmatova, Anna (ps. Anna Gorenko) (1889–1966) Russian poet, wife of Gumilyov (q.v.) and with him and Mandelstam (q.v.) the chief of the 'acmeists'. 'Acmeism' (a name invented pejoratively) is no more than a reaction to the mystical and transcendental symbolist manner; the acmeists themselves were usually visionaries, but they preferred an emotionally hard, 'concrete' surface (cf. imagism, *see* Pound). The term is not useful, except historically, beyond the preceding definition. (Acmeism came into being because the–in Russia, unusually explicit–homosexual Mikhail Kuzmin (1875–1935), a writer of exquisite prose and a trivially overfluent symbolist poet, issued a *pronunciamiento* asking for a return to 'beautiful clarity'.) This urge towards greater exactness of image and eschewal of 'mistiness' has never been forgotten in Russian poetry and Akhmatova herself never forgot it in her erotically and politically unhappy life. She has been overrated, but she is a good though never a major poet. She did not develop; her later, 'public' poetry is distinguished only by the personal content one can discern through it. But she was driven to programmatic indignation by the treatment meted out to her or to her relatives: her son was continuously victimized by Stalin; she was characterized by Zdhanov in 1946 as 'half-man, half-whore', expelled from the Writers' Union and virtually silenced for many years. The long sequence *Poema bez geroya* (1940–62; 1967 in *Slavonic and East European Review*), *Poem Without a Hero,* lacks cohesion and is often impenetrably private, though it contains good individual poems. She attracted attention from the beginning: Blok (q.v.), Mandelstam (q.v.) and Trotsky all recognized her genius. Her first poems, published in a series of volumes between 1912 and 1921, are poems about present love set in a Russia made poignant with the past: reluctant eroticism compounded with and consoled by nostalgia. From 1921, when she published *Anno Domini*—a more sombre set of poems in which violence disturbs the sad serenity of her eroticism—until 1940 she was silent, though she was writing. Her sad poetry had always emphasized the menaces to love—indeed, she believes in these more than in the love relationship itself—and the horrors of Stalinism and war, brought home to her personally, enter too forcefully into the later poetry. The rawness of erotic experience was tempered, for Akhmatova, by a rich past exquisitely recollected; the male foulness of totalitarianism and war shattered her. In 1940 she published a retrospective selection but the 'Requiem' poems, some written in the inter-war period, did not appear until some years afterwards. These and their successors are not—and one remarks this reluctantly—as good as the taut and deliberately thought-denying earlier poems. Translations include *Forty-Seven Love Poems* (1927) and *Selected Poems* (1969).

Alain-Fournier (ps. Henri-Alban Fournier) (1886–1914) French novelist. He was killed at the beginning of the First World War (his body was never found). He is most famous for the novel *Le Grand Meaulnes* (1913; tr. *The Lost Domain,* 1959), although he left an unfinished novel and a collection of sketches and poetry, collected as *Miracles* (1924). His correspondence with Jacques Rivière (1948) is more important than this posthumous creative work. *Le Grand Meaulnes,* a romantic novel of adolescent calf-love and regret at the intrusion of adult realities into fantasy, has been (so to say) written by a thousand young men, but not so well. For Alain-Fournier, as his letters to Rivière reveal, was able imaginatively to distance himself from the subject: it operates, oddly, as both self-indulgent fantasy and objective correlative. The theme of the 'young man' was a predominant one in French letters at this time and *Le Grand Meaulnes* fitted well into the general atmosphere (it first appeared in the *Nouvelle Revue Française*). But it possesses an especially poetic quality: first, because the author conveys, with an uncanny suggestiveness, the haunting countryside of his childhood (near Blois, in Cher) and secondly because, as it unfolds, Alain-Fournier is 'growing up', actually reversing the 'mystic' procedure, sensing the masturbatory flavour of his erotic adventure.

Albee, Edward (1928) American playwright. Albee began as an absurdist (*see* Ionesco) with *The Zoo Story* (1958), but *Who's Afraid of Virginia Woolf* (1962), his most successful play, is a clever amalgam of more traditional influences: the sensationalism of O'Neill (q.v.), Strindberg (q.v.) and others seems to be structurally modified by absurdism, but the play's basic message is that women are horrible, mad and dangerous. Unless Albee is experimenting with oblique protest writing (e.g. *Box-Mao-Box,* 1968), when he produces competent, warmed-through expressionism, he is the reluctant victim of his own misogyny: *Tiny Alice* (1964) and *A Delicate Balance* (1966) both suffer from this. But he is intelligent and is an expert craftsman, as his adaptations (e.g. of Purdy's, q.v., *Malcolm,* 1965) demonstrate.

Algren, Nelson (1909) American novelist, prose writer. Born in Detroit, Algren lived for a long time in Chicago, and with Farrell (q.v.) and Wright (q.v.) was classed as a leading member of the 'Chicago school of realism'. Algren is a neo-naturalist (*see* Zola) with little art: he collected and filed his material on Chicago's north-west side, and produced a series of tough, powerful, shapeless semi-fictions, including *Somebody in Boots* (1935) and *The Man with the Golden Arm* (1949), which is justly regarded as his best work. Algren above all shows how romantic the naturalist impulse really is. His affair with Simone de Beauvoir (q.v.) is well known and has been described by her, fictionally in *Les Mandarins* (dedicated to him), and in her autobiography.

Allen, Walter (1911) English novelist, critic. Allen's criticism (notably *The English Novel,* 1954, *Tradition and Dream,* 1964) is in the very best and proper sense sound: penetrative, considered, affirmative but acutely critical, only occasionally marred by over-generosity. But this activity has tended to distract (his and our) attention from his fictional achievement. The early sociological novels are awkward, but *Rogue Elephant* (1946), about an ugly and egocentric writer, and *All in a Lifetime* (1959), a rueful reappraisal of social change through the eyes of an old man, are major achievements in the context of British post-war fiction.

Amis, Kingsley (1922) English novelist, poet, publicist, whose gifts of comedy, acute observation and delicate moral feeling have been increasingly blunted by a choleric, wilful and artistically ill-advised identification of himself with certain ideological positions. There are, however, other factors: hatred of sham, of the naivety of much extreme left-wing ideology, a warm but too vague and unexplored love of decency. His first book of verse reveals the extent of the basic soft-centredness with which he has had, and still has, to contend. There is also an element of malice which he has seldom managed to contain, except in the brilliant first novel *Lucky Jim* (1954), where it is made innocent as a defiance of academic sham and pretentiousness. When the *Lucky Jim* vein was worked out (*I Like it Here,* 1958), he resorted to a more complexly angled, self-critical type of novel–*One Fat Englishman* (1963), *I Want it Now* (1968)–in which the female is no longer seen as deadly bait for the comically lust-ridden male. This was promising, but *The Green Man* (1969) is disappointingly self-indulgent and slick; ingenuity does not rescue it any more than it does *The Riverside Villas Murder* (1972), which again exploits current themes without irony or true understanding. His satirical poetry, often excellently bawdy, is successful; the rest is somewhat distinguished but inhibited by incapacity to deal with direct feeling.

Anderson, Sherwood (1876–1941) American prose writer born in Ohio. Anderson, though quintessentially American, was one of the first of modern writers to understand that fiction was autobiography and autobiography fiction. He may have abolished the conventional distinction innocently, Americanly, intuitively, but he abolished it for English-language writing. It used to be said that Anderson lost his powers in the early twenties; the definitive *The Memoirs of Sherwood Anderson* (1969), and other properly edited later work has shown this to be less than half-true (the earlier *Memoirs,* 1942, was a misleading travesty). Anderson transformed himself from a hick American in search of success into one of the most beautiful writers of the century.

For him this transformation was symbolized by a single action: he walked out of his job as manager of an Ohio paint-factory (1912): out of commerce into art. In fact Anderson had already discovered himself as a writer: in composing vulgar promotional literature and later, advertising copy, he had seen the non-materialistic possibilities of writing. When he walked out on his job he was suffering from a breakdown brought about by financial difficulties and by his conflicting attitude towards his wife: he felt guilty at wanting to run away from his responsibility towards her, but she—a university-educated middlebrow—patronized his private literary efforts. Anderson went to Chicago soon after his breakdown and was able to make contact with and gain encouragement from the writers of the 'Chicago Renaissance' (they included Sandburg, q.v., and Ben Hecht). He published three books before finding himself, triumphantly, in *Winesburg, Ohio* (1919), sketches about life in just such an Ohio town as the one in which he had grown up. Although this book is compounded of rather obvious influences (Howe's inferior but pointed *The Story of a Country Town*, 1884, was useful; and Twain, Gertrude Stein, q.v., Masters, q.v., and Turgenev had all been digested), the synthesis is original, and the importance of Anderson's anti-dogmatic approach, an example of Keats's 'negative capability' put into strict practice, has been largely overlooked. *Return to Winesburg* (1967), a collection of editorials written by Anderson for his two weekly newspapers (one Republican, one Democrat) between 1927 and 1931, often recaptures the quality of *Winesburg, Ohio,* which is Anderson's only consistently good book. The writers of the Chicago Renaissance had dispersed after the end of the war and Anderson soon found himself isolated: his second marriage had failed (as his third was to do), and those who had learned most from him (e.g. Faulkner, q.v., Hemingway, q.v.) virtually turned against him (Faulkner later repented, Hemingway did not); he was a naked, lyrical writer, and his hard apprenticeship made him over-vulnerable to hostile or snide criticism. He had written *Poor White* (1920), his best novel; *Dark Laughter* (1925), which brought him money, is self-parodic and inferior work. In the short story, however, he produced masterpieces on a level with *Winesburg, Ohio:* the collection *Death in the Woods* (1933) does not show such a degree of falling-off from *The Triumph of the Egg* (1921) and *Horses and Men* (1923) as is generally assumed. All three books are characteristically uneven. 'Death in the Woods' is itself as good as anything he ever wrote and takes its place beside other acknowledged classics such as 'I Want to Know Why', 'The Egg', 'Unlighted Lamps' and 'The Man Who Became a Woman'. Anderson never totally degenerated, and in the thirties, largely as a result of a fourth and happy marriage, he again began to write more consistently well. This is seen not only in the *Memoirs* but also in the underrated *Kit Brandon* (1936). The novel form did not really suit Anderson, but this autobiographical monologue of a woman has not had its due. Since Anderson is beautiful, truthful, lyrically innocent, inspiring, open, he is of course 'embarrassing'. He is puzzling, too, because he was eclectic and sceptical: 'Dim pathways do sometimes open before the eyes of the man who has not killed the possibilities of beauty in himself by being too sure.' . . . Academics are often too sure, and the pseudo-*avant garde* is simply ignorant. We owe much, therefore, to the devoted scholarship of Ray Lewis White who has edited and made available most of Anderson's hitherto inaccessible later prose. Faulkner, who had once used and then (ineffectually) mocked him, said in 1956: 'He was the father of my generation of American writers and the tradition of American writing which our successors will carry on. He has never received his proper evaluation.' *Letters* (1953); *The Portable Sherwood Anderson* (1949).

Andrić, Ivo (1892) Yugoslav (Serbo-Croat) novelist, fiction writer, poet. Nobel Prize 1961. Andrić is not perhaps as psychologically penetrating a writer as his Croatian counterpart, Miroslav Krežla (1893), but he is a very good one–one of the few who can justifiably be described as epic in his scope. Like Krežla, art is for him the one human consolation. His attitude seems so deterministic that one is tempted to call him a neo-naturalist (*see* Zola); but he is too lyrical, too dedicated to beauty, to be classed as a naturalist. He is, rather, a story teller, ironic and lyrical by turns; and always with a remarkable grasp of his material. He was born in Bosnia and his major work is set in the times of Turkish rule there. *Na Drini ćuprija* (1945; tr. *The Bridge on the Drina,* 1959); *Travnička kronika* (1945; tr. *Bosnian Story,* 1958); *Prokleta avlija* (1945; tr. *Devil's Yard,* 1964)–and other work in English translation.

Andrzejewski, Jerzy (1909) Polish novelist. He began (*Ład serca,* 1938, *Harmony of the Heart*) as a Catholic novelist in the tradition of Mauriac (q.v.), though more politically conservative. *Popiól i diament*

(1948; abridged *Ashes and Diamonds,* 1962) is an ambiguous account of the new communist Poland and is not an entirely satisfactory book. *Ciemnosći kryją zemię* (1957; tr. *The Inquisitors,* 1960) is an allegory of Stalinism set in the times of the Inquisition. Andrzejewski has recently written more modernistic novels, clearly critical of the regime. He is not without courage (he resigned from the communist party in 1957 as a protest against censorship), and he can hardly be called an opportunist; but there is something facile and shallowly moralistic about his various attitudes that gives one cause to doubt the validity of his high reputation. C. Miłosz (q.v.) has called him 'Alpha, the moralist', in a devastating portrait of him in *The Captive Mind.*

Anouilh, Jean (1910) French dramatist, filmscript writer (usually anonymously), critic. Anouilh is the best known French playwright both inside and outside his own country; but although a consummate—indeed, an unsurpassed—master of the well-made play and very highly intelligent, he is inferior to at least Armand Salacrou (1899): in the last analysis he almost always sacrifices 'high seriousness' to box-office considerations. The theatre of Beckett (q.v.), Ionesco (q.v.) and others tended to eclipse his French reputation with the critics, but he remains a favourite, and his work cannot under any circumstances be described as simply middlebrow. He is serious, but a certain slickness (as in Wilder, q.v.) almost always underlies his drama: his basic attitudes have not developed and although they were originally deeply felt, they are not really profound. He has, however, cleverly systematized them and his treatments display originality as well as skill. He has divided his prolific work into several categories: *pièces noires* (gloomy plays), *pièces roses* (happier and more romantic treatments of themes which are, however, still 'noires'), *pièces brillantes* (brittly comic plays), *pièces grinçantes* (plays in which comedy and tragedy are mixed in a more deadpan style) and the less important *pièces costumées.* These categories are not very helpful, except to critics of Anouilh—and so they are grist to his mill, as all pronouncements of intention by all writers hope to be. The chief influences upon him have been Scribe (in his adroitness) and, decisively, Pirandello (q.v.), whose achievement tends to demonstrate Anouilh's own ultimate meretriciousness. Although purity remains a sincere obsession throughout Anouilh's work, only his skill is mature: he has nothing at all to say about purity except that it is impossible to attain. None the less he is a superb entertainer and to regard him as reprehensible would be merely to attack him for qualities of depth which he does not possess: meretriciousness is essential to him and he has not tried to feed his boulevard public with optimistic falsehoods (cf. the malign, brilliant adapter of his *L'Invitation au château*, 1947–tr. *Ring Round the Moon*, 1950–Christopher Fry, 1907). Among his best plays are *L'Hermine* (1932; tr. *The Ermine*, 1955), *Voyageur sans bagage* (1937; tr. *Traveller without Luggage*, 1959)–here he comes nearest to a metaphorical representation of his own situation; his own film (1943) of this, with Fresnay, is excellent–and *Pauvre Bitos* (1956; tr. *Poor Bitos*, 1964), a triumph in the art of concealing vulgarity and emptiness. *Pièces noires* (1945); *Pièces brillantes* (1951); *Pièces grinçantes* (1956); *Pièces costumées* (1960); *Pièces roses* (1961). Many of the plays have been translated or adapted. He has been a generous critic of others' drama.

Apollinaire, Guillaume (ps. Guillelmus Apollinaris de Kostrowitzky) (1880–1918) French poet, playwright, pornographer (for money), critic, fiction writer, literary activist. Apollinaire was not French by birth: his mother was Polish and his father was most probably an Italian, a member of a military family, called Francesco Flugi d'Aspermont (Picasso liked to say that he was Pope Leo XVIII, which is certainly untrue; Apollinaire himself enjoyed it). French became his language because his mother (gambler, whore) took him and his brother to Monte Carlo where he received a good education and gained a thorough mastery of the language (assertions to the contrary are incorrect). Apollinaire is of vital importance in French literary history (he influenced painting, and art criticism as well); but his genius is seen at its most substantial and secure in his essentially lyrical poetry, which is a perfect poetic response to his times and which demonstrates that 'modern' poetry, for his is modern, does not need to be alyrical. An excellent short introduction to Apollinaire is by LeRoy C. Breunig (1969); I owe much to it in this account. As Breunig states Apollinaire was congenitally indecisive, but he had an intense, lucid, lyrical energy. One might add that his times in themselves seemed directionless. But Apollinaire had the vigour to search for an identity of his own. Since he was a major poet, Apollinaire's faults are, of course, also strengths. Apollinaire the man was a legend. It was typical of him that he should have spent a few days in jail on suspicion of having stolen the *Mona Lisa*. It was typical of his fate that he should have died two days before the armistice—of influenza and the results of the head wound he had received as a soldier in March 1916—to the sound of a crowd yelling 'Down with Guillaume' (they meant the Kaiser). The legendary man—to whom much of the polemic and fiction and some of the slighter poetry belongs—was wildly inconsistent in all but one thing: he committed himself intellectually to the *avant garde,* the new—and he kept himself so ahead of it that only his delightful nature saved him from being hated by every proponent of every -ism, since this was the age of a thousand isms, and the French are ferocious in their polemical battles. His more serious poems are about his erotic life (his love for the London governess Annie, and for a series of mistresses—including the painter Marie Laurencin—and for his wife of a few months, Jacqueline), and they comprise an unquestionably major achievement and one which has less to do with his polemical activities than might be supposed. After his youthful symbolist experiments, he continuously oscillated between 'new' and more conventional-looking poetry—the 'new' begins to crop up in the early years of the century. He was, of course, influenced by everyone—and in particular by Verhaeren (q.v.). He is as proto-expressionist as he is proto-surrealist, even though (being French) it was by the dadaists (*see* Ball) and chiefly the surrealists (*see* Breton) that he was taken up. It is most appropriate, however, to describe his slighter (though historically important) works separately from his major poetry. His novels, *Le Poète assassiné* (1916; tr. *The Assassinated Poet,* 1923) and *La Femme assise* (1920), *The Seated Woman,* are frankly experimental and do not cohere; but in *L'Hérésiarque et Cie* (1910; tr. *The Heresiarch and Company,* 1965; in UK *The Wandering Jew,* 1967), fantastic stories, he paradoxically achieved a more coherent work, at once mysterious, haunting, lightweight, witty and prophetic. The nature of his connection with cubism (of all kinds) is the subject of controversy; all that need be said here is that he wrote *Méditations esthétiques. Les Peintres cubistes* (1913; tr. *The Cubist Painters,* 1949), and that within ten days of its appearance he renounced cubism for 'orphism'. . . . Certainly one would be unwise to call Apollinaire's own poetry 'cubist' (cubist poetry is explained, appropriately, under Reverdy, q.v.), for he was cubist only in his awareness of the work of art as object, and of its infinite number of simultaneous existences from different points of view (one best gets the sense of this from the paintings of Picasso's cubist period). *L'Esprit nouveau et les poètes* (1946; tr. in F. Steegmuller, *Apollinaire,* 1963) is rather more than less confusing even though it throws light on literary history. The play *Les Mamelles de Tirésias* (1918, but most probably written in 1903; tr. *The Breasts of Tiresias* in *Odyssey,* 1961) is subtitled 'Drame surréaliste' (it was to have been 'surnaturaliste'—we owe 'surréaliste' to the publisher); it is a farce on repopulation and misunderstood genius and yields important clues about the ambivalent nature of Apollinaire's eroticism. The important earlier poems are collected in *Alcools* (1913; tr. 1964; 1965—different, bilingual versions, both of which have their merits). The first great poem, written in 1903, deals with his fruitless courtship of Annie, the puritanical London governess (he had spent time in London): 'La Chanson du mal-aimé', 'The Song of the Ill-beloved'. This long, rhyming, unpunctuated poem begins in a London mist, and proceeds to unite in the most uncanny, powerful and disturbing manner a vast number of moods, observations, images, dreams, historical events and symbols: the unifying factor is a melancholy tinged, here, only slightly with gaiety. *Alcools* contains many more poems of equal distinction, though none is as magnificently sustained as 'La Chanson'. The *Calligrammes* (1918) mix playful poems (in the shapes of their subjects, such as cars, rain or a watch) with some of the later poems written under the impact of the war (most of the other poems are in *Vitam impendere amori,* 1917). Apollinaire has been accused of 'prettifying' this, but the judgement is wooden. Here the gaiety is not slightly tinged with melancholy: the two moods combine. Apollinaire is as 'serious' as Owen (q.v.): there should be no mistake about this. And in the erotic poems, describing the simultaneity of battle action and sexual desire, he displays an insight into the nature of male sexual desire perhaps unique in twentieth-century poetry: 'Two shellbursts/A pink explosion/Like two bared breasts/Snooking their tips/HE KNEW LOVE/What an epitaph.' One view of Apollinaire is that he was a joker (like Jacob or even, in his very different way, Roussel, q.v.) who failed to achieve greatness because he needed to eschew seriousness. Few judgements could be less apt. In the long poem of his early years, in 'Zone', in 'Le Voyageur', in the erotic war poems, in 'La Jolie Rousse', and in much else, he proved himself a major and probably a great poet. The complete poems and theatre are in *Oeuvres poétiques* (1956); the complete works, *Oeuvres complètes,* appeared in 1965–6; there is a *Selected Writings* (1950) in English. Scot Bates's study (1967) is useful.

Aragon, Louis (1897) French novelist, poet, journalist, literary activist. Aragon is not an insincere man and he is certainly a brave one; he has been essentially a superficial, political figure, most interested in putting his technical gifts to immediate use. First he served with the Medical Corps in the war; then he became a frenetic dadaist and, subsequently, surrealist; by 1930 he was a violently committed communist. His *avant-garde* poetry is of little account. His most famous poems were written after he had served with distinction against the Germans in the early part of the war: *La Crève-Coeur* (1941), *Les Yeux d'Elsa* (1942) and others. This poetry brings technical accomplishment to bear on fairly commonplace material, but the impact it made at the time of its publication has not lasted. 'Elsa' was Elsa Triolet (ps. Elsa Brik, 1896–1970), a Russian who began to write in French in the thirties and whom Aragon married. Aragon's greatest achievement has been in fiction. His novels, from the semi-surrealist *Le Paysan de Paris* (1926), *The Peasant of Paris,* have been versatile, shapeless, eloquent and, in their way, highly efficient. None is without serious flaw. Among the best are *Les Cloches de Bâle* (1934; tr. *The Bells of Basel,* 1936), the historical *La Semaine sainte* (1958; tr. *Holy Week,* 1961) and the more overtly modernistic *La Mise à mort* (1965), *Background for Death,* which explores his own romantic and indeed sentimentalist predicament by means of a description of the process by which a writer creates a character, becomes jealous of him, and must finally murder him. An English selection of the poetry is in *A Poet of Resurgent France* (1946).

Arden, John (1930) English dramatist. His earlier plays never achieved commercial success, but he rightly had more prestige than his rivals. The best are *Sergeant Musgrave's Dance* (1959) and *The Workhouse Donkey* (1963), about local council corruption. Since then, although one may admire his personal and strident stand against fashion-conscious producers, his texts have lost all tension–drama is absent.

Arghezi, Tudor (ps. Ion N. Theodorescu) (1880–1967) Rumanian poet, novelist and polemicist. Factory worker, aspiring writer, monk (1899–1904), commercial traveller, journalist, political prisoner, Arghezi is unquestionably the most powerful of modern Rumanian poets of major stature (Bacovia, q.v., Ion Barbu, ps. Dan Barbilian, 1895–1961), although not the most choate. He contains within his astonishingly versatile work (poetry of many kinds; varied types of fiction; polemic political journalism; lurid denunciatory pamphlets) all the numerous threads and influences that make up his country's culture: the oral tradition of the peasants, in which sorrow and death are (often ironically) counterpointed against rough boon-companionship, a natural pantheism, lusty pastoral eroticism, courage and simple praise of God; the sort of acutely sensitive observation of nature that is associated in English poetry with John Clare; satire and hatred of oppressors and oppression; religious pessimism. Arghezi's journalistic career, which led to his being imprisoned twice (after the First World War because he had worked on a pro-German newspaper, but for nationalistic reasons, and during the Second for his socialism), was frenzied, and on the whole it harmed his poetic concentration. Some of the pamphlets are as furious as those of Céline (q.v.) or Léon Bloy. He was forty-seven before he became famous, with the publication of his first collected volume of poems, *Cuvinte Potrivite* (*Suitable Words,* 1927), which was followed in 1930 by *Flori de mucegai* (*Mildewed Flowers*). Arghezi's earlier prose–novels and reminiscences–draws on his monastic and prison experiences, and although entirely his own in style, has affinities with that of the early Gorky, Céline, Eekhoud and even Hasek (q.v.) in its enraptured and lyrical sympathy with the outcasts and dregs of society: *Icoane de Iemn* (*Wooden Icons,* 1930) and *Poartă neagră* (*Black Gate,* 1930). *Tablete din Tara de Kuty* (*Tablets from Kuty,* 1933) is a more elaborately conceived satirical novel of great originality. The poetry of Arghezi's first collections, on the whole his finest, is lyrical in feeling, and is often fluent; but it is complex and dense in texture. The earlier volume combines (in its inimitable Rumanian way) the psalmodic ecstasy of Claudel (q.v.) with the blasphemous bitterness and rage to be found in much Jewish poetry. The second collection reflects more clearly the influences of Baudelaire, whom Arghezi translated, and of life in prison; it has some of the hallucinatory and visionary qualities of Campana (q.v.), and shows the author at his nearest to mental breakdown. The fragments of an assaulted sensibility are always held together, however, by a serene lyricism, which has its roots firmly in the Rumanian soil and the folk literature that has grown from it. The poetry of the thirties, more relaxed, is substantial and shows development, but is lacking in the vehemence and sheer energy of the earlier; one sees in it not only the Rumanian past but also an undeliberate kind of surrealism—or, perhaps, a realism of observation so phenomenological that it looks surreal—that reminds us that Tristan Tzara (q.v.), founder of dada, Brancusi and Ionesco (q.v.) all came from Rumania. The *polisson* element in Arghezi was never allowed to flourish unchecked, and was gradually enveloped by socialist aspirations and by pantheism. The work of his last twenty years—he did not publish for the first seven of them—is markedly inferior: such sequences as *1907* (1955) and *Song of Man* (1956) and their successors consist of poetic flashes in a sea of socialist-realist (*see* Gorky) mud: this has a kind of voltage, but that of professional fluency rather than of imaginative pressure. Arghezi had never been a communist; he was an independent and undogmatic socialist, and the price he paid for his lionization and Nobel candidacy was the loss of this independence. But as he was already sixty-seven when the people's republic was declared, the loss to literature was not perhaps too great. His international stature is confirmed by the fact that he was translated into Spanish by Rafael Alberti (1902) and into Italian by Quasimodo (q.v.). There is no adequate translation, or critical exegesis, in the English language; but Arghezi's poetry may be approached through the translations made into French by André Marcel (*Cahiers du Sud*, XLV, 1958). His best work, in poetry and prose, urgently requires translation into English. D. Mica's book on him, *Opera lui Tudor Arghezi* (1965) has appeared in an English version.

Arlt, Roberto (1900–42) Argentinian novelist, playwright. The nearest writer in the Spanish language to Céline (q.v.). Lack of translations of his work is bewildering. Son of German immigrants, he lived a doomed, neurotic and bitter life, and never acquired a proper education. Yet he paralleled Céline in his excited portrayal of the urban nightmare and anticipated both Cela (q.v.) and contemporary Latin-American experimentalism. His fault is that he could not always find the right words with which to express his terrifying visions, and is not (as Céline is) a 'good' writer. But he is versatile, mixing naturalism, lyricism, hallucinatory purity and the effective crudeness of the early Gorky (q.v.) into a wholly original mixture whose undoubted nihilism is relieved only by his own vitality, prolificity and insistence upon expressing himself at all. This in itself amounts to an affirmation. He is a true *poète maudit* in prose, and there are further affinities which may help the reader without Spanish to place him (and to demand immediate translations): József (q.v.), Lowry (q.v.), Dazai Osamu (q.v.), Joseph Roth (q.v.), Fallada (q.v.): he was, with the obvious reservation that the resemblances are approximate, a writer of this kind. His work is now gaining recognition and there are complete editions of the novels and stories (1963) and the drama (1968), both edited by his daughter Mirta.

Arp (Hans or Jean) (1887–1966) 'The eel of the dunes': German (Alsatian) sculptor, painter, prose-writer and poet. One of the founders of dada (*see* Ball), later a surrealist (*see* Breton), his poetry—mostly in German but also in French (and some, early, in Alsatian dialect)—which he wrote throughout his life—is superior to almost all the radically experimentalist poetry of this century. The secret of its high quality is that although its surface is anti-traditional, dislocated, 'nonsensical', the whole is suffused with a lyrical innocence: it is natural to Arp to approach language as he approaches the material from which he will create sculpture: he takes a practical, plastic view, but this, when he is writing poetry, involves something more than creation of objects: a sculptor's handling of the problem of words-as-things and their relationship, in that capacity, to the apparently other things or states of mind which they denote. The much revised 'Kaspar ist tot', 'Kaspar is Dead', is, for example, as major a poem about death as is Stevens' (q.v.) 'Sunday Morning'. His redeployments of familiar linguistic procedures introduce the reader to an alogical world, but one which has a unique kind of poetic coherence. There are no complete editions of his work, which repays closer attention than it has had outside a limited circle, but *Gesammelte Gedichte* (1963–4) collects most of the poetry, and *Jours effeuillés* (1967), *Pruned Days,* collects his French writings. He wrote stories, reminiscences, essays and the autobiographical *Dreams and Projects* (1952). Of all his work it is his poetry that will prove most durable, though his 'ageometric sculpture' is by no means negligible.

Artaud, Antonin (1896–1948) French playwright, theorist of the theatre, actor, producer. Artaud's own plays were failures, but his 'theatre of cruelty' (though not the fashionable modern one), and his other ideas as put forward in *Le Théâtre et son double* (1938; tr. *The Theatre and its Double,* 1958), are important and valid. They spring from his conviction that words are painfully separated from their referents, and that conventional theatre lacks authenticity. He has exercised a strong influence on the modern French theatre. Artaud, influenced by Balinese dancers he saw at the beginning of the thirties, wanted a theatre that would eschew all realism or narrative, and would concentrate on myth, ritual and magic. It would 'surround' (sometimes literally) the audience and undermine it to the point at which it would, even if unwillingly, participate. . . . He had been a surrealist (*see* Breton), but later formed his own theatre groups (which lost money). Artaud was a drug addict and was in a mental hospital from 1936 to 1946. His voluminous works are being collected. So far there are thirteen volumes.

Asturias, Miguel (1899–1974) Guatemalan fiction writer and poet. Nobel Prize 1967. Of all the recent Nobel Prize winners Asturias is the least read but he is an important, though difficult writer. He spent many years in exile and was the Guatemalan ambassador to France in the late sixties. He studied anthropology in Paris, and translated the Mayan sacred book *Popol Vuh*–accounts of the gods, heroes and people of ancient Guatemala, written in the Quiché language–into Spanish (1927); he worked from the French version of Georges Raynaud, under whom he had studied. This was to have a lasting effect on his fiction, though his most successful novel, *El Señor Presidente* (1946; tr. *The President*, 1963) displays the Indian, mythical influences only in an oblique manner. Asturias had experienced the dictatorship of Estrada Cabrera, but his great novel of the evils of totalitarianism is set in no place at no specific time. God (the tyrant) is shown as the devil and the society over which he presides is a hell on earth in which injustice, hypocrisy and misery prevail. *Hombres de maiz* (1949), *Men of Maize*, is an account of the debasement of Indian life presented in terms of Indian myth, and in a Spanish that intuitively reconstructs the Indian language. It is synchronic rather than diachronic in approach, and is not easy to read, but as an imaginative projection of the *Indian* version of his own degradation it is incomparable. The trilogy on foreign exploitation of the banana trade (*Viento fuerte*, 1950, tr. *The Cyclone*, 1967; *El Papa verde*, 1954, tr. *The Green Pope*, 1971; *Los ojos de los enterrados*, 1955, *The Eyes of the Buried*) is more uneven. *Mulata de tal* (1960; tr. *The Mulatta and Mr Fly*, 1967) demonstrates the still potent power of Indian myths in the story of a modern couple whose relationship is explored in terms of magic. Asturias, who composed some of his books in 'automatic writing' and then carefully re-worked them, was an exceedingly ambitious writer who took risks; but they were worth taking because they explore the nature of the 'primitive' mind, the rediscovery of which he sees as the only hope for mankind.

Auden, W. H. (1907–73) English (later American citizen) poet, critic. He left England for America with his friend Isherwood (q.v.) in 1939; after war-work in the USA he split his life between America, Ischia, and Austria (where he had a house). He was elected Professor of Poetry at Oxford in 1956; and not long before his death his old college there, Christ Church, provided him with a small house. Auden's *Poems* (1930 rev. 1933)—his friend Spender (q.v.) had printed an earlier pamphlet collection—astonished the literary world of the time, and the collection *Look, Stranger!* (1936) was widely held to have maintained his promise. Grigson (q.v.) founded the magazine *New Verse* specifically 'for' him and the attitudes he represented. During these thirties years Auden wrote Brechtian-type poetic dramas in collaboration with Christopher Isherwood—e.g. *The Ascent of F6* (1936)—the 'charade' *Paid on Both Sides* and *The Orators* (1932), a sequence of prose and poetry. The most obvious influences on him at this time were a somewhat superficial Marxism, the rise of fascism (which moved him to write *Spain,* 1937 rev. 1940 and later dismissed by Auden as 'trash'), Groddeck and Freud (q.v.). Later thirties poetry was collected in *Another Time* (1940). *New Year Letter* (*The Double Man* in USA, 1941), a chatty poem (the notes, often in verse, take up much more space than the main text), partly reflects new interests: Kierkegaard, modern physics, Christianity, theology. This is often regarded as the 'transitional' poem between the young, leftish Auden and the later philosophico-Christian one. *For The Time Being* (1945) contained the long works: a sequence on themes from *The Tempest*—'The Sea and the Mirror'—and the title poem, styled 'A Christmas Oratorio'. Then came the 'baroque eclogue', *The Age of Anxiety* (1948), a narrative poem in semi-dramatic form. *The Enchaféd Flood* is his most sustained collection of critical prose, and offers clues as to his intentions at this time. Auden wrote no more long poems but he issued eight more collections of shorter poems. He continuously revised and rejected his poems, a process which displeased nearly all of his many critics; the most recent 'definitive' versions are in *Collected Shorter Poems*

1927–1957 (1966) and *Collected Longer Poems* (1968). *The Dyer's Hand* (1963) and *Secondary Worlds* (1968) collect essays and lectures. Auden was fluent, versatile, inconsistent, but most of the controversy about him has assumed that he is at least a major poet at an international level; the notion of his 'greatness' is now rapidly fading. Auden, partly influenced by Laura Riding (q.v.)–from whose poems he had quite extensively borrowed in the thirties–came to reject poetry as a game, an entertainment which ought not to affect important decisions. Here he showed a degree of conscience, because, in the interests of his ambitions to be a 'philosophical' poet, he threw away both a gift for lyricism and a linguistic gift for engaging his reader's attention at a profound level. His early poems, though exploiting problems of the puerperium and (too) obliquely probing at his homosexual nature, had been exciting–and had contained inspired lyrical lines. His later short poems are stylish light verse; the more ambitious ones show no advance on the ones he wrote at the beginning of his career. But even though he largely wasted his gifts, some residue of the affection (not, I think, respect) that he inspired in his friends remains in all the poetry: he is incorrigible, obsessed with ritualistic ideas about how to behave which he by no means observed (or needed to), frequently trivial–but he loved the English landscape, and never lost the qualities of fascination. When the echoes of the extraordinary phenomenon of Auden have died away, there will remain a handful of lyrics and a large corpus of accomplished *vers de société* without real poetic substance but with some element of the Byronic quality that was his true ideal. The poetic passages are widely dispersed and in no single mature work are they integrated.

Avison, Margaret (1918) Canadian poet writing in English. She completely avoids the coyly 'feminine'; yet, capable of intellectual rigour and with an excellent grasp of form, she preserves her unmistakably female identity. *Winter Sun* (1960).

B

Babbitt, Irving (1865–1933) American critic, teacher. The 'New Humanism' movement of which he was, with Paul Elmer More, the leading light, exercised a strong influence on Eliot (q.v.), who finally rejected it only because Babbitt did not follow him into an explicit Christianity. Babbitt advocates discipline, resistance to spontaneity and unconscious impulse, reason, duty (as against right), and so on. The New Humanist philosophy is narrow and disingenuous, drawing on romantic sources to discredit romanticism, and politically and sociologically naive. Babbitt's own criticism, however, is not as bad as his program suggests (*The New Laokoön,* 1910; *Rousseau and Romanticism,* 1919).

Babel, Isaak (1894–1941) Russian (Jewish) fiction writer, playwright. He fought in the First World War, then (1917) went over to the Bolsheviks. Later he was with Budyonni in Poland (1920–21). He died, perhaps murdered, in one of Stalin's camps. Socialist realism (*see* Gorky) proved altogether uncongenial to him, though he had served the regime wholeheartedly; he eventually, and with great irony, cultivated 'the new art' of silence. His stories—in *Collected Stories* (tr. 1957) and *Llubka the Cossack* (tr. 1963)—about his service with the Cossacks in Poland gain their power and strength because they represent a non-violent intellectual's utterly determined and successful effort to give his impressions of quite fearsome violence, brutality and terror. Raw brutality fascinates *and* repels him; the effect is exceedingly vivid and unusual. The *Evreyskie rasskazy* (1927), *Jewish Tales,* are superbly rendered accounts of Jewish crooks cast in an ironically Old Testament style. The same kind of material is dealt with in the *Odessiye rasskazy* (1931), *Odessa Tales:* Babel was born in Odessa. He was an original writer, whose sense of appalled shock at the nature of his material is rigidly controlled, but he can be characterized to some extent by drawing attention to his affinities with Stephen Crane, I. B. Singer (q.v.) (he was deeply versed in Jewish lore) and with nineteenth-century French writers such as Guy de Maupassant (title of one of his stories). His 'film novel' *Benia Krik,* about the legendary Jewish gangster, has been translated (1935), as have one or two of his plays, which are a less interesting aspect of his art. Babel, who was launched by Gorky, is a visual writer, a 'painter' who worked enormously hard at his prose: one can always see all that he describes. There is much doubt about the chronology of his stories. *The Lonely Years* (1964) collects unpublished writings in translation. Although 'rehabilitated' after Stalin's death, a novel on which Babel was working in his 'silence', and which he considered his masterpiece, has not come to light.

Babits, Mihály (1883–1941) Hungarian poet, critic, editor, translator and novelist. A cautious and intelligent modernist, as editor of the leading periodical *Nyugat* (*West*) from 1929 he went against his own Hungarian passions by trying to create a non-political literature. It was a noble and intelligent enterprise–always accompanied by encouragement to younger poets who were different from himself, but doomed in the long run to failure. It was in an awareness of the advent of Nazidom and of the throat cancer which killed him that he wrote his finest poem, *Jonas könyve* (1938), *The Book of Jonah,* an inspired and tragic poetic autobiography. His earlier poetry had been decadent, then neoclassical; but had never reached this major level and had tended to smother his emotional restlessness. He was a brilliant translator (of, e.g. Dante) and an essayist of sensibility; essentially he was an eclectic, empathetic man, much influenced by his Catholic upbringing, the spirit of pacificism, the psychology of Freud (q.v.) and the philosophy of Bergson (q.v.). *Jonas könyve* alone confers creative greatness upon him but some of his fiction is also of high quality. *Timàr Virgil fia* (1922; tr. in French *Le Fils de Virgil Timár,* 1930) is one of the best of post-Freudian studies of repressed homosexuality: the 'psychoanalysis' is wholly assimilated by the imaginative grasp of character.

Bachelard, Gaston (1882–1962) French scientist, thinker and critic who has wielded an enormous and continuing influence. Sartre (q.v.) has acknowledged his part in the formation of his own thought; Barthes (q.v.), too, regards him as a crucial philosopher. Some have compared him in importance to Freud. Although Bachelard has received little attention in England or America there can be no doubt that his contribution to the nature of poetic thinking is immense. His books (he wrote voluminously, though the earlier ones mostly deal with the philosophy of science) are not easy but they don't have the impenetrability and Gallic humourlessness of such (admittedly important) writers as, say, Lévi-Strauss (large parts), Barthes or Sollers. They have the magic of a gentle, poetic and original personality. He was influenced by Bergson (q.v.), particularly in his criticism of the over-optimistic expectations of science. Bachelard, like all really great thinkers (if sometimes in spite of themselves), was an eclectic and a syncretist: he saw that induction and deduction were inseparable and that the one continuously becomes transformed into the other. Reality, the nature of consciousness, is forever *open:* it unfolds. His psychology, then, explores the continuously developing relationship between the self and the world. As against the *Angst* of the existentialists he demonstrated the pleasures of such a poetic exploration. His 'surrationalisme' teaches us that the poetic enterprise as a whole is one in which the mind can never rest: it continuously questions what it immediately apprehends. And for Bachelard this is not agony but delight. He shows us the advantage of the phenomenological method, of the yielding to a 'newborn poetic image' ('the seed of a world. . . . wonder blossoms forth in all innocence. . . .'), of heeding consciousness as well as unconsciousness. . . . His 'psychoanalysis' is of the nature of images: of earth, fire, water, space. Entry into his work is unlike entry into that of Jung (whose *animus-anima* postulation he used and transformed). The key books are *La Psychanalyse du feu* (1934; tr. *The Psychoanalysis of Fire,* 1964), *La Philosophie du non* (1940; tr. *The Philosophy of No,* 1969), *L'Eau et les rêves* (1942), *Water and* [*Day-*] *Dreams, L'Air et les songes* (1943), *Air and Dreams, La Poétique de l'espace* (1957), *The Poetics of Space,* and, last and perhaps best, *La Poétique de la rêverie* (1960; tr. *The Poetics of Reverie,* 1969). There are a number of other writings of this period.

Bacovia, George (ps. Gheorghe Vasiliu) (1881–1957) Exquisite, if limited, Rumanian poet: he extends, modernizes and exploits the symbolist-decadent style of the turn of the century without in any sense being its prisoner. His poetry meaningfully beautifies his chronic melancholia which it externalizes in the form of urban decay, threat, misery, defeat, doomed erotic projects. In his earlier poems he seems to be in love with death, numbed by cold; snow or rain falls, evenings are gloomy and monotonous. Yet there is always a sense that this world contains, reflects in a Platonic manner, another one: this sense is conveyed by his candour and descriptive precision. At the age of about fifty his poetry developed: a new and more robust note is often found, emerging in the form of a subtly sardonic humanism. He continued (unusually) to write well until his death; throughout his career he remained true to his feelings and apprehensions, creating a superbly memorable body of minor but artistically perfect poetry.

Bailey, Paul (1937) One of the most accomplished of young English novelists. His first novel, a tautly economic, compassionate and restrained study of life in an old people's home, is probably still his best: *At the Jerusalem* (1967); but *A Distant Likeness* (1973), about the crack-up of a hard-line policeman, would have been as good if it were not for its not quite fully assimilated melodramatic element. Bailey is a subtle writer of exceptional gifts and potential.

Baker, Dorothy (1907–68) American novelist. Quite widely read, she never had her critical due and is absent from most surveys. When she is discussed it is as one of Hemingway's (q.v.) disciples but, as she wrote, 'I was seriously hampered by an abject admiration for Ernest Hemingway': to 'grow up', she continued, she had 'to quit writing any direct discourse'. Thus, *Young Man with a Horn* (1938), a study of the kind of man she thought Bix Beiderbecke might have been, is somewhat Hemingwayesque, but in its successors she purged herself of the influence; the last of her four novels, *Cassandra at the Wedding* (1962), is entirely her own. It is a psychologically exact (rather than cold, as has been charged) examination of contrasting twins, the mundane Judith and the more intelligent but self-destructive Cassandra—who must attend her sister's wedding. As well as being a penetrative sociological study, *Cassandra at the Wedding* may be read as an allegory of how sensitive, intelligent, 'neurotic' art may come to terms with coarser, 'non-neurotic' life.

Baker, George Pierce (1866–1935) American academic who influenced American drama and literature through his '47 workshop'

(1905), where he taught drama and allowed his pupils to see their plays in performance. His students included O'Neill (q.v.), Dos Passos (q.v.), Howard and Wolfe (q.v.).

Baldwin, James (1924) American Negro novelist, playwright, polemicist. Baldwin, who shares the capacity with Lawrence (q.v.) to parallel great subtlety, humanity and beauty with 'putridity' (but in his case mostly in public performance—and for reasons less puzzling), has done his best work in his first three novels and in comprehensive essays on Negro problems in *Notes of a Native Son* (1955), *Nobody Knows My Name* (1961) and the validly enraged 'letters' of *The Fire Next Time* (1963). In the first three novels Baldwin dealt imaginatively and movingly with both his feelings as an oppressed Negro and his sexual confusions. *Go Tell It on the Mountain* (1953) is an eloquent evocation of his Harlem childhood; as an adolescent he had sought to destroy his cruel, preaching stepfather by becoming a Holy Roller preacher himself. *Giovanni's Room* (1956) explores simultaneously his fascination with white people and his ambisexual predicament. *Another Country* (1961) memorably and compassionately permutates black-white-hetero-homosexual relationships. The feeble *Tell Me How Long the Train's Been Gone* (1968), reverting to a dislocative procedure that does not suit him, could be read as a desperate and impotent investigation of his own spiritual disintegration. *If Beale Street Could Talk* (1974), another novel about Harlem, exhibits a cooling-down, even though it deals—and for every good reason—with the eroding horrors of racialism; but the price of relaxation has been tragically high, for the book is unrelievedly pedestrian in style and psychology. Baldwin went to Paris soon after the war, in disgust at what American racialism was doing to him and to his people, but he has since returned.

Ball, Hugo (1886–1927) German poet, co-founder of dada, essayist, theatrical producer and (latterly) Catholic theologian. Ball's creative writings are trivial but he is in many ways a seminal figure. His first poetry was expressionist in the manner of van Hoddis (q.v.) and Alfred Lichtenstein (1889–1914), but, significantly, violated traditional forms in a way they did not. A highly intelligent and aware man, he was born too near France (Pirmasens) to feel hatred for it. Futurism (*see* Marinetti) had been the most obviously proto-fascist, non-German manifestation of expressionism; dada, named at random from a dictionary, but meaning 'hobby horse', and with paternal connotations, was German-Alsatian-Swiss and was born of pacifists in Zurich: the most obviously eirenical manifestation of expressionism anywhere, though it looked anything but that. Ball himself soon denounced it (1917) as a fundamentally violent movement. Those involved in it in one way or another included Ball's wife Emmy Hennings, the photographer Man Ray, Hans Arp (q.v.), Tristan Tzara (q.v.)—perhaps the main inspirer of dada—Louis Aragon (q.v.), André Breton (q.v.), who took it over and turned it into surrealism (*see* Breton), the composer Erik Satie, Vicente Huidobro (q.v.) and Richard Huelsenbeck. (The surrealist Georges Hugnet, 'the warbler's trouser', has compiled an invaluable anthology, *L'Aventure Dada, 1916–1922,* 1957.) Ball's verse, and much else like it, carries Marinetti's experimentation one step farther: 'siwi faffa/sbugi faffa/olofa fafamo/fanfo halja finj' and so on. Dadaism, like both the Italian and the Russian futurisms (*see* Mayakovsky), professed scorn for art, literature and culture. It announced that it existed to destroy both itself *and* bourgeois society. In fact it was trying to defend the values of art and humanity—in a manner that was not without some comedy, some element of *épater les bourgeois*—against the barbarisms of middlebrowism and politics. It was influenced by Apollinaire (q.v.), the poetry of van Hoddis (q.v.) and Lichtenstein; and perhaps its chief and most original feature was its combination of literature with other, particularly plastic, arts: Arp (q.v.), Schwitters and Picabia were artists; Satie was a composer (the man without whom, as they themselves well knew, Ravel's and Debussy's music would never have reached the level of achievement it did); and so on. The main dada manifestations were: provocative cabaret (at the Cabaret Voltaire in Zurich), noise (of a generally futuristic kind), anti-sense poetry (see the example from Ball, above) and 'simultaneous poetry'. This last attempted to achieve in poetry what cubism attempted to achieve in art and stemmed in part from the 'dramatism' of H. M. Barzun, a member of the unanimist L'Abbaye group (*see* Duhamel, Romains), and in part from the experiments of Apollinaire; it is at its most serious in Reverdy (q.v.), who had no connections with dada. In addition to trying to present every aspect of a subject *simultaneously*, it employed collage, montage, typographical innovations and anti-literary devices. Ball himself renounced it because he saw sinister aspects in its vitalism, and turned to quiet religious scholarship.

Barker, George (1913) Prolific English poet, prose poet, novelist, critic. Barker is a hit-or-miss poet who has produced exquisite lyrics, an incomprehensibly convoluted magma combining Blake, Smart, surrealism and sheer lack of creative energy, and a number of original, longish meditative poems that are superior to anything by Dylan Thomas (q.v.), with whom he was associated in readers' minds. Barker, a self-consciously *polisson* Catholic, has needed to be the most wildly uneven of all modern English poets in order to stumble upon his true voice. The long poem *Calamiterror* (1937) is a failure, but one of the most interesting ones of modern times. Barker does not mind being feeble with his deliberately atrocious puns and descents into what may be called anti-rhythm: for him this is part of being a poet, the humiliating part of a self-exploration necessary to discover the 'true voice of feeling'; to conceal it would be for him stupid and disingenuous. But he is not altogether ingenuous in his over-indulgent exploitation of the themes of guilt and friendship and is therefore at his most powerful when lyrically inspired (e.g. his version of the *Stabat Mater*) or subdued into contemplativeness (e.g. LIV of the sequence *In Memory of David Archer*, 1973)—or, more occasionally, when transfixed by religious vision. His novels (the experimental *Alanna Autumnal*, 1933; *Janus*, 1935—two stories; *The Dead Seagull*, 1950) repay attention but yield up fewer integrated passages than the poetry, and the last has over-ambitious symbolic pretensions. *Collected Poems 1930–1965* (in America only, 1965) has been followed by three more collections. *Essays* (1970) contains criticism as varied as his other work. It remains to add that he was writing in a 'confessional' (*see* Lowell) style long before Snodgrass (q.v.) and that he substantially influenced both Delmore Schwartz (q.v.) and, almost certainly, Berryman (q.v.). A proper critical appraisal of him would be difficult (it proved too much so for M. Fodaski, *George Barker*, 1969), but is badly needed: his case is unique in modern English poetry and his wide influence has gone unacknowledged.

Barnes, Djuna (1892) American novelist, playwright, artist. Djuna Barnes's work has always been for a minority. It is and always has been thoroughly *fin de siècle* in spirit, but adds to this two elements: a casual and therefore effective notion of humans-as-animals, and an awareness of the efficacy of stream-of-consciousness (*see* Bergson). Her gift (it is beyond a talent) is slight and Eliot (q.v.) made an error in describing her best-known novel *Nightwood* (1936) as having 'a quality of doom and horror very nearly related to that of Elizabethan tragedy'. Actually its sometimes acute sensibility is marred by the sort of Victorian post-Gothic which Darley, Swinburne and above all Beddoes deluded themselves into thinking was 'Elizabethan'. *The Book of Repulsive Women* (1915; 1948), her first publication, illustrated by her, can only be described as butch Firbank (q.v.); later she further toughened her style by concentrating on mentally sick people (the anonymously issued *Ladies' Almanack,* 1928; *Ryder,* 1928); *Nightwood* is a celebration of depravity, transformed into crude relish. *Spillway* (1962) reprinted stories originally published in 1929. *The Antiphon* (1958) is a blank-verse closet-drama presumably intended to prove that Eliot's notion of her as 'Elizabethan' had been correct; it is, alas, less effective than Beddoes' similar attempts to revive Jacobean drama.

Baroja, Pío (1872–1956) Spanish novelist. He was a doctor and a baker before he turned to literature. He was very prolific and a famously poor technician–since he claimed that stylistic perfection is an inaccurate mirror of life. His fiction is uneven, but at its best extremely powerful. Baroja is a picaresque naturalist (*see* Zola) whose main theme is to show, simultaneously, that man has no free will and that he will not accept this. In many respects he is typical of the 'Generation of 1898' (*see* Unamuno). The greatest of his novels is *Laura, o la soledad sin remedio* (1939). He wrote many travel books and essays. Cela (q.v.) has written an excellent book about him. His complete works were published 1946–52. Several novels have appeared in English versions.

Barrie, J. M. (1860–1937) Scottish playwright, fiction writer. Barrie began promisingly as an observant if sentimental prose writer (e.g. *My Lady Nicotine,* the best). But from the beginning, in common with his predecessors of the so-called 'Kailyard School', he treated the manners of his native country as a vehicle for amusing Anglicized gentry and an English audience. Highly gifted as a stage craftsman, he early turned to the drama, and enjoyed enormous prestige in this medium for the rest of his life. The achievement here is artistically though not commercially ephemeral. *Peter Pan* is typical: it conceals relentless infantilism and sadism beneath a skilfully sentimental veneer; *Dear Brutus,* supposedly adult, is no less unserious. His inferiority was discerned and analysed in the late twenties, notably by Edwin Muir (q.v.). *Works* (1929); *Plays* (1942).

Barth, John (1930) American novelist. Barth is a monument to the erroneous notion that fiction can be built out of ideas about what fiction is or should or might be, and out of nothing else. He is ingenious, clever, admirable—and a crushing bore. He cannot tell a story, create a character, or hold the unfeigned interest of the most willing reader. Thus his (invariably) academic admirers use of his work such adjectives as 'marvellous', 'excellent', 'brilliant', 'complex' and 'infinitely malleable'. But Barth is simply a critic who has chosen to express himself in impenetrable fictions, slyly manufactured to accommodate all other critics' predilections. *The Floating Opera* (1956), *The End of the Road* (1961), *The Sotweed Factor* (1960) and *Giles Goat-Boy* (1966) all combine erudition, parody and intelligent questioning of establishment 'values'; no reasons have been advanced as to why he employs or should employ a fictional form.

Barthes, Roland (1915) French critic. His writing is as impenetrably solemn as that of any Gallic critic—which is saying a lot—but is important. His inspirations have been Bachelard (q.v.), structuralism, modern linguistics and Marxism. His systematization of semiology—the quasi-science of signs (clothes, sport, fashion) originally postulated by de Saussure—has been highly suggestive. The point of his complex criticism, in so far as it pertains to literature, might be stated as follows: he seeks to determine not the 'meaning' of a text, but the nature of the system underlying it. For Barthes, as for Bachelard, imagination is the chief instrument of perception. Barthes illuminates texts but he is a bad critic of authors (though his views need to be taken into account) because he traps them in abstract 'structures' of his own making. But, in his own cold manner, he understands one of the reasons why writers are *guilty*: they seek 'some new Adonic world where language would no longer be alienated'. He is thus a champion of Céline (q.v.). The important introductory volumes (he has written much) are: *Le Degré zéro de l'écriture* (1953; tr. *Writing Degree Zero*, 1967) and *Éléments de sémiologie* (1964; tr. *Elements of Semiology*, 1967).

Bassani, Giorgio (1916) Italian novelist, poet. He is a sensitive chronicler of Italian Jews and of what they endured under fascism; this concern culminated in the exquisitely pathetic *Il giardino dei Finzi-Contini* (1962; tr. *The Garden of the Finzi-Continis,* 1963). *Gli occhiali d'oro* (1958; tr. *The Gold-Rimmed Spectacles,* 1960) is a sad masterpiece about a Jewish homosexual. Bassani's finely exact, compassionate and evocative fiction, which is markedly realist, is outstanding in modern Italy. *L'airone* (1968; tr. *The Heron,* 1970), set as usual in the district around Ferrara, is the most complex of his books yet. More recent is *L'odor di fieno* (1972), *The Smell of Hay.*

Bates, H. E. (1905–74) English fiction writer, playwright, poet, critic. Bates's finest work was done in the thirties, when he was the best of the crop of short-story writers thrown up by that decade. He was uninnovatory, and his main master was Maupassant. The strength of the earlier stories lay in their stolid realism, in their unobtrusive, laconic pastoralism and in their broodingly loving descriptions of the English countryside. He was a master at evoking the feelings of inarticulate rural people of both sexes. The thirties novels are weaker: the short form suited him best. As 'Flying Officer X' (he served in the RAF) he wrote a few moving poems and some effective sketches of service life. Then he turned to the popular type of novel and degenerated into an inoffensive, skilful middlebrow writer (e.g. *The Purple Plain,* 1947). He continued to write stories, but only a few approach the old quality. His excursion into the 'comic' novel (*The Darling Buds of May,* 1958, etc.) is best forgotten. *The Modern Short Story* (1941) is a useful straightforward guide. *Works* (1951–).

Beauvoir, Simone de (1908) French novelist, autobiographer, philosopher, travel and sociological writer, playwright, essayist. Simone de Beauvoir, lifelong companion of Sartre (q.v.), is still the predominant woman-of-letters in France but much of her recent activity has been disappointingly journalistic. Her finest work has perhaps been done in the essay and in autobiography rather than in fiction—or drama (her 1945 excursion into this form was a disastrous flop). Her extended essay, the long *Le Deuxième Sexe* (1949; tr. *The Second Sex,* 1960), is still the modern 'feminist' bible and it stands high amongst her achievements. It equals Sartre's account of the male predicament in *L'Être et le néant* in its candour—and may even be read as an anguished response to this. The essays, such as those collected in *Faut-il Brûler Sade?* (1955; tr. *The Marquis de Sade,* 1966), cast a superbly aware female eye on important issues; the viewpoint expressed, whether one agrees with it or not, is always stimulating. Disagreement with Simone de Beauvoir often resembles disagreement with Nietzsche: it opens up new horizons. The series of autobiographies (*Mémoires d'une jeune fille rangée*, 1958, tr. *Memoirs of a Dutiful Daughter*, 1959; *La Force des choses*, 1963, tr. *The Force of Circumstance*, 1965–and successors, all tr.) are magnificent complements to *Le Deuxième Sexe. Pour une Morale de l'ambiguité* (1947; tr. *The Ethics of Ambiguity*, 1948) is among the most lucid of existentialist texts. As novelist, too, Simone de Beauvoir is more than competent; but all but the first two of her six novels fail to cohere imaginatively. For all their superb portrayals of women, they are rather too obviously existentialist theses. *L'Invitée* (1943; tr. *She Came to Stay*, 1949) is about the war years; *Le Sang des autres* (1944; tr. *The Blood of Others*, 1948) goes back to the thirties and then on into the time of the Resistance. Both are penetrating and moving as well as efficient, and are superior to *Les Mandarins* (1954; tr. *The Mandarins*, 1957), which is generally taken to be her major novel. The last, a *roman à clef* (whatever the author declares), is certainly a valuable portrait of post-war French intellectual circles, but it is more diffuse, too long, and too painstakingly explicit. But these–*Tous les Hommes sont mortels* (1946; tr. *All Men Are Mortal*, 1955) is an experiment that conspicuously failed–all contain enough to give their author a high status in European fiction: *Les Belles Images* (1966) and *La Femme rompue* (1967; tr. *The Woman Destroyed*, 1969) are merely worthy thesis novels. The finest of her more recent writing, with the continuing autobiography, has been *Une Mort très douce* (1964; tr. *A Very Easy Death*, 1966), describing her mother's death from cancer.

Beckett, Samuel (1906) Dublin-born novelist, playwright and critic who writes principally in French and who lives in Paris. Brought up as a Protestant. Keen athlete when young, but renounced this for meditative idleness. Began publishing in 1929, knew Joyce (q.v.), but went almost unrecognized by the reading public until the international success of his play *En Attendant Godot* (1952), *Waiting for Godot*, which was published in his own translation in 1956. Beckett is the apostle of nothing (represented for him by dirty, smelly, feeble, utterly defeated tramps and bums); but the often-made charge of nihilism does not stick, or he would never have written at all. His dislike of the vogue of which he has been the centre is notably dignified; when he was awarded the Nobel Prize in 1969 he shunned the publicity. A seminal but not a great writer, he needs to be appreciated as the meticulous expresser of a *malaise* from which all have suffered rather than as the bearer of a message: his message is clearly inadequate as such–or he himself would not have been a member of the French Resistance and would not enjoy cricket and billiards and would never smile (which he often does). Beckett, whose adoption of French (he has been the translator of almost all his works, alone or in collaboration) initially served him as a protection from rhetoric, is the theologian of a void whose inhabitants are mainly concerned to lament the uselessness of *their* theology (language). Beckett is icily comic, but it is as though he always viewed Chaplin, one of his inspirations, in a tragic and earnest light. He has purged his literature of the richness and humour which he undoubtedly possesses because he wants to make the point that literature–a tale told in the dark to ward off the meaninglessness of life and the inevitability of decay–is pointless. In this sense he is an ironic comedian and the man himself is as conspicuously but shamelessly absent from his own work as any modern writer. But he has not written, as Thomas Mann (q.v.) did, any confessions of a confidence trickster. Superb as the laureate of absurdity, Beckett offers no mystery in his work, only despair: the apotheosis of *alittérature,* that utterly contemporary French phenomenon, he is yet a man of a past age, devoted to thinkers of the past–he needs certainty, and if he cannot find it in something then he will find it in nothing, which he dissects with medieval meticulousness and, latterly, monotonousness. His undoubted achievement (one of the chief responses to which, *pace* some over-earnest critics and confirmers of their own despair, is, paradoxically, glee) is a monument to the Robinson Crusoe principle of making do with slender resources–but Beckett has had no Man Friday, only a few seedy tramps and the scratched vision of Chaplin at his hilariously sad antics, and an immense knowledge of European philosophy. He began, at the same time as an excellent essay on *Proust* (1931), with somewhat thin poetry in French and English–his least interesting work. His first novel, *Murphy* (1938), in English (it was hostilely reviewed by Dylan Thomas, q.v., who then, characteristically, stole from it), contains his sole (sporadic) attempts at realism; it is influenced by Joyce, but resembles Flann O'Brien (ps. Briain O'Nualláin, 1910–66) as much, though *At-Swim-Two-Birds* did not appear until later. Beckett had spoken of 'the boredom of living' being 'replaced by the suffering of being'. Murphy suffers from being; Beckett's future characters are to be more bored and even less purposeful than Murphy. But Murphy is already a 'seedy solipsist'. *Watt* (1953), written during the war, owes more to Kafka's (q.v.) *The Castle* than is usually noted: it might well in fact be described as an adaptation of *The Castle* into Beckett's terms, with a K (Watt) who is far too unarrogant, gormless and unambitious to be a con-man. Watt-Beckett is a depersonalized, logical-positivist wanderer into the field of non-trivia; depersonalized because he cannot even accept the Wittgensteinian mysticism that must attend any humanization of the barren reaches of logical positivism. The trilogy *Molloy, Malone meurt* and *L'Innommable* (1951–3), translated as *Molloy, Malone Dies, The Unnameable* (1955–8), begins with Molloy in bed writing an account of how he came to be totally crippled (but he can write) and ends in the irresistibly loquacious prison of his own mind. *Comment c'est* (1961; tr. *How It Is,* 1964), carries this process of rejection of empirical reality even further; the fiction since then has demonstrated a resolutely logical disintegration into silence. Beckett's drama has gone in the same direction. His second play and first success, *Waiting for Godot,* is his own dramatization of the wholly semantic meaning of human history. It is, *par excellence,* the play of a philosopher: for there is as little more than philosophy in it as is possible under theatrical conditions. However, these conditions, like the ones created by fiction, imply an inescapable empiricism: paradoxically, the philosophy is filtered through the reality, if only of illusion, and becomes a parody of itself. Godot is more Charl*ot* (Chaplin: real fun) than 'God', who is conspicuously not there in any form. The play of two tramps who wait for Godot under a tree, and the two other characters who do not wait for him, and the boy who brings them information, are, at bottom, realistic: this farce is happening—on the stage: the author, having with great astuteness excised vitality from his text, draws on the vitality of director and actors. The joke in the end is on the audience, most of whom believe Godot to be 'God', who sit there and take it in and go on to discuss it. This is of course quite legitimate. Similar stage mastery is shown by Beckett in later plays for stage and radio: *Fin de partie* (1957; tr. *Endgame,* 1958) and *Krapp's Last Tape* (1959) are notable. Later work is deliberately pointless, but logically so. Is Beckett fruitfully revenging himself on himself for his initial failure to achieve true linguistic richness in poetry? Or is he, perhaps, simply a happy man whose literary work, however, sadly denies the equally introverted

Valéry's (q.v.) great poetic axiom: 'il faut tenter de vivre' ('we must try to live')?

Behan, Brendan (1923–64) Irish dramatist, autobiographer. Died, like Constant Lambert, from the difficulties presented by alcoholic persistence in the presence of diabetes. His plays *The Quare Fellow* (1956) and *The Hostage* (1959) will hardly survive as texts, but under the kind of intelligent productions they initially had they may persist in theatrical repertory for a few decades. The first is a genuinely compassionate revelation of the moral horror of capital punishment, the second a rumbustious near-farce. His best work is *Borstal Boy* (1958), a good-temperedly subversive account of his early delinquent years and the 'corrective' measures applied.

Bellow, Saul (1915) Canadian-born (of Latvian-Jewish parents who had emigrated in 1913) American fiction writer, playwright, essayist. Bellow has become increasingly victim to the fatal notion of the 'Great American Novel', but has been driven to this not by ambition but by his delicate, humorous sensibility and his passionate and frustrated desire to produce an answer to the twin nihilisms of mindless leftist extremism and faceless bureaucracy. He is anthropologically knowledgeable, which is rare; and while this remained inexplicit it gave strength to his work, but in *Mr Sammler's Planet* (1970), it obtruded, and consequently engulfed the imaginative element. The theme of Bellow's earlier novels was basically existentialist (*see* Sartre): men have the possibility of choosing to be themselves, but are impeded by subjective and objective circumstances. However, he was greatly concerned (and here he has affinities with a very different novelist, Onetti, q.v.) with both the tactics of evasion and the sudden, radiant gushings forth of authenticity. *Dangling Man* (1944) deals with the psychology of a man who does not want to go into the army but does want to escape into its anonymity. *The Victim* (1947) demonstrates the results of urban alienation with great compassion and imaginative power. In both these novels the thesis is secondary: one extrapolates it from the realistic detail. *The Adventures of Augie March* (1953) is longer and less convincing, resorting to the picaresque and to comedy that is excellent but too detachable from the book as a whole. With *Henderson the Rain King* (1959) anthropology begins to obtrude. In *Mr Sammler's Planet* the ravaged central character is an inappropriate vessel for

Bellow's by now over-philosophical concerns. The most beautiful of all his books is the novella *Seize the Day* (1956), in which the central character—another 'victim'—finds himself torn between hatred and love for his impossible father. The end of this is one of the most moving passages in modern literature. Bellow has written plays (e.g. *A Wen*, 1965) and short stories (*Mosby's Memoirs*, 1969), some of which contain work on a level with his best. The novel *Herzog* (1964) was a return to form after *Henderson the Rain King:* its comedy, concentrated in victim-Herzog's attempts to assert his individuality and to discover his place in the scheme of things, is thoroughly integrated. *Humboldt's Gift* (1975) is yet another return to form. It is partly inspired by the tragic collapse of Delmore Schwartz (q.v.).

Bely, Andrei (ps. Boris Bugaev) (1880–1934) Russian novelist, poet, critic. Bely was one of the most influential of the writers of the twenties, even though the Bolsheviks ignored his work in the last decade of his life. Like Blok (q.v.), he was a Russian symbolist whose philosophy derived directly from the mysticism of Vladimir Solovyov (1853–1900), the poet and syncretist who as a young man deeply impressed Dostoievski while he was writing *The Brothers Karamazov*. But Bely, who was at one time (1914–16) a disciple of Rudolf Steiner, savagely satirized every tendency in himself as in others; he was well aware that he might envisage the existence of another perfect world of which this is the caricature (not, in his case, shadow) because he hated this one. . . . He inherited the genius of Gogol without Gogol's ultimate madness. His attitude to the revolution is confused, but he was certainly indifferent to Marxism or its fate. Bely's project is certainly to be a pure Platonic or Solovyovian symbolist, in life as in art, but he could never convince himself of its validity. Hence his wild humour, his frenzy. His poetry is lucid and attractive, his prose carefully contrived and intensely rhythmical. The chief works are the novel *Peterburg* (1913–16; tr. *St Petersburg*, 1960) and the radically experimental *Kotik Letayev* (1917), *Kitten Letayev*, a desperate, autobiographical attempt to give an authentically 'stream-of-consciousness' (*see* Bergson) account, based on the anthroposophical postulations of Steiner, of how the infant becomes aware. *Peterburg*, the masterpiece, is quintessentially Russian: spectral, beautiful, melodramatic, haunted, murderous, irrepressibly mystical. In it Bely approaches Gogol and Dostoievski at their most powerful. Later novels, written after Bely had made another visit to

Berlin (1921–3), where he fell into drinking, are more overtly satirical of the pre-revolutionary Russian scene–but still experimental. He was a subtle and sophisticated critic.

Benét, Stephen Vincent (1898–1943) American poet, fiction writer, historian. Benét's best known works are the long narrative poem *John Brown's Body* (1928), on the Civil War, and the story 'The Devil and Daniel Webster'; he wrote a good deal else. It has always proved difficult to write narrative poetry that will survive for more than a year or two and Benét's still widely read attempt should not be underestimated. *John Brown's Body* has many lapses, but also many triumphs; and Benét's overall approach is remarkably balanced and sophisticated.

Benn, Gottfried (1886–1956) German poet, prose writer, critic (of the origins of expressionism, *see* Stadler). Benn was the son of a Lutheran parson and Swiss-French mother; he became a doctor (serving as such in both wars) specializing in venereal and skin diseases. He was an unhappy man, and much of his poetry is flawed by his deliberately over-cerebral approach; yet it resolutely defies dismissal into the category of 'minor', and has been highly influential. He began in the expressionist ferment (of which his history is useful and attractively idiosyncratic rather than critically reliable), and the influence of expressionism was indelible. He is one of the most puzzling cases in modern literature. Charlatan ('there are worse words', he wrote), poseur, temporary supporter of Hitler ('whom all of us worship without exception', 1934), moral idiot–he is all of these and yet he can sometimes touch the heart and touch it as surely as he can at others repel it. The young Benn delighted (*Morgue*, 1912) in shocking his readers with cynical poems, mostly about his medical experiences, which had been amongst prostitutes and other people defeated by life. These early poems are most distinguished by their stark realism and brilliance, their relish in the pointlessness of life. They are minor, but not, as has been claimed, 'bad': seldom has talent seemed so nearly gifted, so full of poetic potential. The attitude, concentrating on the horrible, is immature, but a cleanness of language compensates. Benn's chief secret is that he was a romantic and a sentimental one. But he was also a clever intellectual, though his gifts in this direction have probably been exaggerated. Soon after the earliest poems, during his war-service as a doctor, came the prose-sketches about Doctor Rönne, clearly a projection of himself.

These, again brilliant in execution, attempt to explain his inner confusions in a clinical manner and are artistically disingenuous inasmuch as their detachment is contrived rather than felt: lyrical feeling is seen as weakness, imagination is emasculated, stopped short; the poet poses as the doctor. Rönne has experienced 'Love, poverty, and X-ray tubes; rabbitpens . . .'; he sees life as pointless and disgusting, but is fascinated by its great flux, the origins of (wasted?) intelligence in 'slime'. . . . The twenties saw Benn move into a new and more lyrical style, expressive of lush yearnings for the rural ('O noon that with hot hay reduces/my brain to meadow, shepherds and flat land. . . .') and for the south; but even this poetry is for the most part marked by neologisms, slick exhibitionistic tricks: a sneering that while it may be partly a self-sneer is none the less obtrusive, anti-imaginative, wilfully (and pseudo-) 'scientific'. The poet avoids all means of immersion into himself as he really is; he does so only in sporadic poems and, more often, sporadic images—outside clinical control. Then he became a spokesman for the Nazis, though he never joined the party. The decision is still a puzzle, though some light may be cast upon it. In any case by 1936 he had become an 'inner emigrant', had had his works banned and had rejoined the army. I offer the following tentative explanation (which is essentially one of Benn as a whole). Benn is always referred to as an expressionist and often as, in the words of one critic, a 'cerebral (Apollonian) poet'—this on the strength of his own pronouncements about the only point of life being the creation of an artistic, metaphysical 'I' independent of the filth of history and the pitiful inadequacy of the brain of man to devise means of living intelligently in harmony. These judgements are not altogether adequate. Benn's poetry until the time of Hitler (compare it with Trakl's, q.v., Heym's, q.v. even the relatively lightweight Lichtenstein's) is not truly expressionist: it is rather neo-romantic-decadent, though cast in clinical, even cubist (*see* Reverdy) forms that may seem expressionist; it is also strictly naturalist (in the gloomy, literary sense) and morbid, two genres that go together more often and more zestfully than is always recognized. Benn's repression of his romanticism, his emasculation of his imagination—seen in the preternaturally hard, sardonic surface of his poetry—had been so severe that it had led him to adopt an *over*-cerebral stance. When Nazism arrived his hitherto stifled hope burst forth, obtusely, stupidly: this hope, so humanly natural, attached itself to the notion of a 'new biological type'. By 1934–5 he already knew better. But because he was

so stubborn, so proud, so used to his *persona* of the quasi-nihilistic-clinician-with-romantic-overtones, he never recanted. 'I will not be de-Nazified', he exclaimed after the war; and indeed he was justified, in the sense that he had already de-Nazified himself long before it. In his private life he suffered much and did much good as a physician. (He quit medicine only two years before his death, and then only for reasons of health.) But because, after a period of being banned by West Germans and Allies alike he suddenly became famous, one or two words might have been in order–out of decency. They were not uttered and yet the later, post-war poetry is his best. Perhaps here, in his proud way, he does apologize. There is a near-Italian hermeticism (*see* Ungaretti) about some of it. And what can one say of his 'Chopin', who 'for his part was unable/to explicate his Nocturnes' and who said 'My endeavours are as complete/as it was in my power to make them'? That is a major poem, even if Benn's own endeavours had never previously been 'complete'; nor, ultimately, even in this superior and reluctantly recantatory poetry, were they ever. But there is much loveliness, truly poetic, in this late poetry. Benn is as fascinating as Eliot (q.v.)–and, ultimately, and more unhappily, rewarding. *Gesammelte Werke*, 1958–61; in tr. *Selected Writings*, 1961.

Bennett, Arnold (1867–1931) English novelist, playwright, widely influential book reviewer. His achievement has been unfairly undermined for many reasons: his streak of cocky (not arrogant) vulgarity inevitably attracted attacks; his capacity to build a credible 'world' made such writers as Virginia Woolf (q.v.)–who lacked it but desired it–jealous; his fiction is wildly uneven, and the hack books seem to (but do not) leave a wide breach for frontal attacks on the excellent ones; he was, in every sense of the word, a success; he did not understand much about poetry, although he tried to write it. He was an odder mixture than most critics suppose and far too much emphasis has been put upon the vulgar solicitor's son from the Potteries who became a London socialite and who boasted about it and made frequent remarks to the effect that art was really all about money. For beneath this much derided *persona* he preserved a subtle sensibility and an artistic integrity quite intact, even if it did not very often surface fully. The best work is no more flawed than is that of, say, Conrad (q.v.); and why is it that he continues, even now, to be damned with faint praise (but Margaret Drabble's, q.v., *Arnold Bennett*, 1974, goes a long way towards correcting this mostly academic habit)? One of the vital keys to Bennett's complex personality is to be found in the *Journals*—not in the self-doctored selection published in the author's lifetime, but in Newman Flower's selection of 400,000 words, *Journals* (1932–3), and in Swinnerton's selection from these, because it incorporates the newly discovered entries between September 1906 and July 1907, and the so-called *Florentine Journal 1910* (1967): *Journals*, 1971. The whole million words, however, should be published without delay. This, and particularly the entries for the period 1902–10, when Bennett lived in France, reveals the private man—one of acute sensitivity, real culture, humour and generosity. The *Letters* (1966–70) are also important. As book-critic of the *Evening Standard* Bennett certainly 'wrote down', and he certainly endorsed some ephemeral rubbish. But his record even here is on the whole good, for he also endorsed many good and then unknown or unpopular writers. The stock academic view is that he wrote some four or five novels of importance (this is true, but there is some much more than competent work amongst his huge and now conventionally rejected *oeuvre*), that (I here quote as a typical example) his 'vision is pathetic rather than tragic'; that he was a good craftsman, but that this quality 'strengthen[s] rather than offset[s] the failure of his art, a failure of the imagination'. Bennett's indisputably major works are *The Old Wives' Tale* (1908), *Clayhanger* (1910) and *Riceyman Steps* (1923)—the also rans are *Hilda Lessways* (1911) and *These Twain* (1916). To this list I should add at least *Anna of the Five Towns*, 1902; *The Card*, 1911—without which the modern British neo-picaresque novel would not exist, and which both anticipates and excels it—*The Pretty Lady*, 1918, 1950; *Elsie and the Child*, 1924, sequel, in a story collection, to *Riceyman Steps; Lord Raingo*, 1926; and perhaps *Imperial Palace*, 1930, deliberately misunderstood. Because Bennett wrote rather awful 'self-help' books, and too brashly pretended to write for profit, it is too widely assumed that he was not self-critical and that his familiarity with the European masters was wide but not deep. This is untrue. He knew his limits. He knew that he could not deal with powerful, directly expressed emotions, and in his best work he avoids them. It was never his aim to be 'tragic'—though *Riceyman Steps* does in fact achieve the status of tragedy and only a snob can fail to see it. But he had feeling: deep feeling and a compassion which he knew how to handle effectively. He also had a rare comic genius (*The Card* is the novel where this is least diluted by other preoccupations).

He dealt with the 'ordinary', and in his realistic manner–he absorbed much from Flaubert–he did so with the acumen of the more modernistic Joyce (q.v.), whose achievement he saluted. *The Old Wives' Tale* is solidly built up and superbly documented; moreover, the documentation is not obtrusive–Bennett had learned from the inferior naturalists (*see* Zola) that no novel can be 'scientific'. As to his 'vision', Bennett's originality as well as his self-critical capacities lay (we are considering the best work) in his avoidance of 'vision'. People's lives can of course be full of pathos, and Bennett records this. But he records much more: his accounts of 'unimportant' lives reveal, extract with a beautiful selectivity, the human–the unselfish, the courageous. Bennett knows above all about drabness–at every social level–spiritual as well as physical; it is his peculiar genius to show the decency in it. He is not only one of the justest of twentieth-century writers, he is one of the most affirmatory. *Clayhanger* and *The Card* scintillate with energy and social accuracy. *Riceyman Steps* (in my view his masterpiece, and a great novel) is one of the last realist classics. Failure of art, of imagination? (And how could these be *strengthened*, except in the eyes of a snobbish hack, by good craftsmanship? Quality of true craftsmanship is part and parcel of success of both art and imagination.) The 'world' Bennett here creates is doubtless a metaphor, but this kind of metaphor, firmly set at the end of a long tradition, can be created by nothing less than imagination–and that creation needed much art at a time when modernism, to which Bennett was not insensitive, had been on the move for many years. Bennett is a case of a very literary man indeed wrapped up in a very unliterary package. Once this has been understood, and the importance of George Moore (q.v.)–as well as the French and Russian novelists–in his development recognized, we should be able to approach the contradiction more constructively, and to dispense with the petty and unjustified strictures.

Benson, Stella (1892–1933) English novelist, travel writer, diarist (her diaries, which may well prove to be her most durable work, became legally publishable in 1973). She died of tuberculosis. *Tobit Transplanted* (1931; 1974), which reflects her experience of the Far East, is the best of her fiction, which is a highly original blend of humanitarian concern, witty observation and understanding of primitive myth and tradition. *Collected Stories* (1936).

Bergson, Henri (1859–1941) French Jewish philosopher, who exercised a huge and deserved influence on literature. Nobel Prize 1928. As a philosopher he anticipates Husserl (the chief exponent of phenomenology) and existentialism (*see* Sartre). He has been much misinterpreted, as by Bertrand Russell (1872–1970). So far as literature is concerned, Bergson helped to expand the notion of reality: he refused to jettison any aspect of actual experience and, unlike Husserl, the general consequences of this interested him. He sometimes wanted to be a Catholic; what is important is that he did not become one (though a priest, with terrible impertinence, said rites over his dead body). One of the reasons for this was that he felt he must keep solidarity with the persecuted Jews. The outlines of Bergson's philosophy are fairly clear; but it is impossible to present even these without being contentious. Like Freud (q.v.), he is a rich thinker. Bergson was anti-positivist, anti-'*scientisme*'. He is often presented as a philosophical idealist; but he was a realist who brought psychology into philosophy. His springboard is the distinction between 'ordinary' clock-time, and *temps vécu,* the time of consciousness (we all recognize this; but the bourgeois version of reality cuts out the notion of *temps vécu*). Clock-time must be, for ourselves, an essentially *spatialized* projection, an artificiality. We have to have it and Bergson knows that we have to have it. But he draws our attention to the 'immediate data of consciousness'. These come to us, whether we realize it or not, as an intuited, *real, duration.* The intellect divides, conceptualizes time for us; the 'intuition' (reflection, not instinct) allows the mind to contemplate itself in its own flux—each 'moment' absorbs the past and is absorbed by the future. Real time is (obviously) a mystery even to Bergson but the key to grasping it (which in his thinking becomes increasingly religious in nature) is memory, 'which prolongs the before into the after' and so prevents there ever being an actual, discrete, moment. 'Some wished', wrote Proust (q.v.), 'the novel to be a sort of cinematographic parade. This conception was absurd.' William James (q.v.) coined the term 'stream-of-consciousness', and he came to almost the same conclusion as Bergson; but it is appropriate to discuss its significance under Bergson because it is the actual starting-point for his thinking. *The present is process,* not a scientifically analyzable concept. Bergson is concerned with artistic creation, rightly seeing it as an attempt of the mind to free itself from determinism by use of the real, submerged self: 'we are free when our acts spring from our whole personality, when they express it, when they have that indefinable resemblance to it which one sometimes finds between the artist and his work.' The fate of pure *scientisme* is to end trapped in a web of determinism. Thus 'stream-of-consciousness', though it often was and is used in a 'narrative' form, can in fact take other forms (e.g. third person narrative). The 'interior monologue' is only one sort of 'stream-of-consciousness'. All Proust (who had, as he says, 'affinities' with Bergson, at whose wedding to his cousin he was best man) is an attempt to use memory as a key; all Proust's diverse approaches are really stream-of-consciousness. . . . Bergson's message is that man can attain free will but he will never (here he resembles Freud on the subject of love) demonstrate an *absolute* grasp of free will (an absolute 'authenticity', as an existentialist would say). He feels (we may well infer) that in some paradoxically mysterious way man's unique symbolizing faculties prevent him from achieving freedom—and so his definition of 'symbol' is never clear, nor are his various suggestions for removing 'symbolization', which he perhaps sometimes confuses with 'conceptualization'. Bergson finally came to believe in 'love'—but not unsubtly. In Shaw's (q.v.) version in *Back to Methuselah* his *élan vital* becomes a vulgar vitalism; actually Bergson's *élan vital* is an elaborate metaphor for an extension of his *durée:* it is non-material (not material, as Shaw would have it), and it projects *la durée* into history and society. Thus the Durkheimian *Les deux Sources de la Morale et de la Religion* (1932; tr. *The Two Sources of Morality and Religion,* 1954) acknowledges the 'religious' as a manifestation but leaves the question of 'belief' open, preferring to consider the matter of the merits of 'open' over 'closed' systems. One might say much more of this great thinker. Enough, however, has been written here to indicate his importance to literature. It comes to the question of how we consider time. 'Dive back into the flux itself . . . if you want to *know* reality, that flux which Platonism, in its strange belief that only the immutable is excellent, has always spurned. . . .' Bergson did not, however, spurn the immutable and he read his friend Proust, who sought it by 'diving into' the indivisible stream of consciousness. . . . He spurned no aspect of experience. We may or may not wish to be told that matter is degraded spirit, or that an Absolute may be attainable by intuition; but the *processes* to which Bergson draws our attention, the account of the *ambiguity* of our sense of ourselves that he gives (cf. Merleau-Ponty)—these are what modern literature has been about. Among his more important works are: *Essai sur les données immédiates de la conscience*

(1889; tr. *Time and Free Will,* 1910); *Matière et Mémoire* (1896; tr. *Matter and Memory,* 1911); *Le Rire* (1900; tr. *Laughter,* 1911)—this is a brilliant, rather Durkheimian, explanation of the comic as social regulator; *L'Évolution créatrice* (1907; tr. *Creative Evolution,* 1911).

Bernanos, Georges (1888–1948) French novelist. Bernanos combines two traditions: that of the impassioned, even furious Catholic (e.g. Bloy), and the anti-Catholic Catholic (e.g. Greene, q.v., the earlier Mauriac, q.v.). He was a writer of power and sincerity, with more control, understanding and compassion than Bloy but, when provoked, of equal ferocity. He became mixed up in the early thirties with unpleasant, anti-semitic elements; but this was accidental: a product of his desire to believe in a system. *Les Grandes cimetières sous la lune* (1938; tr. *Diary of My Times,* 1938) is absolute in its condemnation of Franco and the practices of the Church in Spain. He left Europe for South America in 1938 and returned only after the defeat of Hitler. That his heart was 'in the right place' is certain; the reasons for his furies are effectively worked out in his fiction which demonstrates that they were Furies—and what writer is not haunted by Furies? Bernanos was educated by bad, old-style Jesuits, and although for a time he remained ostensibly indoctrinated by their casuistic rigidities, he quite early began to rebel: he saw that Satan, as well as God, had a firm hold on the world. His first novel, *Sous le soleil de Satan* (1926; tr. *Star of Satan,* 1940; *Under the Sun of Satan,* 1949), is a more ambiguous book than has been allowed. Its priest, Donissan, employs devilish powers to give life to a disturbed girl, Mouchette (who has shot her seducer), from whom he has (he thinks) exorcized devilish powers. . . . The theme of Mouchette (but this is not the same character as the Mouchette of the first novel) was again taken up in *Nouvelle Histoire de Mouchette* (1937; tr. *Mouchette,* 1966); this is in fact his last novel, since the two published after it were revisions of work begun earlier: *Monsieur Ouine* and *Un Mauvais Rêve* were mainly written in the earlier thirties. For Bernanos the human world is certainly a battle between sainthood and devilry; but he knows that human beings are themselves battlegrounds. He is unfair in his criticism of others—as Bloy was—but he reveals his own fierce integrity even in his unfairness, and as a man, with his pipe and his wife and six children and kitchen table (which he also used as a desk) he was genial. We should look carefully for this geniality in his fiction: this compassion and lack of complacency. No one, a non-Christian French critic has written, 'can escape [his] power because it animates with incomparable strength a world simultaneously unusual and familiar, visionary and everyday'. Bernanos looked deeply into the democratic system and found it spiritually inadequate; much of his polemic is directed against it. Yet his motives were–paradoxically, since he loathed all leftism–often Marxist in spirit. He was, basically, against a system that generated capitalism. . . . And in any case his truly democratic motives emerge in his anguished fiction: as so often happens, imagination transcends confusion (the non-imaginative fate of all of us, whether we be readers, writers, or both). After three novels Bernanos attempted to solve his financial problems with a potboiler, a detective story called *Un Crime* (1935; tr. *A Crime*, 1936). Both *L'Imposture* (1927), *The Deception*, and *La Joie* (1929; tr. *Joy*, 1946) present the same torn predicament as the first novel; but, like so many other intended potboilers by serious writers, *Un Crime* has been neglected. *Le Journal d'un curé de campagne* (1936; tr. *The Diary of a Country Priest*, 1937) is regarded as his masterpiece; but major though it is in its account of a poor, weak, sick, anti-Catholic Catholic priest doing his duty in a hateful parish (the 1950 movie, directed by Bresson, is excellent), it is perhaps not his greatest book. The last, *Un Mauvais Rêve* (1950; tr. *Night is Darkest*, 1953), written in 1935, is as good; and *Monsieur Ouine* (1943; 1946; definitive text 1955; tr. *The Open Mind*, 1945–this version should be revised) is certainly his most powerful, ambiguous novel. This *pointilliste* text deals with two of Bernanos's obsessions: the parish oblivious to salvation (cf. T. F. Powys, q.v.) and the anti-saint (Ouine is in part based on Gide, q.v., who was in fact quite as 'saintly', at any rate in his sufferings, as Bernanos). Peter Hebblethwaite, a neo-Jesuit, is at pains to point out in his valuable study of Bernanos (1965) that he was no 'Manichee'. But *Monsieur Ouine* shows that, in one important sense, he was. This strange book, sweated at from 1934 until a year or two before his death, is a modernist, sensitive *tranche de vie*, total in its ambiguity. It is a triumph of agonized scepticism over dogma and a profoundly courageous book.

Berryman, John (1914–72) American poet, critic, fiction writer. Berryman's actual poetic achievement will be the subject of debate for a long time, but the subjective and deliberately egocentric method of his later two-volume work (*77 Dream Songs*, 1964; *His Toy, His*

Dream, His Rest, 1968), a sequence of 385 poems, will continue to fascinate and influence. His early poems were products of the New Criticism (*see* Brooks), and were attacked for this; only in *The Dispossessed* (1948) did he begin to discover his own method. Berryman continued to display the chief early influences on his poetry—Hopkins, the metaphysicals, Empson (q.v.), the intellectual devices recommended by the new critics—but he loosened his forms and learned not only from Barker (q.v.), a fellow-Catholic who had been writing a poetry rather like his for a quarter of a century, but also from the Canadian Abraham Klein (1909–72), who anticipated him in mixing archaisms in with colloquialese. *Homage to Mistress Bradstreet* (1956)—Anne Bradstreet was a seventeenth-century Englishwoman who settled in America and became one of the earliest American poets—simultaneously treats Mistress Bradstreet as Berryman's own mistress and as his *Doppelgänger* (or, more likely, the 'feminine' part of himself). In the dream songs this metaphysical procedure is extended and further complicated. The poems, which adhere, though very loosely indeed in stress or syllabic terms, to an eighteen-line, three-stanza form, are in several 'voices'. The method enables Berryman to range freely about in contemporary history and in himself, but it may also be evasive: in the counterpointed welter of voices his own voice, though not his anguish (he was a severely disturbed alcoholic who fought off his remorse with every desperate energy he could muster), is not often enough distinguishable. But it is arguable that the poem—it is essentially a single poem—is unified by the fact that all the masks, including the one of the white man in black-face called Henry, or Pussycat, are that of the single writer, Berryman; the reality of the suffering of the man, for those who had not gathered it from his text, was made clear when he waved goodbye and tried to jump into the Mississippi at Minneapolis (he hit the bank) in January 1972. Berryman's procedure may be seen as a desperate attempt to achieve a totally phenomenological approach. This necessarily brings in 'bad' poetry as virtuous: the poet, once heroic status has been conferred upon him by a large enough section of the public, may do as he likes. The honest reader will be hit by the power of the poem but will never quite be able to make up his mind about the degree of communication achieved. The crabbed diction, the resort to every sort of utterance, is almost too eclectic; at highly crucial points the poem may tail off into evasive trivialities which fail to reach the epiphanic (*see* Joyce) status they ought to have. This is a poetry that bewilderingly mixes acute sensitivity to all human suffering with specious, rhetorical protestations of friendship—and with moods of wooden insensitivity to any suffering except his own (this is often a feature of alcoholic illness). And yet it is all there: mannered, vital, pained. The poem 'The Facts & Issues' in the posthumous *Delusions Etc.* (1972) is the best introduction to the work as a whole. Its lucidities help to illuminate some of the obscurities of the previous poetry and if, after pondering, the reader finds full response then he knows he rates Berryman highly. But if he sees it as not more than agonized rhetoric then he will know that he must ultimately reject a nevertheless fascinating and instructive poet. Probably Berryman's poetry began to go off when, in the sixties, he decided that 'fame'—his penultimate collection was called *Love and Fame* (1971)—entitled him to be as bad or obscure as he liked, and also fired him with the ambition to become a 'universal man'. *Berryman's Sonnets* (1967) is a set of poems written nearly twenty years before; in these, influences strong in England in the early thirties are yoked to the eccentric, drunken ('I am not', however, 'so think as you drunk I am') manner first fully apparent in *Homage to Mistress Bradstreet*. Berryman's critical biography, *Stephen Crane* (1950), is an important study. *Selected Poems* (1972).

Bethell, Mary Ursula (1874–1945) Anglo-New Zealand poet. Born England, spent childhood in New Zealand, returned there permanently 1924. Published *From a Garden in the Antipodes* in England under a pseudonym in 1929; more under her own name, and, posthumously, *Collected Poems,* 1950. Astonishingly simple and surely controlled in her earlier, garden poems, she gradually brought into her later poems a meditative and religious note; many are preoccupied with themes of love and death. Her lucidity, free-ranging rhythms and poetic use of prosaic detail (as from gardening catalogues) show up the shoddiness of Georgian 'country' verse. She is celebrated in New Zealand but not enough read elsewhere. With Robin Hyde (q.v.) one of the most accomplished woman poets of the century.

Betjeman, John (1906) English poet (Laureate 1972–), commentator on the English scene (e.g. *Ghastly Good Taste,* 1933), radio and television personality. Betjeman became a best-selling poet with *Collected Poems* (1958; rev. 1970), which in Great Britain is unprecedented. He has some 'highbrow' admirers (e.g. Larkin, q.v., Auden, q.v.) but more detractors. His earliest poetry, influenced by Tom Moore and Tennyson, parodied nineteenth-century minor verse and struggled to assimilate Hardy. It seemed a perfectly innocuous and amusing light verse. In later poems he indulges himself in old-fashioned sentimentality and thumping metres but puts in enough that can be taken as parodic by the 'serious' audience. Betjeman has no more than an anachronistic appeal: a man living in the seventies trying to write in the Victorian manner. His (comic-bathetic?) verses on Princess Anne's wedding suggested that he could (or would) not take his duties as Laureate seriously, which is not as surprising as his middlebrow fans would think: he is by no means an 'establishment' man and there is therefore a wilfulness in the persistent archaism of his verse which an individual style does not rescue from triviality.

Blake, Nicholas, *see* **Day Lewis, Cecil.**

Blixen, Karen (1885–1962) Danish fiction writer and memoirist. Karen Blixen married Baron Blor-Blixen Finecke in 1914; they were divorced in 1921; her first book, *Seven Gothic Tales* (1934), written in English, appeared under her maiden name Isak Dinesen. The Danish edition of *Seven Gothic Tales,* which made her famous, *Syu fantastiske Fortaellinger* (1935), differs from the English, and is authoritative. Although all but two or three of her books appeared in English, she regarded herself as, and is, a Danish writer. Her collected works appeared in 1964. She is one of the most original writers of her time: a modernist employing nineteenth-century procedures and exploiting a nineteenth-century kind of narrative skill. She had published a few pieces under the name Osceola in her early twenties; but she devoted the years 1914–31 to looking after her Kenyan coffee farm, first with her husband and then alone—until the Depression forced her to give up. Her roots are in the Gothic, Kleist and Hoffmann; in her tales she understood the individualistic morbidity of the nineteenth century and pushed its decadence over into a valid, new myth-making. Though she exploits the 'novel of terror' (English influences include Walpole and Lewis, q.v.) and the rococo she is always doing so with cunning and high sophistication. She is one of the most delicate of writers, and it is hardly surprising that she should be attracting more and more attention. Her most popular book is *Out of Africa* (1937), a marvellous, affectionate, subtle evocation of the old Kenya and of the world of animals, which she never pretends not to anthropomorphize. She wrote one marionette comedy, but this form, as Robert Langbaum has suggested (his study of her, *The Gaiety of Vision*, 1964, is helpful), helps us understand 'her distinctive qualities': '. . . in responding like a marionette . . . you actually find out . . . who you really are'. One is reminded of Ghelderode (q.v.) but Karen Blixen is wittier. The greatest of her tales, perhaps the most accomplished of all 'modern fairy tales' are in her first book (*Seven Gothic Tales*), *Winter's Tales* (1942), *Last Tales* (1957) and the posthumous *Ehrengard* (1963). All but the first of these appeared in Danish and were first written in Danish. Her anti-Nazi *Gengoeldelsens Veje* (1944; tr. *The Angelic Avengers*, 1947), an allegorical pastiche of late Gothic, appeared under the name of Pierre Andrézel, an 'English' author whom she disowned. She also wrote *Essays* (1965).

Blok, Alexandr (1880–1921) Russian poet, playwright. His personality reverberated and continues to reverberate, yet he was the most pathologically reserved of all the European poets of his generation. He is confused in all but his best poetry. He was a mystic womanologist who was certainly ambisexual. He was an even more fervent follower of the poet Solovyov than Bely (q.v.), and although he accepted the revolution he did so in the most mystical manner, as his famous apocalyptic poem 'The Twelve' makes apparent. The leader of the Russian symbolist movement, he mourned its passing and died—after working himself to the point of exhaustion—a disillusioned, written out man, 'unable to breathe'. He 'persistently tried to turn water into wine' (Zamyatin, q.v.): another way of saying that he needed symbolism, the existence of another world, so that he could sublimate the erotic and alcoholic difficulties which he felt to be evil—and which terrified him—into a spiritual poetry. Yet the poetry may be read as non-symbolist. Though a devotee of the 'Lady Beautiful' (his wife, a Solovyovian notion, music, Russia, other lovers, a vision or hallucination he experienced in 1901—all these), he supported the 1905 revolution and spoke of himself as a social being. Like Yeats and Bely, Blok thought of history in cosmic, 'spiral', terms; and the 'Christ of the Red Guard' in his poem 'The Twelve' may be feminine. (He was as strongly anti-Christian, though, as Rilke, q.v.). His vision is ultimately destructive: he drowns in lushness—but this is not a sentimental lushness. He is desperately sad and sick and it may well be that his poetry does not transcend his neurosis. But it possesses compelling power, and in it true decadence flowers as it never flowered before. He did not achieve emotional or intellectual maturity; but his descriptions of the barriers to this are inimitable. *Selected Poems* (1970; 1972) contains a version of 'The Twelve' and is a useful introduction.

Blunden, Edmund (1896–1974) English poet, autobiographer, critic. Blunden, who fought in the First World War and was badly gassed, spent most of his life as a university teacher (Oxford, the Far East). Like Sassoon (q.v.), he published his first collection (but privately) before the war. Labelled 'Georgian' (*see* Brooke), Blunden partly lived up to this properly pejorative description: he was indiscriminately soft on inadequate as well as unduly neglected (e.g. Ivor Gurney, 1890–1937) poets. His accounts of nineteenth-century literature (*Charles Lamb and his Contemporaries,* 1934, and *Keats's Publisher,* 1936—on John Taylor —are the two best) are informative but not critically sharp. However, there was a period of some ten years during which, under the influence of the horrors of the war, Blunden wrote excellent and original poems which are in no sense Georgian. Nearly all these are in *Poems 1914–30* (1932) and some of the best were incorporated into the prose memoirs *Undertones of War* (1928). 'Report on Experience', a subtle and beautifully stated poem, is one famous example. In this vein Blunden's natural pastoralism, usually over-sentimental, achieves a half-sinister, visionary quality: he sees what his over-indulgent temperament hated to see: the mysteriously evil or violent concealed in the innocently appealing. Around the beginning of the thirties Blunden reverted to his Georgian manner, and wrote little more of poetic distinction. *Undertones of War* is often regarded as a classic of the 1914–18 war, but (poems apart) it is not this: the prose is a little too contrived: clearly Blunden's real energies were going into his poetry. His interest in Clare had been anticipated by Norman Gale, Arthur Symons and G. Claridge Druce, but his selection (1920) was the first scholarly one of the century and he deserves to be regarded as a pioneer in the discovery of a great poet. The fullest collection of his poetry is *Poems of Many Years* (1957).

Bly, Robert (1926) American poet, critic, translator, editor (of *The Fifties, Sixties, Seventies*). Bly is a caustic critic and has even been called 'ill-tempered'. His fault is not, however, ill-temper: about bourgeois hypocrisy, ambitious poetasters and acts of violence he is properly indignant, courageous, acute and often very funny. He has always kept his temper, even though he can be angry. The poetry of *Silence in the Snowy Fields* (1962) is, for a man so acutely aware of foreign poetries, surprisingly original and American in tone. Often dealing with the silences and great open spaces of his native Minnesota, his poems are telluric, blandly laconic, affirmative; and they beat with the pulse of mystery. *The Light Around the Body* (1967) reacts to the involvement of all that Bly loves in the mindless horror of American engagement in the Vietnam war: here shock, rather than outrage, is the key response. Where the poems are not broadly satirical, they exhibit a new sense of disturbance: '. . . the things that we must grasp,/The signs, are gone, hidden by spring and fall, leaving/A still sky here, a dusk there/. . . . where has the road gone? . . .' Bly has translated Neruda (q.v.), Jiménez (q.v.), Vallejo (q.v.), Trakl (q.v.), Machado (q.v.) and others; here, as in *The Morning Glory* (1969), he comes nearest to, though is never imitative of, Trakl: painfully sticking to his 'signs', but now more wearily; still believing that the beholder of mysteries may–within himself, by the quality of his interpretation–pluck them from evil. Bly's strength as a poet depends largely upon his observation in solitude. He looks for the unconscious 'deep image' and regards it as his task to lift this up, clean and pure, into the poem–but this in itself is seldom surrealistically structured.

Böll, Heinrich (1917) German fiction writer, dramatist, poet. Nobel Prize 1972. Böll, a 'left-wing' Catholic in the same mould as Greene (q.v.) and Pope John, is one of the most gifted and intelligent of contemporary European writers. His first fiction is skilfully realist in mode and deals bitterly with the effects of the war (in which he participated and was wounded). *Wo warst du Adam?* (1951; tr. *Adam, Where Art Thou?*, 1955) is one of the most vivid accounts of the Nazi collapse. The short stories of *Wanderer, kommst du nach Spa . . .* (1950; tr. *Traveller, If You Come to Spa*, 1956), with which he first established his reputation, treat the same theme with equal truthfulness and penetration. Böll, having to a certain extent worked the moral and physical horrors of the war out of his system, then turned to an acute appraisal of the *Wirtschaftswunder* ('economic miracle'): *Und sagte kein einziges Wort* (1953; tr. *Acquainted with the Night*, 1954) ironically combines two themes, that of the nerve-shattered returned soldier and the moral realities of West German economic recovery—its most notable feature, however, is its convincing creation of a redemptive character: the soldier's wife, an 'Ich' who truly possesses the capacity, though by no means complete, to see her partner as a 'Du' (*see* Buber). *Haus ohne Huter* (1954; tr. *The Unguarded House,* 1957) is a more direct attack on the post-Nazi bourgeois drive towards 'security', 'prosperity' and the whole non-ethos of the *Wirtschaftswunder*. Here society is seen in its role as destroyer. The novella *Das Brot der frühen Jahre* (1955; tr. *The Bread of Our Early Years,* 1957) returns to what are, in effect, Buberian possibilities of rescue. By the late fifties Böll began to see that a more or less straightforwardly realist technique was no longer adequate to his complex needs. This emerged particularly in the short story, title of a volume, *Doktor Murkes gesammeltes Schweigen* (1958; tr. in *Absent Without Leave and Other Stories,* 1967), 'Dr Murke's Collected Silences', and then in the major novel *Billard um halb zehn* (1959; tr. *Billiards at Half-Past Nine,* 1961), which, though it takes place over the span of one day, traces the history of three generations of a German family. This concerns itself with the barriers created by the absence of a 'Du' (*see* Buber), with the problem of what a viable church might be, and, now with even greater subtlety, the emptiness of the new, prosperous Germany. It is markedly influenced by J. Roth (q.v.) and by the laconic style of Hemingway (q.v.) and perhaps the colloquialese of Céline (q.v.) (an antidote to Teutonic ponderousness). All its modernist devices (flashback, stream-of-consciousness, demotic speech, use of *leitmotifs*) are strictly necessary. In *Ansichten eines Clowns* (1963; tr. *The Clown,* 1965) Böll seems to have been affected both by the existentialist (*see* Sartre) notion of authenticity and by Dostoievski's descriptions of redemption through suffering and his (and perhaps Bloy's) portrayals of how lack of material possessions may bring men nearer to God. It is not today easy for a Catholic writer to convince readers that an anti-Catholic who ends as a beggar is possessed of more grace than the Catholics who populate the novel; but *Ansichten eines Clowns* does so, and its stark power is a reminder of Böll's capacity to deal with exceedingly complicated and contentious material and to make it coherent and moving. This capacity has been interpreted by some of Böll's self-consciously *avant garde* critics as an over-fluency but the study of his texts does not bear this out. Whether he can consolidate his already high achievement remains to be seen: his fiction over the past eight or nine years has become increasingly sparse, literary and self-conscious–this is perhaps inevitable–though also more humorous, and we must hope that we shall be able to follow him as well as we have hitherto. There are comprehensive selections: *Erzählungen* (1958); *Erzählungen* (1961); *Erzählungen 1950–1970* (1972).

Bond, Edward (1935) English playwright and scriptwriter who shocked bourgeois audiences with *Saved* (1966), in which a baby is stoned to death, and *Early Morning* (1969), in which, among other things, Queen Victoria and Florence Nightingale have a lesbian affair. This kind of thing is not new and Bond's sincere sense of outrage is conceived solely in stage, and not at all in linguistic, terms. Consequently his work is ephemeral.

Bonnefoy, Yves (1923) French poet, academic (since 1960 often in America), literary and art critic, essayist, scholar, translator (of, e.g. *Hamlet*), editor (*L'Ephémère*). Highly, perhaps somewhat solemnly regarded in France, Bonnefoy began as an associate of the post-war surrealist (*see* Breton) group; but the chief influences on his work have been Jouve (q.v.) and, unusually, Valéry (q.v.). His mature work begins with the sequence *Du Mouvement et de l'immobilité de Douve* (1953), some of which is in the French-English *Selected Poems* (1968). His essay-collection *L'Improbable* (1959) is a guide to his intentions, and is not without ponderousness. However, it is fair to him to approach his poetry, initially, as he wishes: to eschew the search for 'meaning' and instead reconstitute the experience of the writer. His Douve, half-real and half-imagined, a 'Presence', is a perhaps too heavily loaded feminine dialectical symbol, but the Douve sequence is nevertheless impressive in its sonorous search for the acceptance of death, which alone can confer meaning on life; no one can deny the power of such lines as 'Il te faudra franchir la mort pour que tu vives,/La plus pure présence est un sang répandu': 'You must pass through death in order to live,/The purest presence is a shed blood'. These two lines encapsulate Bonnefoy's project, which might also be seen as an attempt to paganize Christianity, or even to 'atheise' it. *Pierre écrite* (1959; 1964) is one of three later collections. He is the only contemporary French poet to have captured something of the serene tone–concealing mental turbulence–of Valéry.

Boon, Louis Paul (1912) Belgian (Flemish) novelist. The most gifted Flemish novelist now writing; his works, about the proletariat–and by no means the nicest of them–are bursting with energy and fury; Boon often talks to his own characters. Only *De Kapellekensbaan* (1953; tr. *Chapel Road,* 1972) appears in English, but there is a French translation of *Mennet* (1955; tr. *Mennet*). His language can be reminiscent of Céline (q.v.)–a feature he has in common with other Dutch-language writers. He is persistently experimental (one of his novels is in verse) and, despite first appearances, a consummate craftsman and a magnificent storyteller.

Borges, Jorge Luis (1899) Argentinian fiction writer, poet, critic. Borges, who knows English well, was educated in Europe, and there began as an *ultraist. Ultraísmo* was a Spanish movement whose pioneer was the Spanish poet and critic Guillermo De Torre (1900); it was a somewhat violent version of expressionism (*see* Stadler): the image and the metaphor were elevated above the 'story' and above rhetoric or ornament; man was no more than a small part of the universe, not its centre (as implied in nineteenth-century novels). Borges later rejected all this, but it left its mark upon him at least in the sense that he is an anti-realist. He is an exquisite minor writer–minor only because his work lacks the robustness of experience and fails to move because it does so. But then for Borges life *is* escapism: art. In Borges's fascinating and teasing work his own suffering is rejected as being an indulgence. His best poetry (*Selected Poems 1923–1967*, tr. 1972) is about old Buenos Aires. In the thirties he wrote some stories, but was most active as editor and essayist: he was convinced that his inability to confront 'raw' experience had cut him off from creativity (but he did write detective stories under other names). Then came *Ficciones* (1944 rev. 1961; tr. *Fictions,* 1962). The 'fiction' is a short (usually very short) assertion–profoundly playful or parodic or astonishing–of the absolute primacy of the phenomenological: he seeks (ironically) to destroy the reader's confidence (which he knows to be inevitably in 'ordinary' reality) by drumming home the point that neither solipsism nor even absolute scepticism can actually be disproved. Therefore every human effort is a 'fiction'. Borges plays, magnificently, with various philosophical postulations. He knows that as author he is God and enjoys being God in this particular system. If Borges is minor because, ultimately, we miss the psychological in him, still, his enterprise is major, for he carries scepticism to its absolute extreme: he can and will do in his stories exactly what he likes. Hamlet writes Shakespeare, Céline (q.v.) wrote *The Imitation of Christ*, the order in which we read books, not their chronology, is primary. . . . *Labyrinths* (sel. tr. 1962), *El hacedor* (1960; tr. *Dreamtigers*, 1964). *El Aleph* (1949 rev. 1957; tr. 1970) has been translated with the collaboration of Borges himself and will be followed by similarly authoritative translations of all the works, which were collected in Spanish 1954–60. Borges's progressive blindness has undoubtedly influenced his attitude to life but it has not robbed him of his humour. He continues to write.

Bottrall, Ronald (1906) English poet, critic. The most shamefully neglected English poet of the last fifty years. He was of the Cambridge generation of Empson (q.v.), Raine (q.v.), Reeves (q.v.) and others, and was encouraged by the fairly judicious praise of Leavis (q.v.)–a fact which has, quite without reason, been used against him. He has been an academic, a member of the British Council and a diplomat (a fine irony, for his honest straight-speaking is as rare as it is famous). Of the Auden-Spender-MacNeice-Day-Lewis generation, he is beyond doubt the most rewarding poet. He has worked in America, Sweden, Japan, Finland, Brazil, Greece, Italy (where he now lives) and China; he has absorbed all these–and some other–literatures. His poetry is to be found in *Collected Poems* (1961), *Poems 1955–1973* (1975) and in *Against a Setting Sun*, his latest and most highly concentrated collection (now in preparation). Bottrall is not an easy poet: he has a number of distinct manners, ranging from the Blakean through the satirical to the loosely anecdotal; he prints his light verse–giving the uninitiated reader the impression of a great unevenness; he has had some difficulty in dealing with his fluency and metrical facility and is an allusive poet who does not mind his poems reflecting his reading. Although there are good things in *The Loosening* (1931) and the two other collections from the thirties, he has become a better poet with time (which is unusual): *Poems 1955–1973* is better than *Collected Poems*, and *Against a Setting Sun* is better than either. Although his poems are usually reviewed by *literati* who have only too evidently not read them, he has admirers (they include Anthony Burgess, q.v., G. S. Fraser, Robert Graves, q.v. and Charles Tomlinson, q.v.), and it was T. S. Eliot who told New Yorkers in 1932 that Bottrall, with Auden (q.v.), Spender (q.v.) and MacNeice (q.v.), was one of the four most important younger English poets . . . Although Bottrall does not think of Pound (q.v.) as one of the great poets of the century, he was at first influenced by him and particularly by 'Mauberley' and the early cantos. He was also influenced by Laura Riding (q.v.). Although he has great technical energy, humour and verve, Bottrall's poetry is essentially a defence against the rottenness of modern life, of which Pound first made him aware. One of the reasons why his poetry tends to be permeated with allusions to certain other poets is his gratitude towards them for being poets at all in an age of ruin and, as Graves put it in introducing one of Bottrall's collections, 'waste'. ('Why do we hazard that we are sane/When our world is smothered in nonsense . . . ?' he asks.) On the whole Bottrall is at his least effective when displaying his metrical (rather than rhythmical) facility. He is often at his best when telling a story (e.g. in 'Talking to the Ceiling', a long poem about his childhood), or when being meditative or straightforwardly lyrical. He is not a poet who produces great single lines (such as Empson does): one needs to read him through in order to understand him fully. One of the keys to his work is that he goes to the point in a manner to which most of us are unaccustomed. In Bottrall shock, the utmost candour and humour co-exist, and the result is a bewildering versatility: his poems may be bizarre, Blakean, anecdotal or cryptic ('The Ancient Enemies', for example, is as cryptic and as powerful as Vallejo, q.v.). But despite the difficulties his poetry presents, its failure to gain him the major reputation he deserves is one of the most puzzling of phenomena. He has written excellent criticism—on Pound and (in the *Times Literary Supplement*) on modern Italian and Scandinavian literature.

Bourne, George (ps. George Sturt) (1863–1927) English rural writer. He was first a teacher and then took over his family's wheelwright business in his native Surrey. His books on the supplanting of the old village ways were rightly taken up by the Leavis (q.v.) group; essentially, though refreshingly without political, economic or sociological sophistication, he examines the question of what Marx called 'alienation' and what Durkheim called 'anomie' (though not in urban settings). Where is job-satisfaction to come from in a technological age? His picture of the old ways is sometimes over-perfected; but it contains a kernel of truth. *Change in the Village* (1912); *The Wheelwright's Shop* (1923); *A Small Boy in the Sixties* (1927)–under his own name; *The Journals 1890–1902* (1941)–the complete MS is in the British Museum; *The Journals* (1967) is a fuller selection.

Bowen, Elizabeth (1899–1973) Irish (resident in England) fiction writer, who had true, though limited, distinction, but was not criticized enough–to her detriment–because of her literary connections. Like Virginia Woolf (q.v.), whose often saving gift for exploiting interior monologue she could not and did not try to emulate, she was a snob (but this is an over-crude term for a more complex attitude, one inherited from James as much as from her own aristocratic origins) who desperately wanted not to be. Her master was Henry James (q.v.), and she was much influenced by Virginia Woolf. She possessed some of James's capacity to reveal corruption and shared his meticulousness and sense of pity. Her second novel, *The Last September* (1929), may be seen as an over-melodramatic attempt to resolve her social problems (she was good on the wealthy upper class, but always failed not only with the lower classes but also with the poor), but as a portrait of the effect of the Irish 'troubles' on a sensitive landowner's daughter it is prophetic of her finest novel: *The Death of the Heart* (1938). This, the story of a young girl several times betrayed, is one of the major prose works of the thirties. *The Heat of the Day* (1949) reveals her weaknesses most clearly: resort to melodrama, unconsciously patronizing failure to understand the lower classes, lack of sociological subtlety or depth. Her many short stories (e.g. in *Look at All Those Roses*, 1941; *The Demon Lover*, 1945) can be too self-indulgently atmospheric but at their best display her considerable strengths: honesty, serious effort to overcome the limitations she rightly saw as damaging to her achievement, a capacity to convey a sense of erotic loneliness or despair in an apparently unruffled context of moral brutality and selfishness.

Bowles, Jane (1918–73) American fiction writer, playwright. Jane Bowles, who suffered for many years from atrocious health, was a highly original minor writer who deserves to be classed with Firbank (q.v.) because she made an achievement out of a slightness. Her work derives from Gertrude Stein (q.v.) but eschews the non-sense for an oddly-angled realism: what she observes she observes in a singularly meticulous, lucid manner. Her play *In the Summer House* (1953) is her most accessible work. Her writing is essentially a demonstration of the continuing existence of the utterly helpless, though she is not concerned with politics or social themes. *Collected Works* (1967).

Bowles, Paul (1910) American fiction writer, translator, composer. After studying music and meeting Gertrude Stein (q.v.), who advised him to abandon writing for music, in Paris, Bowles has spent most of his time abroad (mostly in Morocco and Ceylon). Although he is well known he has had comparatively little critical attention. He wrote a good deal of music (for film and theatre–and an opera in 1941) before devoting himself to writing. He married Jane Bowles (q.v.) in 1939. Bowles's earlier fiction 'existentializes' (*see* Sartre) Poe's Gothic in (mostly) African settings. His later novels, some tape-recorded from non-literate Moroccans, are superior, for they provide unique insights into mentalities of which the Western world has no knowledge: *A Life Full of Holes* (1964), *Love with a Few Hairs* (1966). As Walter Allen (q.v.) observed, the characters in the earlier novels have no value as human beings; Bowles has now rectified this. *Up Above the World* (1967), set in the Latin-American jungle, is his best wholly original novel.

Boye, Karin (1900–41) Swedish poet, fiction writer, editor (*Spektrum,* on whose editorial staff she was, was an important Swedish radical and modernist magazine–and publishing house–of the thirties), critic. Karin Boye is one of the foremost European poets of the century; but this has not been recognized. After publishing a precociously brilliant book of poems, *Moln* (1922), *Clouds,* and two more collections, she became associated, 1928–32, with the Barbusse-inspired 'Clartéist' group, which was both Marx- and Freud-oriented, but her own work, haunted by her complex erotic defeats and psychiatric uncertainties (she was a trained psychologist), is entirely original and, at its best, independent of the Christian, Freudian and quasi-Marxist phases through which, intellectually, she passed. She used the phrase 'drabbad av renhet' in one of her starkly candid poems, and this, *Struck Down by Purity,* is the title of her friend Margit Abenius's invaluable biography of her. She had something of Simone Weil (q.v.) in her: a dedication, a natural capacity to suffer for others. She was torn between (eventually non-Christian) religious certainty and political hope. But sexual purity was not an issue for Simone Weil (who was in any case exceedingly plain and wanted to look it: her radiance was never sexual); for Karin Boye each desperate erotic entanglement represented a sullying of her independence—and yet a necessary experience. She was unlucky and it was her last affair, together with her generally depressed state, that led her to walk into a winter forest to die alone. Her poetry combines extreme sensuousness with a strict and dedicated purity; at her best she is an expressionist 'nature poet' with affinities with the German Wilhelm Lehmann (1882–1968) but she is more intensely personal and feminine (though not in any cloying or 'male' sense). Of her four novels the underrated dystopia *Kallocain* (1940; tr. 1966), the name of a greenish drug dispensed to the citizens of a police state in order to force them to reveal their inner secrets (a brilliantly ambivalent symbol for the poetic urge) is the best; *För lite* (1936), *Too Little,* reveals the difficulties of the creative life at a more realistic level. The neglect of Karin Boye outside Scandinavia is not short of scandalous. Her works were collected 1948–50.

Boyle, Kay (1903) American fiction writer, critic. Kay Boyle, who is the widow of Baron Joseph von Franckenstein, spent thirty years in Europe, mostly in France, and is one of the few writers of her generation who did not treat it as, in John McCormick's words, an 'American suburb'. Much of her early fiction, influenced in style and manner by James (q.v.), deals with love threatened by 'culture shock' and disease (e.g. *Plagued By the Nightingale,* 1931), death or social ostracism (*Gentlemen, I Address You Privately,* 1933, is about inverts). Kay Boyle published poems in Jolas's *avant-garde* magazine *transition,* but she was never a truly modernist writer. Rather she grew up in an atmosphere in which impressionism and Gothicism still looked modern. The chief feature of her semi-autobiographical first novel, *Plagued By the Nightingale,* her best, is the way its youthful lyricism is modified by the facts of the situation with which it deals. Later, in novels as in her many volumes of short stories, this lyricism tended to excess. The best of her later novels is *Generation Without Farewell* (1960), which puts to excellent use her radicalism and her inside knowledge of the nuances of American-European relations (her first, early, marriage had been to a Frenchman). All in all she has not had the critical attention she merits and one wonders why the poetry of a woman who can acknowledge—and demonstrate—the simultaneous influences of Williams (q.v.) and Padraic Colum (1881–1972) has not been more widely read: *Collected Poems* (1962) is a selection. A selection of her best stories would make a substantial volume.

Brecht, Bertolt (1898–1956) German poet, playwright, amateur singer, novelist, dramatist. Born in Augsburg, Brecht began as a medical student and was a hospital orderly during 1918. By the age of twenty-two he had become a freelance writer. His second play, *Trommeln in der Nacht* (1922), *Drums in the Night*, gained him the Kleist prize. He worked in the theatre (notably with Carl Zuckmayer, q.v.) until 1933. Meanwhile (1926) he became converted to an always only apparent Marxism. From the advent of the Nazis he was in exile–in Prague, Vienna, Zurich, Denmark, Sweden and Finland; he visited Moscow in 1935 and clearly did not like it, but did not say so directly. From 1941 until 1948 he was in America, working in Hollywood (*Hangmen Also Die*) and elsewhere; in 1947 he gave a legendary performance at the Committee on Un-American Activities. Refused permission to enter West Germany he then settled in East Berlin and in 1948 the Berliner Ensemble was established under his (virtual) directorship. He got the Stalin Peace Prize in 1954, but his attitude towards the East German regime became increasingly ambiguous and bitter. He died after a heart-attack. Brecht was a great playwright, a greater poet, and an influential and important theatrical theorist. At rock-bottom Brecht was a lyric balladeer of genius, a lusty *polisson,* a happy celebrant of the socially outcast but vibrantly alive. But his passion for social justice, his intellectual gifts (of which he was impatient), the threat of fascism from 1923 and his own disapproval of his socially nihilistic tendencies thrust him into a Marxism that he reluctantly held on to throughout his life. His lyrical poetry quite transcends, although it contains, the conflicting elements in his personality; his dramatic work derives its tension from his conflicts; and–despite his own efforts as producer to undermine this aspect–is essentially a tragic dialectic between an inhuman Marxism seen as necessary to the future and a deeply felt compassion that is, to varying degrees, reinforced by his temperamental anarchism and zestful cynicism. He could never successfully suppress his distaste for authority and bureaucracy and knew very well that his theory of theatre (which, however, he regretted having outlined) could be used for ends other than those of hard-line communism. In a defiant poem of 1921 he wrote that he would be 'mistrustful, lazy and content' to the end, and there is a sense (allowing for the *épater le bourgeois* element) in which this remained true. Thus, he was throughout his life fascinated by Hašek's (q.v.) character and even wrote a play called *Schweyk im zweiten Weltkrieg* (1957), *Švejk in the Second World War*. He wrote more than forty plays, some of them adaptations (e.g. Marlowe's *Edward II*, Shakespeare's *Coriolanus*), of which the finest, perhaps, are *Mutter Courage und ihre Kinder* (1941), *Mother Courage and Her Children*, *Leben des Galilei* (1943), *The Life of Galileo*, *Der gute Mensch von Sezuan* (1943), *The Good Woman of Setzuan*, *Der Kaukasische Kreidekreis* (1949), *The Caucasian Chalk Circle*; *Die Dreigroschenoper* (1928), *The Threepenny Opera*, after Gay's *Beggars' Opera*, is a superb musical *tour de force* in which Brecht worked with Busoni's gifted pupil, Kurt Weill, as he did in *Aufstieg und Fall der Stadt Mahagonny* (1929), *The Rise and Fall of the Town of Mahagonny*. Brecht's theory of drama has been taken over-seriously by many American and European–though not so much by British–critics: it is inconsistent and its apolitical aspects had been anticipated, notably by the Russian Leonid Andreyev (1871–1919), Pirandello (q.v.) and Synge (q.v.). The theory rests on the belief that the play must arouse the spectator to wish to alter society; he called it 'anti-Aristotelian' and substituted, for his understanding of the Aristotelian key-term 'catharsis', the concept of *Verfremdung*–which simply meant that the content of the drama should be made to seem 'strange'. This was called 'epic theatre'. The audience were to be made critical, to examine the characters rather than to accept them, to reason rather than to feel. All this was no more than a reflection of modernist tendencies but obviously it could be used as a political implement. In his finest plays the theory functions as little more than an element of modernism, for Brecht was quite unable to toe any line for long; but in his propagandist plays, his most inferior though not least clever work, it is deliberately used as a political weapon. The best of these, almost certainly prompted by the Nazi threat that became immediately apparent with the rise of Hitler's fortunes in the 1930 elections, is *Die Massnahme* (1930), *The Measures Taken*. Four communist agitators are sent to China to incite a classically Marxist revolution. One of them–he is played alternately by each of the four actors–puts the others into danger by yielding to immediately charitable impulses, and so agrees to his own execution: this is Brecht the poet trying to commit suicide in favour of Brecht the Marxist. But the poet would not die. Mother Courage is supposed to be evil and Brecht struggled to make her so in his production; but her vitality shines through as a decidedly human quality. And so his later drama gains in strength because, in its cunning and, indeed, Švejkian way, it explores his own predicament. His compassion is never in doubt. This emerges in his poetry, where energy of language—and therefore of mystery—often takes charge. The influences on the poetry are evident: Rimbaud, Villon and (more oddly) the colloquial and proletarian element in Kipling (q.v.). The famous 'Mack the Knife', from *The Threepenny Opera,* combines Kipling with Švejk, but adds a new, sinister and disturbing note of aggression. Elsewhere Brecht resembles, but never imitates, Rimbaud—as in 'Ballade von den Abenteuern', 'Ballad of the Adventurers', where he speaks of one with 'a looted wreath in his matted hair', 'seeking in absinth seas', 'strolling through hells and lashed through paradises'. He could be satirical, roughly balladic, tenderly lyrical and 'Chinese' in manner—he was an admirer of Waley's (q.v.) translations from the Chinese: 'On my wall hangs a Japanese mask:/A gilded devil's face./Watching the swelled veins on its brow/I sympathize with how/Evil prostrates'. Even in his last unhappy years in East Germany, his plays enfeebled, looked at askance by a vicious regime, his money in Switzerland and his nationality Austrian, he did not lose his poetic gift and after the workers' uprising of 1953 wrote an unequivocally self-accusatory poem, 'Böser Morgen', 'A Bad Morning'. Much of his work remains locked up in archives; but the charge (made by Hannah Arendt) that he ever wrote sheerly party verse is false. He enjoyed sly equivocation as he enjoyed vivacious low life but he had no streak of the cruel in him and his work as a whole is as unmarred as that of Pirandello (q.v.) who, like him, utilized totalitarian cash to run a theatre. Almost all Brecht's plays are translated and much of his best poetry. There are several collected editions in German, notably *Gesammelte Werke* (1967), which has been edited by E. Hauptmann.

Breton, André (1896–1966) French surrealist, fiction and 'automatic' writer, poet, manifestoist. Breton is mainly important as the progenitor and tenacious upholder, until his death, of one of the most vital and long-lived movements in modern literature, but also as a prose writer (chiefly in *Nadja,* 1928; tr. 1963—and in *L'Amour fou,* 1937, *Mad Love*); his poetry is of little intrinsic value. Although surrealism is expressionist (in my special general sense: *see* Stadler) it grew immediately out of Freud (q.v.), who was half-shocked, half-amused, by it, dada (*see* Ball) and the futuristic, and other -istic, climate of French letters typified by Apollinaire (q.v.), whom Breton met and acknowledged. But it was Breton, 'the glass of water in the storm', both authoritarian and reconciler, who launched it and held it together. Breton studied medicine and psychiatry, and from 1915 served as a psychiatrist with the Army Medical Corps. In 1921 he met Freud in Vienna. Jacques Vaché (1896–1919), who committed suicide for a joke, was also an important personal influence on Breton, as, earlier, was Valéry (q.v.), who, with Gide (q.v.), Rivière and others gave his approval to the newly developing movement. One must take the inauguration of the movement *per se* as dating from October 1924, with the appearance of Breton's *Manifeste du surréalisme;* but its ancestry may be traced back into the remotest past—it stems, essentially, from the *irrational.* Naturally, the surrealists proclaimed themselves against literature and art altogether. Their greatest heroes were such as Jacques Rigaut (1899–1929) who condemned himself, in 1919, to die on a certain day in 1929, and duly carried out the sentence, or Arthur Cravan (1881–?), the boxer and stripteaser who disappeared in Mexico in 1920 after taking up the teaching of gymnastics. Actually, since most of them were compulsive writers, they sought truth in nonsense, in the gratuitous act (hence Gide's interest), in the phenomenological reality of the dream, in madness—and, of course, in baiting the bourgeoisie with its demonstrably false belief in rationality. The leap from this attitude to a politically revolutionary one was short, and was taken—though the degree of ideological commitment of each of the group gave rise to fierce quarrels. Aragon's (q.v.) and later Eluard's (q.v.) 'defection' to communism were but two of the more serious blows to Breton's own program, which rejected *political* activism—although he himself was in the communist party 1927–35, and was subsequently influenced by, and met, the exiled Trotsky. Useless, unless you are a polemicist, to attempt to define surrealism. Though an extreme aspect of expressionism, it absorbed the whole of 'modernity': the physics of Einstein, the discovery of the inexplicable sub-atomic world, the collapse of bourgeois values and both the violence and the reactive pacificism which this collapse inaugurated, the ferocious wildness of futurism (*see* Marinetti), the discovery of the subconscious—now made sovereign—the phenomenological experience of time. . . . Yet it was in itself a symptom, not a cure, a deliberate sickness rather than a treatment. Its influence was all-pervasive, reaching even to such comparatively 'traditionalist' English poets as

Graves (q.v.), who in the twenties was obsessed with the nonsensical, and in the thirties wrote such poems as 'The Terraced Valley'. It was also sheer fun, as the dada (over which Breton himself 'presided' between 1921 and 1924) that preceded it had been. It is still with us: 'il est partout', a critic has written. Our statesmen and our bureaucrats, the targets of the surrealists, believe they are awake, 'responsible'; but are they not actually in a violent surrealist dream? Surrealism was a movement of which most writers needed to be aware, but they passed through it. For if art is of any value at all then it must pit a *new* kind of coherence against the disguised surrealism of a world that has produced Stalinism, Nazism, economic ruin and all the other familiar ills. . . . This coherence must acknowledge the quotidian, 'clock-time' *and* the phenomenological (cf. Bergson, q.v.). Breton himself, as others, did have an answer outside the essentially superficial program—and this answer has proved of more value than the one resorted to by other surrealists: militant communism. 'The marvellous alone is beautiful', he wrote in the first manifesto, and in *Nadja* and occasionally elsewhere he sees the marvellous as a woman, the 'beginning of hope'. *Nadja*, significantly, is 'true' (although it has been disputed): Breton really did meet the strange woman Nadja, and in his account of his chance encounters with her he apprehends the marvellous. Woman, for him, is the key to the irrational. She is 'mad', hallucinated, shattering to others, absolutely living her dream, which is mysteriously connected with Breton's own apparently independent experience. Here indeed is a series of extreme 'epiphanies' (*see* Joyce). But the conflict in Breton is never resolved: *Nadja* reveals this failure at its most anguished and intense. For Breton was surrealist because intellectually he was convinced of the disorder, the entropic nature, of the cosmos; yet *Nadja* continuously searches for a secret coherence. Eventually the necessarily fluid, submissive, receptive surrealism in Breton hardened into a polemicism as pointlessly rigid as the bourgeois code against which he rebelled. The poetry is for the most part a foredoomed attempt to construct a totally anti-rational poetics: 'even in the freest of his poetry', writes Marcel Raymond, '[he] feels really at home only in prose'. Yet his project and his persistent efforts to keep his brand of surrealism alive are of extreme historical importance. His own work is full of contradictions rather than fruitful paradoxes, but his vain search for truth in love for woman contains invaluable masculine insights into her nature. *Selected Poems* (1969) contains English versions. *Les Champs magnétiques*

(1921), written with Philippe Soupault (1897)–expelled from the group in 1926 for acknowledging the value of literary activity!–is an important document in the history of 'automatic writing', a writing allegedly dictated by the subconscious (based on the Freudian principle of free association), and containing much bright, extraordinary imagery. There is still a surrealist group in France; but it is not influential or much heeded.

Bridges, Robert (1844–1930) English poet (-Laureate 1913), critic. Originally a doctor. This honest master of technique never achieved poetic power; his intelligence and love of experiment were too muted by an innate conformism. His essays on metre are important. His love poems are exquisitely feeble gentleman's exhortations; his descriptive anthology-pieces (e.g. 'London Snow') skilfully polite impressions. The effects of his influence on his friend Hopkins (q.v.) are debatable, though his presentation of him to the public is to his credit. *Poetical Works* (1953); *Collected Essays* (1927–36). For a useful introduction, capably putting forward the necessarily conservative case: John Sparrow's *Poetry and Prose* (1955).

Bridie, James (ps. O. H. Mavor) (1888–1951) Scottish playwright. He was a practising physician until the age of fifty. A late starter, but author of over fifty plays (not all published; there is no collected edition), Bridie was the first truly indigenous modern Scottish playwright (founder of the Glasgow Citizens' Theatre, 1942). He was ingenious, full of ideas, a master of stagecraft (though his construction is often criticized), but failed through lack of emotional substance and a tendency to whimsicality (the main Scottish fault). However, his theatrical achievements were many: *The Anatomist* (1932), on Burke and Hare, *Dr Angelus* (in *John Knox and Other Plays,* 1949)–a crime play, his best of all–and the comedy *Daphne Laureola* (1950), a perfect vehicle for Edith Evans. His more specifically Scots plays (e.g. *Mr Bolfry,* in *Plays for Plain People,* 1944) are too fey.

Brinnin, John Malcolm (1916) American poet, critic, biographer. As a poet Brinnin is versatile, making use of a number of recognizably 'modern' manners ranging from the tightly formal, 'metaphysical' to the neo-romanticism of Dylan Thomas (q.v.) (of whom his scarifying account, *Dylan Thomas in America,* 1955, is his best known book). His most successful poem is 'The Worm in the Whirling Cross', a religious meditation in which he disciplines his verbal excitement without diminishing it. *The Sorrows of Cold Stone* (1951); *Selected Poems* (1963).

Broch, Hermann (1886–1951) Austrian novelist. He began as a businessman; then gave this up to study science and philosophy. He was one of the most reluctant writers of the century but was finally forced to express himself imaginatively–though he questioned the value of fiction. His outlook was that we live in an age of 'no longer, not yet' (cf. Cardenal, q.v.). He could not believe in the Catholicism which tempted him, but felt mankind to be doomed without religion. His masterpiece is *Der Tod des Vergil* (1945; tr. *The Death of Vergil*, 1946), a novel which is both important and yet–undoubtedly–very difficult to read. It reflects his concerns with the value of art, the necessity of employing phenomenological technique (at the end he describes the transition of Vergil from life into death) and tormented social conscience. He also wrote *Die Schlafwandler* (1931–2; tr. *The Sleepwalkers*, 1932) and other fiction, drama and poetry. He was imprisoned by the Nazis in 1938, but was able to emigrate to America. He died in poverty in a cold-water flat.

Brooke, Rupert (1887–1915) English poet, critic. He has become the apotheosis of Georgianism, and it is appropriate, though unfair, to discuss this phenomenon under his name. Sir Edward Marsh invented the term 'Georgian' with the first of his anthologies *Georgian Poetry 1911–1912* (1912; further instalments appeared in 1915, 1917, 1919, 1922). Marsh was a pleasant and cultured man of no very great critical discernment; he also had a penchant for handsome young men (e.g. Ivor Novello), and Brooke was the handsomest and most genuinely charming of his generation–he also attracted Henry James (q.v.), who was even more sentimental about him than about Walpole (q.v.). By 'Georgian' Marsh meant nothing more specific than that something he thought new and exciting was happening in English poetry: that Edwardian post-Victorianism was vanishing. This, as it happens, was true: imagism (*see* Pound) had begun to develop (some 'imagists' appeared in Marsh's series of anthologies), and there were already–in the work of, for example, Monro (q.v.)–the seeds of a new approach. Further, Brooke himself had (at the very least) a freshness that the most admired poets of 1911 entirely lacked. The mantle of Edwardian dullness was being thrown off. There was never a Georgian manifesto, or a real Georgian coterie, and many good poets have been called Georgian either because they lived at a certain time or appeared in Marsh's anthologies. So the term is now meaningless except in one useful sense. Since the movement itself, inasmuch as it ever existed, was amorphous, sentimental, uncritically motivated, we may fairly reserve 'Georgian' as a pejorative term for inadequate post-Victorianism, where escapist fancy –always conservative–is used in an attempt to achieve a valid response to the times. Thus Georgianism is still with us, either as the absurdly 'poetical' or, more often, as the bathetic structure underlying much verse that is tricked out to look modern. The more complex history of the word and of the 'movement' may be traced in R. Ross's *The Georgian Revolt* (1965). But my proposed use of the term (essentially an attempt to give more precision to a widespread one) is justified: by 1918 it had been made clear that as an attempt to develop an adequate response to a new set of conditions, it had failed. The Georgian element fails in Graves (q.v.), Sassoon (q.v.), Blunden (q.v.), De La Mare (q.v.), W. H. Davies (q.v.), Edward Thomas (q.v.), but it is as pointless to denigrate them as 'Georgians' as it is to denigrate Wordsworth for beginning by writing in a late-Augustan vein. . . . Georgianism is still a vice in English (less in American) poetry, and no amount of spurious modernism can remove the problems it presents: we have yet to overcome these. As to Brooke himself–he has incurred blame for which he is hardly responsible. There are three views: that he was a potentially great poet; that he would have become a good 'modern' poet (rather of the type of Graves, q.v., than of Eliot, q.v.); that he represented all that was most disgusting (sentimentality, false patriotism, fake pastoralism) in the pre-1914 age. None of these is correct. But when Brooke died on a hospital ship on his way to the Dardanelles–before seeing action–a promising life was cut short. That he would ever have been a 'great' poet is untenable. But his attitude to the war was that of the young Graves (to whom he seemed original in 1912), Sassoon (q.v.), Péguy (q.v.), Max Weber, Durkheim. . . . He was a typical youth of his generation, but more intelligent than most, and a member of the Fabian Society–he might well have been a socialist prime minister, and, in politics, he might even have changed the course of history. Certain of his poems have a wit and lightness of touch, but his love poetry has dated, his 'Grantchester' is feeble mock-pastoral (emphatically not saved, as

G. S. Fraser has claimed, 'by a delicately poised wit and fantasy'), his patriotic verse, as poetry, is specious. His appreciation of the Elizabethan dramatists and of Donne was not anticipatory of Eliot's but was part of an academic reappraisal (Chambers, Grierson, Bullen and others) that had begun before he went up to Cambridge. He was, however, tolerant and curious: he was interested in Pound's modernism and would have appreciated modern poetry. But there is no evidence that he would have had the linguistic resources to express his recognition of the real nature of the war in his poetry, which is still at its best Georgianism, but hardly more. *Collected Poems* (1952); *Prose* (1956).

Brooks, Cleanth (1906) American critic. A number of writers might be chosen as appropriate representatives of the new criticism. But Brooks is perhaps most appropriate because although he is non-creative (cf. Tate, q.v., Ransom, q.v., Warren, q.v., who are creative), he is not as monstrously in opposition to creation as Wimsatt (q.v.). His own close criticism in *Modern Poetry and the Tradition* (1939) and *The Well-Wrought Urn* (1947) is markedly eclectic and useful. His textbooks, with Warren, on poetry and fiction have been influential in sending students to the texts; yet, as he demonstrates in *William Faulkner* (1963), he is not unaware of social or political problems. The term 'new criticism' is not exactly definable; it came into general currency, though it had been employed previously in a different connection, when Ransom published *The New Criticism* (1941). This in fact criticized Richards, Empson (q.v.), Eliot (q.v.) and Winters (q.v.) and postulated the need for a new 'ontological' critic who did not yet exist. Brooks was not involved–all the more reason here, then, for treating him as representative. For the term implies, essentially, a criticism that will treat literature *as* literature: as organized language. Thus poetic theory became paradigmatic, since the poem may so much more easily be treated as an organic whole than fiction or an entire *oeuvre*. It is more useful to see the new criticism as consisting of various ways of looking at literature as a special kind of language than to try to define it exactly. Eliot concentrated on an objective approach; Richards tried to formulate a *scientific* approach to poetry, which he regarded as non-scientific but *emotive* (and explicable); Empson demonstrated that the emotive effects of poetry arose from complexities inherent in language itself. Brooks's own contributions included the introduction of such important concepts as *paradox* and the *heresy of paraphrase*. He showed, in effect, that poetry of direct statement, of simplicity, which is moving and affecting (e.g. Wordsworth–his own notable example; Blake), actually rests on types of paradox. The attack on paraphrase may have been over-ingenious, confused and over-theoretical, but it did show (to put it at its simplest) that a poem cannot be exactly rendered in prose. After the slackness of the criticism of the early part of this century the new criticism was essential, though it could often degenerate into an over-academic aridity. Its insistence on the primacy of the text should persist and it has itself contributed to the subsequent attacks (notably by the neo-Aristotelian, 'Chicago School') made on it.

Brophy, Brigid (1929) Irish (resident in England) novelist, critic, journalist. An odd mixture of Shavian rationalist castigator of folly, polemicist, optimist, defender of animals' rights and (concealed) modernist, Brigid Brophy's greatest achievement to date is her subtle, lively defence of fiction in the person of Ronald Firbank: *Prancing Novelist* (1973). In her best novel, *The Snow Ball* (1964), the social settings are observed with an acute satirical humour. Sometimes operating under the mask of a virago, she is democratic, hard-working and useful to most socially harmless minorities.

Buber, Martin (1878–1965) Austrian-Jewish thinker, born in Vienna, who prophetically recognized the fundamental (and, very broadly speaking, existentialist) theme of the best modern literature: how to realize religious impulses without surrendering to dogma or rhetoric. He had contacts with almost every Austrian and German writer of importance. He left Germany in 1938 for Jerusalem, where he was disliked by orthodox Jews; his work had previously been influential among theologians, but misunderstood. He wrote many books; the classic is *Ich und Du* (1923; authoritative tr. *I and Thou,* 1973). Buber favoured a this-worldly type of Judaism, Hasidism (cf. Singer, q.v.), and his 'Thou' is really a non-theological concept: God, whatever 'God' may be, does exist, but could only be discovered in totally naked dialogue between people when they are completely 'opened up'. The density of Buber's prose, which is sometimes impenetrable, may make him seem to be a mystic but his message–anguished though it is–is not mystical. It heals the breach between atheist existentialism (*see* Sartre) and the Christian existentialism of such as Gabriel Marcel, between rationalism and faith, and it heals even the 'Cartesian split'. Buber is a religious humanist who will never offer comfort, who agonizes, who sees that undiscovered love is 'God' (not, in the pious cliché, God love); his 'Du' was his wife. . . . 'When *Thou* is said, the speaker has for his object no thing. For where there is one thing there is another. Every *It* is bounded by other *Its; It* exists only because it is bounded by other *Its.* But when *Thou* is said, there is no thing and so there are no bounds. . . . As experience, the world belongs to the . . . *I–It* . . . *I–Thou* creates the world of relation. . . . The act [of artistic creation] involves a sacrifice and a gamble. . . . The work does not suffer one . . . to turn . . . and relax in the world of *It:* but it commands. . . . the exalted melancholy of our fate is that every *Thou* . . . must become an *It*'. *Ich und Du* and its successors, together with his demolition of the Pauline pseudo-Christian pretensions, amount to a huge achievement; his relevance to the work of almost every major writer of the century and to the historical situation he confronts is indisputable. His work casts brilliant, even if unspecific, light on the present literary predicament.

Bukowski, Charles (1920) German-born American poet and prose writer. Bukowski is an extreme representative of the anarchic, individualist element in modern American literature. He is, says an admirer, 'explosive gas', who 'drinks and brawls as wildly as ever'. His aim is to force 'the hidden psychopath in us back to reality'. What is interesting about Bukowski, therefore, is the relative mildness of his verse and prose which might well have been jotted down by any half-cut middlebrow. But his titles are fun: *Confessions of a Man Insane Enough to Live With Beasts* (1965); *All the Assholes in the World and Mine* (1966); *Poem Written Before Jumping out of an 8-story Window* (1968); *Notes of a Dirty Old Man* (1969).

Bulgakov, Mikhail (1891–1940) Russian dramatist and fiction writer in whom a new interest, outside Russia, has developed in the seventies. He was not a reactionary, but he was a natural dissident, and his sympathetic treatment of White Russians and his satires on Soviet bureaucracy brought him into disrepute. His works remained unpublished for many years. His chief themes, often expressed in a form which owes much to Gogol, are the nature of the opposition to Bolshevism and (later) the artist in subjugation to the ignorant (socialist-realist) bureaucrat. He was a kind of magic realist in reverse; Zamyatin (q.v.)

well described his method as 'fantasy rooted in actual life, rapid, cinematic succession of scenes'. The play, based on the novel *Belaya gvvardiya* (1925), *The White Guard, Dni Turbinykh* (1926; tr. *Days of the Turbines* in *Six Soviet Plays*, 1935), is about White Russians. *Beg* (1936), *Flight*, performed in 1927, is on the same theme. His unpleasant experiences of being produced by the director Stanislavsky at the Moscow Arts Theatre provided him with the theme for the unfinished novel *Cherny sneg* (tr. *Black Snow*, 1968). He wrote a play on his favourite author, *Molière* (1936), as well as a superb biography of him (1962). His masterpiece is the novel *Master i Margarita* (1966–7; tr. *The Master and Margarita*, 1968), a multi-layered piece of 'realist magic' about two critics, Berlioz and Bezdomnyi, and the devil, Pilate, Christ and the crucifixion—all in Moscow. Other works now translated include *Sobacheye Serdste* (tr. *Heart of a Dog*, 1968), another fantasy, and *Diary of a Country Doctor* (tr. 1975)—Bulgakov was a qualified doctor. These are fictionalized autobiographical sketches in the well-established Russian style. There is also a great deal of straightforwardly autobiographical material not yet translated. Bulgakov is one of the most interesting of writers to survive (one wonders how he did it) the horrors of the earlier Stalin years. His fictional procedures are among the most original of his time.

Bunin, Ivan (1870–1953) Russian fiction writer, poet. Nobel Prize 1933. Bunin is a little unlucky to be known only for *The Gentleman from San Francisco* (tr. 1922; 1934), a collection in which D. H. Lawrence (q.v.) had a hand. For though this is an original (title) story, Bunin wrote much other good prose—and poetry. As is always remarked, Bunin is unusual in twentieth-century Russian literature in that he belongs to the realist tradition of the nineteenth century (as practised, for example, by Tolstoy and Chekhov, whom he knew). But he did not simply perpetuate this tendency: he developed and adapted it to produce a precise, evocative, nostalgic melancholy prose that is quite unlike anyone else's, especially in its power to evoke mood. Though he had been associated with Gorky (q.v.) and his group in the early years of the century he rejected Bolshevism and lived in France from 1919 until his death. Only recently has he been 'rehabilitated' in the Soviet Union. As a poet he entirely ignored the symbolist movement and wrote tender descriptive lyrics, rather in the tradition of Fet, which afford the key to his later poetic prose. His theme is almost invariably the beauty and the transience of love; all is seen as in a mist or dying away, vanishing–'in deserted museums the gods of Homer were getting cold and bored'; the great consolation is nature. In the prose a brutal and critical realism is deliberately tempered by an intensely aesthetic style (sometimes this becomes intolerably mannered) and by an innate romanticism. His main theme (e.g. 'The Gentleman from San Francisco'), that death is appalling and yet meaningless, seems trite but his best prose does convey a powerful and oppressive sense of this paradox. The love-death theme is present in his best writing: he remained obsessed with the decay of the Russian rural life of the latter part of the nineteenth century and continued to study it beneath an exquisite mask of objectivity, coldness and aloofness. His masterpiece is the unfinished *Zhizh Arseneva* (1928–33), *The Life of Arsenev,* fictionalized autobiography of which only the first part has been translated: *The Well of Days* (1933; 1946). There are numerous other translations, including the novel *Derevnya* (1910; tr. *The Village,* 1923), his most socially critical account of peasant life, *The Dreams of Chang* (1924), exotic stories–some based on his Oriental travels–dating from his period in Russia, the love-story *Mitina Lyubov* (1924–5; tr. *Mitya's Love,* 1926)–and more stories in *The Elaghin Affair* (1935) and *Dark Avenue* (1949). Bunin's Nobel award, for which he worked as hard as Quasimodo (q.v.) was to do twenty-six years later, was the subject of much controversy; but he is a unique writer.

Bunting, Basil (1900) English (Northumberland) poet who was virtually ignored–except by Ezra Pound (q.v.)–until 1965, when *Loquitur* was published; this added to the now rare *Poems* (1950), published in Texas, which passed unnoticed. Since then Bunting has become the centre of a small, appreciative cult, and has published *Briggflatts* (1966), a relatively long poem, and *Collected Poems* (1968). He was for a time Ford's (q.v.) helper on *The Transatlantic Review* in Paris; but he has spent most of his life (some of it in Persia) in non-literary occupations and entirely away from coteries. Read (q.v.), Tomlinson (q.v.), MacDiarmid (q.v.), Creeley (q.v.) are among his admirers. Although more appreciated in America than in England, and himself an admirer of Pound and Zukofsky (q.v.), Bunting is a very English poet; he is also an original one, both in his integrity and in his refusal to try to be more than the minor which he calls himself. Some of the major influences on him have been Wordsworth, the dialect of his native

Northumberland, his early discipleship to Pound, his knowledge of music (he has been a professional music critic), his sense of Arabic, Latin and Greek classical poetry. Bunting has in common with American poets such as Olson (q.v.)–his gentleness contrasts sharply with the latter's largely self-destructive aggressiveness–and Williams (q.v.) a feeling for quantity (duration) in the English language; but he is not dogmatic, and would not seek to deny the existence of accent. Poems for him are 'dead on the page' unless they have a living voice. His poetry, every aspect of which is unobtrusive, combines regionalism, learning and much lyrical feeling of a deliberately unsensational sort. He can be exquisitely moving and the more so because of his heroic modesty. Bunting is special, but in his case it is because he does not try to be, which is most unusual in any writer and more so in a poet.

Burgess, Anthony (ps. John Anthony Burgess Wilson) (1917) English novelist, critic, journalist, translator. A late starter (1956), he has become the most prolific as well as most gifted and versatile novelist of his generation. Not one member of it approaches his fluency, energy, inventiveness, effrontery. This has led, inevitably, to unevenness within his *oeuvre* and within single books. *Nothing Like the Sun* (1964) is a brilliant fictional reconstruction of the life of Shakespeare and its daring is a positive virtue (it seems to be based, and for many good reasons, on Fripp's rather than Chambers's biography); but some important episodes are marred by haste–as, in the recent, extraordinarily complex *Napoleon Symphony* (1974), sometimes the writing fails to do justice to the fantastically treated theme of vulgar, erotic ambition in possession of absolute power. Burgess is an expert musician (and composer) and here he models his tragi-comic life of the ridiculously vulnerable emperor on Beethoven's *Eroica* symphony (with far-reaching implications, in view of the history of Beethoven's attitude to Napoleon). As in other of Burgess's increasingly sophisticated novels, such as *MF* (1971), the dazzling (but in no sense exhibitionistic) use of modernist techniques is somewhat undermined by an almost novellettish kind of dialogue. However, Burgess, though a devotee and splendid interpreter of Joyce (q.v.), has a nostalgia for the past and even for the old 'realism', though he knows this to be totally inadequate. To some extent, then, his frantic prolificity–and this specific fault–reflect not only a nicely old-fashioned gusto and relish for enjoying his work, but also a despair. One should not underrate his relatively sober beginning or its significance for his work as a whole: *The Malayan Trilogy* (1956–9). This is a painful account of how inhumanity and injustice can ruin the old, and is at one level a sustained meditation on the whole subject of social change. Here Burgess is in the half-mellow, half-pained Tory (no allusion whatever to any government of our century is intended) tradition of Johnson, Disraeli, Ford Madox Ford (q.v.), the expatriate Conrad (q.v.), Anthony Powell (q.v.). But, born later than them, he has increasingly turned to 'elephantine fun', the comic, the celebration of the human and the ludicrous, even within the husk of evil (*Napoleon Symphony*), or to the semi-mock symbolic (*The Eve of St Venus,* 1964), or to the parodic spy-SF (*Tremor of Intent,* 1969). His great book, his *Parade's End* (see Ford), is yet to come–if, now, such a book can come from anyone at all. For sheer intelligence, learning, inventiveness, imaginative capacity, writer's professional cunning–no English novelist comes near him. This leads us to expect from him, perhaps, more than he or anyone else can give. Among his many other novels *Honey For the Bears* (1963) is especially worthy of attention. *Clockwork Orange* (1962) is a relatively minor dystopia. *Urgent Copy* (1968) collects reviews.

Burke, Kenneth (1897) American literary and music critic, fiction writer, poet. Burke resembles Empson (q.v.) in that he combines brilliance and breadth of critical perception with frequently poor performance, but where Empson is recondite, Burke tends to be rhetorically abstruse. His approach, influenced but not dominated by Marxist theory, is based on the true psychological status of the literary text. He is thus very important. 'He has', wrote Stanley Edgar Hyman in an admirable summary, 'developed the concepts of *form as the psychology of the audience,* of *symbolic action* for the poem-poet relation and *rhetoric* for the poem-audience relation. . . . [He changes] his terms ceaselessly while his preoccupations remain constant. . . .' In Burke's criticism we have continual discussion of texts as living objects for both writer and reader, both of whom employ 'strategies' to deal with situations. He can also be an excellent close critic. Burke is indispensable because of his recognition that literature actually comes from and works, like a yeast, within the texture of 'life'. But his very width of scope–'the main ideal of criticism . . . is to use all there is to use'–has involved him, somewhat ironically, in an *un*realistic neglect of the 'evaluative' factor in criticism. None the less, Burke is the most rewarding English-language critic of this century and the serious reader needs to know his way around his books. Sorting out one's attitude to Burke is an exciting matter. The major books are: *Counter-Statement* (1931 rev. 1953); *Attitudes Towards History* (1937); *The Philosophy of Literary Form* (1941), the key work; *A Grammar of Motives* (1945); *Language as Symbolic Form* (1966). His poetry is surprisingly ineffective, and reflects his main weakness (*Collected Poems,* 1968); but the prose in *The White Oxen* (1924) and *Toward a Better Life* (1932) is intricate and fascinating.

Burroughs, William (1914) American fiction writer. He has been described by Eric Mottram as 'undoubtedly a major force in 20th-century literature', but this is a grotesque overestimate. Burroughs's first book, *Junkie* (1953), published under the name of William Lee, is his best; it is a straightforward account of what it is like to be a drug-addict and is one of the better books on this popular subject. Burroughs's subsequent work may most conveniently be discussed in terms of Mottram's rapturous claims for it. *The Naked Lunch* (1959), *The Soft Machine* (1961 rev. 1968), *The Ticket That Exploded* (1962) and *Nova Express* (1964) 'extend certain methods of Joyce, Gertrude Stein [q.v.] and dada [*see* Ball] into a new prose', writes Mottram. The experimental form of this tetralogy is important because it 'extend[s] 20th-century fictional innovations into a more thorough expressionist medium'; it is also a 'radical and cosmically pessimistic analysis of [Burroughs's] vision of the Death of God and the universe given over to the licence of uncontrolled technological power groups'. Burroughs's methods, none of which is new, are simply various aleatory devices for stimulating him into making surreal connections. He combines narrative by himself (he is obsessed with hanging and its famous physiological effects, with sodomy, with police action, with violence, with 'mind-extending' drugs and with science-fiction ideas) with other material by 'cut-up', 'fold-in' and other permutational methods, and then rewrites. These methods are perfectly acceptable but they 'extend' nothing because, fundamentally, Burroughs has no coherent imaginative 'vision' of anything. He relies on his aleatory procedures to give, first himself, and then others, the illusion that he possesses linguistic power. He has experimented with drugs; he has also soaked in 'orgone energy' through sitting in a Reichian (q.v.) box, and shown interest in 'scientology', once called 'Dianetics'. These and other such activities, together with pronouncements made in interviews, offer a clue as to the nature of Burroughs's quality. He is a spoiled child, mildly funny when dealing with the most obvious deficiencies of the modern world, but mostly an exploiter of his own obsessions with homosexuality, violence and policemen. His prose style, where one can get at it, is undistinguished. If his plan for the salvation of humanity—an all-male test-tube community—is serious then he is himself an authoritarian. But nothing about him is serious: his 'vision', although sick and loveless, is a pathetic reconstruction of his own experiences under drugs.

Butor, Michel (1926) French novelist, critic, writer, poet. He is associated with the *nouveau roman* school (*see* Robbe-Grillet), but his work transcends the category in a way that Robbe-Grillet's does not. Unlike Robbe-Grillet he is, in philosophical terms, Kantian as well as phenomenological: he is continually seeking meaning, hidden order; he even confesses to want to discover order so that he might help to teach it to humanity. He was deeply influenced by one of his teachers, Gaston Bachelard (q.v.). He began as a confused poet and has for some time now been trying to create, perhaps ill-advisedly, a new kind of poetry. He was a teacher in various countries, including England (Manchester), before he emerged as a writer, and it is clear from his first novel, *Passage de Milan* (1954) that he had read widely: the title puns on the name of an imagined alley in Paris where his characters live, on the Italian city, and on the kite (*milan*). This is a variation on a unanimistic (*see* Romains) theme: the life of people in a block of flats and the currents that pass between them. *L'Emploi du temps* (1956; tr. *Passing Time*, 1960) is set in Manchester ('Bleston') and is the diary of a Frenchman trying to find himself amidst the stiflingness of the industrial city (Butor was born near Lille, a veritable Manchester of France). It is clear from this that Butor was already attempting to trace the hidden nature of reality, even though he simultaneously questions the form and validity of the novel. *La Modification* (1957; tr. *Second Thoughts*, in USA *A Change of Heart*, 1958) was the *nouveau roman*'s first popular success; the narration is in the second person singular—the veteran Fleming Herman Teirlinck (1879–1969) had published a novel, his last, employing the same technique just two years earlier. This is a study of the development of a tragic self-awareness in a man who is situated, between wife and mistress, in a position of 'bad faith' (Sartre has influenced Butor and each has praised the other). *Degrés* (1960; tr. *Degrees*, 1962) is a more complex study, a dissection of a *lycée*. Since then Butor has become increasingly experimental and has in particular exploited alinear and typographical possibilities in books such as *Mobile* (1963), an accurate presentation of American society that must not, however, be read in the order in which it is presented. To impose a chronology on the reader is of course a tyranny but so is to force the reader to make his own way. . . . *Mobile,* a 'poem' rather than a novel, is not as informative or as powerful a work as it might be and demonstrates the risk Butor takes in his admirably principled project. One watches Butor drifting into hyperexperimentalism with a certain dismay: it is all excellent and intelligent criticism, of course, and accounts of it are valuable, but it lacks the vitality of literature and the optimistic Butor seems to be retreating from his sense of other people in the interests of creating a kind of futurological literature. *Histoire extraordinaire* (1961; tr. 1969) is revealing criticism.

Buzzati, Dino (1906–72) Italian fiction writer, dramatist, art critic and journalist. A versatile, always experimental writer, and a quite outstandingly independent journalist (for *Corriere de la sera*), Buzzati wrote at least two minor masterpieces: *La famosa invasione degli orsi in Sicilia* (1945), *The Famous Invasion of Sicily by the Bears,* a tale for children and their parents, and *Il deserto dei Tartari* (1940; tr. *The Tartar Steppe,* 1952), one of those novels that the existence of fascist censorship actually made possible: its necessary lack of explicitness is exactly what gives it its ironic power. Kafka (q.v.) influenced him, and this is perhaps never wholly an advantage (though Lukáks did remark, when imprisoned after the 1956 revolution in Hungary, 'so Kafka was a realist after all'); but he assimilated and exploited this more fruitfully than any other European writer. Even where he fails, he is consistently intelligent and entertaining. At the time of his death he was showing signs of a new lease of creative energy. There is now an excellent selection from all his works, including *Il deserto dei Tartari: Romanzi e racconti* (1975).

C

Caldwell, Erskine (1903) American fiction writer most of whose best work is early and deals with the squalid and degenerate world of Georgian 'poor whites' and Negroes. His method, rather like Algren's (q.v.), is straightforward, simple reportage; but he has a cunning eye for what is both funny and sexually titillating in his bleak and depressing material; none the less, he has a humane outlook. Before becoming a writer he worked as mill-hand, cotton-picker, seaman and in other such occupations. He is a prolific writer who has not really developed; but as late as 1967 he produced in *Miss Mamma Aimee* one of his best and funniest books: its 'Gothic' is shockingly real and casts some shadow over the achievement of Purdy, Capote (q.v.) and other such writers younger than Caldwell. Apart from his most famous books—*Tobacco Road* (1932), which ran for seven years in its dramatic form, *God's Little Acre* (1933), *Georgia Boy* (1943)—attention should be given to *Journeyman* (1935), *Close to Home* (1962) and to some of the stories in *Complete Short Stories* (1953), especially to 'Kneel to the Rising Sun', title story, about a lynching, of a 1935 collection. Caldwell's method is deliberately crude but his selective capacity, his humour, his humanity and his sociological sense often combine to make him into a good writer. He is brilliantly discussed by Burke (q.v.) in *The Philosophy of Literary Form*.

Callaghan, Morley (1903) Canadian novelist, short-story writer and memoirist whose fictional work has not received the international attention it deserves. *That Summer in Paris* (1963), with its revealing portraits of Hemingway (q.v.), Stein (q.v.) and others, was well reviewed outside Canada but his fiction remains largely unread. As a Roman Catholic novelist he is in the class of Greene (q.v.) and his Canadian backgrounds in no way distract the non-Canadian reader. Supposed to have been a disciple of Hemingway's (q.v.), the latter only approached his quality in some short stories and in *Fiesta.* Like Greene, but employing a more laconic and non-lyrical style, he is above all passionately concerned with the painful moral ambiguity of man's existence—and his best novels and short stories (*Stories,* 1959) live up to this ambitious theme: Edmund Wilson's (q.v.) comparison of him to Dostoievski is not far-fetched—and is made less so by his neglect in America and Great Britain. His first important novel, *Such is My Beloved* (1934), is about a priest who tries to redeem two prostitutes and destroys himself in the process. Callaghan deals with crime, with relationships between white and Negro in Montreal (*The Loved and the Lost,* 1951) and, chiefly, with sexual involvements—which he sees as the tormented heart of human ambiguity, and whose seemingly inextricable elements of love and lust he sensitively and compassionately attempts to separate (e.g. *A Passion in Rome,* 1961, the most elaborately symbolic of his novels). Callaghan certainly has a place in the difficult and important modern Catholic tradition (cf. Greene, q.v., Bernanos, q.v., Jouhandeau, q.v., Green, q.v., Mauriac, q.v., Waugh, q.v.) and it is high time that this was properly assessed.

Calvino, Italo (1923) Italian novelist; born in Cuba, lives in Paris. He began as a so-called neo-realist (*see* Pavese), with a novel about the Resistance seen from the eyes of a young boy: *Il sentiero dei nidi di ragno* (1947; tr. *The Path to the Nest of Spiders,* 1956). He later became influenced by the eighteenth-century French *conte* and produced the three tales collected as *I nostri antenati* (1960), *Our Forefathers:* all separately translated into English (e.g. *The Cloven Viscount,* tr. 1962). This was his most inventive phase; later novels are ironically set at a cosmic level and demonstrate the influence upon him of Italian fables: in these (e.g. *Le cosmicomiche,* 1965; tr. *Cosmicomics,* 1969) elegance is sometimes achieved at the expense of substance. But he remains an important and intelligent novelist of great potential.

Cameron, Norman (1905–53) Scottish (mostly resident in England) poet, translator (e.g. Rimbaud, Villon, *Candide*). Cameron was at Oxford with Auden (q.v.), who admired his poetry, but this did not receive much attention until some ten years ago. He suffered from high blood-pressure, which led to his early death. Grigson (q.v.) published him in *New Verse,* and he was associated with Graves (q.v.) and Laura Riding (q.v.); he spent some time in Mallorca in the thirties. He distrusted but was fascinated by Laura Riding's ideas and by her insistence on absolute dedication to poetry. (He had formed his lucid, metaphysical, often humorous style, which did not change, before he met Graves and Riding.) Although he usually held a job there was always a poem clicking over at the back of his mind. Yet he was not prolific and the *Collected Poems* (1957) contains not many more than fifty poems: he knew his own work off by heart and what he rejected he would not write down. To Graves, then dedicated apostle of Laura Riding's prescriptions, he characteristically wrote: 'Forgive me, Sire, for cheating your intent,/That I, who should command a regiment,/Do amble amiably here, O God,/One of the neat ones in your awkward squad.' At the end of his life, feeling mentally lost and weak, he tried psychoanalysis and then, when this failed, became a Roman Catholic: this was not, perhaps, for 'religious' but for 'personal' reasons—but he devoted himself to mastery of the dogma with typical Calvinist rigour. Graves wrote him a savage little poem in French (unpublished) on the subject; and others of his friends were somewhat puzzled and even distressed. He lost the energy to write further poems. He is an important minor poet, anti-romantic in mood and diction, very conscientious about exactly communicating his meaning, ironic and detached in his attitude. All this hid and modified a fiercely romantic nature, a deep, puzzled unhappiness, and a sense of failure. He knew almost everyone in the literary world and was respected by them. He was a 'pub man', but he also, at any rate at certain periods, had a 'secret life', when he would squander himself in despair. His best poems, such as 'A Winter House' (the title of his first, 1935, collection), deal with the (partially erotic) sources of the anguish he concealed so well in his life: this is imaginative, profound, dense in feeling and extremely moving. In this category may be included, among others, 'Nunc Scio Quid Sit Amor', 'The Successor' (less perfectly realized in terms of language), 'All Things Ill Done', and 'The Wanton's Death' (about a sort of triangle that developed between himself and Graves and Laura Riding). Despite his slender output and his absolute trust in the old forms, he is one of the most rewarding and pure poets of his generation.

Campana, Dino (1885–1932) Italian poet. Campana at his best—in some fifteen poems—is hardly surpassed in twentieth-century poetry. He was mad—his disease was diagnosed as *dementia praecox*, the old name for schizophrenia, but it seems likely that a more modern diagnosis would be manic-depressive. Until 1918, when he entered the mental hospital at Badia a Settimo (Florence) where he died without writing any more poetry, he led a wandering existence, travelling in Russia, South America, Scandinavia and elsewhere, working at all kinds of jobs (cop, fireman, bouncer, triangle-player, soldier) and spending periods in prison and in mental hospitals. He never finished his education but remained obsessed with the notion of qualifying in chemistry. Associated with the group around the important Florentine weekly *La Voce* (*Voice*), he published only two books in his lifetime: *Canti orfici* (1914) and an edited reissue of the same collection, with additions, in 1928; the most convenient modern edition, from Mondadori, has the same title (1972). Not long before his final collapse he fell despairingly in love with the poet Sybilla Aleramo (ps. Rina Faccio, 1876–1960), who later became a notable antagonist of the fascist regime; their correspondence (*Lettere*) was published in 1958. He is most usually described as an Italian Rimbaud and inasmuch as he modelled himself on Rimbaud and indulged in total disorder of the senses, the comparison is valid. But it is misleading in the sense that Campana lived later and was of a different and (medically) less fortunate temperament; there is also a greater sweetness in his poetry. Sanguineti is right to regard him as one of the few utterly authentic poets of the past seventy years and to point out that he questioned the 'ultimate reason of poetry', continually testing it (as, he could have added, Rilke, q.v., Vallejo, q.v., and Riding, q.v., did) for the moral weight it can bear. Much of his work is marred by incoherence and D'Annunzian (q.v.) febrility, but the best reflects not only his own anguished inquietude but also that of a whole age. His apprehensions are lush but always modified: 'spring' is 'doubtful', 'words' 'broken'; his poetry, containing serenity, is fractured by terror and regret; its dedication and honesty are absolute. To Sybilla Aleramo he wrote, characteristically (and with the repetitions which are a feature of his work): 'In a moment/The roses withered/The petals fell/Because I could not forget the roses/We sought them together/They were her roses they were my roses/We called that search love/With our blood and with our tears we made the roses/Which glowed a moment in the morning sun/We withered them beneath the sun among briars/Roses not our roses/My roses her roses/P.S. And so we forgot the roses.'

Campbell, Roy (1901–57) South African poet, translator, autobiographer. Active in South African letters until 1928, he left in that year and came to England where his reputation had already been made with *The Flaming Terrapin* (1924). He spent much time in France, and, a militant Roman Catholic, fought for Franco. Later he fought in the British army. He died in a car accident in Portugal. Campbell founded the satirical magazine *Voorslug* (1926–7), *Whiplash*, with Plomer (q.v.) and many of his early poems energetically disposed of the literary and political sloth of his contemporaries. He had already developed a bold, vigorous, fluent and colourful lyrical manner and although his control over this weakened, the gift never quite left him. His satires—on the English Georgian poets, on their thirties successors and on the 'reds' in Spain—are technically highly capable: well-handled couplets packed with fury. But they lack subtlety, taste or compassion and the attitude they embody is ultimately that of an envious and gifted schoolboy drunk with violence (rather than that of a 'fascist', as has been charged). His best poetry had been written in the twenties; probably the best of all is 'Tristan da Cunha', a prophetic and haunting examination of his romantic solitude and his inability to inhabit it quietly. None of his later lyrical poetry, which ranges from the embarrassing celebration of sexual exuberance to the vividly evocative, reaches this level. Some translations, which are included in *Collected Poems* (1949–60), from St John of the Cross, Lorca and others provide inspired and poetic paraphrases. Campbell, who never lacked courage, had in South Africa been prepared to consider struggling with the modern world; after he left he abandoned this and tried to become an aggressive man of the past, but megalomania and intellectual incapacity—though humour and self-criticism occasionally crept in—slowly throttled his genius and finally he became more interesting as a character than a writer.

Camus, Albert (1913–60) French (born in Algeria) novelist, essayist, playwright, journalist, short-story writer, *moraliste*. He died in a car-crash. Camus, whose friendship and subsequent polemical quarrel with Sartre (1952) is an important debate (see the latter's generous obituary tribute to him, however, in *Situations*), is one of the most seminal figures of this century; he deserved his Nobel Prize (1957) at the early age of forty-three. He was immensely gifted and as immensely serious-minded. His chief subject is the 'absurd', but his treatment of it is markedly different and much more demonstrably humanistic and constructive than that of Sartre (q.v.), Beckett (q.v.), Ionesco (q.v.) and others. He was born into difficulty and poverty—his father was killed on the Marne in 1914; his Spanish mother was uneducated—and was ill from tuberculosis in his youth; but before the war he had established a modest reputation as co-founder of a theatre (director, actor, writer, theorist) for the proletariat, and as an essayist. He travelled in Europe, was active as a journalist in the Resistance and for a time after the war edited the newspaper *Combat.* Although his thinking developed considerably, he was consistently an activist rather than a dialectician. His entire career, even though he was before and during the war sympathetic to communism, may be seen as a search for a valid liberal humanism. Many see him as the profoundest and subtlest of all such seekers of our century. Others, such as neo-Marxists and existentialists have, however, attacked him. Camus was never a 'party' man. Almost from the first he worked to discover a positive solution to the problems presented by the notion of the 'absurd' (i.e. the meaninglessness of man's existence on earth); this is already apparent from a volume of early essays of 1937. In Camus, the dedicated pagan and lover of sun, the sense of contingency was opposed by a lyrical love of life—he blamed Christianity, not altogether logically, for the introduction of the notion of original sin. It is easy to understand why he was so devoted to the poetry of Char (q.v.). To put it simply, his 'absurdism' was intellectual—but reinforced by the injustice he saw around him—and his dedication to life and candid hatred of death was temperamental. At the basis of everything he wrote is the sense of moral responsibility; he explores and sympathizes with those who reject it (Meursault, the anti-Christ of *L'Étranger*), he cannot discover it, but he always hates Christ for his sacrifice—for that sacrifice involved such pain. His anti-Christianity is one of the most absolute of modern times (he was courted by some Christians and has—naturally—been described as ultimately Christian). Camus's fiction (his drama—though not his dramatic adaptations from such as Dostoievski, Buzzati, q.v., and others—is a failure) has occasionally been represented as being too tied up with his thinking, but it has an autonomy that makes it most appropriate to discuss, first his thinking, and then his fiction in the light of its connections with his thinking. The final, ambiguous novel surely imaginatively transcends even the finest of his essays. Camus's thinking may be summed up by reference to the two books *Le Mythe de Sisyphe* (1942; tr. *The Myth of Sisyphus,* 1955) and

L'Homme revolté (1951; tr. *The Rebel,* 1953). In the first he gives a portrait of man—not unlike that of the true Nietzsche—who is doomed to perform an absurd task but who may nevertheless learn to be happy in it. This is a paradox: accept meaninglessness but then fight it with every weapon you have. In *L'Homme revolté,* however, Camus refutes communism as an effective weapon: it leads to totalitarianism, which is intolerable; no bad means can justify ends even if these were to prove good. Francis Jeanson reviewed this book in *Les Temps Modernes:* he took issue with Camus's condemnation of Russia, which he insisted was a true communist society, even if a faulty one. Going over Jeanson's head, Camus replied to Sartre himself, who did not defend Russia's concentration camps but did point out that the non-communist bourgeois enjoyed their existence—thus implying that Camus's democratic-socialist solution was in 'bad faith'. Though Sartre's tone was more reasonable than Camus's, plainly the latter had embarrassed him—and plainly, too, the latter's position is less intransigent and to that extent morally superior. Sartre even today vainly but often richly seeks to controvert it; Camus, as the last novel demonstrates, himself understood the sociological and other weaknesses in his humanist position—but, unlike Sartre, he exercised his imagination to the tragic, and ironically absurd, end (a crazy burst of speed by a car he was not driving). His further thinking may be found in *Actuelles* (1950, 1953, 1958) and in the *Carnets* (1962 and 1964; tr. *Notebooks,* 1963 and 1966). There is also a volume of *Essais* (1965). In his three main novels Camus shows considerable development. In *L'Étranger* (1942; tr. *The Outsider,* 1946) Camus laconically presents an Algerian Roquentin (protagonist of Sartre's *La Nausée*), Mersault, who is a Mediterranean sensualist, loving instead of hating his own body. But Mersault is overwhelmed by his senseless sensuality and he kills an Arab. He is condemned because he refuses to conform, to say more than what makes sense to him (which is hardly anything); only the prospect of his death gives him happiness. He is Camus's most straightforward portrait of 'alienated man'—but even he gets pleasure from his vague experiences of the sunlight and its heat; he is not 'nauseated', but simply, as Camus himself asserted, the 'only Christ we deserve'. *La Peste* (1947; tr. *The Plague,* 1948) is wider in scope: a doctor who refuses to accept the fact of death tells the story of a devastating plague in Oran. The novel is less an allegory of the German occupation than a hopeful portrait of the writer-as-doctor—and it is significant that Christianity should, in the person of the Jesuit Father Paneloux, be exposed as an anti-humanism of inescapably totalitarian implications. Dr Rieux exercises his professional skills against the plague, so we may acquit Camus of *ideological* commitment: the chief of the writer's professional skills is his capacity to imagine, and thus perhaps to transform personal into truly ethical imperatives. Camus would have affirmed the moral, purified status of a successful objective correlative. Both these novels are rich in over- and undertones. But the last one, *La Chute* (1956; tr. *The Fall*, 1957), is by far the most complex–and superior. Once again, the lawyer protagonist is an objective correlative for the writer–and, more specifically, for the writer Camus himself. *La Chute* is a masterpiece of self-indictment in which the author 'confesses', to a silent listener in an Amsterdam bar (the very opposite of the sunny sensual places Camus himself loved), his shortcomings. He has been a generous lawyer but also a sexual hedonist, a Don Juan (as Camus had himself been); now, having failed to save a girl from suicide (but any rescue attempt would have been fruitless), he has opened a bar in Amsterdam. . . . It might be asserted that here Camus returns to an absolute nihilism; but the point is that the confession, itself redolent with hidden affirmations–often in the form of apparent negations–is anti-nihilistic. Otherwise why make it? The final versatile and energetic short stories, *L'Exil et le royaume* (1958; tr. *Exile and the Kingdom*, 1958) confirm that Camus had discovered a new vitality. Had he lived he could well have gone on to become the world's foremost novelist. Four of his plays are in *Caligula* (tr. 1958). *Oeuvres complètes* (1962–5) contains his main work.

Čapek, Karel (1890–1938) Czech novelist, dramatist and miscellaneous writer. He is the most internationally known, though not the best, of all modern Czech writers: the typical and anxious product of the First Czechoslovakian Republic, the betrayal of which killed him. His plays–notably *R.U.R.* (1920; tr. 1923) and *Ze života hmyzu* (1921; tr. *The Insect Play*, 1923), both with his brother the painter and author Josef Čapek (1887–1945)–gave him his world reputation; but, as critics agree, his fiction is more important. He was essentially an intelligent and skilful popular author whose approach is often superficial but totally honest; his response to the Czech situation between the wars was genuinely anguished but was decent rather than profound. He is, though, a thoroughly worthy writer. He saw the coming crisis, and warned against it; but a soft-centred romanticism vitiated his awareness of it; this tends to weaken his work. Early books are candidly Wellsian (q.v.): *Továrna na absolutnu* (1922; tr. *The Absolute at Large,* 1927), *Krakatit* (1924; tr. 1925). His chief work, in which he partly rises above himself, is the trilogy of novels *Hordubal* (1933; tr. 1943), *Povètroň* (1934; tr. *Meteor,* 1935) and *Obyčejný život* (1935; tr. *An Ordinary Life,* 1936). Here crisis forces him inwards, to examine the conflict between a cerebral determinism and a rather fuzzy faith in democracy. The balance is resolved in favour of the former but the nature of the inner resources by which the individual may attain peace is not clearly outlined.

Capote, Truman (1924) American fiction writer. Capote began—*Other Voices, Other Rooms* (1948), *The Grass Harp* (1951)—with his own delicate, sweet-sick version of Southern Gothic; it was truly sensitive and truly unpleasant, though the second novel is already too deliberately *soigné*. *Breakfast at Tiffany's* (1958) is clever, modish journalism, tinged with a smooth melancholy. The claims he made for the 'non-fiction' novel *In Cold Blood* (1966) were over-inflated, but this firsthand account of a *cause célèbre,* a peculiarly horrible series of murders, is excellent journalism.

Cardenal, Ernesto (1925) Nicaraguan poet-priest who runs a small commune in a remote part of Nicaragua. His approach is Franciscan and literal; onto his Catholicism, which is revolutionary, he has grafted Amerindian myth and some Buddhist teaching. His guide and spiritual mentor was Thomas Merton (1915–68), the American Trappist poet and religious writer (he died by electrocution in an accident). Cardenal, whose reputation in the USA and Europe is very high, uses the methods of Pound's *Cantos* in his poetry (which has been somewhat overrated), but his message is simpler: in time a new age will arise, an age of peace and Christian brotherhood (this is based in early Mayan rather than Christian thinking on time). He is a most impressive figure, and a notable minor poet. *Marilyn Monroe* (tr. 1975) is a volume of selections in English. *Vida en el amor* (1970; tr. *Love,* 1974) contains selections of spiritual reflections in prose.

Carducci, Giosué (1835–1907) Italian poet, critic, scholar, polemicist; one of the three dominant figures in Italian literature (*see* D'Annunzio, Pascoli) at the turn of the century. Nobel Prize 1906.

Greatly gifted, the 'heroic' Carducci who was the unofficial laureate of the post-*Risorgimento* may now fairly be seen as something of a bore, whose combative intellectualism, albeit democratic, too often blunts his humbler but purer poetic impulses. But as a critic he possessed an underlying robust humanism and sense of balance. Violently anticlerical, he began by founding the *amici pedanti* (pedant friends), opposed equally to the stiff, over-nationalistic classicism of the 'Roman School' and to the 'decadence' of the *scapigliati* ('dishevelled ones') who turned to the Europe of Verlaine and Baudelaire for inspiration—they were in fact too diverse (e.g. Boito and, peripherally, Dossi) to label, but the current they represented is now recognized as having been of great importance. Carducci sought a noble, secular Italian poetry. But the pagan *Inno a Satana* (1865), *Hymn to Satan,* glorifying reason and nature against repressive religion, is altogether too artificial and lofty. Carducci saw himself as a cautious neo-classicist, the poet of Italian history, but it is now evident that he was a muted romantic. The *Odi barbare* (1877–89; tr. *Barbaric Odes,* 1939), the least unsuccessful of his large-scale works, attempt to subdue romantic impulses by the use of Greek and Latin quantitative metres. But his poetic genius is best seen in such shorter poems as 'Alla stazione in una mattina d'autunno', 'One Autumn Morning at the Station', an uneasy, impressionistic love poem (in the *Odi*) which perfectly reflects the mood of his reluctant passion for Carolina Piva ('Lidia'). Carducci was confused and grandiose; but he is a memorable elegiac poet whose achievement is greater and worthier than that of D'Annunzio. There had to be a reaction against him (*see* Gozzano), as against D'Annunzio and Pascoli—but his best poetry, like that of Pascoli, looks forwards. His collected works were published in thirty volumes, 1907–40.

Carpenter, Edward (1844–1929) English Socialist, utopian sexual reformer, pasticheur of Whitman (whom he visited) in *Towards Democracy* (1883–1905). He was a bisexual who worked for tolerance of homosexuality and for women's rights. Mentioned here because his influence, though largely subterranean, was considerable, on 'hippiedom' (he was himself an early hippie) and its offshoots and on the 'permissive' society. He is a figure as important in his own way as Henry Miller (q.v.), and, though a bad poet, he did succeed in extracting the essence of Whitman's democratic and sexual ideas and introducing them to England. His influence was exerted largely through

Havelock Ellis, and, more discreetly, through the homosexuals of the Bloomsbury group (*see* Forster) who could not speak out. *Love's Coming of Age* (1896); *The Intermediate Sex* (1908).

Cary, Joyce (1888–1957) Anglo-Irish novelist. As a very young man he studied painting in Paris, then read law at Oxford. He fought in the Balkan War in 1912–13, and again with the Nigeria Regiment in Africa. In 1913 he had joined the Nigerian Political Service. He resigned in 1920 and lived for the rest of his life in Oxford. He studied writing for twelve years and then brought out his first novel, *Aissa Saved* (1932). Three more novels set in Africa followed, of which the last, *Mister Johnson* (1939), is rightly considered the best. High claims have been made for Cary; he has also been bitterly attacked. Is he a major or a minor novelist? Two preliminary points need to be made. First, he is a hero of tolerant humanist critics (e.g. M. M. Mahood, Kathleen Nott) because his foremost attention is always to try to show that celebration of life can be a means to the achievement of happiness —because, although a rationalist, he is sympathetic to religion as a 'humanizing' force. Secondly, he built his novels from voluminous series of preliminary notes, partly socio-documentary, partly observational, partly fictional (as a social historian he was inaccurate—except in the African novels) and this method did not improve his technique in the finished results. The important novels, apart from *Mister Johnson*, are the trilogy *Herself Surprised* (1941), *To Be a Pilgrim* (1942) and *The Horse's Mouth* (1944); and *A Fearful Joy* (1945). The trilogy deals with Sara Monday (who narrates the first), the senile lawyer Thomas Wilcher (narrator of the second) and the painter Gulley Jimson (who narrates the third). *A Fearful Joy,* like the three novels of the trilogy, is semi-picaresque and presents the history of sixty years of change through the experiences of Tabitha Baskett who is the victim of one of Cary's favourite types, the attractive scoundrel. The trilogy is remarkable for its versatility, for its empathy with characters that most people would regard as sordid, mad, criminal or wasted and for the unusual feat of convincing the reader that Jimson is an artist of genius (though not necessarily of a kind to which everyone responds). This exhibition of creative energy lends a major quality to Cary's fiction but the achievement as a whole (the later novels lack energy) is vitiated by a serious weakness: Cary needed to be able to discern the nature of 'ordinary' reality in order to do anything more coherent than merely create characters—but he was a romantic not even curable by the desperate resort to the building up of those huge piles of 'documents'. Thus Sara, Wilcher, Jimson and Tabitha are alone in a void: for though Cary could not, after the ironic tragi-comedy *Mister Johnson*, create an illusion of quotidian reality, he was also deficient in imagination. His 'message', it is said, is that each is alone in his own world. But this is a weakness rather than a message: if a novelist lacks the power to create *his* 'own world' then he must at least be a capable realist in the old sense. To show human beings alone in their own worlds you must show 'another' world as background. . . . This Cary could not do. He is a major creator of eccentrics, with much feeling; but he is not a major novelist. All the novels up to and including *Prisoner of Grace* (1952) were collected in a 'Carfax' edition with individual introductions by the author (1951–2).

Cather, Willa (1873–1947) American novelist, short-story writer, journalist. Willa Cather is one of the more important American writers of the century; she achieved much from the rather narrow limitations imposed upon her by her personality, and from her (eventual) lesbianism. But she had forced a tough apprenticeship on herself: she rebelled by dressing as a boy and pleasing herself about what company she kept; she worked her way through college, then became a drudge journalist and teacher—until McClure published her story collection *The Troll Garden* (1905), when she became a successful managing editor of his famous magazine. In 1912 she published her first novel and was able to devote the rest of her life to writing. When she was ten years of age her family moved from Virginia to Nebraska, from Southern order—one might say—to a half-explored wilderness settled by pioneers. The spirit of the pioneers took possession of her imagination forever, but so did midwestern stiflingness. She decided that she had been sexually stultified by the complacency and mediocrity of Red Cloud, Nebraska, and this obsession (she often said that nothing important happened to her emotionally after she was twenty) figures largely in her work. It was in part, however, a defence against impulses which she believed would weaken her art: this emerges most clearly in *The Song of the Lark* (1915), in which she uneasily depicts herself as an opera singer. This is a failure as a whole but passages that deal directly or indirectly with the singer's feelings when men try to intrude into her life are finely revealing of feminine sensibility (rather than of anything 'sinister' in Willa Cather's own bruised nature). But her important novels are *O Pioneers!* (1913), *My Ántonia* (1918), *A Lost Lady* (1923), *The Professor's House* (1925), *Death Comes for the Archbishop* (1927), *Shadows on the Rock* (1931)—this brought the author, for the first and only time, into the top-ten fiction-sellers—and the three stories in *Obscure Destinies* (1932). *One of Ours* (1922), her own favourite, but detested by some of her admirers, is at least interesting as an exploration of herself-as-man. *A Lost Lady* and *The Professor's House*—a persistently underrated novel—are, with *My Ántonia* running them a close third, her masterpieces. *A Lost Lady* deals not only with the corrupting influences of commercialism but also, at a deeper level, with the kind of masculinity that can infect and destroy femininity. *The Professor's House,* a beautiful book, explores the vulnerabilities of a sensitive man. The two last novels mentioned above (two comparatively feeble ones followed), which have been her most popular, are lusher and more overtly symbolic elegies for the American past. Dorothy Van Ghent, one of Willa Cather's best critics (*Willa Cather,* 1964), considers them her best work; others find in them the beginning of a failure of creative power. Willa Cather's prose is restrained and, as she revealed, the chief influences on her were Flaubert, James (q.v.) and her friend, the regionalist Sarah Orne Jewett—all fastidious and restrained writers. With her second novel *O Pioneers!* 'the unknown, unpredictable "self" suddenly broke through her carefully trained literary habits'. Alexandra Bergson's recurrent dream, in that novel, of being carried off by an unseen god—of weather, of vegetation, of love—provides a key to Willa Cather's work which, surprisingly, surpasses Lawrence (q.v.) on his own chosen ground. *Not Under Forty* (1936) collects criticism. *Novels and Stories* (1937–41).

Cavafy, Constantin *see* **Kavafis, Konstantinos.**

Cela, Camilo José (1916) Spanish fiction writer, travel writer, memoirist, editor (*Papeles de Son Armadáns*). Cela fought as a very young man for Franco and 'order': his work is an eloquent, truculent, eccentric reaction to this error. His acknowledged master is Baroja (q.v.), upon whom he has written (1958). He is the fictional initiator of the syle called *tremendista*—simply because the readers' reactions to the writer's evocations of horror and brutality are 'tremendous'. This is a neo-naturalism (*see* Zola) prompted by the barbarism of Franco and his supporters although the tendency was always present in Spanish literature. Cela's first novel, *La familia de Pascal Duarte* (1942; tr. *The Family of Pascal Duarte,* 1947), was banned in 1943; it deals, with blatant brutality and yet sympathy, with a man who had no opportunity in life and whose frustrations burst out into paradoxically authentic violence. *La Colmena* (1951; tr. *The Hive,* 1953) gives an account of post-civil-war life in Madrid; though not overtly political it demonstrates the hopelessness and helplessness of the ordinary people. He has written a number of other novels, but has in the main, since his self-exile to Mallorca in 1954, concentrated on eccentric travel writing and somewhat desperate avoidance of his chief concern: his love-hate affair with Spain. His best work, except for *La Colmena,* was done in the forties: *Pabellón de reposo* (1944), *Pavilion of Repose,* and the modernized picaresque *Nuevas andanzas y desaventuras de Lazarillo de Tormes* (1946), *New Adventures and Mishaps of Lazarillo de Tormes,* are both relentless pictures of modern Spain. Since the embarrassment caused to him by *La Colmena* (and especially by the English translation, with its introduction by Arturo Barea), Cela seems to have withdrawn into bitterness or despair: *La Catira* (1955), *The Blond,* already displays signs of disillusion and *San Camilo 1936* (1969) is an unconvincing attempt to deal with the Civil War. Yet Cela, the most gifted living Spanish writer, continues to produce various kinds of books–some of them scatalogical–and to exercise his vitality as an out-of-the-way scholar of Spanish customs and a raffish personality.

Celan, Paul (ps. Paul Antschel) (1920–70) German (Jewish) poet, translator, born in Bukovina; his parents were murdered by the Nazis and he was sent to forced labour. Later he went to Paris and became a Frenchman. He killed himself. His poetry is in the same tradition as that of Trakl (q.v.) and, before that, Hölderlin; but it has certain distinguishing features: it is influenced by French literary cubism (*see* Reverdy)–to escape his longing for death he needed his poems to be 'presences', as he said–and by the fate of his parents and of the Jews as a whole. Further, he uses a fairly unambiguous set of symbols (the chief one is stone), which often weakens his poetry as compared to that of Trakl who cannot be so pinned down. Celan scarcely believed that 'stone' could be transformed in the manner he tried to envisage. His great gifts come most to the fore in such poems as 'Todesfuge', 'Death Fugue', where his torment becomes livid with vital pity and compassionate indignation. As a critic has written, his poetry is a 'desperate search for meaningful communication with the "thou" in whatever form' (for 'thou' in this context *see* Buber); his frequent resort to a deliberate symbolism which is not a part of the expressionism that was natural to his poetic genius reveals, and tragically, his increasing disbelief in the existence of a 'thou'. He found some solace in adaptations from Esenin (q.v.), Blok (q.v.), Mandelstam (q.v.), Valéry (q.v.), Char (q.v.) and others, but at the same time original poetry became more and more difficult for him to achieve, as *Die Niemandsrose* (1963), *Ownerless Rose,* and his three successive collections demonstrate. He becomes increasingly withdrawn, solemnly creating a deliberately absolute verbal isolation, consisting of puns, neologisms and a tone of complete despair. In *Nineteen Poems* (1972) Michael Hamburger does all that can be done in English for this difficult and tragic poet.

Céline, Louis-Ferdinand (ps. Henri-Louis Destouches) (1894–1961) French novelist, physician, writer. Céline, a great modern writer, messed up his life in his heroic attempt to force himself to write a language that would not be a horribly alienated thing: thus, as Barthes (q.v.) writes, his books represent his 'descent into the sticky opacity of the condition which he is describing'. As a man he was a devoted doctor (often treating patients for nothing), a happy companion—and a frenetic critic of politics which led him to adopt an apparently fascistic and anti-semitic position. His novels are, among many other things, 'cubist' juxtapositions and distortions of his own experience; though he found real life 'unbearable' (as he told a critic), yet his representation of his own experience of it makes it worse, not better, than it was. . . . In the war he behaved incoherently: he served Vichy and fled with the Pétain gang (as physician) to Germany, but he did not denounce any individual and in 1951 he was completely exonerated and allowed to return to Paris. This was a correct decision. He was a victim of the war: the severe head wound he received in the First World War, and for which he was awarded a 75 per cent disability pension, gave him vertigo, chronic migraine and a partial paralysis of the right arm—he also suffered from a permanent buzzing in his ears. (Later, in Africa, he contracted malaria, the after-effects of which can be, intermittently, mentally disturbing.) Céline's first novel, built out of an unsuccessful play, *L'Eglise* (1933), was an enormous success: *Voyage au bout de la nuit* (1932; tr. *Journey to the End of the Night,*

1934). It caught a nihilistic mood but Céline characteristically repudiated the prestige it gave him. Instead of becoming a 'literary man', he continued to practise, unprofitably, as a doctor: he loved his patients, and it is puzzling that critics find it hard to reconcile this love with the misanthropy of the fiction—this misanthropy is surely an obvious complement to such conscientiousness (cf. Benn, q.v.). *Mort à crédit* (1936; tr. *Death on the Instalment Plan,* 1938) is a fictional distortion of his earlier years. In 1936 he went to Russia; he was so disgusted that he published *Mea Culpa* in the same year (the book included his first literary work, 1924, on the life and death of Semmelweiss, the nineteenth-century physician who died mad—he had infected himself in order to demonstrate the necessity of hygiene . . .). *Bagatelles pour un massacre* (1937), containing three enchanting ballet-scenarios (untranslated), is a mad diatribe against Jews. Having exhausted himself by the writing of two masterpieces and perhaps made miserable by the inevitable banality involved in good medical practice, Céline's imagination left him: he turned to insane ideas, undoubtedly inspired by his pacificism, about nationalistic 'self-sacrifice', 'pure strains', and so on. Yet the interspersed 'ballets' gently assert his true faith. . . . He stopped writing and thrust himself into medical work (always prophesying the defeat of the Germans). In 1944 he had to leave, first for Germany with the fleeing Vichyites (marvellously described in *D'un Château l'autre,* 1957; tr. *Castle to Castle,* 1969), and then for Denmark. He had heard his own death-sentence pronounced on the BBC. He spent fourteen months in prison in Denmark, but was released to a miserable exile in a hut by the Baltic. Eventually France, which often does its duty to writers (e.g. Genet, q.v.), allowed him to return. Sick, but supported by his second wife—the dancer Lucette Almanzor—he continued to write brilliantly, to practise medicine (usually for nothing), to love animals, and to make confused but often jocose and ironic statements to those interviewers who visited him (his sending-up of Burroughs, q.v. and Ginsberg, q.v., is famous). The two first novels, where he is at least in part the character Bardamu, transcend categories; one can only suggest their quality by drawing attention to their affinities with Swift, Breughel and Rabelais. They are certainly misanthropic but there is joy in their demotic vitality—their idiomatic virtues have not yet been equalled. The final novels, a desperate record of his years of confusion, have yet to receive their due. The excellent *Guignol's Band* (1944; tr. 1954), written in the last hectic days in Paris, is 'unreadable slop'–his phrase–about his sojourn in London soon after the First World War; *Le Pont de Londres* (1964), *London Bridge*, its sequel, has not been translated. *Normance* (1954), *Nord* (1960) and the posthumous *Rigodon* (1969) deal with the post-1939 period; all are remarkable. *Normance*, in particular, is a typically irreverent account of an air-raid on Montmartre; the grotesquely fat and enfeebled eponymous market-porter is clearly Dr Destouches himself. Seldom has a writer kept up his courage as Céline did; writers at least will realize this, and will reserve their judgment on the anti-semitic sickness that overtook him in the thirties–when his decent scorn for public acclaim forced him into the use of a metaphor not merely unacceptable but horrible. Céline (it was his grandmother's maiden name) is still an absolutely modern writer: doctor, absurdist, anguished protector of his own privacy (a point too often missed), traitor to the point of actual near-treason. . . . More will be written of him. A properly documented biography is badly required. The best and fullest study is E. Ostrovsky: *Céline and his Vision* (1967). See also the Céline numbers of *L'Herne*: 3 and 5, 1963.

Cendrars, Blaise (ps. Frédéric Sauser Hall) (1887–1961) Swiss novelist, poet, traveller, writing in French. His mother was a Scot. He regarded himself as quintessentially cosmopolitan, which in many ways he was. A part of his fictional *persona* consisted in telling agreeably fantastic lies about himself, in which many believed, but he lost an arm fighting for the French in the First World War, a fact of which he did not boast. He cannot be categorized; one can only point out that he was violently anti-literary, sophisticated in a highly literary manner, versatile and uneven. He tried business, study and even horticulture before becoming a writer and the background of even his inferior books is well informed; he never stopped trying to make money by extra-literary means and the theme of wealth runs through much of his work. But his true anchor was his friend Apollinaire (q.v.), himself an ambiguous enough character. He considerably influenced Dos Passos (q.v.), who made early and good translations (*Panama*, 1918; tr. 1931) of his wild, rushing, panic-stricken, impulsive poetry, which was effortlessly '*simultanéiste*'. But the poetry (*Poésies complètes*, 1968) is not more than effectively exciting and does not linger in and affect the mind as Whitman's or Apollinaire's does. The best novels and the autobiographical prose are a different matter and have not had the general acknowledgement they deserve. The chief novels are *Dan Yack* (1927–9; 1946; tr. *Antarctic Fugue,* 1948), *Moravagine* (1926; tr. 1969) and *L'Or* (1925; tr. *Sutter's Gold,* 1926). One cannot be sure of the time or order of composition but it is possible that the third of these came after the first two. *Dan Yack* deals with a receptive personality capable of sacrifice, *Moravagine* ('Death to the vagina') with a destructive one incapable of it. *L'Or* is a subtle adventure story, a major historical novel, of wide implication, which urgently needs to be reissued in English translation. There are some poor novels but the quasi-autobiographical *L'Homme foudroyé* (1945; tr. *The Astonished Man,* 1970), *La Main coupée* (1946), *The Slashed-Off Hand,* and *Bourlinguer* (1948) are incomparable essays in the self-exploration of a 'fictional' man vainly (but he knows it) determined to capture the 'non-fictional' elements in his adventurous life. The best studies are by J. Rousselot (1955) and J. Buhler (1962). *Oeuvres complètes* (1963) is useful but not complete. *Selected Writings* (n.d.) is a bilingual American edition.

Cernuda, Luis (1904–63) Spanish poet, fiction writer, translator, critic. A number of younger Spanish poets now consider him to be a more important poet even than Lorca (q.v.), Guillén (q.v.), Jiménez (q.v.), Hernandez, or Machado (q.v.). He is certainly a unique poet whose work has been uneasily dismissed or emptily praised by the regular critics. As Octavio Paz (q.v.) has written: 'His book [*La realidad y el deseo,* 1936, 1940, 1958, *Reality and Desire,* the third and final edition of this title collecting all his poetry] does not point a moral . . . none the less, it puts before us a vision of reality that is a threat to the fragile edifice that goes by the name of Good and Evil.' Cernuda is not a comforting poet, for he offers no consolation whatever. His integrity is absolute. In his earliest poems he turned to Gustavo Béquer (1836–70), Spain's best poet of the nineteenth century, and to Jorge Guillén as models. Both these poets are exceptionally refined in their style, clipping the wings of their romanticism with a neo-classical purity of utterance. This suited Cernuda, the theme of whose poetry is the conflict between reality and desire, between the real world, with which he could not come to terms, and his 'desired' world of beauty and homosexual reverie. He learned from Gide (q.v.) to assert his homosexuality, to treat it as a choice: this took courage in a Spain 'infected', as Paz remarks, 'with *machismo*'. But Cernuda did not like the unhappy destiny his erotic nature forced upon him. He went to England with the advent of Franco, with whose regime he would have no truck, and taught for a while in a well known Surrey public school; later he became a lecturer in America; finally he went to Mexico where, in a state of extreme bitterness and disenchantment, he died. His acute criticism, with much comment on his own work, is in *Poesia y literatura* (1960). Prose poems are in *Ocnos* (1942 rev. and enlarged 1949). Cernuda's poetry is not bleak because no integrity is bleak and because beauty and its passing affected and tortured him, just as did love and its betrayal. It is a record of a man's lesson to himself that life is wonderful and that it leads to nothing whatever: perhaps, he says to the dead in his famous poem about a Glasgow cemetery, God is forgetting you. . . . As he grows older his voice becomes more acerb: even his old friends are attacked (in *Desolación de la quimera,* 1962, *Desolation of the Chimera*), and the world is condemned, especially the horrifying city. No modern poet is as uncompromisingly non-Christian. *Selected Poems* (1972) is a set of translations into English.

Césaire, Aimé (1913) Francophobe Martinique poet and playwright. Martinique, one of the Windward Islands, is an overseas territory of France and Césaire was elected as its Deputy in 1946. He is Mayor of its capital, Fort de France. He broke with the communists in 1956 ('we cannot delegate anyone to think for us') and, although deeply influenced by the surrealists (*see* Breton), no longer considers himself one of them. He was an associate of Senghor's (q.v.) in the thirties, but his *négritude*—a word first coined in print by him—has become different from that of the Catholic Senegalese, though both concepts have common elements. Césaire's *négritude* is more that of his compatriot, Frantz Fanon, whom he anticipated by many years. Senghor's father met kings; Césaire, member of a race of slaves, grew up in dire poverty. Thus, while with Senghor he glories in the beauty and directness of the Negro, his *négritude* is more bitter, ironic, subtle, aggressive, complex, convoluted: he takes an ironic pride in the myths invented by the whites and he can thus also castigate the Negro as some Jews (e.g. Hannah Arendt) castigate their own race. But another element is present: an attitude that oscillates between hatred for the white mentality and one that, at its most generous, insists on the full humanization of both whites and blacks; concomitantly there is an aggressive rejection of white capitalism (not only the 'free' world's naked capitalism but also the cynical state-capitalism of the Russian Empire) as inevitably corrupt—the Negro has something new, authentic and different to offer. Thus does the paradigmatic *assimilé* turn upon his masters. All this and much more emerges in Césaire's most famous work, *Cahiers d'un retour au pays natal* (1939; revised 1960; tr. *Return to My Native Land,* 1968; 1969). Césaire gained his feeling of freedom from his involvement with surrealism but this work is not surrealistic—rather it employs surrealist techniques to achieve wild evocation of his past and his anticipation of his future return to its scene (for he wrote it on the Adriatic coast in 1939 just before making the actual return to his land which events forced upon him). A mixture of poetry and poetic prose, it is an artistically and humanly articulate expression of the predicament of a black man insulted simultaneously by his oppressed history and the sinister events of 1939—and of course of the poet himself. It is, retrospectively, perfectly comprehensible; but until Breton (q.v.) found himself in Martinique on an escape route from the Nazis in 1942 few readers knew of it; it became famous, as it deserves to be, only after the war when the leader of the surrealist movement publicized it. But Césaire's international reputation was not established until towards the end of the fifties. The successors to *Cahiers* have tended to become submerged in its great fame (e.g. *Cadastral,* 1961, *Cadastral Survey*), just as his form of *négritude* (which, as his poetry makes clear, is fully aware of its contradictory elements—it is, for example, a more viable attitude than that of, say, James Baldwin, q.v.) has not been sufficiently distinguished from that of Senghor. Senghor's constructiveness is to be applauded; but, as he himself has now almost acknowledged, white inhumanity—symbolized for Frenchmen by the Black victims of French *assimilation*—has not truly diminished. Césaire's poetry explores his difficult position with more subtlety than seems to be generally recognized: his presentation is stark, his language carefully and eloquently extreme; but he possesses an exquisite sensibility, and is always in control. His plays (e.g. *La Tragédie du Roi Christophe,* 1963, *The Tragedy of King Christophe*) deal with the same theme, dramatically opposing the sophisticated point of view to the native one. He has also written many essays, and the best book on Toussant-Louverture (1962); *Lettre à Maurice Thorez* (1957), *Letter to Maurice Thorez,* explains his break from the communist party. It is evidently not well known that much of Césaire's later poetry is as good as the *Cahiers*. One must add that it is Césaire's *négritude* rather than that of Senghor (who is not as substantial a poet) with which conscientious white people must learn to come to terms.

Chandler, Raymond (1888–1959) American crime writer who began, at the time of the Depression, to write 'hard-boiled' (*see* Hammett) short stories for pulps and for *Black Mask* (from 1933). Previously he had been a journalist and businessman. Rather too much is now made of Chandler as artist but, after Hammett, his acknowledged master, he was the best crime writer of his time. As a critic wrote, Chandler's prose is 'image-laden', 'raw-coloured', Hammett's 'all-bone'. The early stories (some in *Killer in the Rain*, 1964 and *The Smell of Fear*, 1965) are not distinguished, but with his first novel it became clear that Chandler was more than an entertainer. His detective Philip Marlowe is not a convincing character—he is a masochist projection of Chandler himself—but he acts as a perfect vehicle for his creator's wit, acutely critical sociological viewpoint and ear for dialogue. Of the seven novels the first four (*The Big Sleep*, 1939; *Farewell My Lovely*, 1940; *The High Window*, 1942; *The Lady in the Lake*, 1943) are badly plotted, but they are superior to the last three—*The Little Sister* (1949), *The Long Goodbye* (1954), *Playback* (1958)—which are cleverly constructed but more sentimental and less deeply felt. They are collected in two omnibuses (1953, 1962).

Char, René (1907) French poet, art critic, from Provence. His friend Camus (q.v.) believed him to be the greatest twentieth-century French poet (an exaggeration). He was in the surrealist (*see* Breton) movement from 1929 until 1937 and was initially influenced by Eluard (q.v.), with whom (and Breton) he published a volume (*Ralentir Travaux*, 1930). But surrealism did not really suit him (*Le Marteau sans maître*, 1934 rev. 1963, *The Masterless Hammer*, contains the truly surrealist poems), since his inspirations are his profound and therefore undogmatic humanism (he was a leading Provençal Resistance fighter), the precise qualities of his native landscape (L'Ile-sur-Sourge in the Vaucluse)—and Heraclitus. Thus his poetry, admittedly obscure—too often the 'deep images' fail to connect, or the note of aphoristic confidence is unjustified—has a distinctly non-surrealist solidity. Like Heraclitus, Char believes that the unifying nature of the 'Logos', the real 'material' of which all objects are constituted, has been forgotten. In modern terms he is a kind of pantheist, intensely anthropomorphic. His 'fascinators' are Gallic 'epiphanies' (*see* Joyce): moments or observations which illuminate the workings of the Logos. He is thus essentially a religious poet. The extent to which his work, some of which is in poetic prose, succeeds in passing beyond a too vague mysticism is debatable; but of its sensual impact and frequent beauty there can be no doubt. Further, his Camusian sense of man's nobility undoubtedly acts as a valid antidote to the (equally valid) nihilistic view of such as Onetti (q.v.), or Gombrowicz (q.v.): that there are too many 'trivia' in the way of the attainment of an authentic existence. He is at his best when at his most simple, as in 'A Deux Enfants'. Much of his poetry is collected in *Poèmes et prose choisis 1935–1957* (1957) and *Commune Présence* (1964). An English selection is *Hypnos Waking* (1956), in which one of the translators is W. C. Williams (q.v.). *Feuillets d'Hypnos* (1946), inspired by his Resistance exploits as 'Captain Alexandre', is his most immediately accessible work.

Chayefsky, Paddy (1923) American stage and television playwright. He has never improved on *Marty* (1953, TV; filmed 1955) and *The Bachelor Party* (1954, TV; filmed 1957), sensitive and moving plays about ordinary people which just avoid the sentimental. Later work is skilful but more ponderous (e.g. *The Tenth Man*, 1960). *Television Plays* (1955).

Cheever, John (1912) Competent American fiction writer of the smooth *New Yorker* school. He has produced several volumes of stories; his best work is in the novel *The Wapshot Chronicle* (1957) and its sequel *The Wapshot Scandal* (1964), in which he painfully, if never profoundly, combines an elegy for the old America with lively satire on the susceptibilities of the new. With the novel *Bullet Park* (1969) he becomes mannered and influenced by the over-praised 'baroque' black humorists.

Chesterton, G. K. (1874–1936) English fiction writer, journalist, editor, poet, critic, miscellaneous prose writer, Catholic (converted 1922) apologist. Friend of Belloc from 1900. Chesterton was a prolific literary professional; his Catholic onesidedness, for which the influence of Belloc was largely responsible, has possibly robbed him of some of the serious consideration he deserves, though he has never lost his popular appeal. His poetry is attractive but never (as Eliot, q.v., said of the best of Monro, q.v.) 'the real right thing'. His criticism is uneven and inaccurate but often contains more than enough insight to make it valuable, especially to the as yet uninitiated: *Browning* (1903), *Chaucer* (1932), and others. As a purveyor of paradox and in some fiction, however, he displayed genius. Chesterton's belief in God is partially based in his fear of an undefined evil; but by turning to Catholicism and then later to Rome, he found an acceptable means of exercising his basically disconformist and subversive attitude towards conventional morality. He is often a writer saying something very different from what he thinks he is saying, though the notion of God in his best fiction is certainly a religious one, and an acknowledgement of the mystery of creation. The novel *The Man Who Was Thursday* (1908) is rather more than 'excellent light entertainment' (a standard judgement) and so are the best of the Father Brown stories (*The Father Brown Omnibus*, 1947; the collection of the same title, USA only, 1951, adds one more story): they are the best of a writer who could never develop—but who has all the promise of genius. Chesterton was unreliable and dogmatic, but wisdom and compassion slip through, and one of his own remarks serves him well as an epitaph: 'If a job's worth doing it's worth doing badly'. *Collected Poems* (1933); *Chesterton* (1970) is Auden's (q.v.) selection from the non-fictional prose; *Chesterton Reprint Series* (1960–) collects most of the fiction except the Father Brown stories.

Claudel, Paul (1868–1955) French poet, playwright, diplomat, Biblical exegetist. Few have had much nice to say about the man Claudel and his reputation is larger than it should be, but he cannot, unlikeable though he was in most respects, be written off. Stripped of his self-inflationism and his pretensions, Claudel is a minor writer. As a diplomat he was an ambitious opportunist and a coward; as a friend he could be poisonous tyrant (as Jammes, q.v., allowed him to be) or vicious betrayer (as Gide, q.v., discovered and forgave). His letters—mostly from diplomatic exile—have been called warm, but lines may be read between. His roots were less in intelligence than in self-aggrandizement. But truth operated in him, though deviously: a sexual guilt, arising from his convoluted adopted Catholicism, acts in his best works as a kind of self-examination. Claudel's Catholicism, upon which he based his characteristically enormous and suspiciously coherent system of being, was from the beginning both grandiose and equivocal. At the age of nineteen he was converted (in Notre Dame on Christmas night); Rimbaud, who was not a Roman Catholic, was instrumental in this conversion. Claudel needed certainty to continue to exist: one can grant him anguish. But the paradox of Rimbaud's being his religious mentor gave his large ego convenient scope (later Thomist reinforcements are less important than some critics think). From that time his poetry became a form of praise of God and of his creation. He used a chanting 'verset' instead of a line (cf. Senghor, q.v., Saint-John Perse, q.v., Whitman). The main direct influences on this choice of form were the Bible and the works of the seventeenth-century orator Bossuet, but Claudel evolved it as a compromise between the, for him, too exact demands of French versification and the lack of tension of ordinary prose: it is a heightened spontaneity of the naturally God-worshipping mind. It is one of his greatest achievements, and his attempts to explain it (and his entire theory) in *Art Poétique* (1907) and other writings (conveniently collected in *Réflexions sur la Poésie* and other criticism in a two-volume Pléiade edition in 1968) are scarcely helpful. For Claudel the 'word' is sacred; to the extent that it is *the* word he is powerful; to the greater extent that it is *his* word it fails. The poems were collected, *Oeuvres Poétiques,* in 1957. His many plays are more important. They succeeded in stage productions only in the last thirteen years of his life. These are candidly archaic and aloof in that they employ the 'grand' forms of old Spanish drama and are hardly in a French theatrical tradition at all. The majority of them are theological and possess no kind of dramatic life, but there are exceptions, the chief three of which are *Partage de midi* (1906; 1948), *L'Annonce faite à Marie* (1910 rev. 1912; tr. *Tidings Brought to Mary,* 1927) and *Le Soulier de satin* (1928–9; tr. *The Satin Slipper,* 1945). The first deals with the theme that haunted Claudel throughout his creative life: how to transform the love and lust aroused in men by women into a Christ-like renunciation. It is based on personal experience. The second is a 'miracle play'. The third, written 1919–24, is set in a fantastic Renaissance Spain and is on the simplest of themes: the old husband, the young wife, her lover. These three powerful plays put Claudel into serious reckoning. He cannot really deal with woman but he makes an interesting attempt to persuade us that she is a devil-saint. On the subject of the ultimate failure of erotic projects he is more successful. Claudel forces the question of 'belief' too strongly, indeed monstrously, upon us, and the tension in his work is between forces in the authoritarian opportunist Claudel rather than between belief and unbelief; he is minor because he must defend himself against the disaster of contingency—he will not face this. Of Sartre (q.v.) and his followers he could only whiningly ask, in his old age, how could existentialists live and talk in vile cafés, and so on. His stance is intransigent; his world is rigidly finite; his vision is blinkered; he cannot afford humour. But within his limitations he is original and exuberant. His final seven works on scriptural matters are properly ignored. *Théâtre* (1956). Among other plays in English translation are *Tête d'or* (1890 rev. 1901; tr. *Tête d'or,* 1919), *L'Otage* (1911; tr. *The Hostage,* 1945) and *Le Livre de Christophe Colomb* (1933; libretto for opera by Milhaud his former secretary, 1929; tr. *The Book of Christopher Columbus,* 1930). There is a version of his *Cinq Grandes Odes* (1910; tr. *Five Great Odes,* 1967) and there are some other translations in anthologies. A good and intelligent introduction, taking a more sympathetic view than my own, is by W. Fowlie (1957).

Cocteau, Jean (1889–1963) French playwright, novelist, literary personality (he knew everyone of account), poet, critic, filmmaker, craftsman (in glass, ceramics), composer, illustrator. Is his 'genius for talent' (as a critic has tentatively suggested) or is he a great writer? If so, in what forms? His versatility alone doubtless qualifies him as a genius—or is it suspicious? But he was certainly also a charlatan, a spellbinder. At certain times one is apt to judge him as lacking in substance, as not really having much to say. But at others one feels forced to reconsider this judgement. As a man Cocteau was somewhat mysterious: a drug-addict (intermittently) and a homosexual, he was possibly not very secure in his gay but pallid decadence. This may explain why most of his works can fairly be described as, among other things, precious, meretricious, modish, and even pretentious. Under the mask of the Apollinaire (q.v.) -like fast mover from one movement to another (Cocteau tried everything: futurism, 'modernism', surrealism, neo-classicism. . . .) there is a definite sadness, a regret perhaps at not being sufficiently loved, at not being worthy of such love. (He was, it should be noted, Apollinaire's friend and may well have been influenced in his career by Apollinaire's public shifts of allegiance.) Does this pathos ever find true expression? Certainly not in the pyrotechnic poetry, which simply leaps skilfully from one mode to another. His films (the best is

Orphée, 1949) are fantastical and cluttered but undeniably powerful in their impact. His drama is brilliantly effective (e.g. *La Machine infernale*, 1934; tr. *The Infernal Machine*, 1962) and skilled, but tends to fade in the mind and lacks linguistic power. *Les Parents terribles* (1938; tr. *Intimate Relations*, 1962) is an exception: family relationships brought out something more profound than the merely agile in Cocteau—one wonders about the effects upon him of his own childhood (he was the son of a rich notary). But if Cocteau is major in any sense other than that of personality and as a collaborator (e.g. his great ballet *Parade*—with Massine, Picasso and Satie) then this is in the novel *Les Enfants terribles* (1929; tr. *Enfants terribles*, 1930; *Children of the Game*, 1955), which is not limited by artificiality and does, without question, possess substance. It is a story of disturbed adolescence and through its theme Cocteau found the perfect objective correlative for the exploration of his own lifelong compulsion towards fantasy; it is his most convincing statement of his own torment—and it works perfectly on a realistic, psychological level. Cocteau wrote other novels, many plays and many miscellaneous books (e.g. *Opium*, 1930, tr. 1932, the 'journal' of a cure). *Oeuvres complètes* (1946–51) collects much of his work, and the plays are in *Théâtre complet* (1957).

Colette, Sidonie Gabrielle (1873–1954) French novelist, memoirist, music-hall entertainer (1906–12). Colette is incomparable; but the legend of her excellence is not quite consonant with her actual excellence and her best books have been somewhat neglected in the interests of one's good, but less good (e.g. the famous *Chéri*, 1920, *La Fin de Chéri*, 1926; both tr. *Chéri and the Last of Chéri*, 1951). She married, at twenty, the initially attractive but parasitic music-critic 'Willy' (Henri Gauthier-Villars), and her first novels appeared under his name—but they were essentially her own memoirs of Burgundian childhood and of her early married years. She got rid of Willy in 1906, and subsequently made two more, happier, marriages. *La Vagabonde* (1911; tr. *The Vagabond*, 1954), and *L'Entrave* (1913; tr. *Recaptured*, 1931) describe her life in the music halls with great simplicity and a lucid, penetrative charm. Her most beautiful books, however, are about the countryside and animals (the early Claudine series is not more than a rehearsal for these). As a storyteller Colette was a kind of naturalist (*see* Zola) with an important difference: her characters are certainly victims, but of their own instincts rather than of the environment.

They are often brave but they are eventually helpless and their lives are inevitably sad. Even those who come to terms with life do so only by way of a return to childhood and innocence. These novels are excellent, but slight–and, as in *Mitsou* (1919; tr. *Mitsou,* 1930) and *Gigi* (1945) they can tend towards the self-parodic and fey. The best of the memoir-novels are in a different and higher class. They include *La Maison de Claudine* (1922), *Sido* (1929; tr. 1953) and *La Naissance du jour* (1932; tr. *A Lesson in Love,* 1932). Here Colette is actually a part of nature and the world of childhood; but she detaches herself from them to tell us what it is like to be such a part: flowers, animals, her mother, feature largely in this section of her work, which has a magical quality. Later books, on cats and dogs and on Paris in the Occupation, are professional and sensitive but not on a level with the earlier. In *La Chatte* (1933) Colette writes a successful novel on jealousy in which the husband's cat is an important character. Colette celebrated instinct above all and–because it is now scientifically a disputed term–her best work might usefully be taken as a paradigm of what the word could mean in literary contexts. *L'Enfant et les sortilèges* (1925), *The Child and the Enchanters*–familiar to most as the title of Ravel's opera–is one of the most beautiful children's stories ever written. A few more books by Colette (e.g. *Belles Saisons,* 1955, *Summer Months*) appeared after the issue of the complete works, *Oeuvres complètes,* in 1950.

Compton-Burnett, Ivy (1892–1969) English novelist. Author of eighteen extraordinary novels (they were preceded by an immature one) in which a fierce grudge against the world is transmuted into deadly art. The civilized Miss Compton-Burnett, a student of the classics, experienced a traumatic youth: she lost two brothers and her two youngest sisters committed suicide (or accidentally took an overdose of veronal in the course of a 'transcendental' experiment) together in 1917. She was lesbian by inclination, a condition which she accepted but which she knew, with her withering intelligence, that the crass post-Victorian world did not. She knew the narrowness of her limitations–she had not the capacity to write a straightforwardly realist novel –but used this very narrowness to achieve a criticism not of society (though all her work, set in the nineties, carries an implied protest against the emotionally stifling nature of 'Victorianism') but of life. She said, acidly, 'Real life seems to have no plots. And as I think a plot desirable and almost necessary I have this extra grudge against life.' With *Pastors and Masters* (1925) she began a series of novels which are, at bottom, ferocious comedies—carefully based on the principles of Greek tragedy as set forth by Aristotle—of the Freudian *Id*. That is to say, her stories are eventually dreams: in them desire becomes or is revealed as action. Ivy Compton-Burnett's subject is always the family and there is always a family tyrant. Her 'plots' are at once parodies of the neat plots of conventional novels and Graeco-Freudian revelations: every kind of crime, including murder, forgery, incest and theft, is committed. Thus Ivy Compton-Burnett is the opposite of a realist; she merely remarks, with her usual sarcasm, 'I believe it would go ill with many of us, if we were faced with a strong temptation, and I suspect that with some of us it does go ill.' This does not mean that Ivy Compton-Burnett thinks that there is as much actual crime amongst the middle classes as her *oeuvre* suggests, but simply that there is more crime than most people think—and that there is no such thing as innocence. She is one of the most alyrical novelists of our times; one wishes that she might have written a novel about the family of a police commissioner. She comes into the category of a great minor. *Collected Works* (1948–72).

Connell, Evans S. (1924) American fiction writer, poet. Connell's *Mrs Bridge* (1958) and *Mr Bridge* (1969), novels written in the forms of cunningly interwoven short sketches, do exactly what Sinclair Lewis (q.v.) and his admirers wrongly thought he was doing with Babbitt. They are deceptively simple, but exceedingly perceptive and well written. *The Diary of a Rapist* (1966) is more overtly ambitious and less successful. *The Anatomy Lesson* (1957) collects stories. The long poem *Notes from a Bottle Found on the Beach at Carmel* (1963) is learned, curious and readable, but does not cohere as poetry.

Conrad, Joseph (ps. Teodor Józef Konrad Nałęcz Korzeniowski) (1857–1924) Polish-born English novelist. He did not learn English until he was a young man. In his youth he was a sailor, gun-runner, adventurer and would-be suicide. He became a naturalized Englishman at the age of twenty-nine and did not quit the sea until 1895. He thus had plenty of material to draw upon for his fiction, the best of which—it is usually though not always agreed—was written in the first decade of the century. But he could not gain financial independence until the publication of *Chance* (1913), not one of his major books. He had written five books of fiction (*Almayer's Folly*, 1895, is the first) before he collaborated with Ford (q.v.) on *The Inheritors* (1901) and *Romance* (1903), but Ford had published his own first novel in 1892 and Conrad undoubtedly learned much from him, though critics are anxious to suppress the fact. When Conrad is at his best his understandably clumsy style is as 'right' as Hardy's; but when he is not it presents an insuperable barrier of wordiness, rhetoric, romantic cliché. Even his great short story 'Heart of Darkness' (in *Youth*, 1902) is marred by such passages; *The Secret Agent* (1907) is in this (as perhaps in other) respects his best novel. Two themes dominate Conrad's fiction: the desirability but impossibility of achieving fidelity to a decent, simple standard of conduct, and a terror of anarchy arising from his imaginative awareness of the claims of revolutionaries and the counterclaims of autocracies. One serious weakness in Conrad is his failure to handle women or love; he was unhappily married and only in a character who is basically a portrait of his wife Jessie (an unattractive woman, but he was difficult to live with) did he really succeed in depicting a woman: Winnie Verloc in *The Secret Agent*. Winnie 'felt profoundly that things do not stand much looking into' and this was Conrad's fundamental position towards all women. It prevented him from achieving or depicting sexual relationships and it represents a serious flaw in his greatness because it is a misinterpretation: it assumes that because women are not men they do not have their own ways of 'looking into things'. Conrad is a 'man's writer'. But on men, on tests of courage and endurance, revolutions and revolutionaries, the elemental sea, the equally elemental jungle as tests of human morality ('Heart of Darkness'), on loneliness (Conrad was amongst the loneliest of writers), he was magnificent. The blackness of his pessimism is sombrely lit by the richness of his vision, by the power with which he conveys his fascination with and dedication to the existence of the human effort to attain to virtue and brotherhood. The chief works are *Typhoon* (1902), 'Heart of Darkness', *Nostromo* (1904), *The Secret Agent* (1907), *Under Western Eyes* (1911), 'The Secret Sharer' and 'The Inn of the Two Witches' (in *'Twixt Land and Sea*, 1912). In these we learn much of men (nothing of women): of how their characters and behaviour are tested by the inexorable sea, by political upheaval, greed, sexuality (Verloc's motivations are at heart sexual, and *The Secret Agent* is probably Conrad's best novel because here he comes nearest, in a metaphor of espionage and counter-espionage, to examining his sexual bad conscience). . . . The tragic dehumanizing uselessness of politics, the desperate search for the 'natural order' as a necessary alternative to anarchy: these are two more themes that emerge. In these works Conrad gives his fullest and justest picture of the nature of politics at the beginning of the century; *The Secret Agent* is also profoundly prophetic of the pseudo-revolutionary extremism of today. His understanding of political aspirations is profound; his analysis of them is simultaneously empathetic and devastating. *Works* (1921–7); *Complete Short Stories* (1933).

Coppard, A. E. (1878–1957) English short-story writer, poet. Had he kept his literary roots in his native Kent, Coppard's considerable achievement would have been even greater. After a hard first forty years (tailoring, professional athletics), during which he studied and made literary contacts while working as a clerk in Oxford (1907), in 1919 he was able to devote himself to writing. His poetry (*Collected Poems*, 1928) is weak but his stories are distinguished. He was a true professional who learned most from Chekhov; but his technical expertise seldom robbed his stories of their lyricism and psychological exactitude. He is at his best in 'Dusky Ruth' or in the supernatural 'Adam and Eve and Pinch Me' (title of his first collection, 1921). His range is very wide: from the comic to the tragic, from the town to the country, from the starkly realistic to the magical. Where he is faulty it is often because he attempts to tie himself up to a general rather than to a specific English rural tradition. *The Collected Tales* (in USA only, 1948) was followed by two more collections, an autobiography *It's Me, O Lord* (1957) and *Selected Stories* (1971).

Cortázar, Julio (1914) Argentinian fiction-writer. Cortázar, like García Márquez (q.v.), believes the *nouveau roman* (*see* Robbe-Grillet) to be a dead end but his work is highly modernistic. *Los premios* (1960; tr. *The Winners,* 1965) is an 'open' novel inasmuch as the reader may take the allegory as he likes; *Rayuela* (1963; tr. *Hopscotch,* 1966) may be read in any order–and for once the experiment works. *End of the Game* (tr. 1967) contains selected stories. Cortázar is one of the few novelists to have been fruitfully influenced by Kafka (q.v.).

Couperus, Louis (1863–1923) Dutch novelist. Couperus remains the most translated of modern Dutch writers; he deserves his international reputation though Arthur Schendel (1874–1946) is superior and Vestdijk (q.v.) as good. His fiction, dealing with many aspects of life, both past and present, but most notably with turn-of-the-century life in his native The Hague, blends a decadent lushness with an Oriental sense of 'destiny'; his style is elegant, his psychological mastery unobtrusive because his pace is calculatedly slow. Most of his novels were translated and some have been made re-available. His masterpieces are the tetralogy *Boeken der kleine zielen* (1901–4; tr. *The Small Souls, The Later Life, The Twilight of the Souls, Dr Adrian,* 1914–18) and *Van oude Meschen, de dingen die voorbijgaan* (1906; tr. *Old People and the Things that Pass,* 1919; 1963). These alone, reflecting his childhood in the East and the long periods he spent in Italy, amply justify his claim to classic status. There is much truly good reading to be had from Couperus.

Crane, Hart (1899–1932) American poet. Crane, the son of unpleasant parents (his father made bad chocolate), is one of the most important English-language poets of the century, though this assessment rests on some twenty poems and a large number of dispersed passages. Except as a poet—and sometimes even as a poet—his life was an unmitigated disaster: alcoholic, compulsively homosexual in behaviour, damager of his friends' susceptibilities and purses, he suffered from increasing bouts of shame and remorse, the last of which (he felt he had betrayed the woman with whom, at last, he had learned to share love, and also that his poetic powers had left him) drove him to drown himself while on his way back to America from Mexico where he had been unsuccessfully trying to write an epic poem on Montezuma. Crane had little formal education and his grasp of French symbolism and even of English metaphysical poetry, both of which heavily influenced him, is in one sense dubious. Yet he was not a 'non-literary' poet in any sense and, as his *Letters* (unfortunately they exist only in an incomplete, expurgated, over-edited form: 1952; 1965) show, he could be a most perceptive critic. Two of the best poems of his first and most important volume, *White Buildings* (1926), make extensive use of verse by the Austrian-born American poet Samuel Greenberg (1843–1917); his understanding of what this nearly illiterate, inchoate and yet powerful pauper poet was trying to do is demonstrated by his masterly modifications and revisions (he ought, however, to have made his indebtedness public; later Tate, q.v., edited a selection from Greenberg's ms: *Poems,*

1947). Crane is so important because he is one of the few English-language poets of his time to have been excited by the extra-materialistic—or 'magical'—potentialities of language. He understood the Blakean paradox (made by Ouspensky, who influenced him) that what can be expressed cannot be true. He was thus, although he usually kept within fairly strict verse forms, wholly modernist in spirit: he saw that the true relationship between the inner man and the external world was a cipher not a chaos and in his poetry tried to find a lyrical metaphor for this cipher. It is curious that so unhappy a man should have been neither absurdist/atheist nor pessimist. In fact, although his poetry is shot through with tragedy, he was one of the great affirmative—and in the truest sense religious—poets of his century: he believed in meaning and sought for it. He burned himself out by exciting himself with alcohol, which is a dangerous depressant, and—notably in his epic *The Bridge* (1930)—he lapsed into rhetoric when his attempts to create a 'new *word* . . . [an] organic principle of a "logic of metaphor", which antedates . . . pure logic, and which is the genetic basis of all speech' collapsed. Indeed, it was only by their framework of form that his great poems survived at all. He needed to alienate himself from mundane reality in order to pursue his project: his crass, stupid, cloying mother and commercially minded father—their marriage was breaking up as he grew up—gave him his first impetus to do this. As a frenziedly artificial homosexual (his eventual success with Peggy Baird, and what he wrote about its having been a 'great consolation to a loneliness that had about eaten [him] up' prove this to be a correct judgement) he made himself an outcast. Then, trying to deal with his strange sexual predicament in 'For the Marriage of Faustus and Helen' (1922–3; in *White Buildings*) he found it necessary to go increasingly to the bottle. The poems collected in *White Buildings* are his most confident work: fusing together the influences of the Elizabethan poets, Rimbaud and Blake into something entirely his own, they do elevate what is nonsense in 'normal' language into poetic lucidity: 'A goose, tobacco and cologne—/Three-winged and gold-shod prophecies of heaven . . .'; 'In alternating bells have you not heard/All hours clapped dense into a single stride?/Forgive me for an echo of these things,/And let us walk through time with equal pride.' But the price proved too high. With help from a banker, Otto Kahn, Crane (now suffering seriously from alcoholism and its remorses) tried to find a more-than-linguistic metaphor for his keen apprehensions: he became desperate and he became ambitious. *The Bridge*, Brooklyn Bridge, must not be seen as an epic of America as a future Utopia or even as a synthesis of American myths: it is a ragbag of mostly wrecked lyrics, many of which are attempts to explain his homosexual behaviour to himself. Crane tried to recover himself and one or two of his last batch of poems, such as 'Postscript' and 'The Broken Tower' are as good as those in *White Buildings* (*The Complete Poems and Selected Letters and Prose*, 1968). But despite his discovery of heterosexuality, he could not go on, and only in the complex 'The Broken Tower', a great phallic poem, his last, could he leave a wholly truthful record of the failure of his heroic quest. Opinions differ about Crane—some call *The Bridge* a masterpiece; others denigrate 'The Broken Tower'—but the general consensus is that he is one of America's five or six greatest poets.

Creeley, Robert (1926) American poet, fiction writer. Creeley lived for a time in Europe, then returned to America and to Black Mountain College (*see* Dewey). He is essentially a product of influences exercised by W. C. Williams (q.v.) and by that institution, of which his true mentor, Olson (q.v.) was a rector. Most of his poems (*For Love: Poems 1950–1960*, 1962; *Poems 1950–1965*, 1966) are unmemorable, and are in short, imageless lines, broken, unmusical, rigorously pragmatic, faithful to their moment alone. 'Creeley's poems are short; they are not short enough', one critic has written. One sees what he means in that their author will have no truck with anything but the expression of his solipsist ego *now*. Can such moments be of interest to others? Is it not unrealistic to see life only as a series of isolated and private moments? The procedure may, however, be defended as a kind of prose stream of consciousness (there is usually no rhythm in Creeley: his poetry denies a principle of poetry); and there are moments in his earlier work—his most recent is more diffuse, giving an impression of a personality softening or breaking down (*The Finger*, 1968; *Pieces*, 1969)—when one responds to him as a poet, and one who has strayed into rhythm. . . . As novelist (*The Island*, 1963) and storywriter (*The Gold Diggers*, 1954; 1965) Creeley's method is more tortuous; in the novel he doggedly pursues, however, his perceptions of a past time, one which he is trying to destroy in the interests of *nowness*. The stories are more inventive and humorous—they are the only place in his work where an angry sourness, an obstinate (and logical enough) refusal to budge from his desperately limited, limiting, philosophy ('My work is what I am doing *now:* take it'), is not apparent. There is a sullen and fascinating strength in all this and it took courage to pursue it but it cuts out everyone except the author. The author hates patterns and so his poetry rejects patterns by its form and by its content; but there are patterns in nature: physics is not patternless, nor is still water when you throw a stone into it. Creeley's work and its quality and fate are uniquely illustrative of a certain important strand in American literature: the (intelligently) philistine cubist (poem as object for its own sake), but always self-defeating urge to *live* rather than to *use* life. . . . But in Creeley, so far, the brutality of his procedures seems to have gone unacknowledged: love exists (in his work) as a generalization that is taken for granted with an odd and disturbing ease.

Cummings, E. E. (1894–1962) American poet, prose writer, critic, painter. Cummings was educated at Harvard, served with an ambulance unit in the First World War and was imprisoned (*The Enormous Room,* 1922)–through an error–by the French authorities, lived in Paris for a time, travelled in Russia (*EIMI,* 1933), and spent the rest of his life (as a popular, supposedly modernist, poet) in or around New York. Cummings invented, meticulously, an effective typographical method which appeared modernistic but which was not: he is not only perfectly easy to follow but his system actually makes the task even easier. He is a minor poet, but at times, especially when he is being comic or bawdy, a substantial one. His fault as a satirist is that he relies too often and too self-indulgently upon the human diminishment of his targets; as a lyric love poet he is an almost complete failure, a sentimentalist who has an image of himself as lovable individualist and marvellously whimsical lover–yet he appeals to this, so to say, to justify his cruelty: he fails in compassion. Thus the vast majority of his comic or satirical poems are slight. Yet they are intelligent, well-made and immense fun. There is nothing offensive in 'grin/hooray/hooray for the large/men who lie// between the breasts/of bestial Marj/for the strong men/who// sleep between the legs of Lil' or with 'twentyseven bums give a prostitute the once/-over. fiftythree (and one would see if it could)/eyes say the breasts look very good:/firmlysquirmy with a slight jounce. . . .'. But it is in the pure bawdy that Cummings is really at his best, as in the famous car-virgin poem 'she being Brand/ -new; and you/know consequently a/little stiff i was/careful. . . .' But this is hardly epoch-making, merely (at its best) an anti-puritanism admirably perfected: a celebration of the pure and proper bawdiness of pre-puritan times. The whole satirical attitude is, if not 'reactionary', then certainly disappointingly traditional. And the key to this over-romanticism is in the love poems which are simply commonplace. In prose Cummings is perhaps superior: *The Enormous Room* is a classic exposé of cruel bureaucracy and authoritarianism, and had its recognitions of the limitations of official language been fully worked out in the poetry then this might have achieved more. *EIMI* is similarly excellent on Russia. The best of his plays is *Him* (1927), which is more original in form than the poetry. *Six Non-Lectures* (1953) is criticism. *Complete Poems* (1968).

D

Dagerman, Stig (1923–54) Swedish fiction writer, playwright, poet, journalist. Dagerman, who not only possessed but could express some of the tragic psychopathological intensity of Strindberg (q.v.), was for a few years Sweden's literary prodigy; his suicide at thirty-one was as symbolic for the Swedish intelligentsia as those of Crane (q.v.) or Pavese (q.v.) had been for their countrymen. He was a writer of unquestionable genius, power and versatility but finally, feeling under pressure from an intellectual public too eager for more–and resenting its pretentiousness–he gave in to his depressive terrors and fear of losing his literary direction. His attempt to solve his problems by marriage (1953) failed. His suicide may be compared to the earlier one of Karin Boye (q.v.), another whose genius transcended the Swedish literary context, which is generally over-complacent, derivative and secretly resentful of true originality. Dagerman absorbed the work of Eyvind Johnson (1900) and the more interesting Vesaas (q.v.), but was mainly influenced by non-Scandinavian writers: Kafka (q.v.), Camus (q.v.), Faulkner (q.v.), and French existentialism (*see* Sartre). His best writing is an impressive synthesis of symbolism, expressionism and realism, all shot through with a violently melancholy suspicion of social processes. He began as a syndicalist, wrote bad propagandist verse and towards the end tried to counter his self-destructive impulses by adopting a 'proletarian' attitude (there is strong precedent for this in Scandinavian literature); but he was too subtle. He first emerged as a young star of the so-called 'forties' group (*40-taliter*), all of whom (guiltily uninvolved in the war against the Nazis) would have subscribed to his stipulation that we must 'keep fear living in us like a permanently ice-free harbour which helps us to survive the winters. . . .' One cannot but recall Nietzsche, who would surely have approved of the first novel, *Ormen* (1945), *The Serpent*, which terrifyingly demonstrates the existential necessity of keeping fear alive and of attempting to overcome it. *De dömdas ö* (1945), *Isle of the Damned*, is more allegorical and less successful: Dagerman was at his best when dealing with individual psychological situations. *Bränt barn* (1948; tr. *A Burnt Child,* 1950) is a memorable study of a young man's over-attachment to his mother; in its laconic, detached style Dagerman found his own voice. He later dramatized it. *Nattens lekar* (1947; tr. *The Games of Night,* 1960), stories equally convincing and assured in presentation, displays Dagerman's expressionist genius. His plays, many of them successful on the Swedish stage, are equally versatile. The best are *Den dödsömde* (1948; tr. *The Man Condemned to Die,* 1950) and *Streber* (1949), *The Climber,* which although flawed by syndicalist ideology offers superb insights into working-class life. There was every reason for the Swedes to feel traumatized by Dagerman's suicide (by inhalation of car-exhaust fumes): he had fought with courage and intelligence against his pessimism and tendency to over-introspection—and he had lost.

D'Annunzio, Gabriele (1863–1938) Italian novelist, short story writer, dramatist, poet, orator. The most exotic of the three poets (Carducci, q.v., Pascoli, q.v.) in Italy at about the turn of the century. The vast edifice of D'Annunzio's work, much of it based on a crude misreading of Nietzsche, has rotted away. Vastly energetic, courageous, rhetorically gifted, flamboyant, mindless, the national hero who opened the way to fascism (but his attitude to it when it came was more equivocal than is often supposed), egoistic and egotistic, shameless, destructive, D'Annunzio appealed to all that is worst in the Italian character. A crass sensualist for whom an unconsidered death was the final ideal (this is already apparent in the pseudo-Nietzschean novel *Il trionfo della morte,* 1894; tr. *The Triumph of Death,* 1898), he did clear the air of Italian letters—but he also made it uninhabitable. Reaction to him had to be subdued: crepuscular (*see* Gozzano). But the short-lived futurism (*see* Marinetti), although opposed to the influence of D'Annunzio, contained much of his ferocity and egotistic blindness; the first poet entirely alien to D'Annunzio was Ungaretti (q.v.) and Ungaretti did not even visit Italy until he was twenty-six. Still, there is something worth saving from the ruins of D'Annunzio's work: some of the poems written in the eighties, and others from *Alcyone* (1904). Here, his delirium and over-voluptuousness are quietened by his pantheism and profound desire and feeling for the natural world, with whose more sensational characteristics he could effortlessly identify himself. *Al-*

cyone was a product of his long liaison with the Italian actress Elenora Duse, who exercised a fortunate influence on him. There are good selections of his poetry in *The Penguin Book of Italian Verse* (1965, with tr.) and in Sanguineti's *Poesia italiana del Novecento* (1969), *Italian Poetry of the Twentieth Century.*

Darío, Rubén (ps. Félix Rubéli García Sarmiento) (1867–1916) Nicaraguan poet and prose writer, who was a leading figure in the Latin-American movement, *modernismo,* which was strongly to influence Spanish poetry. A prodigy as well as an opportunist, he established himself very early. He lived in various countries in Latin-America and travelled widely in Europe, where (in Mallorca) he had intended to settle—but he died, virtually from the ravages of drink—on his way back to his native country. He himself coined the term *modernismo.* It is now fashionable to dismiss his poetry while acknowledging his enormous influence, but he left a number of good poems and some excellent prose. *Modernismo* has not been—and cannot be—satisfactorily defined. It was a reaction against positivism; it took the form of a Spanish-American nationalism but its style was European. Darío dominated it, though he did not invent it. It began in the eighties and ended with the First World War. Its most important prose document is the essay *Ariel* (1900) by the Uraguayan José Enrique Rodó (1872–1917): this is an intelligent exploration of and prescription for a great Latin-American civilization; Rodó puts the emphasis on spirituality (Ariel) rather than materialism (Caliban). This was oversimplified; Rodó cannot be blamed for a movement which failed in its political aspect because of its excessive cultural hermeticism. But Darío himself was the poet chiefly responsible for bringing his and his fellow-poets' innovations to a moribund Spanish poetry; and that is the real achievement of *modernismo.* The poetry of the *modernistas* is much more flexible than that of their predecessors. His mature poems oscillate decadently between visions of erotic bliss and erotic guilt (he was a womanizer); the best, most candid and least mannered are in *Cantos de vida y esperanza* (1905), *Cantos of Life and Hope.* His complete works appeared 1950–5; the fullest collection of the poems was published in 1967.

Davie, Donald (1922) English poet, critic, academic; for some years has lived and taught in California. Davie is well-endowed with talent and intelligence but has also a nagging didactic quality which mars even his best work. Although fascinated and influenced by modernism (he has written a book on Pound, q.v.), and by the poetry of Charles Tomlinson (q.v.), he is fundamentally a neo-Augustan who distrusts the self-exploratory, spontaneous, unconscious element in romantic poetry—and wishes he didn't, even to the extent of sometimes trying to imitate and simultaneously 'improve' it. He has certain kinds of feeling but in his poetry does not quite know what to do with it, so that he is almost always over-literary, ingenious, contrived: he has hardly succeeded in discovering the true voice for it. He believes in eighteenth-century reasonableness and has sometimes admirably controlled his passionate indignations about atrocity and stupid extremism to produce a decent neo-Augustan minor verse. But one senses two frustrations working away at each other: the furious and exasperated conviction of the didact that a temperamental anti-romanticism is *right* and ought not to be challenged (the very existence of views dissimilar to those he holds does not help Davie's critical or poetic tone); and the yearning to possess a 'romantic' temperament upon which he could put in some hermeneutic Augustan work. Davie's lack of eclecticism and his anti-scepticism weaken his appeal. The poetry is sometimes ingenious; it is never (except in a few very early poems) *moving*—and anti-romanticism, which must, like romanticism, function in all poets, is not a device for subtracting this mysterious quality from poetry. The matter is all summed up in Davie's cunning, intricate, stimulating, disingenuous critical book *Thomas Hardy and English Poetry* (1972). This is on the Yeats versus Hardy theme—and it is a very confused work. His convolutions have quality. *Collected Poems* (1972). *The Shires* (1974) is his most inferior volume of poetry.

Davies, W. H. (1871–1940) Welsh poet, autobiographer, novelist. The young Davies, penniless and without education, became a tramp in America, lost a leg, returned to London and began to sell his pamphlets of verse on the streets. Shaw (q.v.) discovered him, wrote a preface to *The Autobiography of a Super-Tramp* (1907)—the best of his prose books—and established him. Davies wrote far too much (*Complete Poems*, 1963). Fortunately this presents no problems: his poetic genius was not diluted—it either presented itself or simply failed to surface—in hundreds of self-consciously poetical verses. At his best he is lucid but not, as he is too often characterized, 'simple'. 'Scotty's Luck',

'The Inquest' and 'I am the Poet Davies, William' all have a Blakean directness tinged with Davies's own Welsh sense of cunning or mystery; 'The Bird of Paradise' enigmatically makes heart-rending poetry out of what ought to be Georgian cliché (the dying prostitute cries in her delirium 'Don't touch that bird of paradise,/Perched on the bedpost there!'). There are perhaps some thirty poems of this quality in the 749 by Davies that appear in *Complete Poems:* a notable achievement.

Day Lewis, Cecil (1904–72) Irish poet (-Laureate 1968) novelist, critic, verse-speaker, translator, detective-story writer as 'Nicholas Blake'. Day Lewis was a much liked man, associated with Auden (q.v.), MacNeice (q.v.), and Spender (q.v.) in the public mind, whose poetry—especially that of *Word Over All* (1943)—had in his lifetime a wide appeal. He possessed what often looked like poetic energy and lyric power but was fundamentally soft at the centre, whereas even the most 'ravishing poetry', as Housman (q.v.) would have put it, is hard at that point: he achieved his best effects in translation (Valéry, q.v.; Vergil) or in pastiche (Hardy, q.v., Emily Brontë and others). Under examination his poems fall to pieces; are held together only by his own sentimental, indeed Georgian (*see* Brooke) notion of lyricism. The best of his detective stories is *A Tangled Web* (1956). *The Lyric Impulse* (1965) gives a popularized, simplified, Gravesian (q.v.) view of poetry. His unfortunate lapses into 'public poetry' may be forgiven and forgotten. *Collected Poems* (1954) was followed by several more volumes.

Dazai Osamu (ps. Shuji Tsushima) (1909–48) Japanese novelist. A mentally unstable left-wing alcoholic and drug-addict, he managed to produce the finest psychological novels of his generation. He has affinities with Lowry (q.v.), and Fallada (q.v.). The chief influences on him were Akutagawa Ryunosuke (1892–1927), and Ibuse Musuji (q.v.). He attempted to commit suicide three times in the thirties; finally, at the height of his fame, he succeeded (though some believe he was murdered by the woman who died by drowning with him). *Gyakko* (1935), *Retrogression, Doke no hana* (1935), *A Clown's Flowers* and *Ningen shikkaku* (1937; tr. *No Longer Human,* 1938) are savagely self-critical autobiographical novels, full of detached irony and portraits of himself. *Shayo* (1947; tr. *The Setting Sun,* 1950) is his most mature and satisfying novel. He was the son of rich parents who had been deeply grieved by his dissipated life and his opposition to the militarists; now he paid poignant tribute to their lost way of life in an acute and nostalgic study. A number of his excellent stories have appeared in translation in magazines.

De La Mare, Walter (1873–1956) English poet, fiction writer, anthologist (*Come Hither*, 1923 rev. 1928, has been the best English anthology for children of the century), essayist. De La Mare defies classification: he had little critical intelligence, great editorial acumen, his work could be feeble in the worst Georgian (*see* Brooke) sense and yet he is an original poet whose best work is uniquely his own. Strangely, in a man wedded to the past, he often seems as fiction writer and even poet to be the nearest English equivalent of the German expressionists (*see* Stadler)–and certainly he is an expressionist in the wide sense of the term. He seems to have been oblivious to anything but his own supernatural view of reality; this view is sometimes distorted in an English-expressionist manner but at others by a fondness for the lush excesses and the fancifulnesses of hyper-romanticism (as, notoriously, in the anthology-piece 'Arabia'). He wrote poetry and prose 'for children' but it is for adults too; as 'children's writer' he is in any case unapproached by anyone in the century. In his refusal to be deflected from his own attitudes and procedures he resembles Hardy (q.v.) rather than the more ambitious Yeats (q.v.) and so he has not been popular with academics. His poetry needs to be taken all together and is now available in a single volume: *Complete Poems* (1969). Many of De La Mare's long poems that do not come off are intensely interesting; one that does come off is 'The Feckless Dinner Party', which shows him at his bland and humorous narrative best. His poems written for children (e.g. 'Peacock Pie' itself) seem to resemble 'nonsense poetry', but are procedurally closer, despite their Englishness, to the 'uprooted metaphors', the self-generating images, of Goll (q.v.) and Trakl (q.v.), whose work he would doubtless have thought inferior to Brooke's (q.v.). . . . At other times De La Mare is simply a rustic English poet: like Hardy, though differently, he can directly express the spirit of English rusticity, as in 'The Quartette'. Another type of poem he wrote invests the commonplace with a sinisterness, an uncanniness, a mystery. In his stories and novels (notably *Memoirs of a Midget*, 1921) De La Mare achieves the same effects in a prose of rare distinction (Graham Greene, q.v., has cannily compared it to Stevenson's). There is a *Collected Stories for Children* (1947) but as yet no complete stories: some of the best are in *Some Stories* (1962) and in the misleadingly entitled *Collected Tales* (USA only, 1950), a selection. De La Mare is often put forward as an escapist writer and in his inferior writings he may so be described; but at his best he is not an escapist but an expressionist, an unconscious modernist using archaic trappings with consummate skill.

Deledda, Grazia (1871–1936) Popular Italian (Sardinian) novelist who won the 1926 Nobel Prize. The novel has been weak in Italian literature and Italian critics tend (if guiltily) to make too much of Deledda because of the Nobel accident. But she is more than competent. Her best work, all of which is lyrical-naturalist-decadent, is set in Sardinia, which she evokes well: for example, *Cenere* (1904; tr. *Ashes*, 1908). Her imagination is limited and she did not succeed in curbing her romantic excess but she shirked none of the issues of which she was aware.

Desnos, Robert (1900–45) French poet, novelist. He died of starvation and typhus after having been imprisoned by the Nazis for his Resistance activities. He began as a leading member of the surrealist movement but was 'expelled' by Breton (q.v.) in 1930. Of all the so-called 'automatic' poetry of the twenties Desnos's is the most consistently beautiful and suggestive; the later poetry is more consciously controlled and less powerful, but occasionally it achieves a magnificent and moving simplicity. The best poems, however, are in *Corps et biens* (1930) and in the delightful 30 *Chantefables pour les enfants sages* (1944), written as a relief from his dangerous work and his understandably 'committed' poetry. Desnos wrote two other books for children that have not been published. He is 'delirious' in his best poetry but not as 'spontaneous' as he seems. *Choix de poèmes* (1946) is edited by his fellow-surrealist Georges Hugnet. *Le Vin est tiré* (1943) is a novel. An excellent selection from all his poetry is in *Domaine public* (1953).

De Vries, Peter (1910) American novelist. One of the most interesting of the *New Yorker* stable of writers (he has worked on the magazine since the mid-forties). He is best described as a lunatic parodist; he has been at his most serious when he is not trying to be serious. Sometimes he sees life as contingent, sometimes as created by an indifferent or 'dead' God, but this does not disturb him. His first batch of novels (1940–61), including *Tunnel of Love* (1954) and *Mackerel Plaza* (1958), are hilarious comedies of manners often in forms parodic of major twentieth-century American writers. De Vries is laughing, validly and without ill humour, at literary seriousness. *The Blood of the Lamb* (1962) initiated a more confused phase, and misguidedly attempts to give body to an *oeuvre* which already–in its inimitable, deliberately light, way–possessed it.

Dewey, John (1859–1952) American philosopher. He is an important representative of a key element, pragmatism (*see* William James), in American literature and life. The original pragmatism of C. S. Peirce (1839–1914)–he called it pragmaticism to distinguish it from James's–has also been influential e.g. Creeley's (q.v.) poetry is Peirce's and not Dewey's pragmatism carried to solipsist extremes. Dewey tried to transform philosophy into heuristics and called psychology into service in this project. James Ward Smith thus summarizes the first step of his theory of the function of thought, called 'instrumentalism': '. . . Given the breakdown of habit, the organism nonetheless presses on to further action . . .' (cf. Creeley's broken lines). Dewey's influence on American education was enormous (and led to a simplistic reaction). J. A. Rice founded Black Mountain College (1933–56) in North Carolina with the object of providing a heuristic type of creative education; Dewey was a visitor. Those associated with this liberal enterprise included Olson (q.v.), Paul Goodman, Creeley (q.v.), Robert Duncan and Ginsberg (q.v.); Creeley edited *The Black Mountain Review* from 1954 until 1957. Dewey, a resolute anti-Platonist, would doubtless have disapproved of the later Black Mountain movement as excessive and above all as static; but he stands squarely for the concept of learning by action, for democracy as a learning process, and as squarely against religious (or other) systems that create stultifying dogmas which act against the 'creative intelligence' that is mankind's only hope. As Dewey's interesting *Art as Experience* (1954) shows, he did not entirely understand the relationship of his position to artistic practice. As educator he did more or less directly influence novelists and poets but of course he stood, too, for a strain in the American nature. The 'intelligent philistinism' (G. S. Fraser) from which much American literature springs is a result of the traditional Anglo-American view that 'literature' contains immutable truths (like religions); the importation of European modernist procedures into America is frequently through a filter of Dewey-like, tough, 'isolate' empiricism and even when it isn't (e.g. Bly, q.v., Ashbery) it is as frequently understood through that filter.

Dickey, James (1923) American poet, novelist, critic. America's most successful poet of his generation (largely on the strength of an abject novel, *Deliverance*, 1970, which used every ingratiating device from sodomitic rape to large-scale allegory to attain its ends, and which has not enhanced his reputation with critics). His earlier verse (*Into the Stone*, 1960) compounds a Roethkean (q.v.) tone with pseudo-Orphism to produce an unconvincing kind of mysticism expressed in curiously clogged rhythms. In later work (*Poems 1957–1967*, 1967) he synthesizes this with recollection of his war experiences (as an airman), with a more intimate, buttonholing manner, and with the styles of Bly (q.v.), James Wright (q.v.), Rilke (q.v.) and many others. It is a grandiose concatenation and Bly's own savage attack on its self-indulgence and irresponsible use of themes of suffering is a memorable one. Richard Howard, though, refers to his 'titanic choice'. . . .

Döblin, Alfred (1878–1957) Versatile and (outside his own country) underrated German novelist, essayist, who was a practising psychiatrist. A socialist, he left Germany in 1933 and went into exile to France and then the USA, returning to Germany after the war. He became a Christian at the time of the fall of France. His first short stories examined methods of bourgeois self-evasion in a stridently expressionist (*see* Stadler) style. He then turned to many different types of novel, exploring–by means of various applications of depth psychology, and with acute awareness of social conditions–the reasons why individuals lend themselves to mass-movements that destroy their self-identity (e.g. *Die drei Sprünge des Wang-Lun*, 1915, *The Three Leaps of Wang-Lun* and the futurological satire *Wadzeks Kampf mit der Dampfturbine*, 1918, *Wadzek's Struggle with the Steam-Machine*, which deserves a higher status in its genre than it has). His most famous book, *Berlin-Alexanderplatz* (1929; tr. 1931), which makes free use of stream-of-consciousness techniques, collage, montage and Dos Passos's (q.v.) simultaneity, is one of the most comprehensive portraits of a fundamentally decent but socially corrupted and dim-witted proletarian ever written (Döblin had practised in the Berlin slums); it also deliberately and prophetically lays bare the seed-ground of Nazism. His later novels (e.g. his last, *Hamlet*, 1956) do not reach this level, but are almost all of high quality and require renewed critical attention and translation. A somewhat inferior but revealing novel, *Pardon wird nicht gegeben* (1935), is his only other book to appear in English: *Men Without Mercy*, 1937. *Ausgewählte Werke, Selected Works,* has been in process since 1966.

Dobson, Rosemary (1920) Australian poet; better than her grandfather, Austin Dobson. Regarded as second only to Judith Wright (q.v.) amongst Australian women poets, she is in fact considerably superior: she has more effectively, less cosily, contained her sense of religious and erotic disturbance than Wright and her development is more convincing. But she is unhappy in the tight forms that she employs: if she could move into the metrically (not rhythmically) freer territory of Anne Sexton (q.v.) she would be a more substantial poet than either. *Selected Poems* (1963); *Cock Crow* (1965).

Doderer, Heimito Von (1896–1966) Austrian novelist. There is much controversy about Doderer, whose chief novels are *Die Strudlhofstiege* (1951), *The Strudlhof Steps,* and its sequel *Die Dämonen* (1956; tr. *The Demons,* 1961). *Ein Mord, den jeder begeht* (1938) has also been translated: *Every Man a Murderer* (1964). Many readers may well find themselves unable to decide; certainly he did himself little good by his polemical *Grundlagen und Funktion des Romans* (1959), *Foundation and Function of the Novel.* Doderer was in theory a sort of absolute realist: art, he insisted, cannot impose patterns on life. But of course it has to, which is where Doderer as self-critic is so vulnerable. He may also have made an error in trying to rival Musil (q.v.) and in his intermittent use of modernist techniques that were not natural to him. However, his story of the Vienna of the twenties, culminating in the burning of the Palace of Justice in 1927, has humour, great scope, irony and a gallery of convincingly realized characters. He may be a potentially major writer whose achievement was spoiled by an over-theoretical, indecisive approach—or he may be a writer of major achievement who did enough to transcend his confused ideologies. It is some testimony to his readability and creative intelligence that there should be so much controversy on the subject and that we can return to him, without effort, to try to form our own judgements.

Donleavy, J. P. (1926) American-Irish writer who has lived in Ireland. Donleavy's only substantial work, his first novel *The Ginger Man* (1956), is already threatened by a tendency to float about aimlessly in the picaresque and by over-indulgence in whimsicality. But it is a genuinely comic book which has at the same time a moral point to make. After this Donleavy, though the subject of an enthusiastic cult, slid into a pseudo-poetic exponent of the picaresque: in *The Saddest Summer of Samuel S.* (1967) and others.

Dos Passos, John (1896–1970) American novelist, playwright, travel writer, translator, journalist, poet. Dos Passos is of major historical importance and is a major technician but intrinsically a minor writer. He served in the Medical Corps in the First World War. Thereafter he lived in America but travelled extensively, usually on journalistic assignments. The key to Dos Passos' failure to achieve a major fiction in its own right, and to his subsequent decline, lies in his feeble imaginative powers: he can never reconcile his confusions. Ironically, he had by the time of *Manhattan Transfer* (1925), a portrait of New York City, devised a brilliant technique. The massive trilogy *U.S.A.* (1930–6; 1938), though it finely develops this technique, is a less successful work: it is too sprawling, too hard to follow and it magnifies the chief fault of the earlier book, which is that it ignores people's inner motivations. In general terms Dos Passos moved from a leftist to a rightist view of affairs, from a critical socialism to a Jeffersonian conservatism (*The Head and Heart of Thomas Jefferson,* 1954). But he never fully accepted any system and he was never, in any sense of the term, 'radical chic'. He was, rather, a consistent pessimist. Though weak in imaginative power, Dos Passos was the English-language writer of his generation most aware of foreign literatures, particularly French, Spanish, German and Portuguese (his half-Portuguese father fought in the American Civil War). In five books–three novels, a volume of unsuccessful poems and a collection of mannered dialogue-essays exploring Spain and its temperament–he tried to find himself imaginatively, but failed. His solution to his creative problems, which included low but persistent creative pressure (with the obvious corollary of tendency towards pastiche), was fascinatingly intelligent. Feeling crippled himself, seeing no hope in the present and less in the future, and unresponsive to the hope in others, he decided to take absolute control of his material. He exploited *unanimisme* (*see* Romains) not as a message of hope but as a means of attaining objectivity, of passing casually from character to character. He took over Joyce's (q.v.) interior monologue, and the drab, naturalistic aspect of his writing. He allied himself to Baroja's (q.v.) seething anti-institutionalism, really a nihilism. *Manhattan Transfer,* centered around the experiences of an actress, is a panoramic study of a city, uses cinematic and 'newsreel' as well as stream-of-consciousness (*see* Bergson) techniques, and although it fails in psychological terms—its characters are garish puppets—it is successful as a prophecy of urban nightmare and doom: not a realistic novel, but a sociological dystopia. In *U.S.A.*, whose time-span and scope are so much greater, technical triumph is also creative failure. Now the technique has been perfected: newsreel, biographies (of real people), the 'camera eye'—the prose poem into which Dos Passos concentrates his own imaginative perceptions—and straight, objective narrative. Parts of the trilogy are excellent, but—above all because the crucial 'camera eye' passages are impressionistic and not expressionistic and are thus inadequate to deal with the enormous theme—the whole fails. It is written from the point of view of a committed, socialistic anti-capitalist but this point of view is not its conscientious author's true one. He is a pessimist, even at times a nihilist. His people tend to be doomed and, like him, to despair. They are unexcited by all extra-material impulses (this is not 'true to life'). Yet, though his literary gifts had evaporated by the mid-fifties, Dos Passos remained consistent. He had always turned his despair, not enough compensated for by creative excitement (as his single volume of poetry, 1922, shows), into something else. His second trilogy (*District of Columbia,* 1939–49; 1952) is less energetic, and it shows him progressing from disillusionment with communism to an uncomprehending and unshrewd distaste for the New Deal. But his targets are the same: men of power, institutions. Subsequently he became increasingly populist but this is not important because the change is only superficial. Dos Passos is minor because his own 'camera eye', abandoned after *U.S.A.*, is not modernist, is not fitted to deal with modern times, but he invented a technique that *is* modernist, one which has influenced, notably, Döblin (q.v.) and Sartre (q.v.), and one which may legitimately be imitated again. This is in itself a remarkable achievement.

Douglas, Keith (1920–44) English poet and prose writer who, after going through the desert campaign, was killed on his third day in Normandy. He had just time to mature into a poet of considerable originality and achievement. He sensed that he was not going to survive the war and this tempered his romanticism with the result that his later, maturer poems are quite different from most of those written in the over-romantic forties. His profound erotic bitterness is reinforced by his conviction that his life would be wasted, and his irony is thus strangely detached and authoritative in so young a man. He struggled successfully against sentimentality and a neatness of form which he felt to be an inadequate goal. His weakness is that he did not often find a technique in which he could be truly confident—but which of his British successors, of this potentiality, has done so since? His powers of poetic concentration are seen most clearly in such poems as (the relatively early) 'The Marvel', 'Dead Men' and the superb 'Egypt'—perhaps the best of all comments on that strange country—beginning 'Aniseed has a sinful taste: /at your elbow a woman's voice/like, I imagine, the voice of ghosts/demanding food. . . .' and ending (referring, of course, to the late Farouk): 'My God,/the king of this country must be proud'. *Alamein to Zem Zem* (1946), well illustrated by Douglas himself, describes the desert campaign. *Collected Poems* (1966).

Douglas, Norman (1868–1952) Scottish (with German blood) prose writer. His best books are *Old Calabria* (1915) and the shrewd *Looking Back* (1933), which contains many valuable and just observations on writers; his most famous book is the novel *South Wind* (1917). Douglas was a depthless hedonist who could take unworried pleasure in what he called 'time-honoured bestiality' (thus he used to buy young girls for his use from their poor families in Italy; one day a group of youths gave him a beating for doing this and interested him in buying youths. . . .), and his antagonism towards Christianity, puritanism and socialism is strengthened, so to say, by a perfectly undisturbed sincerity. He can convey his delight in the physical features of countries, especially of his beloved Italy, as almost no other travel writer—but, though he can be kind as well as malicious in his retrospective estimates of friends, he lacks consideration or the capacity to stand and stare, is in too much of a hurry to go on and achieve his hedonistic goal. The contents of *The Norman Douglas Limerick Book* (1969), printed privately by him in 1928, give some indication of the scope of his aesthetic. *South Wind,* written to please, sometimes pleases—but its insistence on the virtues of hedonism make it boring. As a critic remarked, Douglas should have been a 'writer of notes'. He killed himself.

Doyle, [Sir] Arthur Conan (1859–1930) Scottish fiction writer, spiritualist, publicist. He was originally a practising doctor. He wrote lively historical romances in the manner of Stevenson, pioneer science-fiction featuring Professor Challenger (e.g. *The Poison Belt,* 1913) and histories–and he created Sherlock Holmes. Holmes is Doyle the decadent, projecting himself into the role of impeccably 'logical' pseudo-scientist (Holmes calls induction 'deduction'); the novels and stories are very skilful and refreshing for they are at once sinister and escapist. They can hardly lose their popularity.

Drabble, Margaret (1939) English novelist and critic. Her earlier novels–*The Garrick Year* (1964), *The Millstone* (1965)–were technically conventional but intelligent, critical and sensitive accounts of the tribulations of young women. Latterly she has become more ingratiating, both in style and content, towards her audience. Her book on *Arnold Bennett* (1974) is, however, an excellent study.

Dreiser, Theodore (1871–1945) American novelist, playwright, writer, journalist. He was born of poor, piously Roman Catholic parents in Indiana, the eleventh and penultimate child. For many years Dreiser was a newspaperman; at Butterick Publications, as editor of the women's magazine *The Delineator,* he achieved remarkable financial success. In 1900 he published *Sister Carrie,* which flopped because, despite Frank Norris's enthusiasm, the prudish publisher failed to back it, but he still believed in himself as a novelist, and with *Jennie Gerhardt* (1911), he succeeded in establishing himself as one. There followed the first two novels in the 'trilogy of desire' about the career of the financier Frank Cowperwood: *The Financier* (1912) and *The Titan* (1914). Then came *The 'Genius'* (1915), followed ten years later by *An American Tragedy,* which, though it was never in the 'top ten' best-sellers, went on selling steadily, and made Dreiser rich. Some non-fiction, such as *Dreiser Looks at Russia* (1928) followed and he became increasingly interested in socialism and engaged in some political activities. He joined the communist party shortly before his death, which assured him of critical obloquy for some years. *The Stoic* (1947), mostly written years before, is so unsatisfactory that it hardly qualifies as the third of the Cowperwood trilogy; *The Bulwark* (1946), with which Dreiser had struggled at intervals over the last thirty-five years of his life, is indispensable to an understanding of him, but a failure. Dreiser wrote plays (*The Hand of the Potter,* 1918, is the best), many non-fiction works (e.g. *Tragic America,* 1931; *Dawn,* 1931; *Newspaper Days,* 1931), free verse (better forgotten) and three volumes of short stories, later selected in *The Best Short Stories* (1947). Dreiser has been regarded, and not without good reason, as the major American representative of naturalism (*see* Zola). But this is to over-simplify and has eventually led to serious misinterpretation of his texts. Of his works *Sister Carrie* and *An American Tragedy* are great, *Jennie Gerhardt* nearly so; the first two Cowperwood books are major; *The 'Genius'*, though flawed, has not received its due; the two posthumous novels are revealing failures. The judgment that Dreiser was an atrocious stylist needs modification. As a man Dreiser was powerful but confused; driven by an excessive sexual appetite, he at first generated creative tension by putting himself between women eager for him, but later he became a more aimless womanizer. Hardy (q.v.) was an important formative influence but unlike Hardy Dreiser did not have the gift of posing the large questions that troubled him in an exquisite way. His genius consisted in the capacity to explore the relationship between contingency and purpose in terms of imaginatively invented character. He was not, however, as unsophisticated or indiscriminate a *reader* as we have been led to suppose. He studied the ideas of Loeb and of Freud (q.v.), and he probably understood them. Dreiser's deterministic view of life and his own experiences of poverty and cheap success gave him a starting point. But one of the secrets of his immense power is his fascinated curiosity about the real nature of what we call chance. Another, more universally acknowledged, is his genius for selecting significant detail, which he accumulates with great skill. In *Sister Carrie* Carrie 'wins' and Hurstwood 'loses'—both by 'luck'. But what is the nature of luck? The novel raises this question. Jennie Gerhardt, by a certain sensitivity in her character not possessed by Carrie, is destroyed. In *An American Tragedy* Clyde is executed. But it is impercipient to assert, as is so often asserted, that 'society is to blame' for his fall. This is a crude misreading. Dreiser's true theme, in his greatest fiction, is the exploration of the possibility that a person's being—his whole state, itself a mystery, and much illuminated by Dreiser's own building-up of detail—'attracts his life' (i.e. his destiny or fortune). As Ellen Moers has shown

(*Two Dreisers*, 1969) the attention devoted to Clyde's *eyes* in *An American Tragedy* is significant and is related to this theme. He shared with Hardy, James (q.v.) and only a few other male novelists the capacity to portray women convincingly and unpatronizingly. As to his style: it can be extremely clumsy and without compensatory factors, but it can also be majestic, as in the closing chapters of *An American Tragedy*, in which a commonplace enough theme is invested with the dignity and pathos which it deserves but too seldom gets. After this, when Dreiser chose to resolve his bewilderment by espousing the socialist cause (some of his actions in the cause of justice were creditable), he was to all intents and purposes written out. The process of his decline had begun, in fact, with the two Cowperwood books, good though these manage to be; *An American Tragedy*, the theme of which had been in his mind for over thirty years, is the culmination of another process. Dreiser was fascinated with the manner in which some people (himself included: the size of his salary at Butterick's was legendary) can claw their way from the bottom to the top—and he was never quite certain if he approved or not. Only in *An American Tragedy* does his position become clear—although it may not have been clear to himself. Social Darwinism is a fallacy, but the Cowperwood books fail to penetrate to its heart. Cowperwood's personal relationships are well handled; the rest wavers between two theses—the notoriously simplistic 'philosophy of life' tends to drag at this work. But Dreiser's achievement is unquestionable and his survival as a classic writer assured. 'Dreiser can feel,' wrote Mencken (q.v.), 'and, feeling, he can move.' It is a fitting epitaph.

Drummond de Andrade, Carlos (1902) Brazilian poet, prose writer, critic. He is the most important Brazilian modernist, though his achievement is relatively independent of the rather frenetic Brazilian modernist movement inaugurated in São Paulo in February 1922. (This *modernismo* movement must not be confused with the Spanish American *modernista* movement [*see* Darío], with which he was, however, associated.) He is an anti-rhetorical poet who deliberately exploits the commonplace but his sceptical, ironic, humorous poetry is imbued with a tender and wistful nostalgia for the past. Of living poets, he is certainly among the first dozen. He has been a journalist and civil servant; literary men have found him an exceedingly elusive person. Drummond de Andrade's poetry does, as has been remarked, concern itself with the 'fragmentation of experience'. But it is held together by a bland unsentimental feeling for the past. Drummond de Andrade's complete works, *Obra completa,* appeared in 1964.

Duffy, Maureen (1933) English novelist, poet. She explores 'abnormal' sexual relationships, the sexual and social underworld of London, the universe of the subvert or the 'drop-out', in an often fragmentary prose that can achieve power, understanding and compassion. In *The Single Eye* (1964) she examined the break-up of the marriage of a young photographer and took considerable and brave risks with her technique in order to convey her sense of the omnipresence of a kind of Bergsonian (q.v.) *élan vital.* Sym of *The Paradox Players* (1967) is the same kind of character but he is more confidently realized and the sense of his physical existence vividly conveyed. Maureen Duffy struggles to discover an affirmatory attitude but rightly refuses to leave her chosen territory of the outcast, in whom she sees some visionary quality that she has not, as yet, been able to integrate with her keen sociological sense. Her poetry is lucid and direct.

Duhamel, Georges (1884–1966) French novelist, essayist, playwright, poet. His great gifts matched his compassion. His work, considering these gifts, has been neglected outside France. The son of a chemist who qualified as a doctor at the age of fifty-one and who was an odd mixture of persistence and fecklessness, he had an unhappy childhood. In 1906 he founded, with others, a community; they rented a house at Créteil and called it L'Abbaye. Here—Romains (q.v.) joined them early—the doctrine of unanimism (*see* Romains), which was already in the air, was formulated; books (including one of poems by Duhamel) were published. But the enterprise collapsed and Duhamel's idealism, already hurt by lack of harmony in his own family, was shattered. He continued to write poetry, and became interested in the theatre (his wife was an actress): it was his plays that first brought him to the attention of the public but they are not his best work. He qualified as a doctor and served as one throughout the First World War. His two volumes of war stories reflect both his horror and his vivid skill: *Vie des Martyrs* (1917; tr. *The New Book of Martyrs,* 1919)—this was published under the pseudonym of Denis Thévenin—and *Civilisation* (1918; tr. 1919). These, like Barbusse's *Le Feu,* come very early indeed in the books that seriously and comprehendingly protest at war; most were written from the late twenties onwards. Duhamel wrote a number of single novels, and many volumes of essays and polemic (the most famous was the excellent *Scènes de la vie future,* 1930, tr. as *America: The Menace* in 1931) but he is most famous for the novel-sequences *Salavin* (1930–2; tr. 1936) and *Chronique des Pasquier* (1933–41; tr. *The Pasquier Chronicles,* 1935–46). *Le Voyage de Patrice Pétiot* (1951) is a late novel that has been underrated because of its pessimism. Clearly the *Pasquier* sequence tells—more or less—Duhamel's own story (as Laurent Pasquier); but so, in its way, does the earlier *Salavin.* It is strange that this masterpiece should not have received the critical attention it deserves: it combines exquisite comedy with pathos, it is undoubtedly proto-existentialist (*see* Sartre) in that—for all its technical conventionality—it describes a man who, though in a state of 'bad faith', wishes to attain authenticity. *Salavin* is at once a great comic novel and a tragedy of Dostoievskian proportions—its subject is, indeed, a 'superfluous' and self-defeating character. It is a book of subtlety, humour and psychological depth; those who have not read it have a profound experience ahead of them. In Salavin Duhamel had found an objective correlative for his failure to achieve humanness without belief in God; in *The Pasquier Chronicles* he describes, with some irony and regret (one volume deals with the Créteil fiasco), the 'success' of Laurent Pasquier. This, again, is an underrated masterpiece. Duhamel was a pessimist who lashed out at verbal imprecision, at the absurd notion of progress (though he never joined the right), at man's misuse of machinery. But Duhamel was no Giono (q.v.): he knew that any attempt at a return to the past would be doomed. All that he 'hated' (he has most consistently been attacked for his 'hating') *is* hateful and his warnings of the thirties were prophetic. Part of the interesting *Lumières sur ma vie* (1945–50) is translated as *Light on My Days* (1958). He is a most lucid and loveable writer.

Duras, Marguerite (ps. Marguerite Donnadieu) (1914) French novelist, scriptwriter, playwright, born and brought up in Indo-China (which she left in her late teens). She has enjoyed both popular and critical success. Her chosen subject has been said to be 'duration', specifically the nature of waiting, *and* the nature of modern women in love (cf. Rosamund Lehmann, q.v.). . . . There is undoubtedly an element of pretentiousness in her rather prolific fiction (and drama); as even most of those who praise her admit, her subject matter is exceedingly limited—her characters, one might assert, are more banal than 'ordinary' people are and her deliberately muted style is frequently tricksy and mannered. Yet she has intelligence and the ability to hold the intelligent reader's attention. She is not insincere, but rather (perhaps) misguided in her overall approach. Her first novels, though on American rather than French models, are perhaps her best (e.g. *Un Barrage contre le Pacifique,* 1950, tr. *The Sea Wall,* 1952). Later successes such as *Moderato Cantabile* (1958; tr. 1966) and *Le Ravissement de L. V. Stein* (1964; tr. *The Rapture of L. V. Stein,* 1967) conceal vacuousness by manneredness; yet, frustratingly, a keen feminine intelligence is obviously present.

Durrell, Lawrence (1912) Irish novelist, poet, humorist, travel writer. Durrell is in some ways a sort of semi-spiritualizing Norman Douglas (q.v.), though he lacks Douglas's exactitude: he looks east (where he has mostly lived) and his hedonism is muffled only by his intellectually unsatisfactory 'relativistic' manner of viewing events. His poetry (*Collected Poems,* 1968), much influenced—though not sexually—by Kafavis (q.v.), can be fastidious and display classical virtues; it can also lapse into vulgarity. His fiction, in particular 'The Alexandria Quartet' (1957–60), has excited some critics but its popularity has aroused serious misgivings in others. It is narrated from different points of view, and its theme could be claimed to be the nature of art, the nature of love (for Durrell, simply sex properly experienced), or both. Technically Durrell is here doing nothing that Pirandello (q.v.) did not do better; the Joycean influence, as in the early *Black Book* (1938), is obtrusive. There is some lush overwriting, 'purple passages' in fact, which not even Durrell's admirers can overlook. It is indeed generally conceded that Durrell, both in this book and its successors *Tunc* (1968)—anagram of 'cunt'—and *Nunquam* (1970), is competing for attention in the language of the uncritical, perhaps pop-conscious, reader; the question is whether he is a master or a fraud or a mixture of both. . . . He is in fact a semi-erudite popularizer with a knack, and with a considerable streak of vulgarity; his chief expositor, G. S. Fraser, is genial on his behalf but evidently does not place him very highly. . . . The *Quartet* is a feat but it is likely that it will become dated and be seen as a glib mixture of popular Einsteinian physics, Milleresque (q.v.) sex-as-pure-knowledge and cut-price Joyce (q.v.).

Dürrenmatt, Friedrich (1921) Swiss dramatist, novelist, critic, writing in German. Dürrenmatt is a gifted sensationalist and a showman whose work is inferior to his compatriot Frisch (q.v.). But the plays *Der Besuch der alten Dame* (1956; tr. *The Visit,* 1962) and above all the famous *Die Physiker* (1962; tr. *The Physicists,* 1963) are not only ingenious but also suggestive, even though they fail—in common with most modern drama—to resolve the serious issues they raise. His less ambitious detective novels are excellent (e.g. *Der Richter und sein Henker,* 1950; tr. *The Judge and his Hangman,* 1954) and *Das Versprechen,* 1958; tr. *The Pledge,* 1959). His critical polemic is slick and tiresomely superficial where it need not be.

E

Eberhart, Richard (1904) American poet who spent some time at Cambridge University in the days when Bottrall (q.v.), Empson (q.v.) and others were there. He has done many jobs: tutor to the son of King Prajadhipok of Siam, schoolmaster, businessman (the Butcher Polish Company, Boston), naval officer, cultural advisor, professor. . . . This versatility is reflected in his poetry (*Collected Poems,* 1960; *Selected Poems 1930–1965,* 1965; *Shifts of Being,* 1968) as a kind of uncertainty of direction. A fair general criticism of the body of his work is that he can neither curb his innate lyricism nor properly concentrate his equally innate metaphysical ingenuity but there are some impressive exceptions. His weakness, a tendency to fall back desperately on to the now inadequate techniques of the past, is seen most clearly in *Collected Verse Plays* (1962), which none the less also display an interestingly overcrowded mind and sensibility. He finds his own voice too rarely–'The Groundhog' is the most famous early example–but the war sharpened his faculties, and drew from him some flawed but often deeply moving poetry. Some find him 'tremendously' powerful and authoritative in his contemplative and meditative poetry; others are touched but deplore his lack of control and diffuseness. Yet he remains as capable of producing almost good poems, such as 'Evil' from *Shifts of Being,* as he is of rank bad ones ('Nothing is so magnificent/As the sun descending. . . .' from the same volume). The key to this gifted poet's disappointing performance lies in his failure to find a personal rhythm–and he is therefore most successful when he uses tight metrical forms, against which something at least like a ghost of this personal rhythm is counterpointed.

Edwards, Hugh (1878–1952) English novelist. Born Gibraltar of naval family. Educated Sandhurst, served with West India Regiment in West Indies and West Africa. Invalided out before First World War; retired to a remote fisherman's cottage at East Prawle in

Devonshire where he remained for the rest of his life. Edwards is the persistently forgotten author of a periodically revived masterpiece, *All Night at Mr Stanyhurst's* (1933; 1937; 1963), much praised by leading critics (especially Graham Greene, q.v.), successfully adapted for radio, but never securely established as the classic it is. Edwards, once a full-blooded young Edwardian rake, was soaked in eighteenth-century lore and customs, and had seen the West Indies in their last blaze of 'barbaric splendour'. He wrote four other competent novels, but *All Night at Mr Stanyhurst's*, a tale within a tale, is unique: its rapport with the late eighteenth century is uncanny, every word counts, the final effect is hauntingly poetic.

Eich, Günter (1907–72) German poet, fiction writer and radio playwright. Eich was the world's leading master of the *Hörspiel* (radio play), but this is an ephemeral form and his many exercises in the genre, while effective, have dated. Two appear in translation as *Journeys* (1968). His stories are good but it is as a poet that he will endure. He is lyrical and feeling without resort to rhetoric or sentimentality and his appalled social conscience is expressed without distortion and with a powerful honesty. He has been influential in Germany, but largely ignored—often in favour of inferior poets—outside it. He worked hard to achieve coherence without falling back on inadequate techniques and his example is important. His collected works appeared in 1974.

Ekelöf, Gunnar (1907–68) Swedish poet, essayist, translator; now the most highly regarded Swedish poet of this century. He was throughout most of his creative life resolutely *avant garde,* though not in the usual faddish Scandinavian manner: what he wanted to communicate—a sense of total insecurity—was very difficult; he at first felt it to be impossible. Ekelöf was always attracted by the Orient—he studied Oriental languages in London as a young man—and particularly by Sufism; other influences, most of them eventually rejected, are Swedenborg, the Swedish mystical romantic poet Stagnelius, Eliot (q.v.), Desnos (q.v.) and surrealism (*see* Breton). His first book is his best (this is a heretical opinion): the self-styled 'suicide book' *Sent på jorden* (1932; tr. *Late Arrival on Earth,* 1967). It is unique in European poetry for its expression of a sense of absolute alienation from all external objects and people. The thirties successors to this collection contain sharp attacks on certain forms of 'bad faith' but are more uneven. In the forties and fifties Ekelöf concentrated more on technique; the poems vainly explore various possible modes of self-discovery and search for meaning out of the meaninglessness that always haunted the poet. The best later volume is *En Mölna-elegi* (1960), *A Moelna Elegy*, in which he communicates most powerfully the psychological and affective implications of his highly cerebral motivations–which are here seen to be absolutely sincere. The volumes published in the preceding twenty years had contained, in their desperation, some merely trivial experimentalism. His final 'Byzantine trilogy', *Dīwān över Fursten av Emgión* (1965), *Sagan om Fatumeh* (1966)–these are translated in *Selected Poems*, 1971, which contain nothing else–and *Vägvisare till underjorden* (1967), *Guide to the Underworld*, have been much praised. In them Ekelöf set out to create a 'pure poetry' of the kind proposed by Ostaijen (q.v.) and, after him, Bremond: a depersonalized poetry in which only the images would speak. The poems are set in medieval Byzantium and are deliberate pastiche of Arabic poetry. In the first book–and, indeed, in many poems published after it–Ekelöf demonstrates that for him thought is the main experience; here he gives way finally to a 'system', even though that system is cunningly paradoxical and mystical. Like Pessoa (q.v.), Ekelöf was fascinated by numerology, the occult and mysticism. But unlike Pessoa he did not make provision for the full expression of his other voices or desires: his subject-matter is narrow. He rested his case, he wrote in a posthumously published poem, on 'nothingness'. In Swedish terms he is a major poet; whether he is in European terms is by no means certain. *Dikter* collects poems 1932–51. *Partitur* (1969) collects unpublished poems 1965–8. *Selected Poems* (1967) is a comprehensive introduction, in English, to his whole output.

Ekwensi, Cyprian (1921) Nigerian (Ibo) novelist and children's author writing in English. *People of the City* (1954) was the first Nigerian novel to reach an international public. He is possessed of fewer literary skills than Achebe (q.v.), but is as intelligent and aware. His first novel is a vivid if sensational description of Lagos; his most controlled and carefully written book is *Burning Grass* (1962). Unlike Achebe he began as a popular writer; since then he has developed rapidly. *Burning Grass* is set in Northern Nigeria (where Ekwensi was born) and is on an African theme: it tells of a chief bewitched by wandering sickness who is finally cured by the 'witch-doctory' of an ex-slave. In *Beautiful Feathers,* again set in Lagos and dealing with urban problems, his style is similarly more assured.

Eliot, Thomas Stearns (1888–1965) American poet, critic and playwright. Born of a New England family in St Louis, Missouri, Eliot studied at Harvard, the Sorbonne and Oxford. Settled in London in 1915, married an Englishwoman, was a schoolmaster for a year and then (1917) entered the Foreign and Colonial department of Lloyds Bank where he remained until 1925. In 1927 became a naturalized British citizen; by 1928 confirmed himself in the position towards which he had long been tending: that of an English, High Anglican, royalist gentleman. His marriage was 'nerve-wracked'; eventually his wife was admitted to a mental hospital where she died in 1947. Meanwhile he entered (1935) the distinguished publishing firm of Faber and Faber, of which he was still a director when he died. He was awarded the Nobel Prize for Literature and the Order of Merit in 1948. In 1957 he made a second marriage, to a younger woman, which enlivened his last years. T. S. Eliot was an influential and pioneer poet, a seminal critic, and a successful reviver of the verse-play as a popular vehicle in Great Britain. He has been widely acknowledged as one of the century's great international literary figures–his poetry has been translated by Seferis (q.v.), Montale (q.v.) and many others almost as distinguished. His sway during his lifetime was immense and as the architect of Faber's famous poetry list he was responsible for introducing the works of Auden (q.v.), Spender (q.v.), MacNeice (q.v.), Barker (q.v.) and many others. His importance as a critic of sensibility, style and insight, and as a master of sensitive craftsmanship in verse, is unquestionable. The question of his poetic achievement remains, despite the enthusiasm of his many admirers, open. The sensibility is never in doubt; the human *sensitivity,* the ultimate sophistication (in a man of high outward sophistication)–these are. Yeats (q.v.) was intellectually vulgar and politically misguided; Eliot was intellectually fastidious and, at least publicly, cautious on political matters. But if Yeats carried it off, he did so because he had, in his own phrase, a 'passionate intensity'. Eliot lacked passion. He also lacked warmth. His adherents can pretend it in him as courtesy, kindness and other qualities; but they cannot point to it triumphantly and decisively, as they can to Yeats's. What in Rilke (q.v.) and Vallejo (q.v.) is literally existential agony, is in Eliot only disgust, exquisite rhetoric, literary awareness, self-relieving liturgical nostalgia. It is very fine but its status as major poetry is difficult to maintain without a kind of special pleading (religious, philosophical, or based on such claims as that style, historical influence or other extrinsic factors must of themselves guarantee intrinsic value) that should not need to be made. Eliot's spiritual-mindedness was genuine but his attempts to translate this into psychological terms are unconvincing: he never integrated his fear of the physical, the robustly sexual, the squalid—from which his spirituality arose—with his Anglican mysticism, which is a beautifully contrived patchwork of tradition, and not affirmative except of a Christian heaven that many admire but few can believe in. A modernist in technique, a true revolutionary in prosody, Eliot has exerted, paradoxically, a conservative influence; as his poetry lacks the firmness of experience so even his acute sensibility failed to recognize the *fact* that the Catholic past (enshrined for him in Dante) has vanished. But contemporary poetry and criticism are indebted to Eliot. In each case he took over tendencies already apparent but wayward and ill-formulated. Late Victorian and Edwardian critics were drawing haphazard attention to the merits of Elizabethan poetry and drama; he wonderfully sharpened this into an instrument that eventually cut through the slack, self-indulgent, iambic verse of the period and into its shoddy, undisciplined, impressionistic criticism. He drew attention to those poets (Davidson, Dowson) who were occasionally able to write in original rhythm, who could break away from the thud of the iamb or the monotonous trot of the triple metres. Meanwhile he had his own emotional wilderness to explore and he did this in early poetry, some sketched at Harvard (worked on assiduously for many years afterwards) of dazzling promise. In *The Love Song of Alfred J. Prufrock* (published 1915; repr. *Prufrock and Other Observations*, 1917) the homoerotically tinged, emotional numbness and sexual frigidity are subtly and self-critically equated with urban decay and social decadence. The main obvious influences, brought into English-language poetry for the first time, are Baudelaire and Laforgue, the symbolist and the ironic decadent; but Edwin Arlington Robinson's (q.v.) wryness is there, too; and an influence so far unnoticed may well be that of the Italian *crepuscolarismo* (Govoni, q.v., Gozzano, q.v.). The free but precisely controlled rhythms come, not from Whitman (anathema to Eliot), but from Eliot's own daring development of tendencies, slight shifts from conventional metres, in nineties poets. Eliot, nurtured on the philosophical idealism (it acted as a vehicle for his natural asceticism) of F. H. Bradley (upon whom he wrote his doctoral thesis) as well as Irving Babbitt's 'new humanism' (*see* Babbitt) was turning, via a long affair with European culture, from commercial America to the England of his forbears. A young man still, he brought an exactness to these processes; all that was lacking was emotional substance—but then the subject of the best poems was, in part, just that lack. His friend Ezra Pound (q.v.), long settled in London and a leading literary figure there, championed his cause and became his mentor. The satirical, precise, self-made-European-looking-at-America vein was continued in *Poems* (1919). *The Waste Land* (1922), still regarded by many as his greatest achievement, was composed in scraps between about 1912 and 1921 when a first draft was complete. It was composed under various pressures: a sense of hopelessness, desire to abandon philosophy for the concreteness of poetry, sexual difficulties, awareness of his wife's unstable mental state, estrangement from his family, psychiatric breakdown. . . . It retains at least, as Richard Ellman declares, 'the air of a splendid feat'. It was ruthlessly cut by Pound; and this version is preferable to the original restored by Eliot's widow after his death (1971). But it might perhaps have been even better had Eliot cut and revised it himself. . . . It is a highly personal poem, interpretable at many levels; certainly it is a record of a sensitive and sexually defeated man adrift in a civilization he loathes. But it is not personal enough; it is unfinished, the best that Pound (with only a few insistences from Eliot) could do. Where Eliot might have painfully pushed the personal through until it attained a universality of communication, he chose to rely on Pound, ellipses, an elegantly rendered satirical negativity, richness of literary allusion, a half-mocking long set of notes at the back (here smiling behind the hand). All that remained—apart from the long series of conservatively oriented but always occasionally illuminating books of criticism—was the fabric of a conversion to mystical Anglicanism (announced in *Ash Wednesday*, 1930, a well-arranged sequence that attempts, unsuccessfully, to convey the sense of a transcendental experience). This reached its peak of expression in the *Four Quartets* (*Burnt Norton*, 1936; *East Coker*, 1940; *The Dry Salvages*, 1941; *Little Gidding*, 1942), four long poems in which personal experience of place is counterpointed against the mystical and the symbolic in finely contrived but almost monotonously falling rhythms. Admiration quite swallows excitement of response although some isolated lines and passages remind the reader that Eliot was, after all, a poet by nature as well as by intent. The dramatic fragment 'Sweeney Agonistes' (1932) had expressed the destructive, satirical, socially and poetically observant side of Eliot; it has greater spontaneity. This vein was not to emerge again. His plays, reprehensibly unrecognizable as being in verse, exploit Greek themes in increasingly drawing-room settings; there is no characterization, little vitality, but a clever imitation of profundity. The exception is the first: *Murder in the Cathedral* (1935), which conceals its essentially non-dramatic nature by skilful use of liturgy and contrasting vaudeville and which performs effectively. It is hardly possible to overestimate Eliot's influence on his own century. As a critic he may have been inconsistent (who isn't?), occasionally foolish (as on *Hamlet*) and disingenuously conservative but he was seldom irresponsible; he interested his reader in his subject. As a young poet he saw what he could see–not the very basic things, like the suffering of others, or the anguish and impossibility of loving–with a piercing clarity. He is endlessly fascinating. *Collected Poems and Plays,* 1969; *Selected Essays,* 1932; *On Poetry and Poets,* 1957.

Ellison, Ralph (1914) American Negro novelist and essayist. Ellison's reputation rests on a single novel, *Invisible Man* (1952); the only other fiction is the fragment 'And Hickman Arrives' (1960, in *The Noble Savage*) from a second novel-in-progress, and some stories; *Shadow and Act* (1964) collects essays on aspects of Negro culture. Ellison was originally interested in jazz and art but contact with Richard Wright (q.v.) prompted him to turn seriously to writing and he produced some promising stories (uncollected). *Invisible Man* owes much to Wright (including, in particular, one important incident in which the nameless hero literally goes underground) but perhaps surpasses anything by him. The theme, presented with great verve and a deliberately disconcerting good humour, is that of the black man's search for his own human identity in a society that mechanistically denies it to him. But Ellison is well aware that this is, in lesser degree, the predicament of all human beings and he takes full account of it. *Invisible Man* combines social criticism, comedy and exploration of total alienation with an uncanny exactitude and it follows Wright in attacking, if only by implication, the North's pretensions to non-racism. The hero is Negro and he cannot discover in anyone, or find anywhere, a reflection as himself as a human being. Yet the hero, despite his symbolic lack of a name, is seen in depth. The hero (and anti-hero) stands, too, for the artist, trapped between his inevitable commitment to society and his commitment to work that subverts society and therefore himself. Ellison's essays are serious and responsible and illuminate their subject-matter more fully and fruitfully than the angrier and more confused commentaries of some recent Negro activists but Ellison has had to work hard to retain his iron control and the moderation of his tone is ultimately more effective protest than the noisier sort.

Elsschot, Willem (ps. Alfons De Ridder) (1882–1960) Flemish novelist, poet, who has exercised a strong influence on Dutch literature (not always receptive to its Flemish neighbours). Three of his comic, laconic, faintly grotesque novels have been translated in *Three Novels* (1963): *Lijmen* (1924), *Soft Soap, Het Been* (1938), *The Leg* and *Het dwaallicht* (1946), *Will-o'-the-Wisp*. The first two satirize the business world and introduce his characters Laarmans and Boorman, the apotheosis of the bourgeois con-man. The last, Elsschot's most poetic book, finds Laarmans trying to help three Indian sailors discover a girl who never appears. *Kaas* (1933), *Cheese*, is also worthy of note for its comedy and unsentimental pathos. Elsschot, a superb stylist, is one of the best of tough-tender European novelists of his time. The complete works were issued in 1957.

Eluard, Paul (ps. Eugène Grindel) (1895–1952) French poet. Eluard, after serving in the First World War, became associated with the dada (*see* Ball) movement; he was one of the founders of the surrealist (*see* Breton) movement, from which he broke in 1938 owing to his communist sympathies. Despite his various affiliations, however, he is a 'natural', an absolutely unanimist (*see* Romains) poet—though he never subscribed to specifically unanimist notions about form and he is always lyrical in tone. The early poems search in the world of dream and reverie for an erotic purity that is beyond his reach; he appears sometimes to believe that he has discovered this but his great appeal lies in the ecstasy of his search. He is a meandering poet but sincerity gives his meanderings a certain direction, though a vague one. His very best poetry is often one of defeat and loss: 'Yet I have never found what I write in what I love.' Reading his work as a whole one is most struck by his failure to discover what he sought; yet the lack of tension, the loose form, functions in his case as an authenticity. His later poems, inspired less by communist dogma than by his sense of identification with the humble or oppressed, the 'slaves', are not as convincing but some of them are luminous with faith in man. He was active in the Resistance and his clandestine Resistance poetry (as 'Jean du Haut') is at least as good as that of Aragon (q.v.). But it is his man-searching-for-woman poetry of the twenties and thirties that will be chiefly remembered. He was not altogether lucky in love: his first wife, Gala, left him in 1924 (he, too, disappeared—to take a trip round the world); his second wife, Nusch, died in 1946; his third wife, Dominique, survived him. His First World War injuries (gassing) contributed to his early death. The complete poems appeared in 1962: *Oeuvres complètes.* There is a *Selected Writings* (1952) in English.

Empson, William (1906) English poet, critic: a figure of great importance in Anglo-American criticism and in British poetry. His *Poems* (1935) reflect the concerns of his first book of criticism, *Seven Types of Ambiguity* (1930 rev. 1961). Drawing on the theories of his teacher at Cambridge, I. A. Richards, and on an analysis of a Shakespeare sonnet by Graves (q.v.) and Riding (q.v.), Empson drew attention to the effect the various types of ambiguity had in poetry. This was a fruitful crystallization of a current critical tendency towards metaphysical poetry and Jacobean drama and was very influential in America. In *The Structure of Complex Words* (1951) Empson comes nearest, in his criticism, to dealing with the passionate though complex socialism that underlies almost all his vigorously recondite writing—though it may seem to be no more than a study of how words can obtain connotations that are not justified by their denotations; it is a bitter and ironic work, whereas *Milton's God* (1961) is a broadside aimed directly at Christianity, the tradition of which Empson finds cruel and evil. The reaction that this attitude has provoked has been strange and (in conventional terms) unChristian: it has varied from convoluted rage to such comic remarks as 'Undermining a man's faith is not the work of a gentleman'. No one has answered him except by describing his views as 'tedious' or 'obsessional'. Empson's critical prose and poetry are often marred by his excited over-ingenuity in making out a case or working out an argument, but as often rescued from it by a depth of feeling and an intuitive power that not all his readers seem able to detect. Empson wants lyricism and simplicity and has (perhaps ironically) pleaded for it—and for a 'story' element in poems; but he is tormented by the cruelly heedless over-sophistications of his age and is too subtle to turn to crudely 'revolutionary' statement. His poetry, in which the early influence was strongly metaphysical and the later weakly Augustan (he has written little over the past thirty-five years), struggles to strike a balance between tradition and justice (when it is not concerned with the erotic) and its intellectually rococo surface should not distract the reader from the rather wide vein of 'human sympathy' that runs beneath this: 'Manchouli' may be reticent, but it is moving and its implications are clear; and 'This Last Pain' explains all, especially in its famous last line, 'and learn a style from a despair'; the lighter 'Autumn on Nan-Yueh' again makes the political/poetic position quite clear. But the influence of the romantics on his poetry has so far been wanting—the poetry has not been written (or, at least, not published), although he has introduced a selection from Coleridge. For so highly influential a poet Empson's output is very slender; yet the 'sympathy' does get into much of this, and in a few major poems, such as 'Aubade', the entire range of a sensitive, extraordinarily intuitive experience is clearly revealed in the perfect guise of an amorous comic 'story'. *Some Versions of Pastoral* (1935); *Collected Poems* (1955).

Enright, D. J. (1920) English poet, novelist, critic. Enright is an anti-sentimental, accomplished and witty recorder of the cultural and urban scene which he cynically distrusts; his poetic energy, already evident in *Season Ticket* (1948), has become somewhat diluted, as *Selected Poems* (1968) shows but he is both comic and tolerant and writes excellently within what he feels are his limitations. He is one of the best of contemporary literary reviewers.

Esenin, Sergei (1895–1925) Russian poet. Esenin, one of the most popular of Soviet poets, was the truest 'peasant poet' of our century; yet it was the exposure of his peasant sensibility to sophisticated literary life that produced his finest poems. He has been compared to Dylan Thomas (q.v.) and Hart Crane (q.v.) but in both cases the comparison is inept: he is incomparably superior to the shoddy Thomas and Crane, though ill educated, was no peasant and was far ahead of Esenin in critical intelligence. Esenin's pure lyricism was steeped in the paganized Christianity (or Christianized paganism) of the Russian peasantry and it incorporates its residual experience and wisdom. His earliest poems are better than is generally allowed; that he came to Moscow salons dressed in a smock to recite them was his personal if not his poetic undoing. They are religious without affectation and their visionary nature (the fruits of the rowan are 'kissed' on the tree by the 'monkish wind', and are 'scarlet ulcers of the unseen Christ') is unforced, as though the young poet were a perfect instrument for recording the essence of rural quietude. He welcomed the revolution in some less good poems. It was, he felt, to inaugurate a peasant millennium, but he entirely failed to understand it, though he knew in his bones that it was not what he wanted: 'I'm not a *new man!*/Why hide it?/I've got one leg in the past,/And trying to dress in steel/I'm slipping and falling with the other.' He fell victim to alcohol and drugs and began to behave in a delinquent manner with those to whom he now felt closest: the lumpen-proletariat inhabitants of urban bars. He made three marriages, the middle one to the dancer Isadora Duncan with whom he was unable to communicate as neither spoke the other's language. After writing a farewell poem in his own blood, he hanged himself in a Leningrad hotel. The Soviet establishment condemned his 'hooliganism' but his poetry remained widely read. His later poetry describes the dislocation of a *naïv* (in Schiller's sense) personality under the pressures of the hideous city, of the temptations of pretentiousness, artfulness and temporarily relieving debauchery, and of a *sentimentalische* attitude which the poet knows he cannot attain. During one of his numerous hospitalizations he wrote 'And you, my headstrong head, oh say,/What have you led me to at last?' In the crucial 'Confession of a Hooligan' (written in 1918) he sums up his situation, his head like a 'kerosene lamp on his shoulders': 'I came like an austere craftsman/to sing and celebrate the rats.' There is a selection from this astonishing poetry in Geoffrey Thurley's *Confessions of a Hooligan: Fifty Poems* (1973); there are a few errors of translation, but it is unlikely that anyone will do better.

Evans, Caradoc (ps. David Evans) (1878–1945) Anglo-Welsh novelist, short-story writer, playwright. Evans offended puritanical, respectable Welsh opinion with his first book of stories, *My People* (1915), and has never been forgiven. He had learned his style from the Bible they claimed to revere. His target was as much himself, however, as the hypocrisy and puritanized lust of his countrymen: his tender sensibility, moulded by Welsh bleakness, turned him into a 'black' and 'cruel' writer; he was not only a satirist but also an exponent of the grotesque. His Biblical style is a kind of parody of itself, of his own

Welshness. His play *Taffy* (1923) caused riots when it opened in London. He wrote four novels (e.g. *Wasps*, 1933) and six books of stories (e.g. *The Earth Gives All and Takes All*, 1946), which should be collected into one volume.

Evtushenko, Evgeny (1933) Russian poet, prose writer. Evtushenko has enormous vitality and passion but is—as most good critics insist—no more than a poetaster. Despite this he has been over-exposed in the West (there are at least four sets of translations: *Selected Poems*, 1962; *Selected Poetry*, 1964; *The Poetry*, 1966; *The Bratsk Station*, 1967—and *A Precocious Autobiography*, 1963, which appeared in France but not Russia). He is essentially a poet of the 'thaw', the period of comparative relaxation of literary censorship following Khrushchev's denunciation of Stalin. His volumes have been best-sellers. He has been in trouble on two or three occasions for speaking out; at other times he has toed the line. He does have energy, but his procedures are too clearly derived from Mayakovsky (q.v.): there is no tension in his poetry; he is a pasticheur.

F

Fagunwa, Daniel (d. 1963) Nigerian novelist; a Yoruba chief. The first important writer in Yoruba. *Ogboju ọdẹ ninu igbo irunmale* (1938; tr. *The Forest of a Thousand Demons,* 1968) is his first and best book, though its successors enjoy enormous popularity. In this book Fagunwa began the literary process of building up an account of the Yoruba cosmogony that was completed (in English) more poetically by Tutuola (q.v.). He died in a boat accident.

Fallada, Hans (ps. Rudolf Ditzen) (1893–1947) German novelist, autobiographer. Fallada's extraordinary life would make–is (one is tempted to say)–a great modernist novel. Versatile, greatly gifted, luminously aware of his environment, he was prolific, successful as writer, farmer and non-collaborating survivor of the Third Reich–and thief, killer, alcoholic, drug-addict, would-be suicide, wounder of his first wife, and mayor. *Falada* is the legendary severed horse's head that tells the truth and Fallada told a good deal of it despite his world and his own self-terrifying actions. Probably the tension between his self-destructive impulses and his gift for survival killed him early as much as the ravages of drink. *Der Trinker* (1950; tr. *The Drinker,* 1952) is his most self-revealing novel; there are also three volumes of autobiography, of which the last, post-Nazi one, *Der Alpdruck* (1947), *The Nightmare,* is the best. Seldom can shrewdness have co-existed as consistently with near-psychotic disturbance as in Fallada: his books published under the Nazi regime avoid trouble more neatly than any other writer's, but are also more subtly critical; in them the sure instinct of self-preservation is kept within the bounds of decency by sheer love of everything that lives. Partly he was kept safe by his concern with 'the little man', through whose immediate feelings Hitler had gained power; *Kleiner Mann–was nun?* (1932; tr. *Little Man, What Now?*, 1933) an international success, could hardly have prompted the Nazis to silence him but it truly depicted a despair which the Nazis had merely climbed to power upon. He exploited his theme (e.g. *Wolf unter Wölfen,* 1937, tr. *Wolf Among Wolves,* 1938), suspected but not seized until after the war had begun; in 1947 came the novel *Jeder stirbt für sich allein, Each Man Dies for Himself Alone,* by far the best account of the anti-Nazi German resistance. His masterpieces, though, are *Bauern, Bonzen und Bomben* (1920–30), *Peasants, Bosses and Bombs,* as sociologically meticulous as it is compassionate an account of a Holstein farmers' revolt, and *The Drinker.* Fallada's writings are truly miraculous interpolations between his episodes of moral degradation; his essential theme is religious: the weakness of man's compassionate will against his circumstances; but he expresses this through a paradoxically ecstatically loving, violently exact observation of all his fellow creatures. He is neither comic nor ironic, though under Nazi pressure he could be Teutonic-whimsical and this reduces, too, the value of *Little Man, What Now?*; his literary strengths lie in his lack of self-pity, his insistence upon concreteness and his utter dedication to his craft. Like all conspicuous sinners of an intellectual hue, Fallada is a savage moralist; but he is an attractively oblique one. Certainly an offshoot of naturalism and influenced by it, he reverses its procedures by devoting his books to hope and his life to a predetermined hell. He is a highly original writer whose affinities with Arlt (q.v.), Lowry (q.v.) and Dostoievski help to explain his subtleties but hardly do justice to his doggedly realist techniques. He was a master of the colloquial.

Fargue, Léon-Paul (1876–1947) French poet, famous among his friends for his telephone calls from bistros and bars all over Paris. He had the priceless opportunity of being taught by Mallarmé (who could not keep order and as a teacher was a wretched failure); later he became his friend. He was an exquisite minor poet. He has been called 'escapist', but is not. He was a bastard, which did not help his earlier years. He is consistently underrated, for his best poetry is both penetratingly original—on the subject of his own half-humorously adopted pose of late-decadent poseur—and delicate. He has huge feeling but knows that it cannot, in his own case, be expressed except in meticulous, modified, anti-grandiose, mock-elegant forms. He began under the influence of Verlaine, Rimbaud and Baudelaire, then of Mallarmé; Gide (q.v.) influenced him; then, discovering the nature of his originality, he turned to the quieter sweetness of Jammes (q.v.) and to the music of Satie and Debussy; he became an impressionist. Verhaeren (q.v.), with his image of the city as a tentacular monster, must have made a strong impact. He knew almost everyone (Sylvia Beach—who published *Ulysses*—Derain, the surrealists, Ravel . . .) but he did not become a surrealist. The world of his work—which progressed from poetry to prose-poems to prose—is a very real one. We are told a sad, true story through a mist of nostalgia, an irresistible Proustian (q.v.) urge towards innocence. There is much delicacy and tenderness in Fargue; but not a great deal of mystery. He was, as Gabriel Bounoure remarked, 'seized by a lucid alienation of the mind'. *Poésie* (1963) is not complete; the late *Lanterne magique* (1944) was translated, *Magic Lantern,* in 1947; there is no selection in translation.

Farrell, James T. (1904) American novelist, short-story writer, critic and essayist. Farrell, born in Chicago, is America's most distinguished continuer of the naturalist (*see* Zola) tradition (Dreiser, q.v., through an influence on Farrell and in part a naturalist, transcends categorization). The trilogy *Studs Lonigan* (1932–5; 1935) is his masterpiece but his other fiction, especially some of his short stories (of which he has written fourteen volumes—*Short Stories,* 1937, collects the first three of these; *Omnibus,* 1956), stands in some danger of neglect. Farrell paid for his own education at the University of Chicago (1925–9) and lived in Paris in 1931–2. He played an honourable part in the political controversies of the thirties, supporting socialism but opposing communist dogma (*A Note on Literary Criticism,* 1936). An ex-Catholic, he was deeply influenced by Dewey (q.v.); he had also made himself aware of the contemporary literary and intellectual currents before he published *Young Lonigan* (1932), his first novel. The most decisive influence, however, was Sherwood Anderson (q.v.). In the mid-thirties, with the completion of his most famous work, Farrell was at the height of his fame; since then his reputation has tended to ebb, although he has some defenders. *Studs* is the brilliantly written study of the defeat (he dies at twenty-nine) of a tough young man of Chicago. It combines realistic narrative with a modified stream-of-consciousness method and it is especially distinguished for its accurate use of the vernacular. This poignant novel-cycle was to a certain extent deterministic but it was a new kind of naturalism: a naturalism that utilized such new techniques as Farrell—who understands his limitations—found would help him. In the Danny O'Neill pentalogy (1936–53), beginning with *A World I*

Never Made and concluding in *The Face of Time,* the same kind of Irish-Catholic, ambitious character as Studs resolutely rejects the driftless life Studs, in effect, chose; we do not see Danny succeed, but he does not fail. The cycle is not as good as *Studs,* but as a critic has perceptively commented, 'these novels are richest in major characters'. In the Bernard Carr trilogy (1946–52: the first novel was called *Bernard Clare,* but a person called Bernard Clare brought a libel suit and Farrell changed his hero's name to Carr) we see for the first time a successful Irish-Catholic: Bernard, like Farrell, achieves himself as a writer. This, like much of the preceding cycle, is set in New York, and deals brilliantly and sympathetically with the leftist thirties. In *The Silence of History* (1963) Farrell began yet another cycle of novels about a Chicago man, Eddie Ryan; and in *A Brand New Life* (1968) he writes as well as he has written in any book since *Studs.* Farrell does have limitations and it is easy enough to spot flaws in all his books but the habit of dismissing or patronizing him disgraces the practice of criticism. At least one other novel should be noted: the experimental *Gas-House McGinty* (1933), a prophetic and semi-surrealistic treatment of the nightmare world of bureaucratic commercialism. There is some substance in Leslie Fiedler's (q.v.) accusation that Farrell has gone on repeating himself with 'diminishing vigour': his theme is certainly rigid. But this is not the whole story: there is much added detail, and the occasional exception, which refutes the charge as a whole. *Selected Essays* (1964).

Faulkner, William (ps. William Falkner) (1897–1962) American novelist. He grew up in Oxford, Mississippi, and lived there—with intermissions for travel, work in Hollywood—for the rest of his life, until in his last months he moved to Virginia. He is the most violently uneven and complex of all the great non-intellectual novelists of the century: for he worked essentially from intuition and passion and never from what an educated man would call thought. In Faulkner it worked, probably because what he believed was creditable mentation acted as a true objective correlative for his complicated emotional and moral concerns. If anyone believes that he possessed a mind in the usual sense, let him read the text of the Nobel Prize speech (1950): cliché-ridden, naive, its words as flatly fail to do justice to its portentous theme as do the speeches of politicians. But, in what is rightly conceded to be his great period (1929–40), Faulkner possessed something more precious than a mere mind: an imagination outraged both by his own violent impulses and by the tragedy of how decency (in the American South) becomes misdirected into a starkly anti-human terrorism itself arising from an irrational fear. His best novels, almost all of which are set in the fictional Yoknapatawpha Country, attempted to heal this wounded imagination both by exposing the raw truth (it is not less than he depicts it) and by painfully, and with astonishing integrity, groping for and discovering his compassion. He never abuses this compassion (as he did in some inferior work) by relying on stock phraseologies or situations. Yoknapatawpha does recreate North Mississippi but Faulkner is no mere regionalist. This haunted and beloved place, peopled by the enraged, the idiotic, the emotionally crippled, the unaccepted Negroes, is given mythological and timeless status. Deficient in education (as he always was—but to the important extent of almost escaping it), Faulkner had found himself driven by an inexplicable urge to write. He read avidly, and poured himself into verse: *The Marble Faun* (1924) is a collection of pastiche of Keats, Swinburne and the then current conventional modes. *Soldiers' Pay* (1926), the first novel, has a style as badly loaded with cliché. Its successor *Mosquitoes* (1927) is a *jeu d'esprit;* but Sherwood Anderson (q.v.) had befriended Faulkner and helped him—as doubtless did his marriage (1929)—to discover his own voice in *Sartoris* (1929), his first good novel, a re-creation of the history of the Faulkner family. The major novels now followed in fairly quick succession, building up the Yoknapatawpha myth by means of evocation of the landscape, its buildings and towns and chronologically wrenched histories of various families and self-destroyed men: *The Sound and the Fury* (1929, in which Faulkner projects himself, the necessarily crippled writer who must none the less express what he feels), affirms the humanity of the oppressed Negro in the person of the servant, Dilsey and tells the story of Quentin Compson's suicide; *As I Lay Dying* (1930), *Light in August* (1932), *Absalom, Absalom!* (1936) and other novels followed, as well as some fine short stories (e.g. 'Barn Burning'); but he fell off in power and only *Intruder in the Dust* (1948) comes up to the level of the earlier work. *The Wild Palms* (1939), not part of the Yoknapatawpha cycle, is perhaps the last wholly successful major novel. Faulkner never wrote well all the time, and *Sanctuary* (1931), deliberately written to make money by the employment of a sensationalist theme, had already demonstrated how easily Faulkner could mix his near-best with his worst. The culmination of his bad vein is *A Fable* (1954), a pretentious and rhetorical Christian allegory set in France. Faulkner was not a Christian (not, that is, a 'believer'), but his best work is shot through and through with Christian symbolism and the figure of Christ's passion obsessed him. Horror, the handling of which he learned partly from his reading of Jacobean drama, operates in his work as (among other things) a reaction to his sceptical failure to accept Christ as truly redemptive. But when he tried consciously to make such an acceptance, or a penitent substitute for it, he failed badly. There is no doubt, however, of his high stature; and doubtless the poor work was part of the price—heavy and exhausting drinking-bouts were another—that he had to pay for his achievement. All the best stories are in *Collected Stories* (1950) and there is a mass of critical material, much of it helpful. He gained early recognition in France, from such as Malraux (q.v.) and Sartre (q.v.), and deeply influenced Claude Simon (q.v.). But international recognition did not come until after the Second World War.

Fearing, Kenneth (1902–61) American poet and novelist. Born, like Hemingway (q.v.), in Oak Park near Chicago. Fearing is famous for the outstanding thriller, *The Big Clock* (1946) and his other crime novels did well but his poetry has been unduly neglected. By use of a long line (which he handled with more skill than some better known poets), techniques like those of Dos Passos (q.v.) and with a mastery of speech-rhythms, he satirized and denounced the evils of urban life in a strikingly original and effective manner: *New and Selected Poems* (1956).

Ferlinghetti, Lawrence (1919) American poet, publisher (City Lights). He was one of those at the centre of the Beat (*see* Ginsberg) movement in San Francisco in the fifties; he is an excellent performer of his own poetry, which is influenced by Prévert, whom he has translated. He is an ineluctably minor light poet, drawing on familiar material; his main talent lies in the effective business management of the unrespectable but he can be funny and his satire is felt. *Penguin Modern Poets 5* (1963) and *An Eye on the World* (1967) are selections.

Ferreira de Castro, José Maria (1898–1974) Portuguese novelist, journalist, miscellaneous writer. Ferreira de Castro is the great social (not 'socialist', *see* Gorky) realist in a country which, under dictatorships for most of the century, has badly needed one. He wrote penetratingly and never with political crudity of the lives of working people in Brazil (where he spent many of his early years in bitter poverty and with fierce ambitions) and in Portugal. His first great success was *Emigrantes* (1928), *Emigrants*, about Portuguese emigrants to Brazil. This, like his masterpiece *A Selva* (1930; tr. *The Jungle*, 1934), is written in an admirably objective, 'photographic' style, masterful in its selection of significant detail. He wrote many more novels, including a memorable study of the Corvilhã wool industry, *A Lã e a Neve* (1947), *The Wool and the Snow*.

Fiedler, Leslie (1917) American novelist, critic, poet, teacher. Fiedler is an idiosyncratic, infuriated, ingenious literary and sociological critic whose judgements and theories always make his reader reconsider. He is clever but unreliable on pre-modern literature; in his main field of American literature he tends to make judgements on individual writers that will fit into his general analysis of the American neurosis which he believes (with justice) arises from a frantic desire to escape from female domination. His insights, particularly into the true value of the fiction certain fashionable writers are producing, and into its motivations, can be piercing; and his eclecticism is admirable, though he is less critical than he should be of his sources. His fiction (e.g. the novel *The Second Stone*, 1963, the stories in *The Last Jew in America*, 1967) has been unduly neglected. His major critical works are *An End to Innocence* (1955), *Love and Death in the American Novel* (1960), *No! in Thunder* (1960)–his weakest book, because he does not take the trouble to find out more than he wants to know about myth–and *Waiting for the End* (1964).

Firbank, Ronald (1886–1926) English novelist. A minor precursor of Waugh (q.v.), Powell (q.v.), Huxley (q.v.), William Gerhardie (1895) and others. He presents a paradox: he had genius, but its essence is, strangely, idle homosexual fatuousness. He did what he could with his decadence and lack of robustness, so that his best stories are not merely homosexual in-jokes but elegant wisps of fantasy graced with wittily absurd dialogue (he had a superb ear for the inconsequential). He is at his most typical in *Concerning the Eccentricities of Cardinal Pirelli* (1926), in which the hero dies while chasing a choirboy. For a brilliant and spirited defence and higher valuation, see Brigid Brophy's (q.v.) *Prancing Novelist* (1973). *The Complete Firbank* (1961).

Fitzgerald, F. Scott (1896–1940) American novelist, short-story writer. He came from a rich, aristocratic, Catholic family and achieved success at Princeton and with his first, autobiographical novel, *This Side of Paradise* (1920). At Princeton he became friendly with Edmund Wilson (q.v.) and John Peale Bishop. Fitzgerald was at heart a moralist, of the generous Catholic sort (he lapsed from the religion), and he knew he had been spoiled and that he was spoiling himself. The conflict in him between the need to waste substance, characteristic of his generation–the 'jazz age' which he above all defined so accurately and damningly–and the need to discover responsibility produced the best books (some short stories–*The Stories*, 1951–*The Great Gatsby*, 1925, *Tender is the Night*, 1934, rev. 1948, *The Crack-Up*, 1936, 1945, and, in part, the unfinished *The Last Tycoon*, 1941) and killed the man. But the matter is not as simple as this. Fitzgerald, whose reverence for decency–in its important and scarcely defined sense of what we lack–shines through his writings, had himself to live through the wrecked life, the twenties life of the *nouveau riche* in which all decency and responsibility somehow leaked out into a spoiled absurdity, in order to know it. He married Zelda Sayre in 1920 and they began to live like characters in his own books. He satirized all this and pointed nervously to Zelda's extra vulnerability in *The Beautiful and Damned* (1922), but without artistic or popular success; not until *The Great Gatsby* could he get the twenties scene into its complex perspective. The ex-crook Gatsby's genuine love is corrupted by his moral irresponsibility and in this sense he stands for Fitzgerald himself; but the novel is also prophetic, especially in its portrait of the proto-fascist Tom Buchanan, and, more generally, in its forecast of the results of the moral decay it depicts. Gatsby is wicked and lives in a world of illusions; he thinks he can buy love with ill-gotten gains, but he has a strange integrity since he dies preserving his dream. This was how Fitzgerald saw his own artistic predicament: he was still drawing artistic material from his life as playboy. *The Great Gatsby* is Fitzgerald's most technically accomplished novel (he owed his method, probably, to Conrad's, q.v., use of Marlow in *Heart of Darkness* and elsewhere); but *Tender is the Night* (1934), though less successful, goes deeper and is more sombre. Fitzgerald now underwent a breakdown which he movingly described in three articles for *Esquire* in 1936 (Wilson collected these, with other material, as *The Crack-Up* in 1945). He went to Hollywood as a scriptwriter and began, in effect, to drink himself to death. A last attempt to pull himself together produced most of *The Last Tycoon*. This is not his best novel as some have claimed but it might have been had he not died of a heart-attack before he had completed it. It is, as one would expect, on the theme of the destruction of creativity by external and internal factors. It is a commonplace that Fitzgerald was destroyed by the very things he most feared and despised—money and dissipation—but his sensitivity as a human being is less fully acknowledged. He certainly behaved with a stupid extravagance which probably cost him his life (his drinking in the late thirties was legendary), but the anguish Zelda had earlier caused him by simultaneously trying to compete with him and depending on him—putting him into the famous 'double-bind' situation—was not initiated by him. Yet, conscientious artist that he was, he took full responsibility for it. He never achieved the polish of the early Hemingway but his books reach much further down. *The Great Gatsby* was the first American novel which made thorough use of modernist techniques; *Tender is the Night* transcends its flaws, for its profound concern for the state of others shines through.

Ford, Ford Madox (formerly J. L. F. H. M. Hueffer) (1873–1939) English novelist, prose writer, critic, editor, poet. Ford's life was a mess both sexually and financially, and he could be a boastful romancer; only a few remained loyal to him in his lifetime (e.g. Pound, q.v.) and even now that he is enjoying some revival this is often called 'fashionable'. Yet despite his lack of practical self-knowledge, his capacity for stupidity and what one of his mistresses called his 'unfairness', he was a great novelist, a great editor, a shrewd and sometimes marvellously perceptive critic, an invaluable and entertaining autobiographer and travel writer, and (in the late group, *Buckshee,* in *Collected Poems,* 1936) a delightful minor-minor poet. He founded *The English Review* in 1908 and edited it until 1910; during these two years it was perhaps the best English-language magazine of the century, publishing Hardy (q.v.), Wells (q.v.), Lawrence (q.v.), Wyndham Lewis (q.v.) and many others. He had already written the historical *Fifth Queen* trilogy (1906–8), one of the best of his minor works but his great fiction was written between 1915 and 1928. The sequence of *The Good Soldier* (1915) and the Tietjens tetralogy–*Some Do Not* (1924), *No More Parades* (1925), *A Man Could Stand Up* (1926) and *Last Post* (1928)–was interrupted only by war service and *The Marsden Case* (1923); *When the Wicked Man* (1931) is the best of the five later novels. *The Good Soldier,* certainly the most technically perfect of Ford's books, is the story of two married couples, one English and one American, and is narrated by the American husband. On the face of it this 'saddest story' is a simple one of corruption and lust: but Dowell, the narrator, and Ashburnham and his wife, are more ambiguous characters, whose motivations are complex. Ford is in perfect control from first to last and his story of weakness and evil has something of the impact of *Madame Bovary,* except that it is impossible to infer any sort of moral or message from it: it is a masterpiece of characterization and pointed plotting and it simply exists as, in Dowell's own opening words, the 'saddest story'. The tetralogy–there is controversy, with something to be said for both sides of the question, as to whether *Last Post* is to be regarded as an unfortunate or a necessary epilogue–is a work on an altogether more ambitious scale. More flawed, it is none the less as great an achievement. It concerns the 'last English Tory', Christopher Tietjens. *Parade's End* is an Englishman's (neater) equivalent to Musil's (q.v.) *Der Mann ohne Eigenschaften* (*The Man without Qualities*) inasmuch as its general territory is the collapse of an old order. It has been remarked that the old-fashioned qualities of Tietjens are laid on a little too thickly but his convincingness implies an ironic frustration and despair. No summary of this work can do it justice: even if Tietjens himself is found unconvincing (though this seems to amount to a failure to discern Ford's subtlety), it provides a rich, accurate and often comic picture of its period–of opportunism, heroism, dishonesty and honesty. Its tone is unique. Meanwhile Ford had started, from Paris, a new magazine, *The Transatlantic Review;* unfortunately it lasted for only twelve numbers. After *Parade's End* he continued to turn out fiction, travel books, reminiscences, and critical works: one would hardly guess that when he wrote the remarkable and lively *The March of Literature from Confucius to Modern Times* (1938) he was already a dying man. Ford has always been read, but only in the last ten years has he been taken seriously by critics. He deserves at least this, for as novelist, editor, critic (e.g. on James, q.v., in 1913, and on Conrad, q.v., 1924, and in his account of world literature) and personality he is remarkable. There are now a number of critical studies, a full-scale biography (by Arthur Mizener, 1971), and a selection of *Letters* (1965).

Forster, E. M. (1879–1970) English novelist, short-story writer, critic, essayist, humanist. Although Forster's last novel appeared in 1924, he for long had (and for some still has) the status of a modern classic. Lately there has been a reaction. However, for *A Passage to India* (1924) at least, Forster is assured of his position as a major twentieth-century novelist. That much of his writing (e.g. his radio talks in war-time) which was effective at the time now seems dated or mannered should not be allowed to distract attention from this novel, in which Forster most successfully resolved his mental conflicts. The influences on him were manifold: from his family he inherited an evangelical sense of morality; at Cambridge he was in the circle—the 'Apostles'—around the philosopher G. E. Moore, and although he never read *Principia Ethica* he was aware of its spirit; he was deeply affected by his friendship with the classicist and humanist Goldsworthy Lowes Dickinson (he wrote his biography in 1934), and particularly by the latter's rejection of Christianity in favour of the spiritual—if not supernatural—values inherent in all religions. The chief literary influences on him were Samuel Butler, Kafavis (q.v.), Proust (q.v.) and Jane Austen. What drove Forster into his forty-six years of creative silence was above all his inability, in the social and literary climate, to deal with homosexual themes. (He had tried in an early novel, *Maurice*, not published until after his death, but must have realized that this is a feeble failure.) Forster has for long been regarded as the apotheosis of 'Bloomsbury', and while the so-called 'Bloomsbury Group' is one of the most amorphous and nebulous of all literary groups (it was not a movement), this association is helpful to an understanding of him. The Bloomsbury Group never, as its best historian, Quentin Bell, has pointed out, represented any consistent body of thought. But there are people who may be considered as having been at the centre of a certain group of writers, artists, economists and others who thought in rather the same way and who thought of themselves as 'Bloomsbury': Forster, Garnett, Desmond MacCarthy, Roger Fry, Virginia Woolf (q.v.), Lytton Strachey and Keynes were the leading writers—and Duncan Grant and Vanessa Bell the leading artists; James Strachey, Lytton's brother, was a lay analyst and later a translator of Freud. (The daughters of Sir

Leslie Stephen, Vanessa and Virginia, had moved to Bloomsbury after their father's death.) If one were challenged to produce two statements as a pointer to what the Bloomsbury Group had in common (they had many differences, and were never a concerted voice) then these would probably be Sir Leslie Stephen's paradoxical dictum (1856) that he believed in nothing but that he still believed in morality, and the non-Bloomsburyite G. E. Moore's assertion that the most desirable objects in life were 'love, the creation and enjoyment of aesthetic experience and the pursuit of knowledge'. (One should add that 'love' here usually implied a love for suffering and underprivileged humanity as well as sexual love.) Forster, then, was a humanitarian aesthete, a gentle élitist who believed in, as he wrote, an 'aristocracy of the sensitive, the considerate and the plucky. . . .' For anyone under fifty his essays will certainly seem dated in manner and sometimes naive but until his imaginative powers were finally crippled he had a more complicated and permanent message—and even in his essays he is often more ironic than some of his detractors have discerned. *Aspects of the Novel* (1927) remains an important and stimulating source book of ideas about the realist novel; and *The Hill of Devi* (1953) is an excellent book on India and on his visits there (in 1912 and 1922). His dislike of Christianity was in its way as fierce as Empson's (q.v.) but he was not singled out for special attack on this score. The early novels—*Where Angels Fear to Tread* (1905), *The Longest Journey* (1907), *A Room With a View* (1908) and *Howards End* (1910)—are of high quality but suffer from the author's desire to impose upon reality, so to say, a mutually balanced type of man in whom he did not truly believe. His stories (collected in 1947) are even more obviously designed to an end. His view of life was tragic and he felt as guilty about this as about his homosexuality. But he had the intelligence and staying-power to produce one greatly superior novel, which he began before the war but did not publish until many years later: *A Passage to India.* The motto of *Howards End* had been 'only connect'; *A Passage to India* demonstrates how the desire to connect, to establish humane personal relationships, is frustrated and soured by fear and ill will. In this complex book which functions effectively at several levels, he allows his tragic imagination full rein and therefore brings in the element of mystery. Much of the novel revolves around the question of what happened in the Marabar Caves: did Aziz assault Adela Quested or not? And it thus revolves around an ambiguity, which is echoed in the almost wise Mrs Moore's anguished realization that 'everything exists, nothing has value'. *A Passage to India* is a beautiful and poetic novel, incomparably superior to its predecessors; it outweighs everything else achieved by Forster, who without it would be an agreeable man of letters who once wrote four novels in which he demonstrated a considerable gift but failed to fulfil it. But the existence of his masterpiece pulls his life and the rest of his achievement into a truly poignant pattern.

France, Anatole (ps. Anatole-François Thibault) (1844–1924) French novelist, critic, poet and writer. Nobel Prize 1921. France moved from Parnassian preciosity (some of this in verse) and mild Christianity through a fashionable porno-scepticism to an unconvincing socialist (even quasi-communist) commitment. He was skilful and professional but usually superficial: his heart was in the right place and he enjoyed being non-conformist but he too readily identified with established positions, even though these were ostensibly subversive. France was brilliant, not deep. Each time he comes near to saying something of true interest (a revelatory self-examination or a shrewd appraisal of a manifestation) he sheers away into the pleasantly trite. He wrote a great deal. Most memorable are the sharp *Histoire Contemporaine* (1897–1901; all four volumes are available in English: *The Elm-Tree on the Mall,* 1910, *The Wicker-Work Woman,* 1910, *The Amethyst Ring,* 1919, *Monsieur Bergeret in Paris,* 1921), and, above all, *L'Île des Pingouins* (1908; tr. *Penguin Island,* 1909), his major satire. He never escaped artificiality of style or over-contrived unoriginality of content; now he is an absolutely dated writer. *Oeuvres complètes* (1925–35), *Complete Works,* has been supplemented.

Freud, Sigmund (1856–1939) Austrian neurologist and founder of psychoanalysis. This is not the place to discuss his theories—only his influence on literature (which, he conceded, had for long contained the insights into the human mind that he introduced into psychiatric medicine). His formulation of the mind as divided into an ego, a superego ('conscience'), an unconscious which contained a violent id (mass of uncontrollable instincts), and his demonstration (anticipated in particular by Diderot) that infantile life is not sexually 'innocent' profoundly influenced writers, who began to deliberately investigate motivations that could not be explained in rational or polite terms. He thus indirectly or directly influenced neo-romanticism (mysterious, hidden, exotic inner possibilities), decadence (opportunities for morbidity) and expressionism (*see* Stadler; the true reality is internal, and the old 'realism' must reflect this and not try to depict the false and rational world of appearances). The developments and modifications of and reactions to his astonishingly rich and suggestive mass of writings have increased rather than diminished his influence. All his work is available in English translation (Hogarth Press) and serious students should read it—and not digests of it.

Frisch, Max (1911) The leading Swiss writer in German. Dramatist, novelist, memoirist. He began as an architect and was also a journalist. He met and became friendly with Brecht (q.v.) after the war and was influenced by him. Whether or not *Biedermann und die Brandstifter* (1953 for radio; 1958 for stage; tr. *The Fire Raisers,* 1962) was occasioned by the softness of the 1948 Czech government towards the communists who destroyed them, it is a subtle tragi-comic critique of bourgeois complacency and ruthlessness, and one of the finest plays of the 'Absurd' (*see* Ionesco), which category it transcends. In *Andorra* (1961; tr. 1962), perhaps his greatest achievement, Frisch deals with his main preoccupation, which is a fundamental theme in existentialism (*see* Sartre): the confusion of public with private identity, the attaching of false labels to people, thus robbing them of their right to seek for personal authenticity. He had already turned seriously to fiction (he had written some earlier, immature novels) in order to explore this theme in greater depth: *Stiller* (1954; tr. *I'm Not Stiller,* 1958) and *Homo Faber* (1957; tr. 1959) are the most successful. *Mein Name sei Gantenbein* (1964; tr. *A Wilderness of Mirrors,* 1965) collapses under the weight of its own despairing complexity, though it is an impressive attempt to coordinate all possibilities, realities (cf. Pirandello, Musil) in a single book. His *Tagebuch 1946–1949* (1950), *Diary 1946–1949,* is a substantial and fascinating 'workshop' account, deliberately impersonal, of his impressions and beliefs. Its successor, *Tagebuch 1966–1971* (1972), characterized by a more experimental presentation (collage, typographical devices), reveals the dilemmas of a leftist who rejects both East and West; it is particularly valuable on Brecht.

Fromm, Erich (1900) German (now American) psychoanalytical and sociological thinker. He was associated with and trained by Freudians, and then worked with Adorno at Frankfurt. His main theme has been in the field of the psychology of modern totalitarianism and its roots in Puritanism (e.g. *Escape from Freedom*, 1941; *The Dogma of Christ*, 1966). His most influential book is *The Art of Loving* (1956), a more popular work which has proved beneficial to many people. *The Forgotten Language* (1951), about the 'hidden' world of dream, folk-tales and myth, is a good alternative to wild Jungian (q.v.) speculations on the same subject, though it needs to be read critically. *The Sane Society* (1955).

Frost, Robert (1874–1963) American poet who became, in the last decade of his long life, the unofficial laureate of his country: the first poet to be so honoured. His work is much and often indiscriminately loved; it is also much and, again, indiscriminately, hated by rediscoverers of 'pure' Americanism—those writers and critics who found, consciously or unconsciously, their American roots in Dewey's (q.v.) pragmatism or in versions of it. For Frost did not publish his first book, *A Boy's Will* (1913), until he was thirty-nine, and when he did so it was in England and partly under the influence and by the encouragement of English friends (Brooke, q.v., Abercrombie, Gibson, Thomas, q.v. and others). He may thus seem to be in the Anglo-American tradition. But he had been writing poems since adolescence and had published fourteen of them before he ever considered coming to England. He was born in San Francisco but moved to New England at the age of ten. His early life was difficult and full of self-doubt; he was always a depressive and probably only his function as poet—and, by extension, stance as famous poet—saved him from mental disintegration. Of his children, the son committed suicide; one daughter died of puerperal fever and another became insane; the third almost disowned him because of her disgust at his behaviour towards his wife, who died in 1938 after forty-three years of marriage. By 1912 Frost had tried farming, egg-selling, factory-work and teaching, and had been near to death from pneumonia and to complete mental breakdown. He went to England for the purpose of risking all on poetry. When he returned to America in 1915, having in the interim performed the service of re-starting Edward Thomas as a poet, he was well known: his first book, and the second (*North of Boston*, 1914), were already published there and were widely read. These volumes, and *Mountain Interval* (1916), contain most of his best poems but he went on writing well until the end (*In the Clearing*, 1962, is his last book): he retained the capacity to produce the odd true poem. Development is one, though only one, of the tests of a major poet. By that standard Frost is a minor: he never developed. His movement toward satire and the philosophically epigrammatic, first seen in *New Hampshire* (1923), is part of his public stance. It is well done, but no part of his poetic process, though this continued intermittently. Frost intimately knew grief and fear of madness very early; his later misfortunes, which were considerable, matched this inner knowledge and he did not change his method of poetic response or learn any new wisdom. Frost's mock-development, from the satirical through the philosophical to the cosmic, is interesting in only two ways: as the history of the intellectual aspect of a therapy against total withdrawal, and as the dutiful response of a public man to an audience. It has little to do with his achievement. After the first three collections we need always to look for what Jarrell (q.v.) called the 'other Frost'. Frost is almost as limited as Housman (q.v.) but not as constricted. By his constitution he found relationships with other people, even his own family, extremely difficult: he was an isolate. The real Frost, the 'other Frost', confronts these problems in his poetry, which may (at least this is a useful indication) be related to the individualist aspect of the American Puritan tradition. The most famous of his poems, 'Mending Wall' (in *North of Boston*), is about 'boundaries': 'good fences make good neighbours'. This Frost, the one independent of 'thought' (he knew and stated that poems cannot *begin* in thought, but he came to break his rule), works out the extent to which the private and lonely man can relate to others. There are astonishing successes: certain beautifully specific revelations of unaloneness in a solipsist desert. The failure is in rhythmic originality. This may be traced, again, to Frost's sense of isolation: his over-distancing of himself from others. Only at his very best does he transcend these limitations, as in 'The Tuft of Flowers', which ends '"Men work together," I told him from the heart,/"Whether they work together or apart".' He could come near to this even in his eighties, as in 'Peril of Hope' from his last book. At his finest Frost gives affirmation out of a deep pessimism, a black despair of loneliness and perhaps even a neurotically Calvinist conviction of 'non-election'. His observation of the New England scene is meticulous though not as detailed as some of his admirers insist and people *as people* simply don't exist in his poetry (the 'book of people' he claimed *North of Boston* to be is not that, but an exploration of his own difficulties of communication and capacity to relate); but at its best it deserves, as Jarrell declared, 'the attention, submission and astonished awe that real art always requires. . . .' *The Poetry* (1969) is complete; *Selected Letters* (1964); *Selected Prose* (1966).

Fuchs, Daniel (1909) American novelist and scriptwriter. With Henry Roth (q.v.) and to a lesser extent Nathanael West (q.v.) Fuchs was a pioneer of the Jewish 'ghetto' novel, which has since become a lucubrated form. He is not on the level of Roth, but his three novels *Summer in Williamsburg* (1934), *Homage to Blenholt* (1936) and *Low Company* (1937), are excellently observed, unsentimental, comic, detached and affecting. They have been republished as *Three Novels* (1961), having previously failed commercially. They are set in New York's Lower East Side, and contain, in more concise form, almost all that their successors of the fifties and sixties contain—less some hysterical or pretentious elements. Fuchs then went to Hollywood where he continued to write excellent short stories.

Fuentes, Carlos (1929) Mexican novelist, critic, playwright, one of the most prominent Latin-American fiction-writers outside his own continent, as well as highly thought of within it. Like his friend Garcia Márquez he has read deeply in English-language literature but its influences are more evident in his fiction, which is distinctly more cosmopolitan in style—even though it deals, and highly critically, with Mexican themes. Most of the translations of his work into (American) English have come under especially heavy fire from critics. After a volume of stories, he produced his first novel, *La región más transpartente* (1958; tr. *Where the Air is Clear*, 1960), a paranomic novel of Mexico City which counterpoints the urban present against the hidden past as represented in the character of Ixca Cienfueges, who has no part in the action. *Aura* (1962) is a super 'horror' novella, and is in many ways Fuentes's most powerful work. *La muerte de Artemio Cruz* (1962; tr. *The Death of Artemio Cruz*, 1964) is an outstanding study of a revolutionary who has become corrupted by power. *Cambo de piel* (1967; tr. *Change of Skin*, 1968), which has brilliant passages, is more experimental and on the whole less substantial. Fuentes has acute intelligence and great potential; it would be a pity if his gift were to be shattered by his facility.

Fugard, Athol (1933) South African playwright, actor, director (he is half-Afrikaans) who has deservedly established an international reputation. He is angry but controlled, and fully translates political horrors into human ones. *The Blood Knot* (1963) is about two brothers, one light- and the other dark-skinned; the censors smelled out its decency and distress and reacted accordingly. *Boesman and Lena* (1969) is more ambitious in scope and as successful. Plays were published in Berlin: *People Are Living There* (1969). *The Island* was produced in London in 1974.

Fuller, Roy (1912) English poet, novelist, critic. He was a building society solicitor by profession until retirement. Fuller began as a self-consciously left-wing poet, influenced chiefly by Auden (q.v.); unlike Auden he has remained more or less faithful to his early Marxism, though never in any way rigidly, stridently or uncritically. His best poetry is in *Collected Poems 1936–1961* (1962): this is limited by his inability to express or to deal with emotion, the existence of which Fuller appears to resent; but it is dry, laconic, civilized, sour, intelligent and well made. Since then the influence of Yeats has crept in, much to the detriment of the poetry. His novels are well observed and plotted; *Second Curtain* (1953) is an excellent thriller. As a critic he is an intelligent expositor of the virtues of traditional craftsmanship, and he may have wielded a good influence as Professor of Poetry at Oxford (1968–73)–*Owls and Artificers* (1971) is the best of the volumes containing his lectures–but he does not understand the nature of poetic or linguistic excitement.

G

Gadda, Carlo Emilio (1893–1974) Italian fiction-writer. He was an engineer (designer and describer of the Vatican power-station) who fought in the First World War and was taken prisoner, when he met Ugo Betti. He made his literary début in 1926. From the beginning he was weary, disillusioned, inclined to solitude, but a streak of energy and outrage also convulsed him from time to time. A mania for listing facts co-existed in him with a satirical impulse that was so impassioned as to be lyrical. As he wrote, his creative effort was largely directed towards 'vengeance': a lyrical or comic vengeance for the awful things that 'fate' does to men, which includes making them stupid or mad as well as subjecting them to the vagaries of weather or barbarians. . . . His writing, owing much to Dossi and through him to the underrated efforts of the *scapigliati* (*see* Carducci), combines colloquialism, archaism and learned reference. Towards the end of his life Gadda issued series of fragments and unfinished novels, sometimes edited by others; these offer important clues to his more important works. These are *Quer pasticciaccio brutto de via Merulana* (1957; tr. *That Awful Mess on Via Merulana*, 1965), *La cognizione del dolore* (1963; tr. *Acquainted With Grief*, 1969), which was written over twenty years before its publication in revised form, and *Eros e Priapo:da furore a cenere* (1967). Gadda–solitary, obviously a severely candid self-analyst whose furious indignation and resentment is perfectly balanced by his propensity to the secret, narcissistic belly-laugh–is a true modern: utterly without pretensions, not dependent upon his writings for his earnings, he has concocted a style that perfectly expresses his sophisticated engagements with reality. His indictment of fascism and its acceptance by a corrupt society and the warmth that infuses his often recondite work both give the lie to the claim of proponents of the *nouveau roman* that he belongs to their camp. Although an 'atomizer' rather than a psychologist, he lacks frigidity or much interest in philosophico-literary theory: characters, such as that of Ingravello in the mock-detective story *That Awful Mess . . .* , tend to emerge; nor does he deny love because a part of him feels that it ought not to exist. He is an original, one of the most readable of 'obscure' authors. It is said that Gadda hates and excludes his reader, that he is 'fundamentally a moralist, and that he does not believe in the possibility of human progress'. The last judgement is true; but he would like to. As for his hatred and exclusion of his reader: this ploy is to drive the pretentious, the *bien pensants*, the 'liberal' acceptors of fascism (the equivalent of our own self-styled 'moderates'), from his work. As for his 'morality': that is simply unstable criticism. His superb short stories are collected in *Accoppiamenti giudiziosi* (1963), *Judicious Connections*.

Galsworthy, John (1867–1933) English novelist, playwright, poetaster. Nobel Prize 1932. Most famous for *The Forsyte Saga* (1906–22), a never penetrative or stylistically interesting novel-sequence which soon turned from mild social criticism to 'worthy' but morally sleazy celebration of the *status quo*. The plays (e.g. *Strife*, 1909; *Justice*, 1910), well-made but not psychologically dense, are keener, revealing an admirable sense of fairness though no insight into human nature. Dominated by his atrocious, hypochondriac wife, the honest, depthless Galsworthy was a paradigmatically genteel, 'decent chap' of his times whose work was for long grotesquely overvalued. His mediocrity and basic complacency were discerned by D. H. Lawrence (q.v.). His main writings are unceasingly available in every shape and form.

Garcia Márquez, Gabriel (1928) Colombian fiction writer. He was brought up in a sleepy and decaying town, Aracataca, and this ('Maconda'), though in a mythologized form, provides the setting for most of his fiction. An admirer of Neruda (q.v.), Borges (q.v.), Guillén (q.v.) and Cernuda (q.v.), and a despiser of both the *nouveau roman* (*see* Robbe-Grillet) and the structuralism of Lévi-Strauss, he has steadfastly gone his own way. *El coronel no tiene quien le escriba* (1961; tr. *No One Writes to the Colonel*, 1971) is a compassionate novella about a retired colonel who awaits his bureaucratically over-delayed pension in a murderously hostile town. The longer *Cien años de soledad* (1968; tr. *A Hundred Years of Solitude*, 1970) is deservedly regarded as a masterpiece: it counterpoints the realistic decline of a

'Maconda' family with the fantastical and poetic inner lives of the inhabitants of the remote region in which they live. It seems bleakly pessimistic but, as Garcia Márquez has himself remarked, 'In good literature I always find the tendency to destroy that which is established, that which is already *imposed* [my italics], and to contribute to the creation of new forms of living . . .' *A Hundred Years of Solitude* draws upon the 'myths, ghosts, solitude and nostalgia' upon which Aracataca (says Garcia Márquez) lived by hinting at their fecundity; the peculiarly ironic tone of the book is established by the realism with which the *deadness* of these 'myths', in the lives of the people, is established. Garcia Márquez is also an important writer of short stories: *Leaf Storm,* a selection, was translated into English in 1972. He has lived outside Colombia for much of his time, and has worked with Fuentes (q.v.) on a filmscript.

Gascoyne, David (1916) English poet, novelist (*Opening Day,* published when he was seventeen, is the most successful precocious novel of our times). Disturbed, versatile, at times genuinely hallucinated in a manner rare in English poetry, Gascoyne's work never quite reached the apogee it continuously promised: had it done so, he would be the single English poet to have wholly assimilated modern French awarenesses into a truly Anglo-Saxon context. As it is he is deeply interesting but his poetry as a whole displays a tortured, fragmented vision which is too often debilitated by sudden losses of rhythm and simplicities that are curiously ineffective and weightless in effect. The positive pole of his inspiration is a Platonic contemplativeness, but while this gives or gave him strength to write, it also robs him of energy; the element of robustness is almost absent, and one gets a sense of a man who is a too intolerable nuisance to himself for being alive. He thus fails as a 'religious' *poet,* though his religiousness may very well not fail. None the less, he is important, serious and original. He turned from beautifully presented and relatively placid surrealist trivia (*Man's Life is This Meat,* 1936) and thirties leftism to self-consciously Christian-Platonist poetry during the war and lost his linguistic verve and nerve except in some pellucid, sweetly simple lyrics (e.g. 'The Goose Girl') and in some lines of 'Night Thoughts' and 'Megametropolitan Carnival', where the world crowds in to haunt, with its cacophony, his Platonism. But despite the bewildering failure of his ear–revealed in particular by his failure to handle a long line–none of his later poetry is less than distinguished. He has published nothing new since 1963. *Collected Poems*, 1965.

Gatsos, Nikos (1915) Greek poet, translator. His surrealist (*see* Breton) poem *Amorgos* (1943; 1963), composed in one night by 'automatic writing', has been highly influential. In translation it can read comically ('. . . one lost elephant is always worth much more than the quivering breasts of a girl'), but its combination of ballad tradition, Biblical rhythms and Heraclitian philosophy has attracted some readers. Gatsos has since made some good translations of poems and plays by Lorca (q.v.), and written words for popular songs.

Genet, Jean (1910) French playwright, poet, essayist. A bastard, Genet (this is his mother's name) was abandoned by his mother; his life and work may be seen, at one important level, as his revenge for this. His Burgundian foster-parents branded him as thief and he accepted this and all the punishments meted out to him in the various reformatories and prisons in which he spent his time until (1948) Sartre (q.v.), Gide (q.v.), Cocteau (q.v.), Mauriac (q.v.) and even Claudel (q.v.) and others petitioned the President to annul his life-sentence; this Auriol did–and invited Genet to dinner. Genet wandered Europe and France in search of degradation, terror and punishment: he was self-confessed thief, pimp, coward, homosexual, prostitute, admirer of Nazidom, betrayer of his friends, professional masturbator and excremental narcissist, police informer. He was pardoned, as is possible in France, for being a genius (he had published seven books: two plays –one had been produced by Jouvet–two poems in one volume, and four autobiographical or semi-autobiographical novels); but this shocked him into six years of silence and he has since kept out of the public eye. Married and with an adopted child, he apparently leads a somewhat puritanical and bourgeois existence–but then this pose fits well into the role for which, in his original 'filthy' project, he frenetically and masochistically sought. There is no longer anything for him to write about: he has earned the money, the respectability, for which he has always yearned. The screenplay for *Mademoiselle* is as bad as the film (1966) itself. Genet is an important writer and an excellent and effective dramatist. The first volume of his *Oeuvres complètes* consisted, curiously, of Sartre's ironic eulogy, *Saint Genet;* two more volumes have followed (1951–3) but they omit some prose and contain none of the plays. Sartre's 'existentially analytic' estimate of Genet as a saint and martyr is over-elaborated but is essentially correct. Genet chooses to become what 'society' has made of him. His poetry is poor: it imitates the neo-classicism of the later verse of Cocteau, who befriended him and probably illustrated the clandestine edition of his best novel, *Querelle de Brest* (1947; tr. *Querelle of Brest*, 1966). But in his prose he adopts a parodically academic, 'beautiful' French—the kind to which the bourgeois pay lip-service—to express an equally parodic indulgence in narcissistic degradation. The two best books are *Querelle*, in which he is able to diagnose his own condition as Seblon, the sodomite who is absent from the action and who merely fantasizes over the murderously evil sailor Querelle and the non-fictional *Journal du voleur* (1949; tr. *The Thief's Journal*, 1964), in which he reconstructs a fantasy autobiography of himself in the years 1932–40. These and the stylistically less successful *Pompes funèbres* (1947 rev. 1948) most clearly embody not a kind of ethic (as some critics insist) but rather anatomize a certain type of chosen, voluntary, masochistic homosexuality: as a system it would be an obscene and ritualistic advocation of power; but the notion of a wheel of fortune in which the man at the top initiates those below him, by process of sexual humiliation, into evil is a noble enough account of Genet's own project. The plays, influenced by English Jacobean drama and (surely?) by Pirandello (q.v.)—or Anouilh's (q.v.) popularization of him—are powerful and effective. The subtlest is *Les Bonnes* (1948 rev. 1954 rev. 1963; tr. *The Maids*, 1954), which was intended to be, but has not been performed by males in drag. *Le Balcon* (1956 rev. 1962; tr. *The Balcony*, 1958 rev. 1960), set in a brothel where men pay to enact fantasy-roles (general, priest, queen, chief of police and so on) adds nothing to Pirandello, but does ask, in crisply contemporary terms, the question, What is reality? There are three more plays, all available in English. Genet's 'pornographic' film *Un Chant d'amour* (made c. 1948), which is frequently sentimental in a lucubrated homosexual manner, provides the best demonstration of why—even though he is so intelligent, and, indeed, in his way, heroic—he is not a major writer: his true obsession is masturbation, his goal fantasy, his God (after all) a 'good' bourgeois existence, as sexually unauthentic and solitary as masturbation. True, it is not possible to know whether Genet has now purged himself of fantasy, and lives as a privately authentic man behind an ironic bourgeois mask. But if he has gained such freedom he has written nothing remotely suggesting that he has. He has been, however, a fascinating and illuminating man and writer, well worthy of the serious attention that has been accorded him. Novels by him not mentioned here are available in English.

George, Stefan (1868–1933) German poet. After symbolist beginnings, George evolved a highly idiosyncratic form of 'pure poetry'. His life-style was certainly original: repulsively autocratic, narcissistic, frigid, naively idealistic. Idolized by a small circle, all but the most mediocre of whom became estranged from him, he constructed a mystico-homosexual cult around the figure of a youth, Maximin (who soon died), who seems to have been an idealization of himself. But his fundamental project—to free the language of poetry from the taint of history—was not so original, although he (unlike Ungaretti, q.v.) was less interested in the possibilities of self-discovery to which such a process might lead, and more in the creation of a 'new Reich' of pure spirit. Like Laura Riding (q.v.) he identified his own personality with his ideal, so that the poetry of his final phase lacks tension: its author's exaltedness is unquestioned and the holy boy is—for all the high tone—an essentially vulgar reflection of his lost youth. But George cannot be disposed of because he wilfully misinterpreted Nietzsche or because he can represent Teutonic portentousness at its worst. He was a very gifted craftsman, a learned man, and that is not all. In a few poems, of which 'Der Herr der Insel', 'The Lord of the Island', is one of the most characteristic, he surpasses his 'philosophy' and becomes a major poet. There is a translation: *The Works* (1949).

Ghelderode, Michel De (ps. A. L. M. Martens) (1898–1962) Belgian (Flemish) playwright, fiction writer. Ghelderode, a very eccentric man in the Flemish manner, wrote in French but some of his plays were first performed in Flemish translations by other hands. His theatre—most influenced by the Belgian puppet tradition, which mixes tragedy and farce, as well as by the Elizabethan and Spanish traditions—seems less grotesque in his native land than it does outside it. He worked closely with the Théâtre Populaire Flamand. He has claimed that many of his plays are no more than 'documents of folklore'. One cannot possibly understand them without some acquaintance with the strange worlds of (Pieter I) Breughel, Hieronymus Bosch—and also such less famous painters as Dieric Bouts. The modern painter who was his idol was the visionary, half-English James Ensor. The plays exist in such grotesque, crowded, esoteric worlds; and yet Ghelderode, because he was steeped in the theatre, also often strangely evokes the world of the actors themselves: poor, humble, uncomfortable, victims of the public, dedicated. His viewpoint is a luridly distorted Catholicism: the world is a battleground between God and the devil but all the participants are debased, animated by instinct. In Ghelderode the crowded canvases of Bosch begin to move violently but there is little apparent juxtaposition at the end. At the centre of each play is a figure (e.g. Christ, Faust, Don Juan) who is a distorted surrogate for the burdened playwright himself. This drama is abundant in stage directions, the action is frenzied–Flemish-surrealist–and the language wholly rhetorical. It is language in fact that is Ghelderode's weakest point; his strongest is his capacity to arrange plays which so vividly mix in all the elements of the ancient tradition of which he is the representative. Lust, greed, terror of death: all these are taken for granted; puppets become people and people puppets; yet vitality so informs the best of the plays that it gives them a humanity that overcomes the frequently cliché-ridden dialogue. There are nearly fifty of them, and seven of the best, including *Barabbas* (1928), *Fastes d'enfer* (1929; *Chronicles of Hell*) and *Sire Halewyn* (1934; *Lord Halewyn*) have been translated in *Seven Plays* (1960). *Escurial* (1927), also notable, is translated in *Modern Theatre V* (1957). *Hop Signor* (1935) has not been translated. There are novels (e.g. *Histoire comique de Klizer Karel*, 1923), theoretical works (*Les Entretiens d'Ostende*, 1956), chronicles (*La Flandre est un songe*, 1953, *Flanders is a Dream*) and short stories (*Sortilèges*, 1962, *Spells*). *Théâtre* (1950–7).

Gide, André (1869–1951) French novelist, diarist, autobiographer, essayist, playwright, prose-poet, critic, editor, correspondent (with, e.g. Jammes, q.v., Rilke, q.v., Claudel, q.v., Valéry, q.v.). Nobel Prize 1947. One of the most influential and controversial of French writers of this century. His *Journals* (1885–1949; tr. *Journals, 1889–1949*, 1947–51; 1953; tr. sel. 1967) are indispensable. Gide was an ambisexual who early sought and obtained sexual pleasure from other men. He explored Africa partly for this purpose and while there met Oscar Wilde. He possessed a brilliant intelligence, much energy, and a multitude of talents (for languages, music, friendship and much else); all this in the undoubted presence of creative genius, although the degree of his imaginative powers has been debated. Since, as his critics agree, his work oscillates between the two almost equally strong poles of a natural puritanism and a natural 'pagan' zest for physical pleasure and since his intelligence is so acute and honesty so absolute he is a crucial writer for our times. He will ignore nothing that happens to him, that he feels, that excites him, that constrains him. 'I let the most antagonistic proposals of my nature gradually come to agreement without violence. Suppressing the dialogue in oneself really amounts to stopping the development of life' (1927). If Gide was influenced by Nietzsche, then he was equally influenced by the scriptures and, indeed, by Christianity. Seldom has a man attracted so much hatred and ill will for such wrong reasons: for Gide was, in the main, a most tolerant, good-tempered, eclectic, gentle, empathetic man—his shrewd remarks about his contemporaries are almost invariably truer than they are malicious. His heart always pointed towards truth. Not that he was always right: he was, in particular, taken in by Stalinism for a time. But in the bitter days of Vichy, as his *Journal* reveals, he identified himself with the decay of France—there is no note of self-righteousness, only of bitter regret. Gide married his cousin (the 'Em.' of the diaries) in 1895 (he had a daughter by Elizabeth Van Rysselberghe in 1923); she was a religiously devout woman and because she was the one consistent love of his life, his ideal, she considerably sharpened the conflict in him between the spiritual and the physical. The pagan side of Gide is revealed in his first significant work, *Les Nourritures terrestres* (1897 rev. 1927; tr. *Fruits of the Earth*—with *Les Nouvelles Nourritures*, 1935–1949). The chief value of this early work lies, however, in its plea—through a series of exhortations to a young man—for liberation from puritanism; its prose, though excellent in an academic sense, has not worn well. Gide was a fine stylist in the specifically Gallic sense but as a prose-poet he failed. Again, in *Corydon* (1911, in limited anonymous edition; 1923; tr. 1950), a plea for homosexuality, the importance lies not in the work but in the message. One has in fact to separate Gide into several compartments: the influential educator—the anti-colonialist, the legal and sexual reformer, the independent fellow-traveller (Gide, as will have been gathered, thrived on paradox); the self-analyst (in the *Journals*); the friend and correspondent; the translator (Tagore, q.v., Shakespeare—notably—Whitman, Conrad, q.v., Blake and others); the critic—and the imaginative writer. He referred to *Les Faux-Monnayeurs* (1926; tr. *The Coiners*, 1927 rev. 1950, in USA *The Counter-*

feiters) as a novel; the rest of his (shorter) fictions he called *récits.* All these are of a high quality; *Les Faux-Monnayeurs,* the most ambitious, is usually regarded as flawed. This is perhaps true, since it tends at times to subordinate its psychological material to problems concerning fiction-writing. But it holds its own on the imaginative plane and is one of the most acutely intelligent novels of the century. It is an immensely complex work, which on the whole successfully creates a 'world' of people, but also deals with some of the problems which obsessed Gide: bastardy and its supposedly liberating effects, homosexuality, the equally liberating 'gratuitous act' (*acte gratuit*), the nature of fiction. His other, shorter novels are simpler. *Les Caves du Vatican* (1914; tr. *The Vatican Swindle,* 1927, *The Vatican Cellars,* 1952) is on the theme of the gratuitous act, and stems—though exuberantly—from Dostoievski: it is brilliantly ambiguous in its approach. *L'Immoraliste* (1902; tr. *The Immoralist,* 1930) and *La Porte étroite* (1909; tr. *Strait is the Gate,* 1924 rev. 1948) are both 'conflict' novels, more serious in tone, demonstrating Gide's obsession with the phenomena of sacrifice, chastity, 'Platonic' love. *La Symphonie pastorale* (1919; tr. with *Isabelle,* 1911, in *Two Symphonies,* 1931), perhaps his most radiant and perfect single work, studies the effects of the sort of Calvinism which his nature possessed and courageously rejected. As playwright Gide was not successful, though he wrote many plays; one may sympathize with his view that the theatre is a non-literary place (it largely is)—but it is not a view that helps produce good drama and his *Oedipe* (1930) and others are superior to the think-pieces of, say, Shaw (q.v.) only in the matter of artistic integrity and intelligence—they are not as entertaining. His autobiography *Si le Grain ne meurt* (privately published 1920; 1926; tr., *If It Dies . . .* , 1935 rev. 1962) is an indispensable guide; his influential books on the maladministrated (French) Congo are both translated in *Travels in the Congo* (1930); his criticism of the French legal system, *Souvenirs de la Cour d'Assises* (1913), was translated (1941) as *Recollections of the Assize Court.* He was a co-founder (1908) of the magazine *La Nouvelle Française,* and exercised a powerful influence on it. As well as the more famous correspondences (referred to above), those with the strange Jouhandeau (q.v.), published in 1958, and the almost equally odd crook and pseudo-scholar (but author of *Father and Son*), Edmund Gosse (1960) are important and revealing. *Et nunc manet in te* (privately issued 1947; 1951; tr. *Madeleine,* 1953) is about his early relationship with his wife. His friend, the novelist Jean

Schlumberger, has written the authoritative account of Gide's marriage: *Madeleine et André Gide* (1956). The best biography is by J. Delay, though it deals only with the earlier years (*La Jeunesse de André Gide*, 1956–7; abridged tr. *The Youth of André Gide*, 1963). The complete works, *Oeuvres complètes* (1932–9), are being supplemented. Gide is, yes, deficient in imagination at the highest level—but his creative work stops only a little short of that level and to all but those certain of their righteousness he is a great and good man.

Ginsberg, Allen (1926) American poet, 'self-prophetic master of the universe' (Ginsberg), philanthropist and public performer. The reaction to the involute American poetry written in the atmosphere of the new criticism (*see* Brooks) was bound to come; Ginsberg's *Howl*, (1956) did not begin it, but it apotheosized it and gave it, for many, authenticity and authority. A poem 'badly made' (in the sense that the poems of Lowell, q.v., the paradigmatic 'post-new critical' poet, are 'well made'), it has its roots in Ginsberg's early Jewish environment (his father is a poet, his mother was a left-wing Russian emigrant), in his avowed homosexuality (exploited here as a minority 'right'), in Whitman, and in his experiments with drugs. It is not a satisfactory poem but it has passages of rhetorical power and it will be remembered and read as of some historical importance. It has, as a whole, authenticity and so do some of the poems that accompanied it. For some Ginsberg then became a kind of saint, a major poet 'expanding the frontiers of consciousness'. But after *Howl* Ginsberg rapidly declined. He is now even worried about his influence, recognizing perhaps that drug-taking can and usually does threaten just what he values: heightened vision. Ginsberg combines a liking for the visionary and personal kindliness with shrewdness. He almost invented Burroughs (q.v.) and he is a skilful publicist. What was genuinely rhapsodic in him has become tiredly self-inflationary; the little that was visionary has become exhibitionistic. Looked at dispassionately *TV Baby Poems* (1967), for example, consists of inept collages of commonplace notions in commonplace though inflated language. Ginsberg was born of the 'Beat' generation: 'beatitude', 'beatific', and 'beat' (weary of the environment). This was sociological: a fifties protest against puritanism, politeness, respectability. Ginsberg was a part of all this, but he knew more and he exploited the situation with some shrewdness and skill. Jane Kramer's *Allen Ginsberg in America* (1969) is a fair portrait of him.

Giono, Jean (1895–1970) French novelist from Provence; his father was a cobbler. His work falls into two main sections: the pre-war novels (the best), and the post-war neo-picaresque romances, commercially successful but comparatively shallow. Giono fought through the First World War and the experience turned him into an ardent pacifist. He went to prison for a time after the 1939–45 war, but his behaviour was soon forgotten—he had, despite his journalistic indiscretions, kept clear of all politics. Giono's inspiration was, first and foremost, his environment: the *gens simples* of Manosque—he was always more friendly with the 'ordinary' folk of his home town than with Parisian literary figures. He early learned from Homer, from the Old Testament (he was not a Christian), from the stories current in his native region: he became an epic storyteller. But, partly of Italian blood, he never became imbued with the spirit of heroism so implicit in Homer. His appreciation of Homer, the Bible, Whitman, Melville, Kipling (q.v.), Hesiod and the great Greek dramatists was not critically profound but he learned his craft from them. He knew in his bones that whatever he had to say must be said in the form of a story. Despite his political naivety he had much to say. The earlier novels are mysterious, ambiguous, lyrical accounts of what Unamuno (q.v.) called *intrahistoria:* the unrecorded life of the 'folk', a story which may be good or bad, but which—despite the 'historians'—exists. Most of these have been translated. The undoubted masterpiece is *Que ma Joie demeure* (1935; tr. *Joy of Man's Desiring,* 1940); in Bobi, the con-man saviour, Giono found a perfect surrogate for himself and his pastoral project. The whole work is alive with an epical sense of men living under the spell of, and sometimes in accordance with, the strange laws of nature. In *Batailles dans la montagne* (1937), *Battles within the Mountain,* the zany prophet has, for the most part, taken over. Other of the earlier books that deserve reading for their powerful evocation of the rural way of life and its relationship with natural forces are *Colline* (1920; tr. *Hill of Destiny,* 1929) and *Le Chant du monde* (1934; tr. *The Song of the World,* 1937). After the war Giono cleverly switched to a new, stylish, 'historical' type of novel. The *Chroniques* (e.g. *Le Hussard sur le toit,* 1954; tr. *The Horseman on the Roof,* 1954—the fifth in the series), largely modelled on Stendhal (but not remotely achieving his status) are laconic, energetic, psychologically without interest—slick. The cataclysm of the Second World War and his own humiliation clearly robbed Giono of his inchoate power; the achievement of creating a popular, new, and by no means simply vulgar genre is a tribute to his vitality and native cunning. These post-war novels add nothing at all to his stature; yet one cannot but admire the project. The Raimu film, *La Femme du Boulanger* (1938), directed by Pagnol—from an episode in the autobiographical novel *Jean le Bleu* (1932; tr. *Blue Boy*, 1946)—is an unforgettable comedy and conveys much of the essence of the good Giono: the Giono who knew and did not try to explain. M. A. Smith's study (1966) is useful.

Gippius, Zinaida (1869–1945) Russian poet, novelist, critic. Married to the insipid and better known Dmitri Merezhkovsky, famous, not wholly undeservedly, for her 'unpleasantness', this bitter-tongued *émigrée* is probably the greatest of all Russian woman poets. Her only rivals are Akhmatova (q.v.), Tsvetaeva and Pavlova (1807–93); but none of these matches her intellectually and she is technically ahead of all of them. Her Dostoievskian novels are efficient; her criticism is less devastating or 'spiteful' (as it is usually called by male critics) than splendidly revealing of the many important writers she met in pre-Bolshevik Russia (e.g. Blok, q.v., Sologub, upon whom she is both invaluable and gentle); but her earlier poetry is as extraordinary as it is neglected and untranslated. She began as an associate of the symbolists, but was most influenced by the poetry of Innokenty Annenski (1856–1909), who was a symbolist hailed by the acmeists (*see* Akhmatova). . . . Her poems, written only under extreme compulsion, are diabolical, feline, and entirely without tenderness. More than one critic has called her 'perverse', a poet of 'viscosity'. She is perverse because she evidently enjoys unnerving her reader by evoking a metaphysical experience that he/she has certainly had. Gippius (whose name is sometimes spelt, by her wish, Hippius) hated daily life and was certainly a Platonist; but she seems to have hated the Platonic world as well. She is an uncanny poet and she could never be popular. One of her plays has been translated: *Zhelonoye koltso* (1916; tr. *The Green Ring*, 1920). Her entire poetic output was collected, in Germany, in 1973.

Giraudoux, Jean (1882–1944) French dramatist, novelist and critic. He was a diplomat by profession. The sentimental, clever novel *Siegfried et le Limousin* (1922; tr. *My Friend from Limousin*, 1923) established him, though he had written much before it. His theatre was immensely popular in the thirties. The first play, *Siegfried*, based on the novel, is typical, and states Giraudoux's own problem: it is about a French prisoner-of-war who loses his memory and thinks he is a German—and Giraudoux himself could never resist the desire to 'be German'. Jouvet made Giraudoux as a dramatist; his whimsical, brilliant, shallow plays need above all skilful direction. Giraudoux does have a genuine vision of life: a frothy, foamy, delicate, curious, over-enchanted one, in which the divine is a certain sort of woman—intuitive, dazzling, necessarily the object of male love. Unfortunately he is usually too precious: the spell is in the performance rather than in the recollection of it. Famous plays by him include *Amphitryon* 38 (1929; ad. 1938) and *La Guerre de Troie n'aura pas lieu* (1935; tr. *Tiger at the Gates*, 1963). The best is *La Folle de Chaillot* (1945; ad. *The Madwoman of Chaillot*, 1949).

Golding, William (1911) English novelist—one of the most original, powerful and yet perplexing of his generation. *Lord of the Flies* (1954) is a savage moral fable, but written realistically, that parodies Ballantyne's Victorian children's classic *Coral Island*. Its premise—that boys stranded on an island would degenerate from rational beings into Hobbesian 'savages'—is false and much genuinely felt gloom spills over and is, so to say, wasted: the book needs to be anthropologically satisfactory and it is not. But it is powerful and, at least immediately, convincing; moreover, it can reasonably be argued that Golding uses boys to stand for men in a hideous Hobbesian metaphor: that he is a black theological fabulist whose subject is original sin. In *The Inheritors* the basic premise—that *homo sapiens* arrived on the scene after Neanderthal man and overcame him—is questionable, but it serves as another suitable metaphorical framework for the description of the loss of innocence from the world—and Golding's narration from his (if not *the*) Neanderthal viewpoint is brilliant. In *Pincher Martin* (1956), describing the death-agonies, recollections and hallucinations of a sailor clinging to a rock, the reader is bound to lose his way; the attempted symbolism is hopelessly unresolved though the physical impact of the writing is again powerful. The same applies to the even more symbolically inspired *Free Fall* (1959) and *The Spire* (1964), though these are at the same time more realistically written. The fault of these novels is that the subject-matter—of good and evil, free will and predestination—is presented to the reader in two ways: confusedly, in the form of Golding's attempt to impose a conscious symbolism on to his material and imaginatively, in the form of the story plus its narration. But the first tends to vitiate and enfeeble the second. It is hardly a pretentiousness, however, but a genuine creative difficulty. *The Spire*—symbol of symbols!—was about as far as Golding found he could go, and in *The Pyramid* (1967) he turned to a more overt realism, though there is no dearth of symbolic intent. It remains to point out that Golding is still the most naturally creative of English novelists of his generation and that he has attracted a large amount of non-creative criticism.

Goll, Iwan or **Yvan** (ps. Isaac Lang) (1891–1950) Franco-German writer (of Jewish-Alsatian parentage). He wrote poetry, drama, novels and criticism in French and German until his fortieth year, after which he wrote mostly in French until his last years. He was in America in the war but returned to Paris, where he died of leukaemia. He also made efforts to write in English. He had contacts with expressionists (*see* Stadler), dadaists (*see* Ball) and surrealists (*see* Breton), and his own later poetry (his main achievement) both draws upon and transcends the theories of these writers. He also passed through these movements as an active adherent. He was much influenced by Joyce (q.v.)—he was responsible for the first translation of *Ulysses* into German—and in particular by his use of stream-of-consciousness (*see* Bergson). His German plays, including *Die Unsterblichen* (1920), anticipate the Theatre of the Absurd (*see* Ionesco). His wife Claire (*née* Studer), herself a poet and magnificent autobiographer, played an active role in his creative life, and translated and edited some of his works. He is the most cosmopolitan of all modern poets, and said of the 'landless John' (himself) of one of his masterpieces, the French sequence of seventy poems *Jean-sans-Terre* (1936–44; tr. *Landless John,* 1958), 'he died with a French heart, a German spirit, a Jewish blood and an American passport'. Although he and his work helped to found surrealism as an acknowledged movement, Goll's own brand of it was nearer to literary cubism (*see* Reverdy). In *Jean-sans-Terre* he sees himself as the Jew wandering in an earth that is hell: the style is lyrical, sometimes approaching balladry and the imagery almost Blakean. The two final collections, in German, *Traumkraut* (1951) and *Abendgesang* (1954), *Song of Evening,* are almost certainly his most outstanding: based on the nature and hallucinatory effects of his illness, the poems consist of a series of vivid images which grow inexorably into one another and which, all together, form a mysterious, haunting vision of the inner self's confrontation with the external reality of appearances. *Fruit from Saturn* (1946) is a collection of unsuccessful poems in English. Among his novels, which are not significant, is *Le Microbe de l'or* (1927), *The Gold Bacillus*. His French poetry has not been collected, but *Poèmes d'amour* (1925; tr. *Love Poems*, 1947) should be read as well as *Jean-sans-Terre*. The German poetry and drama is edited by his widow in *Dichtungen* (1960). The revealing letters to her are in *Iwan Goll-Claire Goll: Briefe* (1966). Goll is perhaps the only indisputably major bilingual writer since Gil Vicente.

Gombrowicz, Witold (1904–69) Polish novelist, playwright, diarist. Gombrowicz, who came of a wealthy family, studied law and philosophy in Paris, but early took to literature with the collection *Pamietnik z okresu dojrzewania* (1933), *Memorials of the Period of Growing-Up*, which contains the themes, in embryo, of all his later work. His best known novels are *Ferdyduke* (1938; tr. 1961) and *Pornografia* (1960; tr. *Pornography*, 1966); he has also written *Trans-Atlantyk* (1953) and *Kosmos* (1963; tr. *Cosmos*, 1967), more short stories, plays and a diary, his most revealing work (*Dziennik*, 3 vols., 1957–66, published in Paris)—some of this has been translated into German (*Tagebuch*, 1961) and French (*Journal Parisien*, 1965). Caught in Argentina in 1939, he lived there until 1963 when he returned to Europe and settled in Vence until his death. Two of his surrealist plays have been translated into German (1964). Though Gombrowicz, whose influence is growing, has been called 'absurdist', 'surrealist', 'existentialist' and 'expressionist', and though all these epithets are justified—for he is unrelentingly modernist—his work as a whole is best characterized as quintessentially Polish. It reflects the agonized Polish historical experience and blackness of temperament; it is somewhat weakened because it continually over-cerebralizes this. Gombrowicz sees bizarre trivia as an impassable barrier to self-realization; he also, more specifically, diagnoses both infantilism (in the recessive Freudian, q.v., sense) and senility as the inevitable causes of *Angst*. Yet he struggles against these obstacles: the bleak Polish literary callousness is softened by humanist concerns and by sheer surrealist-inspired fun, as in *Ferdyduke*, his central fiction.

Gordimer, Nadine (1923) South African short-story writer and novelist who concentrates her sense of outrage into studies of the human predicaments of white liberals and black or coloured people under the

South African regime. Her deliberate lack of polemicism gives her strength; but her novels (e.g. *Occasion for Loving,* 1963) tend to consist of short-story situations linked by weak and even bored narrative. The stories (e.g. *Not for Publication,* 1965) are quiet, sensitive, subtle analyses of often superficially commonplace situations but she has some of the acuteness of Stead (q.v.), though her style is more muted.

Gorky, Maxim (ps. A. M. Peshkov) (1868–1936) Russian fiction writer, dramatist, critic, literary theorist. After humble and rough beginnings Gorky became a provincial journalist; by 1900 he had become as famous in Russia as Chekhov or Tolstoi. The best of his early stories are grimly naturalistic, revelling in the brutality they depict; others are lushly idealistic (e.g. the selection *Twenty-Six Men and a Girl,* tr. 1902). *Foma Gordeyev* (1899; tr. 1928) is a novel about a commercial family which is revolutionary in implication and yet often sympathetic. After being imprisoned and in exile several times, the prolific Gorky became the chief spokesman for socialist realism (1932). He died, perhaps on the orders of Stalin, in 1936. From 1921–31 he was in Italy (but he returned for a time in 1928); his relationship with the regime was never happy. Russian literature had become thoroughly Stalinized by the early thirties, and Gorky's advocacy of socialist realism must be seen as a despairing lapse—his own practice was hardly ever socialist-realist. Officially, socialist realism simply means that the artist must be an activist (not a humanist or a humanitarian): he must portray man as he ought to be (in a socialist society), not as he is. In fact this means either that the artist does as he likes or that he falls victim to his enemies on charges of writing against the wishes of 'communist' dictators. The theory fitted in well with Russian nineteenth-century criticism, since this persistently advocated the creation of a literature that would *change* men. Actually, any theory of how writers *ought* to write hamstrings them. Some neo-Marxist critics in the West point to certain attempts to reconcile a 'free' literature with socialist realism: such attempts are disingenuous or rhetorical. All one can say in favour of Gorky in this sorry affair is that he did his best to be positive and flexible—and that he personally saved many writers from starvation, imprisonment and possible death (e.g. Zamyatin, q.v.). The extent of his own achievement is a matter of contention. He had immense vitality and his sympathy with the proletariat was always burningly sincere but he was a confused thinker and an indifferent stylist—nor did his political convictions often allow his imagination much rein. None the less, he deserves his place as Russia's greatest proletarian writer. The view that his post-revolutionary work is vastly inferior is not accepted by all readers; indeed, almost every aspect and phase of his creative work may be said to have merits—though his raw drama (e.g. the celebrated *Na dne*, 1902, tr. *The Nether Depths*, 1959) is never more than minor, and his criticism (as I have already implied) is undistinguished (his accounts of writers, however, are brilliant and valuable). Gorky's earliest work shows that, essentially, he hated all authority; his later and compromised career may best be seen in the light of this emotion and of the guilt he felt about it. He was no thinker but his own instincts were sure enough (hence his exile in the twenties—for the tuberculosis from which he suffered cannot wholly explain this). His autobiographical books (e.g. *Ispoved*, 1908; tr. *The Confession*, 1916), written in reaction to a series of ideological works, are vividly descriptive and ambiguous on the subject of Bolshevism. His last tetralogy (1927–36) translated as *Bystander* (1930), *The Magnet* (1931), *Other Fires* (1933), *The Specter* (1938) has been described as 'feeble', 'lumbering' and 'unreadable'. It is true that this panorama of Russian life in the period 1880–1924 is over-long and that it is the work of a weary man; but it has passages of interest. Most of his works have been translated into English, but some are hard to find.

Gover, Robert (1929) American novelist. His first novel, *One Hundred Million Dollar Misunderstanding* (1962), about an experienced Negro child prostitute, became a best-seller. *Here Goes Kitten* (1964) and *J. C. Saves* (1968) are on the same theme. *The Maniac Responsible* (1963) is an overwritten account of a murder.

Govoni, Corrado (1884–1965) Italian poet, playwright, novelist. In the ever-playful, sad ('I have always loved sad things' he wrote in an early letter) Govoni we have the strange phenomenon of a poet who passed through almost every phase of twentieth-century poetry and yet who never lost his individuality. He seems curiously weightless, yet he has substance. He began as a follower of D'Annunzio (q.v.), passed into crepuscularism (*see* Gozzano), then into futurism (*see* Marinetti), then into the group around the eclectic Florentine periodical *La Voce* (*Voice*), which ran from 1908 until 1916. The most enduring influence on Govoni was Pascoli (q.v.), than whom he is, however, more visual and more consciously experimental. His most deeply felt poetry is in *Aladino* (1946), the name of his son, killed in the war. *Poesie 1903–59* (1961); *La ronda di notte* (1966), *The Night Watch.*

Gozzano, Guido (1883–1916) Italian 'crepuscular' poet; with Corazzini the chief exponent of this school, which included Moretti, Oxilia, Govoni (q.v.) and Palazzeschi (q.v.). Crepuscular poetry was in general sad (or jokingly casual about sadness—a common mask), 'twilit', shabbily decadent—just, in fact, like Eliot's Prufrock. Gozzano, doomed to die young of tuberculosis, is the ironic poet of decay: determinedly against D'Annunzio, he resembles him in his decadence, but not in his treatment of it. Influenced by Jammes (q.v.) and Verhaeren (q.v.), he affects a consistently flippant attitude towards his own romanticism, creating a memorable gallery of female figures to relieve his sense of despair: the mood is tortured, the act of writing relaxed. *Poesie* (1960).

Granville-Barker, Harley (1877–1946) English playwright, critic, theatre producer. Granville-Barker's plays (*Collected Plays,* 1967) are efficient and humanitarian, his translations and adaptations from foreign drama valuable. He rendered great service to the British theatre. His *Prefaces to Shakespeare* (1927–48) are the best theatrically oriented criticism of Shakespeare, and cast much incidental light on the texts.

Grass, Günther (1927) German (-Polish: born Danzig) novelist, poet, dramatist. He fought in the war and was taken prisoner. He is now as well known in Germany as an active supporter of the Social Democratic Party as he is for his writings. His artistic training plays an important part in his writing. He was well known in Germany before the novel *Die Blechtrommel* (1959; tr. *The Tin Drum,* 1961) gave him international fame: for his sculpture and drawings, his self-illustrated poems, and his 'absurd' plays—all this work was minor, but grotesquely and comically distorting in the most intelligent German manner, and with an underlying commitment to life and to human courage. One of the virtues of Grass's best writing is his capacity to control his anger and despair, to submit it to the influence of his gentler sense of the quotidian, the comic. The first two novels remain the best. *Die Blechtrommel* traces German history from the post-war years through Hitler to the society of the *Wirtschaftswunder* through the eyes of a mad dwarf (Grass; the artist; the author's-eye-view of the historical events of his lifetime) who remains attached to the tin-drum of his stunted childhood: his 'simple-mindedness' is a brilliant distorting device for revealing the over-sophistications of the terrible period under survey. *Hundejahre* (1963; tr. *Dog Years,* 1965) again covers this period. As in the earlier playlets, the influence of Beckett (q.v.) is apparent. Complex in construction, and shot through (as always in Grass) with grotesque incidents, *Dog Years* is especially conspicuous for the sanity and justice of its attitude toward Nazidom in the person of Matern, who, with his childhood friend Amsel, is the chief character of the book. Here Grass is more astringent about the nature of the aftermath of National Socialism. His third full-length novel (*Katz und Maus,* 1961; tr. *Cat and Mouse,* 1963, is a *novelle*), *Ortlich betäubt* (1969; tr. *Local Anaesthetic,* 1970) is wholly contemporary and more specifically autobiographical; Grass dramatized part of it as *Davor* (1969). This novel is not as successful as its predecessors, though it contains passages of equal quality: Grass is in the process of working out his own position, which involves personal assessment as well as consideration of how protest can be effective and his themes do not interrelate altogether effectively. His play *Die Plebejer proben den Aufstand* (1966; tr. *The Plebeians Rehearse the Uprising,* 1967) uses Brecht's (q.v.) type of drama to attack Brecht's attitude to the 1953 East German uprising. It scores polemical points but fails to illuminate Brecht himself, who, unlike Grass, combined the possession of lyrical genius with a love of low-down trickery. . . . There is a useful *Selected Poems* (1966) in English.

Graves, Robert (1895) English (but he is Irish-Danish-German by ancestry) poet, novelist, critic, autobiographer, essayist, translator. His father was the notable minor Irish poet A. P. Graves. Graves was one of the best known of the young Georgian (*see* Brooke) war poets, but his war poems, though realistic, did not have the power of Owen's (q.v.) or Sassoon's (q.v.). He began to discover his own voice only in about 1924, when his war-shattered nerves had experienced the excitements and disillusions of married romantic love. In 1925 he became aware of the work of Laura Riding (q.v.); her then dedicated approach to poetry—though not her procedures, more rhythmically free than his—deeply influenced him. A hack book on his friend T. E. Lawrence and the success of his candid autobiography *Goodbye to All That* (1929 rev. 1957) enabled him to go with her to Majorca (where he still lives) and to set up the Seizin Press. Their relationship there was by no means what is usually termed a 'liaison'. In 1936 he left Majorca for England, Rennes in France and, finally, America, where he and Laura Riding parted company. He settled down in Devon with a new family and then returned to Majorca (1946). Graves has rejected as alien to his temperament any kind of freedom of verse form but he is not a mere continuer of the Georgian tradition. His best poetry, written between about 1928 and 1943, is far closer to the metaphysicals than to the Victorians. The 'story' traceable in his much revised poetry (*Collected Poems* 1938 rev. 1948 rev. 1955 rev. 1959 rev. 1961 rev. 1965 rev. 1975) is one of reluctant but dogged devotion to a romantic female figure; in itself it is simply a late manifestation of the 'romantic agony'. But he was the best love poet of his generation and as such could challenge comparison with Pound (q.v.), Eliot (q.v.), Auden (q.v.) and others who gained more critical and public attention in the thirties. Graves's metrical schemes allow for as much personal rhythm as does Pound's looser technique and Graves is as resolutely contemporary as any poet within his deliberately narrower field. The way in which lyricism is challenged (not blunted) by the stresses induced by a series of temporary romantic defeats is as fascinating as, and less equivocal than, the large, ambitious vaguenesses of *The Waste Land* and *The Cantos*. . . . When Graves combined his love of mythology (which he adapts to his purposes with a confidently scholarly air) with a pseudo-critical rationalization of his romantic concerns (especially of his attitude to his relationship with and ultimate rejection by Laura Riding) to produce the 'historical grammar of poetic myth' called *The White Goddess* (1948 rev. 1952 rev. 1961) he reduced the tension in his poetry, and weakened it. The book is lively, ingenious, fanciful-empiricist; but it 'explains' the mystery of the attractions of the romantic female prototype, and so sets its author to producing formula-poems. Thus his later poetry, with some powerful exceptions, has become increasingly lapidary: it beautifully versifies an ideology. In prose Graves has written distinguished historical and mythological novels (the most famous is *I, Claudius*, 1934), of which the best is *The Golden Fleece* (1944), an excellent sociological study of Great Britain between the wars—*The Lost Weekend* (1940), with Alan Hodge—and many volumes of essays. *The Nazarene Gospel Restored* (1953), with Joshua Podro, anticipated important developments in theology by a decade. As a critic he has not done full justice to his invaluable insights, but he cannot be ignored.

Green, Henry (ps. Henry Yorke) (1905–74) English novelist. Green went to Eton and Oxford and then joined his family's Midlands industrial business, with which he remained all his life. He is one of the most independent, original, comic and consistent of all modern English novelists. His subject, like his famous 'recreation' as listed in *Who's Who*—'romancing over the bottle to a good band'—was deliberately non-literary and unpretentious: 'the everyday mishaps of ordinary life'. This is a characteristic understatement, but it remained his aim; his art he kept largely secret. He could be trivially veristic to the point of boredom, but at his best (*Living*, 1929; *Party Going*, 1939; *Loving*, 1945; *Back*, 1946; *Concluding*, 1948) he is a rich, moving and quintessentially English novelist. One can best describe his unique qualities by suggesting how he gains his effects. The titles of all his mature novels (*Pack My Bag*, 1940, is a 'self-portrait') are gerunds or participles—with the exception of *Nothing* (1950). By this he implies that as a novelist he withholds all theory, judgement: he seeks a true 'objective correlative'—but with an emphasis on the first word and an absolute withdrawal from, but not denial of, the second. Thus artificially (artfully) detached, he eschews description as much as possible, since this might involve a lapse into morality; he also deals impartially with all social classes (he had a good working knowledge of them). He then allows himself a measure of latitude: having established his imaginative 'world' (it is when this is not sufficiently substantial that he fails, as in the over-documentary fire-service novel *Caught*, 1943, and in the final two, *Nothing* and *Doting*, 1952, which are almost entirely in dialogue), he moves into it, concentrating on the 'ordinary', the 'everyday', the 'mishaps'. This proved a devastatingly successful formula. The sensuous detail he reports is always pertinent to his subject and he is thus often called a symbolist. Green's relaxed objectivity finally failed; the gift of imagining situations left him; he remained silent for the last twenty-two years of his life. But at their apogee his intelligence had collaborated with his imagination to produce some of the most affirmatory and lyrical fiction of our time; while he extended the range of the comic novel of society, he never abused comedy by taking sides, or shrank from unsentimentally recording anyone's moments of joy or courage. It was an extraordinary achievement.

Green, Julien (1900) American novelist, playwright, diarist, memoirist, born in Paris; he has lived in France, except for the war years and some sojourns, and he writes in French. The autobiographical *Memories of Happy Days* (1942) is in English. Although influenced by Anglo-American literature (particularly by Emily Brontë and Hawthorne), he is certainly a 'French' novelist–French enough to be elected to the Académie Française (1971). Green, a Catholic (1939; before this he had been Protestant, teenage Catholic convert, Buddhist) who, unlike Mauriac (q.v.) has not renounced his Jansenism, is a violent, neo-Gothic and tormented novelist throughout all whose work, however, there runs a note of simple lyrical affirmation of nature (this is often missed). His themes are the metaphysical anguish of 'man without God', homosexuality and impassioned, melodramatic acts such as self-destruction, suicide or murder; in his novels the characters are near to madness or collapse, but also, we feel, to a kind of grace. The hidden world suggested in the novels until *Moira* (1950; tr. 1951) is both fearful and yet delicious–as he has confessed. The Oedipal nature of his conflicts is made most explicit in the two volumes of memoirs of his early years, *Partir avant le jour* (1963) and *Mille chemins ouverts* (1964), where he tells of his homosexual and narcissistic impulses, and of his attachment to his mother. As he has said, he is 'crucified in sex'. The earlier novels, set in France, concentrate on atmosphere at the expense of style (which has never been a strength in Green's writing); their plots are as sadistic or neo-Gothic as those of any contemporary 'horror' movie, but they are impassioned and point the way towards the mature Green's conviction that eroticism, God-given, is the way to salvation (though he refuses, to the dismay of many fellow-Catholics, to elaborate on this concept), even though it is evil as well as good. The sadistic element in sex is made explicit in every Green novel and the shyness of some of his characters is often connected with their dread of their own violence. The best of the earlier novels is *Epaves* (1932; tr. *The Strange River*, 1933). Here Green's strangely lyrical evocation of a stifling landscape and his sense of man's moral powerlessness, are most lucidly and imaginatively set forth. He has been prolific; his weakest novels, published in the forties, are influenced by his interest in Buddhism; *Sud* (1953), which was well received, is a play in which he deals with a homosexual theme that he had tried but failed to treat in a novel–it is professional and effective but too pat. His two most highly thought of novels are his best: *Moira* and *Chacun Homme dans sa nuit*

(1960; tr. *Each in His Darkness,* 1961). Each is set in America and each deals, now with more sureness and conviction, with the problem of the ambisexual who is thrown headlong into an erotic situation and who wants, therefore, both to murder and to die (the notion of death in Green has as much orgasmic power as it has in any contemporary writer). These are outstanding books: the mature author re-creates the world of his parents' original home through his mother's eyes (for she it was who first told him of Virginia, whose university Green later attended). Much may be learned about Green's mother and therefore Green from his sister Anne Green's (1899) novel (in English) *The Selbys* (1930). Anne Green shared a Paris apartment with her brother between the wars and she has translated some of his books. The *Journal* (1928–58; tr. *Personal Record,* 1940–the first three volumes–and in a selection, *Diary,* 1962), essential to an understanding of him, is included in the *Oeuvres complètes* (1954–).

Greene, Graham (1904) English novelist, playwright, essayist. As has been remarked, although Greene is a converted (1927) Roman Catholic, he is at heart a 'romantic anarchist'. The one does not necessarily preclude the other and both function in Greene's best fiction, in intelligently and humanely modified forms. His Catholicism, once accepted as part of his subject matter, usually presents little problem to the reader, since it may be seen by the non-believer (or, indeed, believer) as a metaphor for compassion: his 'Grace' is not a dogmatic concept, and could apply to a number of immediately recognizable psychological states of spiritual enlightenment. His own division of his work into 'novels' and 'entertainments' is somewhat arbitrary and misleading, since almost every one of his full-length stories is, at least in its framework, a melodrama and a thriller. His approach to the problem of how to create an 'objective' morality by withdrawal of personal judgement has been very different from that of his contemporary and namesake Henry Green (q.v.): more prolific, self-indulgent, romantic, more immediately lyrical or sordid (the sordid sends Greene into lyrical flights). His obvious strengths, some of them leaving him vulnerable, are extreme fluency and professionalism, power, the ability to create clear-cut characters and sound plots. His capacity to convey atmospheres of oppression has hardly been equalled in English. Further, his fluency has not been effortlessly achieved: he has learned constructively and never plagiaristically from Stevenson, Ford (q.v.), Mauriac (q.v.), Bernanos (q.v.) and many others. His most serious deficiency is his failure to portray women 'in the round'. As a Christian novelist he seems less interested in Christ than in men's relationship to their priests or to their God: to have faith in the redemptive powers of a God who can best be defined as the exact opposite of a moral tyrant is the all-important factor. The sins of the naturally faithful are certainly more important to him than the virtues of conformists. In his early taut and well-constructed thrillers Greene brilliantly explored his hatred of authority and unhappy awareness of political corruption. In 1938 he published *Brighton Rock,* his most serious novel (though styled in the USA edition as an entertainment) to that date. Here the anti-hero, a depraved teenage gangster, is defiantly presented as a possible hero. From this novel onwards Green's serious books have been set in hell and he has usually chosen appropriate settings—Mexico for *The Power and the Glory* (1940), West Africa for *The Heart of the Matter* (1948), Vietnam for *The Quiet American* (1955), a leper-colony in Central Africa for *A Burnt Out Case* (1961), the Haiti of 'Papa' Duvalier for *The Comedians* (1966), the last substantial novel—in which heat, corruption, disease and constriction of movement are omnipresent factors. All of these novels are more subtly stated, psychologically more complex, variations on the theme of *Brighton Rock.* Greene's world, 'Greeneland', is a hideously negative and at the same time vividly realized place. It can be charged that his unorthodox Catholicism is merely a sop, for us as for the author, to offer against an essentially nihilistic and pessimistic vision. But this ignores the vitality of the presentation, which reinforces the compassionate and affirmatory 'message' of grace, of the existence of the miraculous and of its morally paradoxical nature. Greene has been an excellent film critic (and scriptwriter for many of the films of his novels), an urbane essayist with a taste for good neglected writers, an observant travel writer, a penetrating biographer (*Lord Rochester's Monkey,* 1974, though written in the early thirties when information on its subject was scarcer, is the best life) and a skilful playwright and short-story writer. *Collected Edition* (1970–); *Collected Essays* (1969).

Grieg, Nordahl (1902–43) Norwegian novelist, playwright, poet. He was killed on a bombing mission over Berlin. In certain respects he resembles Saint-Exupéry (q.v.), since he was essentially a man of action but he was more genuinely intellectual—and somewhat less gifted as a writer. He led an adventurous life: at sea, in extensive travel—

including a substantial period in Moscow–as war correspondent in China and Spain and finally as war hero and airman. In Grieg we see the virtues, the confusions and the defects of patriotism. He was much admired and even imitated by Lowry (q.v.) in the early thirties. His two best books are the collection of poems *Rundt Kap det Gode Haab* (1922), *Around the Cape of Good Hope,* and the vivid sea novel *Skibet går videre* (1924; tr. *The Ship Sails On,* 1927). The chief influences on him were Kipling (q.v.)–whose imperialistic outlook both fascinated and repelled him–Jensen and the notion of 'young death' (*De unge døde,* 1932, *The Young Dead,* is a fervid volume on English poets who died young, from Keats to Brooke, q.v., and Owen, q.v.). His drama (e.g. *Nederlaget,* 1937; tr. *Defeat,* 1945) reflects his political concerns but does not resolve them. He was briefly a communist, but seemed to turn against it with his magazine *Veien Frem* (1936–7), *The Way Ahead,* which rejected all totalitarianism. His last important book is the novel *Men ung må verden ennu vaere* (1938), *But the World Must Be Young,* which is one of the earliest intelligent critiques of Stalinism. His last patriotic poems were effective at the time, but have been overrated: *Friheten* (1943; tr. *War Poems,* 1944). His works were collected in 1947 and again in 1952; there is a separate collected poems, *Samlede dikt,* 1948.

Griffin, John Howard (1902) American writer, most famous for the remarkable and moving *Black Like Me* (1961), his adventures in the South disguised as a black man. He has also written accomplished novels, including *The Devil Rides* (1952).

Grigson, Geoffrey (1905) English poet, man-of-letters, autobiographer, critic, editor, anthologist, topographer, bookmaker. Grigson, a writer as versatile as he is uncompromising, first made an impact as founder-editor of *New Verse* (1933–9), an aggressive magazine formed as a homage to Auden's (q.v.) promise and as the scourge of Georgianism (*see* Brooke) and hyper-romanticism. This is historically important and discovered good out-of-the-way poets but it was somewhat disfigured by the frequency with which invective descended into vituperation. The autobiography *The Crest on the Silver* (1950) puts the record straight and is required reading for students of the inter-war British literary scene. Grigson's closest criticism is in *The Harp of Aeolus* (1947), a subtle study of romantic poetry and its excesses; there are also revealing essays on some of the poets he admires—for example Clare, Hopkins (q.v.)—in *Poems and Poets* (1969). As a reviewer he is sharp, (now) courteously hard-hitting. His earlier poetry (*Collected Poems,* 1963) reveals his interest in craftsmanship, in all kinds of natural objects and in the various ways that people have chosen to represent them; his more recent collections (e.g. *A Skull in Salop,* 1967; *Sad Grave of an Imperial Mongoose,* 1973) are more confident, wider in scope and deeper in feeling. Acute observation of flora and fauna is still at the centre of his poetry, but this carries (without effort) a wider range of application: satirical, erotic, self-analytical. Age seems to have conferred on Grigson an added energy, an epigrammatic gift and a graceful ferocity. But, whatever his earlier failings, he has always been a true and fierce keeper of standards.

Guillén, Jorge (1893) Spanish poet, critic, translator. He came to the fore in what is known, most misleadingly, since none of its writers supported the right wing, as the 'generation of the dictatorship' (of the shoddy Primo de Rivera—who exiled Unamuno, q.v.,—in the twenties), which included such other poets as Lorca (q.v.), Salinas (q.v.), Alberti and Vicente Aleixandre (1898). The single collection *Cántico* (1928 rev. 1936 rev. 1945 definitive edition 1950), continually augmented, took up the first thirty-two years of his writing life, which began in 1918. His early poems owed much to the examples of Jiménez (q.v.) and Machado (q.v.), and were also influenced by Valéry (q.v.), Huidobro's creationism and surrealism (*see* Breton). Guillén's *Cántico* poems do not reflect the horrors of the Civil War or the Second World War which followed it. They have thus been condemned as 'cold'; but his later work shows that he has never been oblivious to evil. *Cántico,* whose final edition contains 334 poems (in the first there were 75), is, in Guillén's own words, 'an act of attentiveness' to the fact that 'It's a well-made world'—though composed (and this is where hostile critics have gone wrong) in the shadow of the parallel fact that 'nothing is truer than that "this world of man is badly made"'. Thus *Cántico* is 'in praise of living', an act of affirmation made absolutely without that 'sentiment' which Guillén's contemporaries and friends abhorred. Like Jiménez he searches for the 'true names' of things, which are 'exactly what they are'. But he knew that after this sequence 'there had to come a work in which . . . evil, disorder and death' were dealt with. Hence *Clamor* (1963), followed by *Homenaje,* more occasional poems. His whole output appeared in Milan in *Aire nuestro* (1968), *Our Air*. Guillén's poetry is uneven: his joy can become cliché-ridden, his modified surrealism monotonous. But at his best (as in 'Muerte a lo lejos', 'Death, from a Distance') he is unquestionably a major poet. *Cántico* (sel. tr. 1965); *Affirmation* (sel. tr. 1968).

Guimarães Rosa, João (1908–67) Brazilian fiction writer. He was a doctor and then a diplomat. At his death he was regarded by many as Brazil's leading novelist, though his approach was resolutely non-realistic. Brazil has an area called the *sertão*, the 'backlands' of the north, which has persistently refused to yield its autonomous 'primitivism', its mythology, to all governmental pressure. Euclydes da Cunha (1866–1909) recognized this in his epoch-making study of an early uprising (1896–7) there: *Os Sertãos* (1902; tr. *Rebellion in the Backlands*, 1944). This was followed by a number of other more sophisticated works on the same subject, notably by Alberto Torres and Gilberto Freyre. Brazilian writers, despite the obscene idiocy, psychotic sexual perversity and cruelty of their rulers, know that the loss of the mythology and way of life of the *sertanjos* would threaten not only Brazilian, but by implication human, survival. In the nine stories of *Sagarana* (1946; 1961) Guimarães Rosa attempted to assert the dignity of the *sertanjos*, relating their geographical to their human fate in a language which at once re-creates their predicament and explains–and justifies–their attitudes. This, which created his reputation, is not wholly successful; but *Grandes Sertão: Veredas* (1956; tr. *The Devil to Pay in the Backlands*, 1963) is a triumph, the logical imaginative outcome of Da Cunha's *Os Sertãos*–which is, indeed, *a*logical. This novel, which uses a language akin to that of Asturias's (q.v.) *Hombres de maiz*–an intuitive reconstruction, this time in Portuguese, of native language–synthesizes the mythology of the whole (huge) Brazilian area in the telling of a tale about a bandit, Riobaldo, who in order to revenge the death of another must make a pact with the devil. This is a difficult book because it is difficult for 'civilized' peoples to understand the force of ancient wisdom in societies whose civilization is merely superficial; but carefully read–perhaps most helpfully in the light of Da Cunha's classic, which is easily available–it will be seen to amount to an eloquent statement of a situation common to all of us: we imagine we are sophisticated, but we have lost contact with the *lyrical* sophistication that is still in our bones. . . . *Primeiras Estórias* (1962), stories, have also been translated into English: *The Other Side of the River* (1969).

Gumilyov, Nikolai (1886–1921) Russian poet. With his wife (1910–18) Akhmatova and Mandelstam (q.v.) he was the leading acmeist (*see* Akhmatova). His earlier poetry, inspired by his travels in Africa and the imperialistic aspirations that flowed from them (he loved Kipling, q.v.), is only interesting, though *Zhemchuga* (1910), *Pearls,* is exceptional because it reflects his dissatisfaction with his symbolist beginnings and anticipates his foundation, in 1911, of the Poet's Guild, the acmeist 'school'. He was shot, despite Gorky's (q.v.) last-minute attempt to save him, on a trumped-up charge, in 1921. The early poetry had been stylistically distinguished and exciting, though inchoate; the later is inspired by a vision of his own death (which he clearly saw as arising from a romantic frenzy), and concentrates his wildnesses into exactness. He bought this poetry at the expense of his life, which he could easily have saved. *Ognenny stolp* (1921), *The Pillar of Flame,* contains the famous 'Zabludivshisya tramvai', 'The Runaway Tram', on to which he leaps and from which he watches his life and his imminent death. He is yet another of the astonishingly large number of major poets who came to maturity in Russia in the first quarter of this century. *Selected Work* (1972) is a valuable selection, in English, from his poetry and prose.

Gunn, Thom (1929) English (now resident in America) poet whose *Fighting Terms* (1954 rev. disastrously, 1962), though clearly by an undergraduate, marked him out as a promising, energetic newcomer. His promise has hardly been fulfilled in *The Sense of Movement* (1957) and its successors, of which the most recent is *Moly* (1971). He inhabits two worlds and has not been able to reconcile them. One is that of the post-Beat (*see* Ginsberg) American male pop-culture, with its leather-jacketed inverts and Beatles-lovers (Gunn regards the Beatles as important poets); and the other is the academe of the late Yvor Winters (q.v.), under whom Gunn did post-graduate work, and who was the most ardent of all champions of consciousness and conscious control. He lacks sensibility (for example, the ironies of his own situation as a neo-classical admirer of Elvis Presley appear to escape him) and humour. But some critics admire his intellectual 'agility' and it must be granted that he puts much solemn and careful effort into his poems and that they bear the marks of this—but they remain curiously unconvincing, as if, with their painstaking, almost painful, use of unassimilated Sartrian concepts, they were the wooden products of an obstinate emotional immaturity. The breathlessly earnest desire to make the poem 'click' was attractive in the younger poet; in the older it is perhaps touching, but poetically bathetic.

H

Hagiwara Sakutaro (1886–1942) Japanese poet. Only one or two critics have recognized that Hagiwara is a major poet, of the standing of Lorca (q.v.) or Jozsef. Fortunately there exist some outstanding translations of his poetry, made by Graeme Wilson in the selection *Face at the Bottom of the World* (1969), which has an informative introduction. Wilson, one of the finest of all contemporary translators, is working on a version of all Hagiwara's work. His poetry is unique, and was the first (important) Japanese poetry to abandon archaic language and employ the oral colloquial. A contemporary brilliantly characterized his poetry as a 'razor soaked in gloomy scent'. It is extraordinarily thrilling work, by a man with naked nerves: sinister, menacing, and yet set against a background of fluid beauty. Threatening, lyrical, absolutely dedicated, Hagiwara's poetry is unquestionably of major proportions, much more deeply felt than that of any of his contemporaries. His neglect by translators of anthologies is puzzling.

Hamilton, Patrick (1905–62) English novelist and playwright. Hamilton, an alcoholic 'communist' very similar in spirit to Dashiell Hammett (q.v.), has never had his due from critics; though most of his novels stayed in print, he did well with his radio plays, and *Rope* (1929) and *Gaslight* (1938) became staple repertory fare. He is a most distinguished and original writer, whose *The Duke in Darkness* (1942), a stage failure, is worthy of Montherlant (q.v.). As a man Hamilton was a half-puckish enjoyer of what he regarded as his human failure, a bitter quasi-Marxist critic of inequality, a self-acknowledgedly 'weak' man; as a writer he is at his best tender, subtle, strong and detached. His subjects are human frailty, deliberate evil and the hypocrisy of the pseudo-gentry, of whom he is the century's finest satirist. *The Duke in Darkness*, a toughly romantic allegory of the imprisoned soul which works perfectly at the realist level, is his subtlest play; *Rope* and *Gaslight* are tributes to their genre: the intelligent thriller. The novels are more versatile than is usually conceded. *Hangover Square* (1939), the best, explores his own predicament in near-Gothic, melodramatic terms and is a minor masterpiece. The early trilogy *Twenty Thousand Streets Under the Sky* (1935) is a part-lyrical, part-naturalistic tale of moral degradation. Here his superb ear for the conversation of the middle classes in pubs first manifested itself; this was brought to perfection in the trilogy about his Heath-Haigh character–*The West Pier* (1951), *Mr Stimpson and Mr Gorse* (1953), *Unknown Assailant* (1955)–which is perfect within its carefully limited territory of a murderous, innocent-evil con-man and his stupid, greedy or pitiful marks. Looking at the fashionably acclaimed novels of the sixties and seventies, one laments Hamilton's last drink-racked, sterile years and relatively early death. Like Hammett, he died of wrecked decency.

Hammett, [Samuel] Dashiell (1894–1961) American crime novelist. Born in Maryland, grew up in Philadelphia and Baltimore. Left school at fourteen, took a variety of humble jobs, then joined Pinkerton's Detective Agency as an operative. Served as a sergeant in the First World War, in which he contracted tuberculosis; this was later cured but his health was permanently impaired. Married, had two daughters, returned to Pinkerton's (he served them for eight years in all), but then separated from his family and began his slow, hard apprenticeship as a writer. His first prose consisted of tough, short, detective fiction. His four best novels, *Red Harvest* (1929), *The Dain Curse* (1929), *The Maltese Falcon* (1930) and *The Glass Key* (1931), made him–as a scarred ex-detective who had experienced the harsh world of which he wrote–the social darling of the fickle Hollywood and New York world. Despite his meeting, personally crucial, in 1930 with Lillian Hellman (q.v.), who remained his dearest friend (off and on) until his death, he began to drink more heavily. The comic *The Thin Man* (1934), written in an interlude of sobriety in the hotel mismanaged by Nathanael 'Pep' West (q.v.), shows a falling off. Then came a period of increasing drunkenness, gambling and scriptwriting. Hammett then went to war as a private (at forty-eight), edited an army magazine in the Aleutians and was discharged with emphysema–and worse health than before. The drinking continued until 1948 and an attack of delirium tremens; he then gave his word to his doctor that he would not touch a drop again–and kept it ('I guess because I gave it so seldom'). Always left-wing, he now devoted himself to political work; served six months in jail in 1951 (the era of McCarthy). He was worried by communism, but was loyal to it and was probably a member of the American Communist Party—he always refused to confirm or deny it. In his last years, sick to the point of disablement, he tried his hand at an autobiographical novel, but it remained unfinished (what there is of it is printed as 'Tulip' in *The Big Knockover and other Stories,* a posthumous collection edited by Lillian Hellman, 1966). What defeated his hope to begin a new career as a writer, apart from ill-health, was his conviction—unhappily held—that 'it is impossible to write anything without taking some sort of stand on political issues'. He died, after long suffering, of lung cancer. The biographical details are important because they explain why Hammett, an author of originality and genius, and by no means merely a good crime writer, stopped at forty. The main keys to his writing, as to his character, are apparently contradictory: personal reticence and a raging passion for justice that took the form of an uneasy Marxism. The innate, rigidly suppressed romantic idealism behind that passion is evident in his first efforts at writing: the tough detective wrote inept verse. Hammett is important. The toughness is authentic and purged of Hemingway's tendency to sentimentalize. The anonymous or near-anonymous narrators make no moral claims for themselves but are ruthlessly dedicated to their jobs—and in that, at least, are honest. The observation of people, rich and poor, and of social milieux, is acute and just. Above all, colloquialese is rendered with a brilliance almost equal to that of Céline (q.v.), though Hammett is neither as wide in range nor as poetic. No imitator, even Chandler (q.v.), came near to Hammett in artistry or achieved the supreme, disciplined detachment by which he represented the corruption, greed, duplicity, naivety—and occasional decency—of the America of the twenties. *The Glass Key,* apparently a simple murder story, is an indictment of American urban politics only because it sets out *not* 'to take a stand': it nags away relentlessly at facts—and facts (whether about gangsters, Chinatown, birds, fish, eighteenth-century guns or crossbows) were always Hammett's obsession. He and Simenon (q.v.) are the only two twentieth-century writers to have consistently raised the 'crime novel' to the level of literature. The most successful novel is *The Glass Key,* but this is closely followed by *The Dain Curse.* There is much excellent, too, in the short stories, even though he himself refused to republish them. Lillian Hellman writes movingly and revealingly of him in *An Unfinished Woman* (1969). His paramount position as crime writer is generally acknowledged; his literary originality, as social observer and stylist (despite recognition by Graves, q.v., Gide, q.v., and many others), is not.

Hamsun, Knut (originally Knut Pedersen) (1859–1952) Norwegian novelist, playwright. Nobel Prize 1920. He is the most unpleasant major writer of the century and is usually completely misunderstood. It is generally asserted that the novel which got him the Nobel Prize, *Markens grøde* (1917; tr. *The Growth of the Soil,* 1920), is his best. It is not; it is not even a good novel, though it possesses a persuasive power of style. Like Hauptmann (q.v.), Hamsun lived too long. Until almost his thirtieth year he knocked about in Norway and later America: a vagabond, he performed almost every kind of menial task and must, from time to time, have come near to starvation. By origin, however, he was a 'peasant aristocrat'; his ancestral farm was called Hamsun. His first novel, *Sult* (1888 in a Danish magazine; 1890; tr. *Hunger,* 1967), though it already shows the brutal egocentricity and insensitivity that were eventually to lead Hamsun to embrace wholeheartedly the false Nietzsche presented by the German philosopher's Nazi sister, to admire Prussian militarism, and to welcome the Nazis (and visit Hitler in 1943), is vibrant with instinct. Hamsun was as *naïf*—in Schiller's sense—as it is possible for a modern writer to be but in his two best novels (the other is *Mysterier,* 1892; tr. *Mysteries,* 1971) it is impossible not to be reminded of Nathalie Sarraute's (q.v.) tropisms: involuntary, instinctive movements. In Hamsun, however, the movements are uncannily towards the self. In *Hunger* Hamsun was taking issue with the social concerns of his Scandinavian contemporaries. *Mysteries,* about the 'outcast' Johan Nagel, who rejects civilized values and kills himself, is his masterpiece. The processes by which he proceeded to evolve a 'system'—anti-materialist, with an eventual emphasis on the virtue of the 'rooted' as opposed to the 'wandering' type—are of great psychological interest; but Hamsun's later ambiguities and ambivalences are involuntary. He never surpassed *Mysteries,* a book in which he catches the quintessence of the Nietzschean project of 'self-overcoming' and of its paradoxical consequences. After the war he was arraigned, but went to hospital for a while instead of facing trial. He was almost ninety and senile, as his apology for his conduct (1949) clearly shows. Today his work is back in favour. The key to his best fiction (he began to decline with *Pan*, 1894; tr. 1956)—the two novels discussed above, and certain later passages—lies in his truth to his instinct: this has heroic qualities. His collected works appeared in 1954–5. His plays and verse are negligible.

Hanley, James (1901) Irish (resident in England) fiction writer, essayist, playwright. Hanley's family was poor and he spent ten years at sea and in menial jobs before he was able to devote himself to writing. Although he is a clumsy and uneven writer, with no apparent interest in construction or style, Hanley has been neglected. He could be called a naturalist (*see* Zola) but for the residue of hope and affirmation of courage that informs even his gloomiest books. He made his name with *Boy* (1931), the scarifying—partly autobiographical—story of a boy's endurance on his first sea voyage; this was banned. The sea figures largely in his *Furys Chronicle: The Furys* (1935), *The Secret Journey* (1936), *Our Time is Gone* (1940 rev. 1949) and *Winter Song* (1950). Hanley's mixture of raw realism, Melville-like visionary poetry and sheer clumsiness has produced some very curious writing; perhaps these various elements coalesced most successfully in *Say Nothing* (1962), about the despairing inhabitants of a boarding-house. *Collected Stories* (1953) is a selection. *Plays One* (1968) contains two plays. His television plays have been outstanding.

Hardy, Thomas (1840–1928) English novelist, poet. Hardy belongs to the nineteenth century but his work, especially his poetry, has persisted as an influence, and a powerful one, into the twentieth, which is why he is mentioned here. The perennial 'Hardy or Yeats?' question is not an altogether absurd one, for although one can have both one is tempted to be forced into a preference. Hardy's sensibility is as modern as that of Yeats (q.v.) and he did not flinch from any issue in the complacent Georgian (*see* Brooke) way, but he is less deliberative than Yeats and his Dorsetshire blandness of manner is the very opposite of Yeats's well-oiled Irish blarney. It is interesting, too, that both were effective verse playwrights—the only effective ones, writing in English, of the century. Yeats wrote for the stage, and ended by writing his best play in prose; Hardy wrote the once revered, now neglected, *The Dynasts* (1903–8) either for a radio that had not then come into being —or for the mind. This work, never adequately examined, is arguably the greatest verse play written since the death of Ben Jonson—and that it is unplayable on the stage is greatly to the point. Neither Yeats nor Hardy was a great articulate thinker, but Hardy stated fundamental problems with moving simplicity, while Yeats dabbled in rubbishy occultism. Hardy had not Yeats's surface sophistication, but his rustic cunning is a match for this. The fashionable view is that Yeats was more 'profound' than Hardy but here one must measure the lyrical power of Hardy's utterance against the rhetorical power of Yeats's. Hardy's bequest is not simplicity (he was not simple, though he could achieve massively simple statement) or traditionalism (he used, like Yeats, traditional forms, but his rhythmical variations within them were as original as Yeats's). It is something more subtle: partly a cast of mind, partly a reliance on pure sensibility unadulterated by theory or rhetoric or public consideration, mainly a beauty of spirit. He is inimitable; but his essentially anti-literary attitude of reticently ironic reserve, scepticism towards programs and movements, distrust of the over-*sentimentalische,* will be essential to the survival of English poetry in this century. This poetry will look very different from Hardy's and it has come to a point where it once again needs genuine fertilization from foreign poetries—but it also needs Hardy's Englishness if it is to remain faithful to its own language. *Works* (1919–20); *Collected Poems* (1952).

Harris, Frank (ps. James Thomas Harris) (1856–1931) Welsh (born in Galway) novelist, journalist, editor, miscellaneous prose writer, pornographer, liar, blackmailer. Harris, who knew everyone of note in his time, and who wrote 'biographies' of most of them, was both an engaging and a pathetic rascal. He lacked sensitivity and integrity but he was coarsely shrewd, usually blackmailed hypocrites or polite establishment rogues, and was more agreeable and honest than most of his counterparts, the respectable journalists. He wrote one good, generally underrated, naturalist (*see* Zola) novel, full of acute observation and genuinely discriminatory feeling: *The Bomb* (1908; 1963, with a good introduction by Dos Passos, q.v.), about a celebrated anarchist outrage—and subsequent miscarriage of justice—in America, where he spent some years of his youth. This novel is by no means perfect, but its description of the anarchists is excellently done. *My Life and Loves* (1922–7; 1963) is good only in the non-sexual passages; the sexual detail is unconvincing, unstimulating and boastful—'Walter's' *My Secret Life* is a more important document. Harris's biographies (Wilde, 1918;

Shaw, 1931) are only useful to the reader who is in a position to sort out fact (there are facts, and he knew his subjects) from fiction; but the series *Contemporary Portraits* (1915–30) are not less inaccurate and are more acute than run-of-the-mill journalism. Apart from his first novel and a few of his stories, it is Harris's exotic life that is of most interest: Hugh Kingsmill's *Frank Harris* (1931) and Vincent Brome's *Frank Harris: The Life and Loves of a Scoundrel* (1949) are amusing though perhaps necessarily incomplete accounts. He was a discerning and generous, if capricious, editor (especially of the *Saturday Review*, 1894–9), second in English letters only to Ford (q.v.).

Harris, Wilson (1921) Guyanese novelist, critic and poet. The outstanding West Indian writer of his generation. His one volume of poems (*Eternity to Season*, 1954) is worth study: it sets out the approach taken in the novels. The usual West Indian approach is sardonic, satirical; Harris takes a more 'African' and anthropological view of his material: rejecting conventional sequence and the finite nature of the nineteenth-century novel, he seeks to explore his characters in their non-finite roles–as an embodiment of their past, as in their present relationship to their geographical environment, and as extensions into their imagined future. His novels (e.g. the 'Guiana Quartet', 1960–3: *Palace of the Peacock, The Far Journey of Oudin, The Whole Armour, The Secret Ladder*) are complex but not unnecessarily so: they seek an optimism without flouting the difficulties, and are remarkably reconciliatory in spirit. His poem 'Troy' ends by speaking of a West Indian Hector: 'his roots serve/to change illusion and forsake/blossoming coals of immortal imperfection'.

Hartley, L. P. (1895–1972) English novelist. Considering that Hartley's understanding of human nature was limited and that he held almost comically unsophisticated and simplistic views about 'permissiveness', he achieved much. He inherited something of James's (q.v.) ability to detect and reveal moral evil or corruption–and he probably achieved this ability through the speculations of an exquisite sensibility rather than through experience. But he was a much thinner writer than James and his short stories (particularly those on supernatural themes) are, like his last two novels, surprisingly poor (*Collected Short Stories*, 1968, includes most of the stories and his first short novel, the over-Jamesian *Simonetta Perkins*, 1925). But his knowledge of the art of the

English and American novel was extensive and put to excellent use. *The Novelist's Responsibility* (1967), critical essays, has some interesting if sometimes fanciful interpretations of the novelists who have influenced him (Jane Austen, Hawthorne, L. H. Myers, q.v., as well as James). The element of cruel stupidity in the man becomes, in the novelist, refined into a posture more subtle and imaginative, and built into that posture is a rueful acknowledgement of Hartley's own sadistic interest in punishment and of his own sexual frustrations. The trilogy consisting of *The Shrimp and the Anemone* (1944), *The Sixth Heaven* (1946) and *Eustace and Hilda* (1947) is best when it is comic: Eustace is beautifully done, except that he should have been overtly homosexual–and Hilda is misogynously manipulated into a villainess. Most of Hartley's novels concern children (the first of his trilogy deals with Eustace and Hilda as children) and examine the tenuous relationship between their interpretations of reality and reality itself. And about children he is ambivalent: he sees how they suffer as they move into adolescence, but discerns no element of innocence in them: in *The Go-Between* (1954) the thirteen-year-old Leo may be seen as a sympathetic character or as the precipitator of a tragedy. Here Hartley makes genuine creative capital from his basic conviction that all sexuality is evil. In *The Hireling* (1957), one of his best books, he is more successful with the chauffeur Leadbitter than he was with Eustace, since his complexities of character may be fully and convincingly explained by reference to his disastrously unresolved Oedipal feelings. Hartley was a minor writer, for his gift either failed him altogether (as in the bulk of the stories) or was extremely fragile. But at his best he is highly individual, and as a relaxed comedian of manners he has hardly been surpassed.

Harwood, Gwen (1920) Australian poet. A slow developer, Gwen Harwood emerged around 1960 as a writer of powerful and often humorous lyrics, much influenced by her musical vocation (she has been an organist). She is an odd, strong poet, owing a debt to Morgenstern (q.v.)–especially in her 'character poems' about Professors Kröte and Eisenbert. She is superior to any of her male contemporaries except Francis Webb and many doubtless find her refreshing after too strong a dose of Judith Wright (q.v.). She uses a number of pseudonyms for magazine publications. *Poems* (1963) and *Poems. Vol II* (1968) are rewarding collections.

Hašek, Jaroslav (1883–1923) Czech novelist, short-story writer, journalist, anarchist, dog-thief, trouble-maker, cook, editor. Hašek drank heavily, calculatedly pretended to commit suicide, invented animals which do not exist (e.g. werewolves) when editing a serious magazine called *The Animal World* and founded a party called 'The Party of Moderate and Peaceful Progress Within the Limits of the Law'. He was drafted for service with the Czech army, was captured by the Russians (1915), volunteered to join their Czech Legion—and ended as an *apparatchik* working for the communists. He was for a time a commissar. He returned to Czechoslovakia in 1920. He wrote at least two obituaries of himself, one of which was headed 'A Traitor'. He wrote his famous novel *Osudy dobrého vojáka Švejka za své ove valky* (1920–3; tr. *The Good Soldier Švejk*, 1973) in the last years of his life, but was unable to finish it. Karel Vanck's completion of it is feeble. *Švejk* is probably the bawdiest, most disrespectful and apparently 'immoral' novel of this century. Sergeant Švejk, for whose exploits and experiences Hašek drew on many of his own, is a blasphemous, coarse, hard-drinking trickster who, although well-educated, pretends to be an idiot and manages to manipulate the higher authorities by praising them, agreeing with them—but never unironically—and hindering their plans. He acts stupid, but never is stupid. Many readers feel that the book is disgusting: not only because it is blasphemously anti-Catholic and apparently displays a total disregard for decency and honesty, but also because it seems to put the Czech character in a bad light. Some aspects of *Švejk* are unpleasant. Furthermore Hašek's way of life did not make for consistent stylistic excellence: he was obviously drunk when writing certain passages and he padded out others (for money). But *Švejk* is the most thorough-going attack on bourgeois values ever launched. Like the author, Švejk is a moralist underneath; he is capable of loyalty; he simply rejects as ridiculous any order which he is given. He is, in a curious way, 'authentic' (in the existentialist sense): he invents an image of himself which he cynically and rightly expects will be accepted and lives his own life, privately, with surprisingly good cheer. He exploits the truly stupid by the strategy of adopting an overt stupidity; this gives the book an extra, ironic dimension. Max Brod was right in seeing Hašek as a writer of the calibre of Rabelais or Cervantes. *Švejk,* though the Sergeant himself is a warm creation, is not a sentimental book; it does not suggest that human nature is capable of flowering into anything very beautiful. But it is now—in the age of stifling bureaucracies both totalitarian and democratic—an increasingly relevant book. Švejk is the paradigmatic victim of idiocy, ill will and bad faith. And he battles back. The book is, above all, an indictment of modern war; the quality of its indignation has a special humanity about it that makes it into a major work, a comedy against a tragic background. Hašek wrote much else, but little of this has appeared in translation. He is a writer who requires more international attention—the issue of the unexpurgated *Švejk* in 1973 was an important development.

Hauptmann, Gerhart (1862–1946) German dramatist, novelist and poet. Nobel Prize 1921. Hauptmann is most famous for his earlier dramas which were influenced by naturalism but by no means dependent upon it. The first of these, *Vor Sonnenaufgang* (1889; tr. *Before Dawn,* 1909), is dramatically effective but dominated by its theme of tainted heredity; here alone Hauptmann is over-dependent on the ideas of Arno Holz (1863–1929). The best mature plays of his earlier period are classics: *Die Weber* (1892; tr. *The Weavers,* 1961 in *Five Plays*), the linguistically brilliant *Florian Geyer* (1896; tr. in *Five Plays*), on the Peasants' Revolt; *Der Biberpelz* (1893; tr. *The Beaver Coat* in *Five Plays*), perhaps the best pure comedy in the German language. Then Hauptmann abandoned his earthy realism and healthy straightforward dislike of bureaucratic authority to become a pseudo-mystic, a modern Goethe: he attempted to reconcile Christianity and paganism, compromised with Nazism (he later courageously recanted) and at the same time essayed a modern revival of a Hellenistic classicism which he did not understand. Such works as the epic poem *Der grosse Traum* (1942) are entirely valueless. Hauptmann had neither intellect nor the capacity to forge a poetic language. However, the judgement that it is only for his early drama that he deserves to be remembered is as wrong a one as that which accords the ponderous dramatic tetralogy of his old age, on the theme of the House of Atreus (1941–8), the status of great tragedy. Amongst the welter of epic verse and drama there is some memorable fiction, in which imagination takes over from Nobel grandeur and Teutonic pomposity: notably *Der Ketzer von Soana* (1918; tr. *The Heretic of Soana,* 1923; 1960), which is a convincing critique of orthodox Christianity because Hauptmann forgot his theories and became obsessed with his chief character, a priest who breaks with the Church—and whose psychology is more interesting than the pantheism to which he is converted. Whenever Hauptmann is giving rein to his basic subversiveness (the play *Indipondi*, 1920, is a fascinating treatment of the incest theme) or concentrating on human behaviour, he is a major writer. His failure to realize the whole of his immense imaginative potential is based in his inability to understand the developments of his own times. Much of his drama is translated in *Dramatic Works* (9 vols., 1913–29), and several of his novels have been translated.

Hawkes, John (1925) American fiction writer, playwright. Hawkes is uneven, but one of America's most outstanding experimental writers. His fiction has been called surrealistic; this is a misnomer. He has been influenced by surrealism (*see* Breton) but none of his work is confined to it. Hawkes is inclined to over-write: he can also appear excessively bookish. Actually the influences on his fiction are simpler than one might immediately infer: Sir Thomas Browne (via Melville), naturalism-cum-absurdity, Faulknerian (q.v.) brutality, and (probably) certain European writers such as Roussel (q.v.) and Gadda (q.v.). One of his books, *The Lime Twig* (1961) uses Greene (q.v.) as a starting-point, as Golding (q.v.) used *Coral Island* in *Lord of the Flies*. It is about the blitzed London of the Second World War and deals with the effects of violence on its protagonist. Hawkes had not been to London. *The Beetle Leg* (1951), the most explicitly brutal of his novels, is about a construction worker trapped beneath a collapsed dam: resilient man against brute nature. Here nature gains the upper hand, but in *Second Skin* (1963) the apparently doomed hero asserts himself by self-discovery: this may have been influenced, to a certain extent, by *Pincher Martin* (1956): Hawkes has affinities with Golding, though his prose is more mannered. He is a writer who has developed in a most interesting way and he can produce long passages of sustained power. *Lunar Landscape* (1969) collects stories; *Innocent Party* (1967) consists of four plays. Hawkes is prepared to take the risks involved in diving into his imagination, and the price (pretentiousness, near-pastiche) has been worth paying.

H D (ps. Hilda Doolittle) (1886–1961) American poet, novelist, memoirist and translator. She married Aldington in 1911 (later she left him) and she spent most of her subsequent life in England and Switzerland. Earlier, in America, she had connections with Marianne Moore (q.v.), Williams (q.v.) and Pound (q.v.). She was, until after her death, a somewhat neglected writer, associated over-closely with imagism (*see* Pound), a movement which in her best work she transcended. She was more versatile than her reputation has hitherto allowed. The early poems were truly imagist: economic, deliberately minor, visual, 'intellectual and emotional complex[es] in an instant of time' (Pound's words about the imagists' aims). Her Greek world was artificial and pastoral and her poems can be painfully studied, even escapist. But in her later poetry, largely ignored, she tries to come to terms with the modern world. It is uneven (*The Walls Do Not Fall*, 1944, is a conspicuous failure), but in some passages achieves the complexity she desired–especially in the posthumous long poem *Helen in Egypt* (1961). The *Tribute to Freud* (1956), perhaps her finest work, makes it clear that she was more than an escapist. She wrote technically interesting novels (*Bid Me To Live*, 1960, is a re-creation of her life in London in the First World War) and an excellent translation of Euripides' *Ion*. *Collected Poems* (1940).

Hecht, Anthony (1923) American poet who works within traditional techniques but is ceaselessly experimenting in order to express his (apparently) Manichean view of creation. His teacher Ransom (q.v.) has exercised a residual influence but Hecht is a very different sort of poet. One of his persistent themes is the sufferings of the Jews. He can be both over-elegant and over-rhetorical but he can also inject a fine minor metaphysical poem into a series of more evidently ambitious, even mantic, poems. He is intelligent and technically gifted, which occasionally inhibits his spontaneity. He can be trite–as though giving up in despair–but can also thread his way through complex subject-matter with a linguistically impressive, hard lucidity. *The Hard Hours* (1968).

Heller, Joseph (1923) American novelist: *Catch* 22 (1961), a play, and *Something Happened* (1974) are his only works. The question of his real status has worried critics: is he a brilliant middlebrow or a serious writer? *Catch* 22, a savage satire on the air-force as a mad bureaucracy, was well made and deeply felt but its message was not new and its technique was less original than brilliantly executed. It is certainly an excellent answer to Cozzens's subtly horrible *Guard of Honour*, in which service-life is portrayed as the height of human achievement. *Catch* 22, with its lunatic humour (this is sometimes tiresome) and its deliberate looseness of structure, coincided with a phase of disenchantment and offered a rather easy way out: 'be crazy, it's all crazy anyway'. It may, therefore, not survive. In its successor, basically on the same theme but this time set in the commercial world, Heller paints a validly lurid picture of American success but his protagonist, Slocum, fails as psychological portrait: he cannot carry the implications Heller wants him to carry. Yet *Something Happened* raises serious questions in a serious way: 'are we all going mad?' is one of them.

Hellman, Lillian (1905) American dramatist, autobiographer; she was, off and on, Hammett's (q.v.) companion and has written beautifully and candidly of him. Her plays have been criticized for being too 'well made' and it is true that her painstaking technique is often over-obtrusive but she cannot work in any other style, and we should be the poorer if we didn't have her best plays. She is acute, she will not manipulate character in the interests of her audiences and she holds the attention without resort to trickery. The best plays are *The Children's Hour* (1934), a scarifying account of the results of a charge of lesbianism against two teachers in a girls' boarding school, the marvellously funny, Jonsonian, *Another Part of the Forest* (1946), one of the best presentations of a set of horrible people to be made in half a century, and *The Autumn Garden* (1951). She has written many plays (e.g. the famous *The Little Foxes* (1959), and the adaptation of *Candide* for the Bernstein musical). She would not give away the names of friends in the 'communist' witch-hunts of the early fifties, though she herself had become strongly anti-Soviet. Her autobiographies–the first is *An Unfinished Woman* (1969)–are clearly the work of a modest and exemplary woman. She obviously believes her life to have been more important than her plays, which are excellent representatives of their type.

Hemingway, Ernest (1898–1961) American fiction writer, traveller, journalist, hunter and killer of animals, perpetrator of semi-accurate reminiscence. Nobel Prize 1954. Hemingway has been seriously overrated but in some of his work he achieves a high level of originality and achievement. One should first separate the self-publicist and exhibitionist from the writer–though the two gradually and inexorably coalesced into the mentally wrecked man who shot himself in 1961. Because Hemingway made a cult of toughness, courage and the ability to hunt, fish, box, bull-fight and sail (etc.), some have accepted his own valuation of himself as physical hero, while others have called him a coward. The truth is that Hemingway, who certainly had courage, was a versatile but not particularly gifted practitioner of various sports—probably he was best at fishing. He was inept (when he went to Spain in the Civil War he nearly blew himself and several other people up), and he knew nothing about bull-fighting, as *Death in the Afternoon* (1932), which purports to be about it, makes painfully clear. In this respect Hemingway never grew up. Even though he could enjoy his outdoor life, prowess in it was an all too obvious means of maintaining his never secure self-confidence. People have loathed the famous Lillian Ross *Portrait of Hemingway* (1961, developed from an earlier *New Yorker* profile) and it is true that it is in some respects slickly malicious journalism; but the impression it gives of Hemingway's mental state in the fifties, and of his general unpleasantness, is of the correct intensity. For Hemingway had few personally endearing qualities: he was a liar, he was treacherous (as to Sherwood Anderson, q.v., in the pitifully unfunny *The Torrents of Spring,* 1926, an attempt at satire) to those to whom he owed most and his decent qualities mostly came out in an area of which he refused to be conscious: he repressed the homosexual element of himself, temperamentally convinced of the 'non-virility' of homosexual feeling; his tendernesses and decencies leaked into his books in the form of accounts of male companionships, observances of codes of behaviour, and so on. Hemingway was never consistent. He wrote nothing of any great value after about 1940; before that he was inconsistent. His best novel—and a very good one it is—*The Sun Also Rises* (*Fiesta* in Great Britain) was published in the same year as *The Torrents of Spring.* Hemingway, who came from near Chicago, was badly wounded (in Italy) in the 1914–18 war and his father killed himself. These two experiences formed him as a writer. Some of his best stories are in his first book: *In Our Time* (1924 rev. 1925). Many of these deal with Hemingway's *alter ego,* Nick Adams, who also figures in many of the later stories (*The Fifth Column and the First Forty-Nine Stories,* 1938, collects them all—*The Fifth Column* is a play of little interest). Hemingway formed his famous, laconic style from three main sources: Sherwood Anderson (q.v.), his experience as a newspaper reporter, and Gertrude Stein (q.v.). Ring Lardner (q.v.) also influenced him. In the stories of the twenties (*Men Without Women* appeared in 1927), in *The Sun Also Rises,* and to a lesser extent in *A Farewell to Arms* (1929), Hemingway wrote his best books. They are on simple themes: fear of death, courage, the necessity of cultivating a stoicism that could preserve a man from despair in face of the vacuum of the twenties. Hemingway got his admirable directness from Anderson, whose lyricism, however, he subdued (he didn't have the great Andersonian outflow of feeling towards others), his lucidity from newspaper reportage, and his manner from Stein. He was also indebted to Twain and to Ford's (q.v.) *The Good Soldier*. No writer had more encouragement from more people (in Paris after the war). Hemingway was by no means intelligent, but he was truly sensitive and very vulnerable. In *The Sun Also Rises* he finds the perfect objective correlative for himself in Jake Barnes, a man who has been (literally) emasculated in the war: Hemingway, himself recovering from the effects of a severe head wound, found it difficult to relate to women (he is weak in depicting male-female relationships) and was plunged into a menacing world of males. In this novel occurs the one satisfactory man-woman relationship in Hemingway's fiction: Jake loves Brett, but he is not a 'man'. What holds all the brilliantly portrayed characters together, or what casts a man or woman beyond the pale, is the observance or non-observance of a certain kind of unspoken stoical code: we feel deeply, we have erotic emotions, but we must appear cynical, endure. The special quality of *The Sun Also Rises* is seen in many stories; this quality may be summed up as a capacity to give the significant detail of learning a 'style from a despair'. For Hemingway the writing was therapeutic—that it wasn't more is one of the keys to his non-greatness—but for the reader it communicates bravery. With *A Farewell to Arms* the rot began to set in: there is a superb description of the retreat from Caporetto and of the vicious panic which possessed the Italian forces, but the psychological element in the book is a failure. The deficiencies of this novel are brought into sharp relief by *Across the River and into the Trees* (1950): that he could publish this self-parody at all is an indication of his deteriorating condition, though in the posthumous *Islands in the Stream* (1970), puerile and without even the old stylistic professionalism, there was worse to come. Apart from some stories, Hemingway's work in the thirties is of little account. *For Whom the Bell Tolls* (1940) contains isolated passages of great beauty but the central figures and the dialogue (now self-parody) fail abjectly. *The Old Man and the Sea* (1952), a short novel, is a portentous and pretentious analogy, though Hemingway managed to maintain his professionalism. It was his last attempt at a 'great' novel and is a treatment of the *Moby Dick* theme on a smaller scale: an old Cuban fights a big marlin. In so far as it is not merely disingenuous it is about Hemingway's struggle with old age and mental illness. Later in the decade he underwent periods of treatment at the Mayo Clinic but he preferred, finally, to kill himself rather than to ask the doctors to pull him, once again, out of his acutely depressive state. Hemingway is often called great because he could so effectively express both the pleasures and the terrors of life. But his expression of pleasure is mostly neurotic and manipulated—even *The Sun Also Rises* has to revolve around the central theme of impotence, and Hemingway's 'tough', stoical refusal to 'go beyond' a certain point is a device to conceal his limitations. One admires Hemingway's early search, made from a position of insecurity (and blank meanness—this emerges in the monstrous posthumous reminiscences of twenties Paris, *A Moveable Feast*, 1964), for a form of decency; but the decency he found is limited and answers little.

Henry, O. (ps. W. S. Porter) (1862–1910) American short-story writer whose uncanny technical skill is not sufficiently matched by his imaginative capacity. He grew up in poverty; but learned enough to buy up and run a comic magazine (1894). When this failed he became a bank-teller; subsequently he was charged with theft and fled. His wife was ill; on his return he saw her die and was then sentenced to five years (of which he served three). Probably he was shielding the real thief—at any rate, the trial was a travesty, the missing amount small. His first story appeared in 1899 and from then until his death (from the effects of alcoholism) he poured out a ceaseless flow of tales. The pleasure one gets from O. Henry is nothing to be ashamed of: though a minor writer, he is too often too easily dismissed. His grasp of his material came from close contact with it; though the acknowledged master of the 'magazine story' of his period, and though often sentimental, he was not genteel. His experiences made him into a determinist (or 'fatalist'), and his tales are crudely determinist (without being naturalist). But the basic formula he almost always used (a beginning calculated to arouse curiosity and provoke a guess; a demonstration that this—stock—guess is wrong; a surprising ending with the famous ingenious 'twist') casts a certain light on the workings of 'fate' amongst the more-or-less will-less; and the urban picture is, as far as it goes, accurate. O. Henry's first, and many of his subsequent, tales deal with South America (he ran away to Honduras when suspected of theft); these are exciting and authentic. O. Henry's status is most aptly indicated by describing him as one of the best purveyors of *yarns* who ever lived. He is sentimental but he is also funny. *Complete Works* (1953).

Herbert, Zbigniew (1924) Polish poet, dramatist. He is generally regarded as the most articulate and powerful of the poets of the new Russian Empire; however, he translates particularly well, which may partly explain his very high reputation outside Poland. He would not publish a volume in the Stalinist period. He is learned in the Polish and the classical past and his conscience-stricken poetry is permeated with his sense of this. He was in the Polish underground during the war. The poetry of the 'Second Vanguard School', eclectic and deliberately wide in scope, helped to form his lucid poetic manner but he impresses so much because of his capacity to convey his humanist concern–and his acknowledgement of a tension between inner and outer life even under difficult external circumstances–without stridency ('I should like to describe courage/without dragging a dusty lion behind me/and to describe anxiety/without shaking a water-filled glass'). One important aspect of the Polish literary genius is the ability to describe collective experience–this is naturally torn out of writers who have hardly ever been able to live securely in their own country; Herbert exemplifies this. *Selected Poems* (tr. 1968).

Hesse, Hermann (1877–1962) German (later, 1923, Swiss) writer of fiction, poet, essayist, water-colourist. Nobel Prize 1946. His early background was pietistic and to discover the nature of his religious impulses he was obliged to run away from a seminary at an early age. Hesse always aroused interest among intellectuals, but it was not until the sixties that he was taken up–first by young Americans because of his interest in Oriental religions and then by the general reader. He is more versatile than is generally recognized and his beautiful minor poetry has been seriously underrated (*Poems*, tr. 1970). It is misleading to describe him as a mystic, though he did have the German tendency towards massive syncretism: he was a man with an acute sense of reality –personal and political–who wanted to translate his strong religious and aesthetic impulses into concrete terms and so he took some wrong turnings. Hesse remained consistent and yet developed. Now one side of his nature would come to the forefront, then another. The conflict, expressed most sharply in the novel *Der Steppenwolf* (1927; tr. 1963), may be defined at its most basic level as the familiar one between *Natur* and *Geist,* nature and spirit, body and mind—and so on with all the innumerable parallels and ramifications. What is remarkable is the extent to which Hesse, in his last novel, achieved a reconciliation without either over-simplification, over-complexity or pseudo-mysticism. He wrote many novels and short stories—and his poems must not be ignored, for they provide a key to the quality of lyrical serenity, the love and understanding of the natural world, that seldom altogether left him. His earlier novels are for the most part on the theme of how philistine life can stifle creativity (e.g. *Peter Camenzind,* 1904; tr. 1961, which made him well known), though his view is not one-sided. But in *Gertrud* (1910; tr. 1955) he showed the other side of the picture: how art can destroy life. Soon after his first success he had married a woman nine years older than himself and during his happy years with her produced some of his most charming and least important fiction. But *Gertrud* was a hint of what was to come, and in *Rosshalde* (1914; tr. 1970)—written soon after a journey to India, in 1911, in search of a solution of his problems—he probed his own erotic and marital predicament when he portrayed a painter too committed to his art to be able to love his wife and who, by a stroke of irony, is released from her by the death of the only bond between them: their child. His own marriage soon broke up (he married again twice). Now, forced by his hatred of German militarism, he settled in Switzerland. Hesse was still, for all his reservations, the dedicated artist, the man apart. But in 1916 he broke down, lost confidence in his creative powers—and went to an undogmatic disciple of Jung (q.v.) who seems to have helped him not so much by 'individuating' him as by introducing him to psychoanalytical ideas. *Demian* (1919; tr. 1958) ushers in what may be called his middle period: now the values of art (culture) and life (ruled by violence and darkness if deprived of culture) are more subtly balanced. This culminated in the mysteriously powerful crisis-novel *Steppenwolf:* here Hesse stripped himself of his own personal saving graces of capacity for serenity and humour and thrust himself into the world as Harry Haller who regains his faith in the spirit by plunging himself into nature with wolf-like gusto: finally he even learns acceptance (perhaps), which includes humour. This is an epic of 'magic realism', squarely based on the German fairy tales and on E. T. A. Hoffmann. This, though a success, is a disturbing and ambiguous book: Hesse was himself disturbed and he felt ambiguous. He tried to repeat the theme in *Narziss und Gold-*

mund (1930; tr. 1959), but over-simplified it and thus falsified it to produce the most inferior of his mature novels. *Steppenwolf* imaginatively reflects the agonizings of his essays of the twenties, in which he had condemned technocracy and had groped helplessly towards a means of banishing chaos (*Blick ins Chaos* had been the title of his book of essays collected in 1920–tr. 1923–and which had led T. S. Eliot, q.v., to visit him and to quote him in the notes to *The Waste Land*); *Narziss und Goldmund,* for all its occasional charm, is a contrived reflection of these agonizings. Yet it is one of the sketches for his masterpiece: *Der Glasperlenspiel* (1943; tr. *The Glass Bead Game,* 1960). This novel contains multitudes, and is one of the most difficult of modern classics but it is also one of the most approachable. It is at once a Utopia, a dystopia, a *Bildungsroman,* an autobiography, a uniquely arranged encyclopedia of learning and history, a treatise on music–and a fable as magical as it is philosophical. Nor, though it may totter from time to time, does it collapse under its own enormous weight. This is not one of the greatest novels of all time but it is one of the greatest of ours. *Gesammelte Schriften* (1957), *Collected Writings.*

Heym, Georg (1887–1912) German expressionist (*see* Stadler) poet, short-story writer, who was drowned in a skating accident on the Wannsee. Pathologically shy, confused, greatly gifted, he affected both 'decadence' (skull on desk and so forth) and a healthy, open-air life. His dream was to be a Van Gogh of poetry. His poem of poems was Rimbaud's 'Le Bâteau ivre'. Dragged by his friends into the eyes of the intellectual public, he delivered his poems atrociously. But, cast in tight and controlled forms derived from French symbolist models, they are full of explosive visions of urban ruin and the best perfectly reflect his and indeed his generation's mental conflicts. His correct sense of the nature of the coming catastrophe, the powerful sense of evil and loneliness that haunts his poetry, arose not only from his socio-political awareness but also, perhaps, from some disturbance of sexual origin. His works, including his revealing dream-diary, are collected in *Gesamtausgabe* (1960).

Hidayat, Sadiq (1903–51) Persian novelist, short-story writer, satirist, essayist. Without doubt Persia's greatest twentieth-century writer. Some of his stories have been translated into German and French; in English only his masterpiece *Buf-i Kur* (published in Bombay in stencilled copies in 1937, then as a book in Tehran in 1941; tr. *The Blind Owl*, 1958) has appeared, and in a translation that is said to be over-literal (thus, the Persian title, *The Recluse*, is translated literally). Hidayat, who came from an important family, was a student of dentistry, then of engineering and finally of the ancient culture of Iran. Vegetarian, animal-lover, recluse, drug and alcohol addict, he gassed himself in Paris leaving a note to a friend 'See you on Doomsday'. His doom-shot fiction, as black as any of this century that is not merely crude, reflects the depressing political circumstances of his country as well as his own melancholy and partly decadent temperament. He was influenced by Kafka (q.v.) and has some affinities with Céline (q.v.) and Sartre (q.v.); but he was no one's disciple. *The Blind Owl* is essentially autobiographical: its narrator's project is to investigate the relationship between his 'real' life and his fantasy life, which is fuelled by drugs and drink. At the same time *The Blind Owl* investigates the artistic condition usually called 'paranoid', though this might often better be described as 'pseudo-paranoid': highly anxious and aggressive. It is more substantially pessimistic than anything by Beckett and yet it is full of poetic excitement, as though the author (unlike Beckett) retained his faith in at least language. Magic, the mystery of life, is what the death-haunted narrator in fact consoles himself with. Hidayat, wrote an American critic, possessed 'that terrible Persian awareness of time, of the past, of the direct burden of a great and unique culture'.

Highsmith, Patricia (1921) American crime writer of high calibre now resident in France. Highsmith's speciality is to put the murderous obsessional psychotic into opposition to the masochistic or weak character and to add an element of chance. But Ripley, her *tour de force*, and the protagonist of a number of her books, is a wickedly amoral variation on this: she succeeds in enlisting the reader's sympathy for his essentially monstrous projects. Her various backgrounds are painstakingly and effectively built up.

Hikmet, Nazim (1902–63) Turkish poet: the only one to have gained a worldwide reputation. He also wrote plays and a novel. He was born in Salonika (then Turkish). He studied French and science in Moscow 1921–5. The Turks imprisoned him in 1928, 1933, and in 1938 sentenced him to thirty-five years for his communism; he was released in 1951 and went to the Soviet Union. He is very widely translated in Europe (especially in France, Greece, Russia and Italy), and the Turkish Cypriot Taner Baybars has introduced him to readers of English in *Selected Poems* (tr. 1967), *The Moscow Symphony* (tr. 1970) and *The Day Before Tomorrow* (tr. 1972). A communist, and much influenced by Mayakovsky (q.v.)–especially in his stepped line and his deliberate up-to-dateness–he made radical innovations in Turkish poetry, which was at the time moribund. Hikmet's Marxism was genuine, but what characterizes his poetry is its humour, its humanity and the somewhat surrealistic form of its structure. For example, *Moscova Senfonisi* (1952), *Moscow Symphony*–originally intended as a part of a projected sequence, *Memleketimden Insan Manzaralari* (1966–7), *Human Landscapes from my Country*, which Hikmet left unfinished–has little to do with Moscow. It is a poem about freedom, in which a rich landowner listens to a symphony while 'stretched at the bottom of the Atlantic', and often talks to a stork. A large number of his shorter poems are about his imprisonment and his love of his wife; they are consistently lacking in self-pity, though often ironic about his captors. There are five plays, and the revealing autobiographical novel *Yaşamak Güzel Şey Bekardesim* (1962; 1967) appeared in French as *Les Romantiques* in 1964. His work has been published in Turkey since his death.

Hoddis, Jakob van (ps. Hans Davidsohn) (1887–1942) German expressionist (*see* Stadler) minor poet, whose famous 'Weltende', (1911), 'World's End', though only slight, is justly regarded as being, procedurally, the first expressionist poem. He was prominent in the expressionist clubs and cabarets and a contributor to the magazine *Aktion* (in which his most famous poem appeared). Johannes Becher wrote that the eight lines of 'Weltende' 'seem to have transformed us into different beings'. The poem ('The bourgeois' hat flies off his pointed head,/the air re-echoes with a cry. . . . Most people have a cold./Trains fall off bridges') had an impact far beyond its intrinsic merits. Van Hoddis, a Jew, 'dwarflike, bedraggled, grey, unshaven, pimply . . . wrapped in a . . . scarf which desperately needed washing . . . already [1911] a little mad . . .', suffered from a passion for Emmy Hemmings, later to marry Ball (q.v.) and this was the immediate cause of his incarceration in a mental hospital in 1914; he remained mad until 1942 when the Nazis sent him away to be murdered. His single collection is *Weltende* (1918; 1958).

Hodgson, Ralph (1871 or earlier–1962) English poet who lived in America for the last thirty-odd years of his life. He was a most remarkable man and is very much a 'poet's poet'. He edited a popular magazine, hated cruelty to animals, enjoyed prize-fighting, drew cartoons, bred bull-terriers–and gave away very little about himself. He possessed both originality and an extraordinary integrity–in certain respects he resembles the composer Percy Grainger but he was more secretive. His work did not fall off, even when he reached ninety years. There are poems better than the relatively innocuous well-known anthology pieces such as 'Time You Old Gipsy Man', and careful exploration of his *Collected Poems* (1961) is vital for anyone who cares about poetry. One of the most remarkable of his longer poems is 'Song of Honour', which is influenced by but not pastiche of Christopher Smart. Berryman (q.v.) wrote of 'good Ralph Hodgson': 'The man is dead whom Eliot praised. My praise/follows and flows too late'.

Holan, Vladimir (1905) Czech poet, translator. Holan began as a member of the 'poetist' school, but abandoned this Czech surrealist manner when Czechoslovakia was betrayed to the Nazis. From 1945 until the communist coup Holan published a 'socialist realist' (*see* Gorky) type of poetry; but the communists accused him of 'decadence' and he retired into seclusion for fifteen years. His poetry of the sixties brought him the reputation at home and abroad of being the best poet of his generation. This later poetry, in which he employs free verse and seeks for what he calls an 'atonal harmony', is not as difficult as is frequently asserted: it is full of melancholy and despair, somewhat hermetic in manner, but explicit as to his feelings of exile from others and from himself. His greatest achievement is the long poem *Noc s Hamleten* (1965), *A Night with Hamlet,* in which he has a conversation with Hamlet (this was written in the fifties, when he could not publish). He is an over-prolific poet, frequently too influenced by Eliot (q.v.) but taken as a whole his work conveys a sense of loneliness and gentleness which is as impressive as it is authentic. *Selected Poems* (tr. 1971) gives a representative selection from the later poetry.

Hollander, John (1929) American poet, critic, editor, teacher. Hollander, an academic of high distinction, is, as Richard Howard has implied, a temperamentally 'confessional' poet who locks up his impulses in an over-glossy impenetrability. He is an allusive, professorial poet and his affinities with Stevens (q.v.) are deliberate. Hollander's poetic energy looks depleted but is in fact merely misplaced: it goes into his neo-scholasticism (it is appropriate that he should have edited the massive *Oxford Anthology of English Literature* with Frank Kermode, a fine critic who sometimes undermines his excellence by a sort of secular theologizing). There are fragments in his poetry which cause one to hope that he will discover a way through to a more sustained kind of directness. *Crackling of Thorns* (1958); *Types of Shape* (1969).

Holub, Miroslav (1923) Czech poet. He is a distinguished research chemist and, regarded as the leading poet of his generation, has been overrated. Like every other writer, Holub supported Dubček; his 'recantation' since—which reads like a string of dictated clichés—has presumably been gained by the application of pressure. His poetry reflects his scientific training, and, for those who like this kind of thing, 'shows us, concisely and eloquently, the *uni* in the universe'. But it is over-cerebral, glum (or, occasionally, whimsical) and lacking in substance. There is a *Selected Poems* (tr. 1967) in English.

Hopkins, Gerard Manley (1844–89) English poet. Hopkins was Victorian, but is included here because his poetry (apart from a few individual poems) did not appear until 1918 and because it exercised a strong, anti-Georgian (*see* Brooke) influence on development and taste. To be properly understood Hopkins must be seen in his Victorian context but he was an innovator, and those who, when Bridges (q.v.) published him, saw him as offering something new and vital to English poetry were right. He is therefore modernist and all the more so because his poems appeared at a time when the Georgian 'revolt' had been revealed as wholly inadequate. It must be remembered that in 1920 the *general* poetry reader admired such poets as Brooke (q.v.), Drinkwater or Freeman more than Owen (q.v.) or even Hopkins, who in effect was one of the spearheads of a real revolt, one which got under way some thirty years after premature death from typhoid. It is significant that a factor in every one of Hopkins' lonely innovations is past practice. His theory of *inscape* and *instress,* which underlies his poetry, anticipates expressionism (*see* Stadler) in its widest sense (representation of inner reality), but is ultimately based on the much misunderstood medieval theologian Duns Scotus's concept of *haecceitas, thisness* (cf. Joyce's, q.v., 'epiphanies'). *Inscape* refers to the 'individually-distinctive' quality of things, perceived through a combination of keen observation and intense introspection. *Instress* generates inscape: it is for Hopkins a divine energy, actualizing inscape in the mind—for others it may be related to a secularized pantheism, or seen as the outcome of what Grigson (q.v.) well describes as a 'passionate science'. Again, the tension between the Jesuit and the poet in Hopkins, while it anticipates the twentieth-century phenomenon—or obsession—which I have elsewhere described as *Künstlerschuld* (artist-guilt), also reflects an ancient tension between the spirit and the flesh. Because he is continually trying to cast new and intense light on reality Hopkins needed a new and intense technique: he saw, earlier than nearly any other poet (but Doughty attempted the same kind of thing—less successfully, but independently—at almost the same time) that the current language of poetry was becoming worn out. In order to bend his words into the shape of the subject, he turned, however, to the past: to an intensification and elaboration of what he called the 'sprung rhythm' of nursery rhyme and Old English accentual verse, to alliteration, to the complex techniques of Welsh verse. His 'sprung rhythm' is fundamentally a highly flexible kind of pure stress approach, in which an unconventional syntactical manipulation plays a vital part. Technique was no longer to be external, decorative: it must be moulded by meaning. Hence Hopkins's use of stress and other marks to indicate how he wanted his poetry to sound, and at what speed it should be taken. (He was, incidentally, a gifted musician and draughtsman.) All this was extremely experimental at a time when experiment was totally unacceptable and Hopkins was fortunate to have Bridges, R. W. Dixon and Coventry Patmore as friends and correspondents. Bridges, crippled by his conservatism, was less aware than the others but he did in time release Hopkins's poetry (the best edition is now *Poems,* 1967). It was inevitable that Hopkins, operating often guiltily and without a public audience, should from time to time fail in his experiments but when he succeeded he produced a poetry at once tragic, exact, beautiful and quintessentially 'modern' in the sense that it dispensed with clichés of eye and ear and substituted for them obstinately intense personal observation and sound. His *Notebooks* (1937), *Journals* (1959) and *Letters and Correspondence* (1955; *Further Letters,* 1956) are of intense importance. Pastiche of his own inimitable manner is always disastrous but his example is now even more vital than it was in 1918.

Hora, Josef (1891–1945) Czech poet, fiction writer, journalist. He is one of the most important of the inter-war Czech poets. He began as a communist, then moved to socialism; then, in his poetry, away from both into a less political and more specifically Czech kind of poetry. The influence of Verhaeren (q.v.) is apparent in *Svdce a vravra sveta* (1922), *The Heart and the Tumult of the World,* but his rejection of urban life is already evident. With *Máchovské variace* (1936), *Variations on a Theme of Mácha* (Karel Mácha, 1810–36, nationalist-romantic who is regarded as the greatest Czech poet), Hora showed the fundamentally non-political nature of his genius: nerve-racked, haunted by poisonous dreams and lush melodies, he begins to look for some reconciliatory element. He wrote a notable if ephemeral poem on the betrayal of 1938; in his last years he struggled with ill health and despair for his country. *Jan houslista* (1939), *John the Fiddler,* is a narrative poem of exile and return which many see as his greatest achievement. As he left the communist party in 1929 the communist regime tried to relegate him to oblivion but his works were allowed to be collected (1950–61) and his influence has been pervasive.

Housman, A. E. (1859–1936) English poet, classical scholar. Housman was an immensely popular poet whose work has some of the ingredients of bad poetry, yet at least a quarter of his output is of high quality, giving him the status of a substantial minor. The poems are short and usually set in a mock-pastoral world of suicidal or condemned young men who are either crossed in love or join the army as cannon-fodder. Housman's view of poetry was simplistic and uncritically romantic but his gift for epigram and naked statement, developed from his reading not only of the classical poets but of Blake and Heine, often rescues him from sentimentality. The secret lies partly in the fact that his outwardly respectable atheistic pessimism was charged with guilt: he was a homosexual and hated being one. Consequently there slashes across the artificially pastoral world of his poetry a profound and wholly impolite bitterness born of frustration–and, at the same time, a tenderness. This bitterness–Housman's poetry tastes of aloes–is a complex enough emotion; the tenderness is even more so, for it is in part a rationalization of guilty lust: human considerateness gives it an extra dimension. Thus Housman is moving, for somehow this gets into the texture of his poetry–along with the deadly innocence of the beloved's character (one needs only to recall Shakespeare's sonnets) that invariably accompanies it. These factors, then, expressed in brilliant epigrammatic form, save some of Housman's characteristic poems. But he is at his most powerful when he is uncharacteristic. The poem numbered XVIII of the 'Additional Poems' in *Collected Poems* (1939; 1956), naturally enough never published by him in his two small collections—*A Shropshire Lad* (1896), *Last Poems* (1922)—sums up his life: 'Oh who is that young sinner with the handcuffs on his wrists. . . . Oh they're taking him to prison for the colour of his hair. . . .' It ends: 'And between his spells of labour in the time he has to spare/He can curse the God that made him for the colour of his hair.' His irony here is reinforced by guilt: '. . . hanging isn't bad enough and flaying would be fair/For the nameless and abominable colour of his hair.' Critics have made much of Housman's pessimism, as over-wilful, and of the ferocious malice displayed in his classical editions; they should remember the case of Oscar Wilde (in which Housman took much interest) and the social difficulties confronting anyone who in those days found himself to be constitutionally inclined towards his own sex. The excessively reticent Housman bore the whole brunt of this, as he did of his disappointment and shame over his feelings for his undergraduate friend Moses Jackson. In the poem preceding 'Oh who is that young sinner. . . .' he speaks of having only 'two troubles': brains and heart, and envies the 'birthright of multitudes': 'That relish their victuals and rest on their bed/With flint in the bosom and guts in the head.' The epigrammatic bite is more than neat. But Housman was not invariably a poet concealing unhappy and frustrated passion behind a veil of epigrammatic skill and atheistic bitterness. 'Ask me no more', he wrote in yet another posthumous poem, 'for fear I should reply;/Others have held their tongues, and so can I.' But occasionally he did reply. The third poem in *Last Poems,* 'Her strong enchantments failing. . . .', which so puzzled and fascinated Eliot (q.v.), is not so puzzling—though it is mysterious—when read as a homosexual's view of the female: the boy-as-girl, bitch-mother, phantom-lover, muse. . . . It is a great lyric, as explicit as it could be. 'The Culprit', XIV of *Last Poems,* has a direct, exact power in the light of the suppressed poems; it hinges on the subject of erection and ejaculation (its theme is hanging, for Housman both a metaphor for his own socio-erotic situation and a subject of sexual fascination), and goes beyond bitterness or epigram in its magnificent close. One must, indeed, read much of Housman in the light of erotic metaphor. His work, when taken in at one sitting (and this is easier than with most poets), strikes one as amounting to a good deal more than its surface suggests. Knowledge of his tragic sexual isolation is a necessary ingredient in this response. Most of the biographical facts are in G. L. Watson's *A. E. Housman: A Divided Life* (1957). *Selected Prose* (1961) includes the text of the 1933 lecture 'The Name and Nature of Poetry', which demonstrates both Housman's intuitive understanding of the nature of poetry and his refusal to acknowledge that it has roots in meaning. It is not critically helpful except as a guide to his own poetry. Housman's brother Laurence, another homosexual and the author of some popular plays about royalty which A. E. despised, issued *More Poems* posthumously (1936), but the most complete edition is the *Collected Poems.*

Hoult, Norah (1898) Irish novelist whose best work has been seriously neglected. Her books since the war have been more than competent but do not match up to the short stories of *Poor Women* (1928) or to the two-volume study of Irish life *Holy Ireland* (1935) and *Coming from the Fair* (1937). These, and the vivid account of an old woman's last years in the London Blitz, served by a wicked young servant, *There Were No Windows* (1944) are outstanding. Norah Hoult learned much from Henry Handel Richardson (q.v.), and the books already mentioned, together with some other novels of the thirties (*Time, Gentlemen, Time!,* 1930; *Apartments to Let,* 1931), are of almost the quality associated with Richardson herself, and with Christina Stead (q.v.). She is psychologically sharp, somewhat naturalistically (*see* Zola) inclined, but lyrical (she has a tendency to slip into sentimentality, as in *Four Women Grow Up,* 1940) and she possesses a feline humour. The socio-economic background is always carefully and effectively drawn in. The best of her later books are the story-collection *Cocktail Bar* (1950) and the alarming novel *A Death Occurred* (1954). Her stories and some four of her novels should be put back into print without delay: she is one of the most gifted writers of her generation. *Selected Stories* (1946).

Hrabal, Bohumil (1914) Czech fiction writer. Hrabal was forty-eight before he took up writing; he was soon a celebrity. Before that he had done a variety of jobs, all of them more or less menial. He is a modern Hašek (q.v.) inasmuch as he treats of 'ordinary' people swallowed up in events they do not understand but he has been considerably influenced by modernist procedures, in which Hašek was not interested. The short, sardonic *Ostře sledované vlaky* (1965; tr. *A Close Watch on the Trains*, 1968) is internationally known.

Hughes, Langston (1902–67) American poet, fiction writer, playwright, anthologist, Negro man of letters. He was the leading figure in the twenties Negro renaissance, and his successors owe more to him than they sometimes acknowledge. Prolific, knowledgeable and versatile, he expressed both Negro bitterness and Negro energy. His character Jesse B. Simple (*The Best of Simple*, 1961, and other collections), a comic social commentator, was first introduced in racy newspaper sketches; but the play *Mulatto* (1936, developed from his poem 'Cross') is a fierce and serious account of the Negro predicament. He has been one of the most effective and discriminating of all delineators of Negro cultural resources, and his vast knowledge of jazz, folk-lore and speech-nuances gets into his best poetry (*Selected Poems*, 1959, and later volumes), the surface rather than the content of which is important. His fiction (e.g. the novel *Not Without Laughter*, 1930) is similar but its themes are more significant. His popular poetry (blues, lyrics) is among the best to be written in this century. Famous, appreciated, he has still not had his full critical due. His autobiographies *The Big Sea* (1940) and *I Wonder as I Wander* (1956) are vital documents.

Hughes, Richard (1900) Welsh (but born in Kent) novelist, playwright, poet. Hughes began as a playwright and poet and although he has himself disowned his poetry (*Confessio Juvenis: Collected Poems*, 1926), it has an originality and cleanness of tone which clearly distinguish it from the Georgianism (*see* Brooke) of the twenties. His first success, *A High Wind in Jamaica* (1929), is a novel in which the Victorian 'wicked pirate'–'innocent children' formula is reversed. *In Hazard* (1938 ed. and abridged by author 1953; 1966) is a deceptively simple story of a storm at sea; once again Hughes takes a popular formula and turns it, with a very Welsh appearance of innocence, into an original and subversive commentary. His next major fictional project, a trilogy, is unfinished: to be entitled *The Human Predicament*, so far only two volumes have appeared: *The Fox in the Attic* (1961) and *The Wooden Shepherdess* (1973). This is more ambitious–a history of the inter-war period from the public point of view as well as from that of a single family and, in particular, one member of it–and on the whole, so far, somewhat less successful. *The Fox in the Attic* is the better of the two volumes; in its successor the perhaps not needfully frustrated poet in Hughes tends to take over in the actual writing, which is at times mannered. But by contemporary standards the first two volumes of *The Human Predicament* achieve much: real-life characters (e.g. Hitler) are made more credible than ever before in twentieth-century English fiction and the sense of an uncomprehending observation of events moving towards disaster is beautifully conveyed. *A Moment of Time* (1926) collects stories. *Plays* (1966). Children's stories, which deserve attention, are in *The Spider's Palace* (1931), *Don't Blame Me* (1940) and *Gertrude's Child* (1966).

Hughes, Ted (1930) English (Yorkshire) poet. Hughes has always been overrated but as a young man he combined a certain raw power with a simple-minded but sincere dedication to the project of becoming a major poet (*The Hawk in the Rain*, 1957). His poetry, influenced by the cruelty of folk-tales, undigested popular anthropology and the D. H. Lawrence (q.v.) of *Birds, Beasts and Flowers*, celebrated aggressive persistence and life-force in animals and its (more fuzzily observed) presence in man. Hughes enjoyed Hopkins (q.v.) but never learned from him to look closely at nature. His technique was poor and has since deteriorated. After *Lupercal* (1960), in the poems of which his mindless search for the animal in man became more evident, came *Wodwo* (1967), a mixture of prose and poetry. It now became clear that he had failed to extend his genuine gift of empathy with animals. The points that admirers of his cruelty want to miss are that, for a poet who all too clearly intends to deal with 'profound' themes, both his technique and his intellect are deficient. This became fully evident in the poem-sequence *Crow* (1970), a best-seller (in terms of verse). *Crow*, with its apparently impressive outbursts of linguistic violence (the writer's ear for vowels is extraordinarily lax), is more offensive to some critics than Dylan Thomas's (q.v.) similar early magmas: the figure of Crow falsely unifies the sequence and does not stem from any thoughtful consideration of anthropology, either physical or social. There can be no doubt of Hughes's energy and savage relish; there is doubt about his sensibility, the quality of his understanding, his technique and his intellectual equipment. His recent activities, which include the invention of a 'language' fashionably called Orghast, reinforce these doubts. 'The playgoer who has entered deeply into [sic]

Orghast [a play scripted by Hughes, produced by Peter Brook] has passed through fire, and can never be the same again', a columnist wrote. One remembers similar remarks about Christopher Fry. Hughes, who has written verse and prose for children, was married to Sylvia Plath (q.v.).

Huidobro, Vicente (1893–1948) Chilean poet, novelist, critic, literary polemicist, editor, liar. Huidobro is, as Paz (q.v.) has stated, 'admirable'—he is also neglected, perhaps partly because, though always anti-authoritarian, he possessed a Latin-American boastfulness and flamboyance which bear within themselves the seeds of obscurity—if only temporary. In 1934 he stood for the presidency of Chile. He fought against Franco. He also fought with the French in the Second World War and claimed to have been in Berlin within days of Hitler's suicide; in the course of this he received a head wound from which, eventually, he prematurely died. Not too much is certain about him. He is now largely unread, but rather remembered as the initiator (if he was) of *creacionismo*, 'creationism', and as a 'surrealist' poet. *Creacionismo* was an essentially cubist notion: anti-mimetic, it insisted that the poem—or work of art—be a new creation in its own right, an addition to nature. 'Why sing of the rose? . . . bring it to flower in the poem.' To what extent Reverdy (q.v.) was involved in the formulation of this theory is not known. But it flourished for a short time in France and then in Spain, whither Huidobro went in 1917, after quarrelling with Reverdy. Much of Huidobro's poetry is in French. He later became an ultraist (*see* Borges). As Huidobro said, creationism was not really a movement but an aesthetic theory: a necessary counter to moribund nineteenth-century procedures. His typographically arranged poetry is clearly influenced by Apollinaire (q.v.). The neglect of Huidobro in Spain and elsewhere is a matter for shame. His semi-surrealistic poetry is often less simply good fun than appears: 'You've never known the tenderness-tree from which I take my essence/It grows on any floor/In the middle of a conversation about pianos/it's as charming as a sixty-metre lake.//Circumstance's eyes/look at time riddled/by pistol shots. . . .' Huidobro's startling juxtapositions are often full of meaning. But in *Altazor* (1919; 1931) he wrote an important pioneer poem on a level with Neruda's (q.v.) *Residencia en la tierra;* and in the novel *Satyr o El Poder le las palabras* (1939), *Satyr or The Power of Words* he demonstrated how Nabokov (q.v.) might have made *Lolita* into a truly serious book, as well as questioned his own fierce excitability. His collected works appeared in 1957 and, in another edition, in 1964. There is no full-length study in English.

Hulme, T. E. (1883–1917) English critic, philosopher, poet. He was killed after serving with the Artillery for nearly three years in France. Hulme has been called the true father of imagism (*see* Pound), though it was Pound who organized it as a movement—and the influence of Ford (q.v.) was considerable. His 'Autumn' could be claimed as the first imagist poem but, though Pound printed five of his poems in 1912 as an appendix to his own *Ripostes,* he was not a member of the 1912 group. He left only a few poems (collected in A. R. Jones: *The Life and Opinions of Hulme,* 1960), and published no original book in his lifetime. His work was posthumously collected in *Speculations* (1924), *Notes on Language and Style* (1929) and *Further Speculations* (1955). Hulme, who was friendly with Read (q.v.) and most of the other writers of his age group, is an important but puzzling figure. Has he been overrated? Has even his influence been overrated? His ideology served as a model for Eliot (q.v.) and in that way his influence was considerable. Again, although an anti-romantic, he deeply influenced the arch-romantic Read (q.v.), who may be more important as an influence and a critic than as a creative writer. . . . His writings are often forbidding, and have not unreasonably been called 'sinister' yet he himself was a 'humorous and libidinous man' (Frank MacShane), who was sent down from Cambridge (1904) for some now undiscoverable offence, and who after gaining readmittance (1912) through the good offices of Bergson (q.v.), left again of his own accord. His friend Epstein, whose bronze head of him is so revealing, said that he 'was as capable of kicking a theory as a man downstairs. . . . Abstract art had an extraordinary attraction for him: his own brain worked in that way'. Hulme thought of himself as an anti-romantic neo-classicist but the chief influence on him, Bergson, was an anti-classical neo-romantic, as well as an anti-abstractionist. . . . The truth is that Hulme, though undeniably brilliant and gifted, was immature: his style is aggressive, often abominable, and his failure by the age of thirty to have produced more than a few badly written articles and a series of scrappy notes towards an ambitious program (six books: on modern theories of art, on Bergson, on Epstein and sculpture, a collection of anti-humanistic, anti-romantic essays, and a philosophical allegory whose central character,

Aphra, would be an 'imagist') suggests that he suffered from some serious block. His poetry is the best work he left but the rest has, in itself, been overrated. His influence, however, has not. He became, perhaps mainly because of his aggressive attitude and his complete—somewhat romantic—disregard for fame, one of the central figures of twentieth-century anti-romanticism (which, seen retrospectively, is of course no more than a modification of romanticism). Hulme's own critical writing is poor and often badly argued but its spirit, well epitomized in the man, in his intuitions and in his startling assertions, is important. Hulme did not mince words: 'I object even to the best of the romantics'. In that mushy age, Hulme is generally on the 'right' side but he over-states and over-simplifies his case. His 'pairs' of opposites are: classicism versus romanticism, religion versus humanist rationalism, royalist-autocratic versus democratic, abstract 'geometrical' versus realism, precision versus 'softness', fancy versus imagination (this he conspicuously failed to work out, but he knew himself, perhaps, to lack imagination), pre-Renaissance versus post-Renaissance, discipline (he was an ardent militarist) versus self-expression (seen as self-indulgence), original sin versus socialist or 'liberal' faith in man. To explain this series of pairs would mean to delve into the psychology of a not very articulate critic and of an unattractive man; but if the political implications and the historical over-simplifications are ignored, Hulme's polemic may be taken as an intuitive expression of the anti-Georgian movement (this was not anti-romantic, but merely corrective of romantic excess and sloppiness). A more lucid, mature and humane exposition of this position is to be found in the criticism of Eliot (when he is not playing to the gallery), or, later, Grigson (q.v.) and Empson (q.v.), or in the poetic practice of Graves (q.v.), who was, like Hulme, a good soldier but never a willing one and who conducted his own war against sloppiness.

Hunter, Evan (1926) American novelist. His 'serious' novels e.g. *The Blackboard Jungle* (1954) are well-made, essentially conservative, middlebrow dramatizations of fashionable issues. His many entertainments, thrillers written under the pseudonym of Ed McBain, dealing with policemen of the 87th Precinct of an anonymous American metropolis, are sentimental but largely accurate accounts of crime and detection with good, exciting plots.

Huxley, Aldous (1894–1963) English novelist, essayist, playwright, critic, poet, writer on miscellaneous subjects. Huxley's intention to become a doctor was foiled by bad eyesight but he managed to retain reasonable sight for most of his life by use of the Bates method. His high reputation began to slip badly soon after the war; his rehabilitation as a major creative writer is unlikely, but his failure is large and cannot be ignored. He combined the blood of T. H. Huxley and of Matthew Arnold, and though he could not reconcile the 'two cultures' except through an unacceptable mysticism, he for long carried on, aloud, an intelligent dialogue within himself and graduated from a cold, clever practitioner of fiction to an unsuccessful, but substantial, tragic novelist. He developed; only the final results are lacking in conviction. His twenties novels were masks to conceal his complex nature, more sentimental than he wanted to acknowledge: they were influenced by Firbank (q.v.), Peacock and perhaps, though not initially, even by Coward (who appears in caricature in one of them): slightly icy country-house romps, clever but vacuous fun (*Chrome Yellow*, 1921; *Antic Hay*, 1923; *Those Barren Leaves*, 1925). The short stories of this period (four volumes were issued 1920–6) are better, and contain some of the best work he did: here he often explores areas left untouched in the novels (*Collected Short Stories*, 1957). Then he wrote *Point Counter Point* (1928), which is the nearest he came to a major novel. But *Point Counter Point* is not a major novel. One can feel the author's seriousness and despair but this does not get into the texture of the book, in which manipulated puppet-characters clash unreally and in which the influence of Gide's (q.v.) *Les Faux-Monnayeurs* is altogether too obtrusive. Huxley was always over-derivative, and in his brilliant dystopia *Brave New World* (1932), which is however more speculative than imaginative, he drew heavily on Zamyatin's (q.v.) *We*, translations of which had appeared in English (1925) and French (1929). His denial that he had read it was not characteristic—or was it? Huxley is moving only because we gain a sense of his concern; his novels become in themselves more and more imaginatively sterile. This is ironic, for it is types of spiritual sterility that he wishes to demonstrate and analyze. His thirties essays—and his anthology with commentaries, *Texts and Pretexts* (1932)—are more stimulating than his fiction for this ruthlessly exposes his deficiencies and fails to bring out the undoubted warmth of the man. None of his later novels is an exception. From the late thirties until his death he dedicated himself to mysticism and, finally, to psychedelic drugs; the adventure was all too clearly undertaken as a retreat from a reality too hard to bear: Huxley's writings on these subjects become increasingly vulgar, but he continued to produce some good books: *The Devils of Loudun* (1952) is a penetrating treatment of a medieval *cause célèbre* and many of his essays have a similar quality. His poetry, written early in life, is witty and often successfully epigrammatic: *Collected Poems* (1971). Huxley will be remembered for sinking much of his acute intelligence into a sensationalist mysticism and he will doubtless be read by eager adepts; he will be valued for his integrity, intellectual shrewdness and for the poise of the best of the essays (*Collected Essays,* 1959, is a fair selection). But the book for which he will be most remembered as well as valued is one he did not plan: *Letters* (1969).

Huysmans, Joris Karl (ps. Georges Charles Huysmans) (1848–1907) French (half-Dutch) novelist, art critic. Huysmans began under the influence of Baudelaire, which he early transformed into a kind of decadence, but he then became interested in the novels of Zola (q.v.) and he was instrumental, through his first novel *Marthe* (1876; tr. *Marthe,* 1948; 1958), and through his personal defence of Zola, in the creation of the actual naturalist (*see* Zola) school. This is yet another indication of the all-important romantic-decadent element in naturalism. For when Huysmans 'broke' with anti-romanticism and naturalism with his most famous novel, *A Rebours* (1884; tr. *Against Nature,* 1949), he did not reject his former work or outlook but used them as the soil for a new one. *Les Soeurs Vatard* (1879), *The Vatard Sisters,* which remains untranslated, is certainly a (good) naturalist novel but Tibaille may clearly be seen as one of the line leading to Des Esseintes and Durtal of the later decadent and Catholic novels. The chief of these are *A Rebours, Là-Bas* (1891; tr. *Down There,* 1935; 1958) and *L'Oblat* (1903; tr. *The Oblate,* 1924). Huysmans himself went through periods of decadence, spiritualism, a kind of Satanism, and, finally, a Catholicism which absorbed all these tendencies. His heroes are ambiguous self-portraits: self-punishing aesthetes, over-refined, bored, eventually driven by the devil into the arms of God. Thus he is important to our century in a number of ways: he directly influenced George Moore (q.v.); he is one of the sources of modern agonistic Catholic anti-Catholic fiction (e.g. Bernanos, q.v., Julien Green, q.v., Greene, q.v.); he is not only a prophet of *le néant,* but also his characters consistently seek to alleviate their existential disappointment. Zola accused him of doing a terrible thing, with *A Rebours,* to naturalism (which, though it hardly matters, he did); but in doing so, he became a more decisively modern writer than Zola.

Hyde, Robin (ps. Iris Wilkinson) (1906–39) New Zealand poet and novelist whose early death robbed New Zealand of a major writer. Born in South Africa, she went to New Zealand and then on to China and England, where she died of benzedrine poisoning. Her poetry (the posthumous *Houses by the Sea,* 1952, and three earlier books) is tender, regretful, subtle and often dramatic; it sometimes refers, without sentimentality, to a tragic sense of unfulfilled eroticism. 'The Beaches' is a superb example. *Passport to Hell* (1936) and *Nor the Years Condemn* are perceptive impressions of New Zealand in the first thirty-five years of this century; *Check to Your King* (1936) is correctly praised as the finest historical novel to come out of New Zealand. Her versatility and potentialities were immense but the poetry (at least) that she left is a positive and exciting revelation of genius: she has the intensity of Karin Boye (q.v.).

I

Ibuse Masuji (1898) Japanese fiction writer. Ibuse is both popular and highly regarded by critics. He has written fiction on both modern and historical themes. *Honjitsu kyushin* (1949; tr. *No Consultation Today* in *Japan Quarterly* VIII, 1, 1961) gives a vivid and witty portrait of a Japanese town. *Kuroi ame* (1966; tr. *Black Rain,* 1969) is the restrained and tragic story of a girl who was exposed to fall-out in the attack on Hiroshima. Many of his stories have been translated in periodicals (e.g. *Japan Quarterly, Encounter*).

Ionesco, Eugène (1912) Franco-Rumanian dramatist, critic, fiction writer, memoirist, diarist. He was born in Rumania but his mother was French and French was his first language–as his parents moved to France soon after he was born. He returned to Rumania at the beginning of adolescence and played some small part, as critic, in Rumanian letters in the thirties; in 1938 he permanently left Rumania for France, in which he stayed throughout the war. He loathed the representational theatre–he liked fiction more than 'reality', but hated 'real' actors–but in 1948 he began to learn English from a textbook (*L'Anglais sans peine*). From the mundane absurdities of this he wrote 'the tragedy of language' *La Cantatrice chauve* (Ionesco's published plays have been tr. in seven volumes, 1958–68; the four plays in the first volume are in different versions in the American editions; the rest are identical: I give the English titles from this collected edition), *The Bald Prima Donna,* which was performed in 1950. At first he failed but Anouilh's (q.v.) praise in 1953 gained him his high reputation. Ionesco's theatre, which draws freely on surrealistic effects, is paradigmatically 'absurd' in Martin Esslin's definition (a sensible 'working hypothesis') in his valuable *The Theatre of the Absurd* (1961 rev. 1968): he quotes Ionesco himself: 'Absurd is that which is devoid of purpose. . . . Cut off from his religious, metaphysical and transcendental roots, man is lost; all his actions become senseless, absurd, useless.' This condition causes man to feel *Angst;* the 'theatre of the absurd' openly abandons 'rational devices and discursive thought' (Esslin) –other drama, by writers also obsessed with contingency (e.g. Sartre, q.v.), presents this *Angst* in more traditionalist, rational terms. One may disagree with Esslin in the choice of some of the dramatists he chooses as fundamentally absurdist but Ionesco unquestionably belongs to this category. Ionesco's plays are exceedingly effective in the theatre: he is the master-craftsman of his limited genre. But, although he is brilliant, he is not–in the drama–at all profound. His main theme is commonplace: bourgeois language is meaningless (the first play's dialogue is based on the dialogue in *L'Anglais sans peine,* though the title comes from an actor's slip of the tongue in rehearsal); since words become trite clichés, based in a mechanistic logic, love, meaningful communication, is thus impossible. However, Ionesco can be successful at demonstrating the processes by which such dehumanization takes place; the weakness of his plays is that they contain little convincing demonstration of the exercise of the fully human which, though perpetually menaced in all of us, does take place. As dramatist he is an absolute nihilist, though he is also an excellently barmy funster at certain isolated points. His approach to the theatre is logical: it must be *theatre,* illusion, distortive. Bérenger, who appears in several plays, is his 'saved character'; but what a critic has called his 'distraught perseverance in his human condition' is unconvincing because it is always made explicit by a slick over-gimmickry. Even *Rhinoceros* (1960), an allegory of a people's surrender to totalitarian hysteria, ends badly. Ionesco knows that subjectivity is the only answer to alienation or anomie but no sense of what it might consist of is, on the stage, ever present. As dramatist he is indeed extremely limited: he still 'loathes' theatre and uses it to express this loathing: his theatre is one of simple negation. Yet this is because he is not really a dramatist, only a skilful arranger. Thus his later longer plays (the early ones are in one act) are markedly inferior. He is not heartless, as his best work–his diaries and occasional writings –show. His stories have been collected in English as *The Colonel's Photograph* (1967). *Notes et contre-notes* (1962; tr. *Notes and Counter-Notes*) collects criticism. The diaries, sensitive and often beautiful, are in *Journal en miettes* (1967; tr. *Fragments of a Journal,* 1968). *Théâtre* (1954–66). *Découverts* (1970). Claude Bonnefoy's *Entretiens avec Eugène Ionesco* (1966; tr. *Conversations,* 1970).

Isherwood, Christopher (1904) English (now an American citizen, 1946, resident in California) novelist, playwright, scriptwriter, popularizer of mysticism. Isherwood, until 1940 a close associate of Auden (q.v.) and co-author with him of several verse plays, is distinguished for his lucid prose. But he has failed to take the creative opportunities offered him by his capacity to write it. His first novels, *All the Conspirators* (1928) and *The Memorial* (1932), are full of promise and they remain his best. They are influenced above all by Forster (q.v.), Virginia Woolf (q.v.), Groddeck and Freud (q.v.), are structurally elaborate and in some ways original, and are courageous explorations of a non-conformity about which Forster could not be explicit. The two thirties successors are good, but not so good. *Mr Norris Changes Trains* (1935) is a brilliant series of Firbankian (q.v.) in-jokes, but abandons the novel form in favour of a series of episodes which in *Goodbye to Berlin* (1939) becomes a series of stories held together only by a deliberately passive 'camera-eye', 'Issyvoo'. Both are set in Germany and both record the decline of the quality of German life under the Nazis but this is more in the nature of superb journalism than of imaginative fiction. Isherwood then went to Hollywood and simultaneously turned out filmscripts and devoted himself to Vedanta. *Prater Violet* (1945), self-styled a novelette, combines a sharp journalistic look at the film industry with an idealized portrait of a director. He at last returned to the novel form, after a lapse of twenty-two years, with *The World in the Evening* (1954)—but this, and its successors, amount to little more than isolated, tortured little scraps of personal misery held together by the (in imaginative terms) cheap cloth of competence and journalistic skill. The attempt to treat homosexuality and Eastern religion fails, it seems, through some sort of mental debility. The best of the post-war books describes a visit to South America: *The Condor and the Cows* (1949). The title of a study of Isherwood by Pérez Minik is unhappily apt: 'Un novelista famoso pero frustrado' (a famous but frustrated writer).

J

Jacob, Max (1876–1944) French (Breton) poet, novelist, painter, art-critic, biographer, palmist, astrologer, professional mystic, clown, drug-taker, who died in the Nazi concentration camp at Drancy. He is often taken as more of a catalystic literary personality than an achiever but this must be qualified in the light of his abundant self-description. . . . He puzzled everyone by his mysteriousness: was he serious, was he joking? The answer is simple: he did not know. A Jew, he had a vision of Christ in a cinema, turned Roman Catholic (*circa* 1915), and eventually went to the presbytery of Saint-Benoît-sur-Loire as a recluse. At first he travelled, spent time in Paris and succumbed to 'temptation'; after 1931 he did not leave the presbytery except to see his family and Saint-Pol-Roux (1861–1940). Perhaps only his friend and fellow-Breton Saint-Pol-Roux, who was a splendid poet, fully understood him. His own work is (deliberately) not serious, since he could not be serious in it (see *Art Poétique,* 1922): he needed someone to love and to love him, and his homosexuality, which horrified him, precluded that possibility. But he is delightful: sadly parodic of poetry inspired by passion, pleasingly idiotic (rather than surrealist), an accomplished dissolver (in his literary work) of the causes of his disturbance. There are interesting books on him by André Salmon (1927) and André Billy (1945). Jacob's personality, combining buffoonery, anguished sexuality, self-indulgence, saintliness (his piety in the thirties was strict), sophistication and primitive Breton 'mysticism' (if it is that), is one of the most puzzling of this century. He knew everyone ('that dear gang'), and it was Apollinaire (q.v.) in particular who learned from him. The clue to his enigmatic character lies in his evasion of the deep emotion which he felt—but which he was convinced was evil. He tried to kill himself three times in childhood. An important document is the novel *L'Homme de chair et l'homme reflet* (1924), *The Fleshly and the Meditative Man.* There is a selection of letters, *Lettres* (1966), a selection in English, *Drawings and Poems* (1951); and the most characteristic poetry is in *Poésie* (1955). A substantial biography is badly needed, as is an *Oeuvres complètes*. Some works remain unpublished.

Jahier, Piero (1884–1966) Italian poet. Born Genoa; died Florence. Apart from war service with the Alpine troops in the First World War Jahier spent most of his life as a railway official in Bologna. He began as a student of theology. Even amongst the many deliberately subdued or mannered Italian writers who reacted to the egomania of D'Annunzio (q.v.) and the proto-fascist frenzy of Marinetti's (q.v.) futurism, the unprolific Jahier was an odd man out, a genuine original and, at his best, an exquisite minor. He was an independent socialist–observed carefully by Mussolini's policemen–who combined in his work a modified chant in the style of Claudel (q.v.) with a rough colloquialism; the result, when not merely puzzling, is unlike the language of any other contemporary European writer. The actual technique–the interspersing of verse and prose, the persistent and stubborn adherence to his own way of seeing and feeling–resembles David Jones (q.v.); but Jahier is small-scale and modest where Jones is epic and ambitious. *Gino Bianchi* (1915) is a prose satire on a bureaucrat, and, when not overdone, brilliantly catches the flavour of Italian officialdom. *Ragazzo* (*Boy*, 1919, rev. with early poems, 1939) is his best book: an account of boyhood, his father (a Protestant priest), and the impact upon him of the latter's death. *Con me e con gli alpini* (*With Me and the Alpini*, 1919), in a mixture of prose and verse, became one of Italy's most popular war books. For the last forty-seven years of his life Jahier, apart from publishing revisions of earlier work and *Qualche Poesia* (*Some Poems*, 1962), remained silent. He was always an admired writer. He has been called Calvinist but this is to mistake for puritanism an insistent sympathy with the underdog. In certain early poems Jahier anticipates the 'hermeticism' of Ungaretti (q.v.).

James, Henry (1843–1916) American novelist, short-story writer, critic, playwright, essayist; brother of William James (q.v.). James, though a realist with his roots in the nineteenth century, has none the less been a dominant force in English literature in this century; his last three great novels, *The Wings of the Dove* (1902), *The Ambassadors* (1903) and *The Golden Bowl* (1904), were published at its beginning; these have in particular exercised an influence and a fascination that has, arguably, changed the face of the modern novel (the two unfinished posthumous novels are not in the same class). First, James may be seen as the writer who developed what we call the technique of realism to its farthest possible point: in other words, to that point at which the choice must be expressionism (in its most general sense; *see* Stadler) or silence. In his work we may find adumbrations of almost every major theme of twentieth-century literature: the creative predicament; the urge towards expressionist techniques (as revealed in the final tortuous complexities—almost fantastical elaboration of motive and intricacies of style; and in the 'single point of view', the resolve to combat the 'omniscient narrator' and cut out the Victorian 'aside' by never allowing in anything that is not representative of the experience of the characters), the concern (and/or obsession) with the feminine mentality, the increasing use of types of metaphor, the awareness of the problem of the nature of the 'world' of a book. . . . The last three novels, immensely and increasingly complex, are explorations of over-sophistication (which is counterpointed against simplicity in the sense that the germinal situation of each novel is elementary), of the nature of fable; they also subtly work out the important ideas of James's father: a Calvinist turned quasi-Swedenborgian—and of his brother William. James's pushing of structure to its utmost limits is pre- and not proto-expressionist; but, while incidentally making it impossible for a new realist to do better, it has also influenced the modernist novel by demonstrating the impossibility of rejecting modernism and thus encouraging radical experiment. James, who defended his failure to assert himself sexually by turning a back-injury into an 'obscure hurt', was a homosexual; he was aware of this, yet instead of repressing it he transformed it—a complex psychological process, lasting many years—into a reinforcing factor in the 'femininity' in which he rightly felt his creative powers to reside. Above all, James fought for the absolute integrity and organicism of the work of art, for the primacy of the imagination under intensive scrutiny: he turned over-sophistication into control. All he did within the limits of tradition points ineluctably forward to the future. *Novels and Stories* (1921–3; 1961–6); *Complete Tales* (1962–5); *Complete Plays* (1949).

James, William (1842–1910) American philosopher; elder brother of Henry James. Most of his work was done against a background of constant ill-health, which included bouts of serious depressive illness.

James was influential in many spheres: personally on his brother and on Gertrude Stein (q.v.) and more generally as a 'pragmatist', and as the coiner of the term 'stream-of-consciousness' (for which, however, *see* Bergson). James was a qualified doctor and then a teacher of physiology but his main interests were in psychology and in an eclectic kind of philosophy. He was a versatile, generous and wide-ranging man: the remarkable brother of a remarkable brother. James as psychologist propounded, with the Danish physician and psychologist Carl George Lange, at least one idea that was to influence, if unobtrusively, the art of fiction: the James-Lange theory of emotion (although this is not valid as originally formulated, it remains a central topic in psychology and has not been discredited): that we do not (say) run away because we are frightened, but rather are frightened because a primary stimulus has caused us to run away. James anticipated most subsequent developments: the inevitability of subjectivity (existentialism), the primacy of the will (phenomenology, in the sense that he held the mind to be intentionalist), the necessity of seeing truth as relative in practical interests—from which the later, full-blown pragmatism developed. He could also be regarded as one of the founders of modern pharmacological psychiatry. An innate scepticism and creative honesty explain his refusal (which irritates some philosophers) to attempt to develop a consistent system. He was, at once, one of the founders of decently conducted behaviouristic experimentation—and an introspectionist whose work proved the invalidity of the silly inferences of such as Skinner and Eysenck. But, a ceaseless mental adventurer, James finally developed his introspectionism into what he called a 'neutral monism'. This is not a reversal, a denial of the existence of introspection; it is a viewing of 'consciousness' as *physical* process: it is not (as Bergson agreed—but many 'Bergsonians', alas, have asserted that he did not) 'stuff'. You cannot reduce experience either to 'consciousness' or 'matter': they are abstractions from flux. One can see the affinities with Bergson (the two men certainly reached their basic conclusions independently: an astonishing fact) and one can see why the co-propounder of the James-Lange theory of emotion took over C. S. Peirce's pragmatism, later to be elaborated more fully by Dewey (q.v.). James meant by his pragmatism that concepts were under no circumstances whatever to be regarded as anything except as *what was done with them:* truth is not more or less than *function.* 'Now however beautiful or otherwise worthy of stationary contemplation the substantive part of a concept may be, the more important part of its significance may naturally be held to be the consequences to which it leads'; 'What is it to be "real"? The best definition is . . . "anything is real of which we find ourselves obliged to take account in any way".' James is a very superior philosopher: a vital thinker—and a master of literary style. Important books by him include *The Principles of Psychology* (1890), *The Will to Believe* (1897)—one of the most courageous books ever attempted by a man in a state of acute (medical) depression—*The Varieties of Religious Experience* (1902), still the classic study of religious psychology, and *Pragmatism* (1907). For some readers we may, in this discussion of James, have seemed to have strayed from modern literary matters but we have been in the thick of them.

Jammes, Francis (1868–1938) French poet, novelist. Jammes was a simple and original poet until the influence of Claudel (q.v.) turned him, in the middle of the first decade of the century, into a patriarchal Catholic mage: Claudel, in fact, distorted the religious, the naturally Franciscan in him into the pious—which did not suit him. He became (Gide, q.v., noted it) self-consciously 'simple'. His works after this are repetitious and mostly without interest. The earlier poetry, by consensus his best, has been variously described as being one of 'sentiment' and 'symbolist'. It is not, however, categorizable. The Jammes of *De l'Angélus de l'aube à l'angélus du soir* (1898), *From the Dawn to the Evening Angelus,* has a disconcertingly clear gaze into 'nature' but he would have remained relatively minor had he not been disturbed by an odd eroticism—all his life he retained a mystique about girls, girls poised between adolescence and adulthood. Alain-Fournier (q.v.), who expressed his mood in a rather more sophisticated key, loved him because he did not separate life from art. . . . C. A. Hackett feels that all 'unpleasant disturbing elements', as well as depth of emotion, are excluded from this early poetry; but Jammes's friend Gide is closer to the truth when he refers to his 'aromatic' quality: these simple poems arise from an erotic disturbance and, though they *are* simple, the juxtaposition of simplicities within them is resolutive. The famous 'J'aime dans les temps Clara d'Ellébeuse' offers an excellent example: the guiltiness is enshrined in an unfalsified past; the imaginary world is phenomenologically precise to the point that it glows; the deliberate touches of realism are perfect; the final line, in which he asks his dream-girl (he wrote a novel, *Clara d'Ellébeuse*, 1899) to come to him 'quite naked' is not evasive: he can now ask the question without anxiety. He is seen at his best in prose in the charming *Le Roman du lièvre* (1903), *The Book of the Hare.*

Jarrell, Randall (1914–65) American poet, novelist, critic, journalist, teacher. His service in the air force in the Second World War was a decisive experience and may have been a factor in his suicide (he was not 'killed in a traffic accident'). Few poets in either war have shown such a degree of tormented compassion for the fighters (Jarrell himself flew for a short time, but was for most of the war an instructor), and it is arguable that his war poems are his best. Jarrell, not (outside the war poetry) altogether as fulfilled a poet as either he or many others could have wished, had a special quality: he cared desperately about other people in general–he was the reverse of Swift, who said he could tolerate Tom, Dick or Harry, but did not care for mankind. Of course he was an enemy of philistinism and the bourgeois non-ethic but he still cared, with an almost Weil (q.v.) -like intensity and this fact operates, even in his unsuccessful poetry, with an astonishing purity. Yet Jarrell was a merciless reviewer of bad verse (*Poetry and the Age*, 1953, collects many reviews and essays) and a sharp satirist of the groves of academe (in the novel *Pictures from an Institution*, 1954). However, his mercilessness has purity: he is always castigating a self-indulgence which he has either purged from himself or which is a threat to decency. He chose to work in an obscure girls' college in the South (he was born in Tennessee) rather than in a prestigious university–and he loved teaching above every other activity; he must have been one of America's most effective teachers of poetry. *A Sad Heart at the Supermarket* (1962) contains some excellent literary essays and shows that Jarrell's critical powers were deepening right up to the end. But the poems themselves, which never had the attention they deserved, are at the heart of his work. The best of the war poems express the piteousness of human vulnerability with a piercing exactitude which recalls Owen (q.v.), though Jarrell lacks Owen's confused, morbid relish. The pervasive theme of the rest of his work is his feeling of having been violated by birth: of the anguish of a world of creatures possessing sensibilities that must of necessity be violated. 'Sin' means nothing in Jarrell: suffering, which he can effortlessly project into masks (especially in his last book, *The Lost World*, 1965), is all. Among his favourite writers were the Grimms, Proust (q.v.), Rilke (q.v.), Wordsworth; and from the Grimms and their later, more literary successors (such as Hoffmann) he finds some consolation. Childhood *is* Pelagian, he tries to convince himself, and in his poetry he continually pushes his characters, his masks, back into childhood reverie or adult reverie of childhood. Technically he found the problem of form almost insurmountable, for he knew the Lowellian fluency to be, at its heart, vain, artificial and ambitious. The earlier poems are traditional (he had graduated from Vanderbilt, then very much under the influence of Tate, q.v.), the later looser—but while he needed to escape from 'tightness', the relaxation afforded him by the freer line refused to reflect his mounting tension. In the last poems he turns, his terror reinforced by his poetic modesty and his empathy, away from himself to monologues by various people, mostly women, which frequently recall childhood or search for simple pleasures. The end of one of his earliest and best poems, '90 North', is a fitting epitaph for a man whose poetry, mostly flawed though it is, will always be studied, and who was one of the greatest appreciators and close critics, of the poetry he loved, of his time: '. . . I see at last that all the knowledge// I wrung from the darkness—that the darkness flung me—/Is worthless as ignorance: nothing comes from nothing,/ The darkness from the darkness. Pain comes from the darkness/ And we call it wisdom. It is pain.' *Complete Poems* (1969); *The Third Book of Criticism* (1969).

Jarry, Alfred (1873–1907) French dramatist, novelist, writer. Jarry is important as a precursor of 'absurdity' but he has not always been fully understood. His individual genius has been overrated. When his famous play *Ubu Roi* (1896; tr. *Ubu Roi,* 1951, and in *Four Modern French Comedies,* 1960) was performed it was Yeats (q.v.) who (famously) exclaimed 'After us the savage God' ('. . . What rough beast. . . ?'). Gide (q.v.), like Yeats not a violent or overt innovator, was also present and he regarded it as an important event. Jarry anticipated surrealism (*see* Breton) as well as the 'absurd' (*see* Ionesco) but he was himself no more than a gifted child: more of a socio-anthropological phenomenon of intelligence than an intrinsic master. The effectiveness of *Ubu Roi* today depends on the nature of its audience: if this is aggressively anti-bourgeois (or imagines itself to be) then the play merely acts as a reinforcement of a subversive (or pseudo-subversive) attitude; if the audience should consist of conventional bourgeois, then it would shock and nonplus them, as it was originally supposed to do, with its crazy plot, its sixth-form dirty language and puns, and its implication that whatever is, is not right. The fact that it now satisfies the pseudo-subversive indicates that its text is dated; but that judgement in no way detracts from the reactions of Yeats or Gide, both of whom saw in it far more than Jarry himself did. . . . *Ubu Roi* 'was a brief but correct summation of a particular climate', as a shrewd critic (David Grossvogel) has remarked. Jarry, with others, had originally composed a loose farce sending up a chemistry professor at their school: he was called Père Hébé, which got turned into *Ubu Roi* by Jarry, who continued, as an ex-pupil, to elaborate the myth. The language of the play is feeble in quality and it ultimately fails (as do its successors, dealing with the same character) because Jarry lacked the cunning of the true playwright, who understands that the audience—whatever its nature—forms an essential part of the drama itself. Jarry, at bottom, loathed life so much (and not very maturely) that his project was to prove that the hideous mask was the *only* reality. But Ubu *was* Jarry, and Jarry himself—who died of a tubercular meningitis aggravated by alcoholism and his growing sense of emptiness—became more and more the part that not only he but also other schoolboys—such as Charles Marin—had created back in 1887–8. Jarry's literary début had been seriously made, in fact, under the auspices of the decaying *symboliste* movement (his chief mentor was Marcel Schwob): the poems of *Les Minutes de sable mémorial* (1894) are insignificant and unsuccessful and Jarry's failure as poet is an important factor in his choice of direction. His 'science' of 'pataphysics', which provided imaginary answers to unanswerable questions, has led to the foundation of a *Collège de 'Pataphysique'* in Paris—Queneau (q.v.), the excellent cabaret poet Jacques Prévert (1910), Ionesco (q.v.) and many others are 'pataphysicians'. 'Pataphysics' is an example of extreme scepticism; it is seen most clearly in the posthumous 'néoscientifique' novel *Gestes et Opinions du Dr Faustroll, Pataphysicien* (1911; tr. in *Selected Works*, 1965), which in form is chiefly influenced by Rabelais and Lucian. The best of his several novels, though, is *Le Surmâle* (1902; tr. *The Supermale*, 1964 rev. 1968): in this proto-surrealist science fiction Jarry was able to discover a language with which to destroy his own earnest tendencies towards ornamented, decadent *symbolisme* and to undermine his masculine false pretences. The complete works, *Oeuvres complètes*, appeared in 1948; *Tout Ubu* (1962) collects the Ubu material; *Ubu enchaîné* (1900) has been translated as *King Turd* (1953); and there is a *Selected Works* (1965) in English which contains Cyril Connolly's translation of the posthumous *Ubu Cocu* (1944). The complete poetry is in *Oeuvres poétiques complètes* (1945).

Jeffers, Robinson (1887–1962) American poet, playwright. Jeffers, born in Pittsburgh, was the son of a Presbyterian minister who was also a classical scholar. The themes of his rhetorical poetry, almost all of it narrative or dramatic, rest on an artificially wrought philosophy based on fundamental, though not unlearned, misunderstandings: of the nature of Greek religion and the Greek dramatists, of the nature of incest, of the people of California around Carmel, where he chose to live in a granite house built partly with his own hands (he imagined this society to resemble that of 'Homer'). The conviction behind virtually all the poems is of a humanity wholly rejected by God: doubtless a morbid, but partially theatrical, extension of the Calvinism instilled into him by his father. This was carried further: into the lucubrated notion that God exists but is not concerned with humanity. However, Jeffers hovers unconvincingly between this concept of God and his notions about the Greek dramatists' concept of *moira*, 'fate'. Jeffers's sensationalist response to his strident pessimism is, briefly, to learn to endure the pain of rejection of humanity from the magnificent peace of the 'strong' things in non-human nature: rocks, large swooping birds, horses. It is an immature philosophy, expressed in an ineffective verse form: a ponderous, monotonous adaptation of Whitman—not at all solid like granite, but rather cluttered with cacophonous clichés and pseudo-stoical asides. Thus Jeffers's one real strength, a limited ability to evoke desolate landscape and to describe action, is an isolated factor, quite meaningless in its grandiose context. Among his poems are *Tamar* (1924), *The Women at Point Sur* (1927) and a free adaptation of Euripides's *Medea* (1946). His use of the sea as a symbol of cruelty has been admired but it is confusedly anthropomorphic. *Selected Poems* (1965).

Jennings, Elizabeth (1926) English poet. She was taken up by the critics when she published *Poems* (1953) and some ten years later rather cruelly dropped. The chief influence on her has been Edwin Muir (q.v.), whose religious preoccupations she extends to accommodate her Catholicism. She resembles Muir, too, in that her poems are often metrically correct but rhythmically flat. Between the mid-fifties and the late sixties she tended to look for subjects rather than let them find her and her poems in this period tend to be weaker than her early ones, which were distinguished by a bare, desentimentalized lyricism and a natural feeling for fable. After *Collected Poems* (1967; 1971) and a series of, unfortunately, banal though affectingly sincere poems about mental ill-health and hospital treatment (*The Animal's Arrival*, 1969), she has fought her way back—with notable humility and courage, and clearly at a high price—to a new and poetically more effective plainness that has involved the kind of harsh self-appraisal that lies somewhere behind all true poetry (*Lucidities*, 1970). The strength of her best poems is that, although they could not possibly have been written by a man, they avoid the traditionally 'feminine'. In this way, though her procedures are quietly traditional, she is an eminently modern poet. *Growing Points* (1975) is a fine new volume.

Jiménez, Juan Ramón (1881–1958) Spanish poet, prose writer. Nobel Prize 1956. Jiménez, though a non-political recluse (he suffered throughout his life from depression which was much alleviated by his understanding wife), never returned to Spain after the Civil War. He was the most internationally famous of the Spanish poets in between the wars—but for his most inferior work, which in fact obtained him the Nobel Prize. He accepted Darío's (q.v.) *modernismo*, but refined and extended it. He drew on the French symbolists and on folk lore. The faults of his sometimes lush, over-ornamented, sentimental earlier poems spring mainly from his inability to cope with his bouts of depression: his decisive change of style (but some earlier poems anticipate the later in their linguistic austerity) is coincidental with his marriage to Zenobia Camprubí Aymar, who translated—with his help—Tagore (q.v.) into Spanish. Tagore came to be an important influence on him. Although regarded as of the 'Generation of 1898' (*see* Unamuno), Jiménez was also deeply influenced by *krausismo*, although he developed and modified this. Unamuno was a bitter opponent of this movement which was a syncretist system based on the philosophy of K. C. F. Krause, a German, and brought to Spain by an educator called F. Giner de los Riós. What was important in this to Jiménez (and to Machado, q.v., and Azorin) was its tolerance and its 'panentheist' scheme of reconciling theism and pantheism. We can see its influence persisting in Jiménez to the very end, in his desperate and dedicated search for the 'precise name of things' which would link him to the 'divine universal essence' (not his phrase). Tagore's views, though Oriental, fit in with this. In 1917 Jiménez published his classic *Platero y yo* (tr. *Platero and I*, 1956), about himself as a child accompanied by a donkey. With *Diario de un poeta recién casado* (1917), *Diary of a Newlywed Poet*, Jiménez enters into his second phase of 'pure' poetry. He discarded everything—conventional form, ornament, rhyme—in the interests of capturing the naked, 'timeless' moment. The result is an abstract, almost solipsist poetry; clearly it is a kind of love poetry but Jiménez will not allow himself to be distracted by personal details. His later poetry, of exile, is somewhat more personal and the 'real world' is more apparent in it. Jiménez's is not a serene poetry, even though it accepts the existence of serenity and it is more full of violent and disturbing imagery than seems to be generally admitted. One critic has well written of how his 'savage pessimism' is 'crossed by tense belief'. He can at any time lapse into preciosity but at his best is exquisite. He wrote well on poetry; his distinction between *voluntaria*, works composed deliberately out of a decision to make them, and *necesaria*, works which demand to be born, is particularly knowing and valuable. *50 Spanish Poems* (tr. 1950); *Selected Writings* (tr. 1957).

Jones, David (1895–1974) Anglo-Welsh writer and artist. Jones's paintings, water-colours, drawings and inscriptions are exquisitely lucid as well as beautiful, whereas his writings (chiefly *In Parenthesis*, 1937, about his experiences as a private in the Royal Welsh Fusiliers in the First World War and the even more difficult *The Anathemata*, 1952) are not 'immediately accessible—although . . . can be read by the light of [his] prefaces and notes', as an admirer has written. None the less, the two must be taken together—at least for the sake of the writing, which is overrated, while the artistic productions are probably underrated. Jones, a devoted Roman Catholic, is distinguished by his absolute integrity. The main inspiration of his work—as his graphic art suggests—is his innocent vision (that of a natural recluse) and his faith in the liturgy. He is a simpler man than he has been taken to be (and this is not intended as a critical slur: on the contrary), but his lack of interest in fame, eccentric in a writer, has led him, especially in *The Anathemata*, into too private territory. Jones has gone back, for his method, to an ancient aural Welsh tradition and one can gain a distinct and valid effect from the *sound* of even his most obscure passages of verse or incantatory prose. This is reinforced by his integrity. But the sense is sometimes inaccessible. The spirit of his literary work, which consists of Pound-like verse interspersed with prose, may be gathered from the famous drawing of a muzzled bear that he made as a child: tender, tragic, irradiated with an almost angelic intelligence. Art, for Jones, is continuously revealed proof of human free will, a reflection of the divine gratuitousness of the Creation. He is a craftsman descended from craftsmen. (All this and much else he explains, often curiously, in his selection of critical writings called *Epoch and Artist,* 1959.) In *In Parenthesis* the war becomes too transformed: inevitably the sense of it, our knowledge of it, moulds the work and yet its hideous actuality is somehow muted. Cockney and Welsh intonation are well reproduced but when the experience of the men is related to the Welsh and English past (recorded in Aneirin's *Y Gododdin,* in Arthurian myth, in Malory, in chronicles of Henry v, in the Charlemagne cycle–all is grist to the mill) an element of artificiality is let in. That it is not artificial to Jones is beside the point. *In Parenthesis* is as much about what Jones says *The Anathemata* is about: 'one's own "thing" . . . part and parcel of the Western Christian *res.* . . .' His own 'thing': 'conditionings contingent upon . . . being a Londoner, of Welsh and English parentage, of Protestant upbringing, of Catholic subscription'. In the face of the raw actuality of the first major traumatic event of this century, the First World War, Jones's vision is too narrow for most–except as radiant scraps of autobiography. *The Anathemata* is, as Jones himself says, a 'heap of all that I could find': of what Michael Alexander calls an 'unearthing of the British deposits in our racial memory'. It has beauty, its tone is consistent: liturgical Celtic. But it is still, for the general reader, a 'heap'. Yet Jones's failure in this respect is large: ironically, it questions the liturgy.

Jones, LeRoi (now Amiri Imamu Baraka) (1934) American Negro writer, poet, playwright. 'He will change us, and he will use force as necessary', writes Carol Bergé. LeRoi Jones, 'Black African-American', has moved from an integrationalist (he married a white wife by whom he had children; he divorced her in 1965 and soon after changed his name) to a fiercely aggressive 'Black power' position. He has been jailed for his part in uprisings. This is the background and his admirers talk of how he writes or speaks 'truth as if it were the sex act'. He will certainly be important in the history of the American Negro literature, for the abrupt termination of his Black Arts Repertory Theatre (Harlem, 1964–5) by withdrawal of supportive funds drove him into a more extremist position and has immensely increased his influence. His thinking is confused–as well it might be. His plays–*Dutchman, The Slave* (1964), *The Baptism, The Toilet* (1967), *Slave Ship* (c. 1964, n.d., duplicated edition)–are his best: they are angry, but the form by its very nature distances him somewhat from his own bitterness–they have an unquestionable power. His poetry and fiction (*The System of Dante's Hell,* 1965; *Tales,* 1967) are less controlled.

Jonker, Ingrid (1933–65) Gifted Afrikaans poet and writer who drowned herself and whose death is seen by many as a tragic protest against the violent and frightened evil of the South African government. Her tragic intensity and end are inevitably reminiscent of Plath (q.v.) and Boye (q.v.) but she is superior to the former (though hardly more powerful) because not psychotic and more clearly concerned with the realities of evil external to herself. *Selected Poems* (tr. 1968).

Jouhandeau, Marcel (ps. Marcel Provence) (1888) French novelist, memoirist, miscellaneous writer. He was a schoolmaster in Passy from 1912 until 1949. He was born, a butcher's son, in Guéret (Creuse), which he has often depicted under the name Chaminadour in his versatile, indefinable writing (e.g. *Chaminadour,* 1934–41; *Mémorial,* 1948–58). Apart from some potboilers (on saints and so on) Jouhandeau's work is essentially autobiographical. He is a strange mixture: exhibitionistically sincere (about his marital difficulties, his homosexuality and other intimate matters), puritanically strict in his treatment of the world as a battleground of the forces of good and evil (cf. Bernanos, whose Roman Catholicism he shares), cynical, tender towards animals, quite uninterested in consistency or in writing well constructed books. His diaries, which tell all, continue to appear at very frequent intervals. His *M. Godeau marié* (1933) and *Chroniques maritales* (1938 and 1943), and other similar stories of his life with the dancer Caryathis, or Elise, have been his most popular books. His method in his books about Chaminadour is to concentrate on the chief features of his characters rather than to subject them to analysis. There is an ambiguity at the heart of all his work: simplicity, sweetness, tenderness, humour are paralleled by complexity, bitterness, cruelty, terror. Many of his novels have been neglected (e.g. *Le Parricide imaginaire,* 1930) and, astonishingly, there has been only one translation into English: a selection, *Marcel and Elise*, 1955). During the war he collaborated to the extent of visiting Berlin but no one remembers this now. He published some early novels under his own name. He is an author eminently worth study and (much) more extensive translation. J. Gaulmier's *L'Univers de Jouhandeau* (1960) is a useful study. The novelist Claude Mauriac (son of François, q.v.) wrote a book on him in 1938: *Introduction à une mystique de l'enfer.*

Jouve, Pierre Jean (1887) French poet, novelist, literary and music (particularly of Mozart, an important influence, and Berg) critic, writer of condensed autobiographies. Though Jouve has subjected himself to many influences, he cannot be categorized and is France's most independent modern major poet. Though he has been a Roman Catholic since about 1924, Jouve's work is characterized by his refusal to take easy options. But his early and fierce attachments had been over-dogmatic, religious; he eschewed them in favour of a commitment which, even in Gallic terms, is indefinite. It has been as artistically necessary a compromise to him as it has been for Greene (q.v.), Green (q.v.) or Neruda (q.v.)–the first two are 'Catholic', the last was 'communist'; but in the light of the autonomous imagination none of these commitments functions other than strategically. We may be intellectual sceptics but we cannot live without making judgements and these–from wherever we may convince ourselves they derive–are ultimately our own. Jouve had above all *energy*. His powerful intelligence early saw the necessity of attempting to control this: to control his dreams, his Bachelardian (q.v.) reveries. Hence his series of 'solutions', of which he transformed the ultimate, 'Catholic', one, into the constructive scepticism it most properly is. He began as an unanimist (*see* Romains), then turned to the analogous but more socialistically inclined 'L'Effort Libre' movement (freedom for the proletariat to express themselves), then to Rolland (q.v.) and pacificism. All the work previous to 1925 and his 'conversion', resulting from an Italian sojourn, was then 'proscribed' by him. It is hardly paradoxical that this earlier work (e.g. *Présences, Parler,* 1913; *Tragiques,* 1924) poses the questions that the later cannot answer; one can only remark that the equally prolific later poetry usually poses these questions with more pain, precision and power. An honest man can hate his certainties with a peculiarly penetrative power and Jouve is above all honest. He has been a major poet because he possesses a linguistic power to which he has resolutely applied a morally responsible but always eclectic, cerebral control. His fiction, persistently underrated and inexplicably untranslated, is important both in its own right and as a guide to the direction of his thought. The crucial novel is *Pauline 1880* (1925): this is more Freudian than Catholic and aptly demonstrates Jouve's conflicts. Freud (q.v.), with proper reservations, regarded religious certainty as a type of insanity: so does Jouve. He writes a poetry in which an extreme, 'id-ish' sexual violence (à la Freud), seen as catastrophic but nevertheless accepted, conflicts with a desire for spiritual redemption that is (convincingly) seen as natural. He is by no means a Catholic poet but rather *the* Freudian one, *par excellence,* of our times. And out of this net he richly attempts to struggle. In Jouve's poetry two notions fight: that of mutual orgasm as divine and that of all erotic projects as spiritually destructive. Combining these is a kind of analogy to the familiar existentialist 'leap' which Jouve has called *nada* (Spanish for 'nothing'). He hardly acknowledges this in his essay (in *En Miroir,* 1954) on the subject; but the ambiguity of an early poem he quotes makes it clear enough: 'Nothing will be attained except in absence/In a night a renunciation of light/A mixed beauty in where nothing exists'. Jouve spent the Second World War in Switzerland, from which he wrote a poetry clearly though never over-explicitly opposed to the Nazi barbarism. Since then he has broken through to his serenest and linguistically richest poetry. An old man, he refuses to disremember sensual delight and his spiritual hope is increasingly reinforced by its imagery. *Poésies* (1962–8). *An Idiom of Night* (tr. 1968) is a useful introductory English selection from the poems of *Le Paradis perdu* (1929) onwards. An excellent study is M. Callander's *The Poetry of Pierre Jean Jouve* (1965); Starobinski's book (1946) is regarded as the standard earlier exegesis, and is invaluable.

Joyce, James (1882–1941) Irish fiction writer, playwright, poet. He was born in Dublin and educated by Jesuits. After considering the priesthood he rejected Roman Catholicism but remained obsessed with it for the rest of his life. He decided to become a writer around the turn of the century and left Ireland in 1902 (his last visit was in 1912). He entered into a union with Nora Barnacle, by whom he had two children, in 1904 (they married in 1931 in order to safeguard their children's interests). Joyce lived in Trieste, earning some money as a teacher of English, from 1905 until 1915. It was here that he met Svevo (q.v.). He had been writing poems and stories since an early age (his first publication, which has not survived, was a poem: 1891); in 1907 he published *Chamber Music*, poetry, and, after censorship difficulties, *Dubliners* (1914), stories. He spent ten years writing the novel *A Portrait of the Artist as a Young Man*, which finally appeared in New York in book form in 1916. But from 1907 he had been contemplating a 'sequel' to this. It became *Ulysses* (1922), over the publication and rights of which he had continual difficulties. In 1915 he had written a play, *Exiles* (1918). Meanwhile the family had moved from Trieste to Zürich, then (1918) back to Trieste–and finally to Paris (1920), where they remained until 1940 when he returned to Zürich; he died there after an operation for a perforated duodenal ulcer. Joyce had always been myopic and subject to eye trouble; in 1917 he developed glaucoma and from that time onwards his sight progressively deteriorated, causing him much pain and frustration. Worse than this, his daughter Lucia (born in 1907 and named after the patron saint of eyesight) began to show signs of schizophrenia in 1929–and, to Joyce's sensibility, probably long before that. Like his eyes, her condition, for which he blamed himself, continued to deteriorate. She stayed with the family until Joyce's death. Joyce began his last major work, *Finnegans Wake* (1939; 1964), in 1923, quite possibly as a considered answer to the combined pressures exerted by financial difficulties, an intuition of Lucia's mental constitution, and failing eyesight. During his life he had extensive though never truly close contacts with leading literary figures: Pound (q.v.), Ford (q.v.), Eliot (q.v.) and many others. He was more likely to be boon-companion to 'ordinary' people. But only one person knew him well: his wife, a non-literary woman who suited him and who wanted to know why he wouldn't write 'ordinary books' (though she would have hated it if he had). The keys to the understanding of Joyce's achievement up to and including *Ulysses* are his posthumously published *Epiphanies* (1956), which he wrote between 1900 and 1903, and which were his means of preparing a literary method. The epiphany is, in Christian terms, the 'showing forth' of Jesus Christ's divinity to the Magi. Joyce's epiphanies are non-Christian, though religious, and may profitably be compared to Hopkins's (q.v.) *instress* and *inscape:* they are 'sudden revelation[s] of the whatness of a thing', 'sudden spiritual manifestation[s]'–'in the vulgarity of speech or gesture or in a memorable phase of the mind itself'.

But whereas Hopkins in his best poetry concentrates on nature, Joyce concentrates on *ordinary people:* it is a compensation for devoting himself to 'art'. One of his roots is in a naturalistically (*see* Zola) tinged realism. Another is in his religious education and a concomitant decadent symbolism, later transformed. A third is in his poetic capacity to perceive 'epiphanic' relationships, 'moments of truth', 'showings forth'. In *Dubliners* Joyce concentrates mostly on realistic protrayal but he becomes progressively more 'epiphanic' in his treatment. In *Ulysses* he combines realism with what may loosely be called symbolism (but 'expressionism' in the general sense is probably a more appropriate term) largely by means of 'stream-of-consciousness' or 'interior monologue'. Joyce did not see the possibilities inherent in this by studying Bergson (q.v.) or William James: he had read the French novelist Édouard Dujardin's novel *Les Lauriers sont coupés* (1888) and discerned that this pioneering but prosaic and tame use of the method could be extended and developed. Doubtless his knowledge of Freud's (q.v.) psychoanalysis, which he (like others) anticipated, and of Croce's philosophy, contributed to this process. *Ulysses,* a tragi-comic, passionate affirmation of life, is also a series of astonishingly effective literary *tours de force:* parodies, epiphanies, fantasies, *tranches de vie,* jokes. . . . It rumbustiously despairs of finding a literary method and in so doing discovers one. It retells a single story in many different ways, simultaneously demonstrating its insignificance and its significance. It is Jesuitical and anti-Christian; a series of paradoxes contained within a paradox. Bloom is like Ulysses, but Bloom is also a ridiculous parody of Ulysses, far removed from such classic dignity. It is one of the richest books of this century, Falstaffian in scope and, for all its profound learning (for Joyce cannot be described as less than learned), a celebration of *l'homme moyen sensuel* and his—not intellectuals'—predicament. *Ulysses* is well established as a triumph and rightly so; the fate and the true status of *Finnegans Wake* is another matter. This cannot ever be in the domain of the general reader and the extent to which it can be absorbed by anyone, however dedicated, is a matter of debate. It is at once too private and too universal (too ambitious): a gorgeous failure, to be saluted as wild loving repentance for a daughter's suffering: a desperate attempt to cure Lucia (and the sick world itself) of madness by codifying madness, explaining it—bringing the starer into space (Lucia, ill; but Joyce, writer, too) back into joyful-sad reality. *Ulysses* is humble, quotidian, ends on a lyrical note. The too huge world of *Finnegans*

Wake, which tries to show a Dublin publican and his wife as Everyman and his Muse, slips out of control, becomes inaccessible, too free: the centre, as Joyce's friend Yeats (q.v.) wrote in a famous poem, cannot hold. There is much academic writing on it, but the finest tribute is that of Anthony Burgess (q.v.): *A Shorter Finnegans Wake* (1966). This sort of project is seldom worth while, but Burgess's abridgement, together with his general book on Joyce, *Here Comes Everybody* (1965), is the best introduction. Another invaluable book on Joyce is Richard Ellmann's biography, *James Joyce* (1959). *Letters* (1957–66). *Collected Poems* (1936)—Joyce is, surprisingly, a somewhat underrated lyrical poet. *Critical Writings* (1959). *Giacomo Joyce* (1968) is a long story written towards the end of Joyce's stay in Trieste.

József, Attila (1905–37) Tormented Hungarian poet, regarded as his country's greatest of this century. József was a manic-depressive, an 'impossible' man most of whose goodness and acute awareness went into his poetry; he was terrified of the madness that encroached upon him and brilliantly (though, for him, sacrificially) identified it with his rotten and menacing age. In his poetry he heroically sought to discover and to purge his sense of guilt (which was partly of erotic origin, but also arose from his inability to form stable relationships) and to achieve some form of affirmation. But he finally threw himself under the wheels of one of the heavy freight trains whose iron industrial world he had explored in his earlier poetry—a victim of a cruel century as much as of his own unfortunate chemistry, which he had after all dedicated to a search for meaning. He quarrelled with most people; only in his poetry did he pursue a coherent path. Influenced by Marx and Freud (q.v.), he embraced for a time a sort of nonconformist communism, but he was too intelligent to adhere for long to any single political dogma. Like most death-ridden poets he was a prophet: implicit in his poetry is not only a realization that the more or less oppressed proletariat would eventually gain control but also a vision of a tyrannical 'Marxist' future —embodied in a realization of the importance of the integrity of the individual. His psychoanalysis collapsed when he fell in love with the analyst and was rejected by her. He was influenced by Ady (q.v.) and by French poetry ('A Tired Man', in *Selected Poems,* tr. 1973, clearly shows the influence of Rimbaud's 'Sensation') directly when he spent a few months at the Sorbonne. The Marxism that succeeded his youthful anarchism did not much encroach on his poetry: he describes the urban world of the workers with a sympathy that is basically apolitical and the huge impersonality of industry both repels and fascinates him; he anticipates, in such a poem as 'A Fine Summer Evening' (also in *Selected Poems*), the helplessness felt by the liberal socialist trapped within extremisms and enmeshed in a corrupt capitalism that he cannot now be certain is humanly replaceable. József was profoundly influenced by his country's folk-poetry but (in the manner of the mature Bartók in music) this is absorbed in his best poems. He is seen at his greatest in such late poems as 'Ode' (in *Selected Poems*), in which the folk element is wholly and fruitfully assimilated and in which a serenity of mood emanates from a masculine erotic anguish. Though deeply disturbed, as a man József is intelligent and—one can only thus state it—violently sensitive; he well understood, as Rilke (q.v.) did, the existential price paid for artistic heroism. His command of form and handling of Hungarian are masterly and enable him to achieve the combination of pellucid lyricism and deep thought that only a very few other twentieth-century poets (cf., e.g., Vallejo, Hagiwara, Rilke, Riding, Lorca, Guillén, Machado, Quasimodo, Valéry, qq.v.) have attained. In his poetry all the seminal threads of our century are gathered together and he is still a poet of the future. Against his death must be measured the 'miraculous' (Gömöri) last poetry.

Juhász, Ferenc (1928) Hungarian poet regarded as the best of his generation; he has achieved international standing. He has great power and passion but is recklessly uneven and seems sometimes to be straying into an inchoate rhetoric. Veins of cruelty and tenderness mix interestingly in his poetry (of which there are a number of selections in English), but are not resolved or examined. His best poems—usually short—draw on folklore, and retain a lucid visionary coherence. The precariousness of existence in Hungary helps him to struggle against the sense of ugly violence that sometimes possesses his poetry.

Jung, Carl (1875–1961) Swiss inventor of 'analytical psychology'. At first he cooperated with Freud (q.v.) but soon broke away. Although safe in neutral Switzerland, he took a pro-Nazi and anti-semitic line for a short time after 1933. His confused system is essentially an uncritical and ill-digested *mélange* of Oriental mysticism, medieval alchemy and other such manifestations (all of importance in themselves) grafted onto an over-simplified 'classical' Freudianism from which the concept of a libido as sole source of life-urges has been removed. His very early work is brilliant; his later is ill-written, ill-organized, interesting and with more than a dash of charlatanism. Nevertheless, some of his own concepts (developed out of his vast and not always deep investigations into past systems) have influenced writers: 'anima', female-in-the-male; 'animus', male-in-the-female; 'shadow', a reformulation of Freud's dysfunctional id; 'archetypes', perpetual symbols of the truth about the psyche of man (racial, historical, religious and so on)—this 'truth' is that there is a 'collective unconscious', with which the individual has to learn to come to terms by 'individuation', which process (many have become incurably insane by trying to achieve it with the help of medically unqualified quacks) involves harmonization of opposing elements in the personality and the full acceptance of the psychic collective. The system as a whole is incomprehensible; many of the concepts are valid. The voluminous works are mostly available in English (1953–).

Jünger, Ernst (1895) German novelist, prose writer. He ran away from home at seventeen to join the Foreign Legion, spent a few weeks in Africa and was then brought back by his father, a prosperous chemist and later the owner of a pharmaceutical factory. These youthful adventures were recounted in *Afrikanische Spiele* (1936; tr. *African Diversions,* 1954). At nineteen he joined the German army and saw four years of active and heroic service. His popular *In Stahlgewittern* (1920; tr. *The Storm of Steel,* 1929; but definitively revised, 1942—this version not tr.) is vitalist, glorying in the ecstasy of violence, but in a precise, aesthetic, candid, freezing prose. After the war he studied zoology (1923–5) and interested himself in botany and geology—in stillness. Jünger is, as a critic has rightly claimed, concerned above all 'with the exclusion of pain'. He is an important, instructive, skilful, humourless and repulsive writer. Part of his skill lies in the completeness of his disingenuousness: his project is to turn men into *things,* to establish a rigid order that he pretends is a 'truth' beyond the nihilism and chaos that have all but destroyed our century. But that 'truth' involves a ripping-out, from the body of existence, of the human heart. He was involved in politics until 1933, as the advocate of a fascist-communist movement in which idealized 'workers' would form a disciplined élite, subduing by technocratic power and force the disturbances of instinct (*Die Arbeiter,* 1932, *The Workers*). He also advocated 'freedom' as a part of this plan.

But this was simply obtuse: the system is totalitarian. The Nazis (also advocates of 'freedom') took over his ideas and he did not object, though he was too aristocratic to join their party. *Das abenteuerliche Herz* (1929; rev. 1936), *The Adventurous Heart,* and *Blätter und Steiner* (1934), *Leaves and Stones,* contain his most original writing: essays on things and dreams in which he uses a de-anthropomorphizing technique to bring himself, not to peace, but to indifference. The attempt is intellectually remarkable and in many ways anticipates Robbe-Grillet and the *nouveau roman* (*see* Robbe-Grillet) by more than twenty-five years. But though Jünger has no heart, no love, little pity, he has a kind of intellectual conscience. The intellect, if it could function alone, has an inevitable consistency: a type of honesty. He therefore turned to the novel form in *Auf den Marmorklippen* (1939; tr. *On the Marble Cliffs,* 1947), to produce what is usually taken as an allegorical protest against Nazidom, which, but in a peculiar sense, it does amount to being: in 1940 the Nazis stopped it being printed after 35,000 copies had been sold. Jünger rejoined his beloved army, was in Paris 1940–2, in Russia for three months 1942–3, and then back in Paris again. In July 1944 he refused to take part in the July Plot against Hitler; in October he was discharged from the army; in the following month his son Ernestel was killed. He then completed the clandestinely circulated *Der Friede* (1943; tr. *The Peace,* 1948), anti-Hitlerian but still totalitarian in spirit; in one of his diary collections, *Strahlungen* (1949; French tr. *Journal,* 1949), *Rays,* he tries to discuss the problem of pain, but more cleverly than movingly. Like Benn (q.v.), he refused to be 'de-Nazified'. *Heliopolis* (1949; French tr. 1952) is a portentous Utopian failure on the same allegorical theme. *Gläserne Bienen* (1957; tr. *The Glass Bees,* 1961) seems to continue an ostensible movement towards Christianity, but this is specious. Even in the memoirs, *Subtile Jagden* (1967), *Subtle Fighter,* Jünger has to invent all feeling. His most recent novel, *Die Zwille* (1973), *The Slingshot,* a (doubtless) semi-autobiographical account of the childhood and adolescence of an orphan boy, tries to bring in humour and colloquialese and to avoid the portentously allegorical but characterization—as always—fails, and all that is really convincing is the bestial act that provides the title. As a whole, his non-fiction is superior to his fiction, which is not convincing at any level; a courageous man, a vile writer, he is also evilly seminal. It is fair to say that he ultimately opposed Nazism; it is equally fair to say that he never opposed it except with an essentially totalitarian ideology. He is an aristocratic enemy of all life, unmellowable: ripeness for him could never be more than either nothing or the ecstasy of carnage—a rottenness while the fruit is still hard and sour. *Werke* (1960–3).

K

Kafka, Franz (1883–1924) Czech novelist, diarist and short-story writer. Kafka, of a German-speaking Jewish family, was a subject of the Austro-Hungarian Empire until 1919, born in Prague and lived and worked there for most of his life. He published more (seven small books, and in magazines) and was rather better known (at least among writers) in his lifetime than is generally supposed: in 1915 he was awarded the Fontane Prize for 'The Stoker', which became the first chapter of his novel *Amerika*. Two other legends, more misleading, should also be corrected at the outset: he had a fairly varied sex-life, including whores and mistresses and he also had a lively, companionable, non-neurotic social side to him, which often manifested itself. Kafka allowed his strong-willed, self-made father, the owner of a wholesale haberdashery warehouse, to dominate his life (it is usually put the other way round). Had he survived the tuberculosis that struck him in 1917, he would perhaps have suffered the fate of his three younger sisters, all murdered in Nazi camps. Kafka studied law ('a profession which will give the widest scope for . . . indifference'); in 1908 he became employed by a Workers' Accident Insurance Institute–this involved morning work only but most afternoons were spent in his father's warehouse instead of at writing. Kafka's own spinelessness against his authoritarian father drove him near to suicide. But he was not to escape from clerical drudgery until death had marked him out. He became engaged to a girl, broke it off, became engaged to her again; then he became engaged to another girl (1919), which he also broke off and only in 1923 did he meet Dora Dymant, twenty years his junior, who lived with him in Berlin and Prague and stayed by his side until his death in a sanatorium near Vienna. It is safe to assert that Kafka is so seminal a writer because he lacks serenity to exactly the degree to which his century lacks it. Yet his prose style is best described as serene: calm to a terrible degree. He asked his close friend and future biographer, the novelist

Max Brod (1884–1968), to destroy all his unpublished work (all but one volume of the six that made up his collected works, *Gesammelte Schriften,* 1935–7, later superseded by the nine-volume edition of 1950–8), yet all of it is concerned with what I have elsewhere characterized as *Künstlerschuld,* artist-guilt, and with the huge implications of this theme. All his writings–letters and diaries as well as fiction–are deliberately creative; his real guilt quite transcends his Oedipal feelings, expressed in the undelivered letter to his father, *Brief an den Vater* (1919), translated in 1954 as *Dearest Father, Stories and Other Writings* (1954). Although, as Georges Bataille shrewdly observed, 'what he really wanted was to live within the paternal sphere–*as an exile*', although he desperately desired his uncomprehending father to comprehend him, although he desired his approval–still, despite the 'father = Father = God' equation (as Heinz Politzer has put it) in his work, despite his bug-like dependence (he thus depicts himself in his famous 'Die Verwandlung', 'The Metamorphosis'), his true project is to examine why literature is a crime. The subject of his own literature, which he wanted blotted from existence, is literature. Like all originals, he subtly but fully reflects the spirit of his time–a nerve-shot one. He was influenced by Flaubert, Jewish fables, the magnificence of Prague, Freud (q.v.), Goethe–and above all by his quadruple alienation: from his Jewishness, his Czech identity (as a German speaker), his family and from his own potentiality to lead a full life. The best of his work is in the shorter fiction, particularly that of the last years ('Investigations of a Dog', 'A Hunger Artist', 'The Burrow'); and in the unfinished *Das Schloss* (1926), *The Castle.* Like the German-speaking Czech Rilke (q.v.), his near contemporary, he is torn between art (which reveals life) and life (which rejects the solitariness, selfishness, lovelessness of the dedicated artistic condition). Unlike Rilke, however, he cannot find full faith in his writing: therefore his life, for all but a few brief moments, is even more wretched and guilt-ridden. Everyone in Kafka is functional, he is tragically uninterested in character: all are mysteriously in the right, trying him for the crime of human insufficiency, for dedication to inadequate words. Josef K in *Der Prozess* (1925), *The Trial,* is being tried for nothing he can specify but he feels guilty and is executed. Karl Rossmann in *Amerika* (1927), *America,* is punished for *allowing himself to be seduced;* and despite the relatively comic surface of the book, it remained tragically unfinished because Kafka wanted to end it on a note of reconciliation and could not do it. As for the castle in the again unfinished novel of that name, Kafka's greatest: ultimately this, too, is reconciliation: the possibility of being a writer *and* being a full human being, who has a family and a human function. K, the protagonist who is an arrogant imposter, a liar (for the people at the castle have never sent for him and do not know him), an erotic confidence man, would (had he ever reached the castle) have had to become not a letter, a symbol, a fraudulent official (land-surveyor), but a whole man with a name: Franz Kafka. But the castle is unknown, mysterious: it is death (to be real), it is God (to believe in whom is the death of artistically autonomous scepticism), it is the stupid father appealed to as wise, the father of the child. Kafka reveals to us, with the wistful and terrifying quality of dreams, the nature of the fabulous. He remains a child but is too serious to play: he is in terrible earnest, he who could see himself only as adult, real, in the form of a beetle—or as mere letters denoting men guilty, afraid, insufficient, incomplete. Almost all Kafka's work has appeared in English; the best brief introductions are by Walter H. Sokel, *Franz Kafka* (1966) and Günther Anders, *Kafka* (1960). See also Elias Canetti's *Kafka's Other Trial* (1974).

Kaiser, Georg (1878–1945) Prolific German expressionist (*see* Stadler) playwright; also novelist, poet. His once famous characterless dramas (e.g. *Die Bürger von Calais,* 1914, *The Burghers of Calais;* the trilogy *Gas,* 1917–19, pt. tr. *Twenty-Five Modern Plays,* 1931) have now dated badly, but he was a skilful theatrical technician. He went to Switzerland in 1938. His first staccato plays (he wrote seventy in all) are influenced by Wedekind (q.v.) and Sternheim; in the later ones he abandoned his stridently 'artistic' and socio-critical attitude (himself an ex-businessman, in 1921 he sold his landlord's furniture and put forward the excellent but unsuccessful defence that he was an artist and needed the cash) for a more subjective one but the results were conventionally 'well-made' rather than self-revelatory because his limitation was that, despite his own wishes, he could as a writer only interest himself—usually naively—in ideas, and never in human psychology. He remains an important historical figure. There is a selection from his massive output in *Stücke, etc.* (1966).

Kassák, Lajos (1887–1967) Important Hungarian poet, editor and novelist, born in what is now Czechoslovakia, he wandered about Europe as a young man—for example, he came under the influence of

Marinetti (q.v.) in Italy. Called both a 'working-class author' and 'chief representative of Hungarian abstract literature', he is a more complex personality than either judgement immediately suggests. He was also a painter. To the liberal humanism of Babits's (q.v.) *Nyugat* group he opposed principles of expressionism, socialist-futurism and political activism. His Whitmanesque verse extols the world of the proletariat, yet he is not a real Marxist and was never a socialist realist (*see* Gorky). His massive autobiography *Egy ember élete* (1927–34), *Life of a Man,* is possibly his most enduring work. His critical polemic, in his various magazines, is abstract; but his best work is concrete.

Kavafis, Konstantinos (1863–1933) Greek poet (often known as Cavafy or Kavafy). Kavafis, the greatest Greek poet of the century and one of the greatest in any language, never spent long in Greece. He spent much of his childhood (1872–8) in England—his English was perfect—and lived his life, a homosexual with a 'dishonourable' code, in Alexandria as an Egyptian civil servant. His early poems were romantic, pessimistic, and disowned by him. In 1896, however, he began to produce sets of small pamphlets for private circulation. A really good text of all his poems was not produced until the *Poiemata* of 1963. There are translations into French (*Poèmes,* 1947; *Poèmes,* 1958; *Présentation critique,* 1958), Italian (*Poesie,* 1961), German (*Gedichte,* 1953) and English (1951; 1961; sel. in *Six Poets of Modern Greece,* 1960—the best—and *Passions and Ancient Days,* 1971). Kavafis was a lonely, disgusted, learned man, much prone to beauty and sadness at its passing; he was not at all influenced by the Greek poetry of his time. His work as a whole, which brilliantly mixes elements of the archaic and the demotic, is a blend of his ironic philosophical determinism, his (again ironical) historical sense (he often invents characters, and the period he concentrates on is classical) and his utterly candid homosexuality. He first became internationally famous when Forster (q.v.) wrote on him in 1919. His technique is free but his lines are so carefully weighted that no one could describe them as free verse. His attitude is pagan, resigned; his theme is, astonishingly exactly, himself: a lonely homosexual in Alexandria describing his interest in Byzantium and Greece, his own (aristocratic) forbears, his memories of his nocturnal love-encounters with beautiful youths, his guilt at his erotic propensities—from which he insisted, however, that not only his own but all good poetry emanated. He was a great holder-forth, often on the oddest of ancient subjects, at café-tables. He found a disturbing correlation between his own sexual decadence (his particular approach to his homosexuality, which was paedophilic, was decadent) and the decline both of the societies he loved and of his own family. He was perhaps the most unrespectable poet of the century yet in his work memory, regret, function as a profound guilt. 'Immersed in terror and suspicion,/with mind deranged, and cringing eyes,/we liquefy, we scheme actions/to evade the ineluctable danger/so horrifyingly threatening us.' His poetry is often paradoxical in this manner; at other times it presents, often dramatically, a view of history in which, beneath a cynical and stoical mask, there is a sense of great grief. His acceptance of his sense of self-nausea, magnificently styled, is heroic.

Kavanagh, Patrick (1905–67) Irish poet and miscellaneous prose writer. Kavanagh, one of Dublin's great drinking characters, rejected his earlier literary self, but in his prose (*Collected Prose,* 1967) he was never altogether able to cast off the stage-Irishry for which he condemned himself. The exception is the autobiographical novel *Tarry Flynn* (1948; 1965), a commercial failure but a convincing and moving picture of the Irish countryside from which Kavanagh, once a farmer, had come. His first significant poem was the long and bitter *The Great Hunger* (1942), a powerful and indignant account of the privations of an Irish farmer and his sister. His earlier poems are mostly lyrical and often trite but it is mistaken to assert that he failed to develop. The poems he wrote in the last decade of his life (he long suffered from precarious health, having had a lung removed as a result of cancer) are, though uneven and sometimes self-indulgent, more mature and reflective, and intelligently and wittily explore his sexual predicament and his partly frustrated desire to disengage himself from his stage-Irish past. These later poems are less 'simple' than they appear and at their best are a notable statement of his loneliness and poetic pride. Usually Austin Clarke (1896–1974) is taken to be the best of the Irish poets after Yeats (q.v.), but Kavanagh at the height of his power is as good: not as critically intelligent, but more direct, less pointlessly eccentric and less narrow. *Collected Poems* (1964).

Kawabata Yasunari (1899–1972) Japanese fiction writer. Nobel Prize 1968. His suicide was but the culmination of his death-haunted fiction and was, in Japanese terms, entirely logical. He deals delicately in the hopeless-erotic (often in its fantasy form) and the nostalgic; in his fiction the love-project is either ineluctably swallowed up in tender memory or is doomed by its own bizarre form, which none the less possesses mysteries which, always nebulously, hint at fulfilment. He sees reality as a rose which, still perfectly formed, is actually just about to collapse into its individual petals: he will contemplate it lovingly, but then apply the single destructive touch. *House of the Sleeping Beauties* (tr. 1969) collects three of his more grotesque stories: sexual desire is here reduced to a helpless perversity, an incurable sickness in the male, or, if he rejects that, an involuntary evasion. There is a strong Western influence (Kawabata studied English literature), but this is unobtrusive. The early story 'Izu no odoriko' (1925; tr. 'The Izu Dancer', *Atlantic Monthly*, CXCV, 1955) examines his own infatuation for an itinerant dancer with a tremulous, detached psychological precision. For Kawabata atmosphere and landscape—in his longer fiction—evoke mood, and mood is almost always death-obsessed. *Yukiguni* (1937; tr. *The Snow Country*, 1957) obliquely hints at regret for the old Japan but concentrates on a straightforward description of a love affair. *Sembaruzu* (1949–51; tr. *Thousand Cranes*, 1959), which is the first part of an unfinished work, once again hints that sexual neuroticism (if not unrelieved by contemplation of landscape) lies at the heart of all behaviour. Kawabata is a cunning, perverse, lyrical writer, who deliberately adapts Western techniques (e.g. surrealism, *see* Breton) to make them seem innately Japanese—he had a point. His fiction is uniformly melancholy and depressed and only its insistence on the human capacity to enjoy transitory beauty prevents it from being wholeheartedly decadent. He lacks the substance and the versatility of Tanizaki (q.v.), to whom he owes much, but his sad and gossamer touch is unique. He was the mentor of Mishima Yukio (q.v.), whom he overrated; the latter's suicide may have been a factor in his own.

Kazantzakis, Nikos (1883–1957) Greek (Cretan) novelist, poet, playwright, critic, translator (e.g. Dante), essayist, journalist, travel writer, philosopher, politician. Kazantzakis outdid even his friend (and sometimes enemy) Angelos Sikelianos (1884–1951) in his syncretism, for in his enormous and ever-changing philosophy he incorporated more or less all known strands of thought. He was in particular influenced by Bergson (q.v.), under whom he studied. For most of his life he was on the move. He could well grasp the nature of a people, a system, or a religion, but he could never express himself with any great depth. Although influenced by Marx and Lenin, and perpetually anxious to reconcile communism with other political systems, he himself was a socialist. Just after the Second World War he was a minister for a short time. The chief influence upon him, as on so many, was Nietzsche, whose unbelief and fascination with the person of Christ he shared. His *chef d'oeuvre* is his massive poem *I Odysseia* (1938; tr. *The Odyssey,* 1959), which is in 33,333 lines. In this colourful 'modern sequel' he attempted to bolster up the nihilism towards which he always tended by a complete and intuitive reinterpretation of the Homeric experience in modern terms. It is better read in scraps, together with such an analytical synopsis as Kimon Friar gives in his translation. For Kazantzakis's conception of Odysseus is not uninteresting: he sees him in varying aspects, as crook, hero, existentialist wanderer, religious man, nihilist robot–in short, as confused modern man uneasily trapped in the lost certainties of his past and finally driven into a repudiation of his human identity. It is a pity that Kazantzakis could not discover an acceptable linguistic means of presenting this. His best books are his (generally) later, popular ones, such as the famous *Vios Kai Politeia Tou Alexi Zorba* (1946; tr. *Zorba the Greek,* 1952), which, though in some ways sensationalist, has genuine vigour and understanding of its subject. This and the autobiographical *Anafora Ston Greco* (1961; tr. *Report to Greco,* 1965) are his finest novels, though there is much excellent material in his many travel books. He has been extensively translated. Kazantzakis is a complex man, but he was not a fulfilled artist, because he found it necessary to harness a too great degree of too coarse energy to enterprises planned to neutralize the despair at the core of his existence: his complexity is never fully crystallized in his work.

Kemal, Yaşar (1922) Turkish realist novelist. He is the best known Turkish writer outside his own country for *Ince Memed* (1958; tr. *Memed, My Hawk,* 1961) and *Ortadirek* (1961; tr. *The Wind from the Plain,* 1962). The first is about a man who tries unsuccessfully to rouse his village into revolt, the second describes the lives of the poor peasants of the Taurus Mountains who descend into the valleys for the cotton harvest. Kemal is well versed in folk-lore, and is an excellent storyteller. *Ince Memed II* (1969; tr. *They Burn the Thistles,* 1973) is a lurid sequel to *Ince Memed.*

Kerouac, Jack (ps. Jean-Louis Kerouac) (1922–69) American (of French-Canadian parentage) novelist, writer. Kerouac was one of those at the centre of the Beat (*see* Ginsberg) movement–really, then, an exploiter of an already well established sociological phenomenon–and he was another of those (cf. Burroughs, q.v.) to be partially 'invented' by Ginsberg. His first novel, *The Town and the City* (1950), pastiche of Thomas Wolfe (q.v.), is his best, and it is poor. The self-consciously Beat narrative, *On the Road* (1957), was typed on long rolls of art-paper and reads like it. He then turned to a vulgarized 'Zen' (this reaches its low in *Satori in Paris,* 1966) and to an unfortunately sustained series of self-indulgent reminiscences in both fictional and non-fictional form. None the less, Kerouac became a cult-hero, and the nature of his unhappiness is disturbing. He went back home in order to drink himself to death. *Doctor Sax* (1959); *Big Sur* (1962).

Kesey, Ken (1935) American novelist, LSD preacher, felon. He was a wrestler, then took to nursing in a mental hospital. He, Neal Cassady–the erstwhile associate of Kerouac (q.v.) and Ginsberg (q.v.)–and the 'Mad Pranksters' started up an LSD cult. His *One Flew Over the Cuckoo's Nest* (1962) is an ill-organized but comic and energetic satire on bureaucratic attitudes; the over-large *Sometimes a Great Notion* (1964) is a pretentious and surprisingly simple-minded attempt to write a heroic-naturalist (*see* Zola) saga set in the North-West. Kesey, although ignorant and socially dangerous on the subject of drugs, is a gifted comic writer. In 1966, after he had been on the run for some time, the FBI arrested him and he was, unfortunately, sent to prison.

Kesten, Hermann (1900) German novelist, critic, memoirist. One of the few distinguished writers who emerged out of the 'Neue Sachlichkeit' ('new objectivity') movement of the twenties. He left Germany in 1933, took American citizenship, and now lives in Rome. He is a skilled, relatively straightforward writer, with a strong sense of character. *Die Zwillinger von Nürnberg* (1947; tr. *The Twins of Nuremberg,* 1946), about the fortunes of a family between the ends of the two wars, is outstanding amongst his intelligent, ironic fiction. *Gesammelte Werke* (1958) collects some of his output.

Keyes, Sidney (1922–43) English poet who failed to return from the famous raid in which Rommel was nearly captured. For a time Keyes was believed to have been the greatest loss sustained by English poetry in the Second World War, but he was inferior to Alun Lewis (1915–44) and Douglas (q.v.). It is impossible to tell what he might have achieved but his surviving poems (*Collected Poems*, 1945) are mostly overderivative (e.g. Eliot, Rilke, the mythological interests of his friend Heath-Stubbs), ill-accomplished and immaturely neo-romantic in the forties manner. There are, however, some striking lines, such as the conclusion of the poem about Timoshenko, who 'made the pencilled map alive with war'.

Khlebnikov, Velimir (ps. Viktor Khlebnikov) (1885–1922) Russian poet, critic, dramatist, wanderer, founder of (Russian) futurism (*see* Mayakovsky). He was initially inspired by the painter David Burlyuk, who later went to America. By 1913 he had become concerned with the foundation of a new 'transrational' language: in the so-called *zaum* new meanings would be created simply out of the sound of each element of the word. There is an affinity with symbolism here, though Khlebnikov would have vehemently denied this; it is in any case an element in all true poetry, even if it exists as only a kind of ghostly entity, a hint of an extra meaning. Khlebnikov worked closely with Alexei Kruchonykh (1886), but was vastly more serious and gifted than that lively innovator. He did not work out his system fully until after the revolution. Khlebnikov is probably the greatest of all genuinely *avant-garde* poets; he believed, interestingly, that *sound* had a definite relationship to *meaning*—and, strangely, his poetry (a good deal of which is lost) seems to prove that this is indeed true. He was an admirer of H. G. Wells (q.v.). At heart he was a Platonist with a vision of the achievement of a perfect world in which people would understand one another; but even anti-Platonists can hardly resist his poetry, which eventually became quite lucid—because he saw that his experimentation had been no more than a gloss on the omnipresent properties of poetry. His vision—scientific, sophisticated, Slavic, pre-historic, anti-Western, pagan, primitivist—is transcended by his imaginative achievement and his courageous poetry continues to exert a strong influence. He was found dead of starvation at the side of a lonely country road, after having made an exhausting journey to Persia. Vladimir Markov's *The Longer Poems* (1962) is a loving selection, with introduction, in English; much authoritative information on him may be discovered in Markov's exhaustive *Russian Futurism* (1968).

King, Francis (1923) English novelist, poet and travel writer. King travelled extensively as a British Council representative, and his delicate and sometimes atmospherically menacing novels are usually set outside England. He is one of the very few English novelists to have been influenced by Japanese writers; Soseki (q.v.) is the most evident of these. He first became noticed as a poet (*Rod of Incantation*, 1952). One impulse behind his writing is the kind of terrified conservatism that L. P. Hartley (q.v.) made too explicit, but King is more reticent and exercises a more intelligent control. He deals with wounded, vulnerable, puzzled people who are quiet in their suffering; with sexual ambiguity, which pervades his books; with the effects of foreign atmospheres on the English. His unobtrusive strength lies in subtlety. One of the most moving of his novels is *The Last of the Pleasure Gardens* (1965), about a middle-aged mother and her relationship with her defective child. *The Man on the Rock* (1957) is a memorable portrait of a man made morally vulnerable by his very attractiveness. King has published three collections of short stories, including *The Brighton Belle* (1968).

Kinnell, Galway (1927) American poet, novelist. Kinnell is a deeply serious and self-critical poet, continually in search of a valid style: one which would combine his native lyricism with his quasi-mystical sense of the true American tradition, whose mysteries press continually on his consciousness. He began by writing in traditional forms, then he broke these up and tried to re-combine them in 'concealed' forms of his own. Later, in the fifties, he came under the influence of French poetry (he has translated not only the whole of Villon but also some of Bonnefoy, q.v., who has influenced his own practice). He now uses free verse, and seems to be in a process of dissatisfied wandering: he seldom achieves the sustained concentration he seeks, although there are powerful passages in his poetry, and much of the 'deep imagery' one finds in Bly (q.v.) and others. *What a Kingdom it Was* (1960); *Body Rags* (1968). *Black Light* (1966) is a novel.

Kinsella, Thomas (1928) Irish poet (now resident in America as Professor at the University of Southern Illinois), regarded as the most important of his generation. He is a highly accomplished and thoughtful poet, who has much genuine feeling. But he has not yet been able to shake off sufficiently the influences of Eliot (q.v.), Wilbur (q.v.) and other Parnassian-type poets. He can produce exciting and moving lines but the reader is too often bogged down in a sly, unobtrusive, muted-Bardic rhetoric. His early poems (*Poems,* 1956; *Another September,* 1958) are to be preferred, since his need to probe at his romantic feelings produced an energy that compensated for his over-literary deliberation (*Nightwalker and Other Poems,* 1968).

Kipling, Rudyard (1865–1936) English (born in Bombay) fiction writer, poet, journalist. Nobel Prize 1907. Kipling was sent to England in 1871; he spent seven miserable years in the care of a sadistic, pious female relative, which left an indelible mark on him. It was a relief when he went to school at Westward Ho! At seventeen he was back in India, working for a Lahore newspaper. By 1892, the year of *Barrack Room Ballads,* he was already famous for his poems and stories of Indian service life (e.g. *Plain Tales from the Hills,* 1888; *Soldiers Three,* 1888). He married in 1892 an American woman with whose brother he was (unconsciously) in love; he lived unhappily in America until 1896. His confused sexuality disturbed Kipling, causing him to experience an undefined sense of guilt which is partly responsible for the strange power of his finest short stories. In 1895 he refused the Laureateship and later he refused the OM. From 1902 until his death he lived in a Jacobean house in Sussex, suffering for much of that time from bad health and bad nerves. After the First World War (in which he lost, in 1915, a son) his reputation began to decline and at the time of his death he was detested by most critics (though not readers) as an arch-imperialist. Kipling's political ideas, when he makes them explicit, need not be taken seriously: they hardly have the status of ideas. Kipling worshipped the idea of action, and longed to be 'in' on every kind of male 'mystery': how to run trains, boats, machines, empires and so on. This made him feel safe. He tended to see women as destroyers (as in his unsatisfactory novel *The Light that Failed,* 1890, in which he revenges himself on the cruel female guardian of his childhood and obliquely protests at his obligation to 'fall in love' with a member of the opposite sex). But when Kipling's women are imagined from the feminine side of himself, which in life he fiercely protected, they are magnificent, as in the great short story 'Mrs Bathurst'. His racism is innocent enough–but few of his detractors can believe that a man of genius can also be a blind idiot when his genius is not working. As a poet Kipling is a minor, much of whose work is spoiled by a crude and over-simplifying rhetoric. But it often has a *frisson:* there is an energy, sometimes macabre or sado-masochistic, behind some of the most unacceptably jingoistic of his ballads. He had metrical skill but seldom showed any delicacy of rhythm. There are a few interesting poems of bare statement in Kipling, some tender celebrations (not observations) of the countryside, and such repulsive, horrifying but fascinating ballads as 'Danny Deever'. His poems on the whole profit from being read aloud. He is not, as is so often stated, Britain's greatest master of the short story–George Moore (q.v.), for one, is superior–but he comes near to it. His children's books (e.g. *The Jungle Book,* 1894; *Puck of Pook's Hill,* 1906; *Rewards and Fairies,* 1910) display a gift for significant anthropomorphism and a capacity to make the supernatural seem natural (which, of course, it is). The novel *Kim* (1901) is excellent only so long as one does not question the Indian framework in which it takes place. This leaves his 'adult' short stories, amongst which his greatest work is to be found. As his ideas became fiercer and increasingly naive (from the Boer War onwards), so his fiction strengthened in intensity. The finest stories appear in *Traffics and Discoveries* (1904), *Actions and Reactions* (1909), *Debits and Credits* (1926), *Thy Servant a Dog* (1930) and *Limits and Renewals* (1932): the real, imaginative Kipling of these volumes, when (but only when) the artist is in control, has little to do with the imperialist. His method is the opposite of crude or cruel: it is both mysterious and experimental. 'Mrs Bathurst' (1902) is a famous, familiar and appropriate example of his highly effective method of 'suppressed narrative'. Kipling acknowledges the limits of his art: if there is a complete explanation, then this is resident in the complex symbolism (often including the names of the characters) of his tales. Kipling was a real poet, almost all of whose poetry presents aesthetic difficulties. But he is a major prose writer. He preserved within himself the innocence and oneiric commitment of a child; with this he could bring the world of the unconscious into sharp focus. Since he was intellectually wanting, and sometimes even loathsome (but this no longer matters), his complexity may surprise some readers. But the unconscious is itself complex. *Collected Works* (1937–9) is the definitive edition, as is the separate *Verse* (1940).

Koestler, Arthur (1905) Hungarian-Jewish (now English, 1945) novelist, playwright, autobiographer, prose writer, thinker. Koestler grew up in Vienna, went to Palestine and became a Zionist, joined the German communist party, left for France (1933), was condemned to death by the fascists while reporting the Spanish Civil War (*Spanish Testament,* 1937), and was then interned by the French (*Scum of the Earth,* 1941 rev. 1955) before escaping in 1940 to England. He was an active journalist and science writer in the late twenties and thirties. All Koestler's work until the novel *Arrival and Departure* (1943) was written in German, but was immediately translated. He saw into the nature of Soviet communism before most other members of the party, as his chief work, the novel *Darkness at Noon* (1940), amply demonstrates. This is the central and best of the trilogy of novels dealing with revolution: *The Gladiators* (1939) and *Arrival and Departure* form its outer layers. *Darkness at Noon,* perhaps initially suggested by the fate of Bukharin, is more imaginatively satisfying and therefore all the more terrifying as an analysis of Soviet (specifically Stalinist) inhumanity. It is a novel with overtones that can fairly be described as Dostoievskian; its tragic diagnoses remain topical. *Thieves in the Night* (1946) is a more documentary account of the fight of the Jews—the 'exposed nerve[s] of humanity'—for a country of their own. Since this time Koestler has mostly devoted himself to an acute examination, in a series of essays, of the differences and the resemblances between science, technology, and art, mysticism, the apparently paranormal. He has studied, among other things, ancient cultures damaged by a sudden access of technology (Japan, India), parapsychology, scientific dogmatism run wild into persecutory cruelty and inhumanity (*The Case of the Midwife Toad,* 1971) and the psychology of the British addiction to hanging (*Reflections on Hanging,* 1956). He has also written a play, *Twilight Bar* (1945). Some of his non-fiction writing is hurried and journalistic but he is an important thinker and a badly needed influence, whose painful experiences and sensitivity to cruelty have made him neither hysterical nor histrionic. His intellectual scope and grasp, and his sympathy with both rational and irrational approaches, make him a seminal and stimulating writer. *The Yogi and the Commissar* (1945) reflects on communism and democracy. *The Lotus and the Robot* (1960) is on East and West. Other important essays are in *The Sleepwalkers* (1959; pt. 4, *The Watershed,* 1960), a highly original historical study of the nature of scientific discovery, *The Act of Creation* (1964), *The Ghost in the Machine* (1967) and in the retrospective *Drinkers of Infinity* (1968). *Arrow in the Blue* (1952) and *The Invisi-*

ble Writing (1954) are autobiographical. His works, sometimes in revised versions, and with prefaces or postscripts, are being reissued in a 'Danube' edition (1965–).

Kraus, Karl (1874–1936) Austrian (a Jew born in mid-Bohemia) anti-journalist, playwright, poet, aphorist, essayist. He spent his adult life in Vienna. He is one of the most shamefully neglected of modern prophets and writers; in England Auden (q.v.) and Grigson (q.v.) have been almost alone in championing his work. There are four main reasons for his neglect: his major drama *Die letzten Tage der Menschheit* (1919; pt. tr. into English in *Poems*, 1930), *The Last Days of Mankind*, is immensely long, though never boring; he was a savagely effective satirist and parodist, who hurt permanently; he was fiercely independent, a journalist–he edited and wrote most of his own magazine *Die Fackel* (1899–1936), *The Torch*–who castigated his own profession; and he supported Dollfuss not because he liked him but because he thought he might save Austria from Nazidom, which lost him many friends (his attack on the Nazis, written 1932–3, was not published until 1952). The expressionists (*see* Stadler) regarded him as a mentor but he satirized their movement (though not those who were passing through it and were not merely a part of it). As a critic Kraus was concerned above all with the abuse of language by cliché, rhetoric and lack of imagination–and it was the so-called 'liberal' or 'moderate' writers who were his main target. He saw this as leading to just the kind of cataclysm to which it did lead. The highly colloquial and original language of *Die letzten Tage der Menschheit* tries to counterbalance this within the ironic framework of the history of the war years. He never questioned the value of a true language and is in this sense a rueful counterweight to later authors such as Beckett (q.v.); at the same time he is perhaps limited, as an imaginative writer, by his lack of curiosity about its real nature–he simply assumed that if it were properly handled (though he was not optimistic about this possibility) then it would be efficacious. Language was for him the 'crystallized spirit of the spirit of man', and his own native language he brilliantly characterized as the 'most profound of languages' but the 'most shallow of speeches'. His smashing-down of the Austrian equivalents of the Bernard Levins of his time resembled, F. M. Kuna has written, 'public executions'. And here perhaps he set his sights too low and, like

Wyndham Lewis (q.v.), with whom he has some affinities, he paid for it posthumously. *Gesammelte Werke,* 1952–66.

Kristensen, Tom (1893) Danish fiction writer, critic, poet and polemicist. Regarded as Denmark's leading expressionist (*see* Stadler) Kristensen, who was born in London but educated in Copenhagen, is essentially noisy and superficial—though he has exercised a beneficial influence and is a worthy figure. His novel *Hæværk* (1930; tr. *Havoc,* 1967) hardly deserves its 'classic' stature, though it is an accurate enough reflection of the unhappy and existentially directionless lives of Danish radicals and social rebels in the twenties. He began in the obvious enough vitalist ambience of the Nobel Prize winner Johannes Jensen (1874–1950) and Lawrence (q.v.), but his poems are empty. *Hæværk* is rather monotonously vitalist. His memoirs, *Fortielser* (1963–6) are an interesting and attractive source.

Kunitz, Stanley (1905) American poet whose considerable reputation has been confined—oddly—to a relatively few poets and critics; the recent publication of a volume—a retrospective selection, 1940–70—in Great Britain should make him more widely known: *The Terrible Threshold* (1974). *Selected Poems 1928–1958* (1958) appeared in Great Britain in 1959 but made no real impact. Much of Kunitz's life has been taken up with the editing of the H. W. Wilson bio-critical series of reference books such as *Twentieth Century Authors* (this began with *Living Authors,* 1931, in which the editor's name was given as 'Dilly Tante'; he once wrote 'I suffer the twentieth century . . . the nerves of commerce wither in my arm'. . . .); more recently he has made authoritative translations of important Russian poets, such as Mandelstam (q.v., see *Poets on Street Corners,* ed. Olga Carlisle, 1968). He has also been a university teacher. Kunitz is a poet superior to Lowell (q.v.) and one perhaps even more frightening (and more controlled) than Berryman (q.v.); he is less vain and more original than Lowell. From his first volume, *Intellectual Things* (1930) onwards, he was, for all his firmness and control, expressing the nightmarish jitteriness or agitated gibber seen, in various forms, in the more familiar poetry of Roethke (q.v.) and others. Later he was able to write in a more affirmatory manner—a manner won through the personal struggle with despair that the earlier poems movingly record. Kunitz's scope is wide but his viewpoint is always personal and even at their most dense and complex his poems have a lyrical charge. He has not, like Wilbur (q.v.) gone in for an essentially reactionary elegance; his own rhythms dominate the metrically impeccable lines. He is slowly but surely getting the recognition he deserves.

L

Lagerkvist, Pär (1891–1974) Swedish novelist, poet, dramatist. Nobel Prize 1951. Scandinavians overvalue their literature (this is not inevitable: the Dutch, for example, underrate theirs) and no better example of this habit could be found than in the vastly inflated reputation of Lagerkvist. He has styled himself a 'religious atheist' and the fault of his work is that it attempts to justify such grandiose philosophical conceptions when its author's undoubted gifts lie in quite another and more modest direction. He is markedly inferior to a number of Swedish writers of this century (e.g. Söderberg, q.v.). He began as a highly self-conscious expressionist whose ambition was to be Sweden's and the world's new Strindberg (q.v.); his example has been disastrous. His best work, written after a series of poems, plays and experimental prose, is *Gäst hos verkligheten* (1925; tr. *Guest of Reality,* with other works thrown in, 1936): this describes, often with sincerity, his upbringing and the conflict set up in him between love for his parents and rejection of their Christianity. This is in strong contrast to the opportunist, programmatic *Ordkonst och bildkonst* (1913), *Verbal and Visual Art,* a strangely confused but cleverly strident mishmash of modernist ideas, including cubism, Oriental religions and Icelandic sagas. After writing *Guest of Reality* Lagerkvist produced a large number of works in which, with various fashionable aids (e.g. *The Golden Bough*), he presented mankind as a battleground for good and evil. His most famous novels are *Dvärgen* (1944; tr. *The Dwarf,* 1953) and *Barabbas* (1950; tr. 1952). These are violent allegories in historical settings; the best passages, as in the earlier 'Bödeln' (1933; tr. 'The Hangman' in *Guest of Reality,* 1936), depict human bestiality. When writing of this aspect of existence Lagerkvist can attain great power but the 'vision' he constructed around his sense of it is specious and false. Seven of his plays are translated in *Modern Theatre: 7 Plays* (1966). *Ahasverus' död* (1960; tr. *The Death of A.,* 1962) is a novel.

Lagerlöf, Selma (1859–1940) Swedish fiction writer, educator, Nobel Prize 1909. Her early prose is enchanted and enchanting, though perhaps minor by international standards. Her best books are her first, *Gösta Berlings Saga* (1891; tr. *The Story of Gösta Berling,* 1898) and the children's travelogue (on the back of a goose) *Nils Holgerssons underbara resa* (1906–7; tr. *The Wonderful Adventures of Nils,* 1907; *Further Adventures,* 1911). Nearly all her novels and stories were translated into English. The strength of the early work lies in its combination of sociological accuracy and folk material. She possessed an intuitive understanding of the people of Värmland, where she grew up and although her capacity for complex symbolism has in recent years been exaggerated, her evocation of this world of the province towards the bottom of Eastern Sweden, on the border with Norway, is masterful. Later work, while entertaining, is vitiated by too great a reliance on the supernatural. In her last thirty years, the shrine of a foolish cult, a wavering and confused devotee of spiritualism, she declined into a defused sage—as the unfinished tetralogy known in England as the trilogy *The Ring of the Löwenskölds* (1925–8; tr. 1931) clearly demonstrates. A collected edition appeared in 1933. Her *Dagbok* (1932) was translated as *The Diary* (1936).

Lampedusa, Giuseppe Tomasi di (1896–1957) Italian (Sicilian) novelist. He came of a rich and aristocratic family and was a prince. He spent the kind of wild youth often associated with aristocrats, but later devoted himself to assiduous study. He wrote *Il gattopardo* (1958; tr. *The Leopard,* 1960) at the very end of his life and never knew the enormous fame it was to bring him. It is a brilliant historical novel set in the Sicily of the latter half of the nineteenth century and is based on extensive and deep knowledge. To its violent and decadent subject matter it brings a keen, detached intelligence, but not one which ever interferes with its enthralling atmosphere. *Racconti* (1961; pt. tr. *Two Stories and a Memory,* 1962).

Lardner, Ring (1885–1933) American fiction writer, humorist, sports writer, playwright, journalist, from Michigan. Lardner died young of tuberculosis (and of drink and heart complications), but had the extreme prolificity often associated with sufferers from this disease. His gifts were great; he anticipated many later literary developments; he has exercised a considerable and often unacknowledged influence. Lardner became famous through his *You Know Me, Al* (1916 rev. 1925) letters: these purport to be written by a moronic, vicious and mean 'busher' (newcomer to baseball), 'Jack Keefe', to his best friend. They are not more vile than human beings can actually be and Lardner's ear for midwest vernacular is masterly. He is on the whole a better short-story writer (*Collected Short Stories,* 1941) than even Hemingway (q.v.), who learned much from him. It is true that his scope is narrow: he seldom goes outside the realm of the horrible-as-funny—but his attack on the bourgeois mentality is so concentrated and so effectively sardonic as to compensate for the violence of his misanthropy. However, he was by no means as rancorous as is usually supposed and in some of his writing one can sense a feeling of real pity for a situation in which each sucker (one of his collections is called *Gullible's Travels,* 1917 rev. 1925) believes that life, and the other suckers, will really give him a break . . . There is present throughout an implication that an authentic self at least *ought* to exist. He hated sham because he loved the feeling honesty can generate. Much of his work is over-hasty and although he could not always solve the problem of working for two audiences (the undiscerning, who took him as a kind of Bill Nye; the discerning, who knew better), he remained close to life. Edmund Wilson (q.v.) asked: 'What bell might not Lardner ring if he set out to give us the works?' This question was asked in 1924—and Lardner did succeed in ringing a rather loud bell: his revisions of earlier work indicate that he was becoming aware of his problems. Unfortunately he spent much of his last decade in states of alternating alcoholism (of a type specific to TB sufferers) and suicidal depression; his achievement is therefore all the more remarkable (his friend Scott Fitzgerald—'Ring is my alcoholic'—who helped him as he helped so many others, said of him that he had 'stopped finding any fun in his work ten years before he died'). His autobiography, written just before he went into his final decline, is one of his best books: *The Story of a Wonder Man* (1927). Collections of stories followed it. Lardner's playlets (uncollected), once called 'skits', fitted in with a type of nonsense humour then popular in the USA (Fitzgerald himself wrote such a playlet in 1923); but, while one should not be solemn in drawing attention to their part in the ancestry of the Theatre of the Absurd (*see* Ionesco), they are amongst the best of this genre. *The Portable Ring Lardner* (1946); *The Ring Lardner Reader* (1963).

Larkin, Philip (1922) English poet, novelist, jazz critic. Larkin's early work, *The North Ship* (1945) and his novel *Jill* (1946), gained the admiration of his Oxford contemporaries Wain (q.v.) and Amis (q.v.), but no general attention. *The Less Deceived* (1955) suddenly established him as the most important of post-war English poets. It appeared at the height of the anti-romantic, anti-rhetorical reaction to the often inchoate poetry of the forties. This has been followed by *The Whitsun Weddings* (1964) and the slim *High Windows* (1974). His *Oxford Book of Modern Verse* (1973) was generally regarded as a disastrous potpourri; and while it certainly demonstrated his critical shortcomings, it also contained good poems that more fashion conscious editors might well have ignored (e.g. by Reeves, q.v., Sisson, q.v.). Clearly he is critically over-insular at a time when English poetry needs an infusion from abroad, and as clearly he lacks nerve. He wrote another sensitive novel: *A Girl in Winter* (1947). *All What Jazz* (1970) collects record reviews written in the sixties. Larkin's subject is self-deprecation, sexual defeat, decay. His most obvious masters are Hardy (q.v.) and Graves (q.v.). He is an authentic poet but a minor one—not, as has been claimed, of the calibre of Hardy or Graves. If he rejects foreign poetry and post-symbolism then this is because he does not critically understand them, or because, like most English poets, he cannot work theoretically. His subject-matter is narrow: the inadequacy of culture to sustain a sense of personal identity ('Books are a load of crap'), rueful contemplation of the emotional adventurousness of other people's sexual commitments—which are candidly envied though at the same time seen as sordid folly—the triteness of contemporary life. He cannot write a love poem and seems sometimes to write about himself as one constitutionally unable to risk loving, but he can be moving, as in 'High Windows', a poem which summarizes his own regrets but also beautifully affirms the necessity of confronting life. His output has dwindled considerably but the quality has remained consistent. It is true that Larkin as a critic has not realized that traditional procedures are no longer adequate; but he has the distinction of being the last Englishman to write a viable non-expressionist body of poetry. We should be grateful to and for him.

Lawrence, D. H. (1885–1930) English novelist, poet, critic, writer of miscellaneous prose, playwright. Lawrence has been one of the most influential figures in Anglo-American literature and life of this century.

Much in his writing is lovable and irresistible on any terms but his tiresomeness as a man also intrudes damagingly into it. He is full of insights, but as full of neurotic and unpleasant idiocies. Seen as a visionary, a 'visceral' thinker, Lawrence's wisdom, though incidental in a sea of wrong-headedness, does balance with his absurdities; but the best of his stories (with some poems) are on an eminence that rises above the rest. He was 'awful'–and he was 'marvellous'. His father was a rough Nottinghamshire miner; his mother had ambitions towards gentility, but both shared a bourgeois background. Lawrence never resolved his Oedipal feelings for his mother and it may be that her lack of intellectual quality infected his entire life-style. He studied to be a teacher, and taught for a while in Croydon. He even wrote, as 'L. H. Davison', a school textbook: *Movements in European History* (1921 rev. 1926). It was Ford (q.v.) who first encouraged him, by accepting some of his poems for *The English Review*. His novel *The White Peacock* appeared in 1911. His first important, and incomparably best, novel appeared in 1913: *Sons and Lovers*. All Lawrence's full-length novels are more or less flawed by sudden angry intrusions of *opinion* into the *imaginative* texture; this is the least so flawed. In it he attempts fairness to his unpretentious father–but his mother's (innocent enough, in all conscience) pretentiousness is less satisfactorily dealt with–and demonstrates, more convincingly, the destructiveness of technology; the pains of adolescence in a provincial setting are conveyed with tenderness and understanding. Lawrence's later novels are major failures: *The Rainbow* (1915; 1949), *Women in Love* (1920), *The Lost Girl* (1920), *Aaron's Rod* (1922), *Kangaroo* (1923), *The Plumed Serpent* (1926), *Lady Chatterley's Lover* (1928; 1961. *John Thomas and Lady Jane*, 1972, is the preferable second draft). The reasons for this are complex, for every one of them (even the notorious last-named has some excellently observed non-sexual passages) contains magnificent sections but are all marred by his own intrusions. Two of Lawrence's novels were suppressed (*The Rainbow, Lady Chatterley*) because they were reckoned to be over-explicit about physical sexual relationships. Lawrence's general explicitness about sexual matters had a vast educational and liberating value in the twenties and thirties. Unfortunately, however, his sexual program in itself was nagging, inept, ignorant and –ironically–puritanical. He was not, as some have asserted, constitutionally homosexual, nor was he what could truly be called ambi- or bisexual. But he found women difficult to understand and accept; this problem, exacerbated by his conflicts over his mother and father, caused him to become what might fairly be described as a man whose agonized heterosexuality was from time to time interrupted by bouts of homosexual feeling. Had he not been the self-styled 'priest of love' who intended to 'preach [his] heart out' (his great weakness was that he preached), and consequently a *soi-disant* sexual lawgiver, things might have turned out differently. He can hardly be called a misogynist; but misogyny is an element in his life, his feeling and his work. In 1910 his mother died of cancer—it is likely that he eased her passing by an overdose of morphine, thus taking upon himself a terrible psychological burden—and in 1912 he ran away with Frieda Weekley (*née* von Richtofen), the German wife of a Nottingham University professor; they married in 1914. Lawrence had left teaching and from now he began to travel almost ceaselessly. He lived in many places, including Italy (where he died) and Mexico. His health was always delicate, and from the early twenties (if not earlier) he suffered from the tuberculosis that killed him. His married relationship had its rewarding moments, but was strained and violent, and was by no means what Lawrence wanted or believed it to be; his novels, from the fourth *The Rainbow,* onwards, are all flawed by his false view of it and by his rationalization of his own inadequacies. Lawrence in his novels wrecks his often beautifully imagined world with raw, tiresome obtrusions: he suddenly preaches, he is exasperated, he wants to assert his sexual superiority over other men and men's (Lawrence's) sexual superiority over women. But at his best he is a uniquely beautiful and tender writer. His genius persisted until his death and when it surfaces it is intact: thus his best writing is in short compass—the story and the poem. His intellectual deterioration dates from the crisis of his mother's death. It was during the war that he began to go mad. From this time onwards he was always searching for what he had made his mother: as he told his first sweetheart, Jessie Chambers, he had always loved her 'like a lover'; no other woman would ever 'plunge her hands through [his] blood and feel for [his] soul, and make [him] set [his] teeth and shiver and fight away'. His sexual project was always to make his women into his mother, so that he could 'fight' them . . . Thus Lawrence's most moving writing in the area of human psychology is done in relaxed, undogmatic contemplation of his personal Oedipal situation—as in the poem 'Sorrow' (an experience also related in different form in *Sons and Lovers*) where his cigarette smoke reminds him of the 'long grey hairs' of his mother, 'a reprimand/To my gaiety'. But if Oedipal anxiety provided the more or less solid core of Lawrence's prose and poetry the scope of his sensibility is wider. 'The core of his mind was unsophisticated', wrote Norman Douglas; and so he saw and felt exactly the nature of the harm inflicted by industrialization on the old agricultural ways. When, as in many of the stories, he is relaxedly observing people he understands them marvellously, sympathetically, humorously, robustly, unpatronizingly. He has naked sensitivity and the language to match it. There are flashes of this in the novels, but each is a *roman à thèse*, and the thesis becomes progressively more pathological (this appears most clearly in *The Plumed Serpent*, a farrago of sick, protofascist mysticism). His earlier poems are his most substantial, but *Birds, Beasts and Flowers* (1923), though often marred by mawkishness and lack of technical control, contains much of permanent value. His plays, some of which have enjoyed recent stage revival, have been underrated at the expense of over-praise of *The Rainbow* and *Women in Love*. Not much of the abundant criticism of Lawrence presents a clear picture: critics are either hagiographers (there is, critically, more than a trace of this in Harry T. Moore's definitive and invaluable biography *The Priest of Love*, 1974), or Lawrence's ideas offer them personal erotic succour, or, less reprehensibly, they remain so entranced by the beauty of his trees that they cannot see the diseased wood. But if he is a tragic figure he is an indispensable one, who gave much that is inimitably precious to literature. *Works* (1954–7) includes three volumes of the stories. *Complete Poems* (1964). *Complete Plays* (1965). *Collected Letters* (1962). *Selected Literary Criticism* (1956) is a valuable selection.

Laxness, Halldór (1902) Icelandic novelist, essayist, poet, dramatist. Nobel Prize 1955. Laxness has been traveller, Roman Catholic convert, monk, and finally communist (of the Icelandic variety: Iceland accommodates the occult as easily as Marxism, which is well represented in its political life). He has been influenced by expressionism (*see* Stadler), Upton Sinclair (q.v.) and above all by the long history of his country. His fiction mixes the epic with the lyrical, the parodic, the symbolic and the satirical–and is not wholly integrated. He early broke away from the archaic tradition in Icelandic literature–and owed much to the example of the untranslated '*ofviti*' (overwise) Þórbergur Þórðarson (1889), who is perhaps the superior writer. Many of Laxness's novels have been translated into English. They vary from meticulous and moving accounts of twentieth-century fishermen or farmers (e.g. *Sjálfstætt folk,* 1934–5; tr. *Independent People,* 1945), through historical sagas–of these only the semi-parodic *Gerpla* (1952; tr. *Happy Warriors,* 1958) has been translated–to overtly satirical political novels, of which *Atómstoðin* (1948; tr. *The Atom Station,* 1961) is typical. Laxness has never produced a single wholly satisfactory major work but he has been successful in each of the many genres he has chosen, and his fundamentally sympathetic grasp of the past and present situation of his country is firm.

Laye, Camara (1928) Francophone West African (of the Malinka tribe) novelist. He is undoubtedly the leading French-language African novelist. Laye was the son of a goldsmith renowned for his magical powers; *L'Enfant noir* (1953; tr. *The Dark Child,* 1955) is an autobiographical novel telling of his growing up and of the distorting effects of Westernization. His masterpiece, *Le Regard du Roi* (1954; tr. *The Radiance of the King,* 1956), is one of the very few novels to have successfully absorbed the influence of Kafka (q.v.); it is a parable–delicate, comic, heartrending, alarming, sinister–of a white man's quest for authenticity in the form of an African King, and (contrary to the opinions of Laye's detractors) it is one of the profoundest accounts of 'Africanism' in existence; further, it demonstrates how the white man may cancel the component of hatred in the radical *négritude* of such as Césaire (q.v.). *Dramouss* (1966; tr. *A Dream of Africa,* 1968) draws on Laye's experiences when he returned to Guinea in 1955. Although he entered politics and held important posts, his relations with the changing authorities became strained and he now works as a university teacher in Senegal. Laye's second novel is a major one, an achievement of great imaginative penetration; his potential remains great, though he has written little in the past few years.

Leavis, F. R. (1895) English critic, teacher, editor. Fellow of Downing College, Cambridge, from 1936 until 1962. Leavis has exercised a powerful influence on English literature and has become a highly controversial figure. He is fundamentally an educator: his thesis is that the study of English in institutions should produce an élite morally aware of the technological threat to society. His chief inspiration is Lawrence (q.v.), not in his capacity as (would-be) sex-educator but as prophet of the doomed old rural ways. He is not a scholar: the object of his close scrutiny (*Scrutiny*, 1932–53, 1963, was his magazine) of texts is twofold: to counter the feeble impressionistic and biographical criticism prevalent at Cambridge when he began to teach there in the twenties and, more importantly, to demonstrate that works of art—poems, novels—are organic, moral, educational instruments. His earlier criticism was stimulating: *New Bearings in English Poetry* (1932), *Revaluation* (1936), the *Scrutiny* essays collected in *The Great Tradition* (1948), on Jane Austen, George Eliot, James (q.v.), Conrad (q.v.) and Lawrence (q.v.). He intelligently advanced the claims to attention of Eliot (q.v.) and Hopkins (q.v.) and his appreciative essays on Keats and others contributed greatly to the thirties reappraisal of the poetry of the past. He helped many to read with greater attention and deepened response and directed them to good writers: a notable achievement and one which cannot be diminished. But he has faults so serious that his status as a major critic and, indeed, as a generally effective educator, is dubious. His political philosophy is vague, naive and insular. He is totally oblivious to the possibility that any of his judgements might be wrong and as oblivious to the notion of critical relativism. For an educator his range of interest is absurdly (this is not too strong a word) narrow. Leavis has fought for standards; but these are ill-defined and narrow. His criticism of fiction—for example, his exegesis of Conrad (q.v.)—owes much to his wife, Q. D. Leavis, who wrote the important *Fiction and the Reading Public* (1932; 1965). *The Common Pursuit* (1952) collects more *Scrutiny* essays; *English Literature in Our Time and the University* (1969) is a full general statement of his views.

Lehmann, Rosamond (1903) English novelist, playwright. Rosamond Lehmann's fiction deals exclusively in female anguish and is set in the upper echelons of society; she has learned from Henry James (q.v.). Her work has become increasingly misandrous, but this is hardly a fault, for her women really are of the sort who are destroyed by their love for certain kinds of men. In *The Echoing Grove* (1953), however, her genius has become diluted into too much talk. Her two best novels are *The Weather in the Streets* (1936), a memorable and sensitive period piece, and *The Ballad and the Source* (1944), a subtle observation of an old tyrant through the eyes of a child. The latter is by far the best written of her novels, the prose of which generally tends to hover between extremes of self-consciously 'feminine' over-sensitivity and bathetic reportage and dialogue. Of the quality of her understanding there can be no doubt but she has perhaps done less than justice to herself except in the unpretentious, moving *The Weather in the Streets* and, more fully, in *The Ballad and the Source.*

Leroux, Étienne (ps. S. P. Daniel Le Roux) (1922) The leading Afrikaans novelist, best known for his 'phantasmal' trilogy (highly praised by Graham Greene, q.v.), which has appeared in English as *To a Dubious Salvation* (1972). Leroux, a trained lawyer but now a farmer, is a highly gifted but disconcerting and certainly sometimes pretentious writer. He mixes black comedy, concepts from every kind of psychoanalysis, a convoluted metaphysicality of a kind peculiar to Afrikaans writers, satire, caricature and a hatred of technology and commercialization that is interestingly balanced by a reluctant fascination with its mathematical qualities. Leroux is difficult and over-cerebral; but one has to persevere, because underlying all the pyrotechnics and complexities is a vision of imaginative power which, should it ever find a lyrical expression, could well produce major writing. The three volumes of *To a Dubious Salvation* were followed by *18-44* (1967) and *Isis Isis* (1969).

Lésmian, Bolesław (ps. Bolesław Lesman) (1878–1937) Polish (Jewish) poet, claimed by some to be the most original of all the modern poets of his country. He was also a translator (e.g. Poe). He was educated in Kiev and some early poetry is in Russian. Influenced by symbolism and neo-romanticism, he is essentially a Platonist in the sense that he aims in his elegant poetry, in traditionalist forms, to create an autonomous, verbal metaphor—a kind of denial of objects. But this is only his project, for in his ballads, using folklore and mythology, he bitterly reflects upon crippling, harsh experience. His haunted and haunting poetry was collected in 1957.

Lessing, Doris (1919) Rhodesian novelist, playwright and short-story writer (born in Persia) who left for England in 1949. Lessing is interested in left-wing activism (she was a communist, but was disillusioned), female psychology and (increasingly) in certain kinds of mysticism (for example, Sufism). Her best work is in her first novel, *The Grass is Singing* (1950), *The Golden Notebook* (1962)—a candid and sensitive record of a woman writer's failure to achieve a successful novel–and in short stories (*Five*, 1953; *African Stories*, 1964). She is an honest writer who is really at her best when dealing with individuals; but she cannot altogether escape from political concerns, and while this (and the unimaginative detail that clogs the action) flaws the Martha Quest tetralogy (gathered into two volumes: *Children of Violence*, 1965–6) it lends strength to the experimental frankness of *The Golden Notebook*, in which she is able to attain a remarkable degree of Stendhalian 'crystallization'. Life, she sees bitterly, is too complex for politics–and here, for all her crudities elsewhere, we can only sympathize with her efforts to simplify it by change. All her work conveys a strong sense of the predicament–in a patriarchal society–of the woman of intelligence and goodwill. *Going Home* (1957) is a searing documentary account of Welenski's Rhodesia.

Levertov, Denise (1923) American (1955) poet born in the horrible suburb of Ilford, Essex, England, of Welsh-Russian-Jewish parentage. Here Denise Levertov grew up, was a nurse in the war, and published (1946) her first collection, *The Double Image*. This was a typical English forties product: romantic, lush, and with few hints of the direction she was to take. She went to America in 1947. In the following decade, under the influence of Williams (q.v.), Olson (q.v.), Creeley (q.v.), Pound (q.v.) and others, she became a thoroughly 'American' poet. Or did she? Behind the objectivist (*see* Williams) and unconsciously pragmatist methodology there was still the same romanticism of *The Double Image;* but in time (*The Jacob's Ladder*, 1962) this became transformed into a half-self-acknowledged mystical element, Jewish in flavour, and often powerful and individual. But in later poetry this has so far seldom been more than fragmented. It is as though Denise Levertov, all of whose poetry conveys a strong sense of her acute sensibility and compassionateness, were too modest: too respectful of some of her influences (which are not all good ones), afraid of her own originality. But her integrity and imaginative power are always in evidence and she bears careful study. *Penguin Modern Poets 9* (1967).

Lewis, Sinclair (1885–1951) American novelist born in Minnesota. Nobel Prize 1930 (the first to an American). Lewis is only of socio-anthropological interest; as a writer he is almost worthless, and, in the light of Sherwood Anderson's (q.v.) achievement, the notion that 'without [him] one cannot imagine modern American literature' is wrong.

Lewis lacked imagination, his characters are nearly all journalistic 'types' and he subscribed to what he thought he was attacking. He began as a plot-seller (to, among others, Jack London, q.v.), and began writing novels in 1914. *Babbitt* (1922) was accepted as an *exposé* of middle-class banality and hypocrisy, but, like its predecessor *Main Street* (1920), it reinforced it: Lewis's so-called iconoclastic fiction does not criticize, but enviously celebrates, both big- and small-town success. Of his many novels only *Elmer Gantry* (1927) has merit. It probes his own predicament by describing the rise and fall of a successful but corrupt preacher. The notion that Lewis is in any sense important as a writer should be resisted. *Arrowsmith* (1925); *Dodsworth* (1929).

Lewis, [Percy, a name he disliked] **Wyndham** (1882–1957) English novelist, painter, prose writer, art critic, literary critic, poet. Lewis was born off the American coast on his father's yacht and educated at Rugby and the Slade School of Art. After a period of foreign travel he established himself—with the help of Ford (q.v.) and Pound (q.v.)—in England as artist, *avant-garde* polemicist and writer. The air of mystery with which he surrounded himself made him into a fascinating personality. He founded and edited the aggressive *Blast* (1914–15), and was associated with the 'Vorticist' group. This, including Pound (who invented the name) and the sculptor Gaudier-Brzeska, was a more advanced and continental version of imagism (*see* Pound): influenced by literary and graphic cubism (*see* Reverdy) and futurism (*see* Marinetti), Vorticism advocated a clear-cut, conscious approach, involving geometrical arrangements and striking colours. This episode is possibly less important in Lewis's development than has hitherto been supposed and when the Vorticist painters merged with the 'London Group' Lewis disengaged himself. After taking part in the war he struck out on a more original line; by the beginning of the thirties he had become a largely neglected figure who operated behind the mask of 'The Enemy' (the name of a periodical he edited and largely wrote, 1927–9). He married in 1929. His early stories in *The English Review* (*see* Ford) and elsewhere, his play *The Enemy of the Stars* (1914 rev. 1932; 1966 in the valuable selection *A Soldier of Humour*), other work published by him in a small edition in 1917 (*The Ideal Giant*, a play, and two stories), and the first novel *Tarr* (1918 rev. 1928) had been more influential (e.g. on Joyce, q.v.) than is generally supposed, but in the twenties—and through the thirties—he began to attack the very men whom he had influenced: Eliot ('pseudo-believer', a 'romantic agony' of 'exceedingly low temperatures'), Joyce ('mirthless formal acrobatics'), 'stream-of-consciousness' writing, Stein (q.v.), D. H. Lawrence's (q.v.) 'dark forces'. . . . His critical ideas are most clearly expressed in *The Art of Being Ruled* (1926), *The Lion and the Fox* (1927), on Shakespeare, *Time and Western Man* (1927) and *Men Without Art* (1934). Lewis's attack on his contemporaries was extreme; today it survives more as prophecy of the consequences of their practice, even though it is punctuated with insights of deadly shrewdness. Most of the writers he attacked were expressionist (used in its widest sense) and Lewis, always and profoundly a man of peace by intention, detected the violence inherent in expressionism. But he also detected the violence in himself and sought to purge it. He was, paradoxically, himself producing energetically expressionist creative works: *The Childermass* (1928 rev. 1956 as the first part of *The Human Age*), the massive satire *The Apes of God* (1930), *Snooty Baronet* (1932). In the early thirties he indulged in some journalistic baiting of the left and made the error of collecting articles on the rise of Hitler, which had appeared in *Time and Tide,* in *Hitler* (1931). The views he held in the first half of the thirties were a mixture of uncharacteristic naivety (partly the result of serious illness), inspired prophecy, independence and journalistic carelessness. He then pulled himself together, and in the novel *The Revenge for Love* (1937) entered into a new creative phase: this is a more or less realist study of extremism, and in it Lewis for the first time allowed himself a measure of human compassion. This excellent novel is often hailed as his primary achievement, but it is not: the period of his supreme greatness as creative writer dates from after the war, although it begins here. In 1939 he went to America and thence to Canada, where he spent five miserable and mostly penurious years with his wife. His change of heart first becomes fully evident in the neglected novel *The Vulgar Streak* (1941; 1974), a self-critical work of great complexity. In *Self-Condemned* (1954), about which he began to think in 1943, the second phase of Lewis's fictional activity reaches its apogee and also comes to an end; it is a scarifying novel, in which autobiography is brilliantly transformed into tragic art. (It has been seriously misassessed, notably by William H. Pritchard, 1968.) Lewis, who became totally blind in 1953, had meanwhile returned to the expressionist mode. The tetralogy *The Human Age* consists of the revised *The Childermass, Malign Fiesta* and *Monstre Gai* (1955); the fourth part, *The*

Trial of Man, exists only in the form of a synopsis and a draft of the first chapter. This was successful as a radio adaptation by D. G. Bridson and Lewis himself. It will come to be recognized as the greatest single imaginative prose work in English of this century. The second and third parts are closely related to *The Childermass*, for although this work had more in common with Lewis's writings immediately before and after 1928 than at first seems apparent, it also has a separate, poetic element (the vigorous poetry in *One Way Song*, 1933, 1960, is satirical) which the author virtually abandoned for almost twenty years. *The Human Age* is the most comprehensive and coherent presentation of what is now called the 'human predicament' of our times. 'Life' is presented as hell, but the presentation itself transcends satire (as Swift could and did) because at last the author is able to see himself as involved in the fabric of this hellishness. The meaning of life–the work is set resolutely outside what a realistic novelist (such as the Lewis of *The Revenge for Love*) would call 'real' life–is investigated from a point of view that hovers between authentic visceral disgust, holy awe and agonized scepticism. Lewis handles and criticizes his rhetoric by dividing it up between various characters; his descriptive passages achieve the non-rhetorical originality which he was struggling towards in the earliest stories. Lewis is without question the greatest English-language writer of the century and one of the greatest in world literature. *Letters* (1963) is a sketchy, useful, interim selection; *Wyndham Lewis: An Anthology of his Prose* (1969) selects from non-fiction; short stories are in *The Wild Body* (1927), *Rotting Hill* (1951), *Unlucky for Pringle* (1973); the best short introduction is Grigson's (q.v.) *A Master of Our Time* (1951). The agreeable satire *The Roaring Queen* (suppressed 1936) appeared in 1973. *The Red Priest* (1956), the last published novel–the almost completed *Twentieth Century Palette* has not appeared–has been dismissed as inferior, but it is at the least an indispensable guide to the late Lewis, and Eliot's dismissal of its central figure as 'preposterous' puts the finger on its extraordinary quality. But Lewis had by then gone beyond any of his contemporaries.

Lezama Lima, José (1910) Cuban novelist, poet, critic, editor. His poetry (*Muerte de Narciso*, 1937, *Death of Narcissus*) is hermetic or, later, surrealist in manner, but its images are highly evocative. He founded the review *Origines, Origins*, in 1944, and gave new direction to Cuban poetry. But his most important book is the long novel

Paradiso (1966; rev. 1968; tr. 1974), the story of a poet, José Cemí, of about Lezama Lima's own age. This draws on all the modernist techniques but remains coherent. The prose is highly individual and while all the characters are compassionately viewed and presented, the sense of the mystery of life and death and their only dimly perceived connections with sexuality, are preserved. The writing appears to be surrealistic and has been described as such but in fact it sees things from a fresh angle, incorporating all kinds of myth—Chinese, Latin-American, classical—and learning and musical analogy. The dialogue is not realistic but rather represents what the characters would say if they could say it. Dialogue is used as interior monologue. Honoured by the Castro regime with important cultural posts, Lezama Lima is now out of favour because his famous novel pointedly ignores politics. *Paradiso* most imaginatively solves the problem of how to employ a wide variety of methods without making fiction unreadable or impenetrable.

Lindegren, Erik (1910–68) Swedish poet, critic, librettist (e.g. of Martinson's, q.v., *Anaira,* 1959), translator. Lindegren, with Karl Vennberg (1910), was the leader of the 'forties' group of Swedish poets, who, so to say, established modernism. The chief influences on Lindegren were surrealism (*see* Breton), Ekelöf (q.v.) and—surely—Birger Sjöberg (1885–1929) but his one really good volume, *mannen u tan väg* (1942; 1945; tr. *The Man without a Way* in *New Directions,* 20, 1968; French tr. *L'Homme sans voie,* 1952), a sequence of forty 'exploded sonnets', sprang from his own sense of shock and outrage at war, his own non-involvement in the battle against Nazism and his personal intellectual and emotional anguish at finding himself without direction. This is a successful and remarkable poem in which a sort of direction is found in the bleak similarity of each of the forty poems: seven unrhymed couplets. It represents, to use a phrase of Lindegren's own, 'a catharsis of Angst'. Its language, however, transcends its somewhat Camusian (q.v.) philosophical preoccupations: this is naked, determined in its rejection of lushness or 'beauty' and so starkly simple that the sequence has been described as incomprehensible. After this Lindegren became a useful critic and translator, but his later poetry—apart from certain isolated passages—is more self-consciously 'modern', less original, and sometimes even a compost of fashionable influences. Some poems are translated in *Seven Swedish Poets* (1963).

Lindsay, Vachel (1879–1931) American poet. Like Sandburg (q.v.) and Masters (q.v.) he was raised in Illinois; he and they form a trio of proto-modernist poets–and at his best he is the most achieved of them. Lindsay's main sources were the folkways of Illinois (which by 1879 meant, among other things, a special, by no means simple, reverence for Lincoln the man, Lincoln the myth, and the pre-Lincoln Illinois–myth turned into, invested in, 'Lincoln'), Biblical fundamentalism, the activities of the populist orator and politician William Jennings Bryan (1860–1929), who was in some ways backwards-looking but in others an embodiment of certain vital elements of Americanism (*see* Lindsay's own 'Bryan, Bryan, Bryan, Bryan. . . .'). Lindsay was, in the special Schillerian sense, a *naïv* poet, and one of great originality. He had no intellect but fully absorbed the 'intrahistorical' (*see* Unamuno) element of midwestern America. His family were Campbellites (these fundamentalist 'Disciples of Christ', founded in 1827 by the Scots immigrant Alexander Campbell, believed in the rejection of the creed, baptism by immersion–and the imminent Second Coming), and he retained their crusading spirit and their hatred of drink (he was a temperance man). Donald McCrae, in his fine critique of populism, has drawn attention to its 'poetry': Lindsay is the embodiment of this poetry. And, like the few nations or states that have succumbed to populist or quasi-populist direction, Lindsay fell to pieces–though not in any sinister political manner. He studied art unsuccessfully and became a 'tramp and beggar': his first (immature) collection is called *Rhymes Traded for Bread* (1912). With his next book, *General Booth Enters into Heaven* (1913), he found himself. His poems were a highly original synthesis of folk elements: Negro preaching and vaudeville, fun rituals in black face, evangelism, simplistic Swedenborgian notions ('In Praise of Johnny Appleseed', in *Collected Poems,* 1923, is about his favourite hero of all, John Chapman, 1774–1847, a legendary pioneer Swedenborgian orchardist) and jazz rhythms (he regarded jazz as degenerate). Lindsay held it all together by his own dramatic and effective performances of the poems. His rhythms are as authentic as they are fundamentally simple; but by about 1922 his poetic powers and energies were rapidly becoming exhausted. His last four volumes contain a few pleasant minor poems but are generally feeble: they are the work of a man falling into an increasingly severe reactive depression. That in 1931 he chose the method of *drinking* poison to end it all is perhaps of interest to students of the evangelical 'temperance' mentality. . . . Lindsay is nicely puzzling, because his best poetry defies both literary categories and his own viewpoints (he wrote prose). What Lindsay did for America is no longer possible of achievement: it has degenerated into the pop- and drug-corrupted 'ballad', perpetrated by the creations (and victims) of a vicious commerce. *Collected Poems* (1925). *Selected Poems* (1964). *Letters* (1940).

Lins do Rego, José (1901–57) Brazilian fiction writer. His first five novels were about the Brazilian sugar industry and three of them appear in translation in the single volume *Plantation Boy* (1966). He was a poor stylist but an acute observer and a powerful psychologist. *Pedra Bonita* (1938), *Wonderful Rock*, deals with an incident related by da Cunha (*see* Guimarães Rosa). *Fogo Morto* (1943; tr. *Dead Fires*, 1944), on the changes in the sugar industry, is reckoned to be his masterpiece; though *Eurídice* (1947) is one of the most distinguished studies of a sex-killer in modern literature.

London, Jack (1876–1916) American novelist, 'bastard son of a wandering astrologer whom he never saw', London's raw, crude version of naturalism (*see* Zola) has been most influential on countries encouraging or enforcing socialist realism (*see* Gorky). However, his fiction was and is popular elsewhere: it can vary from the abjectly bad through the authentically entertaining (London had led a tough life) to the genuinely interesting (*The Iron Heel*, 1907; *John Barleycorn*, 1913, a courageous attempt to examine the roots of his compulsion to ingest overlarge quantities of alcohol; *The Star Rover*, 1915). His books have dated; but the best written, which will survive, are *The Call of the Wild* (1903) and *White Fang* (1906): empathy with animals muffles the crude and simplistic political message, and gives the style a moving quality. Despite his stylistic failures and his apparently inadequate intellect, London's fiction is more complex than either his Soviet admirers or his English-language detractors allow.

Lorca, Federico García (1896–1936) Spanish poet, dramatist. He was murdered at the beginning of the Civil War—not precisely for political reasons but none the less by fascist thugs (Machado, q.v., wrote a noble elegy for him). Lorca is the most internationally famous of twentieth-century Spanish writers, for he had the most dramatic (though not lurid) manner of presenting his work. He was also immensely popular with the Spanish people. He knew little about surrealism (*see* Breton) beside what he picked up from his friends of the 'Generation of the Dictatorship' (*see* Guillén); but he naturally discovered that element of the surreal which has existed in the exotic Spanish literature and folk-lore from the earliest times. Although, like nearly all his contemporaries, he was influenced by the metaphysical Góngora, it would be most true to state that his achievement lies in his re-creation of the whole of the Spanish popular tradition (the epic poetry, the ballads, the folk-lore, the customs) in modern terms. He was himself an energetic but tormented and alienated man, a 'natural' who felt out-of-place in the mechanized modern world, the 'global village', and yet one who refused obscurantism. And so in his work we have a dual vision: of the past seen in terms of the present and of the present permeated and menaced by the past. In what, together with the famous elegy 'Llanto por Ignacio Sánchez Mejías' (1935; many tr.), is his finest collection, *Romancero gitano* (1928; tr. *Gipsy Ballads*, 1950), Lorca personifies himself as the gipsy: persecuted, impassioned, pagan, mysterious, a threat to 'law and order'. These poems combine innocence with extreme sophistication in an extraordinary manner: their ambiguity is resolved in the actual gipsy-figures, who are half realistic Andalusian gipsies, but half demonic angels, creatures of Lorca's own heated and disturbed imagination. The nature of the nerve-shot psychological crisis from which they sprang is revealed in the less successful but exciting poems of the posthumously published *Poeta en Nueva York* (1940; tr. in two versions 1940; 1955). Lorca went there soon after the publication of *Romancero gitano*, and, since he spoke no English and was appalled and stunned by the city, was driven to the edge of mental breakdown, reinforced by 'culture-shock' and current sexual difficulties. He found himself again poetically in the elegy for his friend, the bullfighter Ignacio Sánchez Mejías (killed in the ring in 1934): in a poem which not only prophesies his own pointless end but also the catastrophe into which Spain would so soon be plunged. If as a dramatist Lorca is (just) not one of the supreme of the century then this is because his plays are difficult to present, at least outside Spain (he himself produced most of them in his capacity as co-director of La Barraca, the republican government's touring company). He owes much to Valle-Inclán (q.v.) and to the puppet-theatre, but his late tragedies about women, which incidentally incorporate savage criticism of the paternalism and obscurantism of Spanish society, are original. These,

Bodas de sangre (1933), *Yerma* (1934) and *La casa de Bernarda Alba* (1936), have been translated in one volume (*Three Tragedies*, 1947; 1961). It is interesting that in the last one Lorca, as Yeats (q.v.) did towards the end, seems to be moving towards a kind of compressed prose. Lorca, who was a gifted musician and a good amateur painter, has come under some critical fire in the past years for no better reason than that his world-wide fame has eclipsed that of such poets as Machado, who deserve it as much or perhaps more. But, even if his poetic achievement is not as a whole as great as that of Machado, it is impossible to deny him his major place in Spanish literature. *Lorca* (tr. 1960) is a good selection of his poems. The complete works (1938–42; 1954) need re-editing. His important last unfinished play, *El Publico, The Public*, will soon be issued.

Louw, N. P. van Wyk (1906–70) Until his death the leading Afrikaans poet; an academic, he was also a verse dramatist, critic and radio playwright. He led the thirties revival of Afrikaans poetry, whose foundations had been laid earlier by Marais, 'Totius', Celliers and Leipoldt. He was profoundly influenced by Dutch and Flemish poetry (particularly Roland Holst's neo-Platonism and Marsman's expressionism), and may fairly be described as an expressionist poet—but he is Afrikaans through and through, and is certainly the greatest poet in that language (which is, virtually, a slightly simplified Dutch with some English loan-words). He dealt with many large themes and was big enough to do so without overloading himself. His early poetry (*Alleenspraak*, 1935, *Monologue*) reflects Nietzschean individualism and an unresolved, passionate eroticism; *Die Halwe Kring* (1937), *The Semi-Circle*, is more personal and more bitterly nihilistic. But with the narrative poem *Raka* (1941; tr. 1941) he gained new impetus from folk themes and poetry—though the pessimism and the complex double-vision of good and evil, reflected in the figures of Koki and his destroyer, the beast Raka, are still there—and was thus able to enter into a third and more stable phase, in which some affirmation may be discovered. This culminated in *Tristia* (1962). Just as *Raka* is accepted as the greatest narrative poem in Afrikaans, so *Germanicus* (1956), the 'tragedy of inaction' (in certain respects an examination of his own artistic role) is taken as the best play. His many essays directed the course of Afrikaans thought and will remain central in its literature. Some of his poems are in English versions in the *Penguin Book of South African Verse* (1968) and in *Afrikaans Poems with English Translations* (1962).

Louÿs, Pierre (ps. Pierre Louis) (1870–1925) French novelist, poet, critic, scholar, editor. Disciple of Heredia, whose daughter he married. Friend of Gide (q.v.), Valéry (q.v.) and others. *Chansons de Bilitis* (1894), prose poems, purported to be translations from the ancient Greek and deceived everyone. Louÿs was skilled, but his work is spoiled both by its overlushness and the artificiality of his attempts to freeze this into a Parnassian manner. But his novel *La Femme et le pantin* (1898), *The Woman and the Puppet,* an only ostensibly 'moral' study of a man's disintegration under the spell of a 'scarlet' woman, still exercises fascination. *Collected Works* (tr. 1932).

Lowell, Robert (1917) American poet of famous aristocratic American family; regarded by most critics as the best English-language poet of his generation and by certain readers as beyond criticism altogether. For better or for worse, Lowell is the modern poet-as-film-star: his private affairs are apparently carried out mainly in public (this is miscalled 'confessionalism'): his themes have included the personalities and behaviour of his relatives, his various marriages and liaisons, the (presumably) affective disorder which has landed him in hospital many times, and so on. Lowell was and is extremely gifted but the conventional view of his development, even where this judges the most recent poems as failures, is not quite correct, for it mistakes potential for achievement, and overrates him. At first Lowell went, for his poetry, to his Roman Catholicism (later renounced), his pacifism (for which he served a term in gaol), his New England Calvinist temperament and to his teachers (chiefly Ransom, q.v., and Tate, q.v.). His second volume, *Lord Weary's Castle* (1946), took over a few revised versions of poems from the first (*Land of Unlikeness,* 1944), and added more. This was a 'new-critical' (*see* Brooks) poet struggling, under the familiar influences (Ransom, Tate–and Yeats, Eliot and the metaphysicals), to express himself through an intricate tightness of form. Most of the poems had been worked at too hard; they were over-compressed but they displayed genius and originality. This process continued with *Poems 1938–1949* (1950, in Great Britain only), which reprinted most of the contents of its predecessors, but omitted the title poem of *The Mills of the*

Kavanaughs (1951 in USA only). This, a clotted narrative poem, grafts E. A. Robinson (q.v.) on to the other influences, but fails. Lowell later acknowledged these poems of the forties–Christian, Empsonian (q.v.), historical, allusive–as having a 'stiff, humourless and even impenetrable surface'; he was right up to a point–but much of his best work, the minor achievement of a major gift–is here. Towards the end of this phase Lowell, who had remarried (his first wife was the novelist Jean Stafford, q.v.), began a new, twofold, process which might be described as a 'loosening up'. He began to rediscover himself through other poetries, making very free versions of many foreign poets (the final results are in *Imitations*, 1961); and he allowed his concentration on Christianity to lapse in favour of following his intensely liberal and radical impulses. *Life Studies* (1959 rev. 1968) adds a further dimension to this second part of his process of self-liberation: the use of personal experience to create sets of metaphors and images that would disturb and illuminate by their unfamiliarity (less is 'confessional' here than has often been assumed: this is a highly self-conscious, artificial method). Undoubtedly Lowell wanted to make a new and truthful poetry but something went awry. He wanted, he said, to give his reader 'the *real* Robert Lowell'. He had been aware of Williams (q.v.) since 1937, and in these poems he did achieve a valid loosening of form. But he did not pass, as he claimed, 'beyond symbols into reality'. These 'real' poems, despite their relative freedom of form (in some ways exemplary), are as cleverly wrought as the earlier ones. And Lowell does not here, and never does, escape the monotony of the iamb unless in favour of other conventional metres. He is a master of prosody, of fitting the rich line or altered quotation into a metrical context but his poetry has become increasingly *constructed*, spontaneity is overmuffled rather than tamed or filtered through an intuition-powered consciousness (the most difficult part of writing poetry is to get this process right). The famous 'Skunk Hour', too beautifully made, exhibits the inherent, intensified narcissism: the 'poet-as-Christ' is unfortunately as much an assumption as a knowing component of the poem. As for the 'madness' poems: to be afflicted with mental disorder (often a matter of mysterious chemistry) is no joke. But to put such a disorder into the public field is to change it. His poetry after this adds nothing: only an over-introspective self-agonizing with which one can do no more than sympathize. By the time of the *Notebook* (1969 rev. 1969 rev. 1970; drastically revised, cut and augmented as *History*, 1973; this last revision supplemented by *For*

Lizzie and Harriet, 1973) the poet, now sucked into the bog of the iamb, is photographing and re-photographing himself from every conceivable angle. He is trying to show the public that he is as good as Berryman (q.v.)–as is evident and as has been independently noted by others. The desperate desire to be truthful has not vanished but we are asked to judge this work as poetry, and this quality is seen, in the light of such judgement, not only as pitifully unrealized but also tarnished by an element of exploitation. *The Dolphin* (1973), a separate sequence, is actually bathetic, banal, showing signs that even Lowell's skill at inserting his 'rich' lines into a carefully prepared context is leaving him. In this volume Lowell speaks of his 'lifelong taste for reworking the same water'; yet one of his sympathetic critics has spoken of his 'refusal to repeat himself'. Who is right? Lowell's poetry reflects the age and its uncertainties; it can dazzle us into temporary admiration and its statements can remind us memorably of our general predicament. But it is linguistically cold at the centre; it knows about but lacks empathy–ultimately the great words, 'love' among them, are counters. *For the Union Dead* (1964); *Near the Ocean* (1967). *The Old Glory* (1965) contains three plays based on stories by Melville and Hawthorne; *Prometheus Bound* (1969) is a strangely (from a classicist) ineffectual prose re-treatment of the Aeschylus play.

Lowry, Malcolm (1909–57) English novelist, poet. Paradoxically, Lowry succeeded only because he persisted in destroying himself with alcohol; he is consequently a disturbing as well as a tragic writer. As a boy he ran away to sea (*Ultramarine*, 1933 rev. 1963, is based on this experience) but returned to study at Cambridge. He published nothing between 1933 and 1947, but wrote intensively in between savage drinking-bouts. (On one occasion he drank a bottle of shaving-lotion.) *Lunar Caustic* (French tr. of early draft in *L'Esprit*, 1956; 'spliced' version from two mss., revisions and notes by his wife and E. Birney, 1963 in *Paris Review*, 29; 1968), intended as part of *Under the Volcano* but rejected, is about his detention as an alcoholic in Bellevue Hospital, New York, in the thirties after his first marriage (1934) was in process of collapse. His second wife, whom he married in 1940, remained with him until the end. He had lived in Mexico, the setting of *Under the Volcano*, in the thirties and returned there in 1945–6 (this visit is the background of the novel, edited from drafts, *Dark as the Grave Wherein My Friend is Laid*, 1968). From 1940 until 1954 he lived in a shack at Dollarton, British Columbia; it was here that he wrote most of *Under the Volcano*, upon which he had started work in 1936. Lowry was almost always working at several novels at the same time, but he managed to sort out *Under the Volcano* after ten years and in 1947 it was published. When it was reissued in 1962 it was immediately accepted as a classic. Set in Mexico, it describes the last hours in the life of a mescal-drinking former British Consul, Geoffrey Firmin. Like Lowry himself, he maintains a purity of poetic vision only by his self-destructive addiction. *Under the Volcano* is a symbolic novel and yet it transcends symbolism because its realistic detail, however fantastic (but life is fantastic, and life may be taken as symbolic), is convincing. The influences on Lowry were many and various: his close association with Conrad Aiken (q.v.), dating from 1929 and his acquaintance with Nordahl Greig (q.v.); cinematic technique; Buddhism; Freud; Greek tragedy; the Jacobean playwrights; such features of Cabalistic lore as were useful to him; and above all the phenomenon of the 'significant coincidence', called 'synchronicity' by Jung, and usefully investigated in recent years by Arthur Koestler (q.v.). Lowry saw, and stated that he could be accused of monstrous pretentiousness, but he rightly wrote: 'I feel I go clear; because . . . other meanings and danks and darks are not stressed at all; it is only if the reader himself, prompted by instinct or curiosity, cares to invoke them that they will raise their demonic heads from the abyss, or peer at him from above.' *Hear us O Lord from Heaven Thy Dwelling Place* (1961) collects stories. *October Ferry to Gabriola* (1970) is another posthumous novel reconstructed from drafts. *Selected Poems* (1962) shows Lowry as an uneven but by no means negligible poet. *Selected Letters* (1965) contains his important defence (1946) against Cape's reader's assessment of *Under the Volcano*, and much else of interest. Douglas Day's *Malcolm Lowry* (1974) is a useful interim biography.

MacDiarmid, Hugh (ps. C. M. Grieve) (1892) Scottish (but only by a whisker–he was born in Langholm in Dumfriesshire) poet, critic, autobiographer, publicist. MacDiarmid's best creative poetry was written in the twenties but he retains the respect of his fellow Scots for his almost single-handed initiation of a truly *Scottish* modern poetry. His war with gentility and Anglo-Scottish values was not always coherently conducted, but he won it–to the benefit of a host of writers. His early lyrics (in *Sangschaw*–'Song Show'–1925, and *Penny Wheep*–'Small Beer'–1926) revitalized Scottish poetry by smashing through the barriers set up by the pseudo-admirers of Burns, with their 'Burns nights', and going back for inspiration to Henryson, Dunbar and other earlier Scots poets. He writes in English and (better) in a version of his own Border dialect reinforced by manifold borrowings from many other, often obscure, Scottish sources. Not enough effort has been made in England to appreciate these early poems–they do present linguistic difficulties but the *Selected Poems* (1970) shows the reader how to begin to solve them. After these two volumes MacDiarmid wrote his finest poem (in Scots), *A Drunk Man Looks at the Thistle* (1926); this foreshadows the mental breakdown which eventually (1933) sent him to a lonely croft on Walshay in the Shetlands for eight years. It is an impassioned, highly personal, 'drunken' lyric permeated by a sense of intellectual puzzlement about his predicament. It is a poem of despair, of major proportions. The history of MacDiarmid from this time (*To Circumjack Cencrastus,* 1930, contains some good poems, but a diminution of powers is evident) is perhaps of interest only to his devotees. He helped found the Scottish Nationalist Party in 1928 and was in the Communist Party (1934–8; 1957–); he supported Social Credit (*see* Pound); and while campaigning for Gaelic in schools began to write in English. His later poems (e.g. *In Memoriam James Joyce,* 1955) are prosy collages of scientific, literary and other texts, held together by cantankerous, bathetic monologue (e.g. 'In the United States Mark Twain/ Could finally make headway/ Against the Transcendentalists'). The confusions of MacDiarmid over the past half-century are really of little intrinsic interest. But he deserves the respect he still retains for his earlier achievements. *Lucky Poet* (1943) and *The Company I've Kept* (1966) are autobiographies; *Collected Poems* (rev. 1967–the 1962 edition is, through no fault of the author's, a bibliographical disaster) is misleadingly titled, but is useful; *Selected Essays* (1969). The 'collected' edition is supplemented by *A Lap of Honour* (1967), *A Clyack-Sheaf* (1969) and *More Collected Poems* (1970)–but the bibliographical confusion has not yet been resolved. The best introduction is the *Selected Poems* of 1970. For a different and more positive view of the later MacDiarmid the *Festschrift* of 1962 should be consulted.

Macdonald, Dwight (1906) American radical, editor, critic. He was one of those who supported Henry Wallace, and has written admirably about this tragic, noble and not yet exhausted episode in American politics in *Henry Wallace* (1948) and in *Memoirs of a Revolutionist* (1957). His literary criticism is weaker, but his onslaught on 'mid-cult' literature contained in *Against the American Grain* (1962), while not thoroughly worked out or sufficiently documented, succeeds in touching a raw cultural nerve. His demolition of Cozzens, however, was complete.

Machado, Antonio (1875–1939) Spanish poet, critic, dramatist, prose writer. He is usually, and justly, regarded as Spain's greatest poet since Góngora. He was known as the 'good' Machado not only because he was a good man but also because he had a brother Manuel Machado (1874–1947), poet and at one time collaborator with Antonio in plays, who was a skilful dilettante who turned fascist. Antonio, a teacher of French by profession, supported the legal government and died only a short time after fleeing to exile in France. Machado was associated with the 'Generation of 1898' (*see* Unamuno), but was neither a publicist nor polemicist. He married a young girl in 1909 and her death in 1912 was a decisive factor in his unhappy but good-humoured life. He was influenced by Spanish folk-lore (his father was a folklorist), *modernismo* (*see* Darío)–initially by early Spanish ballads and poetry, Bergson (q.v.), under whom he studied in 1911, and French symbolist poetry. Much of his lucid and yet rich poetry is permeated by the

Castilian landscape, of which he is the greatest evoker. Machado is hardly a typical modernist poet: his resonant style remains unaffected by surrealism (*see* Breton), a form of which flourished in Spain in his lifetime; his language seems prosaic even if it is not, and he turned to the past more than any of his contemporaries. Yet the body of his poetry is surpassed only, perhaps, by that of Vallejo (q.v.) in this century. It is quite different, and yet both men ended their lives in despair at Franco's barbaric triumph but still hoping that a new Spain would one day emerge; both men were influenced by Marxism (it would be too much to claim that even the official communist Vallejo was actually a *Marxist*). Machado is an aphoristic, classical poet, employing a deliberately sparse language. Eroticism pervades some of his poetry of the twenties, when he had a love affair. Humbleness (rather than humility) is the key to Machado's work, which is not prolific. In *Juan de Mairena* (tr. 1963), who was one of his alter egos—like Pessoa (q.v.), though less systematically, he had 'heteronyms', such as Abel Martín—he wrote witty, paradoxical prose fragments. His poetry, he wrote, was a 'deep palpitation of the spirit', an 'essential word in time', 'the dialogue of a man with his time'. Thus, ordinary, greedy, inevitable flies 'remind me of all things': of his first childhood *ennui,* his classroom at school—and then of love and death (the equation between these two is a persistent theme). Often his poems take the form of conversations between himself and conceptions of nature (water, dawn), whose nature he seeks to define. There are a number of translations, including *Eighty Poems* (tr. 1959)—the best—and *Castilian Ilexes* (tr. 1963).

Machado De Assis, Joaquim (1839–1908) Brazilian novelist, short-story writer, poet, critic. It may seem odd to include in this book a Brazilian who wrote most of his novels in the last century but Machado de Assis is as modern an author as, say, Hopkins (q.v.), and he is hardly known in Great Britain (though USA readers are aware of him). He is an indispensable writer whether you are a critic or a reader (or, even, a critic-reader). His poetry is not important but at least five of his nine novels are masterpieces, and to these must be added up to fifty of his 200-odd stories (sel. tr. *Brazilian Tales,* 1921; *The Psychiatrist,* 1963). He was born in poverty, an epileptic and a mulatto; yet from printer's apprentice and subsequently journalist he rose to the highest position in Brazilian letters and society—a fact that caused this tragi-comic ironist not a few qualms. Machado knew about the fictional status of fictional characters—and about the novel-as-autobiography. He also knew that people found it difficult to discover an identity until society gave them a false one. He was, at the end, a pessimist who could find refuge only in an art which is as modernistic as that of Unamuno (q.v.) or Valle-Inclán (q.v.). The important novels are *Memórias Póstumas de Brás Cubas* (1880–1; tr. *Epitaph for a Small Winner*, 1952), which begins at the end of Brás Cubas's life (Machado had read Sterne), *Quincas Borba* (1891; tr. *Philosopher or Dog?*, and in USA as *The Heritage of Quincas Borba*, 1954), *Dom Casmurro* (1899; tr. 1953), *Esaú e Jacó* (1904; tr. *Esau and Jacob*, 1966) and *Memorial de Aires* (1908), *Ayres Memorial*. Like Pareto and Schopenhauer (in their very different ways) Machado saw human nature as essentially unchangeable, and the theme of the later fiction is the waste caused by effort to achieve ends, usually sexual. But he is sardonic and good natured; the greatest novelist in the Portuguese language.

Mackenzie, Compton (1883–1972) Novelist, comic writer, essayist, autobiographer. Mackenzie, son of an actor, began as a poet; he turned to the serious novel with *The Passionate Elopement* (1911), which was followed by *Carnival* (1914), *Sinister Street* (1913–14) and *Guy and Pauline* (1915)—perhaps his best. Henry James (q.v.) noticed his promise in 1914. But he never quite fulfilled this. He became a Roman Catholic in 1914, though this was never made evident in his work. His early work is observant, deeply felt and well written. He knew Norman Douglas (q.v.) and Lawrence (q.v.) well, and has written (and, in his famous role as raconteur, spoken) amusingly, maliciously and revealingly of them. In the twenties he turned to lighter fiction and to children's books (e.g. the excellent *Fairy Gold*, 1926); the more serious *The Four Winds of Love* (1937–45) is not at the level of his first works, but *Buttercups and Daisies* (1931) is one of the funniest books of the century. His novels after the Second World War are frankly entertainments (e.g. *Whisky Galore*, 1947). But there is one exception: *Thin Ice* (1956), a highly competent and compassionate study of a blackmailed homosexual politician. Like MacDiarmid (q.v.), he was a founder-member of the Scottish National Party. He founded *The Gramophone* magazine and edited it for many years. His autobiography *My Life and Times* (in ten volumes, 1963–71) is uneven but contains important and well observed passages. He was a versatile and generous man whose early fiction, and comic novels, will survive.

Mackenzie, Seaforth (ps. Kenneth Mackenzie) (1913–55) The best of Australian novelists and poets who remained in their own country in the period 1935–50. Stead (q.v.) had left (1928) before publishing anything, White (q.v.) was not to publish (except verse, 1935, and a prentice novel, 1939) until 1948, Boyd was in England, his contemporary novelists at home were using conventional methods; the poets were trapped in the blind-alley of the Lindsay-McCrae vitalist school or its sillier offshoots, or were struggling to achieve an Australian usage that came to Mackenzie perfectly naturally (though he was influenced by Lindsay, who spoiled his first collection, *Our Earth,* 1937, by adding illustrations to it). Mackenzie's four novels are imperfect but the three best–*The Young Desire It* (1937), *Chosen People* (1938), *The Refuge* (1954)–show up the inadequacies of the Australian fiction then being written in extremely sharp relief; his only serious rival then living in the country was the unprolific Leonard Mann (q.v.), eighteen years older than himself. Not that he obtained recognition, even though his first novel is still one of the most acute of studies of adolescent homosexuality and the strains of school: he became dangerously alcoholic, almost starved, broke up his marriage, cut himself disastrously off from other people and died by drowning. His last three novels are imbued with a sense of hideous evil, and (though flawed in very obvious ways) work so well because the realistic technique by which he holds the terrible motivations of his characters at bay parallels his own attempt to hang on to life. But, though very uneven, he is at his most powerful and original as a poet: his poems, like Lowry's (q.v.), but with greater conviction and confidence, retain a passionate simplicity redeemed from mawkishness by the precise expression of his feeling of living in a beautiful but terrifying and guilt-haunted no-man's-land between life and death. His technical control is remarkable. *Selected Poems* (1961); a complete edition is on its way. Only the fiction appears under his pseudonym.

MacNeice, Louis (1907–63) Irish (son of a Bishop) poet, critic, playwright, translator. He was educated and lived in England. He read classics at Oxford and was friendly with Auden (q.v.) and Spender (q.v.), though his affinities with them were exaggerated. After a decade of teaching classics he joined the BBC (1940) and remained with them until his premature death of alcoholism and pneumonia. MacNeice was a very unhappy and intelligent man, with a gift for superbly vital comic verse (e.g. the famous 'Bagpipe Music'). He has his admirers but his ultimate reticence, his failure to define his anguish, relegates him to the ranks of talented minor poets. At the heart of his work, but too concealed, is a profound erotic disturbance and sense of the tragedy of existence. Instead of expressing this in poetry, he would (towards the end of his life) take himself off to anonymous places and drink himself into a fearful insensibility. Thus the last poems (*Eighty-Five Poems,* 1959; *Collected Poems,* 1966), which have sometimes been admired for displaying a new urgency, are not explicit enough: one knows that they are 'personal' but they somehow evade their real subject. The linguistic excitement is deliberately muffled by inexplicably 'neutral' passages which irrevocably muddy the poems. The earlier MacNeice, who was not politically minded (though he was always committed to decency), adopted an evasive pose: the surface of his poetry, which though sometimes vulgar is glittering, technically brilliant and acutely observant of mood, distracts us from, not an emptiness of content, but a strategy for avoiding self-confrontation. For MacNeice in the thirties was more intelligent and mature than either Auden or Spender–and we may admire his poetry not only for its surface accomplishment but also for the sense it conveys, willy nilly, or moral awareness and impulse to self-destruction (e.g. in *The Earth Compels,* 1938, and *Plant and Phantom,* 1941). *Autumn Journal* (1939), a long narrative of a bad time, is uneven but vivid and memorable; one wishes he could have written like this of his deeper emotions. His translations of the *Agamemnon* (1936) and Goethe's *Faust* 1 and 2 (1951) are outstanding. His allegories for radio (e.g. *The Dark Tower,* 1947) are somewhat overloaded and portentous, though always well made. His poetry will always be interesting but he lacked the ability to commit himself seriously to it–and this, perhaps, more than anything else, led to his early death. The critical *Modern Poetry* (1938) displays this lack of commitment. *The Strings Are False* (1965) is an unfinished and, again, evasive autobiography.

Maeterlinck, Maurice (1862–1949) Belgian (writing in French) poet, dramatist, prose writer. Nobel Prize 1911. Maeterlinck's free-verse symbolist poems, collected in *Serres chaudes* (1889; tr. *Hot Houses,* 1915) and later volumes were extremely influential. He was always lucky, for these dated, oppressive and unrewarding verses caught the mood of the time; he was vastly inferior to Verhaeren (q.v.) and the neglected Georges Rodenbach, who died in 1898. His plays, again, coincided with and reinforced a prevailing mood of gloom and fatalism. *Pelléas et Mélisande* (1892; tr. 1895) is the most famous because Debussy made it into an opera; the best are *Les Aveugles* (1890; tr. *The Sightless,* 1895) and the realistic anti-German *Le Bourgmestre de Stilemonde* (1919; tr. 1918). Later Maeterlinck became a spiritualist, a Count and writer on insects (his book on the white ant was shamelessly cribbed, in the best spiritualist traditions, from one by Eugene Marais). Maeterlinck has historical importance and the play *L'Oiseau bleu* (1908; tr. *The Blue Bird,* 1909), which got him the Nobel Prize, has genuine charm. He is an inexorably minor writer, who is now largely forgotten–but one must recall that Rilke (q.v.) and many others did not think so.

Mailer, Norman (1923) American novelist, short-story writer, versifier, sociological and literary critic, playwright, self-publicist, journalist. Mailer is, as Eric Mottram has written, 'completely characteristic of mid-century America'. The question is whether he has risen, as a writer, above the turmoil of his times. Is he a successful imaginative writer or merely one of the best journalists of our time? He is brilliant, 'confessionally' confused, almost always simultaneously highly intelligent and entertaining, aggressive, rather egocentric; his work has many aspects but its two main themes are the predicament of the heterosexual male and of cultural, social or ethnic minorities (Jew, writer, Negro, cop, gangster and so on). Mailer has not often, in fact, succeeded in letting his imagination work: in finding true objective correlatives. The work of, for example, Bellow (q.v.) helps to demonstrate this quite clearly. But even in criticizing Mailer one must immediately admit that he was at least a necessary man 'to have around'. His two main weaknesses are his immature need to be the 'best' and his intensely neurotic sexuality. It is honest of Mailer to admit that he is fiercely competitive–he is dedicated to the truth, even if often in too much of a hurry to do it proper justice–but in this respect he is like a little boy and the characteristic has continually undermined his more serious efforts. His unevenness–his TV performances can range from the entrancingly intelligent to the embarrassingly bizarre—is simply part of him. But his competitiveness is intolerable in the context of a mind of his quality. As to his other weakness: Mailer's obsession with sexual violence, his anxiety ('the great ocean of the fuck'), suggest an intensification of the mass male sexual neurosis which may be too individual, too particularized, to allow him total empathy. The sense of alienation that his stark fear of and love for women gives him may very well help to build up the tiresome self-image of a champ intimidating his 'opponents'. To be neurotic is to be characteristic of mid-century America (and elsewhere) but imagination must clearly preside, in creative work, if not in life, over neuroses; and this is where Mailer usually fails. His first novel, *The Naked and the Dead* (1948), was a best-seller and a *tour de force* for a young man; an army novel set in the Pacific (where Mailer had served), it is more seriously intentioned than it appears. Its weakness is that in trying to probe the nature of authoritarianism Mailer is unknowingly also probing his own tendencies toward violence and his complex feelings towards women. Few of its less conventionally written successors are superior (I include stories) and in all of them the same kind of struggle is taking place. The best of the fiction is in *Advertisements for Myself* (1959), a self-appraisal consisting of early work connected by a fascinating commentary. This contains 'The Time of Her Time', once part of a novel, now a story, which is the best of all Mailer's prose: it deals with his central obsession, the male-female sex-relationship, and with great fierceness; but the usual deliberately over-sophisticated context is lacking. This is a spill-off from Mailer's self-conscious efforts, in the fifties, to emerge as Prophet-Writer: to be a Blake or a more sophisticated Lawrence (q.v.). *Advertisements for Myself* is the point at which Mailer tacitly acknowledges his need to discover a technique by which he could extricate his imagination from the existential concerns that press upon it; it is an account of the twentieth-century conflict between the Schillerian *naïv* and *sentimentalisch* which is made all the more alarming by the evidence of fragmented creative genius that it reveals. *The Barbary Shore* (1951), *The Deer Park* (1955), *An American Dream* (1965) are all intensely interesting failures, displays of shooting stars of creative energy fading away against a background of anxious political commitment, yearnings for Reichian (q.v.) release and the doomed attempt to create a valid hero-figure, the White Negro, the hipster, the purged Mailer . . . . *Why Are We in Vietnam?* (1967) is a disaster in which Mailer desperately attempts to liberate himself from his sense of ideological commitment by wholly inhabiting it. Since then Mailer has produced a stream of uneven journalism—the best is *The Armies of the Night* (1967), about the March on the Pentagon in which he took part—on subjects that include the Chicago Democratic Convention of 1968, a moon shot and Marilyn Monroe. Clearly he is becoming exhausted but what has exhausted him has usually had an immediate relevance to problems at the heart of our times. *The Presidential Papers* (1963) and *Cannibals and Christians* (1966) contain essays and fiction.

Malamud, Bernard (1914) American novelist, short-story writer. Malamud has been regarded as, with Bellow (q.v.), the leading American Jewish novelist of his generation; the reputation has not helped him, for although he is an explorer of the Jewish predicament—of the paradox of loneliness and solidarity—he may have forced himself into an over-self-conscious narrowness of theme. *The Natural* (1952), really a novella rather than a novel, examines his own New York baseball fervour with love and detached amusement; his ambivalence towards his baseball-Holy Grail allegory makes a perfect background for the sad story of the rise and fall of a baseball player. *The Assistant* (1957), Malamud's best novel, is the tale of a good, defeated Jew and the ex-gunman gentile assistant he takes on at his pathetically unsuccessful grocery shop after the former has robbed it. It lives on in the mind first and foremost because it is full of warm psychological exactitude and love. In *A New Life* (1961), Malamud's 'college novel', there is a confusion about the main character and the ambivalence here works against the success of the book: the central character *is* a Jew but Malamud has not been really sure throughout the book. In his previous novel the assistant had been, quite certainly, a gentile. The two early collections of stories, *The Magic Barrel* (1958) and *Idiots First* (1963), contain the rest of Malamud's finest fiction: some beautiful modern fables and some excellent realistic studies of urban Jews. The turning-point in Malamud's career (to date) came with *The Fixer* (1966), an attempt to write a 'great' Jewish novel which, for all its skill and scope, is second-rate in terms of what had gone before it. It is based on a famous scandal which took place in pre-Bolshevist Russia, in which a Jew was unjustly accused of murder. The atmosphere of the Russia of the early twentieth century is brilliantly evoked, and anti-semitic attitudes (still, of course, persistent in Soviet Russia) are well analyzed; but the characterization is flat. The connected short stories in *Pictures of Fidelman* (1969) represent the low point in Malamud's writing career but *The Tenant* (1971), about a white and a black writer eating each other up in a tempestuous relationship, shows a fumbling back to the old form. *The Fixer* is a skilful attempt to attain a grand dignity—but its author fails by trying too hard. *The Assistant,* which seems in many ways to develop logically from Henry Roth's (q.v.) *Call it Sleep,* is a major novel—there is no reason why it should not be followed by another. *A Malamud Reader* (1967).

Malraux, André (1901) French novelist, critic, essayist, art historian, politician, man of action, adventurer. Malraux's fiction, which he abandoned for (heroic and dramatic) Resistance activities and then Gaullist politics (he was De Gaulle's Minister of Culture), anticipates many of the themes taken up by somewhat younger novelists: the absurdity of existence, the anguish but necessity of 'commitment', the force of the elliptical within a carefully constructed context . . . . Despite his apparent political *volte-face*—leftist (though non-communist) until 1939, Gaullist (but perhaps not 'right': Gaullism, now dead, was a complex phenomenon, embracing at least radicalism, pragmatism and 'Vichyism')—it is correct to assert that a consistency underlies his work. Essentially he is a neo-Nietzschean: the question he has tried to answer is: What can man achieve? And his final solution, which is underpinned by a profound pessimism, is that only Art—and graphic art at that—can transcend human idiocy. This view is most clearly expressed in *Les Voix du silence* (1951; tr. *The Voices of Silence,* 1953), with which many art critics have quarrelled on technical grounds. The book is unconvincing because Malraux's imagination, though not his courage, has failed: he turns to the only permanence he can see, and later, as Minister of State for cultural affairs, he had some of the historical buildings of Paris cleaned up—but so 'well' that they are almost modernized. This is no satisfactory answer to Malraux's Spenglerian convictions. In the twenties Malraux went, with his first wife, to Indo-China as an archaeologist, and was sentenced to imprisonment for taking statues from a Buddhist temple; this sentence was suspended and he subsequently became involved in the revolution in China (1926–8). His earliest works were short fantastic allegories (e.g. *Lunes de papier,* 1921), *Paper Moons,* influenced by surrealism and literary cubism. *La Tentation de l'Occident* (1926; tr. *The Temptation of the West,* 1961), non-fiction, is a Spenglerian warning, remarkably free of mysticism, for men of the West to turn to the East. His third and fifth novels are his major achievements: *La Condition humaine* (1933; tr. *Storm Over Shanghai,* 1934; *Man's Fate,* 1935–two different versions) and *L'Espoir* (1937; tr. *Days of Hope,* 1938). *Le Temps du mépris* (1935; tr. *Days of Contempt,* 1936), on Hitler's Germany, runs these a close second. *La Condition humaine,* which deserved its success, is a shatteringly detached account–its method approximates to the cinematic one of 'cutting' from one scene to another, so as to bring out the irrationality of the historical process–of the 1927 Shanghai revolution, when the late and unlamented Chiang Kai-Shek treacherously turned on his communist allies. Here Malraux is no Marxist: few books proclaim the tragedy of revolutionary fervour, and the corruption it carries in its wake, more powerfully than *La Condition humaine.* Malraux fought against Franco but *L'Espoir* is one of the most balanced novels to emerge from the Spanish conflict. At this stage the author could still, after tasting action, stand back from it and portray both its heroism and its absurdity. The tension in the novel is maintained by the conflict between man's capacity to discover himself in violent experience and the ridiculousness of violence itself. *Les Noyers de l'Altenburg* (1943; 1945; tr. *The Walnut Trees of Altenburg,* 1952), the last novel, is a part of a longer novel, *La Lutte avec l'Ange, The Battle with the Angel,* the rest of which was destroyed by the Gestapo. It is more autobiographical and philosophical than imaginative–and the reconstruction of Nietzsche's madness contained in it (recollected by the hero's great-uncle, represented as Nietzsche's friend) is significant. Though in this book Malraux largely abandons the scenes of violence in the description of which, in earlier novels, he had excelled, does he not also in this episode record the pointlessness of his own question, and suggest that his therefore pointless answer (the 'permanency of Art') is no more than a destructible artifact? After this he enters De Gaulle's first government (as Minister of Information) and then becomes his chief intellectual propagandist, famous for his frenzied if controlled rhetoric (his clawings at the air have been recalled by rapt watchers). *Antimémoires* (1967) is scarcely revealing: the politician and rhetorician has taken over. In 1972, having left politics with the General's fall, he is in Washington advising Nixon and Kissinger on how to approach the Chinese . . . The man lives behind a mask–but a mask that may be respected. An incomplete *Oeuvres complètes* appeared in Geneva in 1945.

Mandelstam, Osip (1892–?1941) Russian (Jewish) poet, prose writer, critic, translator. With Akhmatova (q.v.) and Gumilyov (q.v.) the leading acmeist (*see* Akhmatova). Some regard him as superior to all other Russian twentieth-century poets, including Blok (q.v.). His life after the Revolution was saturated with apolitical gloom about the Russian future and he ended as one of Stalin's victims (probably he died of a heart attack in or on his way to one of the camps near Vladivostock: he was arrested in 1934, exiled and then rearrested in 1938). Mandelstam was born in Warsaw, but grew up in St Petersburg, whose laureate he certainly is. He was a classicist and he is Russia's only poet to have made the classical style his model. His Russian, a critic has said, 'sounds like Latin', but his greatest love was for Greek poetry, and he shared Nietzsche's belief in the balance of the ancient Greek culture. Of Russian poets he preferred Bativskov (who influenced Pushkin and went mad), Pushkin, and Baratynsky. Mandelstam published three books of poetry in his lifetime: *Kamen* (1913), *Stone; Tristia* (1922); *Stikhotvoreniya* (1928), *Poetic Works.* But he wrote more poetry, some of it reflecting the anguish of his later years; this appeared in America in 1955 and 1961. His prose pieces, which are not important, were collected in two volumes; *O Poesii* (1928), *About Poetry,* collects his excellent and revealing criticism. He translated Romains (q.v.) and others. It has not often been noticed, but Nietzsche was a potent influence on him (he spent two terms at Heidelberg University in 1910): he understandingly accepted, though with great agony, the complex Nietzschean hypothesis of 'eternal recurrence'. In his case this involved an acceptance not of the literal truth of the proposition but of a poetic commitment to pain: 'Everything has been, and everything will happen again;/ for us only the moment of recognition has joy.' Thus poetry was for him a religion, a way of life–but he has none of the mysticism that characterizes so much of this century's Russian poetry. He was fiercely sincere. He will relate nature to metre and he will insomniously mourn the death of Homer and the end of antiquity; but he knows, terribly, that he is poised at a fearful moment of history. At first he had looked at the Russian turmoil with a fascinated horror and compassion; but he would not sacrifice his independence and when history turned against him he repudiated it for an inner life, based in the past, with a huge reluctance. Mandelstam's style became more complex, his poetry more tragic, but he never became numb, or ceased to feel. In the (appropriately) Nietzschean term, he 'overcame' himself despite his terror and the indignities he endured. He had, a friend said, 'an air of just-passing-throughness'. His intelligence, linguistic knowledge and learning are enormous, yet his power–though more subdued–is as great as that of the frenzied Blok (who was, incidentally, a Jew-hater). The French critical work *Osip Mandelstam* (1972) by Jean Blat contains some good translations of poetry and prose, and is a useful introduction. *The Complete Poetry* (1973) gives better versions than the over-ambitious W. S. Merwin (q.v.)–Clarence Brown selection: the former are miserably banal, but leave the reader to work out the poetry for himself: there are copious notes. But Clarence Brown's *Mandelstam* (1973) is an invaluable introduction to this supreme poet.

Mann, Heinrich (1871–1950) German novelist, playwright, essayist, Heinrich's reputation has by now (but once he was more famous) been largely eclipsed by that of his brother Thomas (q.v.); yet he has very considerable merits as well as faults. Thomas was a liberal-conservative, clever but not always ingenuous; Heinrich was always much further to the left, more honest, possessed, in the final analysis, of less profound insight–and he tended to rely in polemic where his brother relied on a sometimes rhetorical but at other times effectively ironic cunning. His early work is promising but has dated because of its calculatedly frenzied D'Annunzian and pseudo-Nietzschean decadence. In the short novel 'Pippo Spano' (tr. in *Tellers of Tales*, 1939), however, he equals his brother by dealing as clearly as he with the problem of the guilt of the artist. In *Professor Unrat* (1905; tr. *Small Town Tyrant*, 1944), which became the famous movie *The Blue Angel*, he institutes a line of psychologically exact satire that he was to continue in the first volume of a prophetic trilogy–*Der Untertan* (1918, *The Patrioteer*; tr. *Man of Straw*, 1947)–the succeeding volumes of which did not live up to the promise of the first. He wrote two more major books: the two novels about Henri IV of France (*Die Jugend des Königs Henri Quatre*, 1935, tr. *King Wren*, 1937 and *Die Vollendung des Königs Henri Quatre*, tr. *Henry, King of France*, 1939), and the autobiography *Ein Zeitalter wird besichtigt* (1945), *An Era Surveyed*. If Flaubert, as some say, 'proved' with *Salammbô* that the historical novel cannot be great, then Mann's eloquent, subtle, and imaginative account of Henri IV as artist-democrat-actor-King might well be put into the other scale of the balance. The autobiography is a model of honesty. There are many other notable novels and some effective plays. Heinrich Mann has now become a neglected author. A definitive *Gesammelte Werke* is in progress (1959–).

Mann, Leonard (1895) Australian novelist, poet. A gloomy post-naturalist, Mann–clumsy, tender and powerful–has been underrated. When mentioned at all the poor quality of his writing is almost inevitably alluded to; but, as with Dreiser (q.v.), his cumulative power could not be achieved without his dogged and inelegant persistence, which is therefore in one sense a virtue. Honesty, modesty, and compassionate puzzlement characterize all that he has written and he is certainly worthy to be called Australia's Dreiser. There are, too, muffled undertones of Dostoievski, especially in the best of the seven novels, *The Go-Getter* (1942). Another writer with whom Mann has affinities is Gissing, but the whining element is absent. *Flesh in Armour* (1932) was, with Manning's *Her Privates We,* the most distinguished Australian novel of the First World War. Mann is a gifted minor poet (e.g. *Elegiac and Other Poems,* 1957). Other novels include: *Andrea Caslin* (1959), *Venus Half-Caste* (1963).

Mann, Thomas (1875–1955) German novelist, publicist. Nobel Prize 1929. Mann is a strange case. His greatness may be undermined, but is indisputable. A man deeply divided between artistic 'decadence' and bourgeois virtue, both of which he saw as necessary to human beings but irreconcilable, he has four main styles (which are often bewilderingly mixed): the pompous and rhetorical publicist, the masterly narrator (more substantially in his early period), the ironist, and the poisonous decadent (e.g. *Der Erwählte,* 1951; tr. *The Holy Sinner,* 1951). His greatness consists in his capacity for deep insight into the creative needs of man and his recognition of the fact that this need, to be exercised, requires the practice of evil; it is chiefly flawed by his failure, except in some three or four *Novellen,* to resolve this problem–which is essentially that of *Künstlerschuld,* artist-guilt. All his novels except the more modest (but excellent) first, *Buddenbrooks* (1900; tr. 1924), suffer from one or more flaws: pretentiousness beyond the perhaps necessary degree, rhetoric, disingenuously ambiguous ironies, over-exploitation of parodic and other stylistic techniques within conventional frameworks. . . . He was dishonest and was not really likeable (in his capacity as Thomas Mann: author and public man); but he knew that these faults arose from his need to be creative and his sense of this self-knowledge had a moral and humane quality of feeling that make him almost forgivable. If he has been overrated, then it has been necessary (for all of us) to overrate him: for all his lapses, he knows so much. He was masterfully intelligent, but both his sensibility and his sensitivity can be seriously at fault. Mann did, however, survive decently as a person: after, unlike his politically more percipient brother Heinrich (q.v.), giving wholehearted support to the German cause in the First World War, he recanted, attacked fascism in various ways, and was amongst the first to be declared *persona non grata* (in 1933, while abroad). He settled in Switzerland, then the USA (he became a US citizen in 1944), and spent the final three years of his life back in Switzerland. He made a happy marriage in 1905. *Buddenbrooks,* though it contains the seeds of his later preoccupations, is in the nineteenth-century realistic tradition; that he always loved it showed both his nostalgia for the old days and his acute awareness that they had irrevocably passed. In a certain limited sense it is his most successful novel: a late masterpiece of its genre, it deals with the conflict between art and life without recourse to techniques of which Mann was never (for all his ingenuity) wholly master—because he hated them. The *Novellen Tonio Kröger* (1903) and *Der Tod in Venedig* (1911) (*Death in Venice*)—both, like nearly all Mann's fiction, are widely available in translation—display Mann at his greatest; both describe the predicament of the sophisticated modern artist in a perfectly balanced, moving and acutely penetrative manner. From now on, however, taking each of his works as a whole and allowing magnificent passages and sections, one admires rather than fully responds (the exception is perhaps the final unfinished novel, *Felix Krull*). The next major work is *Der Zauberberg* (1924; tr. *The Magic Mountain,* 1927), an artful parody of the *Bildungsroman,* which both ironically demolishes it and simultaneously wistfully attempts to perpetuate it. The *Bildungsroman,* 'education novel', dealt (essentially) with a passive hero's capacity philosophically to adapt himself to (not to influence) the true meaning of society; it was an attempt to relate the individual to society. The hero of *Der Zauberberg,* once 'healthy' (nineteenth-century), goes to a sanatorium where he 'learns' the new sophistication; he survives, but it is 1914 and the events of history threaten him. . . . This has marvellous episodes, but its confusions are not resolved: one can say no more than that Mann attempted too much. The Biblical trilogy on

Joseph (1934–43) is invaluable to critics of Mann, but fails badly as a whole, above all because of its pretentiously archaic style. *Doktor Faustus* (1947), on the life of a modernist composer, is a massive failure: massive because of the ingenuity of its complex techniques and its sheer grasp of the problem of art and virtue, a failure not because it fails to solve this problem (who could?) but because this account of it is more calculated than imaginative: intuition is absent, the *real* artist, who can convey the sense of creative pressure even while he cannot explain it, is withdrawn. At the end of his life Mann took up a story of 1922 and expanded it into a novel: *Die Bekenntnisse des Hochstaplers Felix Krull* (1954; tr. 1958). This, though comic and at times even picaresque, is none the less a confession of his bleak pessimism. He had seen very clearly—as clearly as anyone in his century—but after about 1912 he had creatively cheated, he had accepted the 'greatness' conferred upon him without acknowledging that he no longer possessed the capacity to lyricize, the courage to abandon himself to his creative depths.

Mansfield, Katherine (ps. Kathleen Mansfield Beauchamp) (1888–1923) New Zealand short-story writer who went to England in 1908 and settled there. She died of tuberculosis in the Gurdjieff community at Fontainebleau. Married Middleton Murry (q.v.). It is tempting to attack Mansfield's famous 'sensibility' and it has been done not without point (e.g. by Frank O'Connor). But is she over-, or just wrongly, rated? Most of her best stories range back into her childhood and here she shows control and unique insight: shock at her brother Leslie's death in an accident behind the lines sent her into this reverie, which at least is fortunate for posterity. Some stories are cunningly arch, for she could seldom keep her extreme neuroticism within bounds unless she dwelt in the past; the 'sensibility' is sometimes an over-literary pretence at control. A new and fair evaluation is required. 'Life of Ma Parker', 'At the Bay' and 'The Fly' (not set in New Zealand) are supreme examples of her fiction; her *Journal* (1954) and *Letters* (1928; 1951) contain possibly her finest writing of all. *Collected Stories* (1945).

Marinetti, Filippo Tommaso (1876–1944) Italian literary publicist, poet, novelist, playwright, fascist. Born in Egypt, Marinetti spent his youth in Paris; his first writings are in French. For a short time, after the publication of his 1909 futurist manifesto, Marinetti seemed to have synthesized a new spirit in Italian letters. Many Italians (e.g. Palazzeschi, q.v., Papini, Govoni, q.v.) passed through futurism. The program of the special manifesto on literature was inconsistent since it advocated the rejection of the past, of syntax, of rules, but at the same time exalted war, nationalism and machinery (which is, after all, constructed systematically or not at all). Marinetti's own work is energetic but wholly superficial; he alone remained faithful to futurism—which was, more than anything, a rationalization of the D'Annunzionism (q.v.) that Italians only thought they had rejected—and was, logically enough, honoured by the fascists. But he made a real impact on pre-war Europe and his career is more pathetic than repulsive: he could not see beyond his own immediate and frenzied feelings.

Martin du Gard, Roger (1881–1958) French novelist, playwright and letter-writer. Nobel Prize 1937. Close friend of Gide (q.v.). Martin du Gard had many literary connections and friendships, but kept both his private life and his own opinions (despairingly socialistic) as secret as he could. Above all he sought objectivity, accuracy of historical background, fair-mindedness. Ironically, it is his fastidious integrity—perhaps combined with a lack of linguistic intensity—that just robs his work of greatness. He was, as he recognized, a divided man: on the one hand a rebel, an isolate, a zestful tragedian, misanthropist and pessimist; on the other a passionate archivist (he studied history and archaeology between 1899 and 1905), an objectivist, even an apostle of reason. In between: an earthy comedian. Much of his correspondence, which was voluminous, cannot be published until 1983; this, together with other personal material, is perhaps more clearly revelatory of his seminal mind and of his virtue than any of his work—unless the unfinished novel, *Le Journal du Colonel Maumort, The Diary of Colonel Maumort,* on which he worked between 1941 and his death, proves to be a masterpiece. He apparently could not find a satisfactory form for it; an edition is in preparation. Martin du Gard must at present be judged, therefore, on *Jean Barois* (1913), the eight volume *roman-fleuve,* his most famous book, *Les Thibault* (1922–40; tr. *The Thibaults,* 1937–41), the brilliant novella about incest, *Confidence Africaine* (1931), *African Confidence,* and on his three ferocious farces of rural life, of which the best is *Vieille France* (1933), translated as *The Postman* (1955). His plays, of which the most interesting is *Un*

Taciturne (1933), *A Silent One,* on homosexuality, are less successful. *Jean Barois* traces, both inside and outside the mind of its eponymous hero, the great debate between rationalism and religion, and over the Dreyfus affair, that convulsed France in the years before the First World War. It is intelligent and worthy in the best sense of the term and will undoubtedly survive, but is somewhat weighed down by earnestness. *Les Thibault,* profoundly naturalistic in spirit, though by no means enfeebled by naturalistic theories about heredity, is above all about what led to the First World War, what it did, and the hopelessness it stood for. It is the chronicle (cf. Duhamel's *Chronique des Pasquier,* q.v.) of a French family, the Thibaults (and their neighbours the Fontanins), in the years before and during the First World War. Massive in its detail, its grasp of its main characters, its honesty, *Les Thibault* is one of the most tragic major novels of the century. It lacks humour and scarcely compensates for this. Martin du Gard's earthy sense of comedy came out in his three tales and two plays about peasants, whom, however, he undisguisedly and unreservedly loathed: 'that accursed race', he publicly called them. These works are virulent, scatological: pictures of greed, boredom, lust, stupidity, malice and cunning relieved only by a raging humour. Possibly *Confidence Africaine,* a bland first-person account of incest with a sister, is the published novel in which Martin du Gard's gifts are most fully integrated. He is in any case a writer of fascinating sensibility, perhaps one of the few great writers-manqués.

Martinson, Harry (1904) Swedish poet, novelist, playwright, essayist. Nobel Prize (with Eyvind Johnson) 1974. Martinson's father died when he was six, whereupon his mother deserted him for America. He was an international tramp and seaman during the twenties; by the mid-thirties he was an established literary figure in Sweden, the leading member of the so-called 'Five Young Men' who emerged in 1929 (the only other to have survived with as high a reputation is Arthur Lundkvist, 1906, who is a confused and derivative writer, a Swedish sounding-board for all modernist phenomena). Martinson's best work was mostly done by 1945, when the volume of poetry *Passad, Trade Winds,* was published. This showed some evidence of the influence, albeit oblique, of Saint-John Perse (q.v.), perhaps acquired through his friend Lundkvist. Most of his writing since then has been overcalculated, 'cosmic' and hence, ultimately, pretentious, for his genius lies in his spontaneity—and even the earlier poetry and prose fails when Martinson 'takes thought' and becomes mannered, literary, or sentimental. He is thus always uneven. His travel books (e.g. *Kap Farväl*, 1933; tr. *Cape Farewell*, 1934) and the autobiographies of his early life, *Nässlorna blomma* (1935; tr. *Flowering Nettle*, 1935) and *Vägen ut* (1936), *The Way Out*, are objective, affirmative and vivid. His three very best books, however, contain lyrical and loving observations of nature, largely unencumbered by speculation or existential anxiety: *Svärmare och harkrank* (1937), *Dreamers and Daddy-Long-Legs*, *Midsommardalen* (1938), *Midsummer Valley* and *Det enkla och det svåra* (1939), *The Easy and the Difficult*. The poetry is minor, but at its best when it approximates to the smaller concerns of these prose books. Martinson became disillusioned with Russia after visiting it in the thirties and fought for Finland in the Winter War. Thereafter he became obsessed with science—his library is said to contain mostly popular books on the subject—and the attainment of an intellectual 'position'. This does not suit him and the long 'space poem' *Anaira* (1956; ad. 1963) shows it. The best of his post-1945 work is in the novel *Vägen till Klockrike* (1948; tr. *The Road*, 1955), about tramps. This is inchoate, but the central character, the vagabond cigar roller Bolle, is a convincing objective correlative for Martinson himself.

Masefield, John (1878–1967) English poet (Laureate from 1930), novelist, critic. As a young man Masefield stood out from the bulk of his indifferent generation. He had been to sea, and the early narrative poems (*The Everlasting Mercy*, 1911; *Dauber*, 1913) had a force of colloquial language and a realism quite missing from the verse of Phillips, Newbolt or Watson or any other of the poets then in vogue. He was superior to Brooke (q.v.). These poems, and *Reynard the Fox* (1919), are better than the lyrics of *Salt-Water Ballads* (1902), but those are pellucid, vigorous minor poems. Masefield's plays are unsuccessful but not disastrous. His poetry totally collapsed after about 1920, though he went on writing poorer and poorer poems until his death. *Collected Poems* (1923) contains everything worth reading, but there is a *Collected Poems* of 1938. His romantic criticism is not scholarly or subtle but it generates enthusiasm: the best example is the one-volume *William Shakespeare* (1911 rev. 1954), which is among the best introductions. It is in his novels, however, that he did his finest work. The Stevensonian *Jim Davis* (1911) is one of the best children's adventure stories of this century. *Sard Harker* (1924), *Odtaa* (1926), *Eggs and Baker* (1936) and *Dead Ned* (1938) are all good novels in their racy, vigorous, adventurous genre. The autobiographical fragments of his extreme old age, *Grace Before Ploughing* (1966), reveal a man of great sweetness. Masefield's prolificity and his abject official poems have tended to distract attention from his limited but substantial achievement.

Masters, Edgar Lee (1868–1950) American (born in Kansas but raised in Illinois) populist who wrote one important book: *Spoon River Anthology* (1915). With Lindsay (q.v.) and Sandburg (q.v.) Masters formed part of a midwestern trio who were more or less intellectually 'wanting' but who, by their intuitive sense of their roots, subjected regionalism to a radical reappraisal and thus, if only incidentally, pointed towards its national possibilities–in a huge federation of states this is not as paradoxical as it sounds. Masters's friend Lindsay was the most poetically gifted of these men and Sandburg was the least unintelligent. Masters is called a poet, but even in *Spoon River Anthology* he is hardly this. He had studied printing and law and tried literature–without success. Then by a happy accident an editor gave him a copy of a set of J. W. Mackail's translations from the *Greek Anthology*. Masters had taught himself Greek but it was the Mackail versions that inspired him. *Spoon River Anthology* is a set of epitaphs spoken by the inhabitants of the cemetery of an Illinois town (a combination of Petersburg and Lewisburg). These ironic comments on the hypocrisies and defeats inflicted on men by their own selfishness, and by the decay of the old ways are prose effectually cast in the form of free verse. They exactly catch the atmosphere and the psychology of the midwest of 1880–1914–and Masters expressed this perfectly through his new awareness of the affinity, in the matter of lucidity and candour, between Greek and English. But this book was the record of a high point of disillusionment; thereafter Masters collapsed into a naive agrarian. Underlying the portrait of a rotting town given in *Spoon River Anthology* had been a barely grasped vision of an older and more gracious order. That order had never existed in 'Spoon River', but it has the poetic validity of the populist dream (cf. Lindsay). Masters could not go on to face the fact of its impossible remoteness, or like Lindsay, to try to make it real in poetry. He continued to write unheeded books, including fiction and verse. His account of Lindsay is invaluable and his *Lincoln, the Man* (1931), savaged on its appearance because it accuses Lincoln of being an enemy of liberty, deserves another look.

Maugham, William Somerset (1874–1965) English fiction writer, playwright, memoirist. Maugham is one of those writers whose immense success—as playwright as well as novelist—has unjustly affected his reputation. He was read and enjoyed by a middlebrow audience, but only in his clever plays did he pander to their tastes. He qualified as a doctor but did not practise. Maugham was a bisexual and his ambivalent attitude towards women is clearly revealed in his fiction, but this by no means always functions as a distorting factor. His art was not obtrusive and he did not try to be an innovator, but his intelligence has been underestimated. His early novels are influenced by French naturalism (*see* Zola)—he was born in Paris, knew French literature intimately, and lived in the South of France from 1930—and *Of Human Bondage* (1915) was introduced by Dreiser (q.v.), who had written an enthusiastic review on its first appearance, in an American edition of 1938. *Liza of Lambeth* (1897) is an excellent first novel about the London slums and shows a depth of feeling and sensitivity that is absent from Maugham's fiction after 1915. *Of Human Bondage,* a revision of an earlier unpublished novel, intensifies this feeling and the charge that it is flawed by careless writing is not a relevant one: it is a major novel, despite some lapses of structure and style. It has exercised an enormous influence on foreign literatures (e.g. Tanizaki, q.v., wrote a Japanese variation on its theme). The view that Maugham's 'view of women here . . . seems essentially a male fantasy of the ideal lover and mother' woodenly misses the point. Actually Maugham resolves, and partly by a device used by Proust (q.v.)—the portrayal of a man as a woman—some of the problems of his own ambisexuality. He admitted that the novel was partially autobiographical but its fictional elements are perhaps more intimately autobiographical than its reflections of his immediate experience (as medical student and resident of Paris). *The Moon and Sixpence* (1919), suggested by the life of Gauguin, explores the nature of the artistic predicament more romantically and is less successful. Maugham's plays are very skilful and brought him prestige but they do not represent the best of his work. The one-act *The Breadwinner* (1930) is perhaps the best. In 1921 Maugham published his first short-story collection, and it was as a short-story writer that he became chiefly known in the last forty years of his long life (*Complete Stories*, 1951). In this form Maugham's achievement is considerable. He travelled all over the world and his shorter fiction reflects his vivid sense of place (particularly the tropics) with great brilliance. He was a master of the form (he learned much from Maupassant) but it cannot be said that many of his stories fall into the slick, over-well-made category. He combines compassion with irony and his anecdotal approach perfectly suits his informed-man-of-the-world, personally resigned but never indifferent, attitude. His novels after 1915 are readable and intelligent, but only *Cakes and Ale* (1930) comes anywhere near the status of *Of Human Bondage.* His autobiographies (included in *The Partial View,* 1954) and *A Writer's Notebook* (1949) are of great interest. *Collected Plays* (1952); *Collected Works* (1931–); *Selected Novels* (1953). His last book, *Purely For My Pleasure* (1962), was about his superb art collection.

Mauriac, François (1885–1970) French novelist, playwright, critic, poet, biographer, journalist. Nobel Prize 1952. Most of his fiction is set in or around his native Bordeaux, whose atmosphere he memorably evokes. He is a powerful writer but almost all his imaginative work after *Le Noeud de vipères* (1932; tr. *The Knot of Vipers,* 1951) is neutralized by piety. It is an error not to separate the earlier, tormented, superior Mauriac from the later, whose creative conscience is troubled (with consequent and welcome gushes of radiant pessimism) but who is throwing himself into the arms of a malodorous dogmatism. It could be argued that *Le Mystère Frontenac* (1933; tr. *The Frontenac Mystery,* 1952) just stays within the bounds of Mauriac's vision, but it is a weak work; *La Fin de la nuit* (1935; tr. in *Thérèse,* 1947–see below for the Thérèse Desqueyroux saga and its significance in Mauriac's work: the whole is tr. in *Thérèse*) is an uneasy lie in his own teeth, unfaithful to his own view. Mauriac began as a scholar but soon turned to poetry and fiction. As he fell under the spell of Barrès–a weakness he could never overcome–he also fell under that of the pagan, sensual Gide (q.v.). Later, as priests moved in to ensnare his genius, he was to disown Gide but to grant him a 'terrible sincerity'; of his position Gide remarked (1931), with a more savage truth, that it amounted to saying 'that if he were a perfect Christian, he would cease to have any material of which to make his novels'. It is ironic that Mauriac, worried by criticisms of his pessimism, should ever have considered that he had, as one critic has put it, 'underestimated the power of love': the novels of his major period (1922–32) never do underestimate this, since they continually imply it. What they do is to demonstrate the cruelty of God (axiomatic for Mauriac), the power of lust, and the terrible extent to which evil feelings—hypocrisy (Mauriac—with Bernanos, q.v.—is France's most passionate of all haters of the *bien pensants*), greed, jealousy, the desire for revenge—can rule the lives of human beings. These are major novels because they are, like our own lives, our own intentions, our own self-styled loves, ambiguous. It may fairly be charged that Mauriac, in this period, creates characters who fulfill his 'Jansenist' intentions: men and women who do not and cannot possess the will to know God and who therefore lack free will. (The non-Catholic reader may take for 'God', 'love', 'mercy' and so on: a complex of in some way saving externals existent in our world.) But there are such, and a novelist must follow the open choice of his imagination and not that of any closed system. *Le Baiser au lépreux* (1922; tr. *A Kiss for the Leper*, 1950) is usually said to be totally pessimistic; but the anguish of the physically repulsive Péloueyre and of his suffering wife Noémi has its poetry and its episodes of courage. The oneiric *Genitrix* (1923; tr. 1950) confirms that Mauriac had entered into that (creatively) fruitful situation in which as a whole man he was unable to accept the nature of existence; the writer in him could create a terror-theology of lust. It shows that Mauriac's anguished erotic preoccupations ('For a century would I await that second when our bodies/Will insult the sky with their intermingled thirsts . . . ?' he wrote in a bad poem of this period) were in fact based in incest-horror: *Genitrix* is, to all intents and purposes, the story of a man, nominally married to another woman, who is actually (of course metaphorically) married to his own mother—whose pleasure is to destroy him. Mauriac's most powerful fiction is as 'Freudian' (q.v.) as that of anyone in this century: it takes us into the centre of that 'real world' of nightmare in which none of us can quite believe. *Le Désert de l'amour* (1925; tr. *The Desert of Love,* 1949) is more compassionate but it must still be interpreted in the light of the Oedipal situation. With *Thérèse Desqueyroux* (1927) Mauriac wrote a less complex but more committedly 'anti-orthodox' novel. Its sequels (*La Fin de la nuit*—and two stories written in 1933) put him into deep trouble. Thérèse, bored, Lesbian, tries to poison her husband; she is tried, but his false testimony saves her. Eventually she leaves him and goes to Paris. Like Clyde in

Dreiser's (q.v.) *American Tragedy,* she is ready to kill, but finally begins to do so only because of an accidental circumstance. Here Gide's influence is at its uppermost: the central character uses crime to free herself from stifling circumstances. Soon afterwards Mauriac underwent (*circa* 1929) his 'crisis': among the results were *Le Noeud de vipères* and *La Fin de la nuit.* The first presents a 'conversion' (Mauriac's own 'conversion'): the world of most of the book is as black as ever, its central character Louis more deliberately horrible than any other of Mauriac's. But he becomes a 'saved character' and one can say only that while this change of heart does represent a sincere and lyrical hope on the part of the writer, in psychological terms it fails. The revived Thérèse is an artistic disaster: sensationalist, melodramatic, Mauriac tries to write up her salvation as though he were God. Conor Cruise O'Brien, whose study of Mauriac in his *Maria Cross* (1963) is quite the best, rightly accuses the novelist of trying to solve an emotional problem intellectually. Of the later work only *La Pharisienne* (1941; tr. *A Woman of the Pharisees,* 1946) possesses the old touch of genius: the vividness of his portrait of a hypocritical woman undermines his pious intention to write the 'Catholic novel' in which he did not in any case believe. Mauriac's theatre is for the most part dead—only *Asmodée* (1938; tr. 1939) achieved popular success. When all has been said, even the weak Mauriac is a writer of the highest standards, possessed of a lucid and excellent style, capable of unforgettable vignettes. His personal integrity is not in question. The *Journal 1932–39* (1947) and *Journal* (1950) are important. *Le Cahier noir* (1943; tr. *The Black Note Book,* 1944), under the necessary pseudonym of Forez, was written while he was active in the Resistance. All the novels appear in English versions. The *Oeuvres complètes* (1950–) contains almost all his writings.

Maurois, André (ps. Émile Herzog) (1885–1967) French critic, biographer, novelist, miscellaneous writer. Born in Elbeuf (about thirty miles south of Rouen), of Jews from Alsace, he said of it that if you wanted to see people at the windows you had better shout 'fire!' not 'help!'. Though very well known and versatile as well as uneven, he has not had his full due. He was an ardent Anglophile but his biographies of Shelley, Byron and other Englishmen are not his best work: though racy and well conceived, they are over-romanticized and lack psychological depth. But *A la Recherche de Marcel Proust* (1949;

tr. *The Quest for Proust,* 1950) is a magnificent achievement and remains—amazingly, in view of the number of its competitors—the best general book on Proust (q.v.); this is first-class writing from an author generally second-class. The English conflation of two of his books of essays, *From Proust to Sartre* (1967), contains invaluable studies of Mauriac (q.v.), Romains (q.v.), Gide (q.v.), Valéry (q.v.), Sartre (q.v.), Claudel (q.v.) and others. Maurois, a most genial and intelligent man, can be superficial; he can also be surprisingly profound, as on Proust. This is in part due to the influence exerted upon him by his teacher, the philosopher Alain (ps. E. Chartier, 1868–1951), whom Maurois overrated but who nevertheless combined depth with a shallowness that resulted from trying to be over-laconic and paradoxical (cf. Chesterton, q.v.). Maurois's fiction is elegant, minor and ironically observant (e.g. *Les Silences de Colonel Bramble,* 1918; tr. *The Silence of Colonel Bramble,* 1927 rev. 1940; *Bernard Quesnay,* 1926; tr. 1927—the best—and *Les Roses de Septembre,* 1956). *Mémoires* (1970).

Mayakovsky, Vladimir (1893–1930) Russian poet, dramatist, activist. He was the pre-eminent poet of the Revolution but he is always much better (despite the insult of Stalin's admiration) than a merely political poet; he became disillusioned with Bolshevism and killed himself. Mayakovsky is not the best twentieth-century Russian poet, but no twentieth-century poet has possessed more vitality. Even his crassly propagandist poetry is appealing. Early on Mayakovsky became a notorious revolutionary figure (he was three times imprisoned) and he was among the leading Russian futurists. Russian futurism did not accept Marinetti's (q.v.) Italian futurism—when Marinetti visited Russia in 1914 Mayakovsky had already published an attack on him, repudiating his advocacy of war and proclaiming Russian futurism's independence—but had many elements in common with it: the manifesto 'A Slap in the Face for Public Taste' (1912) attacked the whole Russian literary past, especially symbolism, and pleaded for radical linguistic experiment. Mayakovsky, Khlebnikov (q.v.)—the real founder, and a more substantial figure than Marinetti—and their friends also welcomed the age of machinery and looked forward to the Revolution. Mayakovsky's bourgeois-baiting was often amusing and salutary. He threw himself heart and soul into Bolshevism and produced much strident verse but at heart he was an individualist and not a collectivist. His disillusion and his unhappy love affair with Lili Brik (wife of Osip Brik) led him to shoot himself. His best poetry is sensitive, resonant and mostly about love (e.g. the great last unfinished poem, in particular the fragment, found in his pocket, beginning 'It's past one o'clock'). Much of the less good poetry is in 'stepped lines' (cf. W. C. Williams), and even when the content is banal it has an inspired vitality. He is an accentual poet, using (though Russian prosody is different from British) a sort of 'sprung rhythm' (*see* Hopkins); his verse is flexible, laconic, startling and owes a great deal to folk-poetry. His drama is versatile and similarly striking; the last two satirical plays, *Klop* (1928; tr. *The Bedbug* in *The Bedbug and Selected Poetry*, 1962) and *Banya* (1930), *The Bathhouse*, undoubtedly reveal his increasing contempt for the developments under his admirer Stalin. Significantly, he wrote an impassioned poem on the suicide, which he criticized, of Esenin (q.v.). *Mayakovsky and His Poetry* (1965) contains a selection. There is much more in his work than mere propaganda (*agitka*), and he is an exciting poet. But non-Russian criticism of him is not often distinguished or helpful. At heart he was a religious (non-Christian) modernist but with his roots more firmly in tradition than many of his contemporaries.

McAuley, James (1917) Australian poet, critic; founder-editor of *Quadrant* (1955–). McAuley (with Harold Stewart) perpetrated the notorious 'Ern Malley' hoax (1944); he tricked the simple-minded editor of *Angry Penguins*, Max Harris, into accepting as genuine an inchoate, Dylan-Thomas-like, deceased *poète maudit* whose verse had been got up for a joke. This was partly a prank but it indicated McAuley's humour and critical pungency—he remains Australia's shrewdest critic of poetry (*The End of Modernity*, 1959). His poetry has proved to be a disappointment: he shows himself as the doomed heir of Australian traditionalism in the sense that he, like his predecessors, has failed to capture the sound of his own Australian voice; to compensate for this McAuley has adopted an aggressive 'classicism' which belies his critical eclecticism and shrewdness. The result has transformed him from gifted, Rilkean lyrical poet into self-conscious defender of classical light: he has cut the 'blackness' out of himself as though it did not exist: has wrongly equated it with the trivial nihilism of much modern poetry and has turned himself into a demonstrator of the virtues of the past. 'The corruption of a poet is the generation of a critic.' His poetic voice is thus inadequate to voice his despair. The skill of his earlier lyrics suggests that he may still turn back into himself. *Collected Poems* (1971).

McCarthy, Mary (1912) American novelist, journalist, critic, travel writer. She was for a time married to Edmund Wilson (q.v.). Mary McCarthy is an odd mixture; her true category–that of the very 'highest' (but not 'heavy') middlebrow author who is capable of, and sometimes brings off, even better things–is instructive. As novelist she is readable, formally traditionalist, acidulated, witty and a castigator of intellectuals (she is herself *par excellence* an intellectual) and their pretensions. As travel-writer (*Venice Observed,* 1956; *The Stones of Florence,* 1959) she is, stylistically, insufferably pretentious. As critic she seldom goes deeply, though her woman-wit, when she does not indulge it too obviously, is often penetrative. She has always been a radical, though a critical one; her attacks on the Vietnam war (e.g. *Vietnam,* 1967) were useful and well executed. The best novels are *The Oasis* (1949) and *The Groves of Academe* (1952): these satirized the kind of people amongst whom she had moved. The latter is certainly a minor satirical classic and is lacking only in feeling and compassion, which as an author she lacks. But she does have a keen cerebral understanding of sexuality, even though she cannot convey sexually emotional states without deprecating them. The autobiographical *Memoirs of a Catholic Girlhood* (1957) suggests that her shortcomings in this respect are confined to her fiction. *The Group* (1963) traces the fortunes of a group of girls who were all contemporaries at Vassar (her own university). It is intelligent entertainment, with some sharp analyses of masculine attitudes, but, being on a larger scale than *The Groves of Academe,* it is ultimately shallow–and a certain type of ingratiating fluency, and even a cunningly disguised sentimentality are deliberately employed to cover up the superficiality. *Writings on the Wall* (1970) collects recent criticism, much of which, once again, sacrifices robustness for cleverness.

McCullers, Carson (1917–67) American novelist, short-story writer, playwright. Carson McCullers was a Southern (Georgian) writer who struggled, with exuberance and courage, against ill-health and adversity. She suffered from recurrent attacks of pneumonia, a series of paralytic strokes and, finally, cancer of the breast. Her first marriage ended in divorce in 1940. In 1945 she re-married her first husband who, wounded in the war, became an alcoholic drug-addict subject to fits of psychotic aggression. She left him and soon afterwards he killed himself. She worked on until the end, when a stroke killed her, but she had little chance to fulfil the promise of her earlier work. Nothing she did is without quality and she never betrays a sign of self-pity. She had done her best work before she reached thirty. However, *Reflections in a Golden Eye* (1941), her worst novel, appeared in this early period. It is clearly, in part, an attempt to work out her marital problems, and it fails badly. Her three best works are her first novel, *The Heart is a Lonely Hunter* (1940), her third, *The Member of the Wedding* (1946: she successfully dramatized this, 1951), and the story 'The Ballad of the Sad Café' (1943: this is the title of an omnibus volume containing all the novels to date and six more stories, 1951). There are other excellent stories; the last novel, *Clock Without Hands* (1961), does not come off, though it is superior to *Reflections in a Golden Eye*. Albee (q.v.) made a stage adaptation of 'The Ballad of the Sad Café' in 1963. When Carson McCullers wrote within her limitations she transcended them; she crippled her ability when she tried to transcend them. Her fiction does consist of grotesques or cripples set against a decadent Southern background (it has been called 'unromantic', but it is often romantically naturalist); but, as in the first and third novels, she was capable of a precise psychological tenderness—especially in the justly famous portrait of Frankie, in *The Member of the Wedding*, whose 'world' is seen through this adolescent girl's lyrical-innocent eyes. In the best work the lyricism of Carson McCullers irradiates its corrupted setting. Her chief limitation was that she could not go further than this. But she has done something no one else has done in modern Southern fiction: seen the whole putrifying mess, with its beautiful and beckoning colours of decay, through an innocent eye. In what is perhaps her masterpiece, 'The Ballad of the Sad Café', her lyricism is concealed. The plot and the outcome could hardly be more grotesque, tragic and pessimistic. But the manner in which the story is told, as though it were a half-humorous fairy tale, transforms what might have been an exercise in sensationalist Gothic into a classic which evokes wonder rather than horror. O'Connor (q.v.), also the Southern victim of a hateful disease, is undoubtedly ranked higher but Carson McCullers's work stays in the mind in a way which suggests that she is at least as excellent. *The Square Root of Wonderful* (1958) is a poor play in which (gallantly) she tries to push away the trauma of her marriages by treating them as flippant comedy.

McGinley, Phyllis (1905) Canadian-born American writer of light verse. Her position appears to be frankly sentimental and middlebrow-oriented but the poet at the core is as sharp as she is relaxed, because she does not have to care what critics think of her. She is at her best when reporting, unmaliciously, on what her own audience (she is predominantly a *New Yorker* poet) gets up to. At her weaker she is fun; her best poems have been perhaps the best of their difficult genre, as practised over the past half-century by such as Nash (q.v.) and Betjeman (q.v.), to both of whom she is superior. *Times Three* (1960), a retrospective selection, was introduced by Auden (q.v.).

McLuhan, Marshall (1911) Publicist, literary critic, teacher, recently the lynch-pin of an organization run by a man who, among other things, sells literature which tells you how to double your car's m.p.g., live to well over a hundred, achieve mastery over others, get into tune with the universe, etc. 'Midcult's Mr Big' (Benjamin de Mott) McLuhan, a Canadian, became converted to Roman Catholicism in 1937. He has been influential; but there is enough in the symposium *McLuhan Hot and Cool* (1967) and in Jonathan Miller's *McLuhan* (1971) to reveal him for what he is. If he has value then this consists in what Miller has called a creation of a 'possibility of truth' into which the very monstrousness of his contempt for truth may succeed in shocking us. . . . McLuhan's main work is *The Gutenberg Galaxy* (1962); the rest of his output, some of it done in collaboration, consists of a series of repetitions of its theses. McLuhan's 'message' is (briefly) that the spoken word is 'hotter' (in his vocabulary this means richer, more capable of carrying a complex message) than the written word. Therefore the invention of printing not only strained man's limited visual sense but also caused him to believe it to have powers it does not possess. However, despite the wickedness of machinery, mankind may now be saved by the new electronic media, particularly TV. We can give up reading and join together in one (Teilhard-de-Chardin-like) 'nervous system': the electronic 'global village'. A vital corollary is that the medium *is* the message—seldom has the form-content problem been so simplistically solved. This is necessarily a very compressed account of McLuhan's message or medium—though one cannot over-simplify it.

Clearly there is 'something in it', but it is better to go to McLuhan's sources than to McLuhan in order to get the value inherent in it, by going to (for example) William James (q.v.), Bergson (q.v.), Pirandello (q.v.), Wölfflin, and to modern psychology. Critics have tended to take McLuhan seriously as a thinker; they have failed to see that he is merely a user of other people's ideas, which he treats as he treats facts: if they don't fit in he simply changes or ignores them. The consequences of McLuhan's own program, if any should trouble to develop it seriously (it has done its work for him), are politically sinister beyond measure; but he does not seem to have the feeling to see this, or to care.

Mencken, H. L. (1880–1956) American editor, journalist, critic. Mencken is an odd mixture of the good and the atrocious. However, as literary journalist he is incomparably better than anyone now working (in that exclusive capacity) in the English-speaking world. He was above all a newspaperman; this and his lack of much formal education explain the notorious unevenness of his literary criticism. He was a useful and amusing scourge of what he called the 'booboisie' and of the various over-intense expressions of American Puritanism but it must be pointed out that he made no attempt to understand the all-important influence of Puritanism. Many of his rude aphorisms, then, are shallow, yet the *Prejudices* series (1919, 1920, 1922, 1924, 1926, 1927) make excellent reading and there are flashes of insight. He could not see that Sinclair Lewis (q.v.) was not in the class of Dreiser (q.v.) and Anderson (q.v.), but he did draw sensible attention to the merits of the two latter writers. He did 'lack taste and scholarship', he did mis-read Nietzsche—but who can be quite sure if he has not?—but was he, as John McCormick claims, 'first in the modern line of radical reactionaries that leads to the John Birch Society'? This is an unfair judgement: he was an over-busy journalist who ignored certain sinister political developments and made misjudgements (he failed to acknowledge the Depression until far too late), but his faults are not basically those of a reactionary. One can detect a streak of decency underlying all his work, even the too hastily thrown-off stuff. And *The American Language* (1919–48; abridged ed. 1963), though described by some linguists as a mere popularization of their own work, is a useful book. He was a good enough editor (*The Smart Set*, 1908–23; *The American Mercury*, 1924–33), to be discussed in the same bracket as Ford (q.v.),

Harris (q.v.) and Babits (q.v.). *The Mencken Crestomathy* (1949), *The Vintage Mencken* (1955), *Letters* (1961).

Merwin, W. S. (1927) American poet, playwright, translator. Merwin nervously nudges the mysterious but his literary opportunism and excessive skill as pasticheur rob his poetry of authenticity: he seems, in the words of one of his American contemporaries, as 'cold as hell'. He began as an involute new criticism poet, then moved to a style that mixes Williams (q.v.) and French post-surrealist poetry. It is all elegant and intellectually impeccable; but a sense of desperate sexual unhappiness and guilt (common to many poets) comes across as through a filter of insincerity parading as metaphysicality. There are sporadic, sad and appealing gestures towards feeling, but the general impression is of a man curious about, but unable to plunge himself into, contradictory emotional certainties. He has found some compensation in his Neruda (q.v.) translations, but a too perfect solace in his versions of Jean Follain (1969), whom he rationalizes into a deep-freeze landscape-for-emotion poet. *A Mask for Janus,* 1952 (the stanzaic manner), *The Lice,* 1967 (the 'continental plus Williams' manner). Nothing but courage is to prevent Merwin from turning from a model-poet into a poet. His poetry has aroused considerable, though rather defensive, admiration, but seems to excite no one to enthusiasm. The obstacle could be his studied lack of humour: his sometimes vaunted 'dignity'.

Michaux, Henri (1899) Belgian poet, prose writer, artist. He was first discovered and introduced by Gide (q.v.) in a short book (1941). He now prefers painting to writing and has recently concentrated on it—and on experiments with drugs (for a cogent discussion of these and Michaux's books about them see Octavio Paz, q.v., in *Corriente Alterna,* 1967, tr. *Alternating Current,* 1974). Michaux is a versatile, secretive, bewildering, humorous, continually surprising writer. For the majority of readers he is most accessible through his sketches about his Chaplinesque character M. Plume: *Un certain Plume* (1930). Some of these are in the bilingual *Selected Writings* (1952), which contains translations from *L'Espace de dedans* (1944), *The Space Within,* the author's own selection from his earlier work. As a young man he went to sea and his first books are vivid descriptions of his travels. Among his first admirers and encouragers was the percipient Jules Supervielle (q.v.). His work displays an uncanny mixture of shrewd realism, decent compassion—and intensely phenomenological, inner inventiveness. He aims to 'exorcise' (as he has explained) his tensions by 'outbursts'; these are sometimes wildly funny, sometimes tragically serious. His creation, Plume, is perhaps his greatest and most memorable achievement. Gide's (q.v.) appreciation of him, which was unsolemn, has been criticized by over-earnest writers as superficial; but Gide, who was never himself superficial, was in the main correct, and his book is better than other, later and more heavyweight ones. Michaux claims no confidence in the poem or, indeed, in any process of achieving self-sufficiency.

Miller, Arthur (1915) American playwright, fiction writer. Miller is perhaps the most distinguished contemporary author of 'well-made' plays in the English-speaking world. He makes some use of the techniques of Brecht (q.v.) and Pirandello (q.v.), but his chief debts are to Ibsen and (this has not been so fully acknowledged by critics) Shaw (q.v.). Like Bellow (q.v.), Mailer (q.v.), Malamud (q.v.), Wallant (q.v.), Fiedler (q.v.) and other important American writers, Miller is a Jew forced to work from (and therefore away from as well) the initial—and surely unavoidable—premise that the creative or persecuted or alienated minority is paradigmatically Jewish, that the lone rebel is a Jew. But being a playwright he has more easily been able to avoid the direct issue, which is none the less always immediately there and staring the audience in the face—the Jew is, after all, in Koestler's memorable words, the 'exposed nerve of humanity'. Miller began as a fledgling leftist writer and, in the war, shipyard worker; his first play failed, as did *Focus* (1945), an over-contrived novel about an anti-semite who is demoted when he has to wear spectacles, which make him appear Jewish. . . . The first important play, which put Miller on a par with Tennessee Williams (q.v.) as America's leading young playwright, is *Death of a Salesman* (1947). Like all its successors, this is obtrusively theatrical. Miller cannot avoid, it seems, old-fashioned theatre 'business'. But of the later playwrights—none of whom has yet got beyond the trio of O'Neill, Brecht and Pirandello, and the very different, poetic, Synge (q.v.)—Miller is one of the best: he is nobly sincere, and though his characters remain ideas (types)—as Shaw's do—some of their utterances jerk them into sudden, vivid, transitory life. *The Crucible* (1953) treats the McCarthy witch-hunting (of which Miller was one of the victims). *After the Fall* (1964), perhaps his best play, is both a portrait of Marilyn Monroe, to whom Miller was married from 1956 until 1961, and a highly critical self-appraisal of his role in their relationship. Other plays include *Incident at Vichy* (1964), about Frenchmen and an Austrian being investigated as Jews in Vichy, and *The Price* (1968). In the first of these, both of which play well, Miller convincingly portrays an act of self-sacrifice. His script for the Monroe-Gable film *The Misfits* (1961) is a failure. Miller's main themes are collective responsibility, sexual anxiety, parent-children or sibling relationships, and integrity. He does not use humour. *Collected Plays* (1957). *I Don't Need You Any More* (1968) is a book of stories.

Miller, Henry (1891) American writer, educationist. He started to write at thirty-three, and was resident in Paris in the thirties; he has lived at Big Sur in California ever since. He has been an enormously important influence on the anti-intellectual, anarchistic tradition in American literature but his individual achievement is hardly to be considered in this light. He is a strange mixture. *The Books in My Life* (1952) reveals his vulgarity, lack of mind and simple-heartedness. His first book, *Tropic of Cancer* (1934) and its later counterparts (*Black Spring*, 1936; *Tropic of Capricorn*, 1939) reveal his comic verve—partly arising from a suddenly achieved honesty and directness when he decided (1924) to abandon his soulless job as an employee of the Union Telegraph Company of New York—and his sexual confusion. His once notoriously 'obscene' passages are now dated but were of some genuine educational value. But he has never come to terms with his terror of women (in this he is the non-intellectual counterpart of the intellectual Mailer, q.v.), and he can consequently vary from embarrassing sentimentality to boring garrulity. He has no art at all—an advantage and a disadvantage. As critic he is of no value (e.g. *Rimbaud*, 1952), as sociologist (notably *The Air-Conditioned Nightmare*, 1945, a description of the America of 1941–2, and continuation, *Remember to Remember*, 1947), he is over-vehement and on the whole ineffective. He is by no means a major writer but he has major historical importance and is a fascinating American phenomenon. He is at his best as a comic and/or autobiographical writer and some of his recollections of other people, including members of his own family, are exquisitely felt. Curiously enough, he is as a writer conventional: his work has no innovatory value whatever. His absolutely most admired author is Whitman, but he has never achieved Whitman's poetic concentration. One needs to read through all but the purely 'critical' work of this immensely prolific writer, since one may stumble at any moment on some excellent passage. But the trilogy *The Rosy Crucifixion* (*Sexus*, 1945, *Plexus*, 1949, *Nexus*, 1960) is the least rewarding: like his master Whitman, Miller is intolerable when he is being 'philosophical'. Certainly he cannot be ignored. Some of his voluminous correspondence has been published (e.g. *Lawrence Durrell and Henry Miller: A Private Correspondence*, 1963) and there are a number of privately printed editions of memoirs and rambling essays. An affinity that is not often mentioned is with Sherwood Anderson (q.v.). He can achieve Anderson's directness, but is more solidly urban and, of course, much more diffuse—and he lacks Anderson's lyricism.

Miłosz, Czesław (1911) Polish poet, critic, translator, novelist. Miłosz is one of the most intelligent, self-critical and aware of modern European writers. He was the leader of the sensible 'Second Vanguard' movement. He was in the Warsaw underground against the Nazis and served the 1946 Polish government as a diplomat but he broke with the communists in 1951 and is now a teacher in the USA. His criticism of his predecessors and contemporaries is astringent (e.g. *Zniewolony umysł*, 1953, tr. *The Captive Mind*, 1953; 1962; and *History of Polish Literature*, 1969). Miłosz's poetry is torn between a form of hermeticism, an exploration of 'inner space', and a liberal humanism; his forms are generally classical. He has written that his intention is to outwit the 'ineffable' world of symbolism but this bad conscience (usual in a poet) merely demonstrates that he believes in a meaning beyond that of 'commonsense' meaning. He has written two novels: *Doliny Issy* (1955–7; tr. in French *Sur les Bords de l'Issa*, 1956), *The Valley of the Issa*, about his childhood, and *Zdobycie Władzy* (1955; tr. *The Usurpers*, 1955). Miłosz in his criticism can deal with the problem of why poets should gain inspiration from 'catastrophe' (as he did in the thirties); but in his more recent poetry he has moved too self-consciously into an 'assenting' attitude. None the less, he deserves his high reputation outside and inside Poland. *Selected Poems* (tr. 1973).

Mishima Yukio (ps. Hiraoka Kimitake) (1925–70) Japanese novelist, dramatist. Mishima was a remarkable man, capable of great industry and effort of will; the circumstances of his ritual suicide are well known. His literary achievement, however, has been overrated—even if his skill has not. He was an excessively prolific writer, highly intelligent and sick to the core. Psychotic exhibitionism, rather than his obscurantist dedication to the 'emperor', is the explanation of his silly and bungled death. Mishima was finally evil and cruel. But his vision of life was pitiful: he was, for all his gifts and his occasionally expressed sense of beauty, no more than a nasty little boy. His imagination fails at the point where it might take over. It is heartening that his self-destruction has not upset people as did those of Crane (q.v.), Dagerman (q.v.) and Pavese (q.v.). 'By any standards, he is a major figure in modern Japanese literature', asserts a critic. But, and especially because of the crushing dullness of his last pretentious tetralogy *Hojo no umi* (1965–70; *The Sea of Fertility*, now in four volumes, 1975), this judgement is already dated: he is a writer whose enormous, impressive but meretricious brilliance soon encompassed his slight decency–and beside Toson (q.v.), Soseki (q.v.), Dazai Osamu (q.v.), Kafu, Ogai, Tanizaki (q.v.), Kawabata (q.v.) he is merely an incompetent, insensitive, academic minor. His decadent nihilism, as revealed in *Kinkakuji* (1956; tr. *The Temple of the Golden Pavilion*, 1959), is immature–and his Swinburnian precocity of manner and technique should not distract the reader from this evident fact. *Gogo no eiko* (1963; tr. *The Sailor Who Fell From Grace with the Sea*, 1965), is a readable tale, but it depends, wholly, on its disagreeables. In Mishima's fiction decadence is casually exploited; instead of bursting upon its reader's consciousness, awakening his sense of his own immaturity–questioning, indeed, the very notion of maturity–it stinks in the mind like rotten meat and becomes a focus of that terrible point at which individual psychosis coincides with collective evil. There are many translations from his work, of which the early novel *Kamen no kokuhaku* (1949; *Confessions of a Mask*, 1956) is interesting inasmuch as it unwittingly reveals the reasons for his adoption of a homosexual role.

Mistral, Gabriela (ps. Lucila Godoy Alcayaga) (1889–1957) Chilean poet, prose writer. Nobel Prize 1945. She was for some years an honorary ambassador for Chile in many countries, including Italy, France and USA (where she died). Her lover killed himself under mysterious circumstances when she was a young woman, and much later an adopted son also killed himself; these events, and her desire to be a mother, left their mark on her erotically impassioned and fluent writing. She was no experimentalist but the uninhibited nature of her perceptions and her understanding of children (she had been a schoolteacher, and she wrote good poetry for children) are so fresh as to be, in effect, modernist. She wrote about anything that caught her excited and empathetic imagination, so that her work is extremely versatile, though her main themes are her feeling for nature, her frustrated maternal instincts, and her eclectic Roman Catholicism. Her bibliography is in an atrocious state and not all she wrote in prose has been published. *Poesías completas* (1958) has a misleading title. She continually rewrote her poems, which will make the task of gathering them together in final texts difficult.

Monro, Harold (1879–1932) English poet, editor, anthologist, critic, founder-owner of the Poetry Bookshop (which lost him money). His later poetry, written out of physical pain and erotic despair—he was a bisexual, as Aiken (q.v.) makes clear in *Ushant*, which contains the most revealing portrait of the man—has not, despite Eliot's (q.v.) praise, had its critical due. The 1933 *Collected Poems*, with notes by Eliot and Flint, is to be preferred to a later reprint which cuts out the notes and substitutes a feeble essay. Monro's generosity towards every kind of poet—he did perhaps as much as Pound (q.v.) for others—prevented him from concentration on the pursuit of his own considerable genius. This came out only in the last five or six poems (the most famous is 'Bitter Sanctuary'); but much of interest may be found amongst the escapist, Georgian (*see* Brooke) poetry of his earlier years. Had he come to terms with imagism (*see* Pound) he might have reached his own original, tormented manner much earlier. This emerges, precise and melancholy, in the final poems, in which a language born of internal despair entirely takes over from the previous (and evasive) pursuit of trivial themes.

Montale, Eugenio (1896) Italian poet, critic, prose writer. One of the five great twentieth-century Italian poets (the others are Saba, q.v., Ungaretti, q.v., Campana, q.v., Quasimodo, q.v.). He was always an opponent of fascism, and gave up an agreeable cultural post in 1938 rather than join the party. A student of music (especially *bel canto*). This has played a more obvious part in his than in any other of his contemporaries' poetry. He fought in the First World War. Eliot's (q.v.) *Waste Land*, which he has translated, struck a responsive chord in him but too much has been made of his indebtedness to Eliot: there are no real affinities beyond the keen recognition of a collapsing civilization and Montale is a more honest and a superior poet–more naturally accessible because he can both feel 'politically' and express love without the heedlessness and naivety that so shocks one in Eliot. Both poets liked Gozzano (q.v.); Montale wrote on him (1950) and developed from him. Montale can be called 'hermetic' (*see* Ungaretti and Quasimodo) only inasmuch as his poetic world seems 'closed'; the 'word', as word, is less important in his poetry, which is self-consciously musical–and much more frankly referential, if ultimately to inner experience, than in that of Ungaretti or Quasimodo. Like them and like Saba in his different way, he regards poetry as a medium which needs to be stripped of D'Annunzian (q.v.) swagger and rhetoric but he is more content than Ungaretti to make do with what Gozzano and other *crepuscolari* have left him. He is at his best when subdued rather than 'light' or whimsical. His method may be seen in the prose sketches of *La farfalla di Dinard* (1956 rev. 1969; tr. *The Butterfly of Dinard,* 1971): the casual style and insubstantiality are mostly only apparent. Yet readers unused to the colour and brightness of Italian poetry might think of him as comparatively intense–just as they might be puzzled to hear that this author of 'La primavera hitleriana', 'Hitler Spring', was a pessimist and a 'closed' poet. . . . Montale despises politicians and has only resisted, not joined, parties. Montale has succeeded in learning a style–and a most evocative style it is–'from a despair' (as Empson, q.v., put it); his waste land is full of women-haunted and beautiful landscape (he continually harks back to his native Liguria). It is Montale above all who is useful in showing up Eliot's poetic insufficiency at an international level, the thinness of his achievement (and Eliot, indeed, published a translation of Montale's 'Arsenio' in an early number of *The Criterion*). There are four main collections (as yet there is no collected edition): *Ossi di seppia* (1925; 1963), *Cuttlefish Bones; Le occasioni* (1939; 1963), *Occasions; La bufera e altro* (1956; 1963), *The Storm and Other Things;* and *Satura* (1971), which though interesting, shows, for all its cheerfulness, some falling off in linguistic inventiveness: it reflects the author's feelings about life, but the pressure behind its composition has clearly been less; there is a certain philosophical artificiality about it that seems poetically uncharacteristic. Yet what Carlo Bo said of it is true of all Montale's poetry, good and bad: it betrays a 'contradiction between a lucid and ruthless cruelty and a very pure feeling of love'. One needs, however, to amplify this. The early 'Arsenio' clearly isolates poetic loneliness as something that is in effect humanly 'cruel'—and regretfully felt as such—and it does so with an honesty of such intensity that one cannot doubt the poet's conviction of the deadness, to all people, of the universe, or his existential disappointment at having to be—as an 'involuntary' poet forced to be—detached; this poem at once expresses the conviction of absurdity now so familiar as to be a cliché, and the regret that existence, with its beauties, must end absolutely—Unamuno's (q.v.) 'tragic sense'. Montale's is never a poetry of resolution: despair simply co-exists with love; hope may be ironically (*pace* Quasimodo) treated, but is never—in deference to a truth to temperament—falsely 'let in'. Yet 'Dora Markus', however poignant, is one of the most beautiful love poems of all time. . . . There are many English translations from Montale, including *Selected Poems* (with Italian text, 1965), and, a different book, *Selected Poems* (1964 rev. but without Italian text, 1969). Nobel prize 1975.

Montherlant, Henry de (1896–1972) French novelist, playwright, essayist, miscellaneous writer. Montherlant was an aristocratic Frenchman whose attitudes in some ways resemble those of Gide (q.v.), who influenced him; both fully exercised their ambisexuality, but Montherlant's upbringing was Catholic and although he was a pagan, he was a pagan of distinctly Renaissance-Catholic hue. Though a small man (he was squat and powerful, but not much over five feet tall), he was devoted to sport—particularly bullfighting—and he found a certain inspiration in war (he fought and was badly wounded in the First World War), which is expressed in *Le Songe* (1922; tr. *The Dream*, 1962). Montherlant, though never a collaborator (as has been suggested) has been taken to be a 'right-wing' author; but this is to confuse stoicism, an acceptance of the actualities of war (he was not one of those driven into a 'violent' pacificism) and an aristocratic attitude with political conservatism. He was against Franco and his scorn for his fellow-countrymen in 1940 was not altogether unjustified, though it was tactlessly expressed (*Le Solstice de juin*, 1941, essays, was, however, originally banned by the Nazis). It was characteristic of him that he should efficiently shoot himself when threatened by blindness—the sight of one eye had been lost when, over seventy years old, he was beaten up (1968) in the course of a nocturnal homosexual adventure; that of the other had begun to go. It seems usual to rate Montherlant's drama more highly than his fiction; this is an error. It is in his fiction that his great and powerful sense of pity most clearly emerges. His overt 'philosophy'–of Spartan virtue against adversity, of 'masculine' hardness and virility, of lack of 'soft' emotionalism, chivalry based on a code, of pure sensuality–is only half the story; critics have not seen the other half. But the tension set up in his best books–whose style is exemplary in the 'classical' French sense–is between this life-style and his romanticism, intuitive tenderness and compassion. There are many novels, but the notable ones are *Les Bestiares* (1926; tr. *The Bullfighters*, 1927), the best of all novels on this subject, *Les Célibataires* (1934; tr. *The Bachelors*, 1960), the tetralogy *Les Jeunes Filles* (1936–9; tr. *The Girls*, 1968), *Le Chaos et la nuit* (1963; tr. *Chaos and Night*, 1964), *La Rose de sable* (published in part 1954; full text 1968; tr. *Desert Love*, 1957) and *Les Garçons* (1969; tr. *The Boys*, 1974). *Les Célibataires* is a touching tragi-comedy about two old men, exquisitely realized. *Les Jeunes Filles* is an exploration of the theme of the novelist-as-detached-person and has been widely misunderstood. It is an oblique attempt at justification of Montherlant's 'Renaissance' ambisexuality, but one full of self-criticism and pity for the victims of the author-'hero' Costals ('Je ne suis pas Costals', wrote Montherlant); it is also an ironic and often comic critique of romantic love, containing much regret. *Le Chaos et la nuit* is perhaps his most perfect book: the old Spanish anarchist exile at its centre is Montherlant's fullest and most subtle objective correlative for himself. *Les Garçons* is the middle part of a trilogy whose first and third books were written in the twenties; it is also the fictional counterpart of the drama *La Ville dont le Prince est un enfant* (1951), first drafted when the author was seventeen. This is the complex autobiographical story of adolescent and priestly homosexuality and contains a moving portrait of a dying woman. As he became older Montherlant's gifts ripened; not all his work has yet appeared–but when everything is available in its entirety a very different picture from the current one will be revealed: of a consistently developing artist, a tormented and courageous man of great psychological insight. His drama, much of it turning to history for its themes, is effective in technique and often moving. Some of it, including *Le Maître de Santiago* (1947), has been translated into English in a volume under that name (1951). It is mostly 'strong' drama and it usually concentrates on putting forward Montherlant's own ostensibly stoical philosophy. Exceptions are *La Ville dont le Prince est un enfant* and the touching *Celles qu' on prend dans les bras* (1950), *Those Whom One Takes in One's Arms*. There is a *Selected Essays* (1960) in

English. *Théâtre* (1954) and *Romans et oeuvres de fiction non-théatrales* (1959) are useful collections.

Moore, George (1852–1933) Irish fiction writer, autobiographer, playwright, critic, man-of-letters. Moore, an important and original experimental novelist and autobiographer, has been consistently and meanly underrated by academic critics, though recently there have been some signs of a revival of interest. He was a great writer. He studied art in Paris in his youth, and wrote atrocious pseudo-decadent poetry. Then he became aware of naturalism (*see* Zola), and although not himself a naturalist but rather a vulnerable man of exquisite and tender feelings without a 'philosophy' ('life is a rose that withers in the iron fist of dogma'), he gave himself a creative start by adopting a naturalist stance. His account of his Paris years, *Confessions of a Young Man* (1888), is a masterpiece of ironic self-criticism as well as an interesting if not always strictly accurate account of many important French writers and painters. Its subtlety has not yet been fully understood: Moore's defences of his vulnerability were complex, but were impeccable in literary work (except in some of his criticism). He first showed his uncanny flair for portraying women in *A Mummer's Wife* (1885) and *A Drama in Muslin* (1886); with *Esther Waters* (1894) he became famous. This is not naturalistic but realistic; the heroine is a servant girl who has a bastard and who is eventually allowed the consolations of true motherhood. It is a beautiful story, unsentimental, acutely observed, full of the sort of tenderness, robust feeling and decency that leads thin-hearted professors to call it a 'thin enough work'. Following this Moore changed his approach, as is evident in the three stories in *Celibates* (1895), which, though effectively realistic, exploit symbolism in a highly original (and proto-Freudian) manner: the masterpiece here is 'John Norton', in which the author deals, though never overtly, with his own problem of the irreconcilability of sexual love and creative art (to which, as Ford, q.v., recognized, he was as dedicated as any man of his age). The connected novels *Evelyn Innes* (1898) and *Sister Teresa* (1901) explore the same subject, using a woman as objective correlative. *The Lake* (1905) is a novel about Irish life whose style points forward to the 'seamless', melodic prose of the late novels. This and the tales in *The Untilled Field* are astonishing in their psychological scope and sensibility. Moore played a leading part in the Irish revival, and knew Yeats (q.v.) and Synge (q.v.) intimately. His own plays are not successful. The trilogy *Ave, Salve, Vale* (1911–14), often taken as merely malicious conventional reminiscence, is not only an invaluable account of Irish literary life but also another *tour de force* of experimental autobiography. *The Brook Kerith* (1916) marks the beginning of his last period, of a prose with which modernism has not yet caught up; he pursues his 'story' as if it were an unbroken melody, employing a unique method in full awareness of the inadequacy of purely realistic techniques. *Héloïse and Abélard* (1921) is a later and subtler reversion to his old theme of sexuality versus art, and displays an astounding insight into the medieval 'nominalist-realist' controversy. *Celibate Lives* (1927), five very great stories–some are revisions of earlier material–contains 'Albert Nobbs', a tragi-comic tale of a transvestite waiter that ranks in the first dozen short stories of world literature. Moore as literary personality could be extremely foolish and opinionated and he had as abject a band of disciples as any great man ever has had. But his rehabilitation is only a matter of time, for he was an accomplished and profound writer. He was an inveterate reviser, and his bibliography is complicated. *Works* (1937) remains the best general guide to his final intentions, but a new complete Moore is badly needed. The compilation *George Moore's Mind and Art* (1968) is uneven, but a useful general introduction. Hone's life (1936) is again useful, but is polite. The most discerning guide to his art is by P. Noël (1966); this is by a French critic and has yet to be translated.

Moore, Marianne (1887–1972) American poet, editor. Marianne Moore is perhaps the one genuinely modern writer to have successfully made a poetry out of a reactionary puritan conventionalism (she voted for Nixon in 1960, which surely no other serious poet did). She has been much (and rightly) loved, and consequently overrated. She is not more than a minor poet of great distinction, her editorship of *The Dial* (1925–9) was fundamentally poor, and her explanations of her technique are evasive. Yet, curiously, her best poetry (the worst is whimsy) amounts to considerably more than a defence against her narrowness of character–her cultivated 'spinsterishness'. She has the capacity to extrapolate from this narrowness a true fastidiousness of observation and gives her reader a beautifully and originally angled view of the world of animals, places and innocent habit. It is a limited world, and her treatment of exotic or fabulous animals contains no awareness of its absolute anthropomorphism. But it has purity of vision. She early saw that she must discipline her tendency to allow herself to meander and chose to do this by writing in elaborate syllabic patterns (often slightly 'irregular'); thus she invented an illusion of continuity rather than succumbed to the urge to indulge herself in it. There is much art in this. She had no stomach for the realities of human relationships, because these contain savage and 'rude' violences; so her subject was her own life-style, which was one of restraint. This very sophisticated and educated poetry rests on an odd paradox: it is an authentic description of an escapist existence. And so it has its value as a post-Freudian recipe for the rejection of the Freudian 'horrors'. The most perfect poem is 'The Pangolin', a self-description based on a masterfully arranged collage of zoological detail, observation, clippings and fancy: '. . . To explain grace requires/a curious hand. . . .'; 'Not afraid of anything is he,/and then goes cowering forth. . . .' And in 'Silence' she states another central autobiographical fact (this is a poem that really does require 'Freudian' analysis): her *father* [my italics] wasn't insincere in saying 'Make my house your inn' because 'Inns are not residences'. . . . Proper respect for Miss Moore's mental privacy during her lifetime, and liking for her as a person, have precluded satisfactory critical assessments being made; but now the job can be done properly. *The Complete Poems* (1968). *Predilections* (1955) is criticism.

Morante, Elsa (1918) Italian novelist; married Moravia (q.v.) in 1941. Author of three novels: the vast *Menzogna e sortilegio* (1948; abridged pedestrian tr. *House of Liars,* 1951), *Storia* (1974), also very long, and her masterpiece, *L'isola di Arturo* (1957; tr. *Arturo's Island,* 1959). This is shorter: a painful and evocative study of a boy's agonized initiation into love and then into the sexual realities that lie behind it, told in an evocative poetic prose somewhat reminiscent of Alain-Fournier (q.v.), but altogether more mature and confident. Admired by critics as discerning as Lukács (q.v.), she is an original and independent writer; she has disowned some of her earlier published writings and destroyed still more that were unpublished; *Lo scialle andaluso* (1963), *The Andalusian Shawl,* twelve selected stories including some from her first volume, shows her to better advantage than do her two long novels—but these are nevertheless remarkable in the way they combine elements of a baroque and exotic sensibility, nostalgia, psychological penetration and truth to history. Her marriage to Moravia has ended.

Moravia, Alberto (ps. Alberto Pincherle) (1907) Italian fiction-writer, critic, playwright, journalist, film critic. A Jew born in Rome, son of an architect, Moravia had little formal education owing to illness in youth; in 1929 he took the literary world by storm with *Gli indifferenti* (tr. *The Time of Indifference,* 1953), which is not only a criticism of fascism but of the corrupt social situation that allowed it to flourish. Moravia has always been on the left, although critically so. He was harassed by Mussolini's 'Popular Culture' police-clerks, and *La mascherata* (1941; tr. *The Fancy Dress Party,* 1947), which contains a comic portrait of Mussolini, was eventually suppressed. He spent much of the war on the run. Moravia is a prolific writer and an important one; only in the past ten years has his work shown signs of a falling off in quality. His reputation in Italy is at present at a relatively low ebb but he is still one of the best known Italian writers outside his own country and his earlier work enjoys great respect. Moravia, who can employ his sense of humour to great effect, has two main themes: he is a masterful critic of bourgeois 'bad faith', moral decadence (the earlier Moravia has even been called 'Jansenist'), and he explores the strains imposed on males by their loneliness and by their (in his fiction) fruitless efforts to escape from it by the exploitation of women. Only in the writing of *La romana* (1947; tr. *The Woman of Rome,* 1949), a lyrical description of a prostitute and a magnificent tribute to femininity, has he ever been able–it seems–to find peace. It is often said that Moravia is sexually over-obsessed: this is prudish nonsense, for his descriptions of sexual contact are among the warmest in modern fiction. But *La romana* did not release him from his erotic *Angst,* which is certainly 'existential' in its intensity (his first novel influenced Sartre, q.v.), and latterly he has made some unsuccessful experiments. In the short story, of which form he is a master, he shows a rare empathy with his lower- or middle-class individual characters. *L'uomo come fine* (1963; tr. *Man as an End,* 1965) is a notable book of political and literary essays. Nearly all his fiction appears in good English translations, notably *Agostino* (1944; tr. 1952) and *Il conformista* (1951; tr. *The Conformist,* 1952). Short stories are in *Roman Tales* (tr. 1956), *More Roman Tales* (tr. 1963) and other volumes.

Morgenstern, Christian (1871–1914) German 'nonsense' poet. His serious verse is expendable rubbish ('masterly' only in the sense of the word used by prematurely aged and pompous Teutonic academicians).

His nonsense poems, which are by no means nonsense, are major contributions to an important and difficult genre. He anticipated most of the modernist tendencies that came after his early death from tuberculosis: concrete poetry (but really only for fun: an object-lesson to our portentous modern practitioners of this essentially graphic form), the realization that bourgeois 'values' are mechanisms for self-evasion, experiments with words as things-in-themselves as well as (arbitrary?) symbols of what they denote. Unknowingly he was puncturing his own philosophical and anthroposophical pretensions—yet, in some mysterious way, retaining the essence of the ideas he studies. He was trying to solve the German problems of over-reliance on philosophical systems and ponderousness. His characters (Palmström, von Korf and others) are metaphysical but metaphysically untormented clowns because they inhabit a word-world. What is so validly ridiculous is the contrast between their strictly verbal literalness and the reality which is conventionally described in symbolic (verbal) terms. The important poems are collected in *Alle Galgenlieder* (1951; sel. tr. *Gallows Songs,* 1963). There are other translations of varying merit.

Móricz, Zsigmond (1879–1942) Important Hungarian novelist, short-story writer, playwright and editor. At first influenced by nineteenth-century writers, he became an associate of Babits (q.v.) and introduced a new realism into the treatment of peasant life. He was a friend of Ady (q.v.), and shared some of his views. Like Henry Handel Richardson (q.v.) Móricz was influenced by naturalism but transcended its program. He wrote with piercing accuracy of sensitive souls crushed by their circumstances or their temperaments (as in *Úri Muri,* 1928, French tr. 1960); his attitude towards his peasants is just that expressed by Verhaeren (q.v.) in his famous early poem 'Les Paysans', and he has, indeed, affinities with the Belgian, achieving a Rembrandtesque thickness of line in his delineations of coarse, vicious and lustful characters (here, curiously, he resembles another Belgian, Lemonnier—*Sararany,* 1910, *Golden Mud,* is uncannily like Lemonnier's *Le Mâle,* which preceded it by twenty-eight years). Conservative critics tend to find him repulsive, but his vision is truer than their evasion. One of the greatest (and most successful) of his many novels, which include long historical works, is *Légy jó mindhalálig* (1920; tr. *Be Faithful Unto Death,* 1962), in which a child opposes himself to the corrupt adult world. Many of his short stories and novels appear in English or French translation.

Morris, Wright (1910) American novelist, critic. Morris has a devoted following but has never gained true recognition. He is a most complex, gifted writer, who repays close study, but some of his novels appear disconcertingly poor because they try to combine too many themes. The keys to his work lie in his mid-western (Nebraskan) origin —his awareness of the great spaces broken, with bewildering intermittence, by man-made and man-used objects (cf. Bly, q.v.), which theme he explores most lucidly in his early novels—in the novel *The Works of Love* (1952), in his independence of mind, and in his inability to resist the tiresome, cranky repetition, in various forms, of incidents which obsess him. This last characteristic, his chief fault, is intimately related to his tendency to the neo-picaresque, a technique which does not suit his genius. However, his two most fully articulated novels (to date) are major: *The Works of Love* (1952) and *The Deep Sleep* (1953). The former is a variation on the 'saintly fool' theme, and is the tragic and moving story of a man who can give love but find no takers; the latter is a re-creation of the true life of an outwardly respectable and powerful judge in the recollections of those who survive him. Morris is a profound pessimist whose despair is assuaged only by his interest in (and therefore hope for) human beings; and, after all, in the key novel, *The Works of Love,* at least the hero himself has love. He is an accomplished photographer, and the early Nebraska books, *The Inhabitants* (1946) and *The Home Place* (1948), and *God's Country and My People* (1968) are illustrated by his own pictures. Wright's criticism is acute: *The Territory Ahead* (1958) and the splendid *A Bill of Rites, A Bill of Wrongs, A Bill of Goods* (1968), one of the finest of all attacks on the new American pseudo-culture with its Zen, pop, McLuhanizing (q.v.) 'dropouts' and drug-mages. The compact *In Orbit* (1967), one of the best of the novels, is a careful study of a young delinquent and the wake he leaves behind him. Here Morris successfully combines social comment with psychological illumination of a criminal adolescent—and he makes this character's predicament an objective correlative for the artist's. Although still not much read in America, several of his novels have been translated into European languages. He is one of the two or three most original of contemporary American novelists.

Mounier, Emmanuel (1905–50) French writer, critic, philosopher: leading exponent of the philosophy of personalism; others associated with this include the Swiss Denis de Rougemont, Albert Béguin and Jean Lacroix. French personalism has its roots in the philosophies of Lotze and Eucken as well as in Péguy (q.v.), Bergson (q.v.) and Christian socialism. It asserts the primacy of the individual, the necessity of social reform, the importance of the religious impulse. Mounier, who founded the journal *Esprit* (1932), was anti-capitalist and anti-bourgeois and was sympathetic to the spirit of Marxism—he accepted Marx's diagnosis of alienation—but he was opposed to Marxist dogmatism and to its *a priori* assumptions. The personalist, an anti-determinist, believes that a renewal of society will be possible only when men choose to initiate it. There are obvious affinities, here, with existentialism. But Mounier was anti-materialistic and anti-atheistic: suppression of religion, in his view, leads to abandonment of moral responsibility. Mounier is one of the founding fathers of the post-war 'heretical', 'left-wing' Roman Catholicism that has produced worker-priests and rebellion against the hierarchy of Rome. He is important as an influence and a thinker. *Manifeste au service du Personnalisme* (1936; tr. *Personalist Manifesto,* 1938); *Le Personnalisme* (1950; tr. *Personalism,* 1952). Mounier was active in the Resistance and then exhausted himself in the effort to modify and reconcile existentialist atheism, hard-line Marxism and academic philosophy, whose failure to engage with reality he rightly deplored.

Mphahlele, Ezekiel (1919) Important South African critic, novelist and short-story writer; he left South Africa in 1957, lived in various parts of Africa, and now lives in America. He is the most articulate of African critics. As his masterful autobiography, *Down Second Avenue* (1959), demonstrates, he has kept his intellectual balance, under intolerable conditions, extraordinarily well. *The African Image* (1962), on literary and political themes, is the most instructive and intelligent book of African criticism. His fiction, often ironic, eschews none of the squalor of African settings, but is unusually elegant and humorous. Short stories are in *Man Must Live* (1946); *The Wanderer* (1971) is a novel. 'Literature and art', he has written, 'are too big for *négritude,* and it had better be left as a historical phrase.' He has shown courage in his life, and even more (of a different kind) in his defiant assertion that humanity rather than mere 'Africanness' is the stuff of literature. With Achebe (q.v.), he is the most important of African English-language writers.

Muir, Edwin (1887–1959) Scottish poet, critic, novelist, autobiographer, translator (with his wife Willa, of Kafka, q.v., and many others). Born in the Orkneys and then transferred at adolescence to the foulest part of Glasgow, he remained forever shocked by the transition. As he tells in *Autobiography* (1954), he had to fight for his education and a place in literary life. An incisive critic of the Scottish 'Kailyard' tradition, he was both admired and attacked by MacDiarmid (q.v.), who could not discern that the fiery aspirations of Scottish Nationalism were alien to his essentially contemplative temperament. He rejected Lallans (MacDiarmid's synthetic Scots as practised by other younger poets) without effort, but was not the less Scottish for that. He wrote an important and rather neglected book on the novel, *The Structure of the Novel* (1928), which is a substantial contribution to the subject; his own three novels, written at this period, have distinction (e.g. *Poor Tom,* 1932). *Scott and Scotland* (1936), a critique of the feebleness of the Anglo-Scottish tradition, may be preferred by some to MacDiarmid's less reasoned diatribes. His chief work, however, is regarded as having been done in poetry–he began late, publishing his first book in his late thirties. His position *vis-à-vis* twentieth-century literature is a most peculiar one. Though the translator of Broch (q.v.), Hauptmann (q.v.) and Asch as well as Kafka, he seems to have absorbed no continental poetic influences, even though the last-named, whom he misinterpreted as a Christian visionary, turned him towards fable. Yet he remained oblivious to the Scots lyricism of the early MacDiarmid (whom he admired), and to the modernism of *A Drunk Man Looks at the Thistle*–and to the Pound-Eliot 'revolution'. Yet, though acutely aware of the modern predicament, he is not quite as startlingly original –for a poet of achievement–as one might expect. This is because he lacks linguistic and rhythmical 'attack'. His poetry tends towards the metrical rather than the individually rhythmical; yet at his best his quietness is a virtue. He came to believe in a divine order (his later work has heterodox Christian overtones), expressed in the fabulous, which transcended time. Muir's absolute sincerity and quietness are impressive, as is the steadfastness of his vision; but too often in his poetry the tensions of his personal experience are sacrificed to his pursuit of a metaphysical haven—he is slack in the appealing way that Traherne is slack. He has almost ignored the violent, negative pole of himself: the spark between this and the positive, affirmatory pole is weak, as though evil were (decently) shielded by some screen that cuts off three-quarters of the force of the electrical discharge approaching it. There are, however, exceptions. The sequence *Variations on a Time Theme* (1934), his most substantial achievement, does have power and tension, and the characteristic translation of a sense of personal crisis into metaphysical terms is here effective and convincing: the poet is resolving his traumas into a form of healing meditation. And there are a number of short later poems, such as 'Suburban Dream', 'Song', 'The Good Town', and the final '"I Have Been Taught"', which either refer to concrete experience or glow with a true inner light such as we find in Thomas Vaughan. He deserves his growing reputation and his dedication and total disregard of fashion and sensationalism are exemplary. *Poems 1921–1958* (1963) adds a batch of uncollected late poems, and is the completest collection; the American edition of 1965, with Eliot's (q.v.) preface, adds more poems but omits some poems in the English edition. *John Knox* (1929) is a perceptive study, and *The Scots and Their Country* (1949) a helpful introduction.

Murdoch, Iris (1919) Irish (but educated and resident in England) novelist. She is married to John Bayley, a percipient critic who, as an undergraduate, wrote some extraordinarily promising poetry—a vein which, alas though doubtless honourably, he seems to have been unable to pursue. The secret of Iris Murdoch's huge critical success as a novelist lies, ironically, in her inability to write novels: this is an age in which the English of her generation have not generally been able to do so. None of her books can survive: for all the work she puts into them, they have been consistently and unerringly aimed at an audience tuned into fashion rather than to creative achievement. Iris Murdoch, however, is intelligent and aware. What she lacks is a sense of character. She is unable to create a 'world' of her own. Without imaginatively cohesive ability, she has always drawn on the immediate concerns of her literate audience. Iris Murdoch began with a short (overrated) exegesis of Sartre (q.v.) in 1953; in the following year she produced an energetic but wholly fashionable neo-picaresque novel, *Under the Net.*

Its fifties successors were, as even her admirers admit, 'conventional middlebrow'. These admirers, however, claim 'significance' for the sixties and seventies novels. It is a pity that they cannot be more critically explicit: 'Intelligently planned, beautifully written and technically assured' (of *An Unofficial Rose,* 1962) will hardly do if you cannot draw attention as to *why*. And enthusiastic reviews of her ever-increasing stream of books do, alas, tend to generalize: they discuss the fashionable concepts dealt with—sadism, masochism, homosexuality, neo-Gothic, and so on. What are missed are two points: the tawdriness of the writing and the poor dialogue, and the inability to treat goodness except in a helplessly sentimental manner. It becomes increasingly clear that her novels are a concatenation of current ideas and fads, intelligently understood, but cobbled together without any imaginative faculty. *The Sandcastle* (1957); *The Italian Girl* (1964); *An Accidental Man* (1971) and several others.

Murry, John Middleton (1889–1957) English critic, editor, novelist, pacifist. Murry has been described as a 'professional sufferer'; this has point, but he really did suffer much—Katherine Mansfield (q.v.) was not an easy wife, and his third marriage was very unhappy; human unhappiness and stupidity made him actually suffer, which is not as common as might seem. His best books are of literary criticism. These have stylistic faults—he becomes carried away by emotion and resorts to embarrassing gush—but his ability to grasp certain aspects of his subjects' personalities gives them indispensable insights. They have exercised some influence. The best are *Keats and Shakespeare* (1925), *William Blake* (1933), *Shakespeare* (1936) and the more scholarly and sober *Jonathan Swift* (1954). *Selected Criticism* (1960). Murry edited *The Adelphi* and, in the Second World War, *Peace News*.

Musil, Robert (1880–1942) Austrian (with Czech blood) fiction writer, critic, playwright. He was born of an old Austrian family of the kind described by J. Roth (q.v.) in *Radetzkymarsch*. He has been discovered as a major novelist only since the Second World War, though he was fairly well known in Berlin until he left Germany for Austria in 1933; he died in Switzerland, whither he had fled—the Americans refused him—after the *Anschluss*. He was an officer in the First World War. He was able to write, after 1933, only through the financial help of devoted friends. His one play and his farce are negligible, but his short stories (all available in English as *Tonka and Other Stories*), and his two novels, *Die Verwirrungen des Zöglings Törless* (1906; tr. *Young Torless,* 1963) and the massive, unfinished *Der Mann ohne Eigenschaften* (1930–43; tr. *The Man Without Qualities,* 1953–60) are masterpieces. Musil had been trained as an officer (at the same Moravian military school as Rilke, q.v.), and had studied engineering and science (he invented a chromatometer). His first novel is the most terrifying 'school story' ever written; it is a tale of growing up, of adolescent introspection and homosexuality, and of the cruelty and corruption of which boys are capable, particularly under the educational system in Austro-Hungary at the beginning of this century. Besides being a masterly study of character, it is also prophetic of the side of expressionism that led directly into Nazidom. Musil's stories, exquisitely accomplished, are his tenderest work: he allows his lyrical strain, his feelings for sexual relationships, to come to the fore. But everything (including the plays, which are not distinguished as theatre—Brecht, q.v., called one of them 'shit') Musil wrote had been, in a sense, a study for *Der Mann ohne Eigenschaften,* the unfinished and unfinishable novel that combines more themes, perhaps, than any other of the century. Musil's treatment of his material is realistic. Yet one of the aims of this most constructively sceptical of all novels, which was continuously revised, is to show that the *possible* co-exists with the *actual.* Törless, the boy, had displayed an almost repulsive objectivity—but as Ulrich, the 'man without qualities', he has grown into a wholly unrepulsive and sensitive, even though cerebral man. Both Törless and Ulrich are projections of Musil; but Ulrich is not a self-portrait—or an attempt at one. Ulrich is really an objective correlative (in this book used uncontentiously, not in Eliot's, q.v., sense, but to mean no more than any character, situation, etc., which acts as a metaphor for a 'private', authorial situation). Musil was a many-sided man. He was a romantic; he excelled in descriptions of nature; he loved one aspect of the old Austro-Hungarian empire, but hated another; he had moral feelings; he liked to withdraw moral judgements. *Der Mann ohne Eigenschaften* is a 'scientific' treatment of the author's subjective situation, but it is not cold. First, Musil is a great comic writer. Secondly, he is devoted above all to art, and he knows perfectly well that there is no such thing as the novel-as-science. His novel is plotless, but it deals with certain separate sets of facts, which are then interrelated. The reader is not helped by the condition of the author's final drafts: he died suddenly and there are some passages that exist in more than a dozen different versions. It was begun in the early twenties. At one level *Der Mann ohne Eigenschaften* is a marvellously accurate, tragi-comic evocation of a great empire on the blink. But it has increasingly mythological under- and overtones, and it explores the sexuality of what may fairly be called just-post-Freudian Vienna (rather curiously, Musil professed to hate both psychoanalysis and Karl Kraus, q.v.): of a decayed era tottering into another in which over-sophistication will co-exist with the worst barbarisms of history. Haunting the book is the figure of the sex-killer Moosbrugger, by whom both Ulrich and the frenzied woman (wife of his friend Walter) who wants him are profoundly fascinated. There are many other themes, some of the more important of which are Ulrich's hostility to Arnheim, Prussian businessman and successful author, to whom he is in a strange sense bound; his relationship with his sister Agathe, which develops into an incestuous one; and, most curiously of all in a twentieth-century writer, a treatment of music as an apparently evil rather than as a healing form of art—or is this just a treatment of *Wagnerian* music? Musil had undoubtedly been much influenced by the so-called 'thought-economy' of Ernst Mach; *Der Mann ohne Eigenschaften* could even be claimed to be an essentially imaginative application to human life of the principles Mach wanted to apply to science; but this application is also proto-existentialist (*see* Sartre), for one of Musil's most famous metaphors is of man being attracted to life as a fly is by the sweet stickiness (cf. Sartre's viscosity) of a flypaper: to the degree that the fly plunges deeper into the sweetness, so its doom is increasingly sealed. Mach, who influenced Einstein, wanted to get rid of 'medieval' concepts (such as 'absolute space') and to view phenomena in a relativistic way (cf. Pirandello, q.v.). Mach's combination of neo-Kantianism and empiricism was one of the chief inspirers of the logical positivism of the Vienna Circle but Musil's Ulrich, of course, by his artificial project of dispensing with qualities, is in search of qualities—of a kind of, in existentialist terms, *authenticity*. So in Musil the two mainstreams of modern philosophy combine: positivism and its offshoots—and existentialism. . . . Musil's novel is up to such a task, and to much more than this; his gigantic project, though unfinished, is of the utmost originality and importance and the critics who put him alongside the best of the century are right. The section of the collected works, *Gesammelte Werke* (1952–7), edited by A. Frisé, which contains the reconstruction of the third volume of the novel (Musil had withdrawn an earlier version of it from the press) has come under heavy fire from Musil's English translators, Eithne Watkins and Ernst Kaiser. Their arguments seem justified but they have not yet offered their own version. There is a French translation of the whole, *L'Homme sans qualités* (1957–8).

Myers, L. H. (1881–1944) English novelist. His father was F. W. H. Myers, one of the odd, interesting group of Cambridge men and women who set out to 'prove' the soul's immortality in the hard light of reason. Leo Myers, who was able to live without working, thus grew up into a 'Bloomsbury' (*see* Forster) milieu: he did not much like it. He was a man of subtle intelligence and he inherited his father's psychologically curious brand of mysticism. His unique fiction is essentially an attempt to reconcile his transcendentalism, his keen sense of existential disappointment and his hatred of his own class (in the thirties he behaved and spoke like an extremist communist–which he was not). That he killed himself is not in the least surprising. He is one of the only British authors who has written successful 'philosophical' fiction. He suffered from severe depression and was a hypochondriac and it is a tragedy that he destroyed his autobiography and left instructions for his letters to be burned: these would have cast light on many matters, for his eclectic temperament, gift for introspection and acute awareness of himself are rare phenomena. He began with a verse drama: *Arvat* (1908). This is a failure, but contains indispensable clues to his future development. 'I have no natural gift for writing,' he said. Critics have misinterpreted this remark: the emphasis is on 'natural', not 'gift'. His first novel, *The Orissers* (1922), took him some twelve years to write. During that period he had turned himself into an aesthete, reluctantly humorous, tolerant. (He had married in 1908.) When he later put on the communist mask, his friend L. P. Hartley (q.v.) tells us, the change seemed very startling and unpleasant (but Hartley, it must be remembered, had a fascist streak). *The Clio* (1925), which anticipates Golding (q.v.), was his next novel. (G. H. Bantock, one of Myers's critical exponents, is wrong to state that it 'hardly merits serious consideration' and was merely an imitation of Huxley, q.v.). Then he embarked on the tetralogy which was to become well known only when, in 1943, it was published in one volume under the title of the first of the series: *The Near and the Far*. The novels are: *The Near and the Far* (1929), *Prince Jali* (1931), *Rajah Amar* (1935), *The Pool of Vishnu* (1940).

The first three had previously been collected as *The Root and the Flower* (1935). *Strange Glory* (1936) is not one of the series. Every one of Myers's settings is imaginary though *The Orissers* is supposed to happen in Wales, *The Clio* in the Amazon, *Strange Glory* in New Orleans. The India of Akbar (a contemporary of Elizabeth I), in which his masterpiece is set, is 'not . . . historical. . . . I have done what I liked with history . . . an imaginary world.' The fact is that Myers was a misanthropist and he felt guilty about it. He was very nearly, although perhaps not actually until 1941, a mentally sick man. His tetralogy is certainly autobiographical and the writing of it certainly saved his life for many years. For the question that consistently concerned him is 'Why should human beings choose to live?' After he had finished *The Pool of Vishnu* he became really ill: his violent pro-Sovietism and his deliberate breakages of old friendships were pathological acts, arising not only from his lifelong hatred of compromise but also from depressive illness. He was far too subtle to embrace any dogma wholeheartedly: the Marxism was a desperate and angry mask. Myers was taken up by the Leavisites (q.v.) chiefly because part of his tetralogy contains a telling satire on Bloomsbury (*see* Forster)–as the Pleasaunce of the Arts–and critics in that tradition have had some useful things to say about it. But they take his evident intentions too much at face value in their exegeses. They also claim affinities with Lawrence (q.v.), which is bizarre. It is true that Myers thought–and rightly–the spiritual as important in life as is sex. It is true that he divided people into 'Fastidious' and 'Trivial': the committed, the, in existentialist terminology, 'authentic'–and the vulgar, the materialists, the ones who believe that their masks are real. But this 'philosophy' forms only a framework within which his imagination may function; the psychological results are as extraordinary as the atmosphere and are tragic in a way which the rather neat philosophy could not accommodate. In *The Pool of Vishnu* (Hartley saw it as 'communist') Myers does try to present the possibility of an ideal order; but he knows it is illusory, and this knowledge and despair work in the book like a yeast. He was interested in Oriental religion, but he did not believe that Westerners could become authentic Buddhists or Hindus: what fascinated him was the possibility of Westerners being able to make some concrete psychological use of the concepts of *maya* and of detachment. For himself personally, in an age when no anti-depressant drugs had been invented (sometimes amphetamine was prescribed, an eventually disastrous procedure) this fascination was of some practical use. Myers is immensely original—the claim that he was not a technical innovator is shallow—and he needs to be read. He remains highly relevant. We should know much more about him.

N

Nabokov, Vladimir (1899) Russian *emigré* novelist who wrote in Russian until 1937; he became an American in 1945 and was a teacher at Cornell for eleven years; he now lives in Switzerland. He is a distinguished lepidopterist. His Russian fiction was written under the pseudonym of Vladimir Sirin: most of this is available in English. He achieved international fame with *Lolita* (1955). Nabokov is a minor writer of distinction whose showmanship—his flippant defence against the anguish of exile—has much confused the critical issue. He can be a very bad writer indeed (e.g. *Ada or Ardor,* 1969) and he has added nothing of consequence to his work since *Pnin* (1957). He is a man of extreme intellectual brilliance but has a nearly fatal tendency to push this to extremes: imagination in his work is too often distorted (for all the consistently increasing sardonic exhibitionism) by what looks like severe neurosis. The Russian fiction is, on balance, superior to the English, which is none the less a stylistic *tour de force.* His failure to put his superb understanding of the techniques of such as Gogol and Bely (q.v.) to truly substantial use lies not only in his incapacity to adapt to exile but also in his realization that he lacked the linguistic resources to be a poet at a time when Russian poetry was still one of the richest in the world: his first two books were of poetry (1923). Hence the well known flippant games with words: more and more ingenious, more and more empty, more and more triumphantly claiming, as it were, that festering envy of poetic ability can be transformed into success (do not many critics take such books as *Ada or Ardor* seriously?). The best of Nabokov is in the Russian short stories (some of these can be found in various translations, notably *Nabokov's Dozen,* 1958, *Nabokov's Quartet,* 1967 and *Nabokov's Congeries,* 1968: the bibliography is intensely complicated because of revisions of Russian works into English—I give here English titles; if these are translations from Russian then the first, pre-1938, date will indicate their provenance), in *Laughter in the Dark*

(1932; 1938), *The Gift* (1937; 1963) and *Pnin* (1957). The best stories and *The Gift* deal, often exquisitely, with the ironies and agonies of exile; *Laughter in the Dark* is a more successful because more honest treatment of the theme of sexual obsession than the later *Lolita*. *Pnin* is, again, not too desperately and disingenuously 'detached' from the author's own experience: it is a tragi-comic story about a Russian teacher at an American university. *Lolita*, in attempting to probe even more deeply than *Laughter in the Dark* into sexual themes, is an artistically distorted work—though it thoroughly deserves its reputation as a *tour de force*. It is ironic that Nabokov should be famous for having written a successful novel about sexual obsession: the project is essentially a defense against his own inability to write convincingly about sexual relationships (see some of the passages describing sexual congress in *Ada*, that index to his true status). The object of Humbert's obsession is so young as to cause him to appear insane and pitiful rather than tragic. . . . One must admire the cunning of this evasion. Other assessments of Nabokov—highly intelligent ones—differ considerably from mine, and put his achievement at a much higher level: among the most able of these is Andrew Field's *Nabokov* (1967).

Naipaul, V. S. (1932) West-Indian (of Indian parentage) novelist now resident in Great Britain. His reputation, which was considerable in the sixties, has, like his work, rather faded in the seventies. But he still has potentialities. His early novels and stories about Trinidad were brilliant: under the comic surface there was a fine irony and a controlled compassion. The best are *The Mystic Masseur* (1957) and the stories in *Miguel Street* (1959). He achieved a new depth, not yet rediscovered, in the novel *A House for Mr Biswas* (1961), in which the comic-naturalistic description of society perfectly reflects the anguish and defeat of the poverty-stricken protagonist. Since that novel, Naipaul has become more self-conscious, and a lack of pressure to write has become uncomfortably evident. But *An Area of Darkness* (1964), about his visit to India, is indispensable and depressing. He is an excellent journalist.

Nash, Ogden (1902–70) American writer of light verse. Nash is not in any sense a poet and the bulk of his work is reprehensibly designed to appeal to the bourgeois. But his technical trick of relentlessly pursuing the rhyme through windingly massive (learned from famous 'bad' poets) lines of deliberately banal verse occasionally led him into rendering a valid portrait of the banalities, 'moral' and otherwise, of bourgeois existence. At his best, then, this *New Yorker* writer is exceedingly depressing. He is not a satirist, since he lacks moral responsibility or hatred, but he is perhaps the best American light *versifier* of his age. *Collected Verse* (1961); *Marriage Lines* (1964).

Nemerov, Howard (1920) American poet, novelist, critic, teacher. Serious and almost boiling over with potentialities, a certain indulgence in over-versatility has prevented Nemerov from achieving these except in one or two instances. But he could be one of the leading writers of his generation, as his generally penetrative criticism (e.g. *Poetry and Fiction,* 1963) demonstrates. As a poet he is always outside the obviously *avant-garde* or pseudo-*avant-garde* tradition, and he has had considerable difficulties in finding a manner to suit his voice. His philosophical verse is respectable but ponderous, his deliberate slight poems are usually just off-target or trite. He often gives the impression, indeed, of seeking to avoid his own gift by over-intellectualizing it: by becoming too explicit. And his 'style' is frequently *too* impeccable. Yet he knows the 'pretty poems are dead', and in such poems as 'Runes', where he can escape into dream and follow his own bent, if through a sustained, tight form, he is effectively mysterious. The best of his novels is *Federigo, or The Power of Love,* a comic, ironic treatment of the nature of devilishness. *New and Selected Poems* (1960); *The Winter Lightning: Selected Poems* (1968). *A Commodity of Dreams* (1959) collects stories. *Journal of the Fictive Life* (1965) is unclassifiable: an autobiographical novel (as sketches for several novels) interspersed with poetry and criticism.

Neruda, Pablo (ps. Neftalí Ricardo Reyes) (1904–73) Chilean poet. He is the most loved poet Chile has ever had. He took his pseudonym from a late nineteenth-century Czech poet, Jan Neruda, whom he admired. He was for most of his life a diplomat and was Allende's ambassador in Paris until 1972, when he had to return to Chile because of a cancer of the prostate (the prognosis for which is excellent). A few days after the murder of his old friend Allende Neruda 'died' in a hospital and what manuscripts Pinochet's gunmen could get hold of were seized; at his funeral, attended by a huge crowd, uniformed gangsters kept their guns at the ready. Neruda always had an enormous creative energy and his political commitment to communism–arising from his experiences in Spain in the thirties–never vitiated this, although it was responsible for some passages of boring and prosy polemic. His poetry employs surrealist (*see* Breton) techniques, but he is not a surrealist: rather he seeks to explore himself by reference, first, to his feelings of alienation and desire to escape from this, and secondly, to the exotic, 'secret', mysterious, unexplored landscape of South America (an apt symbol for the exciting, dangerous depths of the mind). In the earlier poems, *Veinte poemas de amor y una canción desesperada* (1924; tr. 1969), and the first two parts of *Residencia en la tierra* (1925–31; tr. *Residence on Earth,* 1946), there is a tension between absolute despair –with strong anti-bourgeois elements–and love of the earth. The sheer energy of this poetry acquits Neruda of the charge of 'nihilism' that has been levelled at him. When he joined the communist party he made a conscious effort to become 'committed'; but the finest parts of *Tercera Residencia* (1947) and *Canto General* (1950) are wholly non-political. It is simply that his membership of a cause relieved him of despair and allowed him to indulge his love of life and of the earth upon which it is lived. *Odas elementales* (1954–7; sel. tr. 1961) concentrate, often humorously, on 'humble' and 'ordinary' subjects; once again, the communist ideology (though not the idealism and hope) is irrelevant to the poetry. He can be irresponsible and meandering, but at his most powerful his poetry is incomparably excited and exciting, his language set at an astonishingly high poetic pitch. There are many translations: *Selected Poems* (tr. 1961); *Selected Poems* (tr. 1970)–this is a large bilingual volume–*Extravagaria* (1958; tr. 1972), also bilingual. There was an edition of 'complete' works published in Buenos Aires in 1968.

Nin, Anais (1914) American (but born in France of hybrid descent; her father was a Spanish pianist) novelist, diarist, critic, dancer, psychologist, journalist. She is occasionally absurdly overrated but is by no means without merit. She knew many writers, including Henry Miller (q.v.) and Artaud (q.v.), and her diaries (*Journals,* 1967–70), though ragbags and not 'recognized . . . masterpieces', are interesting and valuable. Her fiction (e.g. *Ladders to Fire,* 1946; *The House of Incest,* 1949; *Seduction of the Minotaur,* 1961) is a compost of various modernist techniques that yields powerful passages but no kind of unity, though she has perpetrated elaborate fictional theories (*The*

Novel of the Future, 1969). Really she wants to turn writing into painting, dancing and feminine self-observation; one may say that she is brilliantly intelligent but, as a writer, all at sea. Had she tried to concentrate on only one or two themes she could have been a major experimental novelist.

Nossack, Hans Erich (1901) German novelist, poet, playwright, essayist. Sartre (q.v.) introduced his work to France, where he has enjoyed much success as a 'German existentialist' 'working in surrealist forms'. Whatever the truth of these claims–they have substance–he is an original writer who deserves more recognition in English than a single translation (*Unmögliche Beweisaufnahme*, 1959; tr. *The Impossible Proof*, 1969). Essentially he is a 'magic realist' and has certain affinities with the Italian Massimo Bontempelli (1878–1960), though his characteristically Teutonic use of archaic and mythical material adds an extra dimension. His early work was destroyed by air-raids on his native Hamburg and he was banned by the Nazis. His chief full-length books are *Nekyia* (1947; French tr. *Nekya*, 1947), *Spirale* (1956; French tr. 1956) and *Der Fall d'Arthez* (1968), *The Case d'Arthez*. The first is a 'report', by a sole survivor of the 1945 German chaos, who discovers in it what Sartre would certainly call the reporter's own 'authenticity'. *Spirale* is subtitled 'novel of a night of insomnia'; its description of a man's re-creation of his past and his self-judgement again bring up typically existentialist (*see* Sartre) themes (solitude, falsity to self, defeat). *Der Fall d'Arthez* is a major dystopia about a state which regards the quest for the true self as treason. *Spätestens im November* (1955), *At Latest in November*, is a more conventionally styled attack on the *Wirtschaftswunder* society. *Das kennt man* (1964), *We Know That Already*, experiments with demotic, and should probably be classed with his major books, though it is somewhat overloaded with recondite detail. *Der jüngere Bruder* (1958; French tr. *Le Frère Cadet*, 1958), *The Younger Brother*, is also notable. His most recent novel, *Die gestohlene Melodie* (1972), *The Stolen Melody*, is about a retired schoolteacher who, after failures at suicide, marriage and work, rejects the external world entirely–the theme is not new for Nossack, but this time the protagonist does not comprehend the nature of his decision. *Dorothea* (1950), the German revision of *Interview mit dem Tode* (1948; French tr. *Interview avec la Mort*, 1948), consists of remarkable autobiographical essays, describing how Nossack watched Hamburg–

and his old self—being smashed to pieces, and what he felt. His poems were collected in 1947: *Gedichte.* There are several volumes of stories, one of which is translated in *Great German Short Stories* (1960). He deserves to be more widely read, for his quest for reality without resort to dogma has high distinction.

O

O'Casey, Sean (1880–1964) Irish (of Protestant family) dramatist, autobiographer. His finest plays are realistic and lyrical; they were driven out of him by what he had seen of poverty, feminine decency and courage, and murder in his youth. Before turning to literature he had done many manual jobs and had been an extreme left-wing activist. He was lucky to have escaped being shot because of his role in the Easter 1916 uprising. The Abbey Theatre took him up in 1919 and put on his three masterpieces–*Shadow of a Gunman* (1923), *Juno and the Paycock* (1924) and *The Plough and the Stars* (1926). These are fiercely exuberant plays, contrasting the savagery of their background with the vitality of its victims–and they show a remarkable sympathy for women. But the last-named, centred on the 1916 affair, infuriated everyone in Ireland; embittered, he moved to England and began to involve himself in Marxist pacificism and to practise expressionist (*see* Stadler) techniques. *The Silver Tassie* (1928), an anti-war play effective in performance but lacking in linguistic vitality, was refused by Yeats (q.v.) for the Abbey and O'Casey became even more enraged and bitter. He continued to exploit his great comic gift in a number of plays satirizing the narrowness of various aspects of Irish life (e.g. *Red Roses for Me,* 1942; *Cock-a-Doodle Dandy,* 1949), but his compassion had vanished. His experimental *Within the Gates* (1934) was a failure and on the whole the theatre critics were (for once) right in their attacks on it. His abortive, crude experimentalism is also shown in the *Autobiographies* (1939–54 in six volumes; 1963 in two volumes). These are ragbags of straight narrative, dialogue and stream-of-consciousness (*see* Bergson) writing; their form is unsuccessful, and they contain too much histrionic material–but, read critically, they are an indispensable guide to the man, to his writings, and to certain aspects of his times. *Collected Plays* (1949–51); *Behind the Green Curtains* (1961) contains three more plays; *Five One Act Plays* (1958); *Blasts and Benedictions* (1967) contains essays and stories.

O'Connor, Flannery (1925–64) American novelist, short-story writer, critic. She is a strange, difficult, mind-haunting case. Born in the South (Georgia), where she lived, she was a member of the Roman Catholic Church and believed intensely in a Christian God. Since her style seems pure 'Southern Gothic' and her Catholicism seems Protestant ('crazy' Southern Revivalist, in fact), these two topics have been much discussed by the critics of her fiction. Two others deserve emphasis. The first is that she was extremely intelligent and the second is that she inherited (from her father) a horrible and incurable disease, disseminated lupus (the rare, generalized form of *lupus erythematosus* which affects heart, spleen and kidneys—and not just the skin), which progressively crippled her and finally, when it was reactivated by a necessary operation, killed her earlier than it might have. The facts of her deliberation as a writer (she is certainly horrifying in her fiction, yet behaved as though she were a genteel lady) and her atrocious health are important. Her characters are all possessed by her vision. The characters in her novels—*Wise Blood* (1952), *The Violent Bear It Away* (1960)—and her stories (the best are 'The Artificial Nigger' and 'Parker's Back': all are collected in *A Good Man is Hard to Find*, 1955, and *Everything That Rises Must Converge*, 1965)—are insane, grotesque fanatics who seek to prove God's existence by various acts of violence. They are believers in the sense that they *will* become or see God, yet unbelievers in the sense that they are tormented by their lack of God. It is said that Flannery O'Connor is a 'religious novelist'; but is it not truer to say that her novels are 'about religion'—incredibly distorted nightmare metaphors, as horrible as lupus, for the anguish caused to all of us by our ignorance of the reason for our unique cortical properties? This ignorance is the non-Christian equivalent of the Christian feeling of being 'cut off from grace': a craving for knowledge as potent in the idiot or moron as in the Pope or an atheist polymath. Haze Motes, the hero of *Wise Blood*, is thus cut off. Having 'lost his faith' (the false, indoctrinated faith of childhood?) he sets out to create a 'church of truth without Jesus Christ Crucified'. The plot is one of the wildest and most fantastic ever conceived. *The Violent Bear It Away*, a superior novel, tells of a boy's mission to baptize a still younger boy (he drowns him), and of his ambiguous uncle; at the end he is drugged and raped by Satan (this was by the lady who refused to read *Lolita* on the grounds that it wouldn't be proper to do so). Again, the 'religious' hero, Tarwater, is 'cut off': his real mission is to purge himself of everything but madness. These novels, and the stories, depend on exceedingly complex and erudite theological symbolic structures, elaborate punning, bizarre comedy reminiscent of German expressionism (but deliberately rooted in 'Southern Gothic') and an atmosphere highly charged with fanaticism. Yet the project of the work seems to be to show that fanaticism is, finally, sanity. One can understand why so sick, crippled, weak and confused a writer should have felt impelled to state that she saw 'from the standpoint of Christian orthodoxy', that 'the meaning of life is centred in our Redemption by Christ. . . .' To have chosen any other life-style (she was a born Catholic) would have meant insanity; she chose to invent insane characters in novels whose unorthodoxy reveals her true state of mind. What is Flannery O'Connor's status? Probably she is too impenetrable (except in a few stories) to have achieved what we call greatness. But her powerful and fascinating fiction does raise the 'question of belief' more startlingly than that of any other writer of her generation. The most useful of her expositors has so far been S. E. Hyman (1966). But for further elucidation of her novels—and perhaps enlightenment—we shall need to analyze both her medical history, which probably explains much of her symbolism, allusion and punning (though at a deep level), and her few articles about being a Catholic and a novelist (e.g. 'The Role of the Catholic Novelist', *Greyfriar*, 7, 1964). I suspect her (contentiously) to have been, as writer, a satirist and critic of the *Christian* religion (so peculiar and intolerant in its exclusiveness) and I read her texts as a deeply reluctant and therefore not quite fulfilled imaginative attempt to point to the existence of a grace freed from dogma.

Odets, Clifford (1906–63) American playwright who began as a communist (1934–5) and ended by bowing to (Joseph) McCarthy. Unintelligent, confused, professional, impassioned, weak, fluent, Odets wrote 'well-made' plays that are ultimately unconvincing, sentimental and rhetorical (e.g. *Golden Boy*, 1937); but they act effectively and are still played and admired. A few passages have real power. *Six Plays* (1939).

O'Hara, John (1905–70) American novelist, short-story writer, journalist. O'Hara's professionalism is admirable but the general consensus that his best, earlier work was overrated and that his later work is fundamentally weak, is correct. His best novels are *Appointment in Samarra* (1934) and *Butterfield 8* (1935), and the best of his many stories are in the thirties collections, *The Doctor's Son* (1935) and *Files on Parade* (1939). These are invaluable guides to the middle-class mores of Pennsylvania, but they are essentially excellent journalism. O'Hara lacked imagination or psychological penetration and he covered up these lacks with a laconic, ironic style that is really a blank sentimentalism. His excursions into sexual detail are more reprehensible. O'Hara had genuine sociological insight into the well-heeled world of business men and their wives, and into the more obviously sadder one of lonely, less privileged suburbanites, but he had not the technical resources to illuminate the psychology of their alienation. In other words, he relied on journalistic prestidigitation because he had no more than nineteenth-century methods at his command—and these are not adequate to treat of twentieth-century material. He is therefore, even at best, a journalist as pseudo-novelist. Still, good journalism has its considerable merits. The later stories lack feeling or insight, but know how to make their readers feel sad. That is trickery of a low order. The best of the later novels is *Ourselves To Know* (1960), ostensibly about a man who gets away with killing his wife but really (though O'Hara didn't know it) about his own murder of imagination.

Olesha, Yuri (1899–1960) Russian fiction writer, dramatist. He fought for the Bolsheviks but soon became disillusioned with their treatment of writers and of individuals in general. He was imprisoned by Stalin in 1938 and again after the war but Khrushchev released him and he was allowed to pursue journalism in his last few years. He is an anti-technological caricaturist, whose most famous novel—a masterpiece —*Zavist* (1928; tr. *Envy,* 1936; 1947) is a clever and exuberant satire on the Soviet way of life. It involves a bureaucratic supporter of the regime, a drunken bum, and a mad machine called Ophelia which will bring the mechanized world into disrepute. It was taken by some as a defence of the Soviet system. Olesha later dramatized it. Soon after this he stopped serious writing, doubtless finding this impossible after the advent of the socialist realist (*see* Gorky) line. But *Zavist* remains one of the best novels to come out of Russia in the twenties, nor does its satire apply only to its immediate context.

Olson, Charles (1910–71) American poet, critic. Until the early fifties, when he became rector at Black Mountain (1951–6), Olson had only a tiny following; he owed his reputation to Creeley (q.v.), whose mentor he was, and who edited his *Selected Writings* (1966). His study of Melville, *Call Me Ishmael* (1947), was his best known work until he became the inspirer not only of Creeley but of many other 'Black Mountain' poets. Olson, who was in many ways a good and generous man, had an excellent education (Yale, Harvard, Wesleyan) which he partially misused. His influence cannot be stated to have been bad, but it was not good. Besides the poetry, the key works (for those who feel Olson holds keys) are 'Projective Verse' (1950), *Mayan Letters* (1953), *Letters for Origin 1950–1956* (1969)—*Origin* was a magazine subscribing to Pound-Olson-Creeley ideas edited by Cid Corman—and *Proprioception* (1965). The third is really an elaboration of the first, which was reprinted in *Human Universe and Other Essays* (1965). The second, which consists of letters written to Creeley from Mexico, with the more general *Causal Mythology* (1969), sets forth his ideas of mythology. The last is a typical Olson 'instruction book'. Despite his education, or because of it, Olson uses a populist-Yankee-professorial style which leads him into over-simplification and vulgarity. 'Projective Verse' grafts on to a lucubrated and confused discussion of the old form-content question (form is an 'extension of content') a more original but insufficiently worked out notion of poetry-as-spoken-voice, syllable, breath: 'all the thots [sic] men are capable of can be entered on the back of a postage stamp. So, it is not the PLAY of a mind we are after, is not that that shows whether a mind is there at all?' Olson does not acknowledge any unknown factor in poetry: he is telling us how to do it, which is intolerable. His 'anthropology' contains incidental insights but has its basis in an agrarianism as simplistic as Masters's (q.v.). As to the poetry (*The Maximus Poems,* 1953–68; most of the rest are collected in *Archeologist of Morning,* 1970): this is a noisy, rhetorical, busily egotistical combination of Williams (q.v.) and Pound (q.v.), irritating in its typewriter-graphical wildness, and with print almost always trying to ape voice. One can say only that inside the great earnest framework there are some light, domestic, humorous passages that express the relaxed private man. . . . So Olson is this: the prophet of a new American fashion, of which his disciple Creeley is the (now declining) leader: the projection of personality through performance of what is called poetry. This is not the same as 'poetry reading', since the vast majority of the audiences do not read the words delivered at all—if they do then they look at them as film-fans look at photographs of stars: to be thrilled, and get good vibes. But Olson, quirky and tiresome though he is, has prose that deserves perusal. He is historically important as a leader and false prophet of the anti-academic American school; he did not do justice to an important role.

O'Neill, Eugene (1888–1953) American playwright. Forms, with Pirandello (q.v.), Brecht (q.v.) and Synge (q.v.), the great quadrumvirate of twentieth-century dramatists. Nobel Prize 1936. O'Neill is frequently the prey of critics because his drama so clearly flouts this or that academics' law—or is it because he is so moving? Our century has not produced a single major play in verse (Yeats's, q.v., best play is in prose, and Lorca's, q.v., moves towards it); and O'Neill really realized that this could not be done, and set to work to make what he could out of this. His great virtue in his best plays is that he entirely and deliberately avoids poetic language. Like good playwrights, he is as readable as he is playable. And, like all artistically successful dramatists, he had cunning: he knew uncannily how to override the gimmicks of directors (and intellectually ambitious actors). His plays, given competent performers, 'play themselves', and for all their flaws, they have behind them a massive voltage of passion and of tragic experience deeply reflected upon. O'Neill's restless experimentalism led him to write some poor (though always interesting) plays; but it also led him to his greatest triumphs. His parents were actors: his father a well known romantic ham and director, his mother a drug addict. He was raised, literally, in the theatre; then, after a year at Princeton, he became a sailor. After contracting and recovering from tuberculosis, he joined Baker's (q.v.) 47 Workshop (1914). His first one-acters were produced by the Provincetown Players (beginning with *Bound East for Cardiff*, 1916—he had previously published four one-act plays, in *Thirst*, 1914, and three others). By the end of the war he had become well known and in 1920 and 1921 he won the Pulitzer Prize for *Beyond the Horizon* and *Anna Christie* (published with *The Hairy Ape* and *The First Man*, 1924). O'Neill's drama developed, but all his plays (with the exception of the uncharacteristic comedy, *Ah, Wilderness*, 1933) have one thing in common: essentially they are searches for a meaning and therefore an affirmation: an answer to his own involuted, brooding anguish. The chief influence on him was the theatre itself and in all of his drama there is a built-in assumption that the theatre is illusion (cf. Brecht, Pirandello, Synge): the rhetoric he constructed is uncynically based on this assumption. No playwright influenced him more than

Strindberg (q.v.), whose extreme neurosis and proto-expressionism he could understand. He was deeply affected by his reading of Greek drama. His work may be divided into three main phases, the first two of which overlap: the early sea-plays, the experimental plays written between 1920 and 1934, and the great last plays worked at during a twelve-year period from 1934, but not finalized or produced until or after O'Neill's death. The one-act sea plays, five of which are in *The Moon of the Caribbees* (1919), culminate in the longer *Anna Christie*. There was no American tradition upon which O'Neill could build and so he had to learn from Baker and then become the Provincetown Players' great 'discovery' (he owed much to both). The sea-plays smash once and for all the old 'sea-dog' stereotype; they are finely constructed, combine naturalism (*see* Zola) and symbolism, and above all present, here as the sea and its fatal attractions, that Greek sense of fate, *moira*, of which O'Neill had so profound and intuitive an understanding. *Anna Christie* sums up, elaborates and extends this sea-*moira* equation. *The Emperor Jones* (1921) introduced expressionism into the American theatre. There followed some fourteen more (produced) plays before O'Neill fell into silence in 1934. In them he experimented with expressionism (*see* Stadler), Freudianism (q.v.), the religion-rationalism conflict, satire (*Marco's Millions*, 1927), symbolism and stream of consciousness (*see* Bergson). The masterpieces are *Desire Under the Elms* (1925), *Strange Interlude* (1928—but this is a contentious view) and the trilogy *Mourning Becomes Electra* (1931). *Desire Under the Elms* brilliantly combines realist illusion with (chiefly Freudian) expressionism; *Strange Interlude* is a study-in-depth (again chiefly Freudian) of a woman, making use of stream-of-consciousness methods (as 'asides'); and *Mourning Becomes Electra* re-creates the Orestes story in a post-Civil War setting. Although in this last we can sometimes feel O'Neill yearning for a poetic utterance (he had, it goes without saying, begun as a poet) to match his grand theme, the trilogy as a whole is a triumphantly convincing and imaginative re-creation of the Greek idea of a family curse (*Ate*), which enriches and not merely employs Freudian concepts, particularly the 'Oedipus complex'. In his twelve years of silence O'Neill struggled with plans and drafts for a huge dramatic cycle to deal with the history of an American family; this was not achieved, but the ending of the war (which, even more than his other troubles, had suffused him with the titanic gloom of which, as we see from his plays, he was capable) gave him the strength to see two of his works into production; four more have followed posthumously. *The Iceman Cometh* (1946), written in 1939, is one of the most pessimistic plays ever written, presenting, with fearful power, man as a creature who has nothing at all except hopeless illusion and death. At one level it expresses his own disappointment at his failure to achieve a poetic language by demonstrating that human beings have proved themselves unworthy of such a thing: its prolixity and its prosiness seem somehow deliberate, an anti-poetry so sombre as to suffuse the mind with its opposite. *A Moon for the Misbegotten* (1952), written in 1943, is a less successful play based on the life of his brother, who was also an alcoholic. The posthumous *Long Day's Journey into Night* (1956), written in 1940–1, was an enormous success at its first production in 1956: it is an apparent return to realism, but actually welds together, without obtrusion, almost all O'Neill's experimental concerns. Dealing with a day in the life of an American family, and clearly a final resolution of O'Neill's fundamental autobiographical problems (the drunk brother, the addictive mother, the ex-matinée idol, O'Neill himself–Edmund–Freudianly trapped in the family constellation), it shows insight and compassion, although it is a tragedy. *A Touch of the Poet* (1957) and *More Stately Mansions* (1964) are the only two surviving plays of the huge cycle he had planned. The first, and the first of the projected cycle, was written in 1936 and reveals the 'forgiving' O'Neill but betrays his weakness of health at the time; the second, probably the fourth in the series, has been published only in an edited and possibly misleading version. It remains only to mention *Hughie* (1959), written in 1941, a one-act near-monologue which strangely disproves what the critics had always accused O'Neill of: lack of verbal sensitivity. For it is an immediately recognizable tragi-comic masterpiece of the colloquial. O'Neill is certainly a puzzle. But at the least he is the single great American dramatist: a man who raised his struggle with his own demons to the point at which it could become a metaphor for the struggles of all human beings. *The Complete Plays* (1934–5); *The Plays* (1946); *Plays* (1922–62, in Great Britain); *Ten Lost Plays* (1964).

Onetti, Juan Carlos (1909) Uruguayan fiction writer, journalist. He has subjected the tradition of naturalism (*see* Zola) to a peculiarly wry, Latin-American existentialist (*see* Sartre) scrutiny. He is aware of man's desire for 'authenticity', but never for a moment presents him as being near to the attainment of it. He is an excellent, humorous, depressing writer. He learned much from Céline (q.v.), whose nausea he shares; but he is better humoured. His novels and stories are all outstanding, but only *El astillero* (1961; tr. *The Shipyard*, 1968) has so far been translated. This and its successor *Juntacádavares* (1965) deal with a Célinesque character called Larsen, whose professional life is fantastically absurd but who nevertheless tries to cling on to self-identification —through his inner life, over which he manages comically varying degrees of control, none of them strong. *La vida breve* (1950), *The Short Life*, deals with a character who is more straightforwardly fantasist and who ruins his life. Onetti is an original and subtle writer, whose psychological pessimism presents an indispensable challenge to all idealistic philosophies and fictions.

Ortega, José (1883–1955) Spanish thinker, critic, journalist. He is more often known by his full name Ortega y Gasset. He was the son of the realist novelist, of the 'Generation of 1898' (*see* Unamuno), José Ortega Munilla (1856–1922). Ortega quarrelled with Unamuno over the matter of the Church, which Unamuno thought essential and he—being a pagan—did not; but he was at least half-formed by him and eloquently mourned his death. Ortega's ideas were influenced by German philosophers at Marburg and he was a professor of philosophy; but his style is unaffected by the German language and he used journalism (which was of a high level in Spain when speech was free) as his main weapon: many of his books first appeared as series of articles. Paz (q.v.) calls Ortega a 'reactionary', though he pays tribute to his perspicacity; this is not fair. Ortega was a reformist (not a revolutionary), who blamed both right- and left-wing authoritarianism, as well as Church and Army, for Spain's stagnation, and he advocated tolerance and mutual understanding between groups. That is not reactionary. He was a member of the Cortes in 1931, but was out of Spain during the Civil War (1936 until 1945, after which he divided his time between Lisbon and Madrid). He is a proto-existentialist who believes that 'I am myself plus my circumstances'; life is a process of becoming. Like Sartre (q.v.) after him, Ortega was influenced by the phenomenologist Husserl; but unlike Sartre he fights shy of revolution and concentrates exclusively on the nature of *Angst:* man is a victim of *naufragio* (shipwreck): he is stranded in a sea of insecurity and he leans on the conventions—only in solitude can he learn to lead his own existence. His ideas about Spain are in *España invertebrada* (1921; tr. *Invertebrate Spain*, 1937).

The elitism of the famous *La rebelión de las masas* (1929–30; tr. *The Revolt of the Masses,* 1932) is as tolerant as elitism can be, and what it prophesies is unpleasantly correct. *La Dehumanización del arte e ideas sobre la novela* (1925; tr. *The Dehumanization of Art and Notes on the Novel,* 1948) is a puzzling, ironic book, and it is not really consistent with Ortega's political views: art must be 'artistocratic', removed from reality (bourgeois reality—his *creencias* are the conventions to which shipwrecked man clings), 'dehumanized', unpopular, expressionistically distorting (cf. Valle-Inclán's, q.v., *esperpento* or Pirandello's, q.v., *grottesco*). Ortega was flamboyant, rhetorical, over-combative, controversial, lucid and indispensable. He had been called a historicist and he was tempted—by his disdain for the 'masses'—in that direction; but he was like Swift in that he loathed the collective masses but not Tom, Dick or Harry, whom he exhorted not to accept circumstances blindly, but to modify them, to create. His collected works appeared 1946–69.

Orwell, George (ps. Eric Blair) (1903–50) English novelist, critic, journalist, polemicist, socialist critic of communism. He was sent to Eton but instead of going on to university he joined the Burma Police (1922–27), an experience which profoundly disturbed him but which he was eventually able to absorb. He set out to be a writer, nearly starved, and wrote of his apprenticeship in *Down and Out in Paris and London* (1933), a little classic which shows the influence of Gissing but which is already flavoured with his own individuality, strongly independent personality, and power of objective description. He settled his account with imperialism with the restrained novel *Burmese Days* (1934). He wrote two more Gissing-like novels (*A Clergyman's Daughter,* 1935, and *Keep the Aspidistra Flying,* 1936), both of which have been somewhat underrated by critics. They are critical of the bourgeois, and show anti-heroes in ineffective revolt; much of their detail is beautifully observed. Then he went to Spain as a journalist and within a few weeks joined the Republican forces. He was seriously wounded in the throat and on his return he wrote *Homage to Catalonia* (1938), in which he describes how Stalin's tactics had succeeded in undermining the loyalist cause. This is one of his most exquisite books, full of sympathy for the genuine anti-Franco spirit then alive in Spain, and extremely fair and accurate in its portrayal of the villains. This made him even more unpopular with the orthodox British left-wing than had *The*

Road to Wigan Pier (1937), which revealed the leftist intellectuals' total lack of understanding of the atrocious conditions which they too abstractly insisted they desired to correct. Like Myers (q.v.), with whom he has little else in common, Orwell believed in commitment: the very substance of his dubieties forced him into impulsive, self-critical, action. This led him into certain confusions: while he certainly did understand the victims of poverty in a way that most of the Labour politicians did not (he never joined a political party), he was highly sceptical of doctrinaire systems. That was right, but he became sometimes neurotically unpredictable in his approaches to personal living and public utterance. He possessed a Weil (q.v.) -like streak of compulsive saintliness, a desire to be utterly identified with the oppressed (he and his first wife gave away their ration-books); but against this operated both his detachment and a certain guiltily concealed scorn for stupidity. In general he resolved these difficulties, though premature death (of tuberculosis aggravated by his wound and overwork) perhaps prevented him from writing a novel of major scope and wide human compassion (he appears at his death to have been pondering on a work of this kind). The nostalgic *Coming Up For Air* (1939) remains his most substantial 'straight' novel. During the war he threw himself into journalism (the *Manchester Evening News*, the *Observer*, *Tribune*) and worked for the BBC; many of his essays and commentaries of this desperate period helped him to resolve his problems (these, on reactionary figures and on vulgar-popular ones, are all collected, with other material, in *Collected Essays, Journalism, and Letters*, 1968: an indispensable key to Orwell, now issued in paperback). The deadly and yet restrained allegory of Stalinism, *Animal Farm* (1945), suddenly made him famous. It is a major classic animal fable, showing great love for the actual protagonists; apart from Swift and Lewis (q.v.), with whom Orwell had strange affinities, no one has produced anything comparable to it in English literature. In this 'fairy tale' Orwell displays his essentially imaginative genius to perfection. But by this time he was seriously ill. He was in despair, fighting a battle against the left from (as he stated) within the left. He produced much engaging criticism and commentary; his final dystopian masterpiece, *Nineteen Eighty-Four* (1949), perhaps reflects his own final anguish as much as it does his terrifying—and partly fulfilled—view of the future. This, influenced by Zamyatin's (q.v.) *We*, but not to its disadvantage, is an indictment of all totalitarianism. It prefers neither right nor left, but rather concentrates on the evils of behaviouristic approaches and on the horrible results of the crushing of individualism. Orwell was forced to write much of his criticism and commentary in a hurry and without due thought; he was less scholarly than his mental quality deserved, but even in his weaker essays (e.g. on Swift) he has remarkable insights. And he is and remains the paradigm of the agony of the left: he best posits the paradox of how a bureaucracy created in the interests of equality can stultify the individuality of human beings. His chief weaknesses as critic and commentator are his lack of an education (with which to educate himself) and his need to rush off copy. But his last two works of fiction transcend these weaknesses: decency, tolerance and imagination carry him above his shortcomings. And he was a master of lucidity, of saying what he meant, of exposing the falsity of what he called 'double-think'. Few writers have been able to go as far as he did beyond their limitations.

Osborne, John (1929) English playwright. Osborne has some real passion and theatrical ability but his plays lack linguistic interest and have become increasingly either personally obsessive or pieces designed to please audiences. He lacks control of himself and has no very publicly conspicuous intelligence. *Look Back in Anger* (1956) was authentic in catching the fifties quasi-nihilist mood and its success was deserved. But Osborne has not proved himself intellectually capable of convincing dramatic analysis of later and more destructive moods. *The Entertainer* (1957) lacks true sociological percipience. *Luther* (1961) is interesting but it is mechanical pastiche of Brecht (q.v.) and its significant lines, from Luther's own utterances, depend on the actor delivering them (it was originally Albert Finney). The later plays are tired neo-Shavian reconstructions (*A Patriot for Me,* 1965, a psychologically feeble dramatization of an Austrian homosexual military scandal of the early nineties) or confused talk-pieces. Osborne is immediately appealing but his self-defensiveness and apparent lack of capacity to think self-critically and lucidly have robbed his work of everything but (occasional) persuasive rhetorical power.

Ostaijen, Paul Van (1896–1928) Flemish poet and prose writer who exercised a strong influence on his own and the post-1945 poetic generation. *Music Hall* (1916) is frenetic unanimistic (*see* Romains) expressionism (*see* Stadler), in which the influence of Verhaeren (q.v.) is promisingly grafted onto a modernistic vitality; *Het Sienjaal* (1918), *The Signal,* is more sober, but *Bezette Stad* (1921), *The Occupied City,* yields to dada (*see* Ball) in the spirit of Apollinaire (q.v.). Ostaijen was a figure of great energy and talent who did not live long enough to realize his gift; his last volume of 'pure poetry', *Het eerste Boek van Schmoll* (1928), *The First Book of Schmoll,* in which he essays a pure poetry he called 'organic expressionism', is still experimental, though some of the poems anticipate the concerns of Francis Ponge (1899) and others in their desperate search for a lyricism in the world outside the poet. His stories, influenced by Kafka (q.v.), Apollinaire and the German expressionists, are slight. His criticism was provocative (e.g. *Self-Defense,* 1933), and he remains an important influence. *Poèmes* (1951) is a French translation. His complete works were issued 1952–3 and are now in course of revision (1963–). There is a valuable English study of the prose: E. H. Beckman's *Homeopathy of the Absurd* (1970).

Owen, Wilfred (1893–1918) English poet, killed leading an attack a few days before the 1918 armistice was declared. Sorley (q.v.) was the first poet to see through the hollow 'patriotism' of the First World War, but he had no time to develop his genius; Owen is generally regarded as the greatest of the 1914–18 war poets and the one who embodied most substantially the horrors of that war. This is partly true, but it was Sassoon (q.v.), author of earlier, more directly satirical poems on the subject who determined Owen's final direction (at Craiglockhart Hospital in 1917)—and Graves (q.v.) had already written, if without the maturity of Owen's last poems, in a similarly disillusioned vein. Gurney and Rosenberg (q.v.), who is superior, knew more exactly than Owen, when they joined up, the nature of what they were going into. Owen was an 'injustice collector' (Joseph Cohen) and somewhat miserably passive homosexual whose poetic genius was inspired rather than simply quickened by his experience of war. Sassoon, himself at this time (and for some time afterwards) a zealous subterranean homosexual, put Owen straight about his erotic inclinations as well as helping him with his poetry (the one action seems as commendable as the other). Such facts are not irrelevant, since they help to correct the still general impression that Owen's famous pronouncement that 'the poetry is in the pity' is to be taken at face value. It isn't. The rightly famous final poems are certainly descriptive, and graphically so, of the extreme hideousness of war. They have behind them a well-defined sense of the cruel futilities that lead to it (had he lived, Owen could have been a socialist politician of distinction, not a poet—there was no more to come). But in those poems there is an extreme naturalist's relish in horror: an indulgence of the decadence that may be traced back to his early and mostly feeble poetic exercises. Owen's new techniques (assonance, dissonance, internal rhyme) are surely owed to shocked horror, to his sense of the inadequacy of the Victorian-mellifluous or superficial-patriotic in the face of war; but careful study of his texts (e.g. the famous 'Strange Meeting') reveals that his true subject is not protest but horrified fascination. His letters (*Collected Letters*, 1967) clearly demonstrate his fear and hatred of women. His 'pity' is sensualized by his lust for boys as well as by his proto socialist passions. In 'Strange Meeting' (no less good a poem because of this interpretation) the deepest level is one of unconsummated pathic love: the poem is not only about the waste caused by war but also about the plight of the homosexual: the dead in hell are the oppressed ones, the homosexuals. 'I would have poured my spirit [i.e. semen] without stint/ But not through words. . . .' says the other man the poet meets in hell. He is notable for his lack of self-pity, for his sarcastic delineation of the staff officers, for his superb destruction of the non-combatant padres' 'encouragement' ('I dreamed kind Jesus fouled the big-gun gears'), for his courage, for the furious pitch to which indignation raised his language; but his poetry, though always truthfully, exploits war to examine his sexuality. *Collected Poems* (1963) was not very competently done by Day Lewis (q.v.)—but a new edition is in preparation by Jon Stallworthy, and this should be impeccable. In his lifetime his poetry was known only to a literary few: Sassoon's edition (1920) made him well known, and later the thirties poets, such as Auden (q.v.), established his reputation. There are studies of him by D. S. R. Welland (1960) and Jon Stallworthy (1974); his brother Harold's *Journey From Obscurity* (1963–5) contains much biographical data.

P

Palazzeschi, Aldo (ps. Aldo Giurlani) (1885–1974) Italian novelist, poet, memoirist. One of the most gifted minor writers of this century—and in his most famous book, *Sorelle Materassi* (1934; tr. *The Materassi Sisters,* 1953), he is a major novelist. Anti-traditional, anti-rhetorical, independent, Palazzeschi is not so much a 'literary entertainer' (as he has been called) as knowing, compassionate and sophisticated. He began, as so many of his generation did, as a follower of D'Annunzio (q.v.), but was soon parodying him. He passed through *crepuscularismo* (*see* Gozzano) and *futurismo* (*see* Marinetti)—exploiting them for his own purposes—and then struck out on his own. He published no poems between 1910 and 1968 (except for two collections, both entitled *Poesie,* of 1925 and 1955, both largely retrospective), when he took it up again. He is a deeper and more serious writer than might be supposed from his deliberately clownish poetic stance. *Il codice di Perelà* (1911; rev. 1954 as *Perelà uomo di fumo, Perelà, the Man of Smoke*) and *Riflessi* (1908; later revised as *Allegoria di novembre, Allegory of November*) describe his personal predicament: the first, prophetic of fascism, has for its theme the detached, sensitive artist—the 'objective' aspect of anyone living in a horrifying world; the second, a strange book, is about narcissism, guilt, homosexuality and the 'decadent' temperament. *Sorelle Materassi,* less personal, is the story of the love of some middle-aged sisters for their opportunistic nephew. Later novels are uniformly excellent. Palazzeschi's poetry is deliberately light-hearted in manner, but contains much substance.

Pascoli, Giovanni (1855–1912) Italian poet and scholar. Not as aggressive or outspoken as D'Annunzio (q.v.) or Carducci (q.v.), Pascoli was ultimately as influential as either, though less directly and immediately. His idyllic childhood on a rich property of which his father, Ruggero, was bailiff, was painfully interrupted when Ruggero was murdered in 1867; his mother died in the following year and his elder brother in 1876–these events left their indelible mark on his subsequent poetry. In 1877 he was imprisoned for socialist activities; but by the early eighties he had already established himself as an academic and when Carducci retired from the post of Professor of Rhetoric at the University of Bologna (1905) he succeeded him. This was appropriate, because Pascoli, before going his own way, had begun as his disciple. He died at the height of his fame of cancer of the liver. The earliest Pascoli seemed to Croce in 1907 to be the perfect modern poet: the poet of intuition, the erudite and skilled expositor who animates and beautifies nature by his ability to remain a 'child'. Pascoli put forward his own theory of poetry in his essay 'Il fanciullino' (1907), 'The Little Child'. His truest poetry, in collections published between 1891 and 1905, is remarkably original. Modern Italian criticism, fiercely polemical, does not quite know how to take him; some critics are put off by his popularity. He is quiet, he feels pastoral and traditionalist and does not wish to be a modernist, yet his poetry of the nineties anticipates in one way or another almost all that was to come: the crepusculari (*see* Gozzano), futurism (*see* Marinetti) and the brand of 'hermeticism' practised by Montale (q.v.). He is, in sum, a perfect proto-modernist. With an unobtrusively brilliant technique and a use of onomatopoeia which (when it comes off) is daring in its absolute innocence (his famous *'scilp'* and *'vitt . . . videvitt'* for the cries of sparrows and starlings respectively pointed the way towards Marinetti's less convincing 'tumbtumb' etc.), he tells of his attachment to simple things, his nostalgia for childhood, his early domestic tragedies. At his worst he is monotonous, childish; at his best childlike and glowing. Death, as in 'Ultimo sogno', 'Last Dream', effectively haunts his poetry as a metaphor for sinister erotic longing: he set up house, devoting himself to certain tasks like a perfect pastoral husband, with his sister Maria. The 'last dream' involves a sense of ecstatic freedom from 'illness' and 'evil' as he sees his mother at his bedside: the innocence counterpoints the sexual longing, robbing it of 'Freudian' guilt in a manner almost unique. One of his 'key words' is 'tremulo' (trembling; tremulous), for not only nature but also his world of words that intuits it vibrate; he will use pidgin Italian, hypocorism, local words; he is a most anthropomorphic poet, investing all objects with individualities and feelings. For him, death alone confers beauty: nothing would be beautiful if it did not pass. Pascoli–who also wrote prize-winning Latin poems of great skill, a contentious and interesting interpretation of Dante, and many fine letters—cannot be categorized. A gentle soul, he is a strange mixture of sophisticate and naïf: in fact strung tensely between anarchism and reaction, spontaneity and learning, life and literature, simplicity and cunning, he refuses not to relax, and so must refuse the gratifications and excitements of an overtly erotic life—his secret longing for which, however, colours his entire *oeuvre* in an extraordinarily honest way. He renewed the language of Italian poetry. There have been some English versions, but a properly executed selection is badly needed. *Poesie* (1974) is a scholarly edition of the Italian poems in a single volume.

Pasternak, Boris (1890–1960) Russian (partly Jewish) poet, translator (e.g. Shakespeare, Goethe), memoirist, dramatist, novelist. Nobel Prize (which he was not allowed to receive) 1958. He possibly owed his life to the fact that he translated Georgian poets into Russian: Stalin was a Georgian. Although the novel *Dr Zhivago* (in Italian 1957; in Russian 1959; never published, though circulated, in Russia; tr. 1958; 1961) is his most famous work and an impressive one, it is not his best—critics other than journalists knew of Pasternak's genius long before *Zhivago* and the persecution that Pasternak endured on its account. His prose masterpiece is *Detstvo Luvers* (written 1918; 1925; tr. *Childhood,* 1941): this Proustian piece—the revised first chapter of a novel that was lost—is short; and it is in short forms that Pasternak excels. But his efforts to write in a longer compass are valiant and include verse epics of some power: *1905* (1926) and *Leitenant Schmidt* (1927), as well as *Zhivago*. His early poetry mixes symbolism with (Russian) futurism (*see* Mayakovsky), but he soon found his own inimitable manner, which eventually led him to a severer and more traditional style recalling that of the acmeists (*see* Akhmatova). As a young man he was influenced by the mystical ideas of the composer Scriabin, and a vein of nature-mysticism runs through all his poetry. He was always politically aloof, though he detested socialist realism (*see* Gorky) and its wider implications. His poetry displays his love of the Russian natural scene, his nervous, tremulous eroticism and his religious outlook; he is also perpetually fascinated by the process of poem-making, which he saw as magical, and perhaps equated with a kind of prayer. His poems are full of, and in themselves search for—with a sort of cubist fervour—'unknown secrets'. Characteristically, a pond is 'like a revealed secret'.

But the quest is lonely and fraught with horrors: there beckons a 'fatal hour,/blacker than monks, more stifling than priests/when madness overcomes'. Pasternak devoted himself mainly to publishing translations during the Stalinist era. The later poems, represented in the English selection *In the Interlude: Poems 1945–60* (1962), are simpler, more tragic, and draw on Gospel themes. Prominent among them is the sequence 'by' Zhivago—this did appear in Russia in 1954. These poems have led people to suppose that Pasternak had turned from revolutionary (his epics celebrate the revolution, though not over-fulsomely) to Christian, but, though Zhivago may be said to be Christian, the relationship between Pasternak himself and Christianity is perhaps tenuous. He accepted the New Testament as a repository of symbols and regarded himself as 'an atheist who had lost his faith'; but whether he literally believed in Christ as redeemer and may rightly be described as a 'great Christian poet' is doubtful. In any case his later poetry is inferior to the earlier, with the exception of certain of the Zhivago poems. He had been working on the novel since 1934. It is not deliberately anti-Soviet: what offended the culture-lackeys, many of whom knew Pasternak personally, was that it gave an account of an existence that was not, so to say, 'socialist realist' (*see* Gorky). It implicitly rejects communist activism in favour of the spiritual but it does not retreat into the kind of mystical obscurantism now, apparently, embraced by Solzhenitsyn (q.v.). It is a formless work, unable to carry its weight—but this weight is undeniable. Nevertheless, it is as a poet that Pasternak will endure. He had suffered a severe heart attack in 1952 but the anguish he bore after the Nobel Prize affair undoubtedly hastened his end. There are a number of translations, of varying merit: *Fifty Poems* (1963) has the authority of the poet's sister, whose translations are competent and accurate; *Selected Poems* (1946; 1959) is useful; *Poetry* (1959) is comprehensive; *Selected Writings* (1949) contains some poems; *The Collected Prose* (1945) has a misleading title but is valuable. Also: *The Last Summer* (1960); *Letters to Georgian Friends* (1967); *The Blind Beauty* (1969), part of an unfinished trilogy of plays at which Pasternak was working when he died.

Patchen, Kenneth (1911–72) American poet, novelist, painter. He suffered, from the late forties, from a severe and progressively incapacitating spinal disease: the symptoms of this illness, against which he manfully fought, had begun many years earlier and they explain the haste which robs his work of its proper concentration: he was always a man in too much of a hurry. The premonition of death can concentrate; in Patchen's case, tragically, it diffused—diluting the work with anger, resentment, decency (peculiarly horrible paradox) and technical recklessness. One can understand his adherents' passion for him but, alas, this is not justified in his texts. (One notes these men's rhetorical refusal to refer to the texts specifically—and mournfully, too: because one knows that he, a man of devoted energy, spent the last twenty-one years of his life on his back, crippled not only by his condition but by the cortisone that kept him alive.) Patchen was one of modern America's many failed Whitmans. His project had been to describe (never to diagnose) and then to heal, with leftist-Blakean passion. His four novels and thirty-odd books of poetry are described by his admirers in such terms as 'apocalyptic', 'talismanic', a 'Bible torn out of America's heart. . . .' He is a part, and doubtless a historically important part, of America's protest against 'America'. *Selected Poems* (1964); *Collected Poems* (1969). *Memoirs of a Shy Pornographer* (1945) is the most instructive of the novels.

Paton, Alan (1903) South African novelist. Celebrated for *Cry, the Beloved Country* (1948), a passionately anti-apartheid novel; but *Too Late the Pharalope* (1955) is better. His best writing, however, is in the short-story collection *Debbie Go Home* (1961); some of the tales are based on his experiences as principal of a reformatory school for boys (1935–8). His novels are sincere, strident and unsubtle and his attempt at an archaic prose that will integrate Bantu and English elements conspicuously fails. His most famous work was filmed (1952) and turned into an opera (*Lost in the Stars,* 1950) by Maxwell Anderson with music by Kurt Weill.

Pavese, Cesare (1908–50) Italian novelist, poet, critic, diarist, translator. Born in Piedmont, grew up in Turin, where he worked as a publisher at the house of Einaudi. He spent some time in the mid-thirties as a political prisoner. His *Moby Dick* is one of the great translations of a classic. He also translated Defoe, Faulkner (q.v.), Joyce (q.v.) and others, which had a marked influence on his own work. He is regarded as a leader of the Italian post-war neo-realist school—but this tendency never had a program, and the label 'neo-realist' is no more helpful in assessing Pavese's achievement than it is in assessing that of Vittorini (q.v.) or Pratolini (q.v.). (Neo-realism was no more than a reaction to that *ermetismo, see* Ungaretti, Quasimodo, which the fascist cultural program had forced on Italian writers. We see a form of it clearly in Quasimodo's own later professed attitudes.) His suicide in a Turin hotel in 1950 was a traumatic event for many of his contemporaries, who rightly saw it as the tragic capitulation of an exquisitely sensitive and imaginative man—but a capitulation that might actually be justified. One may say that he died because he had become convinced of the human impossibility of living for others. He was politically disillusioned and sexually neurotic—but he had a terrible insight into his sexual problem ('I know nothing of the look of recognition a woman can give to a man') which, as we see from his fiction, poetry, letters (*Selected Letters,* tr. 1969) and diary (*This Business of Living: A Diary, 1934–1950,* tr. 1961), transcends insufficiency or self-pity and becomes a nakedly pessimistic statement on the male sexual condition. His poetry (*A Mania for Solitude,* sel. tr. 1969) is minor but distinguished and is indispensable for the full comprehension of his fiction, for which the term 'realistic', as usually understood, is a misnomer. Pavese's main themes are loneliness and human insufficiency to surmount it. In his poems as in his novels—most have been translated—he displays a remarkable empathy for the lonely secrets of ordinary or oppressed people: the childhood behind the façade of the whore and the failure of her clients' imagination, the frustration of those who cannot act unselfishly but can only newly and uselessly and painfully create old moments, the loveliness of landscape which haunts and mocks our aspirations towards harmonious adulthood. His finest novels—among them *La casa in collina* (1949; tr. *The House on the Hill,* 1956) and the final *La luna e i falò* (1950; tr. *The Moon and the Bonfire,* 1952) 'express precisely and definitively', as a critic has well said, 'the dichotomy of contemplative man cut off from the world of action'; they amount also to, tender though Pavese was, a relentless critique of the world of action. Life is anguishing because it is only, for the contemplative man, memory; and so for the writer memory must become words. The last novel is major, gathering up not only all the threads of Pavese's previous work but also many of those inherent in the history of the European and American novel. Anguilla returns, after twenty years in America, to his birthplace (which resembles Pavese's own), to try to find himself with the help of his old friend (and foil) the calm and accepting Nuto. The often violent life of this village–under fascist, war and post-war conditions–is thus re-created; Anguilla's project is indeed a metaphor for that of the novelist. The novel succeeds on every level–as autobiography, as epic, as history, as inspired commentary–but Anguilla fails. And Pavese's own death is thus one more example of that *Künstlerschuld*, 'artist-guilt', which has so characterized our century. Other novels include: *Paesi tuoi* (1941; tr. *The Harvesters*, 1962); *Il compagno* (1947; tr. *The Comrade*, 1962); short stories in *The Political Prisoner* (tr. 1955).

Paz, Octavio (1914) Mexican poet, critic, essayist, editor. He is widely regarded as the greatest living Spanish-American writer. Ceaselessly experimental, immensely learned and eclectic, he has also been called a 'vogue' poet–and in the sense that he has rapidly moved from one position to another, and that his work attracts the attention of people who do not understand him, so he is. But he has retained his own identity, even if his recent experiments with 'concrete' and other experimental forms of poetry are, disappointingly, more theoretical than imaginative. He is an illuminating critic (e.g. *Corriente Alterna*, 1967; tr. *Alternating Current*, 1973) whose main weakness is to judge poets by their *avant-garde* intentions rather than their results. He has moved from Marxism (he was in Spain in 1937) through surrealism to a kind of 'Hindu Mexicanism' influenced by the structuralism of Lévi-Strauss. He was Mexico's ambassador to Delhi until 1968, when he resigned in protest against his government's unnecessarily brutal suppression of the student riots of that year. Paz has always been preoccupied with two facts: his Mexicanness and his solitude; to some extent he identifies these, but he feels and has always felt that in order to function properly as a social being a human being must first look into his or her own aloneness. Although by temperament a genial and optimistic (and sometimes critically over-generous) activist, his position is a pessimistic one: the oversophisticated West is nothing and has lost almost all traces of ancient wisdom; but Latin America–though nearer the primitive–is dominated by brutality and by a spirit contrary to the one of love which made Breton (q.v.) so appealing to Paz when he met him in Paris just before the Second World War. Of his prolific poetry 'Piedra del sol' (1957), a long poem structurally based on the Aztec calendar, is the best: this is incorporated in *Configurations* (1971), a representative selection of his poetry in English translation. 'Enamoured of silence', Paz has written, 'the poet's only recourse is to speak'. 'Piedra del sol' (584 lines) illustrates his dilemma. It is not, as it has been called, a 'great' poem, but is a fascinating attempt to reconcile solipsism with political 'engagement'.

Péguy, Charles (1873–1914) French poet, critic, journalist, editor. Péguy, possessed of enormous intelligence, is a seminal figure. He is somewhat enigmatic because in him an especially noble sense of justice was accompanied by an extreme excitability which, while it is responsible for his best creative work, he hardly had the opportunity to curb or to examine. He threw himself, characteristically, into the anti-German cause in 1914 and within a few weeks was slaughtered in the Battle of Marne, at the head of his troops. Péguy, of Orléans peasant stock, pulled himself up by his bootstraps; he became the first famous pupil of Bergson (q.v.) and his subsequent development may be seen as a particular, and always sympathetic, response to Bergson's teaching. Bursting with energy, he began as an ardent Dreyfusard, socialist activist, and humanist. Certain nationalists like to appropriate the ethically agonized Péguy to their various convoluted causes, but, as his important works show, he was a cunning peasant as well as an intellectual. The one side of him–founder-editor, with Rolland (q.v.), of the *Cahiers de la quinzaine* (1900), conscientious polemicist for this and that–is of immense historical importance and is to be respected, but this importance has tended to obscure the odd originality of his more imaginative work. The early socialist manifestos are less interesting than the first long poem, *Jeanne d'Arc* (1897); the later pleas for the preservation of *mystique* in the face of *politique* are not as substantial as the later long poems, such as *Le Mystère des Saints-Innocents* (1912; tr. *Holy Innocents and Other Poems,* 1956) and the 'tapisseries'. Péguy, undoubtedly a Catholic, was a strange one: he did not marry in a church, he did not attend mass, he disliked priests, he was deprived of the sacraments, he did not have his children baptized, he was devout–a true anticipator of Simone Weil (q.v.). He was *simple* as well as intellectual but the simplicity of peasants does not lack its paradoxically coarse-grained subtlety–and that quality in Péguy is not a part of his intellectualism. Perhaps Péguy, in those long poems which so many have left off reading too soon, is less 'convinced' (of Catholicism), 'old-fashioned' and 'idealistic' than we (no doubt reasonably enough) have been led to suppose. The peasant-intellectual is rare in this century. Péguy did hold forth Faith, Hope and Charity as the ideal virtues (and why not?); he did develop strongly patriotic notions (the nature of these shows up the unpleasant nationalism of Barrès for precisely what it is); but his true message is less of hope than of *the need for it.* Péguy's last and best poems partake desperately of the unanimism (*see* Romains) of the years immediately before the First World War, but they also attempt an original telluric poetry. His Christ, in 'La Tapisserie de Sainte Geneviève et de Jeanne d'Arc' is a matriarchal heretic, a kind of pastoral unanimist, a spokesman against the city. *Eve* (1913), his best poem, is deliberately repetitive; yet it does not really meander through its nearly two thousand quatrains in rhyming alexandrines: it is truly Bergsonian, subjective, a sort of stream-of-consciousness presented in quasi-classical, rhapsodic, liturgical form. We must not take Péguy to mean (intellectually) what he seems to say: we must take him to be exploring the nature of his own chant, to be insistently and with peasant-like doggedness refining the *song* into a *thought* which will not, however, be divested of song. He did not know what he could find, and went into the 'just war'—as did so many at that time —almost gratefully. The complete works, *Oeuvres complètes,* are in twenty volumes (1917–55). The complete poetry is in *Oeuvres poétiques complètes* (1941). English selections include *Basic Verities* (1943) and *Men and Saints* (1944).

Perse, Saint-John (ps. Aléxis Léger) (1887–1975) French poet. Nobel Prize 1960. He was a diplomat by profession. The Vichy government sacked him and he lived for many years in the USA; he went back to France. He writes not in verse but in a highly rhythmical prose (sometimes interrupted by the introduction of classically metrical lines). Perse is a literary, erudite poet; only in his first volume *Éloges* (1911; tr. 1956), *Eulogies,* does he come anywhere near to the demotic. The whole body of his work, which is deliberately epic, rhetorical, exotic (he maintains that he dislikes the exotic, a paradox explicable by the fact that he was born and brought up on a small West Indian island near Guadeloupe, and cared for by a Hindu nurse who was also a 'priestess'—so the exotic is second nature to him), could be described as a sort of lush, anthropological type of unanimism (*see* Romains). Perse, influenced by Claudel in his procedures, is not a Christian poet but his poetry certainly celebrates a grand faith in Man. Despite its pantheistic mode of expression, this faith cannot be described more appropriately than by the term 'unanimistic', though Perse was unconnected with the movement. But criticism of Perse, who is recondite and lofty, tends to be over-servile and muddled by different kinds of mystical preconceptions. He holds the reader by his sincerity (clearly he feels as he writes, which cannot be said of all poets), his eloquence and his wide range of images—evoking great movements of races, ancient things, ordinary things (e.g. salt) in their whole historic perspective—but one may, heretically, wonder if his significance is as great as has been claimed by his few but fervent admirers (e.g. Ungaretti), who may well have taken from him more, paradoxically, than his actual poetic content is able to give. Yet his rhapsody—the different works are all sections of a single vast epic—certainly demands to be read and absorbed. The *Oeuvres poétiques* (1960) collects all his poetry in two volumes. In English: *Anabase* (1922; tr. *Anabasis*—by Eliot, q.v.—1930 rev. 1949), *Exil* (1942; tr. *Exile,* 1954), *Vents* (1946; tr. *Winds,* 1962) and others.

Pessoa, Fernando (1888–1935) Portuguese poet, critic. Pessoa is one of the dozen or so greatest poets of this century, yet when he was writing his best poetry his reputation was slight and he published only one book in his lifetime—though he did publish in magazines. 'Initially he appears the most complex man that ever lived', a critic has well said. His stepfather was a Portuguese consul in South Africa and he was brought up there; his first works—*English Poems* (1921, written earlier) —are in a deliberately wrenched 'metaphysical' English; they deal with youthful homosexual themes in an avowedly Shakespearian manner (especially 35 *Sonnets,* 1918) and his failure to find his own voice in them drove him into personal despair and great Portuguese poetry. By profession he was a typist, commercial translator and heroic solitary drunkard. Eschewing the company of others, he dissected himself into three carefully constructed personalities, 'heteronyms', and another called Pessoa, and held private colloquies with himself. '. . . I upon the world turn round in thought', he had written in English, 'And nothing viewing do no courage take,/But my more terror, from no seen cause got,/To that felt corporate emptiness forsake,/And draw my sense of mystery's horror from/Seeing no mystery's mystery alone' (convoluted and over-Shakespearian though this is, it must be unique in English-language poetry for its date). Pessoa thus did in poetry what Pirandello (q.v.) did in prose and drama. Much of what he wrote is ironic or parodic and has been misunderstood by his critics; none the less he suffered his mystical over-indulgences in the interests of a unique exploration of incoherence—he trusted to his poetry to present an ultimately unified picture, of which he himself, however, was sceptical. To an extraordinary extent it does so. Pessoa also wrote much theoretical criticism, miscellaneous prose and letters. At first quite prominent as an ultra-modernist, he seems to have more or less withdrawn from public life when his friend Sá-Carneiro, the poet and fiction writer, killed himself in Paris. Towards the end of his life a few (notably the poet José Régio, 1901–69) already realized that he was Portugal's greatest poet since Camões. Pessoa certainly seemed to be mad: he had a penchant for occultism and corresponded with Aleister Crowley; he supported the dictatorship of Paes and the fascist takeover of 1926 on the (approximate) grounds that they heralded the approach of a new, Portuguese world (and 'cosmic') order associated with the national myth of King Sebastian; he prophesied the arrival of a new super-poet; he seriously considered (1916) becoming an astrologer; he invented and tried to patent a *Synthetic Yearly Calendar By Name and Any Other Classification, Consultable In Any Language* (1926). Nor was all this mere fun. But in the light of such wilful eccentricity Pessoa's self-knowledge was strangely profound, the intellectual plan behind his poetry is as remarkably lucid and *un*eccentric as that of any in the twentieth century. There is no adequate study in English. An English selection is by Edwin Honig, *Selected Poems* (1971); Jonathan Griffin's *Selected Poems* (1974) is as useful—but Paz's introduction to the earlier selection is superior to Griffin's (who compares Pessoa to Ginsberg, q.v.). There was a histrionic element in Pessoa ('The origin of my heteronyms is at bottom an aspect of hysteria . . .'); but the poet at least had it well under control. He was subject to irregular fits of quasi-mania, depression and 'mixed states' ('I suffer—on the very limit of madness, I swear it—as if I could do all and was unable to do it by deficiency of will'). His antidote was not only drink but also intellectual rigour; his defeat of his manic-depressive condition, and of his ambisexuality (he apparently eschewed all sexual contact), is the most complete and impressive of the century. Once this has been grasped, Pessoa is altogether more explicable. He was a man in whom the religious sense ('manic') struggled with scepticism ('depression') so violently that he had to stop (1914) and, as Paz writes, 'invent himself'. But this invention was intensely sincere. He is a character (Pirandello was unable to be a poet) in a Pirandello drama. For Pessoa was a dramatist who wrote only one (closet) play, *O Marinheiro, The Sailor* (written 1913); thereafter, when (1914) his 'heteronyms' Caeiro, Reis, Campos and Pessoa emerge, he is, as he remarks, a 'dramatic poet'. It was Alberto Caeiro (1889–1915), of no profession or education, not a pagan but 'paganism itself', who first emerged. Caeiro is a supreme *naïf* poet in the Schillerian sense: in him is all Pessoa's 'power of dramatic depersonalization'. He is the 'master', who simply affirms things-in-themselves and blandly accepts the world as it is ('My mysticism is not wanting to know/In living without introspection.//I don't know what Nature is: I sing it . . .'). He writes free verse. Then Ricardo Reis (1887), a doctor living in Brazil, arrives. A neo-classicist, he writes more metrically, and is also a pagan—though Pessoa says that the paganism in him is intellectual and even 'false'. To counter him the futuristic, Whitmanesque Alvaro de Campos is now invented: he is wild, homosexual, writing in a frenzied free verse. Campos (1890) has been a naval engineer in Glasgow but is now retired and living in Lisbon. Pessoa, the symbolist, survives as poet, although he is 'balled up inside'. Pessoa was in turn a decadent, a proto-fascistic futurist under the influence of Marinetti (q.v.), a symbolist—and, until he stopped trying, a frustrated lover. The heteronyms—and there are other 'sub-heteronyms'—are of course connected with aspects of his personality: subtle bindings-together of his affective strands. Caeiro is inspired. Reis is abstract, cold, hellenic. Campos is impulsive (rather than inspired). Pessoa, himself, who writes in a rhymed, metrical form, is himself, but also a metaphysical poet and disciple of Caeiro's—and author of beautiful love poems. Each heteronym writes a poetry of achievement, but I believe (heretically) that Pessoa himself writes the fullest poetry. Caeiro is, after all, impossibly 'innocent' and the other two inventions are artificial in a sense that 'Pessoa' is not. He often repeats that he does not really feel, but all the time he affirms that he does, and the strongest feeling we get is of his existential disappointment, his loneliness. Much of Pessoa's prose is superb; some of it, quoted by critics as by him, is in fact 'by' heteronyms (such as the famous 'Ultimatum' of Campos in 1917), and must be judged as such. He is often more ironic, I believe, than even Paz gives him credit for, but we do, as Paz says, 'need' all his writings. There is a critical study, *Vida e Obra* (1970) by J. G. Simões. The *Obras Completas* (1945–65) is not complete. There is a one-volume collection of the poetry, *Obra Poética* (1960), collections of letters, and other prose.

Pinter, Harold (1930) Leading English (Cockney Jewish) playwright and (now occasional) actor. He made his name with *The Caretaker* (1959). Pinter's greatest asset is his ear for inconsequential (in fact realistic) dialogue. He constructs his plays around the sinister, menacing or ambiguous under- and overtones of this type of conversation and is clearly at his best when he himself is puzzled by its paradoxically vacuous meaningfulness and sense of threat. His debts to Kafka (q.v.) and Beckett (q.v.) are very great, though from the former he has taken no more than an audience-manipulative trick: he amuses himself (as the movie-maker Hitchcock does) by preposterously stretching his audience's attention: it wants an explanation, but the fact is that so far as Pinter is concerned there isn't one. His tramps and scruffy types are straight out of Beckett. He is not really an absurdist (*see* Ionesco), since he merely uses an unstructured realism which appears absurd. *The Caretaker* and *The Birthday Party* (1960) are excellent because they cut clearly across the complacent assumption that bourgeois life is in any true sense purposeful. *The Homecoming* (1965) is more obviously planned as social comedy and lays more emphasis on individual psychology. He has written poetry; but it is the prosaic of which, at his best, he is a master. His movie-scripts (*The Servant, The Pumpkin Eater, Accident, The Go-Between*) are among the finest of our time and display his more conventional powers (of, for example, characterization). He has written good one-acters (e.g. *The Dumb Waiter*, in *The Birthday Party*, 1960). His television plays (e.g. *Tea Party*, 1967) exploit the different medium with similar skill. Although the most gifted and accomplished British dramatist of his generation, Pinter has yet to show that he has the power to move an audience. There is warmth in his intelligence but his presentation of sexual relationships and moments of catastrophe are cold. This is an admirable counter-attack against commonplace theatre rhetoric; but if he is to be a major playwright Pinter must find a means of conveying emotion.

Pirandello, Luigi (1867–1936) Italian playwright, novelist, short-story writer, poet and theatre-director. Born in Sicily. Hugely gifted, Pirandello is one of the four greatest of modern playwrights (Brecht, q.v., Synge, q.v., O'Neill, q.v.), and the greatest short-story writer of the century. He anticipated, without lapsing into incoherence, every aspect of modernism. A seminal figure, he has been widely misinterpreted as a pessimistic philosopher the aim of whose works is to reveal truth as non-existent. Actually his aim, from beginning to end, was to discover what is authentic and his art, though bitter, is affirmative if only of its own redemptive function. His three early books of poor poems (1889, 1891, 1895) contain the kernel of his work—as is frequently the case. Son of the owner of a sulphur-mine, he studied at the Universities of Palermo, Rome and Bonn. His main subject was philology, but he absorbed much formal philosophy: German idealism, French pragmatism and, in particular, the anti-rationalism of such as his compatriot Gentile as well as that of Nietzsche. Pirandello, encouraged by Verga (q.v.), began as a Sicilian *verist* with *L'esclusa, The Outcast,* which was written in 1893 (but was not published until 1901 and did not reach book form until 1908). He wrote six more novels, of which the best are *Il fu Mattia Pascal* (1904), *The Late Mattia Pascal,* and *Uno, nessuno e centomila* (1925–6), *One, None and a Hundred Thousand.* In 1894 he married the daughter of one of his father's business associates: this was an arranged marriage and he had hardly seen his beautiful wife before their wedding-day. They had two sons and a daughter; after the birth of the third his wife's mental health broke down, and in 1903, on hearing of the flooding of her father-in-law's sulphur-mine and of the subsequent ruin of both families, she became an incurable schizophrenic. Her illness took the form of jealousy, but Pirandello kept her at home until 1919, when her suspicions of his relationship with their daughter became dangerous. She survived him by twenty-three years. Pirandello was a Professor of Italian in Rome (1897–1922); he seriously took up with drama only towards the end of this period: the performance of *Sei personaggi in cerca d'autore, Six Characters in Search of an Author,* in Rome in 1921 brought him international fame, sealed by the award of the Nobel Prize in 1934. In 1924 his *Teatro d'arte di Roma* was formed, with his (sporadic) mistress Marta Abba as its leading lady. Pirandello gained state support for this, but when it shut down in 1928 it had lost a large sum of money. Pirandello's attitude towards fascism was ambiguous; he thought Mussolini vulgar, but none the less took his money for his theatre and joined his party by request immediately after the Matteotti murder. After a period of self-exile (1928–33), partly prompted by fascist hostility to his plays, he returned to Italy in time to denounce privately (and sometimes publicly) all the honours that were showered upon him. He died in his sleep, with his last drama *I giganti della montagna* (1938), *The Mountain Giants,* which is set 'at the border between fable and reality', uncompleted. He was a prolific writer: besides the novels there are nearly fifty plays, nearly two hundred and fifty stories (from which he took the bases for twenty-eight of the plays) and two critical works, the important *L'umorismo* (1908 rev. 1920), *Humour,* and the anti-Crocean *Arte e scienza* (1908), *Art and Science.* There is Pirandello and *Pirandellismo:* the works and the way we talk about them. The two need to be distinguished, for although Pirandello was of a philosophically sceptical cast of mind he was always fascinated by individual character. That is why his short stories—dry, compassionate but never sentimental, masterly in execution, acutely observed—are unequalled by any writer after Chekhov. Thus, our total response to reading him, or to seeing his plays, is always more substantial than our ideas about what we take to be his ideas: one mark of a major writer. The central drama of his life was his wife's madness, and it was while he looked after her that he conceived the most important part of his work—for so many of the plays are based on stories written in that painful and economically insecure period. He had, indeed, to some extent anticipated his own involvement with pathological jealousy in the novel he wrote just before his marriage. Pirandello's main concerns are: the falseness of appearances; the apparent absence of a unifying factor in the personality, which is thus simply a series of moods, beliefs, impressions, a multitudinousness of different 'I's; the paradoxical permanence of fictional creations as distinct from real people, who die and are forgotten; the pretence of the human race that it lives by rational principles when it does not. But what is less often added to this list, especially by critics who think of Pirandello only as a playwright, is his passionate curiosity about real people, his strong regional feeling, the ultimate primacy of his imagination over his pessimistic, 'comic' philosophy (humour, for Pirandello, is wryly tragic awareness of the disparity between man as he is and man as he believes he is). His finest characters, such as Henry IV in the play of that name, *Enrico IV* (1922), have an obstinate life of their own and this play, perhaps his greatest, ends on a realistically tragic note—for all the philosophical problems it raises. Pirandello is both a deeper thinker than Shaw (q.v.) and a playwright whose real theme is, paradoxically, to create not types (like Shaw) but characters who do have a constant quality. That gives hope to humanity: for if art redeems, it redeems humanity because it is a human product. Pirandello's lifelong objection to Croce was, indeed, that he was too philosophical, too abstract. Pirandello is always, residually, a realist who clings to a belief in characterological unity; hence the rare lucidity of his absolute modernism: for he anticipates absurdism, the phenomenological approach, the despair with politics (which he carries too far by 'comically' accepting the buffoon Mussolini's money for cultural purposes), and Brechtian 'alienation'—he smashed the 'Aristotelian' theatre, in *Sei personaggi in cerca d'autore,* and even in *Cosí è (se vi pare)* (1918), *Right You Are (If You Think So)*, before Brecht (q.v.) or Artaud (q.v.). His sin is never in fact to prove that truth is non-existent, but rather that relativity is true (Einstein told him, 'We are kindred souls'): that there are many realities and that we can find ourselves only in the light of this. The discovery is tragic—Henry IV makes himself into a murderer—but only because of human unawareness of human irrationality, of the fact that the false—imprisoning—mask imposed upon us by society is accepted ('the manifestation of pain is my theatre'). But such a project in itself implies hope, or the only answer would be silence—and Pirandello was both loquacious and empathetic. Although it is in the *bozzetto* (little scene, episode, anecdote) that he is supreme, he managed to extend this mastery to the best of his drama, and it was imperative that he turn to this form: only here could he fully convey his message about illusion, since theatre is so obviously and acknowledgedly just that. Apart from those already mentioned, some of his more important plays are *Ciascuno a suo modo* (1924), *Each in His Own Way*, *Questa sera si recita a soggetto* (1930), *Tonight We Improvise*—which with *Sei personaggi* form a trilogy of theatre-within-theatre technique—and *Come tu mi vuoi* (1930), *As You Desire Me.* But he did not write a single bad or uninteresting play. Almost all of his work has appeared in English translation, but little of this is more than competent. His collected works appeared in Italian in six volumes, 1956–60. A useful English introduction is Oscar Büdel, *Pirandello* (1966); Walter Starkie's study is obtuse and should be avoided. Pirandello had his faults, aptly revealed in his attitude towards fascism; but he is an endlessly fascinating writer who transcends all prescriptive criticism.

Plath, Sylvia (1932–63) American poet. She left America in 1956 when she married Ted Hughes (q.v.). She had a history of mental illness and had attempted suicide in 1953 after a burst of mania—she was manic-depressive, not, as is usually suggested, schizophrenic—and, some time after her marriage to Ted Hughes had broken up, she killed herself. The failure of a prescription to arrive was a factor mentioned at the inquest. The (then) Third Programme had on that evening broadcast a play by Hughes. The poetry in her first volume, *The Colossus* (1960), did not attract much attention: it consists of fairly quiet poetry about objects, and contains only hints of the later, violent style to be found in the posthumous *Ariel* (1965), which was written in a last burst of mad energy before her death. These have been overrated but they are very impressive and horrifyingly fascinating as the dramatic products of a condition of mania shot through with depression or a terror of it—a condition in which a heightened agitation, partially erotic, is mixed with personal griefs, which are confused with such international tragedies as Auschwitz and Hiroshima. She is undeniably powerful. Yet she has, as I have remarked, been overrated (the reverent tone of such intelligent though over-generous critics as Richard Howard or M. L. Rosenthal is not, alas, deserved): she was sick, and finally she fails to transcend her sickness (as a major poet must). She owed much to Roethke (q.v.), who was also mad (and a megalomaniac)—too much, really, of this influence remained unabsorbed. She tended, under the self-destructive pressures that assailed her in 1962, to speak too much through his voice—and, to a lesser extent, that of Anne Sexton, whose *To Bedlam and Half Way Back* (1960) and *All My Pretty Ones* (1962) covered the kind of personal territory hardly touched by Sylvia Plath in her own first volume. That her poems are about illness does not matter (much poetry deals with human illness), but they are about a terrible *case,* a single one—and while they shock, appal and impress, as articulations of that case, they scarcely transcend it. This means that she is a 'minor minor', possessed both of word-power and of the terrible integrity of the suicide. But the imagery of death-as-second-birth is not convincing: it is tragic delusion. Compare her to Campana (q.v.), who suffered from a, in certain ways, similar type of illness and one sees that her senses of nightmare suffused with beauty, of beauty suffused with nightmare, are far more confined to herself. Sylvia Plath—brilliant, delicate, skilled though she is—is more of an astonishing spectacle, a woman closed in on herself. *The Bell Jar* (1963 under a ps.; 1966 under her own name) is in some ways her best work: it draws on her experiences before her first suicide attempt in 1953 and penetrates more realistically into her mind, seeking clues; it is not ultimately intent upon giving up.

Plomer, William (1903–73) South African poet, novelist, biographer, editor and man of letters. Soon after founding and editing *Whiplash*

(1926–7) with Roy Campbell (q.v.), Plomer left South Africa in disgust (he returned only once), first for Japan and then for England, where he quickly became an established literary figure. A gentle and courteous man of deep feelings, he was particularly well loved by his many friends, who included E. M. Forster (q.v.) and Stephen Spender (q.v.). His early novel *Turbott Woolfe* (1925), on a theme involving miscegenation, made his views clear: '[South Africa] can never be anything but a black, or at least a coloured man's country.' He retained his South African identity to the end. He edited *Kilvert's Diaries* (1938–40) and wrote four more novels, of which *Museum Pieces* (1952), a subtle Edwardian study of people who insist on living in the past, is probably the most distinguished. There are five volumes of short stories and he was the best comic poet of his generation (in this vein he incidentally shows up the ingratiating genteel tawdriness of Betjeman, q.v.). His humorous poems are all in *Collected Poems* (1973), which demonstrates how underrated his poetry has been. He wrote a biography of *Cecil Rhodes* (1933) and two memorably witty, sensitive autobiographies: *Double Lives* (1943) and *At Home* (1966). He wrote the libretti for a number of Britten's works. His poetry ranges from the broadly comic to the tragic and elegiac (as in the moving elegy for the Afrikaans poet Ingrid Jonker, q.v., and for the writer Nathaniel Nakasa: 'The Taste of the Fruit'); he never courted fashion but was an unobtrusive master of almost every one of the many manners he employed. Plomer is a rewarding writer: his beauty of character, sense of fun, passion for justice, delicacy of feeling and hard-earned tolerance of heart all irradiate his many-sided writings.

Pontoppidan, Henrik (1857–1943) Danish fiction writer. Nobel Prize 1917 (shared with his abject, Teutonized fellow-countryman Karl Gjellerup, 1857–1919, the dullest writer of the century, and the least read). Pontoppidan is the greatest Danish writer of fiction and it is a matter for regret that so little of his work has been translated. He is a 'massive' writer, immensely prolific but not pretentious. He fulfilled his intentions: 'to give a coherent picture of modern Denmark (i.e. 1880–1918)'. The years through which he lived were difficult ones, and Pontoppidan's attitude towards his own countrymen is critical. He was much influenced by George Brandes (1842–1927), an agitator and later Nietzschean who acted as the Danish mouthpiece of, first, positivism, and later, 'aristocratic radicalism'; but Pontoppidan soon transcended

Brandes, who, although very influential in Scandinavia, was essentially a superficial thinker. Pontoppidan, whose father was a Lutheran parson, first studied engineering; then in the eighties he married a farm girl and tried to practise a Tolstoian form of idealistic withdrawal; but the marriage came to an end (he remarried in 1892) and with it the experiment. This is reflected in the first of his three great novel cycles, the trilogy *Det Forjaettede Land* (1891–5; first two volumes only tr. *Emanuel,* 1896, and *The Promised Land,* 1896). This, a story selection, *Mimoser* (1886; tr. *The Apothecary's Daughters,* 1890), and the odd separate story, is all that has appeared in English. *Lykke-Per* (1898–1904), *Lucky Peter,* and *De Dødes Rige* (1912–16), *Kingdom of the Dead,* are his major works, although *Mands Himmerig* (1927), *Man's Heaven,* is one of the most memorably accurate hostile analyses of a people by one of its own writers that has ever appeared. The stories of the eighties are more or less naturalistic (*see* Zola), but one can scarcely classify the later cycles of novels; one powerful influence on them, however, was that of Nietzsche, whom Pontoppidan understood better than Brandes. Particularly noticeable in this connection is Pontoppidan's reaction against the Rousseauism which he had once embraced. *Lykke-Per,* in which Brandes appears as Dr Nathan, is the story of Per Sidenius, who begins as a materialist but ends up as a quite certainly Nietzschean would-be 'self-overcomer'. (The hero of the previous trilogy had ended up insane.) *De Dødes Rige* is more sociological: the liberal attacks false liberalism. All these works, executed on a vast scale, are psychologically and sociologically convincing; the deep bitterness Pontoppidan felt about the gap between idealistic illusion and reality, between religion and rationalism, comes across with a great and noble force. A profound fear of death lies at the heart of his work, which is nevertheless a response to it much more subtle and powerful than the critical attention Pontoppidan has had outside Scandinavia would suggest. His late memoirs, *Undervejs til mig selv* (1933–40), *On the Road to Myself,* are more serene, but are revealing.

Popa, Vasko (1922) Yugoslav (Serbian) poet, acknowledged as the finest of his generation. His symbolic poetry, which draws exclusively on Yugoslav legend and folk tradition, is deeply influenced by that of Momčilo Nastasijevič (1894–1938). He combines the literary with the colloquial to create poems that are 'autonomous' in a specifically modernist ('cubist') manner, and yet which are soaked in nationalist tradition. Rather too high claims have been made for him, but the integrity of his vision is unquestionable. *Selected Poems* (1969); *The Little Box* (1970)–a selection–and *Uspravna zemlja* (1972; tr. *Earth Erect*, 1973), which contains invaluable notes on the folk and legendary sources.

Porter, Katherine Anne (1890) American fiction writer, essayist. Born in Texas, she early decided to make herself as independent as possible of her Southern Catholic heritage–which to some extent meant living out of a suitcase. She spent some time in Mexico and Europe and was twice married. The consensus of critical opinion, that her early stories are excellent and that her work shows a decline from *The Leaning Tower* (1944) to the bestselling *Ship of Fools* (1962), is correct. She is fundamentally a short-story writer drawing, with stern and courageous objectivity, on autobiographical material. She wrote because she had to appraise herself–she would not, she has said, have 'chosen' to be a creative writer. Her quest for emancipation from her background, as she imaginatively described it, amounts to a significant record of the frustrated efforts of a self attempting to achieve authenticity through rejection of its environment. Her concern is, naturally, the nature of the Southern environment (she is rightly called a 'Southern writer'). Her sense of Southern maleness she can use as a key to all maleness. Her treatment is generally stream-of-consciousness (*see* Bergson), mixed in with highly compressed narrative; the tone and attitude of the 'voice' telling the story has always been very carefully considered. At her finest she uses 'Miranda', a complex objective correlative for herself, to describe this basic process. But her scope is wider than this suggests, for her observations of men are masterly and deep. *Pale Horse, Pale Rider* (1939) contains three stories, two dealing with Miranda herself and one 'narrated' by her ('Noon Wine', Katherine Anne Porter's masterpiece) and also obliquely dealing with her. Before this she had published *Flowering Judas* (1930 augmented 1935) and the ten stories collected here should be read in conjunction with those of *Pale Horse, Pale Rider*. The two volumes together represent a major achievement in small compass, and 'Noon Wine' works as beautifully at all levels as any novella of its age. With *The Leaning Tower* (stories) Katherine Anne Porter's powers of imaginative synthesis began to leave her and she tended towards the too deliberately allegorical or parabolic. *Ship of Fools* is really a set of failed stories stitched together by an allegorical device; it shows too much evidence of the author's merely journalistic skills, and lacks true concentration. *Collected Short Stories* (1965); *Collected Essays* (1970).

Pound, Ezra (1885–1972) American poet, critic. As a historical influence Pound is, with Eliot (q.v.), the most important figure in English-speaking poetry of this century. But his own achievement does not measure up to this, a fact which is quite rapidly becoming apparent —though there still exists a school of thought (e.g. Davie, q.v.) which argues to the contrary. He was born in Idaho. He left it early in life, but the populist background continued to influence him—disastrously so when, of partially unsound mind, he aggressively applied it to European politics, which he never understood. At the University of Pennsylvania he met Williams (q.v.) and HD (q.v.); in 1908 he left America for London (via Italy), whereupon, bursting with vitality and a zest for the new, he became the leader there of modernist poetry. His own early poetry is more pre-Raphaelite and Browningesque than would seem likely to the student of his ideas and programs, but then his poetic development was perhaps more distorted, from the beginning, by his oddly severe limitations. His first significant act in London was to 'take over' (and genuinely transform) imagism from Hulme (q.v.), Ford (q.v.) and others, but he also to a certain, not altogether determined, extent synthesized this into an active Anglo-American program. The movement was not as revolutionary as it was corrective. Historically it lasted from 1912 to 1917, and its platforms were Harriet Monroe's *Poetry Chicago* and the anthologies of imagist poetry in 1914 (*Des Imagistes*), 1915, 1916 and 1917. Williams and Lawrence (q.v.) contributed but were not members. Pound himself abandoned this 'ism' in 1914 for vorticism, which was a very short-lived English cubism (*see* Reverdy) involving all the arts, and influenced by Marinetti (q.v.) and Lewis (q.v.). Imagism opposed twentieth-century Victorianism, which led it to attack the great Victorian poets themselves (what was really being attacked was the persistence of their influence). Its models were short Japanese poems, Greek and Latin purity of diction, and some elements of French Parnassian elegance. The metrical system was attacked: poetry was to be written in the rhythms appropriate to the impulses behind it; concentration on the *image* was recommended. The poem should be stripped, unornamented. 'In the Metro' is typical of the effect Pound was at this time after: 'The apparition of these faces in the crowd;/ Petals on a wet, black bough.' Here fact is parallelled by an imaginative image: there is a 'leap' from the prosaic Paris scene to (possibly) the mythological underworld of Persephone (or anything else that 'fits in'). As a movement imagism could clearly produce only minor poetry and the more important poets connected with it soon went beyond its requirements. However, in its implications it was extremely important. Technically it pointed to greater freedom: the term 'free verse' was really a misnomer, since the maintenance of discipline imposed by rhythm over a whole poem is harder to achieve (whether counterpointed against a metrical pattern or not) than that imposed by a mere metre (almost everyone can write 'blank verse'). The concentration on the image pointed towards expressionism (*see* Stadler) in its widest sense. This was, then, the Anglo-American beginnings of a new poetry which would make it possible to abandon Victorian-bourgeois in favour of intuitive (cf. Bergson, q.v.) coherence. It was then flourishing in Germany (e.g. Rilke, q.v., Trakl, q.v., and others), but Pound seems not to have been aware of this. Apart from his generous help, throughout his life, to many poets in search of or deserving recognition, or trying to discover a style (e.g. Frost, q.v., Marianne Moore, q.v., Yeats, q.v., and above all Eliot, q.v.), this was Pound's greatest contribution to literature. It remains to describe the rest of his career and to consider the status of his poetry. *The Cantos* were first planned (*c.* 1913) to be a series of poems to educate America and were thus directly in the familiar populist-pragmatist (*see* Dewey, James) American tradition. But Pound kept changing his conception of the series, and eventually came to regard it as an incoherent failure. The history of his conception of it (it is unfinished) is in some sense his own history. In the First World War Pound remained in England, fighting Philistinism on all fronts and behaving in a highly eccentric–perhaps at this time slightly hypomanic–manner. Already the borderline between good, sound, insightful thinking and incoherent antics is a trifle blurred. But Pound's sense of outrage at the horrors of the war led him into his best poetic period. Although he never could begin to understand the causes of war (but this may be disputed), the poetry of *Homage to Sextus Propertius* (1917), a series of free adaptations from the Latin poet, and *Hugh Selwyn Mauberley* (1920), represents the keenest articulation of his struggle against despair. He thoroughly purged himself of 'art-for-art's sake' attitudes, and clearly stated his predicament: that of a poet in a period of cultural rot. He wanted to find from culture a few 'fragments' to 'shore against [his] ruin'. It is a minor poetry of major importance; minor in achievement because linguistically it fails to live up to the expressionist ideal (cf. Rilke, Pessoa, q.v., or Vallejo, q.v., whose poetry does), but major in influence because it gave countless poets a sharp sense of the kind of world in which they were living. Then Pound, after an active period in Paris, went to Italy in 1924 in order, in effect, to construct a defence of culture against contemporary wickedness. But this latter he did not comprehend. He seems to have been partially mad from then until his death. For all his dynamic intelligence, his narrowly populist assumptions helped lead him into the belief that evil stemmed from various conspiracies, mainly of Jews and bankers. He became obsessively and insistently (though not personally) anti-Semitic—there were always Jews behind the conspiracies. Mussolini became his God: characteristically, he seized on the idealistic element in early Italian fascism and ignored both its dangerous results and the cynicism and power-seeking elements also inherent in it from the start. All this was a decidedly sick development out of his earlier interests in Syndicalism and Guild Socialism. It cannot be written off, in a man of Pound's intelligence, as simply a tragic mistake: he was claiming, after all, to have found a solution. It is significant that in the period just preceding his commitment to Mussolini his wife (he had married in 1913; in 1924–5 he entered into a lifelong friendship with Olga Rudge, who bore him a daughter; both women remained, on and off, a part of his establishment) was in a state of mental unbalance, and that he was propounding the interestingly Reich (q.v.)—like theory that the brain is really a 'great clot of genital fluid' and that man is the 'phallus . . . charging . . . the female chaos'. But Pound continued to be friendly to individual Jews (e.g. Untermeyer, Zukofsky, q.v.), to help others with money when he could, and to talk and write sense. *The Cantos* (1925; 1928; 1930; 1934; 1940; 1948; 1955; 1959; 1969; *The Cantos 1–84*, 1948) are basically Pound's attempt to gather together what is good and endures, and to make this into a coherent whole. Some critics project into them ambitions and subtle schemes (e.g. Hugh Kenner, *The Poetry of Ezra Pound*, 1951; D. Davie, q.v., *Ezra Pound*, 1964) which enable them to treat the sequence as coherent. But, in terms of achievement, as Pound himself came to admit, it is too flawed to be anything but a ragbag. It reaches its high point, perhaps, in the 'Pisan' section (74–84): these were written while Pound was held in captivity at Pisa for his pro-fascist speeches to American troops from Rome during the war. He was flown to America, charged with treason, declared insane, spent more than twelve years in St Elizabeth's Hospital in Washington and was finally released, to return to Italy, in 1958. But even to these and other such high points the same criticism must apply as applies to *Hugh Selwyn Mauberley:* there is a mental restlessness that has prevented the poet from concentrating on experience, a complete lack of reflective quality, a fragmentariness. There are lines and passages of great beauty but these are never sustained—or if they are then they have an inexorable slightness. One other aspect of Pound's activities must be mentioned: his translations. These are not accurate from a scholarly point of view, but are not supposed to be. His knowledge of languages was wide but not deep. He needed cribs to understand Chinese. His efforts in translation are usually (the *Propertius* sequence is an exception: he needed an appropriate guide to write his own poem) intended to build up in himself and his reader a sense of the originals: to (again) clarify what will endure. He often got the details wrong, but equally often he created a new imagery, a new music, a new thinking: a new possibility. He translated from the Chinese, the Provençal, the Anglo-Saxon, the Greek and other languages (*The Translations*, 1963). The dust has not yet settled in Pound's wake. There is enormous potential in his criticism and in his poetry; he is a major figure; the view that restlessness ruins or at best reduces his own achievement is undoubtedly contentious and involves the assumption that his madness got more into his writings than his admirers wish to admit. He will continue to gain attention. J. Edwards's *Annotated Index to the Cantos* (1957) is essential to the examination of the sequence's claim to a grand coherence. *Personae* (1926) collects all the important shorter poetry, and remains in print. *Letters 1907–41* (1950); *Literary Essays* (1954); *Letters to James Joyce* [q.v.] (1967). *The Life* (1970) by Noel Stock is an excellent critical biography, and the fullest to date; by an ex-disciple, it takes rather the same view of *The Cantos* as I do, and it has therefore upset many Pound admirers.

Powell, Anthony (1905) English novelist, biographer. Powell has written two sets of novels: the separate ones of the thirties, and the celebrated twelve-volume *roman fleuve* called 'The Music of Time' (at the time of writing, the final instalment has yet to appear): *A Question of Upbringing, A Buyer's Market, The Acceptance World, At Lady Molly's, Casanova's Chinese Restaurant, The Kindly Ones, The Valley* *of Bones, The Soldier's Art, The Military Philosophers, Books Do Furnish a Room, Temporary Kings* (1951–73). He also wrote a biography of John Aubrey (1948), and has worked as a critic on the *Times Literary Supplement* and the *Daily Telegraph.* His earlier set of novels, which include *Afternoon Men* (1931), *Venusberg* (1932) and *From a View to a Death* (1933), owed a certain amount to Firbank (q.v.)—than whom he is, however, much more robust—and their satirical portrait of bohemian high life contrasts strongly with that of Evelyn Waugh (q.v.): it lacks Waugh's blackness but to the farce adds an unobtrusively serious dimension of social criticism. These are perhaps the funniest novels of their decade, yet the background is very carefully and intelligently examined. The *roman fleuve,* candidly Proustian (q.v.) in conception, is a major work. Its action, which is seen through the eyes of the novelist Nicholas Jenkins, covers Powell's own life-span and experience: Eton, Oxford, London life, army service, the post-war life of public relations men, civil servants and artists. Jenkins (as the autobiography Powell plans to write will doubtless make clear) is not simply Powell, but a very highly variable series of self-critical images of Powell-as-artist and, to some extent, as man. The sequence possesses all the humour of the earlier books, but has become more sombre as it has progressed (as life becomes or seems to become, to the artistic observer, more puzzling and more serious). There is much tragedy, and this is given an extra impact because it is seen through the ironic filter of the detached artist (who, as Powell knows, is in one way not detached at all). The greatest tragedy—a bewildered ruefulness—is concentrated into the subtle and complex sense of the actual passage of time as the author conveys it. He does so by an intricate (and essentially innovatory) method of presenting his characters as in a constantly shifting web which is itself inexorably moving forwards in time, to the consternation (implied with beautiful reticence) of Jenkins and of some of those he has known. Despite its classic moments of humour—and these function as the author's perfectly correct assumption that a proper humour is a saving grace, a blessing, in the tragic fabric of human existence—'A Dance to the Music of Time' is a deeply serious work. Only Powell, in English writing, has made major use of the technique of selection from pure realism (cf. Pinter, who is more trivial), which is 'absurd' (hence his apparently grotesque characters), to achieve an expressionist (*see* Stadler) presentation. It is an extraordinarily adroit achievement and its strength lies in Powell's insistence on what seems, so far, to be an

Anglo-Saxon necessity: immediate coherence of surface. Jenkins, the narrator, is an ambiguously reticent figure: wryly, and with an insistence on good manners, he is a man seeking for 'the good' in which all modern writers must be concerned. Haunting his and others' lives is the clever but morally obtuse go-getter Widmerpool. Widmerpool is one of the great comic creations of modern literature; but he is more than that. He represents the bureaucratic rot that eats into decency like a corrosive acid, the concealed philistine, the Iago to society's confused Othello—presented by Powell through his characteristic filter of sad and resigned irony. The restraint of Powell's vision should not be mistaken for absence of feeling; he is subdued but never unmoved or unmoving; time will show the skill and modernity of his procedures.

Powers, J. F. (1917) American fiction writer. Powers, who comes from Illinois and whose fiction is mostly set in the midwest, is best known for his cleverly written, half-loving, half-satirical, stories about Roman Catholic priests: men in *The Presence of Grace* (1956) trapped in quotidian provincial affairs and fund-raising activities. He can be sentimental and trite, but is usually excellent within his deliberately limited subject-matter. His first collection was *The Prince of Darkness* (1947). His best work, however, is in the serio-comic novel *Morte D'Urban* (1962), which deals with similar material but in greater depth and with a more sustained sense of paradox.

Powys, John Cowper (1872–1963) English (of Welsh descent) novelist, critic, versifier, miscellaneous writer, polemicist. He was educated at Cambridge, but spent most of his life until the thirties in America; in 1934 he settled permanently in Wales. He published his first novel (*Wood and Stone*, 1915) at the age of forty-three; two followed, but *Wolf Solent* (1929 rev. 1961), his first substantial fiction, did not appear until he was nearing sixty. This was followed by *A Glastonbury Romance* (1933 rev. 1955), *Weymouth Sands* (1934 rev. in England as *Jobber Skald*, 1935), six more novels, and then *The Brazen Head* (1956). His last novel was *All or Nothing* (1960). There is a cult of J. C. Powys, as there is of his brother T. F. Powys (q.v.); his idiosyncratic work can invite nothing else. While one can admire his integrity, one has (if outside the cult) to deprecate the obstinate prolixity of his massive fictions, which lack, even at best, the ingredient of consistent readability. The key to all his work, much of which is philosophical or critical (e.g. *Rabelais,* 1948), is that while he refused to take up any kind of sceptical position, he failed to realize the coherent philosophy of life which he sought. He mixed realism with pretentiousness without ever really succeeding in examining the latter, an element in himself which he fully recognized (as his *Autobiography,* 1934, his best book, makes clear: the American edition *The Art of Happiness,* 1935, differs interestingly in text). His huge semi-mystical novels, which often use myth as framework (*A Glastonbury Romance,* for example, is based on the Grail legend) are decked out with rhetoric; only the short, realistic passages are at all outstanding. He was always trying to come to terms with a sadistic element in his nature, but this effort is lost in grandiosity. As is often stated, he is essentially an autobiographical writer; unfortunately his autobiographical enterprise failed to purge him of his self-confessed charlatanism. He is consequently an interesting but minor author. A contrary view is expressed in Wilson Knight's *The Saturnian Quest* (1964) and in subsequent studies.

Powys, Llewelyn (1884–1939) English writer. Brother of J. C. (q.v.) and T. F. Powys (q.v.); he died, after a long struggle, of tuberculosis. His first book was in conjunction with his brother J. C.: *Confessions of Two Brothers* (1916). Whereas John Cowper histrionically exploited his sexuality and suffering in all his books, Llewelyn took the opposite approach; he is slight, but superior. *Love and Death* (1939), an odd 'imaginary autobiography', has not had its due; and his travel writings, when not marred by purple passages, are sometimes evocative: *A Pagan's Pilgrimage* (1931), on Palestine, and *Black Laughter* (1924; 1953), sketches about Africa, are outstanding. His fiction is poor. But the autobiographical *The Verdict of Bridlegoose* (1926; printed together with *Skin for Skin,* 1925, also autobiographical, 1948) is the distillation of his small genius.

Powys, T. F. (1875–1953) English fiction writer, brother of J. C. (q.v.), and Llewelyn (q.v.), and also of the writers Littleton Powys, Albert Reginald Powys (an architect), Philippa Powys and Marian Powys. The father was a Church of England Evangelist whose superficial but fierce certainties deeply affected his children (J. C. was a confused idealist-mystic, Llewelyn an atheist, T. F. a heretical Christian). He settled (he was married) in Dorset in 1901 and died—a recluse—in the remote hamlet of Mappowder in 1953. His best writing was done between 1921 and 1933, though he began before he was thirty. Doubtless he would have preferred to be a farmer but his attempts at farming in his twenties proved disastrous—his bitterness on this score is reflected in his work. His grotesque, allegorical prose, usually in the shorter forms, has been widely influential: on, for example, Sylvia Townsend Warner (q.v.) and Dylan Thomas (q.v.). He found his fictional voice through his discovery that he could localize a thoroughly paganized Christianity in rural Dorset, of which his vision is wholly unrealistic. Powys was at his best as a miniaturist and he has an imaginative power his brothers lack, but the 'philosophy' informing his most celebrated works is always spurious. He is at his best as a savage, bizarre pessimist. There are certain (limited) affinities between his treatment of peasant life, as he sees it, and that of a very different writer, Giono (q.v.): both see the peasants' 'ignorance' as embodying final paradoxical truths. But Powys regards death as a Christless God's most precious gift; he is best when describing the horrors of life. Thus, in the novel *Mr Weston's Good Wine* (1927), wrongly regarded as his supreme achievement (but it has superb passages), his offer of 'hope' is specious and his Bunyanesque allegory is ultimately disingenuous. Weston, God, is a wine-salesman, a tradesman rather boastful of his creation, who sells the Light Wine of Love and the Dark Wine of Death. The payments for them are respectively Love and Life. The allegory does not quite work: it is too contrived and, despite the beautifully realized passages dealing with actual encounters, it suddenly strikes the critical reader as wooden, invented—a failure of imagination. Powys's stories (many are in *The White Paternoster*, 1930, *Bottle's Path*, 1946, *God's Eyes a-Twinkle*, 1947, *Rosie Plum*, 1968), on the other hand, contain his truer, uninvented vision. God is there but he is ineluctably, impenetrably malignant: he seems actually to challenge the pattern of moral values that the piggish corruption of the characters throws up. This reflects the atheist vitalism which Powys, in his earlier religious struggles, would have liked to embrace. Here is a Dorsetshire Jouhandeau (q.v.) or Bernanos (q.v.) without hope, forced (because of his failure to achieve atheism) to dread some kind of punishing afterlife. Powys is basically a Manichean (there are hints of this in the character of Mr Weston); perhaps his pseudo-quotidian detail, peculiarly hideous, is an anticipated or dreamed terror of a state in which evil coexists with good—the evil the black details of mortality and cruelty and ignorance, the good only the author's pitiful (in his own eyes) attempt to impose an intellectual structure on the material which his uncontrollable imagination casts up.

Pratolini, Vasco (1913) Italian novelist, playwright. His early experiences of poverty in his native Florence are apparent in his fiction. He began as a progressive fascist but was a socialist before the age of thirty and has remained on the left. He is a gifted and energetic realist, 'committed', but not in any dogmatic way. Many of his novels are available in English. He is vivid, warm and penetrating in his depiction of the family life of the poor. Among his best novels are *Il quartiere* (1945; tr. *A Tale of Santa Croce*) and the successful *Metello* (1955), which is set in the Florence of the nineties. For some his best novel is *Cronache di poveri amanti* (1947; tr. *A Tale of Poor Lovers*), a moving story of the Resistance.

Priestley, J. B. (1894) English (Yorkshire) novelist, critic, playwright, essayist, journalist, broadcaster and miscellaneous writer. Priestley is a mixed writer whose popularity has (generally) prevented critics from both an appreciation of his entire, rather benign achievement, and from his good writing (which exists, but which needs to be separated from his middlebrow exercises: these are seriously intentioned, but sentimental). The first point to make about him, and one not insignificant in these days, is that he is always a professional: nothing he has written is incompetent. As a novelist he has not proved adequate to deal with the complex problems of his century because he obstinately refuses to abandon rigidly traditional forms; as a playwright he has been, on occasions, fruitfully experimental—a fact that is scarcely recognized. He is a useful critic, who has written well on many authors (particularly *Meredith*, 1926); *Literature and Western Man* (1960) is the best pre-modernist assessment of its subject, and is historically indispensable as a guide to what 'ordinary readers' want. Little need be said about his huge success *The Good Companions* (1929): a sprawling picaresque romance, it fails as a whole, but contains some vital and vigorous writing. One regrets that, as an old-fashioned, tolerant political radical, he refused to consider new fictional techniques. But he was good at the old ones. *Black-Out in Gretley* (1942) is a superb thriller. He has written much other fiction: the best is evocative of old-time, simple vigour; the worst is characterized by a refusal to understand that personal relationships are not simple (an assumption not implicit in his drama). His best plays (*Dangerous Corner*, 1932; *Time and the Conways*, 1937; *I Have Been Here Before*, 1937) are influenced not only by the time-theories of J. W. Dunne but also by Ouspensky—and perhaps by Jung (q.v.). They are 'well made' but ingenious and entirely unsentimental. An excellent later play is *An Inspector Calls* (1945). *Works* (1931–7). *Plays* (1948–50; 1950–52). *The World of J. B. Priestley* (1968).

Pritchett, V. S. (1900) English fiction writer, critic, reviewer, travel writer, autobiographer. Pritchett's many stories and novels have lower-middle-class settings and are in the tradition of Dickens and Wells (q.v.), but he has his own individual note, which comes out in his careful, subtle prose style. He captures the grimly comic, often grotesque, reality of lives hemmed in by narrowness—very often of a puritan kind. He has written on Spain (e.g. *The Spanish Temper*, 1954), and his two autobiographies, *A Cab at the Door* (1968) and *Midnight Oil* (1971) are rightly regarded as little classics of evocation of the atmosphere of past days. He is a most reliable and fair critic and reviewer, exceedingly accomplished in describing the quality of the work under consideration. *George Meredith and English Comedy* (1970) is an excellent example of his capacity to deal with difficult cases. His greatest achievement, however, is in the novel *Mr Beluncle* (1951), a masterly and compassionate study of a fantasizing puritan bigot and unconscious opportunist; this far surpasses Cary (q.v), who tried to portray somewhat similar types of eccentric, in psychological depth and human sympathy. *The Living Novel* (1946) and *Books in General* (1953) are two of his critical books. *Collected Stories* (1956); *When My Girl Comes Home* (1961) contains more stories. Pritchett never achieved the acclaim of Bates (q.v.), another thirties story-writer, but his work is wider in scope and his prose more complex.

Proust, Marcel (1871–1922) French novelist, critic. Proust is *the* dedicated writer of the century. He sacrificed his life to 'become' his book; yet, paradoxically, the main theme of this book is the problem (the agony) of the difference, the distance, between Marcel, its narrator, and Marcel Proust, its writer. For Proust experience early became a matter of material for his project. Before he started writing his actual masterpiece, he had been assiduously practising for it. It is the least compromised piece of writing in literature: it was conceived, on a psychological level, as an escape from a too acute sensitivity; it is therefore ironic that it should be so robust, so indelicate (as well as impressionistically elegant), so ultimately and fully human. It is the best answer to itself and the best commentary on itself—and, like humanity, it is unfinished. It has 'faults' but it is uncriticizable. It *is*. It is a unique case in literature and to treat it as anything else is to fall into error: useless to compare it with anything, more useless to measure it against anything, ridiculous to subject it to any kind of 'critical method'. Absurd, as against reading and re-reading it (or ignoring it), to try to comment upon it—which is what I shall now do. We all must do so because, whatever its 'status', it, as I have remarked, *is*. As *are* the devil and deep blue sea, between which we always precariously exist. Admiration. Hatred. Disgust. Ambivalence. Indifference. Any or all of these emotions or attitudes may be aroused by Proust's *A la Recherche du temps perdu* (1912–27; tr. *Remembrance of Things Past*, 1922–31); and it is all the more difficult for us because Proust, though inevitably enigmatic, is not God: we have a text (the best French edition is the *Pléiade* of 1954: nothing after *Sodome et Gomorrhe*, 1921–2, was fully revised, and the bibliographical problems presented by the work are formidable). Proust's imperfections have all the dreadfulness of humanity's—and the splendour. He was the son of a distinguished Roman Catholic physician and a Jewish mother. His mother (she died in 1905) was, as all critics agree, the one great love of his life. His homosexual and sadistic impulses—balanced by qualities of exquisite generosity and sometimes almost insane concern for others—arose from his failure to abandon her (even after her death). Unlike his friend Gide (q.v.), he could neither find justification for nor even temporary pleasure from his homosexual inclinations. And his strange sadism (it mostly concerned the deaths of animals—the notorious example is his orgasmic response to the deliberate torture and killing of rats by hatpins) was perhaps in large part a revenge upon the environment for robbing him of his mother—of her total attention at the early stage, of her absolute understanding at a later, of her very presence, in 1905. His work is Oedipally permeated; yet much of its universality is earned by his heroic and successful attempts to transcend this. The situation is a good deal less unique than Proust. His heterosexual impulses (for he was an ambisexual) were expressed in the lyricism of the earlier books. As a young child he developed asthma and although in his earlier days he was able to attend the Sorbonne, to put in a year of military service, and to become a socialite, he deliberately succumbed to the illness after his parents' death (his father had died two years before his mother) and became a virtual recluse. One senses, however, even in this comparatively active period, a preparation for the great work. The long failure *Jean Santeuil* (1952; tr. 1955) is certainly a rehearsal for *A la Recherche:* written a decade before his mother's death, it is undoubtedly a youthful anticipation of the devastating impact this would have upon him. As he wrote it he haunted the *salons,* minutely studying the habits exhibited therein. He read and translated Ruskin. Previously he had attended Bergson's (q.v.) lectures and had made friends with him. Assiduously, it seems, he was putting together the elements of a style: he was evolving a method which he would be able to manage rather than making a conscious effort to be innovatory. He worked cleverly within his own limitations and those of his age. Bergson's influence (whatever critics may assert) was crucial and is reflected upon almost every one of his pages. That he, like Bergson, was sensitive to a new development in thinking is neither here nor there: Bergson's formulations of it helped him. An expressionist in the wide sense (what is 'Marcel' but an attempt to exhibit and define the whole internal nostalgic life of Marcel Proust?), he used impressionistic methods: in his prose he 'paints' a little, trying to catch the fleeting essences of the Bergsonian (q.v.) 'moments'—but he does not try to paint actual pictures: he is no frustrated painter. *A la Recherche du temps perdu* begins as the child Marcel, the imaginary autobiographer, cannot, sent early to bed, sleep without his mother's goodnight kiss. It is thus universal. But although Marcel always tries to return to his pre-pubertal childhood, his story embraces hierarchies of Parisian society, the vicious jealousies of lovers and others, the magnificent homosexual Baron de Charlus, the amorous experiences of Swann. . . . All or nearly all of these characters, in differing degrees, are self-admired or wishful aspects of Proust (certainly, for example, the writer Bergotte, the musician Vinteuil); but such considerations, for once, do not (at least at first) serve to recommend the book. If this man desired always to be a 'ten-year-old', as so many critics protest, then the writer certainly grew up. Proust's life, as extremely 'good' as it is extremely 'bad', is a dedicated one: he ignores our mundaneness; chooses, even from his famous cork-lined room (eventually he was forced to abandon this), to explore the extremes of his personality. Proust wanted to write a work of art that would approximate as nearly as possible to truth; it is not, indeed, going too far to state that he intended his work to be 'truer' than 'life'. He gives us incomparable comedy; he conveys the anguish of sexual attachment; he writes better than any twentieth-century novelist of the nature of memory. He may be attacked for his *longueurs*—but not every reader agrees—and he may be attacked for mocking homosexuality as fictional homosexuality and acknowledging its anguishes only as fictional heterosexuality. But against this may be argued that he none the less demonstrates the 'pathological' nature of all romantic love: that perhaps what were original defense juxtapositions (e.g. Albertine as woman) become, to a more or less effective degree, explanations of the phenomenon of love itself. . . . He has also been attacked by an academic for the 'inordinate space' he allows for 'the theme of male and female homosexuality', for his 'excessively bleak view of human personality', and for being—even if 'richly endowed'—'sick'. Presumably this gentleman is happy with what he sees about him, especially such as reflects his unsick self. . . . Ultimately we can say no more than that, for all intelligent writers and readers, Proust exists as inexorably as the sun. That Scott Moncrieff's translation is 'better' than the original is a myth. But it is a superb adaptation (though the literary titles of the sections should be dropped), and it is hard to see how it could be bettered. The last section, *Le Temps retrouvé* (1927), was disastrously badly rendered by Stephen Hudson (ps. Sydney Schiff, 1866–1944, whose own fiction, especially *A True Story,* 1930—rev. *The Other Side,* 1937—is unduly neglected) as *Time Regained* (1931); much better are the translations of Frederick A. Blossom (1932) and A. Mayor (1970). Incomparably the best short introduction to Proust in the English language is by Gabriel Josipovici in *French Literature and its Background 6* (1970); the George Painter biography (1959–65) is indispensable for facts, but must be supplemented by Maurois's (q.v.) *A la Recherche de Marcel Proust* (1949; tr. *Quest for Proust,* 1950). L. P. Quint's study (1946) is also perceptive.

Purdy, James (1923) American (Ohio) novelist and short-story writer who began with great promise and power but whose work has since declined into vulgar, silly pseudo-Gothic (*Eustace Chisholm and the Works,* 1967) and latterly, into inexplicable bathos (*Jeremy's Vision,* 1970). He has never been much liked by American critics, but *Eustace*

Chisholm, which ambitiously over-indulged his previously delicate penchant for homosexual Gothic, made a scandal and secured his reputation. Only his first four books need be considered here: in the fifth, the novel *Cabot Wright Begins* (1964), he lost control. Of the important books two (*Colour of Darkness,* 1957; *Children Is All,* 1962) collect stories, and two (*Malcolm,* 1959; *The Nephew,* 1960) are novels. The finest story, included in his first collection, is '63 Dream Palace', which appeared separately in 1956. *Malcolm* is about a lonely lost boy led about a small town by an astrologer. *The Nephew,* by far Purdy's best book, fully expounds his feminine insight: it is the tragic and sympathetic account of a woman's discovery of her dead nephew's real personality. In these earlier books Purdy reproduced Ohio speech with superb accuracy, and portrayed petty urban life with hideous detail but without malice. Tenderness and sensibility were in superb control. With the collapse of this control he has become an inchoate, brash, fashionable, fragmentary writer.

Q

Quasimodo, Salvatore (1901–68) Italian (Sicilian) poet, translator, critic; winner of the 1959 Nobel Prize. The son of a railway worker, he first studied engineering, came to Florence in 1929 and finally settled in Milan where from 1941 he was Professor of Italian Literature at the Giuseppe Verdi Conservatory. Few poets can have been looked at more wrong-headedly than Quasimodo—but the Italian literary climate is fiercely polemical and Quasimodo was himself especially ambitious as well as in certain respects arrogant, snobbish, opportunistic, disingenuous and humourless. He was also led into excessive and unjustified rancour against contemporaries who were as honest as he—as when, commenting on his 'many enemies', he replied: 'the others are poets of convenience'. None the less, these faults do not detract from his poetic greatness and dedication and the doctrine that his poetry is quite certainly inferior to that of Ungaretti (q.v.) and Montale (q.v.) is contentious. He has been referred to (and by one of his English translators!) as 'leader of the Hermetic school of poetry', and as a 'communist'. Both these statements are misleading—the second simply mistakes sympathy with the left, which in Italy is not confined to leftists, with communism. Quasimodo was always anti-fascist, and was arrested by the fascists. He (endorsed, though cautiously, by Montale among others) published his first two books in 1930 and 1932 when the label *ermetismo* (1936) had not been invented. Quasimodo's first collection, *Acque e terre, Waters and Earths,* contained poems written when he was a very young man, but these were subsequently rewritten some years later when he built up contacts with the group associated with the magazine *Solaria* in Florence through Elio Vittorini (q.v.), who had married his sister. So that it seems likely that while Quasimodo's early *ermetismo* (the term is not susceptible of any more precise definition than I have given it in discussing Ungaretti) is more 'native' than that of Ungaretti or Montale, the early poems were none the less written well within the instructive ambience of the poetry of the two older men. Quasimodo's earlier poetry is collected in *Ed è subito sera* (1942), *And Suddenly it's Night;* at this time he championed hermetic poetry. Then, with *Giorno dopo giorno* (1947), *Day after Day,* he appeared to many readers to have 'betrayed' hermeticism—or, of course, to have 'developed' a social conscience. His own polemic contributed somewhat to this situation (he enjoyed fame more obviously than any of his Italian contemporaries), since he repeatedly insisted that poetry, 'not a game', had an ethical and social function, and he announced that his personal task was to 'remake man'. Most of Quasimodo's final poetry, that written after *Il falso e vero verde* (1956), *The False and the True Green,* is inferior—this applies also to the *Xenia* of Montale and, to a lesser extent, to the last volumes of Ungaretti. But there were at all times two Quasimodos: he was not merely uneven (as are all poets), but he wrote at two levels—one markedly inferior, the other astonishingly original and moving. It is thus true to say of Quasimodo's inferior poems that they are over-literary and lack the 'inevitability' of Ungaretti; but it is not true of, say, 'Acquamorta', 'Dead Water'. Right from the beginning Quasimodo, haunted by words-as-objects, morally aware of his poetic responsibility, searched for some faith to pit against his own nostalgia and egotism. To put it at its simplest, throughout Quasimodo's poetry, from 1930 until his death, there is a constant element: a tension between a religiously sought-for oneness in the universe and individual disparateness. Thus his landscapes *are* (as charged by an English critic) 'statuesque', arranged: his native Sicily, its pagan past, its beauty and grandeur at first represents a permanence, however desperate; this is no more artificial than the landscapes of Ungaretti or Montale. Later the utterly contrasting, industrial world of Milan (a centre of the resistance) played an important part in his poetry. There is hardly a 'first' and a 'second' Quasimodo: his poetry developed, became more open and sometimes more accessible and it is true that his famous translations of Greek lyrics, *Lirici greci* (1940)—done as much from cribs as from the originals—did help him to forge a new and less solipsist language; but he remains, in his finest poems such as 'Il falso e vero verde', 'hermetic' in manner but none the less convincing. Addressed to the 'thou' who in Quasimodo's later poetry seems to denote at least himself, a beloved of the past, and some young hopeful, it subtly and movingly discriminates—alluding to both Dante and Lorca—between 'the false and the true green/of April, the unbridled sneer/of certain blossomings'. Quasimodo's poetic faith is summed up in 'Discorso sulla poesia' (1956), 'Discourse on Poetry': this is impressive and eloquent, but not as good as his best poetry, in which may be discerned his struggle from the very beginning. 'Oboe sommerso', 'Sunken Oboe', first appeared in 1932: 'Miser pain defer your gift/in this my hour/of craved abandonment.//An Oboe, chill, restates/happiness of evergreen,/not mine, and scuttles memory;//in me it is dusk:/the water dries/on my grass hands.//Wings against wan sky move/fitfully: the heart transforms/and I am barren soil//the days a rubble.' It is clear here that he can only desire what he later came to feel more deeply. To understand Quasimodo it is more useful to be aware of his ambivalent attitude towards Christianity, of his studies of St Augustine and Spinoza, of his devotion to Tasso—than of the confused history of *ermetismo*. He translated Aiken (q.v.), Cummings (q.v.), Arghezi (q.v.), Homer, Virgil and Shakespeare. *Tutte le poesie*, 1960.

Queneau, Raymond (1903) French novelist, critic, poet. His primary inspirations were surrealism (*see* Breton), Céline (q.v.), Roussel (q.v.), Freud (q.v.), and Jarry (q.v.). He is, with Ionesco (q.v.), the leading 'pataphysician' (*see* Jarry) of modern times. If some of his work is overrated by sterile critics—which it is—then this is because he suffers from the Gallic complaint of dullness resulting from over-concentration on philosophical/theoretical rather than imaginative enterprises. But, as is the case with Ponge, his intellect is formidable: he is a professional encyclopedist (editor of the *Pléiade* Encyclopedia), has an excellent grasp of philosophy, and understands modern mathematics. He is yet one more of those modern Frenchmen whose emphasis on the word-referent problem has tended to vitiate his achievement; but he has abundant energy. His philosophical preoccupations have continually threatened his chief desire: to bring the colloquial back into an over-academized French. Yet his intrinsic humour has on many occasions broken through, to give substance to his books. As a poet he can have charm, but is mostly playing games (especially in *Cent milles milliards de poèmes*, 1961, a 'do-it-yourself sonnet-kit' which has little to recommend it beyond its ingenuity—its attack on the sonnet form is not more valid than that of W. C. Williams, q.v., though Queneau is too sophisticated and humorous to call this 'fascistic', as Williams did). His best work is in certain of his novels, especially those in which his *joie de vivre* and Chaplinesque irreverence are not too much undermined by his erudition. The first, *Le Chiendant* (1933; tr. *The Bark Tree,* 1968), is the best—except for *Le Dimanche de la vie* (1952), *The Sunday of Life,* in which he exploits his genius for hoaxes to an extent so comic that it becomes serious. *Chêne et chien* (1937), *Oak and Dog,* is a fascinating attempt to survive the experience of (French) psychoanalysis. *Zazie dans le métro* (1959; tr. *Zazie,* 1960), is the most meretricious of his novels—and probably the best known outside France.

R

Ramos, Graciliano (1892–1953) Brazilian fiction writer. The best, with Machado de Assis (q.v.) and Guimarães Rosa (q.v.), of the past hundred years in Brazil. He is a superb stylist, mainly realistic in approach—almost a neo-naturalist (*see* Zola), for naturalism flourished in Brazil. His masterpiece is *Angústia* (1936; tr. *Anguish*, 1946), a study of sexual obsession, insanity and murder which uses a phenomenological technique. This, because the protagonist is originally from the backlands, needs to be read in the light of da Cunha's classic work (*see* Guimarães Rosa). *São Bernardo* (1934; tr. *Saint Bernard*, 1940). *Vidas sêcas* (1938; tr. *Barren Lives*, 1965). Ramos was imprisoned by the dictator Vargas in the thirties.

Raine, Kathleen (1908) English poet and critic (mainly of Blake and of the neo-Platonic or alleged neo-Platonic stream in English poetry). She was first married to Hugh Sykes Davies, a Cambridge don who had written a surrealistic work, and then to Charles Madge. Both marriages were dissolved. Although she had some leftist political sympathies in the early thirties, Kathleen Raine soon abandoned these in order to concentrate on her true poetic métier: the visionary nature lyric. Her best poems, assured in diction and technique, are lucid, pure, intense observations of biological phenomena, evocations of the innocently absorbed landscape of the rural Northumberland of her childhood. Later she became a Platonist: she 'discovered', she wrote, 'the roots of the language of poetic symbol within the Perennial Philosophy'. She then took to writing what may be described as a 'transient' (her word) 'soul-poetry': a poetry that searches continuously for the spiritual rapture of Platonic reality, a subject upon which she is extremely dogmatic. She has been much influenced by her study of the Platonic elements in Blake (*William Blake and Traditional Mythology*, 1969, is a contentious but important work), and she expresses her philosophy of poetry in the essays of *Defending Ancient Springs* (1967). For some Kathleen Raine's later poetry may represent a too easy escape from the bonds of the flesh: it does lack the tension between mind and body that is found, in different ways, in Graves and her admired Yeats (q.v.). But there is a visionary quality, a purity of diction, which gives the seal of authenticity to her mystical experience. *Collected Poems* (1956); *The Hollow Hill* (1964).

Ramuz, Charles-Ferdinand (1878–1947) Swiss novelist, miscellaneous writer, who wrote in French. His early fiction is conventional, intelligent and readable. His chief novels, however, were written between the mid-twenties and the mid-thirties. Set in his native Vaud and written in an intensely regionalistic spirit, they transcend their category by virtue of their unobtrusive, inspired artistry; their rugged simplicity of style, eschewing 'literary' graces in favour of the local Vaudois, is by no means unsophisticated. Characteristic is *Derborence* (1935; tr. *When the Mountain Fell*, 1949), which creates a universal myth around the tale of a young man who survives an avalanche. Here Ramuz avoids pretentiousness because his story is absolutely convincing. His collected works appeared 1940–54. He published a journal and other reminiscences and collaborated with his friend Stravinsky on *Histoire du soldat* (1918; tr. *The Soldier's Tale*, 1955). *La Beauté sur la terre* (1927; tr. *Beauty on Earth*, 1938) and *Adam et Ève* (1932) are his two other most important novels. He is one of the most original of European novelists; his style is unique.

Rand, Ayn (1905) American 'philosopher' and novelist who left her native Russia at the age of eighteen. Unfortunately her crypto-totalitarian and ultra-simplistic ideas have had some influence on the conservatively bred young, since they allow people to be ruthless without a bad conscience. Her 'philosophy' is capitalistic-Superman (as in the comic): the 'great' men are those who use others, in the name of 'reason', with an enlightened ruthlessness. Her best known novel is *The Fountainhead* (1943), a projection (as she admitted) of her own aspirations in the form of a travesty of the character of Frank Lloyd Wright. As critics observed at the time, it–like her other books–is offensively ill written ('pedestrian, pockmarked with short, clipped staccato sentences').

Ransom, John Crowe (1884–1974) American poet, critic, teacher. He was born in Tennessee; as a teacher at Vanderbilt University from 1914 to 1937 he was extremely influential in American letters. He was not, as is frequently stated, the real pioneer of the new criticism (*see* Brooks)—though his own criticism and teaching had influenced it—because his book of that name (1941) was fundamentally critical of those who came, through it, to be called new critics. . . . Most accounts of Ransom take him at face value; this is an error. The main key to the understanding of him is that he was a reluctant poet: he disliked and resisted the 'opening up', or abreactive, effect that sudden and powerful poetic impulses have. But Ransom, whose main career as a poet spanned only four years (1921–5), informed his internal struggles with a rare ironic intelligence; his best poems are very good because they reflect these struggles. They are mostly in *Chills and Fever* (1924). *Poems About God* (1919) is prentice work; *Selected Poems* (1945 rev. 1963) adds some more good ones written after *Chills and Fever;* the sonnet-sequence that gives *Two Gentlemen in Bonds* (1927) its title shows his powers on the decline and was dropped by him until curtailed and revised in the disastrous *Selected Poems* of 1970, in which he resumed, with a vengeance, his lifelong process of spoiling his poems by over-cerebral revision. Ransom inherited the full confusions and paradoxes of the South; this inheritance involves strong nostalgia for an old order which had its retrospective virtues—but which was more than unsatisfactory from a contemporary point of view. The conflicts and stresses of being intelligent and Southern produced a crop of remarkable writers; Ransom and his pupils tried to rationalize them in the symposium *I'll Take My Stand* (1930), after he had (virtually) turned from poetry. This defence of agrarianism was based on fantasy, not fact, and demonstrates not the conservatism but the naivety of academics and intellectuals when they try to tackle social problems. But other factors helped drive Ransom to poetry. He had early become interested in escaping from Victorian monotony; he wanted every line in a poem 'to work'. Then he went to the war (he served as an artillery officer), which clearly stimulated him into a more urgent poetic activity. He had also, earlier, come under the influence of a learned eccentric called Sidney Mttron-Hirsh, whose knowledge of out-of-the-way and mystic love must be accounted as one of the bases of Ransom's often recondite and obscure themes. It was Mttron-Hirsh who first thought of founding the poetry magazine *The Fugitive* (1922–5), one of the most famous little periodicals of this century. The Fugitive group comprised, among others, Donald Davidson, Tate (q.v.), Penn Warren (q.v.); Brooks (q.v.), Andrew Lytle and Laura Riding (q.v.) were associated. But most of the best poetry in the magazine was by Ransom. All that needs to be said of the group is that out of it grew the *I'll Take My Stand* symposium—and that the position taken by the contributors to it has mostly been abandoned (Davidson is an exception). Now, as we have seen, Ransom certainly was modernist; but he was so in a mannered, deliberately crabbed, erudite, 'classical' and allusive manner. His best poems circle knowingly around their themes; only a few (e.g. 'Janet Waking', 'Captain Carpenter') are direct. He has marvellous lines; his ironic, metaphysical poetry is confident that its language is doing something that the language of science cannot do. Bergson (q.v.) is an obvious influence—and like Bergson Ransom is a true realist, an anti-abstractionist, an anti-Platonist. There are strong personal themes in the poetry, but these are ironically wrapped up in allusion. Ransom is anti-rational inasmuch as he believes that man has become hopelessly split. To get at his self-criticism on this score means digging very deeply indeed into his poetry: he is a cunning concealer of his own experience. His later criticism (*God Without Thunder*, 1930; *The World's Body*, 1938) is essentially an elaboration of his own poetic method; it is useful but over-academic: in other words, it is a fence around his personality. Briefly, the burden of his criticism is that a poem is an account of a precious object; it is even superior to the object because it cannot be tainted by material use (cf. Platonism!). Ransom's actual critical methods were very influential: a poem has a *structure* (argument, grammar, form: the logically describable) and a contrasting *texture* (the more or less destructive qualities of sound, subject itself, tone, imagery). The poem is a text: a thing-in-itself. This is an excellent formulation: to look at a poet's structure-texture strategy is to find out a good deal about him. Ransom acted as a stimulus to many poets and critics, both in his capacity as Professor at Kenyon (1937–58, subsequently Emeritus) and as editor of the eclectic *Kenyon Review* (he printed criticism by Burke, q.v., Blackmur, Empson, q.v., and many others). From the viewpoint of the more or less Whitmanesque wing of American letters (led by Williams, q.v., and subsequently others) he represents a dead-end tradition; but he is still a highly relevant figure. The selection *Grace After Meat* (1924) was published in England and introduced by

Graves (q.v.), upon whose own verse his has been perhaps the chief modern influence.

Rattigan, Terence (1911) English dramatist, scriptwriter. Rattigan began with highly successful, well-made farces of no consequence (e.g. *French Without Tears*, 1936). Later he went on to write semi-serious but seldom ingratiating plays, excellent and intelligent entertainment, for his middlebrow audience, whom he ironically described as 'Aunt Edna'. He has been honest, and is content with his deliberate conventionality. He is not usually pretentious, though the Lawrence-of-Arabia play *Ross* (1960) showed him in deep water through trying to be experimental. He has, and can convey, feeling. Among his best plays, which give good value for money, are *Flare Path* (1942), *The Winslow Boy* (1946), on the Archer-Shee case, *Separate Tables* (1954). *Collected Plays* (1953–64). His film scripts are more frankly commercial.

Read, Herbert (1893–1968) English (Yorkshire) critic, poet, writer on art, anarchist, polemicist, publisher, essayist, editor (*Burlington Magazine*, 1933–9), teacher. Read was an eclectic, tolerant romantic, whose literary criticism is always stimulating and open-ended (*Collected Essays in Literary Criticism*, 1938; *Selected Writings*, 1963). He used the concepts of depth-psychology extensively, though he never evolved a consistent theory (he scoffed at the notion of consistency). As art-critic and educator he was in favour of abstract and *avant-garde* forms and was a great champion of Henry Moore's work. He wrote one of the best contemporary essays on rhythm and metre in poetry (it is in *Collected Essays*), another outstanding one on Swift's poetry, and a perceptive book on *Wordsworth* (1930). The *Selected Writings* provide an excellent introduction. His war poetry (he fought in the First World War) is original and unlike that of any of his contemporaries: it is 'flickering and intermittent' as poetry (C. H. Sisson), but dignified and lucid. His best poem is the long, retrospective *The End of a War* (1932); this lacks attack, but makes up for it in quietly meditative sensitivity and deliberate lack of sensationalism. In general, however, his poetry is uncertain of its direction, veering between extreme experimentalism and an almost Bridges (q.v.)–like post-Georgianism. Read's best work was in creative prose: *In Retreat* (1925), again on the war, the astonishingly poetic and imaginative romance *The Green Child* (1935)–his most perfect work, the autobiographical

The Innocent Eye (1933) and *Annals of Innocence and Experience* (1940). The best of his criticism is indispensable because of its eclecticism and insight into the creative process; his fiction captures the true quality of the visionary. His most seminal essay is 'The Nature of Art' (in *Collected Essays*). *Collected Poems* (1966).

Reeves, James (ps. John Reeves) (1909) English poet, children's writer, anthologist, critic. As a children's poet Reeves, though not on the level of de la Mare (q.v.), is certainly his natural successor: *Collected Children's Poems* (1973). As a poet (*Collected Poems 1929–1974*, 1974) he has been neglected, and only partly owing to his lack of colour–for in one of his styles, that of exasperated rebellion ('Greenhallows'), his attack thoroughly compensates for this. He has three other modes: the ironic-pastoral, often exquisite; the (more rare) lyric impassioned by guilt; and the weak, wholly metrical, neo-Georgian. At his best he is an original and incisive poet whose main theme may fairly be said to be infuriated criticism of his own sentimental and over-impressionable nature (which floods out into his inferior verse and more feeble criticism). Fear is another theme, and here he resembles Supervielle (q.v.), as a shrewd French critic has noted. His children's tales are poetic in feeling. As a critic he tends either to over-irascibility or, more often, to a slack romanticism (*Homage to Trumbull Stickney*, 1968); but there are golden exceptions, such as his introduction to *Selected Poems of Emily Dickinson* (1958, the best selection in existence, but which is most regrettably robbed of textual value by his orthographic interference). His devotion to literature is always a sustaining factor.

Reich, Wilhelm (1897–1957) Austrian (born in Galicia) doctor, psychoanalyst, writer, crank. He has been highly influential, since his death, on certain American writers (e.g. Mailer, q.v., Paul Goodman, Bellow, q.v., Kerouac, q.v., Burroughs, q.v., Ginsberg, q.v.), though not all of these know much about him. He was at first one of Freud's favoured pupils but in 1927 the latter refused to analyse him, a decisive event in his life. He published *The Function of the Orgasm* in the same year (but this is not the same book that we now buy in paperback: Reich's bibliography is complicated). He became a communist, tried to reconcile Marxism and Freudianism, and finally broke with both. From about his thirtieth year he began to show signs of mental instability. His most important contribution to psychoanalytical thinking is his concept of 'character-armour': man's defence against his spontaneity and true nature. He could be successful as a therapist in breaking this down. None of even the final versions of Reich's many writings are without incidental insights (*Selected Writings,* 1960, is a useful introductory volume), but he became obsessed with an idea and insanely attempted to demonstrate its truth 'scientifically'. His message is that full genital release in both men and women is the key to freedom; that totalitarianism and authoritarianism are caused by frustrated genitality. This may be wrong but is not stupid, and clearly it is a theory pertinent to modern literature (cf. Lawrence, q.v.) and to American literature in particular. Reich's description of the 'ideal' sex act, written in the twenties, is remarkable–and all the more so because of the seemingly impossible task. But Reich's attitudes were extrapolated not only from Freud but also from Bergson (q.v.), whom he misunderstood as a conventional 'vitalist', from his own unconscious puritanism and from his own serious sexual neuroses (he passed fairly rapidly from partner to partner); further, he was himself highly authoritarian. He went to Scandinavia and gathered a number of cranks around him; here he began to 'demonstrate' that sexual energy existed in a bio-electrical form–and that it could be tapped. . . . All this because he could delude himself that the ordinary electric potential possessed by bodies was 'orgone energy', which 'glowed with a bluish light' and so on. Undoubtedly he believed that full mutual genital release *was* love. He went to America, set up an institute, and began to go seriously insane. He developed persecutory symptoms (Eisenhower, however, was defending him), and when he tried to market his 'orgone accumulator' the federal authorities moved against him. He died in prison from a heart condition of long standing. He is a strange mixture of madness and sane insight and an important historical figure. For fuller accounts see C. Rycroft, *Reich* (1971); Paul A. Robinson, *The Sexual Radicals* (1969); M. Seymour-Smith, *Sex and Society* (1975): the first is critical but fair; the second fairly favourable; the third tries to put him in his context.

Remarque, Erich Maria (ps. Erich Maria Remark) (1898–1970) German novelist. His war novel *Im Westen nichts Neues* (1928; tr. *All Quiet on the Western Front,* 1929) is regarded as the best of the war books, but although not bad, compared to those by Ludwig Renn,

Jünger (q.v.), and others, it is no more than competent and crude. A Catholic pacifist, he left Germany (1932) and later became an American (1947). Author of other effective best-sellers.

Remizov, Alexei (1877–1957) Russian novelist, prose writer. Remizov, who left Russia on the day of Blok's (q.v.) death in 1921, lived in Berlin until 1953 (he died in Paris) but did not take the familiar *émigré* anti-Soviet line. His neologistic *skaz* style (*skaz* means narrative incorporating all the peculiarities of the narrator, who is usually a peasant, or lower-than-middle-class: Remizov's speciality was seventeenth-century *skaz*) was highly influential, though he could and did write fairly straightforward realistic prose such as *Olya* (1927; pt. tr. *On a Field Azure,* 1946). His real master was the nineteenth-century writer Nikolai Leskov (1831–95), though he considerably refined and intellectualized Leskov's *skaz.* He was also influenced by Gogol and Dostoievski. His most characteristic writing mixes dream, Russian religion, legend and folk-lore, and present reality. Though he adopts the mask of one who regards the world as peopled by demons, Remizov's humour and fantasy often cut across this attitude in later work. *Prud* (1907), *The Pond,* and *Neugomonny buben* (1909), *The Irrepressible Tambourine,* early works, are notable for their nightmarish accounts of an urbanized Russia. With the exception of *Olya,* only the early and more negative stories have been translated: *Chasy* (1908; tr. *The Clock,* 1924) and *Pyataya yazva* (1912; tr. *The Fifth Pestilence,* 1927). There are more French translations. Remizov began as a symbolist and ended as a sick, purblind, poor, and terrified old man; his books, almost seventy-five of them, became increasingly substantial as his terror grew —games with language which turned into defences against insanity so rich and dedicated as to transcend themselves. *Podstrizhennymi glazami* (1951), *With Trimmed Eyes,* memorably explains all this.

Reverdy, Pierre (1889–1960) French poet, critic. Doubtless the term 'cubist', when used of poetry, is as much of a nuisance as a guide, but if anyone's poetry can be called 'cubist' in a coherent literary sense then it is Reverdy's (though it has been given many other labels, such as 'mystical' and 'surrealist', which it is not). He and/or Huidobro (q.v.) postulated a 'creationist' poetry (*see* Huidobro), cubist in at least the sense that the poem is regarded as object-in-itself. Reverdy had associations with Apollinaire (q.v.) and his circle, but was remarkably independent; in 1926 he went to the Abbey of Solesmes (famous for its choir), where he led a life of meditation but failed (it seems) to find true faith. Reverdy's poetry is essentially phenomenological, a quest for reality. Just as modern physics demonstrates a secret, 'irrational', 'surrealist' sub-atomic world–hidden from positivists by the 'false' skin of atoms–so Reverdy's poetry searches for a reality that lies below the data of given experience. He is cubist in this sense: he 'in-sees' (cf. Rilke, q.v.) each of his situations, which he freezes, from a number of positions–and he combines all these viewpoints into a single poem. He may thus appear to be mystical but he is not. Does not an object indeed so exist? Does not, therefore, an emotion, a feeling? Yet he is not anti-Bergsonian (q.v.): his poems are not cinematic 'frames': they have the sense of moments being carried forward: the process of assimilation of the past, of transformation of the future, is in its (admittedly recondite) manner also recorded. There is one more indispensable aid to the reading of his poetry: his 'subjects' are frequently very 'ordinary'. Though he eschewed the movements he influenced, the surrealist Breton (q.v.) regarded him as of supreme importance. And so he is; for the best of the poetry, far from being merely based on a theory, evokes a response. This is the record of a melancholy man's reactions to his experience. Reverdy tried to capture the exact relationship between the dream–stripped ruthlessly of its unauthentic manifest content, its keen latency revealed–and the wholly engaged consciousness. This was, in his phrase, *poésie brute* (raw poetry). The voice is anonymous. The search fails. But the reality of the search is felt by the sensitive and careful reader. The work before 1920 is mostly experimental (e.g. the proto-surrealist 'novel' *Le Voleur de Talan*, 1917); but the poetry collected in *Plupart du Temps* (1945 rev. 1967) and *Main d'Oeuvre* (1949)–almost all he wrote–is certain of its method. *Poems* (1968) is an English selection. The critical essays and notes are in *Le Gant de crin* (1926), *The Horsehair Glove*, and in two other collections.

Rexroth, Kenneth (1905) American poet, translator, critic, memoirist, playwright, painter. Since 1927 he has been at the unofficial centre of most of the movements that have sprung up in or about San Francisco, where he lives; he was born in Indiana. He has been a pioneer of jazz and of poetry readings to jazz. A vital and exuberant figure of great integrity and generosity, he is for the most part a thoroughly bad poet:

inchoate, prosy, sprawling, self-indulgent, over-prolific, often maudlin, without control. He is literally spawned by Williams (q.v.) but what is passable poetry in this warm-hearted mass of directionless vitalism was learned from the objectivists (*see* Williams) rather than from the surrealists (*see* Breton), who merely made a bad case worse. However, he has an acute intelligence, which finds its expression mainly in translation (e.g. *One Hundred Poems from the Chinese,* 1956; *One Hundred French Poems,* 1970)—the sense of the original curbs his tendency to go in all directions at once—in some of his literary criticism (e.g. *Assays,* 1962) and above all in the mostly excellent *An Autobiographical Novel* (1966), about his youth. *Collected Shorter Poems* (1967); *Collected Longer Poems* (1969); *A Kenneth Rexroth Reader* (1970). He is agreeable and has been a useful catalyst; but he is also sentimental and far too frequently uncritical to an intolerable degree.

Reymont, Wladyslaw (1867–1925) Polish fiction writer. Nobel Prize 1924. The son of a village organist, he spent some years of poverty wandering from job to job (novice monk, railway clerk—this is reflected in *Marzciel, The Dreamer,* 1910—actor, starver-in-garret, tailor) before becoming a journalist. Reymont was self-educated; but voracious reading had been his only solace in a bleak childhood, and he was steeped in Polish lore even before he left home. The poet Słowacki (1809–49) and Henryk Sienkiewicz (1846–1916) were important influences. Journalism taught him how to report crowd scenes, and his childhood (his father was strict, his mother pious) taught him that life was harsh. But he was not a naturalist, and in fact he wrote his masterpiece because he found Zola (q.v.)—in Polish—unrealistic. . . . His first novels drew on his acting experiences, telling of a travelling actress and her fantasies and sexual adventures; then came a savage and powerful portrait of the city of Lodz, *Ziemia obiecana* (1899; tr. *The Promised Land,* 1927). This was a direct reaction to the positivist, pro-industrial movement in Polish literature. The epic *Chłopi* (1902–9; tr. *The Peasants,* 1924–5) is his finest novel, and is rivalled only by Verga (q.v.) in its portrayal of peasants. It is distinguished by the brilliance of its depiction of a whole community (cf. unanimism, *see* Romains), its psychological accuracy, its honesty, its blending of realism with myth—the four seasons act as the framework for the action, which is mainly concerned with a father-son conflict—and by its subtle creation of a peasant idiom which is a kind of concatenation of specific dialects. Reymont's later fiction is less important, though the historical *Rok 1794* (1914–18), *The Year 1794*, is a solid enough account of the Kościuszko rebellion. Reymont became a spiritualist and a medium and his novel *Wampire* (1911), *The Vampire,* is an oddly bad treatment of the subject. Reymont deserves rediscovery outside Poland; the English version of *Chłopi* should be put back into print without delay.

Reznikoff, Charles (1894) American poet who combines the imagist (*see* Pound) principles of the objectivists (*see* Williams) with a strong Jewish streak. As an imagist pure and simple he is one of the best. As an urban-Jewish-American poet he has remained faithful to his 'objectivist' treatment, distancing himself painfully from the *objects* of his sympathy (mostly Jewish people of immediate or nearly immediate European origin). The poet is very much of a painter, though not a frustrated one. As he says, he doesn't aim to state meaning but to suggest it by clear image and rhythm. He should be better known, for there is much that is excellent in his deliberately modest poetry. *By the Waters of Manhattan* (1962) selects from ten previous volumes of poetry; there are *Nine Plays* (1927); the meditative and poetically less successful *Testimony: The United States 1885–1890* (1965)—not to be confused with the prose *Testimony* of 1934—and *Family Chronicle* (1963; 1969), a really remarkable collection of three prose pieces about Jewish life in New York in the thirties.

Rhys, Jean (1894) Welsh-Creole fiction writer who grew up in the West Indies; she writes in English. Lately she has come to public prominence through adaptations of some of her stories on British TV. Her earlier stories and novels reflect her experiences of rootlessness and isolation between the wars, when she lived alternately in Paris and London. The collection in *The Left Bank* (1927) was introduced by Ford (q.v.), whom she knew intimately; *After Leaving Mr Mackenzie* (1931), a novel, is partly about him. She published five books between 1927 and 1939; the last was *Good Morning, Midnight* (1939). She then sank from public sight for many years. The first books are exquisitely rendered studies of loneliness and despair against the background of the great anonymous cities in which the 'life of art' is no compensation. Her woman characters are resigned, sad, helpless—and totally convincing. After her long period of silence Jean Rhys published her novel about the mad wife of Mr Rochester (of *Jane Eyre*): *Wide Sargasso Sea* (1966). This is a new departure and returns to the West Indies of the author's childhood, but the heroine is once again an alienated soul. *Tigers are Better-Looking* (1968) contains more stories.

Rice, Elmer (ps. Elmer Reizenstein) (1892–1967) American playwright, novelist. He is a worthy but crude expressionist (*The Adding Machine*, 1923) who maintained his radicalism through difficult decades (see *Minority Report*, 1963, autobiography). He plays effectively, but his drama declined through the years: it was mechanical, and while upholding individual values, failed to create individual characters. Rice tended to see everything in political terms. *Street Scene* (1929) is his best and most realistic play.

Richardson, Henry Handel (ps. Ethel Florence Robertson, *née* Richardson) (1870–1946) Australian novelist, translator. Born Melbourne, lived in England from 1903. Studied music in Europe, read Schopenhauer and Nietzsche, translated J. P. Jacobsen's *Niels Lyhne* (an inspiration to Rilke, q.v., and countless others). Richardson and Patrick White (q.v.) are Australia's two most important novelists. Influences on Richardson are complex and diverse, but helpful in understanding of her fiction: the mysterious solace to be found in music, observation (as a child) of the disintegration of her father's mind and of his death, Jacobsen's gloomy, nerve-shot ideal of 'flawless work' and (at a profounder level) his refusal of religion on the remarkable grounds that nothing could ever erase sin, Flaubert, Freud, Russian and Scandinavian literature in general. Herself successful, Richardson's persistent theme is failure. Although her name is well known she has not had her critical due in Great Britain or America and is not widely enough read. Though she spent little time in Australia after leaving school (she was there, researching, for a time in 1912), she is both a quintessentially Australian and a major novelist. *Maurice Guest* (1908), set in Leipzig, is not altogether successful, since its components —of Flaubertian realism, naturalism and *fin de siècle* decadence—are somewhat obtrusive, but the withdrawal of moral judgment, the understanding of the erotic quality of Maurice's self-destructiveness and of his lover Louise's sexual confusion and the study of the homosexual Krafft are all notable in their subtle insight. These qualities were to be fully developed in her masterpiece—now unduly neglected—*The Fortunes of Richard Mahoney* (1917–29). Clearly the book has elements of naturalism; but Mahoney, the main character, is no paradigm for all well-intentioned or gifted men and his rise and fall are related to his Australian experiences and to the pattern of his aspirations with great subtlety and insight. Richardson used her father's life as material, but Mahoney is not even an attempt to portray him exactly as he was. With its tragic vision of a doomed imaginative soul, its many sharply etched vignettes of Australian characters, its sociological grasp, its resistance to piffling literary categorization, this complex novel is a worthy predecessor to the later ones of Patrick White, and is certainly the first large-scale Australian classic.

Richler, Mordecai (1931) Canadian novelist, editor, resident in London for many years. Much read by Canadians, Richler also irritates some of them by his long self-imposed exile but he remains essentially Canadian-Jewish. His best books are *A Choice of Enemies* (1957) and *The Apprenticeship of Duddy Kravitz* (1957), set in London and Montreal respectively. He is directionless—but these novels seriously, although technically maladroitly, explore his difficulties and are laced with rich colloquialese and acute observation of Canadians. His latter work (e.g. *Cocksure*, 1968) shows a grave falling-off into near-dead, fashionably rebellious neo-picaresque conventionalese.

Riding, Laura (1901) American poet, critic, thinker, editor, fiction writer. She early married and divorced the history professor Louis Gottschalk (her first poems were published as by Laura Riding Gottschalk); the Fugitives (*see* Ransom) gave her a prize in 1924; after a short period in New York—where she knew Hart Crane (q.v.)—she came (1925) to England. She and Robert Graves (q.v.) were associated —in London, then Mallorca, then Rennes (Brittany) and finally Trenton (near Princeton, USA)—as editors and collaborationists (*A Survey of Modernist Poetry*, 1927; rev. extracts, by Graves only, contained in Graves's *The Common Asphodel*, 1949) between 1926 and 1939. In 1941 she married Schulyer B. Jackson, who died in 1968; new work by her is signed 'Laura (Riding) Jackson'. She renounced poetry in 1939. Since then she has written *The Telling* (1972), the 'story of human beings in the universe', as she characteristically describes it, essays giving her views on poetry (in *Chelsea*, 1962 and 1964); a long book, on which she and her husband worked for twenty-seven years, designed to 'dissipate the confusion existing in the knowledge of word-meanings', has now been completed by her. Even by 1950 few readers had taken note of Laura Riding's poetry (*Collected Poems*, 1938; *Selected Poems*, 1970), although many poets (e.g. Auden, q.v.) had made extensive and not altogether scrupulous use of her techniques. Her influence on Graves's personal life was crucial but he borrowed nothing from her poetic procedures. Now there is a growing interest in her work. Many of the poems in *The Close Chaplet* (1926) and in its eight successors—*Americans* (1934) is a surprisingly facetious failure: a short and ineffective satire in rhyming couplets—are astonishing in their bite, their originality, their precision and their beauty. Her statements about her poetic aims (especially in the introduction to the *Collected Poems*) and about her reasons for renouncing poetry are of the greatest interest and relevance to the modern phenomenon (referred to elsewhere in this book) which I have called *Künstlerschuld* (artist-guilt). In Laura Riding's case, however, the problem is complicated by what has seemed (doubtless incorrectly) to many critics to amount to a puzzling intellectual disorder. From the beginning Laura Riding was a non-sceptical crusader. She impressed some of the Fugitives by her almost naive enthusiasm. She founded (with Graves) the Seizin Press (they, but mostly she, edited the three volumes of the miscellany *Epilogue*, 1935–7), and her thirties activities culminated in *The World and Ourselves* (1938), which consisted of requested contributions on world problems from a host of writers and some others, with acute commentary by her. Like Romains (q.v.) she seems to have thought that she might prevent the war. As to her poetry, at its weakest it is somewhat Steinesque (q.v.) and rambling: she betrayed some signs of envy of Gertrude Stein's reputation, though Seizin published Stein's short *An Acquaintance with Description* (1926). But she is none the less the most consistently good woman poet of all time: an amazing achievement in the context of our century. The astonishing quality of her poetry defies description: it must be read. Her own characterization of it (1970) as 'of the first water' is, anyway, not incorrect; her inability to be modest is characteristic. It is concentrated, movingly based in experience, effortlessly absorbent of the residual qualities of truth-seeking systems. 'Back to the mother breast/ In another place—/ Not for milk, not for rest,/ But the embrace/ Clean bone/ Can give alone. . . .' Her account is that she left poetry because her fellow-poets were 'more concerned with making individualistic play upon the composition-habitudes of poetic tradition than with what concerned me'. What concerned her was that 'poetry seemed where the verbal maximum could be one with and the same as the truth maximum'. She possessed and possesses the faith that truth resides in human language. There are hints at her view of truth in *The Telling;* we must await her (and her husband's) book on words to discover how she relates language itself to this view. She renounced poetry not because she renounced her own efforts in the poetic medium but because she became convinced that this medium did not provide a suitable climate for the more 'far-reaching trueness of word' which she sought. Her own literary and critical achievement (she cannot deny its nature: she published books under an identifiable signature) is immense, as many are now beginning to understand. Her project, because of her intelligence and linguistic power, is immensely significant: one might state it as a project to discover, capture and transmit the reasons for human existence. But can this be done? She continues to publish and to proselytize: the reader, in face of an intransigence perhaps unique in co-existence with such powers as she possesses, is forced to consider the presence of some miraculously controlled 'paranoid' or hebrephenic condition. She has always had devoted disciples but those discipleships have usually come to an end, and always her (public) statements have relegated blame—sometimes at quasi-cosmic level—to the other party. Yet she has given much, including a body of marvellous poetry. She is a major twentieth-century writer and thinker whose very potency and challenge has led to her neglect. *Contemporaries and Snobs* (1928) and *Anarchism is Not Enough* (1928) collect essays. *Experts are Puzzled* (1930) and *A Progress of Stories* (1935) are stories. *A Trojan Ending* (1937) is a poor, wooden, historical novel.

Rilke, Rainer Maria (1875–1926) Austrian (then Czech) poet, novelist. Born in Prague. One of the greatest poets of the century (cf. and q.v. Vallejo, Valéry, Machado, Trakl, Laura Riding, Blok, Mandelstam). He is so original that he can be tied to no school or movement: he could be described as neo-romantic, decadent or expressionist, but his poetry effortlessly transcends all these categories. It is most appropriate to trace his development more or less chronologically. Only two comments need precede this. First, his life was restless: he wandered Europe, had close relationships with women—both with many mistresses and some patronesses, spent a short time in the army during the war, and finally settled in seclusion in Switzerland until his premature death, of leukaemia. His marriage (1901) lasted only a few months; he consistently and guiltily eschewed permanency of sexual relationships. Secondly, despite his dedication to his poetic vocation and his lack of political interests, he worried more about the validity of the poet's calling than almost any other contemporary; but his anxiety was in a psychologically rather than a politically existential context. The crucial influences and incidents are: a mother who treated him as the daughter she had wanted; the trauma of early military training; liaison with Lou Andreas-Salomé, with whom he maintained a correspondence after they parted; visit to Russia (1900), where he met Tolstoy; the sculptor Rodin, for whom he ran errands (1905–6), whose artistic impersonality was the stolid plastic equivalent of the ideal more ambiguously and nervously set forth in the important proto-expressionist novel *Niels Lyhne* (1880; tr. 1919), by the Danish writer Jens Peter Jacobsen (1847–85) which was of enormous importance to Rilke as a sensitive, subtle statement of the problems of atheist conviction versus religious feeling and of free love versus marriage; the expanding city and Verhaeren's (q.v.) poetry about it. His protracted personal crisis or 'creative illness' really lasted from about 1905–6 until the moment of self-revelation that occurred (1912) with the opening lines of the first of the *Duino Elegies*–an existential sickness from which he may be said to have had only some periods of remission for the rest of his life. This personal crisis is most clearly reflected in the novel *Die Aufzeichnungen des Malte Laurids Brigge* (1910; tr. *The Notebook of Malte Laurids Brigge,* 1930), a truly terrifying 'city' novel, enigmatic, confused, of immense power: Malte is a 'decadent' Rilke, insane–an attempt to separate the author from what he most feared; he is also Rilke the thinker and sometimes Rilke the poet. His first, nineties, poetry had been conventional but already bore the marks of his genius. From the beginning he was obsessed with the mythical (never the historical) Christ, who always fascinated him but whose pure spirituality repelled him as in keeping with neither the worst nor the best in reality. He remained resolutely anti-Christian until the end, though it was not altogether people's own fault if they sometimes saw him as an unorthodox Christian, since all that he wrote on the subject was not then available. His rejection of every form of Christianity is of supreme importance throughout each of his poetic phases, though its complexity is sometimes nearly impenetrable. Essentially Rilke's hatred of Christianity, his resentment of the force of the Christ-myth, is based on his independence: man must live and die for himself, suffer for himself, learn for himself, begin in scepticism, not retreat into sexual asceticism. But this hatred, which was consistent (he refused a priest when dying), passed through (early) phases in which attempts are made to transform Christ, or in which Christian symbolism is turned against itself. His first mature collection of poems was written just after the turn of the century and published, in revised form, in 1905: *Das Stundenbuch, The Book of Hours* (all Rilke's mature poetry has been translated, often several times; in Great Britain all the versions are published by the Hogarth Press; the USA versions may be traced from the American *Books in Print*): these contain passages of inspired fluency which anticipate the later Rilke but are still tied to the theme of Christian belief. They reflect both his Russian and his Italian experiences; one could describe them as the poetry Ivan Karamazov might have written had he been of Rilke's nationality and generation. . . . In the *Neue Gedichte* (1907–8), *New Poems,* we catch for the first time more than glimpses of the great poet. He has now learned to dispense with ideas, to surrender to his feelings of the 'inwardness' of things (cf. Hopkins's, q.v., 'instress' and 'inscape') and yet to attain an external coherence, however complex. The hard actuality of Rodin's sculptures helped him considerably here: he saw them as self-contained, isolated from the untruths of worldly discourse, externalized images of inwardness, *things*. There are at once affinities in this attitude with expressionism (*see* Stadler), literary cubism (*see* Reverdy), with the ideals of George (q.v., whom Rilke met in Italy) and with Hopkins, unknown of course to Rilke. More than anyone else at this time of Valéry's (q.v.) silence and of the comparative immaturity of his greatest contemporaries, Rilke was writing not only about the inner nature of his actual subjects but also about the insuperable problems of being a poet. And so the best of the *Neue Gedichte* have a grand, sculptural substance: they are, at a certain level, demonstrations of where, why, how the ideal of 'pure poetry' must fail; also, however, of the necessity of making the effort. They identify the point of Rilke's recognition that life without the poetic is barbarous but that any poetry without life is an impoverished one. Yet: '. . . there's an immemorial antipathy/between life and a great work'. These are among the concluding lines of the requiem Rilke wrote (1908) for his friend the artist Paula Modersohn-Becker; it contains another theme, that of the problem, which he never solved, of why women should want to 'possess' him if he was prepared to allow them freedom. This need of theirs for love as well as understanding gave them for Rilke an irritating quality that was positively Christ-like in its fascination. But, though he may not be called a love poet, he did not shirk the issue. However, his faith in poetry (as *Malte Laurids Brigge* makes clear) was beginning to be badly shaken. He desperately needed to feel that as a man he was as virtuous, as unsullied by 'life', as was his ideal poem, and he could not so feel. He was acutely troubled by the (indeed) acutely troubling old question: 'Why aren't poets more virtuous than grocers?' Thus his faith that 'Gesang ist Dasein', 'song is existence', was hideously undermined. The *Duino Elegies* (there were originally eleven, but the fifth was rejected and published separately, leaving ten), which took ten years to complete, are the result of Rilke's heroic attempt to deal with this problem, with the question of the human position of the man who knows he is in possession of poetic powers: is he humanly dysfunctional or does he have an extra burden to bear? Or both? The *Duino Elegies* are so called because the first, second and some fragments were written at Duino on the Adriatic coast in January–February 1912. Debate about their exact meaning is intense and will continue to be so. All that needs to be said here is that their main subject is the poetic predicament and that they deal with this subject more comprehensively than any other single modern poem. The 'angels' are not Christian angels but ambiguous metaphorical entities which have many functions: they confer structure on the sequence, they represent poetic pressure (the power of vision into the heart of things), they represent, at times, the evil need to 'use' experience of relationships with people in order to achieve this vision; at a personal level they embody Rilke's agonized awareness of his own selfishness and narcissism; they are reconciliatory. . . . The poem might be called, among other things, an analysis and an exploration of the religious element in man, seen as the cult of inwardness. The *Elegies* were completed in February 1922; and just before this time there came to him, as a sudden gift, the *Sonette an Orpheus* (1923), *Sonnets to Orpheus*: this Nietzschean sequence is his least tragic poetry. He finds here the convincing Orphic substitute for 'this Christ who is always interfering in everything', he is able to lose his identity, 'as though', in the words of one of his soundest interpreters, Eudo C. Mason (*Rilke*, 1963), 'Narcissus were tearing himself away from his own reflection'. These are great modern pagan poems, making a less cynical use of Christian symbolism than the Christians once had of pagan: one of the most formidable of modern challenges to the Pauline Christ. The *Sonette* are not superior to the *Elegies;* but without them the latter would mean less. Most of Rilke's poetry after this final effort was in French and he discovered both Valéry (q.v.)–whom he translated–and Cocteau (q.v.). His letters are second only to Keats's: *Selected Letters,* in English, 1946. Most of his poetry and prose is in *Sämtliche Werke* (1955–63), and there are over a score of volumes of diaries and letters, many of which are collected in *Gesammelte Briefe* (1936–9) and *Tagebücher aus der Frühzeit* (1943)–the early diaries.

Robbe-Grillet, Alain (1922) French novelist, often regarded as the leading practising theorist of the *nouveau roman* (his only rival in this respect is Butor, q.v.). He was trained (and worked) as an agronomist and statistician and–whatever he or others may claim–the most consistent features of his work are his positivism and his behaviourism. He is important as an influence in modern fiction but his intrinsic achievement, which is by no means ingenuous, is small. His novels are above all boring; critics (often, in England, dons) who delight in them do so because they respond favourably to his structural ingenuity and to his fictional theories. A highly intelligent, favourable and illuminating account of him, in complete contrast to the one offered here, is given by John Sturrock in his *The French New Novel* (1969). The failure of Robbe-Grillet lies in his exclusively cerebral approach and in the tawdriness of his deliberately parodic 'worlds'. For all the impact the *nouveau roman* has made, Robbe-Grillet is himself an evader of the mysterious and of the imaginative: an escapist *par excellence.* This is ironic, for one of his intentions is to purge fiction of escapism by questioning all its previous assumptions. However, it is necessary to separate Robbe-Grillet the theorist from Robbe-Grillet the putative novelist, even if his fiction may eventually be shown to be no more than theory: dialectically his theories are important, and that he happens to be unable to write imaginatively cannot detract from this importance. On other writers his influence has been valuable and he sums up (*Pour un nouveau roman,* 1963; tr. in *Snapshots,* 1965) many of the aspirations of his predecessors. Robbe-Grillet's 'new novel', actually an abstraction because it cannot exist, is an essentially provocative conception: it is not original except inasmuch as it gathers together nearly all the concerns of fictional modernism into one slick, intelligent polemic. The term had attained international status by the end of the fifties. Most of the points made are eminently reasonable and may be briefly summarized. It must be recognized that fiction is lying: therefore, today, novels are inadequate if they do not dispense with such artificial devices as 'characters', 'plots', 'ideas' and 'clock time' (*see* Bergson). The philosophical assumption underlying this is that the world is indifferent to us, so anthropomorphism is a tragic waste of time. Style must be at 'zero degree' (*see* Barthes): the novelist's eye must be like a camera, for if it is not then the novelist is party to a bourgeois, 'comfortable' conspiracy in which life is supposed to consist of plots. For Robbe-Grillet, who prescribes one of the novelist's tasks as being to record the world of things (*chosisme*), imagination is an illusion: it is simply memory. And so, with a quite proper philosophical rigour, the new novel must be no more nor less than a record of what is going on in the author's consciousness. All novels, of course, must first be that–although they can become something else; but Robbe-Grillet's approach is, notably, not neoteric or fruitful and is over-theoretical. What the pure theory omits or ignores is that: by no means everything, in particular the nature of perception, is at all well known; we do anthropomorphize; in general we do like 'stories'; fiction is not philosophy. Nietzsche wrote (*c.* 1885): 'With a stiff seriousness that inspires laughter . . . our philosophers . . . wanted to supply a *rational foundation* for morals.' For 'philosophers' read 'purist new novelists' and for 'morals' 'novels' and you have an answer to Robbe-Grillet. Sarraute (q.v.), Simon (q.v.), Butor (q.v.) and others have been influenced by this theory but none has been so arid in practice as Robbe-Grillet, and all have used the metaphor and symbol which he wishes to eschew: they cannot be eschewed, even by him. The concept as a whole is quintessentially Gallic and while it is important that novelists in other countries should respond to it, it is equally important that they should not try to write French novels in their own languages. The *nouveau roman*, then, is an over-ambitious and sterile enterprise. Robbe-Grillet's purpose is didactic: to show the reader that reality is inaccessible to him and that books, myths and dreams are worthless. He is thus an authoritarian behaviourist. We do not mind having our plots, characters or clock-time taken from us; we care only that *our* responses, our reconstitutions in consciousness, be respected. In Sarraute or Simon there is tension, whatever either may aim at. Robbe-Grillet's books are a series of sour scientistic instructions and his viewpoint is as reprehensible as those of a Skinner, an Eysenck or even a Watson. His books, which include *Les Gommes* (1953; tr. *The Erasers,* 1964), *La Jalousie* (1957; tr. *Jealousy,* 1959) and *La Maison de rendezvous* (1965; tr. *The House of Assignation,* 1970), all attempt to perform their hopeless critical function of demonstrating that nothing is really patterned or tragic (*Les Gommes* cleverly but quite unconvincingly tries to expose the Oedipus story as an arbitrary piece of nonsense), that the real is only factual and cannot ever be a part of mind. Robbe-Grillet's fiction is immensely clever in its use of puns, time-tricks, and other devices; in human terms it is perhaps even totalitarian –it is certainly dangerously dogmatic and narrow. He claims that his neutralist view of the world as simply 'there' is humanistic; but this is not true because it cannot ever be a part of real *human* experience. Robbe-Grillet's script for Resnais's *L'Année dernière à Marienbad* (1961; tr. *Last Year at Marienbad,* 1962) gave him international fame. All his publications have been under the Minuit imprint: its director, Jérôme Lindon, was largely responsible for the foundation of the alleged 'school'–which includes Georges Perec (1936), Claude Ollier (1922) and J. M. Le Clézio (1940).

Robinson, Edwin Arlington (1869–1935) American poet whose considerable achievement was for long engulfed by the tidal wave of the thoroughgoing modernism of Pound (q.v.), Eliot (q.v.) and others. But Robinson was less old-fashioned than he seemed and there is an interesting parallel between him and the Italian *crepusculari* (*see* Gozzano), of whom he knew nothing–and therefore between him and the early Eliot, who certainly utilized his procedures, whether consciously or otherwise. Robinson was born in a village in Maine; his miserable childhood made him into a poet. His mother died horribly; his brothers went to the devil; his father became a fanatic spiritualist. This, and the then universally prevalent notion that success consisted only of gaining cash and power over others, made him feel an outcast and failure from the beginning. He suffered destitution, almost drank himself to death (alcohol remained a problem for him, and he once put his survival down to the fact that he never resorted to it until darkness fell), and only gained a little critical recognition with *Captain Craig* (1902). Fame, readership and financial security did not come until 1916, with *The Man against the Sky*. But he was forty-seven and the chance of a sexual relationship had passed him by. He is one of the loneliest of poets. Robinson's first masters were Browning, Crabbe, Hardy (who praised his first privately printed volume of 1896: *The Torrent and the Night Before*) and the pre-Raphaelites. He had few other sources. He remained a Victorian living on into a non-Victorian century. But what is fascinating, unique and important about his poetry is that it records aware strategies for such a survival. (At his least good he is compellingly readable.) Out of his misery his acute sensibility made a cogent poetry: the account of a traumatized nineteenth-century childhood turning into a lonely twentieth-century adulthood. He seldom speaks as himself. Instead he describes defeated, puzzling or failed characters (e.g. the famous Miniver Cheevy, Flammonde, Craig, Luke Havergal): men corrupt but spiritually incapable of succumbing to the materialism of their times. 'Flammonde' is a masterly exploitation of the clichés and sentimentalities of the kind of verse that was acceptable in his time; it rests on a relentlessly ironic—though subdued—piling up of such, and on a knife-edge of enigma and paradox. Like many of the earlier poems—before, successful at last, he took to writing longer narrative works—it is exceedingly sensitive and subtle and Robinson's own rhythms slash, to great effect, against the metrical framework. Most of these poems are set in 'Tilbury Town': this is his imaginative reconstruction of the world of the town of Gardiner (Maine) to which his family moved when he was a small child. What he has in common with the *crepusculari* is that his defeated characters, though far more solidly set in a sociological context, are objective correlatives for himself —doomed not to the prospect of early death but to a life of loneliness, solitary drinking and quiet despair. The later narrative poems, which are on the whole inferior, vary in quality. They cannot, in an age in which narrative poetry has conspicuously failed, be dismissed. The medieval ones (e.g. *Merlin,* 1917) are spoiled by over-indulgence in pseudo-Arthurian ornamentation; but some of the 'novels in verse'—*The Man Who Died Twice* (1924), *King Jasper* (1935)—really need their verse form (cf. Crabbe) to achieve their often subtle psychological effects. If one hesitates to describe Robinson as major, one cannot easily call him minor. . . . He is a most courageous, honest and exemplary poet—and a lovable one. *Collected Poems* (1937). *Selected Early Poems and Letters* (1960) contains some poems not in the *Collected Poems*. *Selected Letters* (1940) is an unsatisfactory work, but there are two further collections of letters—*Untriangulated Stars* (1947) and *Edwin Arlington Robinson's Letters to Edith Brower* (1968). A *Collected Letters* is in preparation. The best critical biography is by E. Barnard (1952; 1969).

Roethke, Theodore (1908–63) American poet, teacher. He did not become widely known until the publication of his fourth volume, *The Waking* (1953). *Words for the Wind* (1958), which confirmed his reputation, selects from the first four books. *Collected Poems* appeared in 1968. Roethke is a deceptive poet, not nearly as good as he sometimes looks; he exercised a strong influence on the so-called 'confessional' school; he could even be accused (though wrongly) of initiating it. His admirers claim that he achieved a synthesis but they fail to see that it is a false and rhetorical synthesis. He spent a fair amount of his time in mental hospitals (so, of course, did Clare, Smart and others) and his malady may well have included a form of hysteria. His poetry has many of the qualities we associate with hysteria: there is an emotional shallowness in it, co-existent with an uncanny ability to convince people—by brilliant 'acting out'—that very deep emotions are being expressed; it is egocentric, histrionic and, curiously enough, immature. Furthermore, like many hysterics, Roethke 'had his fans': there were many anxious to protect him from hostile criticism. But he was a clever and intelligent, though gross, hysteric. His early poetry was conventional and mediocre (*Open House*, 1941). Later he developed an undoubtedly brilliant, nervous manner, just on the edge of hysteria, but its effects, as M. L. Rosenthal has pointed out, are 'finally unearned'. It is nearly all manner and no substance, 'acting out'; done to gain baby attention. The famous but minor poem: 'I have known the inexorable sadness of pencils,/ Neat in their boxes, dolour of pad and paperweight,/ All the misery of manila folders . . .' shows him at his best. Roethke's father was a nurseryman and the imagery of the 'greenhouse' poems which made his name draws ingeniously on his childhood experiences in greenhouses. He spoke of his desire to purify his life because he felt 'defiled' by it; and he really did feel defiled by his vulgar competitiveness and far too glib wish to be the 'greatest'. *Letters* (1968) and *Notebooks* (1970) confirm, alas, his shallowness, his egocentricity and his vulgarity. There is no true sense in his poetry of even the existence of other people (I think he felt genuinely ashamed about this). His mellifluous later poems are almost insolently derivative (from e.g. Yeats,

Blake, Dylan Thomas). A fake: but a fake with style and *élan:* as tiresome but as touching as a little boy innocently attempting to become the centre of the universe.

Rolland, Romain (1866–1944) French novelist, idealist, musicologist, biographer, essayist, historian, playwright. Rolland, though he has little imaginative genius, is the exact opposite of Barrès: he is internationalist, orientalist, Marxist-socialist. He wrote learned musical studies and was a scholar of deserved repute. In 1939 he abandoned his pacifism in the face of Hitler. Nobel Prize 1916. His most famous novel, *Jean-Christophe* (1904–12 rev. 1931–4; tr. 1910–13), is a massive and now tedious *roman à thèse* about a German composer who heroically rejects the materialistic and thus artistically triumphs (in France). It well illustrates Rolland's passionate desire to create an understanding between France and Germany and his admiration of Tolstoy, whose later optimism and idealism influenced him all his life. *Jean-Christophe,* like some of Rolland's plays for his 'Theatre of the People', has its virtues; but the author's noble but over-lofty notions about 'heroes' keep his feet well off the ground. He was an able, vital, intelligent and good man but his idealism makes him a minor writer. His best work is in plays such as *Danton* (1900).

Romains, Jules (ps. Louis Farigoule) (1885–1972) French novelist, poet, playwright, miscellaneous writer and polemicist. In Romains, a fascinating and versatile writer, we see embodied in imaginative form the important ideas of Emile Durkheim, the sociologist who put forward the idea of the *conscience collective* and who was among the first to examine the viability of the phenomenon of religion from a 'secular' viewpoint. Romains's claim not to have read him until after he had formed his own 'unanimist' ideas may well be true. His poetry, like his immense novel *Les Hommes de bonne volonté* (1932–52; tr. *Men of Good Will,* 1933–46–Romains was not in France in the war, hence the appearance of the final volumes, finished in 1944, in English before French), has been consistently underrated; he was most universally successful with the play *Dr Knock* (1923; tr. 1935), which was filmed three times (twice with Jouvet: 1933 and 1950). He was a subtle, complex man; the outright political naivety of his late thirties and 1940 polemics must be put down to his passion for peace, to the temporary intellectual collapse to which this may have brought him–and, not least, to a certain grandiosity he (rather inoffensively) possessed, and which was connected with his fascination with the idea of great conspiracies and the important part he might play in preventing or diverting them. Romains had a brilliant academic career and was a professor of philosophy before he gave up teaching for writing. At eighteen, in 1903, he had an overpowering feeling, as he was walking along the street, that he had literally merged with, become a part of, the great crowd. At that moment literary unanimism may be said to have been born; though Romains's sensation was experienced, in one way or another, by many people of his time. It is often stated that Romains was a co-founder or member of the Abbaye community at Créteil (*see* Duhamel): he was neither; but L'Abbaye printed and published his second book of poems, *La Vie unanime* (1908) and he was closely associated with the group. He had already, at twenty-one, published a 'unanimist' work: *Le Bourg régénéré* (1906), about a village that discovers its communal life. Further, it was his book of poems that led Duhamel and his friends (Vildrac, Luc Durtain and others) to call themselves 'unanimistes'. . . . All of Romains's work stems from the themes of this volume (not his best). But the matter is not as simple as it seems: for Romains is a great comic writer and, as well as sending up communities he often sends up himself. This is a point usually missed. Influences on him at this early stage, when he was something of a prodigy, must have included Verhaeren (q.v.), Whitman and Gabriel Tarde, the judge who postulated a kind of dialectic of unanimism (which he called integration) based on the principle of imitation; he also studied biology. The basis of unanimism, which remains valid—though hardly satisfactory as the *raison d'être* of a literary school—is that a procession, a town, even two lovers, have an *independent collective life*. It was left for Romains to work out the difficult implications of this, for as a movement *per se* it fizzled out into *simultanéisme* and other such -isms. It is important to remember that he never related his unanimism to communism or to fascism; he remained a dedicated democrat. In his own words, the 'unanimous life' involves the '*unrestricted living*' (my italics) of 'human groups'. The selection *Choix de poèmes* (1948) shows Romains to be a more considerable poet than is usually supposed: a poet searching for the 'collective' aspects of experience less programmatically than the majority of his critics charge. He remained faithful to the principle of 'accorded' blank verse until the end of his life: this involved rejection of rhyme, ornamentation, allegory and symbol, and a special use of recurrent sounds. Of his earlier novels *Mort de quelqu'un* (1911; tr. *Death of a Nobody,* 1914) and *Les Copains* (1913; tr. *The Boys in the Back Room,* 1937) are the best. Both have 'unanimist' themes. In the first a man dies, lives in the memories of those who knew him for a while, and finally dissolves—but his death becomes a part of another man's life. In the second Romains describes a series of hilarious practical jokes played by a group of young men on the inhabitants of two towns; their hoaxes create a kind of group consciousness. The trilogy *Psyché* (1922–9; tr. *Lucienne,* 1922; *The Body's Rapture,* 1937—the final part is untranslated) explores the 'unanimity' of lovers and is an erotic classic. The major work, *Les Hommes de bonne volonté,* is far better than present-day criticism allows. As a whole it does fail; but, as Maurois (q.v.) has pointed out, it does not do so abysmally. Who has attempted a work on this scale in this century and succeeded (other *romans-fleuves* are considerably shorter)? Romains understands that his Durkheimian intuitions are not simple. A yeast of imagination works through *Les Hommes de bonne volonté* and it provides by far the subtlest and most exhaustive investigation of the *conscience collective* in its relationship to 'individualism' in existence. Later fiction, and some of the many volumes of essays, are of considerable interest. It is sad that such reputations should be allowed to fade: there is more than good reading in Romains and even the long passages of *reportage* in the big work have their virtues.

Rosenberg, Isaac (1890–1918) English poet and artist of Russian-Jewish origin, he grew up in London's East End. He is now recognized by most critics as having been the severest loss sustained by English poetry in the 1914–18 holocaust. Clearly, in his final poems, he was succeeding in working out a lucid presentation of his complex and clashing impulses. He would have become, it seems reasonable to suggest, the major poet of the post-war period. Only Bottrall (q.v.), sixteen years his junior and a very different sort of poet, has had the scope of his vision. Rosenberg was influenced by imagism (*see* Pound), by modern developments in French painting, by Blake (as illustrator and visionary myth-maker) and by his Jewish heritage. His visit to South Africa (1914), where his sister was living, may also have affected and perhaps crystallized his outlook. There are certainly 'cubist' (*see* Reverdy) elements in his poetry, which is so extraordinarily original as to have led many critics to regard it as no more than inchoate and highly promising. As C. H. Sisson has observed, 'Rosenberg was bursting with things to say, as Flint, or Aldington, or even Pound could scarcely be said to be'. He was perhaps the first English-language poet to have been directly and nakedly obsessed with the idea of an *actively* evil God (by no means similar to Hardy's, q.v., view of the 'immortals'); there are important moments when he sees this evil, this vengeful God of the Old Testament given a metaphysical twist, as being opposed or mitigated in some phantasmagoric struggle with women, with the feminine principle as seen through the eyes of a Jew well acquainted with the legends of Lilith and her magical kind. His vision was Jewish in tone but it took a singularly original form. His poetry is full of menace and, although he seldom found the exact form he wanted, has a strange authority which may at first seem rhetorical but which is in fact anti-rhetorical. He writes of war but he does not, as Owen did, write 'war poems': this is a poetry of experience, a poetry which deals not just with the horror of the trenches but with the human disorder lying behind this, as well as with the sinisterly erotic themes that are so intimately connected with that disorder. Most unfortunately Gordon Bottomley, when he came to edit Rosenberg's poetry (1922), destroyed some possibly priceless material; this was to some extent corrected in a 1937 edition (*Collected Works*) and in 1949 in the American *Collected Poems*. But Rosenberg's bibliography remains in a less than satisfactory state. He published only three small volumes in his lifetime, including the play *Moses* (1916), which contains some of his most powerful writing. The high claims that have been made for Rosenberg in recent years have not been exaggerated. The *Collected Works* (1976) is now the best edition.

Roth, Henry (1906) American novelist. He was born in Austro-Hungary, of Jewish parents who emigrated to America when he was an infant. He has written only one novel (he began but was unable to finish another; a fragment was published, and there have been one or two poor stories), *Call it Sleep* (1934; 1963), but it is one of the greatest of this century in any language. It concerns the experiences of a small boy, son, like Roth himself, of immigrants in the slums of New York. All through it is pitched at exactly the right level: it perfectly and lyrically inhabits the terrified mind of the boy, victim of a paranoid father, of a mother cut off–by ignorance of language and her husband's crazed distrust—from reality, of an irritable Rabbi teacher, of the tough and violent life of the ghetto. The speech habits of the people who live in the ghetto are brilliantly rendered. Above all, the novel conveys the sense of a particular kind of modern American Jewishness—acute sensitivity transformed into an anguished ecstasy by a series of tortures and by a sordid environment—as powerfully as it has ever been conveyed. *Call it Sleep* combines absolute realism (down to the most searing details) with absolute poetry—and with a beautiful fairness towards all its characters. Roth, however, broke down. He opted out of literary life, was at one time a poultry farmer and teacher of mathematics, at another an attendant in a mental hospital. Perhaps this was the price for so heroically raising the level of the ghetto novel; as Fiedler (q.v.) has remarked, one can only surmise the anguish behind his silence. He now states that he is writing again.

Roth, Joseph (1894–1939) Major Austrian novelist, short-story writer, critic, who is persistently underrated outside the German-speaking countries despite serious efforts made on his behalf. His father was Austrian, his mother a Russian Jewess. His life was a distressingly unhappy one. He never saw his father, who left his mother before he was born (hence his identification of himself as a Jew); his education was interrupted by the war, in which he served; his wife went mad and he supported himself precariously by intermittent journalism and menial jobs until the thirties, when he became an exile in Paris; he died there, completely destitute, of acute alcoholism in May 1939. And yet he was a prolific writer who resolved his confusions. Like Musil (q.v.), Roth was concerned with the fate of those who had been brought up in the Austro-Hungarian empire, but he linked their alienation with that of the Jewish diaspora and with those who had been destroyed by their war experiences and he was a straightforwardly realistic narrator. All his work (collected in *Gesammelte Werke*, 1956 and *Romane, Erzählungen, Aufsätze*, 1964) repays study; it is extremely versatile within the limits of traditional procedures (he made the right choice for himself). Outstanding are *Die Flucht ohne Ende* (1927; tr. *Flight Without End*, 1930), a description of the collapsed empire seen through the eyes of a returned officer; *Hiob* (1930; tr. *Job*, 1931), on the theme of the estranged Jew, the great *Radetzkymarsch* (1932; tr. 1974), his most popular work—its sequel *Die Kapuzinergruft* (1939), *The Crypt of the Capuchins*, is weaker—and *Die Legende vom*

Heiligen Trinker (1939; tr. *The Legend of the Holy Drinker* in *Heart of Europe*, 1943). *Radetzkymarsch* tells the story of three generations of the Trotta family: the old soldier ennobled for accidentally saving the emperor's life; his son, the dedicated civil servant who is a sensitive man but cannot express himself; and the grandson (really the main character) caught up in the final catastrophe, which despite his intelligence he cannot comprehend. This is an exquisite novel, a gentle, delicate and sad mixture of irony and nostalgia, which perfectly evokes the atmosphere of the last sixty years of the Austro-Hungarian empire. Roth made many political pronouncements and seemed at the end of his life to have become a 'conservative and a Catholic' who 'desired the return of the Empire'; but as has been well said, he was a novelist interested in human beings and not in politics. He is one of the last of the great traditional writers.

Roth, Philip (1933) American fiction writer who gained fame with the 'masturbation novel' *Portnoy's Complaint* (1969), which is often very funny (an over-extended Jewish joke), but which was his least good book to that date. Its successors have been notably poor. *Goodbye Columbus* (1959), six stories, made a promising beginning; and *Letting Go* (1962), though too long and too flippant, is essentially a serious and detached study of Jewish-Gentile conflicts. His best book, though, is *When She was Good* (1967), in which–in a midwestern setting–he convincingly creates a 'man-destroyer', and as convincingly explains her familial and environmental motivations. *Our Gang* (1971) is a rather weak satire on Nixon and his gang. The novella *The Breast* (1973) is intelligent but cannot carry the weight of its surrealist and psychoanalytical implications: a man is turned into a huge breast, whose nipple is of course penile.

Roussel, Raymond (1877–1933) French novelist, poet, playwright. Roussel is one of the most enigmatic of modern writers. He cannot be ignored, but, as an eccentric and as a genuine precursor of surrealism (*see* Breton) his actual work has been overrated. He was a complex ambisexual (probably mostly homosexual) manic-depressive whose case Pierre Janet, his doctor, described in some detail (as 'Martial' in *De l'Angoisse à l'extase*, 1926)–Janet does not cast it in such terms, but this would be the modern diagnosis. At nineteen he suffered an attack of mania during which he wrote a long novel in alexandrines (about

5900), *La Doublure* (1897), *The Understudy:* he believed that his pen actually gave off light as he wrote this tale of a man and his girl (or girl-as-man) progressing through a carnival in Nice, and that he was the greatest man in the world. When the book failed to attract notice his mania became shot with a terrible depression; but he never broke down. He continued to write and publish, and he was able to do his military service (he was also called up during the First World War). There is a sense in which this strange man, always rich (at least until the end), could act perfectly sanely for most of the time: there was a strong histrionic streak in him and he would (apparently) often perform the role of himself-as-mad. The undoubtedly 'paranoid style' of his later years was in part a desperate hysterico-solipsist pose. He is a fascinating man and writer but his writings are much less readable than the surrealists or the exponents of the *nouveau roman* (*see* Robbe-Grillet), who also claimed him as a precursor, will admit. However, they are at the very least technically suggestive. The three important and procedurally mature ones are *Impressions d'Afrique* (1910; tr. *Impressions of Africa,* 1966), *Locus Solus* (1914)–both in prose–and *Nouvelles Impressions d'Afrique* (1932), in verse. Roussel added to the confusion by putting together a book called *Comment j'ai écrit certains de mes livres* (1935), *How I Wrote Some of My Books,* posthumously published. Critics have taken this too seriously, for they tend to interpret Roussel's texts in the light of his own intentions; in fact they must be judged in the light of his mental state, against which they are a series of defences so intelligent (or is 'hysterico-canny' the term?) as to be, perhaps, of universal significance. They may function as 'experimental' but they were not initially intended to be experimental. That is the point most critics have missed. Roussel's fiction proceeds, as it has been put (Robbe-Grillet, q.v.), from 'situation A, to the same situation very slightly modified, A1'. He does it by use of homophones, phonic and punning distortions, and other verbal means. So Roussel says and so Robbe-Grillet likes to think. And it has its importance: as Foucault rightly says, the same word can have two or more distinct meanings and this can suggest an 'abyss' in any picture of reality, and so tormented Roussel. But even more important is what happens on the 'conventional' surface of Roussel's writings. Rayner Heppenstall, in his useful but curious pamphlet on Roussel (1966), likes him because he is 'not serious'. And of course he has spotted the fact that Roussel, like Jacob (q.v.), had to try to avoid seriousness at all costs. There are statements so 'secret' in Roussel that they are glaringly there, on the surface, concealed by his 'procedures' (which in the *Nouvelles Impressions* include a fantastical system of bracketings): his characters, his situations, his 'plots', the persistence of certain themes (masks, acting, understudies, lining—*doublure* means both—and many others). His girls are almost certainly boys, though he may not have been as aware of this as Proust (q.v.), who praised *La Doublure* in modest terms. The treatment of Roussel would have to include the fullest biographical details in conjunction with his writings but his life is wrapped in mystery. The chief authority on him is Michel Leiris, and one would do well to accept and extrapolate from his accounts. Roussel wrote two plays and an adaptation of *Impressions d'Afrique* (this was also, later, adapted by Pierre Frondaie): he paid top actors to play them and they created scandals. He took up chess (1931–2) and exhibited a genius for it in a very short time. Then he took to the bottle, finally succumbing to barbiturate addiction—he killed himself, almost certainly, by an overdose. It is quite possible that his money had at last run out. He is in a way the invention of a century distinguished for its psychosis and its psychotics; a genius, an enigma, an anti-hero; a figure a study of whom would greatly help to resolve the problem of the connection between art and illness. Such a study would also demonstrate the persistence of the 'container myth': that words have no relationship to what they denote, that they are arbitrary symbols. Linguisticians may well have disposed of this myth but we find their proof difficult to believe. There is an eight-volume complete works, *Oeuvres complètes* (1963–4), though because of the quarrels between the post-surrealists and the proponents of the new novel, and because of extensive bibliographical difficulties, this is not regarded as perfect; it is, however, as good as we shall get for some time.

S

Saba, Umberto (ps. Umberto Poli) (1883–1957) Italian (Triestian) poet. Unique in twentieth-century poetry. His Christian father left his Jewish mother and he changed his name to the Hebrew for 'bread'. He had an early spell in the army and was in hiding in Florence and Rome during the Second World War. His poetry seems, at first sight, to be provincial and traditional; it is often called 'homely', an understandable but misleading adjective. Saba had a traumatic childhood and early realized that his native city was effectively cut off from Italian culture; instead of leaving it, however, he took advantage of his isolation to make his own quotidian poetry, which deals, in a language deliberately humble and un-literary, with quotidian joys and sorrows. Saba's type of simplicity, however, is modern: it is, for example, more anti-literary than that of any of his leading contemporaries, all of whom employ rhetorical devices. He stuck closely to his own history: his childhood, his life with his wife Lina, his relations. Since he concentrates so intensely and simply upon his own experience, some features of it acquire a symbolic value–but this is a fact that he wisely ignores. This well-described 'dearest' poet, of 'secret and modest' life, is less innocent than he seems. He was relatively immune to the Italian modernist currents but this does not mean that he is merely an effective traditionalist survivor. He eventually assembled his poetry under a single title, *Il Canzoniere* (1921; 1945; definitive edition 1961) and in 1948 he published his comments on the poems in *Storia e cronistoria del 'Canzoniere'*; this is reprinted in *Prose* (1964). Saba is gentle and subtle; some of his poems are banal because he is so deliberately low-keyed; one of his secrets is that he is an intellectual who has the courage not to take too much thought, but instead to watch the surface of life itself–not images or idealizations of it–and to record it in as candidly intimate a manner as possible. There are many risks involved but Saba remains calm–and his achievement is suddenly revealed. His Hebraic melancholy is balanced by domestic serenity and an off-hand humour; his love of animals is, as has been observed, authentically Franciscan. Lucid though Saba's actual language is, he has a little more in common with *ermetismo* (*see* Ungaretti, Montale, Quasimodo) than is usually allowed: he had known the anguish of the ghetto and he shared his contemporaries' hatred of fascism. 'Il vetro rotto', 'Broken Window', is less sensational and exciting than anything of, say, Montale's, but it is neither less effective nor less complex nor more prosaic: 'Everything's against you. Foul weather,/lights that switch themselves off, the old/house shaken by a hailstorm and dear to you/because of evils suffered, hopes/deluded and some good hours too./Survival seems rebellion/against natural law./And in the crash/of breaking glass you hear the sentence.' This is a very sharply ambivalent poem, whose final grudging message of hope is truly earned by the poet's faithfulness to his own mood; it is most remarkable for its lack of rhetoric. One has only to submerge oneself in Saba (the *Antologia del 'Canzoniere'*, 1963, affords an excellent starting point) to discover his depth and originality.

Sagan, Françoise (ps. Françoise Quoirez) (1935) French novelist, playwright. She writes superficially but skilfully of the transitory nature of love–of which her concept is characteristically limited–for wealthy, bored women moving in a society to whose rottenness she only implies lip-service. Her greatest achievement is the title, *Aimez-vous Brahms?* (1959; tr. 1960). *Bonjour Tristesse* (1954; tr. 1957) and others have been big screen successes.

Saint-Exupéry, Antoine de (1900–44) French novelist, writer, pioneer airman, adventurer and *moraliste*. He is one of the few wholly serious French writers to have achieved immense popularity. He joined the Free French forces in Africa and was shot down–his plane was not recovered–while undertaking a reconnaissance mission from a Corsican base. The posthumous *Citadelle* (1948; tr. *Wisdom of the Sands*, 1954) is a misleading compilation: consisting of aphoristic and frequently portentous notes, it represents Saint-Exupéry as a thinker, which he was not. Saint-Exupéry was notable as a pioneer of early air-mail, flying difficult and dangerous routes both from France to Africa and within the South American continent. Attempts on speed records nearly cost him his life. He was fortunate to survive the air-battles of 1940. His terse second novel, *Vol de nuit* (1931; tr. *Night Flight*, 1932), which brought him fame, is his masterpiece: the real hero is the man who has to order one of his young pilots, newly married, on a hazardous night flight—from which he fails to return (as, thirteen years later, Saint-Exupéry himself was to fail to return). Here as strongly as elsewhere the author makes clear his simple dedication to duty—even at the expense of love. Saint-Exupéry seems a strangely old-fashioned writer: in him almost alone the old spirit of unanimism (*see* Romains) survived: man can only survive by sacrifice and by banding together in a fraternity. But this is no Brookean (q.v.) false patriotism or cliché-ridden political rhetoric—as Gide (q.v.) and Sartre (q.v.) after him recognized. There is much more to Saint-Exupéry than his ideas. First, there is a heroic acceptance of technology—valid for him not merely because he sees it as inevitable but also because he has a fully humanized view of it. Secondly there is always an implied tension between Proustian nostalgia for a happy childhood and the exigencies of the dangerous moment. The pilot in his plane feels like a god but he is also alienated in his splendour. *Terre des hommes* (1939; tr. *Wind, Sand and Stars,* 1939) tells of how the airman is plunged 'into the heart of the mystery', and what its prose poetry praises and explains is not courage but existentialist intensity of experience. *Pilote de guerre* (1942; tr. *Flight to Arras,* 1942) is about flying in 1940; *Le Petit Prince* (1943; tr. *The Little Prince,* 1943) is a delightful children's story. Saint-Exupéry's style, which at first owed something to Gide, has great merit: lucidity, disdain for the 'talkers' (this is why it is a pity that the jottings of *Citadelle* should ever have been allowed to appear), nobility. Most of his work is in *Oeuvres* (1963).

Saki (ps. H. H. Munro) (1870–1916) Scottish short-story writer, novelist, playwright, journalist. Born in Burma, brought up in Dorset by two sadistic puritan aunts, whose example left an indelible mark. Killed by a sniper in France after refusing commission. There is more in Saki than is often supposed; he is certainly more substantial than Firbank (q.v.), yet has never been the subject of a cult—only of a wide readership. Ostensibly Saki is the satirist of Edwardian polish, using its own manner to expose the beastliness it conceals. But there is a streak of the poetic in his use of animals and his icy farcicalness that lifts him out of the merely satiric realm: his shudder is prophetic; his control of it exquisite. His novel *The Unbearable Bassington* (1912) is persistently underrated. Works 1926–7; complete stories 1930; many selections.

Salinger, J. D. (1919) Immensely popular American fiction writer whose work is based so precariously on the knife-edge between fluent sensibility and psychological superficiality that he has lapsed into near-silence. *The Catcher in the Rye* (1951) was, from the beginning, misinterpreted. In it lie the seeds of Salinger's decline into clever pseudo-Zen vulgarity and then silence. Judged by the high standards which have been too confidently applied to his work, Salinger is a minor writer whose first book (the earlier stories are of no account) fitted in with a simplistic mood of alienation from society then prevalent among young people and their older imitators. The Holden Caulfield of *The Catcher in the Rye,* Salinger's version of Huck Finn for the early fifties, has been taken as an embodiment and re-creation of adolescence. Certainly the book has enormous stylistic and idiomatic distinction. But Holden is not convincing as an individual: he is in fact no more than a device for recording a mood and his sense of the people and world surrounding him as *phoney* is expressed in a series of appropriately colloquial notes and impressions. Granted that *The Catcher in the Rye* is a *tour de force,* it must be pointed out that a major writer (and Salinger has often been called this) would have gone on to raise profounder questions. What did Salinger do? In *Nine Stories* (1953; in Britain *For Esmé, With Love and Squalor,* 1953), the first story, 'A Perfect Day for Bananafish', is an account of the suicide of a Seymour Glass. Other Glass characters appear in other of these stories. Salinger's main project from then onwards was, in essence, to explain, or rather to justify, this suicide. In later work (*Franny and Zooey,* 1961; *Raise High the Roofbeam, Carpenters* and *Seymour: An Introduction,* 1963; and its single successor, a letter home written by the seven-year-old Seymour from summer camp–published in the *New Yorker* in 1965) he does indeed explore the whole Glass family; but his obsession is with the 'genius' Seymour, whose brother Buddy investigates his mystical life in order to find an identity. Salinger is clever, fluent and allusive in a manner helpful to enthusiastic critics but the Glass family is unreal (possesses no vitality), and the writing has become increasingly mystical and, in fact, meaningless.

Sandburg, Carl (1878–1967) American poet, biographer, prose writer, folk-song collector. He is rightly associated with Lindsay (q.v.) and Masters (q.v.) as one of a midwestern (he was born in Illinois of Swedish immigrant parents) trio who helped transform the Anglo-American poetic tradition into something truly American—but who did so in an unsophisticated, 'accidental', manner. Of the three, Lindsay is the most poetically gifted and unsophisticated, Masters the least poetically gifted and (in his cranky way) the least unsophisticated; Sandburg, more prolific, comes somewhere in between. He is, overall, the most balanced; he alone could be an unembittered and successful 'man of letters'. Lindsay drank poison; Masters festered in a frustrated populist rage. Sandburg always over-naively believed in the 'people' and he lacked intellectual curiosity; but in his best work his vigour and anti-bourgeois decency come through. Like Masters and Lindsay, he first found a hearing through Harriet Monroe's *Poetry Chicago*. The early poems have affinities with imagism (*see* Pound) and are inexorably slight; his power comes from his superb sense of popular poetic idiom and its speech cadences (he compiled *The American Songbag*, 1927, and *The New American Songbag*, 1950, and his temperament naturally assimilated the poetry in this material). Populism—for all its poetry—is dangerous, and all the more so because power-obsessed politicians can cash in on, or try to cash in on, its potent mainsprings (e.g. Perón); and Sandburg's 'thinking', centred on Lincoln (but his six-volume biography of him, *Abraham Lincoln*, 1926–39; abridged ed. 1954, if critically read, has instructive value), was always basically populist. But this well-intentioned feeling was modified not only by positive radical action (he was an early and active socialist) but also by his magnificent scorn for gentility (which means not politeness or courtesy but cruelty, resistance to truth, greed and hypocrisy) and his capacity to identify with folk articulation. His huge body of poetry, based on Whitman's procedures, is mostly diffuse, rhetorical and eminently readable. Despite his ability to evoke vivid atmospheric images, he lacks—unlike Whitman—real poetic concentration. However, some of his accounts of genteel nastiness have authentic, penetrative bite—and he at least deserves his popularity. There is vitality in his crudity and a certain small grandeur. *Complete Poems* (1950). *Always the Young Strangers* (1953) is an engaging autobiography. *Remembrance Rock* (1948) is an enormous novel (three books in one, in fact) which chases the 'American Dream'.

Sandel, Cora (ps. Sara Fabricius) (1880–1974) Norwegian novelist who lived in Sweden for the last fifty-three years of her life. She is the best modern Norwegian novelist after Hamsun; the English-speaking countries had little opportunity to acknowledge this before 1960, when *Kjøp ikke Dondi* (1958) was translated as *Leech*. She had experienced bohemian life in Paris and an unhappy marriage before she wrote the first of the brilliant *Alberte* trilogy (1926–39). These have been translated as *Alberta and Jacob* (1962), *Alberta and Freedom* (1965) and *Alberta Alone* (1965). They are autobiographical but the author shifted chronology and used other devices in order to gain her remarkable, but never unsympathetic, detachment. As a portrait of an intellectual woman, by a woman, the *Alberte* series is unique; Cora Sandel is as complex as, but less limited than, Virginia Woolf (q.v.). *Kranes konditori* (1945; tr. *Krane's Café*, 1968), which was a huge success in Helge Krog's dramatized version, is another study of a woman—and, incidentally, one of the most memorable and funny of all exposés of small-town hypocrisy and male pretensions. Yet, brilliantly penetrative as she is, Cora Sandel is never cold; her eye seems anything but obsidian. There is much more by this brilliant writer to translate, including many short stories; the collected works of 1950–1 run to six volumes. Her strength lies in her ability to convey, without stridency, and in great depth, the predicament of sensitive women living in a man's world. Her style is lucid and suggestive.

Santayana, George (ps. Jorge Ruis de Santayana y Burrais) (1863–1952) Spanish (though he came to America at the age of nine, wrote in English, and is reasonably thought of as 'American', he significantly retained his native citizenship) philosopher, literary critic, novelist. Santayana is one of the most interesting thinkers of the century: a man whose seminality is only gradually coming to be recognized. His thinking is so complex, his scope so wide, that here it is possible only to draw attention to its importance. He has been widely misunderstood. Of Latin and Catholic (though, *pace* some of his interpreters, he was not Christian: he is buried in unconsecrated ground at his own request) temperament, he saw the limitations of 'philosophy' and consequently he extended them. He tries to reconcile scepticism with a sort of ontology, realism with idealism, conservatism with radicalism (to which he was by constitution antipathetic). He has huge intelligence, and because he is trying to show that (Platonic) essences both do and do not exist—and trying to show it philosophically, since he studied the subject of philosophy under William James (q.v.) and Royce, and then taught it at Harvard for many years—he gets into serious *philosophical* trouble. But he reflects human, not merely academic, uncertainties. He and R. W. Collingwood have the best literary styles of the philosophers of the century. In his prolific work may be found embedded invaluable discussions of most of the important literary-critical concepts of the age, though not often in the terminology of literary criticism. He was a failed though respectable poet (*Poems,* 1922), and he knew it: his life's work is in fact a substitute for his failure to find a poetic language. Thus, religious dogma is not 'truth' but poetry and myth. His novel *The Last Puritan* (1935), which unaccountably became a best-seller—to the extent of actually heading the lists—is an excellent and tragic study of the puritan and the hedonistic temperaments against the background of the developing war situation in the first years of this century. *Lucifer* (1899 rev. 1924) is a play interesting to read. Like Collingwood, though differently, Santayana is a highly critical realist. 'For good or ill I am an ignorant man, almost a poet, and I can only spread a feast of what everyone knows.' The essential philosophical works are *The Life of Reason* (1905–6), *Scepticism and Animal Faith* (1923) and *The Realm of Being* (1927–40). *Works* (1936–7); *Selected Letters* (1955); *Critical Writings* (1969); *The Genteel Tradition* (1969). Santayana left America in 1912, lived in England and Europe and spent his old age (including the war years) as a guest in a convent in Rome.

Sargeson, Frank (1903) Novelist, short-story writer, playwright, Sargeson occupies the same position in New Zealand literature that Patrick White (q.v.) does in Australian: though his scope and depth nowhere match those of White, he is of international stature and, less powerful, he has exercised a more salutary influence on his younger contemporaries. Like White, too, he is the exposer and evaluator of the New Zealand bourgeois scene, which is less bumptious and brash than that of Australia, but more offensively genteel. He is versatile, witty; and, for a lyricism which he perhaps feels strongly but is unable to express uninhibitedly, he has substituted a *polisson* element: a sense of identification with the rough drop-out, crook, outcast. Thus many of his excellent stories (*Collected Stories,* 1964) are narrated by non-literates, who thus recreate an authentic, unbookish, vernacular that sharply challenges the politeness of the respectable. *I Saw in My Dream* (1949) traces the successful rebellion of a son against his bourgeois parents. *Memoirs of a Peon* (1965), a more picaresque novel, resolves the problem created by the rather curious negativeness of the rebel of *I Saw in My Dream,* and is a subtler work than critics have seen: the defeat of John Newhouse (i.e. Giovanni Casanova) in his battle to acquire women and affluence in the New Zealand of the Depression (this bleak background is superbly evoked) lies as much in his disturbed sexuality as in other aspects of his character. *The Hangover* (1967) treats vividly, and with increasing sureness of technique, of the problems of adolescence. Sargeson has developed consistently, and is a writer of unusual independence and integrity.

Saroyan, William (1908) American fiction writer, playwright. Almost all that this author, born in California of Armenian parents, has written fills one with unease. Sentimentality and fantasy jostle with an exuberant vitality and *élan* in his earlier stories, novels and plays. He is an over-excited writer who could have been much better if he had practised some kind of control. His best collection of stories is his first, *The Daring Young Man on the Flying Trapeze* (1934); later collections are less and less consistent—the best is the semi-autobiographical *My Name is Aram* (1940). The play *The Time of Your Life* (1939) is genuinely affirmatory, but is weakened by its lack of depth. Later work (e.g. the novel *One Day in the Afternoon of the World,* 1964) is marred by an over-obtrusive, unearned bitterness. Saroyan has only one source of creative energy: his vigour, humanity and love of life. He is aware of evil but has increasingly confused it with personal disappointments. His work thus lacks tension. But he has written one powerful little masterpiece: the one-act play *Hello Out There* (1949), about the lynching of a tramp.

Sarraute, Nathalie (1902) French novelist, playwright, critic. She was born in Russia of Russian-Jewish parents; until 1939 she practised at the bar in Paris. Regarded, with justice, as a precursor of the *nouveau roman* (*see* Robbe-Grillet), she is superior to all the more rigorous practitioners of this abstract concept because her writing is motivated less by philosophical than by psychological considerations. None the less, she became famous through these novelists and she regards herself as one of them. *Tropismes* (1939 rev. 1957; tr. 1964 as

Tropisms and the Age of Suspicion—the latter, critical essays, *L'Ère du soupçon,* had appeared in 1956), short, acute sketches demonstrating the disturbing gap between the rich, pre-verbal motivations of middle-class people and their ritualistically banal behaviour and speech, at first passed unnoticed. *Portrait d' un inconnu* (1948; tr. *Portrait of a Man Unknown,* 1959) also failed, but Sartre (q.v.) wrote a preface to it in which he gave it some sovereignty in the contemporary process that he rightly described as 'the novel reflecting upon itself'. By 1959, after *Martereau* (1953; tr. 1964) and *Le Planétarium* (1959; tr. *The Planetarium,* 1964), she had gained an international reputation. *Les Fruits d' or* (1963; tr. *The Golden Fruits,* 1964) and two further novels have followed. *Tropismes* provides the clue to her method and to her originality. Tropisms are involuntary turning, curving movements of organisms (or parts of them) induced automatically or by stimulation. Such movements in human beings provide the matrices of her fiction; she boldly goes behind, so to say, stream-of-consciousness (*see* Bergson) to a 'primitive', pre-verbal level. It is mainly Kafka (q.v.) who provided her with the precedent for keying such movements with *terror;* Ivy Compton-Burnett (q.v.) supplied (or reinforced) the consistent preoccupation with *enslavement. Portrait d' un inconnu,* a kind of modernist gloss on Balzac's *Eugénie Grandet,* presents an anonymous narrator creating himself through his observations of the relationship between a miser and his spinster daughter: the novelist inventing the novel—but at the same time providing precious insights into the depths of the mind. In *Martereau* the narrator is related to the action he is describing and the effect is even more powerful. Each of Nathalie Sarraute's novels is in some subtle manner related to the authors she regards as most important to her: Proust (q.v.), Dostoievski and Joyce (q.v.), as well as Kafka. In *Entre la Vie et la Mort* (1968), *Between Life and Death,* she describes how tropisms operate in the life of a writer. Her self-appraisal is inclined to be severely theoretical and conceited—though it is always shrewdly intelligent—partly because for too many years she was ignored. It tends to make her work, which does after all explore a level below that of self-awareness, seem less accessible than it is, and may cause us to underestimate her comic gifts. Although she ostensibly desires the obliteration of 'story', it is—ironically (cf. Simon)—the fact that her fiction does in its unique way preserve a story element that makes it so accessible. If, as she has complained, she is underestimated in Britain and America then this is at least partially because her theories, and the theorizings about her, are better known than her actual work. *Le Silence* and *Le Mensonge* (plays published in one volume in 1966) are translated into English as *The Silence* and *The Lie* (1969). *Vous les entendez?* (1972; tr. *Do You Hear Them?*, 1974) is a novel.

Sartre, Jean-Paul (1905) French novelist, playwright, philosopher, editor (*Les Temps Modernes*), essayist, memoirist, playwright, political activist. Refused Nobel Prize 1964. One of the most important and seminal writers of the century, he has for some years abandoned creative writing, which is a loss to world literature–he has been a major novelist and a playwright of great distinction. His influence, especially as philosopher, has been and still is enormous. Existentialism is by now a term as vague as 'romantic': we can see proto-existentialist attitudes in a huge range of past literature and philosophy. This attitude, however, was first clearly crystallized by Sartre and his friends (who diverged in their views) just after the Second World War. The only chief features of the existentialist tendency that are reasonably safe to enumerate (and even these have been disputed) may be stated as follows: hostility to abstract theory in favour of concrete experience; preference for a phenomenological viewpoint over a mathematical or theoretical one; general contempt for most academic philosophers (while the British school ignores it as irrelevant, it ignores the British school–which it has hardly bothered to examine, and which, one is bound to add, it should examine); *existence* precedes *essence*–it is anti-Platonic in spirit and if its roots are in ancient philosophy at all then they are in pre-Socratic thought; it is either violently atheistic (Sartre) or profoundly religious (Gabriel Marcel, who coined the word)–but it is in any case always underpinned by a passion for the practical that is distinctly non-secular. Ancestors of modern existentialism, in its various forms, include Augustine, Pascal, Nietzsche, Kierkegaard, Bergson (q.v.), Husserl, Bachelard (q.v.) and Heidegger. *Writers* rather than what we ordinarily think of as philosophers are also ancestors: *experience* and its qualities precede *thought*, which is anyway seen–and rightly–as a consequence of experience. Obviously most serious British writers will sympathize with this continental movement and will despise modern British philosophers for their insularity and their barren, nit-picking positivism. Sartre might have gone to Unamuno (q.v.) or Ortega y Gasset (q.v.) for his inspiration: the latter's remark that 'I am myself plus my circumstances' sums up one of the cardinal tenets of all modern existentialism. But, as a young philosopher, he went to Germany and to Husserl and Heidegger. Husserl's phenomenology 'concretized' consciousness; the imaginary situation is as vital, for him, as the 'real' one (cf. Bergson); but consciousness is basically intentionalist. Sartre rejected much of Husserl's later (philosophically idealistic) conclusions, but–influenced by Bachelard–he stuck with his 'intuitions' of the 'meaning' of 'things': *we are what we prefer*. From Heidegger (mainly)–who, ironically, rejected his own master Husserl as a Jew and wholeheartedly accepted Nazism–Sartre took the complementary notions that man *is* his existence and that he is perpetually haunted by *anxiety*. For Sartre man's presence on earth is irrational; he must therefore commit himself to freedom. As a philosopher he is thus in a trap: his phenomenological *description* of man's plight, desperately alone and desperately pledged to destroy the freedom of his neighbours, is excellent (*L'Être et la néant*, 1943, tr. *Being and Nothingness*, 1957, his chief philosophical work, is really as much autobiography as brilliant metaphysics); his *description* of people's attempts to free themselves from their condition is vivid and magnificently penetrative, but his philosophical *prescription* is unconvincing because his own philosophy rejects its self-styledly 'humanist' motives. Sartre's world is not godless–as he, without evidence and without proper regard to a constructively sceptical attitude, insists–it is in fact a world awaiting a God. And that God has always been Marx (one must acquit this most modest and principled of men, as saintly as Augustine himself, of ever imagining that it could be himself). Sartre, however, has always refused to join the communist party and has become progressively disillusioned with practical 'Marxism'. In the enormous and unfinished *Critique de la raison dialectique,* preceded by *Question de méthode* (1960; tr. *The Problem of Method,* 1964), he attempts to create a 'humanist' Marx (for him 'existentialism is a humanism'); but he abandons this to write another massive, and also unfinished, work on Flaubert's (his own?) sexual bad faith. . . . His philosophy is essential reading because it is a splendid demonstration, by a nakedly honest man, of the fact that even the person utterly convinced, intellectually, of the contingency of existence cannot live without hope: his unsuccessful attempt to create a system of freedom without recourse to anything but the closed, subjective world of consciousness, is undoubtedly as heroic as it is intelligent. But its best demonstration of all is in his fiction (and, to a lesser extent, drama). Here he specifically shows us *how* we evade our responsibility (a sense that we possess which his philosophy cannot, of course, convincingly explain); here he demonstrates that the 'nothingness' we feel can express itself in our actuality. French fiction had for some time concentrated on such themes (e.g. Malraux, q.v.); but Sartre's project in his unfinished trilogy *Les Chemins de la liberté,* 1945–9 (*L'Age de raison,* 1945, tr. *The Age of Reason,* 1947; *Le Sursis,* 1945, tr. *The Reprieve,* 1947; *La Mort dans l'âme,* 1949, tr. *Iron in the Soul,* 1950—in USA *Troubled Sleep,* 1951) is to delineate precisely the psychological processes of various kinds of bad faith, and those of the vain attempt to make the 'leap' into, the choice of, 'authenticity'. Sartre himself has never claimed 'authenticity': we are not confronted, by him, with any 'authentic' group. In Sartre himself, in fact, we are confronted by despair: a shifting from one project to another, an abandonment of imagination. But of *les salauds,* the 'dirty swine', the bourgeois gang, we obtain an invaluable account. In *La Nausée* (1938; tr. *Nausea,* 1965) Sartre had written his own spiritual autobiography: set in 'Filthville' (Bouville: the Rouen where he worked as teacher at a *lycée*), it agonizedly dwells on the disparity between the phenomenological, 'intentionalist' consciousness—searching for truth anywhere—and the absurdly apparent solidity of the actual world. We may say, with Bachelard in mind, that Roquentin, Sartre's projection of himself in the novel, cannot discover 'what he prefers'—and so prefers *nausea,* the extremest possible form of anxiety. The stories in *Le Mur* (1939; tr. *Intimacy,* 1956) study similar cases. The trilogy, *Les Chemins de la liberté,* a projected tetralogy (for the hero, Mathieu-Sartre, is *not,* as a published fragment of the last book has indicated, killed at the end of the third of the trilogy), is based squarely on the 'simultaneous' technique of Dos Passos (q.v.), whom Sartre overrated—but to the importance of whose technique his own achievement bears ample witness. Céline (q.v.), too, was an important influence. Since Sartre's philosophy is so famous (or infamous), it is perhaps best to recommend this as a great realist novel, a tale of various different kinds of people's lives as the Second World War approaches: it has compassion; its sense of the approaching disaster is epic; its characters are as convincing as those of any novelist of the century; its sense of atmosphere, its versatility and its scope are unique. Descartes' 'I think therefore I am' is here transformed: to hell with 'I think', to hell with 'therefore': 'I am, therefore it is hell'. But Sartre has the great novelist's capacity to see into others' 'amness'. We may relate the philosophy to his fiction as we will, but the latter, essentially independent, is what really matters: it challenges comparison with the best. All it lacks is humour; but perhaps the late thirties in which it is set also lacked humour. . . . As playwright Sartre is extremely skilful, effective and exciting. In his plays he frequently tries to demonstrate how a reified Marxism might enable men to attain authenticity; in fact he demonstrates the difficulties into which his (and our) specifically political thinking leads. . . . However, the early *Huis clos* (1945; tr. *In Camera,* 1946), set in an eternal hell, gives a bleaker view which is perhaps nearer to that of his own temperament. Even the overtly political plays (especially the dramatically very fine *Les Mains sales,* 1948; tr. *Crime Passionnel,* 1949) tend to demonstrate his disbelief in his own increasingly involute political commitments. But his predicament–for all his shifts and complexities, and his disappointing abandonment of creative writing–is sufficiently near to our own to make him a figure of almost endless fascination and importance. His autobiographical and critical work (e.g. *Situations,* 1947–71; some tr.; *Les Mots,* 1964; tr. *The Words,* 1964) fully exhibits his qualities.

Sassoon, Siegfried (1886–1967) English poet, autobiographer, critic. Sassoon was a strange mixture, 'twisted from birth' says his close friend and then enemy (but they were officially reconciled before Sassoon died) Robert Graves (q.v.): he is by no means a major writer but he is an important and fascinating one. He had enthusiasms (or their opposite) which often turned into lurid obsessions. There is indeed a crippled quality about almost all his writings: he was honest, but his work as a whole lacks the integrity and consistency of the dedicated poet. He was until comparatively late in life a devoted 'underworld', 'decadent' homosexual (young men dancing naked in moonlight to piano music). This decadent side of his nature was doubtless reinforced by his association, before the First World War, with such Edwardian *littérateurs* as Gosse. At this time, having left Cambridge without a degree, he led a respectable life as a country gentleman. He had excellent aristocratic connections through his mother, who had left her Jewish husband and had brought him up as gentry. Possibly his strange and neurotic personality and its written expressions were in part a reaction against his having been deprived of both paternal influence and the Jewishness he knew he had inherited. There are odd hints of real poetry in his gentlemanly pre-war verse (e.g. in *Poems,* 1906; the extraordinary 'parody' of Masefield's q.v., *The Everlasting Mercy, The Daffodil Murderer*, 1913). But it was his experiences in the war which produced the vast majority of his best poetry. He joined up in 1914, was twice wounded, and was awarded the MC. He then returned home determined to make a protest by refusing to serve. Graves (mainly) dissuaded him and he was sent to Craiglockhart; discharged from there, he went back to the war. The war poems, though purely war poems, satisfactorily canalized for the first and only time in his life his capacity for fury: concentrated, laconic, laceratingly ironic, they describe the horrors of the 1914–18 trench warfare and the fearsome, cruel complacency of the staff officers and the awfulness of the silly padres. Tersely enraged though they are, they glow with humanity and indignation. Thereafter Sassoon, after an involvement with Labour politics, devoted himself once more to the pursuit of the life of a country gentleman. His *Memoirs of an Infantry Officer* (1930) is the best of his prose, although it is too literary to rival Graves's *Good-Bye to All That*. His other autobiographical prose—he began with the anonymous *Memoirs of a Fox-Hunting Man* (1928; the 1929 American edition gave the author's name); the other main books may be found in *The Complete Memoirs of George Sherston* (1937, continuing the *Memoirs of a Fox-Hunting Man*), in *The Weald of Youth* (1942) and *Siegfried's Journey* (1945)—has been much praised. It certainly contains much to edify readers who embrace the values of 'country gentlemen', but it is evasive and, in essence, a fantasy-photograph. Sassoon, who continued to issue poor verse, ended as an enfeebled convert to Roman Catholicism. *Collected Poems* (1961).

Schwartz, Delmore (1913–66) American (Brooklyn Jewish) poet, editor (*Partisan Review*, 1943–55), fiction writer, critic, teacher, playwright, translator. His life and work are summed up by some lines from an early poem (in his first book, *In Dreams Begin Responsibilities*, 1938): 'Now I must betray myself. . . . None may wear masks or enigmatic clothes,/ For weakness blinds the wounded face enough./ In this sense, see my shocking nakedness.' He ended in ill-health and despair. His poetry is mostly spoiled by its very nakedness: he displays sentimentalities and uncontrolled guilt that do not, in that form, belong in poems. One can say only that this is an appealing poetry (*Summer Knowledge: New and Selected Poems 1938–1958*, 1959), often skilful, and penetrated by vivid lines and passages in which, movingly,

Schwartz's despair turns into an actual, achieved, poetry. His sensitive stories (*The World is a Wedding*, 1948) of Jews seeking self-fulfilment or false substitutes for it are, on the other hand, successful. In poetry he could not deal with the problem of his own utterance: a kind of honesty about neurosis, guilt and oversensitivity crippled the voice which wished to be nakedly lyrical. His translation of Rimbaud's *A Season in Hell* (1939) is one of the most interesting (cf. Fowlie, Varèse, Rhodes, Paschal). As critic (*Selected Essays*, 1970) he is against American over-academicism, but not deliberately philistine in the Black Mountain (*see* Dewey) tradition. His virtual mental collapse, as gifted man and as intelligent urban American Jew, has a poignant significance. 'He had followers but they could not find him;/ friends but they could not find him. He hid his gift/ in the centre of Manhattan/ . . . in cheap hotels,/ so disturbed on the street friends avoided him. . . . He painfully removed/ himself from the ordinary contacts/ and shook with resentment'; he 'undermined// his closest loves with merciless suspicion'; 'He was out of his mind for years,/ in police station & Bellevue'; 'His work downhill, I don't conceal from you,/ ran and ran out': Berryman's (q.v.) elegy for him (VI of *Dream Songs*) is bad poetry but memorable and instructive prose.

Seferis, George (ps. George Seferiades) (1900–71) Greek poet, translator, critic. Nobel Prize 1963. He was born in Smyrna and was by profession a diplomat (in London in the mid-fifties as counsellor and as ambassador 1957–62). Though disenchanted with Greek post-war politics, he spoke out against the Colonels and soon afterwards died in hospital. His first volume, *Strophe* (1931), an ironic pun on 'stanza' and 'turning point', initiated the modern movement in Greek poetry: a change from the stilted, ornamental, 'poetical' work of the past. He was influenced by the French symbolists and by Eliot (q.v.), whose *The Waste Land* he translated; but the example set by his depressed, gloomy, objurgative contemporary Kostas Karyotakis (1896–1928) should not be forgotten. Seferis from the first decided (as he later emphasized) to be 'simple'. What he really (tactfully) meant was that he was in revolt against the ponderous traditionalist poetry of even such as Sikelianos whom he admired. He did not, as other poets a little younger did, turn to surrealism (*see* Breton). He instead produced a hermetic kind of poetry, in which the ancient Greek experience might be absorbed into a modernist-type poetry. He was perhaps sincere; but his poetry is seldom without pretension, because, despite his concentration on Greek themes, he always seemed to look towards Stockholm —he wanted to be considered as *the* modern Greek who can incorporate ancient themes into a fashionably European idiom. He thus calculatedly adapted Eliot's waste-land notion to his own Greek predicament and he had the skill to make it look good. Sometimes it is. But, studying the bilingual *Collected Poems 1924–1955* (tr. 1969)—see also *Three Secret Poems* (tr. 1969) and the excellent bilingual Italian versions, *Poesie* (1963)—one is continually struck both by his modishness and his desire to be applauded as a perfect contemporary employer of classical 'purity'. He is an exceedingly calculating poet. And thus his most unpopular (second) poem, *I Sterna* (1932), often dismissed as impenetrable, is in certain respects his best. Here anyway he was not looking outwards: it is a poem which has odd affinities with the Italian 'hermetic' poetry of that time (e.g. Ungaretti, q.v., Quasimodo, q.v.): 'Here, in the earth, a cistern's rooted:/ a secret swelling water-nest/Its roof hears steps; its heart/defies the stars. Each day/ripens, opens, shuts —it is oblivious.' At the end, falsely accused by the Colonels of having gained his Nobel Prize by betraying his country's interests, he found himself again more surely: the 'secret poems' reach linguistic heights not achieved for almost forty years—as in such lines as 'You said years ago:/"I'm a question of light at heart". . . .' Generally, though, Seferis is a minor whose use of free verse (dating from his third collection, 1935) is, however, major in terms of technique. Despite his admirable achievement in breaking out of the stifling pseudo-classical traditionalism into which he grew up, he failed to purge himself of a besetting modern Greek sin—he imagined himself to be potentially capable of recapturing the glories of the classical age. Demetrius Antoniou (1906), a sea-captain by profession (and Seferis's friend), is a more rewarding poet, but he is more modest in intention—and considerably less widely translated.

Selby, Hubert (1926) American novelist. *Last Exit to Brooklyn* (1964) is uniquely revelatory about Brooklyn homosexuals and transvestites. It was the subject of a ridiculous obscenity trial in London; the philistine verdict was reversed on appeal. Selby achieves a form of surrealism (*see* Breton) in a most effective and original manner: he studies external and internal reality and strictly records it. *The Room* (1971), written in a (for once wholly effective) super-realist stream-of-consciousness (*see* Bergson) style, describes the fantasies of a tubercular madman who has been casually picked up by two police officers and charged with (in English legal terminology) 'loitering with intent'. It is a searing document, horribly exact. Selby is certainly a Calvinist in spirit if not in fact: the horrors and hopelessness and helplessness he so powerfully describes recall the terrible decree of Calvin's God: some shall be damned. Only in Selby *everyone* is damned: there are no elect. His honesty is as impressive as it is bleak.

Senghor, Léopold Sédar (1906) Senegalese (Serere) poet and essayist writing in French (in which he is more fluent than in his native Wolof); President of Senegal since 1960. Césaire (q.v.) first coined the term *négritude* in print but it is Senghor who is more associated with the concept in the public mind—and who has, in fact, changed it as he has changed from Catholic socialist to (failed) Catholic Teilhardist and advocate of a (Senghor-guided) Federation of self-governing African countries. Césaire's *négritude* is revolutionary, arising from his deprived Caribbean background and aggressive temperament; Senghor's is increasingly political and 'Africanist', and as he has grown older and has scrupulously increased his power over his (economically poor) country he has become more pompous, regal and rhetorical—but his poetry is important, his critique of Marxism and especially of its application to African affairs, is acute and just, and he must be one of the few bigtime politicians in today's world not only to retain a measure of humanity but also to be a possibly major poet. In this he is unique—and furthermore, in his dramatic poem 'Chaka', which was published in *Éthiopiques* (1956), and which is based on Mofolo's famous novel, he has at least tried to face his problem of combining in one man the role of poet and politician: his Chaka dies as poet but is reinstated in death. It is unfortunate, though hardly surprising, that this is not one of his most successful poems; that he should have written it at all is remarkable. His non-Marxist position is not at all understood by the neo-Marxists but they should read his essays on politics, some of which are in *Poetry and Prose* (tr. 1965). His grandiose ideas about federation apart, Senghor is important for the way he has developed *négritude* into (virtually) 'the sum total of the African's cultural values' as well as for his poetry. He has always been a reconciler and if he likes power then his liking for it is in sharp contrast to that of most other dictators or semi-dictators. Senghor is above all a syncretist, wishing to see all differences—particularly, in Senegal, those of the majority religion, Islam, and Christianity—resolved. In his *négritude* the African must learn from the white man—who must also, however, learn to learn from him his directness and his 'co-operation . . . *con-spiracy,* from centre to centre, of hearts'. This is 'reformed *négritude*'; naturally enough, during Senghor's early years as a student in Paris he tended to concentrate on the African virtues more than on those of the white man—but while always sympathetic to certain aspects of Marxism (he well understands his old friend Césaire), he was from the beginning repelled by others. Senghor, with Damas and Césaire, was the pioneer of modern African poetry and his anthology of it in 1948 was introduced by Sartre. His own poetry (tr. *Selected Poems,* 1964) is in a *chant* style reminiscent of Claudel (q.v.) and Saint-John Perse (q.v.); imbued with a serene rhetoric that is at the least very impressive, it combines lush sensuality, a priestly sense of high mission and much celebration of the beauty of African life. He is a positive and affirmatory poet, whose devotion to Teilhardist syncretism may blind him to certain difficulties; the question of to what extent his florid rhetorical power compensates for lack of tension in his poetry is not easy to answer but its impression does not fade in the mind. He is a paradoxical and courageous figure, unpopular amongst most African leaders—who are less far-seeing—for being a 'black Frenchman'; as thinker he is of major stature; as poet he is likely to survive.

Sexton, Anne (1928–74) American poet of the so-called 'confessionalist' school: she used her experiences of her children, her married life, her many hospitalizations for depression, to produce an anti-genteel, dramatic, extremely sensual, domestic poetry. She is a minor poet, often diffuse or trivially over-direct, but she keeps within the limits she sets herself. She began writing poetry as therapy (1957); clearly she wanted to shock herself into a sense of the reality of 'ordinary' experience (children, sex, marriage, etc.), and had faith in truth. It was a heroic project and probably she lived longer because she undertook it. Her poetry is at its very best when she refers to the intrusion into her happy world of the terrible chemistry which dragged her into suicidal depressions. And she can be magnificent: 'Men enter by force, drawn back like Jonah/ into their fleshy mothers./ A woman *is* her mother./ That's the main thing.' *To Bedlam and Part Way Back* (1960); *Love Poems* (1969); *The Death Notebooks* (1975).

Shapiro, Karl (1913) American poet, critic, editor (*Poetry Chicago*, 1950–6; *Prairie Schooner*, 1956–63), teacher. Shapiro is somewhat of an odd-man-out in American letters. He has attacked modern intellectualist poetry (in the satirical blank verse *Essay on Rime*, 1945 and in *Beyond Criticism*, 1953), but has not been much attracted by the non-academic 'schools'. He began as a self-consciously Jewish poet, exploring the predicament of the artist in a corrupt society. He is an expert prosodist but he was unhappy with the generally 'new-critical' forms in which his intelligent early poems were written (some are in the useful *Selected Poems* of 1968; more in *Poems 1940–1953*, 1953). Many of his strictures on Pound (q.v.) and Eliot (q.v.), both rabid anti-Semites, are extremely telling; his attacks on the new criticism (*see* Brooks) even more so. But Shapiro didn't want the crackerbarrel philistinism and distorted pragmatism (*see* William James) of Olson (q.v.) and instead he turned to Whitman and then to (the partly Jewish) Williams. However, some continental influences have been taken over into his later poetry, as the prose-poems of *The Bourgeois Poet* (1964) and the personal erotic frenzy of *White Haired Lover* (1968) clearly reveal. But at any of the phases following his neat, subdued beginnings, Shapiro's voice tends to get drowned in his Jewish primitivism, which finds outlet in various sorts of wildness or simply ineffectuality (he can sound like a writer of light verse). Capable of concentration (as his criticism shows), he refuses, in poetry, to concentrate. He is too intelligent to want to sound like the later Ginsberg (q.v.), but too often he comes quite near to this. He is yet another casualty in the long lists of poets who have found traditional forms inadequate. . . .

Shaw, George Bernard (1856–1950) Irish playwright, polemicist, music critic, reformer. The world would have been a duller place without Shaw, and he has a part in social and literary history. He was witty and very gifted. But he exercised little permanent influence, was gullible (e.g. on the subjects of Stalin and Mussolini), and his plays are psychologically empty—though, because they are clever and amusing, they continue to attract audiences. Shaw was a nice man, but blind to certain cruelties or the existence of certain passions because of deficiencies in feeling. His unconvincing love-letters to the actress Mrs Patrick Campbell (1952) are, alas, an index to his imaginative capacities. But he was a great journalist, splendidly humane within his limitations, and his plays, although they are never more than vehicles for ideas, are brilliant. His brilliance, however, conceals his lack of depth and his imperviousness to the poetic. *St Joan* (1923), often called his greatest play, is a farrago of 'poetical' rhetoric: talent posing as genius where it best can: in the theatre. He received the Nobel Prize in 1925. He was an immense force in his own day but prolonged discussion of him may be left to his many admirers, few of whom are serious literary critics (those who are, are stage-struck). In other words, considerations of his importance are extra-literary. *Complete Plays* (1965); *Complete Prefaces* (1965).

Shaw, Irwin (1913) Popular American fiction writer, playwright. He began quite seriously with radically inspired plays (e.g. *The Gentle People,* 1939) but with the long Second World War novel *The Young Lions* (1948) turned to intelligently superficial, well-made fiction; *The Troubled Air* (1951) is on the anti-communist witch-hunt, while *Two Weeks in Another Time* (1960) deals ambivalently with the film industry. He is, as Fiedler (q.v.) has put it, 'semi-serious'. His many stories are skilful and readable.

Sholokhov, Mikhail (1905) Russian novelist, short-story writer, opportunist. Nobel Prize 1964. His massive novel *Tikhiy Don* (1928–40; tr. *And Quiet Flows the Don, The Don Flows Home to the Sea,* 1934–40), about Cossack life between 1912 and 1922, is certainly balanced and epic in scope; even *Podnyataya Tselina* (1932–60; tr. *Virgin Soil Upturned, Harvest on the Don,* 1935–60), on the collectivization of the same people, has some vigour, and tacitly recognizes the misery caused by Stalin's policy. But did Sholokhov write *Tikhiy Don* which is, despite serious flaws, a masterpiece of fluent narrative? Solzhenitsyn (q.v.) claims that he has evidence that he did not. The truth may be that he obtained most of his material from other sources, but that he understood it and put it into shape. Many authors have done the same. Konstantin Prima's *Tikhiy Don srazaetsja* (1972), *The Quiet Don at War,* gives a fascinating account of the history of Sholokhov's book in the hands of the translators and critics.

Shute, Nevil (ps. Nevil Shute Norway) (1899–1960) English popular novelist who spent his last fifteen years in Australia. Some of his many novels reflect his experiences as an engineer. Great successes include *Pied Piper* (1942), *A Town Like Alice* (1950), *On the Beach* (1957). He is a typically middlebrow novelist of the inoffensive kind: pseudo-serious, fluent, sentimental, well-meaning. *Three of a Kind* (1962) collects three novels.

Sillitoe, Alan (1928) English novelist and short-story writer. He also writes verse. His first novel, *Saturday Night and Sunday Morning* (1958), drawing on his experiences of his Nottingham working-class background, was ill-written but effectively presented the personality of a confused, selfish and violent young factory worker. But Sillitoe's best work has been done in the short story (e.g. *The Loneliness of the Long Distance Runner*, 1959; *The Ragman's Daughter*, 1963; *Guzman Go Home*, 1968), in which form he is usually lyrical and straightforward and can sometimes present anguished predicaments with exquisite precision and delicacy. His later novels have been disastrously poor; what is good in them—such as the presentation of certain highly eccentric characters—is not integrated into their structure, which is distorted by an immature and obstinately unworked-out hatred of authority in any shape or form. Sillitoe has an original and subtle imagination but, it seems, too little intelligence. The keys to his intellectual immaturity may be found in his verse, which is resolutely prosaic, and in his attempt to write an eighteenth-century picaresque novel in a contemporary setting, *A Start in Life* (1970). *The Death of William Posters* (1964) and its sequels attempt to examine the motives of a man who 'walks out', as Gauguin did—but from a working-class and not a bourgeois background—and though the writing is clumsy, it contains several fascinating concepts which show, and this is confirmed by the best stories, that in this novelist there is a truly powerful one struggling courageously to come out. *A Tree on Fire* (1967). *Trees in Nihilon* (1971).

Silone, Ignazio (ps. Secondo Tranquilli) (1900) Italian writer. Silone has had an international reputation as a novelist but his fellow-countrymen do not regard his imaginative achievements as high; their instincts are correct. *Fontamara* (in German 1930; in Italian 1947; in English 1934) is crude, and later novels more so. However, he has gained respect for his courage and sincerity as a communist, and, since the thirties, quasi-Christian socialist.

Simenon, Georges (ps. Georges Sim) (1903) Belgian novelist; the most distinguished psychological crime novelist of his age–though he has not invariably dealt with crime. He has been one of the most prolific and fast-writing authors of his day; he now states that he has stopped writing owing to ill-health (the worst symptoms of which have been brought on by the act of writing). He began as a hack, then created the famous Inspector Maigret–whom he dropped for a while, but then resurrected. He is one of the very few crime writers to have written true novels. He is a masterly evoker of atmosphere and his capacity to reveal motive without making moral judgments is unequalled within his genre. He is a favourite of almost every major writer, from Gide (q.v.), through Ford (q.v.), to Graves (q.v.). Maigret, unlike any other stock detective, works by soaking himself in the psychological atmosphere of the case in which he is engaged. The later books are on the whole less powerful, although Simenon's professionalism never deserts him. Among his masterpieces are *La Neige était sale* (1948; tr. *The Stain on the Snow,* 1953) and *Pedigree* (1948; tr. 1965), which is set in his native Liège. It has been said that his books will not survive, but at least a dozen will.

Simon, Claude (1913) French novelist, playwright, essayist. The inclusion of Simon in the ranks of the practitioners of the *nouveau roman* (*see* Robbe-Grillet) questions the ultimate usefulness of the category, since although his fiction has certain features in common with the 'new' novelists, it owes most to Proust (q.v.), Conrad (q.v.), Joyce (q.v.) and Faulkner (q.v.), and in any case his first novel, *Le Tricheur* (1946), *Trickster,* was written in 1941, long before the advent of the school, and before Nathalie Sarraute (q.v.) had gained any attention. It is more appropriate to see him as modernist refiner and modifier of naturalism (*see* Zola): for him, it seems–though his sense of his characters' human identities works against the conviction–entropy replaces determinism. He first wanted to be a painter and his idol was (and is) Cézanne, who, proto-cubist, attempted to discover the phenomenological meaning of objects: not their Platonic essence, but their existence in the mind as separated from their quotidian, mundane, 'factual' existence. But Simon has other than philosophically phenomenological concerns. His quest is to abolish time (hence his dedication to painting) and to deny 'story', but actually he is haunted by the past-in-the-present (cf. Proust), is highly susceptible to the sensual pleasures of nature, and is obsessed with the very 'story', causal sequence of events, that he seeks to obliterate. There are, after all, stories, even if only in the sense that we tell them, and Simon's novels are always haunted by the ghost of a story. In the best novels the results are impressive: the demonstration of a modern man's effort to seek an artistically valid (even 'cubist', *see* Reverdy) escape from an existence seen as simultaneously threatening to true self-experience and as full of human nobility and helpless effort. His sentences, virtually devoid of punctuation, are often lyrical: he tries to see all people as Faulkner saw Benjy, the idiot; this project fulfils his pessimistic intentions, but also enables him to show non-idiots as plunged into the stream of their own consciousness. Merleau-Ponty said of Simon's fiction that what is felt in it has got to be made to talk. This is an impossible task, yet it is the goal of literature: to match the richness of inner experience with words. Simon has not always been communicative, but he is worth persevering with—and he is fervent and massively sincere. The two most important novels are *Le Vent* (1957; tr. *The Wind*, 1959) and *La Route des Flandres* (1960; tr. *The Flanders Road*, 1962). The first, which has a subject that would have delighted a naturalist—a man cannot succeed at anything, and some vines he has inherited are destroyed by the winds—has as much of a 'story' as the second, which combines the events of 1940 with a variation on the familiar theme of the wife who believes that her husband has died in war and has married again. The non-realist treatment is counterpointed with the possibly parodically 'realist' material: wind or rain destroy all, minds are in wild flux, the explicit is rejected (Simon is an exponent of stream-of-consciousness, *see* Bergson, *par excellence*), time is mixed. Yet it is not so difficult as it seems. Take such a French film as Resnais's *Stavisky* (1974)—his best—and persevere with its insistence on being itself (a film), with its time-mixes and abrupt flashes back and forth, and we can be helped to understand and follow Simon, who is a novelist of great importance. *L'Herbe* (1958; tr. *The Grass*, 1961); *Le Palace* (1964; tr. *The Palace*, 1964); *Histoire* (1967; tr. *Histoire*, 1969); *La Bataille de Pharsale* (1969; tr. *The Battle of Pharsalus*, 1971).

Simpson, Louis (1923) American poet, critic, anthologist, scholar, teacher. He was born in Jamaica and did not obtain American citizenship (in Germany) until the end of the war, in which he fought. He began (*The Arrivistes*, 1949; *Good News of Death*, 1955; *A Dream of*

Governors, 1959) as an over-literary but immensely promising and original poet, then discovered his own voice in a most impressive manner (mainly in *At the End of the Open Road,* 1963)–and then lost his way again as he tried to move too drastically over to the tradition of Walt Whitman (*Adventures of the Letter I,* 1971). *Selected Poems* (1965) is usefully representative. He has drawn on his Jamaican childhood, on the war (notably), and on all of the poets who interest him: chiefly, perhaps, Eliot, Marvell, Whitman. A strong influence on him may have been Jarrell (q.v.). (Mark Van Doren was an influential teacher.) He writes two sorts of poem: lyrics of love or war, or based in personal experience, and longer semi-narrative or dramatic pieces, which are uniformly less successful. He is at his considerable best in such a powerful lyric as 'My Father in the Night Commanding No', in which his own style is perfectly integrated. Lately Simpson has become uncertain of his direction; he works in freer forms, but cannot seem to discover the kind of internal discipline that would suit him. The penetrative intelligence is still there, but his satire has become somewhat feeble and there is a rhythmical slackness which helps blunt even the best of the poems. Still, there is no knowing what Simpson will do next; and he has produced a body of work that invites comparison with most of his post-war English-language contemporaries. His critical study of *James Hogg* (1962) is excellent. *Riverside Drive* (1962) is a novel.

Sinclair, Upton (1878–1968) American polemicist, reformer, novelist, miscellaneous writer, socialist. For this indefatigable Utopian, of fierce energy and finely simple and untormented faith in socialism, the novel was simply a weapon. He is a good journalist; but his fiction lacks psychological depth or humour. He was one of the founders of Helicon Hall, an early cooperative for leftist writers which ended when it burned down. He took part (unsuccessfully) in political campaigns. *The Jungle* (1906) is, however, an exceedingly vivid portrait of the horrible conditions in Chicago meat-packing factories, and it led to reform. He wrote more than 100 books; most famous is the eleven-volume Lanny Budd series, *World's End* (1940–53), a history of the post-1918 world seen as through the eyes of the unbelievably omniscient trouble-shooter Lanny Budd. This is, again, journalism. Sinclair was an admirable man but his achievement is hardly literary. *Autobiography* (1962).

Singer, Isaac Bashevis (1904) Polish-Jewish fiction writer in Yiddish who emigrated to America in 1935. Since then he has earned his living as a journalist on *Jewish Daily Forward:* he signed his journalism as 'Isaac Warshausky' and his creative work as 'Isaac Bashevis'. His first novel, *The Family Moskat,* did not appear in English form until 1950 (I give details of English translations only), since when his reputation has steadily grown. (An abridged early version of the novel *Satan in Goray,* 1955, appeared in an English anthology in 1938 but attracted no attention.) His translators include Saul Bellow (q.v.), Jacob Sloan and himself (as collaborator). Both his brother and sister were novelists; Israel Joshua Singer (1893–1944) was for long better known than Isaac for his own superb novel in Yiddish, *Di brider Ashkenazi* (1936; tr. *The Brothers Ashkenazi,* 1936). Singer himself began writing in Hebrew, but soon turned to Yiddish. In this language he is unsurpassed as a fiction writer. Singer's chief subject is the now irrecoverable world of Polish Jewry between the seventeenth and the twentieth centuries, but his approach to his material is that of a sophisticated New Yorker. He is devoted to Yiddish, but feels that its future is 'very black'. His sense of its rapidly disappearing world irradiates his work, as nostalgia and as (however ironically modified) lyrical plea. Since Singer became popular not only with good non-Jewish or non-Yiddish-speaking critics, but with pseudo-sophisticated American readers, many Jewish (and particularly Yiddish-oriented) critics have become increasingly infuriated with him and accuse him of pandering to non-Jewish tastes and of being indifferent to social factors. Beyond pointing out that he really is devoted to Yiddish (he thinks forty per cent of the value of his books is lost even in the translations made under his guidance), and that his predicament is unenviable, it is difficult to comment on their strictures: most readers must judge him as they find him: in English translation. Here, and especially in the realm of the short story, he is a major writer: we do not feel that he panders to our tastes but that, on the contrary, he enriches both our knowledge and our imaginations. The tension in his work is between the old and the new. He is a rabbi at heart, but he is a realist and while he knows of this conflict, he will not entirely give up his sense of the poetry of the old, even though he knows this involves social obscurantism. His imagination is anchored to the *shetl,* to the ghetto-life of old Poland; his point of view is, in Jewish terms, that of the 'Enlightenment'. He knows that the *shetl* was socially unenlightened–unacceptable–but remembers its desperate and often joyous coherence. Beyond implying the relevance of Yiddish, his work has little 'message'. He describes his vanished people, driven by or in fear of demons, in realist modes. *The Family Moskat* deals with Warsaw Jewry between 1911 and 1939; *The Magician of Lublin* (1960), the best of his novels, uncannily portrays modern man, torn between hedonism and guilt, absurdism and belief, in the nineteenth-century figure of Yasha Mazur. Other novels include *The Slave* (1962) and *The Manor* (1967). But it is as short-story writer that Singer excels. Under the guise of re-creating the *shetl* (though some stories have modern and American settings), and thus able to use the fantastic, the erotic, the perverse, the superstitious, the magical, the bizarre, the violent, Singer in these reflects, in realistic form ('one Kafka in a century is enough'), our own inner disorders and, perhaps, some of the undiscovered coherence of our dreams. His art is thus as expressionist (*see* Stadler) as it is realistic–in fact, given the impossibility of reconstruction of the past, it is predominantly expressionist. The stories are in *Gimpel the Fool* (1957), *The Spinoza of Market Street* (1961), *Short Friday* (1964), *The Séance* (1968) and *A Friend of Kafka* (1972). A good deal of his work remains untranslated, for he is–like Borges (q.v.)–exquisitely sensitive on the subject of the mutilation of his texts. *In My Father's Court* (1966) is a more journalistic, but most excellent, account of his childhood.

Sinyavsky, Andrei (1925) Russian novelist and critic. In 1966 he and Yuli Daniel were sentenced to labour camps. Sinyavsky had published abroad under the pseudonym Abram Tertz (after his release in 1972 he did it again: the experimental *Golas iz chora,* 1973, *Voice From the Chorus,* which incorporates his letters to his wife from prison, the life of Pushkin upon which he worked while there, a diary, and other writings). Sinyavsky's work does, as has been remarked, hark back to the great days of the Serapion Brothers (*see* Zamyatin); but it is none the worse for that–what else can an original Russian writer do? And was not the Serapion experiment frustrated by exile or silence? In fact Sinyavsky is the most gifted of all modern Russian prose writers; he is as brave as the better-known realist and documentarist Solzhenitsyn (q.v.), more intelligent, and a superior writer. Like Voznesensky (q.v.), he learned much from Pasternak (q.v.). Sinyavsky was determined to challenge the crushingly boring tyranny of socialist realism and in effect he carried on where the Serapion Brothers had left off. He collaborated in an important study of Russian poetry 1917–20 (1964). Previously he had written the novel *Sud idyot* (1960; tr. *The Trial Begins,* 1960) and the stories in *Fantasticheskiye Povesti* (1961; tr. *The Icicle,* 1963). The background for these is the Stalinist terror, but the treatment is 'phantasmagoric'; *Lyubimov* (1964; tr. *The Makepiece Experiment,* 1965) is the best dystopia to come from Russia since Zamyatin's *We.* Sinyavsky represents something altogether different from Solzhenitsyn: he is one of the most outstanding upholders of the artist's right to use the freedom of his imagination–wherever it may lead him. He is now in Paris.

Sisson, C. H. (1914) English poet, novelist, critic, essayist and translator. A higher civil servant until 1972. Sisson is a poet whose neglect is hard to explain inasmuch as his procedures are in no way overtly startling. However, he is the most intellectually subtle writer of his generation and his preoccupations may have seemed over-narrow: an impression that should be corrected by the fact that he is a member of the Church of England (in the most serious sense) and by the publication of his collected poems, *In the Trojan Ditch* (1974). No dogmatist is more elastic; few collections of poetry more eclectic. Sisson is utterly, indeed obsessionally, English; but he is also the only English poet of the century to have fully assimilated French culture and, in particular, non-surrealist French poetry. Sisson is an accomplished ironist, whose torn soul is sutured only by reticence, firm and highly personal rhythms, good sense and a deliberatively irrational faith in a redemptive Christ from whom he savagely–and with an admirable absence of self-indulgence–separates his own mortality. Looking a little like Dr Doolittle, enjoying his pipe, speaking not always wholly audibly, ironically 'in' on 'important' decisions of state, he has suffered the blows of neglect (severe to one of such evident potentialities) with monumental good humour and charity. His novel *Christopher Homm* (1965; 1975) reveals his Christianity entirely without vulgarity: told in reverse, and with a revealing epigraph from St Augustine, it has seemed (at least to some) to surpass Beckett (q.v.): by simultaneously exposing human desolateness and yet pointing to a purpose transcending it, in its gently ironic starkness, an affirmative book. *Christ*opher Homm[e] does not finally vanish into his indignity, but back into his mother's womb: to birth. In his poetry Sisson, often in tight and finely controlled forms, candidly explores the nature of what, to him, is (terminologically) sin, corruption—a condition with which all of us, Christian or non-Christian, are familiar—and measures it against Christian hope, always faithful to his human (mortal) mood, which emerges in his exact rhythms. He puts landscape into its sombre historical perspective: exact, evocative, tragic, entranced. He ponders his limitation. More recent poems exploit the very essence of French Parnassianism and neo-classicism, but in an entirely English way: prefigured rhythms call to him and, encouraged by recognition, he responds. Sisson is a modest but powerful poet whose Christianity does not divide him from the pagan or, indeed, from the student of fashion who can be jerked into awareness. This is not an evangelical or a mystical Christianity, but simply (to adopt a phrase from an essay of the author's) a confession of sudden, inspired 'unblinkeredness'—which he finds as puzzling as the reader, whose own sense of mystery, however, will be quickened.

Sitwell, Edith (1887–1964) Eccentric English poet, biographer, critic, anthologist. The victim of a rich upbringing and an unpleasant though amusing father (see her brother Osbert's, q.v., accounts of him), Edith Sitwell slowly developed from an aristocratic fun-raiser and lively minor synaesthetic poet into a megalomaniac who wrote hugely self-inflated, Roman-Catholic-oriented poetry about what she took to be suffering and God. Her best and most serious poem, *Gold Coast Customs* (1929), much influenced by Lindsay (q.v.), is a *tour de force* and a notable exception to the patronizing European pseudo-*négritude* (*see* Césaire) of this period. Many others written before it are gay, skilful explorations of the relationship between rhythm and painting; some verge on inspired nonsense. Still others, less successful, too obliquely examine her Lesbianism. Her poetry remains minor because it is ultimately evasive; in *Gold Coast Customs* and sometimes elsewhere, however, she could unobtrusively eroticize her vibrant fancy to quaint effect. The later poetry is not insincere but simply grandiose and overconfident: it is unlikely that anything written after *Street Songs* (1942) will ever be studied or much read except in quasi-literary devotional circles. Edith Sitwell was a critic whose occasional discernments (for example, she saw Bottrall's, q.v., merits) are almost irretrievably spoiled by her hysterical eccentricity. Her biographies (Pope, Swift—this is semi-fictional—Elizabeth I, and others), many of them written for money, are wildly inaccurate and stridently over-written. *Collected Poems* (1957); *Selected Letters* (1971).

Sitwell, Osbert (1892–1969) English novelist, short-story writer, prose writer, poet, autobiographer. Brother of Edith (q.v.) and Sacheverell (q.v.). His best book is the novel *Before the Bombardment* (1926), a subtle study of the disintegration of Edwardianism. There are some good earlier stories in *Collected Stories* (1953). As a poet he is a distinguished versifier (*Collected Satires and Poems,* 1931). The war filled him with as much indignation as it had Sassoon (q.v.) or Graves (q.v.), but he was too innately aristocratic to transcend his manneredness and old-fashioned (unrealistic) anti-philistinism (the state should support writers, &c.) except in nostalgic works such as *Before the Bombardment.* His series of autobiographies are deservedly popular and are revealing and funny about his early family life: *Left Hand, Right Hand!* (1944); *The Scarlet Tree* (1946); *Great Morning* (1948); *Laughter in the Next Room* (1949); *Noble Essences* (1950). Their style, however, is over-'perfect' and often irritating. Like his sister Edith, he may have been creatively inhibited in later life by his failure to deal with the problem of his homosexuality. He has in him a little of Firbank (q.v.), on whom he wrote.

Sitwell, Sacheverell (1897) English travel writer, essayist, poet. In the First World War and the twenties the Sitwells got up to many anti-philistine pranks (this is all, in retrospect, that they were); Sacheverell was always the least exhibitionistic and the most withdrawn. His poetry was once admired (Michael Roberts included him in *The Faber Book of Modern Verse*); but it soon became apparent that although it resembles no one else's, it is also wooden, dull and lacking in attack. He has written many travel books and biographies; for those whose minds are not clogged by his off-beat, meanderingly learned prose, these have provided entertainment and food for thought. *Collected Poems* (1936); *Selected Poems* (1948); *Poetry Review 58* (1967) printed forty-eight poems. *Spain* (1950 rev. 1961), *Cupid and the Jacaranda* (1952)—essays—and *Gothic Europe* (1969) are among his many prose titles.

Smith, Iain Crichton (in Gaelic, Iain Mac a' Ghobhainn) (1928) Scottish poet who writes in English and Gaelic—but mostly in the former. His Gaelic short stories (collected, e.g., in *An Dubh is an*

Gorm, 1963) are highly thought of, but his English poetry is his chief achievement. This (e.g. *Selected Poems,* 1971; *Love Poems and Elegies,* 1972) is uneven, but at his best Smith is perhaps as original and as rewarding as any poet of his generation. He has consistently developed, and *Love Poems and Elegies* sacrifices none of his admirable plainness in its discovery of new depths. Of all English poets now writing, he alone seems to be seriously aware of the phenomenon of *Künstlerschuld* (*see* Laura Riding, Rilke, Mann and others): he 'trembles' in a love poem, as to 'What love [Scott] must have lost to write so much'. His spare, tense poetry, ironically critical of its own Calvinism, combs his complex personality painfully deeply; its contempt for the lies of the politicians is thoroughly earned and consequently powerful and effective. His theme, as he has stated, is the 'conflict between discipline and freedom': a West Highlander, Calvinism is in his bones, but so is the hunger for a different sort of grace and freedom than that offered by Calvin's inscrutable God, with his terrible decree. *Consider the Lilies* (1968) is a fine novel about the Highland Clearances, although its original version was preferable to the published one. *Survival Without Error* (1970) collects stories.

Snodgrass, W. D. (1926) American poet, translator. Snodgrass's first collection, *Heart's Needle* (1959), contained poems on highly personal themes cast in tight, witty, Empsonian (q.v.) forms. Many readers, including Lowell (who acknowledged his debt) were impressed with the title-sequence, dealing with the poet's divorce from his first wife and consequent separation from their daughter. There is a certain slick complacency in much of his later work. *After Experience* (1968) contains poems in looser or experimental forms which are quite self-indulgently whimsical in so intelligent a poet, but some of the translations are exemplary.

Snow, C. P. (1905) Created Baron Snow of Leicester 1964. English physicist, don, scientific expert, civil servant, government minister and romancer of *The Corridors of Power,* one title in the eleven-novel sequence 'Strangers and Brothers' (1940–70). Snow's heart is in the right place; but he runs in blinkers, since he is oblivious to both religious and individualistic manifestations. His subjects in his chief work are himself (as Lewis Eliot), orthodox ethics, the proper place of science in affairs. His accounts, held by some to be readable and by others to be dull, bear little resemblance to reality. His best book is his first, a detective story called *Death Under Sail* (1932). He enjoys an inflated reputation, but 'Strangers and Brothers' deserves praise for doggedness, honesty of purpose, industry and a certain sympathetic insight into the difficulties encountered by gifted provincials when they make social progress.

Söderberg, Hjalmar (1869–1941) Swedish fiction writer, dramatist, essayist, anti-Christian and anti-Nazi polemicist. Söderberg is an underestimated and misunderstood writer, from whom Swedish writers should have learned a great deal; he should certainly not be relegated to the pre-modernist period—which he usually is, because he wrote little after 1912, and (perhaps) because he lived in Copenhagen for the last twenty-four years of his life. He is not nearly as expressionistically comic as Hjalmar Bergman (1883–1931), but the same ambivalent mood may be found in his fiction. He was soaked in decadence, but his enterprise was from the beginning to counteract this by a sharp and shrewd psychological exactitude. His uncanny ability to render the atmosphere of his native Stockholm—rivalled only by Bo Bergman (1869–1967)—is reluctantly acknowledged by all his critics, who are repelled either by his dislike of Christianity, his alleged 'pessimism', or both. Söderberg was a sceptic, but, like Rilke (q.v.), he was fascinated by the struggle between religious feeling and nihilism which found its richest imaginative expression in the Dane, Jens Peter Jacobsen. His first novel, *Förvillelser* (1895), *Bewilderments,* appalled his contemporaries and immediately distinguishes itself from the *fin de siècle* mood by the cruel keenness of its analysis of its decadent, will-less hero. *Martin Bircks ungdom* (1901; tr. *Martin Birck's Youth,* 1930) is rightly prized for its poetic realization of Stockholm, but its psychological account (largely autobiographical) of its eponymous hero's development from childhood to middle age (which the author had not yet entered) is dismissed as artificially 'decadent'. Such is not the case. Söderberg's lucid, limpid prose ought to have set an example to his countrymen; but it seldom did. *Doktor Glas* (1905; tr. 1963) elaborates the theme of the power of place (Stockholm) by putting in a story of unrepentant euthanasia. *Den allvarsamma leken* (1912), *The Serious Game,* is a tough and subtle study of the nature of modern love. He wrote many acid stories (*Selected Short Stories,* tr. 1935) and some plays, of which

Gertrud (1906) is the best known. The best of his anti-'Christian' essays, many written after he had abandoned creative literature, should be translated. Söderberg's works were collected 1943–4.

Solzhenitsyn, Alexander (1918) Russian fiction writer, historian, dramatist. Nobel Prize 1970. He was imprisoned in 1945 and spent the rest of Stalin's lifetime in camps. His first novel *Odin den v zhizni Ivana Denisovicha* (1962; tr. *One Day in the Life of Ivan Denisovich,* 1963; 1970) was published in Russia; no other book by him has appeared there since, though he published in the magazine *Novy Mir* until 1966. This account of prison life gave him an immediate international reputation. In 1964 he was put forward for the Lenin Prize, but he soon fell into disgrace. His main works since then have been the three novels *V krage perrom* (1967; tr. *The First Circle,* 1968), *Rakovy korpus* (1969; tr. *Cancer Ward,* 1968) and *Avgust Chetyrnadtsatogo* (1971; tr. *August 1914,* 1972), the first of a sequence. Stories are in *For the Good of the Cause* (1964), *Stories and Prose Poems* (1971) and in other collections. There are now rival translations of several of his works. In 1967 he publicly asked for the abolition of censorship. In 1970 he was expelled from the Writers' Union. In 1974 he published *The Gulag Archipelago 1918–1956* (tr. 1974) in France: this consisted of the first two parts of a projected seven-part study of the Soviet prison and labour camp system from 1918 until the present. 'Gulag' is an acronym of Glavnoye Upravleniye Lagerei: 'Chief Administrative Office for Corrective Labour Camps'; the archipelago is a metaphor for the 'islands' that the scattered camps represent in the 'sea' of the USSR. Solzhenitsyn was thrown forcibly out of Russia in February 1974; his family was allowed to join him, and for the time being he has settled in Switzerland. The status of Solzhenitsyn is a matter of controversy. It is likely that we have overrated him, but there is a school of thought that believes him to be a great writer. He is certainly a man of great strength, will and courage. But he may not be 'wholly agreeable', as a critic has put it. Still, who after such an ordeal as his *would* be agreeable? His first and shortest book—and some of his stories—is his best: a well-written third-person account of life in a Soviet camp, incorporating shrewd and astonishingly cool observation and colloquialese. *The First Circle,* about life in a labour-camp for specialist scientists who get certain privileges, is good documentary and includes a splendid caricature of Stalin. *Cancer Ward,* based on the author's own experiences as a cancer patient (his cancer is arrested), has its rich moments, but is not well constructed–or as original as it has been made out to be. *August 1914*, the first of a series on pre-revolutionary Russia, is poor in style, boring and, again, ill-constructed. *The Gulag Archipelago* is very good journalism, but its powerful effect is gained less from the writing than from the ghastly material. Solzhenitsyn has nobility and courage and his various pleas for freedom from a position of grave danger were moving. But he is a naive man, who believes in what Dostoievski wanted to believe in: Holy Russia. He dislikes the West and does not fully understand democracy. His admiring fellow-dissident Sakharov, a physicist who remains in Russia, has sharply criticized his lack of understanding of what his country really needs, which is certainly not a retreat into simple-minded and fundamentally anti-democratic mysticism. Solzhenitsyn is a remarkable man; he is by no means a great writer.

Sontag, Susan (1933) American fiction writer, essayist. Susan Sontag combines extreme intelligence with extreme silliness. Her collection of essays *Against Interpretation* (1966) showed a wide range of knowledge and many insights but its uncritical acceptance of Norman O. Brown's sexual prophecies and its attempt to define 'camp' revealed a girl unable to rise out of a fashionable and trivial life-style which she vainly tried to intellectualize. She confuses what is artistically valuable with what is sociologically interesting. Her novels (*The Benefactor*, 1963; *Death Kit*, 1967) are over-experimental. Later essays show a weakening of intellectual powers.

Sorley, Charles (1895–1915) English poet. He did not have time to develop his considerable promise but he is distinguished for a handful of poems and for his *Letters* (1919), which show that he was among the first to see the real nature of the war. He saw through the pretensions of the public school system and he criticized Brooke (q.v.) for his speciousness. He was a man of conspicuous intelligence and his death in action was a great loss to English letters. *Marlborough* (1919) contains his poetry.

Soseki Natsume (ps. Natsume Kinnosuke) (1867–1916) Japanese novelist, poet (mostly in Chinese: a tradition amongst Japanese), critic, teacher. Soseki was and is one of the most popular and influential Japanese writers; nearly all his work has now been translated, some of it in several versions (the later the better). He was, like many Japanese writers, a mentally sick man and his mature fiction is a magnificent analysis of his neurosis. He gained his fame from the bitterly satirical *Waga hai wa neko de aru* (1905–6; tr. *I Am a Cat,* 1961), in which he looks at the world from the angle of a cat. But this is, in his own terminology, a 'leisure novel'. His next book, *Botchan* (1906; tr. *Young Master,* 1922) is more serious: it is a prophetic variation on the 'holy fool' theme, about a man whose personality is revolutionary but whose intelligence is low. *Kokoro* (1914; tr. 1957) is a study in what Freud (q.v.) would have called latent homosexuality, loneliness, guilt and suicide. It is a great and suggestive novel, all the more potent for its detached treatment of its violent themes. *Michigusa* (1916; tr. *Grass on the Wayside,* 1969) is a terrifyingly accurate study, meticulous in its psychology, of the years Soseki spent making his decision to devote himself to writing. He forced himself, at his desk, to accept the Buddhistic resignation in which he could not, existentially, believe. He is the equal of Toson (q.v.), and we are fortunate to have so many of his books in translation. *Kasamakura* (1906; tr. *The Three-Cornered World,* 1965) deals with the impossibility of love; *Meian* (1916; tr. *Light and Darkness,* 1971) is an unfinished study of a miserable marriage. *Mon* (1910; tr. *The Gate,* 1971) examines, with great honesty, the existential failure of Soseki's Buddhistic aspirations. More of his novels are translated; essays are in *Garasudo no naka* (1915; tr. *Within My Glass Doors,* 1928).

Southern, Terry (1924) American fiction writer. *Candy* (1955; in USA 1964), written in collaboration, is a quite amusing parody of pornography loosely based on *Candide,* but using a modern girl. *Flash and Filigree* (1958) is, like its title, all surface. He is one of the begetters of the 'black humour' school of the sixties, and he has little to offer beyond a certain technical skill. *The Magic Christian* (1959).

Soyinka, Wole (1935) Nigerian (Yoruba) playwright, poet, novelist. He studied at Leeds University and worked at the Royal Court Theatre before returning to Nigeria. He was imprisoned without trial in 1967, owing to his attitude towards the Biafran affair, and was released after the defeat of the Biafrans. He is now director of drama at Ibadan University. Versatile, mocking, angry, intelligent, Soyinka has undoubtedly succeeded in the field of drama; his poetic and fictional achievements are less easy to assess. With *The Lion and the Jewel* (1963), *Madmen and Specialists* (1971) and others he has established an authentic Nigerian theatre in English; his plays are vital and sparkling, and owe this to his use of indigenous material. Imprisonment gave his poetry (e.g. *A Shuttle in the Crypt,* 1973) a darker and stronger tone. But perhaps his controversial prose works, *The Interpreters* (1965) and *The Man Died* (1973), criticized by some as impenetrable and 'sprawling', give the clearest indication of his high potential. As Achebe (q.v.) has pointed out, Soyinka is always a celebrant of life, even at his most pessimistic; the complexities of *The Interpreters,* whose techniques assimilate those of modern European fiction more thoroughly than any other African novel, bring this out clearly to the aware reader.

Spark, Muriel (1918) Scottish novelist (resident in England and then for some time in Italy) whose early verses and criticism were feeble. With *Memento Mori* (1959), a novel about old people, she began to attract attention, but she has been overrated. Her style has lately become conceited and mannered and she has been accused of pointless malice. *The Prime of Miss Jean Brodie* (1961) is her best novel, but it lacks real curiosity about people. *The Mandelbaum Gate* (1965), an attempt to achieve substance, is ingeniously constructed but clumsily written.

Spender, Stephen (1909) English poet, critic, translator, fiction writer, co-editor (*Horizon, Encounter*) and, now, academic. Spender was closely associated with Auden (q.v.) and MacNeice (q.v.) in the thirties. Auden, whose first small and now rare collection of poems he published, influenced him profoundly and may have been partly responsible for the comparatively early 'modernization' of his adolescent Georgian-Shelleyan beginnings. His very early poems (*Nine Experiments,* 1928; *20 Poems,* 1930; *Poems,* 1933 rev. 1934) are extraordinary in that they attain an intensity of romantic yearning (G. S. Fraser has called it 'groping')—this characterizes all his work—without, on the whole, slipping into sentimentality. He has a hard, humorous, sardonic side to his nature, but while this emerges in some of his criticism, it did not come out in his poetry until *The Generous Days* (1971), an interesting volume which has hardly had the critical attention it deserves. While Spender is no orthodox 'existentialist', and while he is not a subscriber to Heidegger's dense (and probably partly incoherent) philosophical prose, the Heideggeran *sorrow*—an anti-dogmatic individual's yearning for his 'religious' relationship to what Durkheim called the *conscience collective* to be in some existential way defined—is at the heart of his poetry, and most surely so in the earlier work. The stresses and strains of sexual life and the international distress of the thirties caused Spender's later poetry to become somewhat blurred; even in later, post-war, love poems (which contain some beautiful passages), the nature of the Buberian 'Du' (*see* Buber) is never sharply defined in the sense that Spender wants: some vaguely androgynous object emerges, and this object is relevant and interesting—but it justifies Fraser's characterization of his work as 'groping'. Norman Cameron's (q.v.) affectionate reference to him as the 'Rupert Brooke [q.v.] of the Depression' has its point (and all the more so for implicitly recognizing him as superior to Brooke), for the erotic component in his verse seems to want to be like Brooke's straightforward one (however inept this may now appear). However, he does not 'grope' for the specifically physical; he metamorphoses the objects of his yearning into delicate metaphors ('Eye, gazelle, delicate wanderer,/Drinker of the horizon's fluid line') or actual descriptions of aspects of landscape ('The sea like an unfingered harp' is only one well-known example). In his autobiography *World Within World* (1951) he somewhat frustratedly fails to come to grips with himself, but this was by no means his own fault. But he had characterized his own position clearly enough in his critical book *The Destructive Element* (1935): here he accepts a 'world without belief', but clearly insists on a constructive, idealistic approach. This has led him into some (not unattractive) naïvety, and also into becoming a public cultural figure—a role which he appears to dislike. His worse poems are lush, vague and technically clumsy but his best have a lyrical openness and nobility that is almost unique in contemporary English poetry. The famous 'I Think Continually of Those Who Were Truly Great' (not his best poem) is ultimately too lush and imprecise to be really good, but it is not rhetorical, it is felt, and it is therefore moving. Who else today could have written it without completely botching it? Spender has written much criticism (e.g. *The Creative Element*, 1953; *The Struggle of the Modern*, 1963), travel books (e.g. *Learning Laughter*, 1952, on Israel) and has translated from Rilke (q.v.), Lorca (q.v.), Éluard (q.v.), Wedekind (q.v.), Toller (q.v.) and Schiller. He wrote one good novel about the miseries of a boy at a nasty preparatory school: *The Backward Son* (1940). *Collected Poems*

(1955) is a revised selection; earlier books include *The Still Centre* (1939), *Ruins and Visions* (1942), *The Edge of Being* (1949)–and *Selected Poems* (1965).

Stadler, Ernst (1883–1914) German (Alsatian) poet, killed at Ypres after winning an Iron Cross. The most substantial of the early German expressionists, and one of the most severe losses sustained by literature in the First World War. Stadler had an unusually wide cultural and linguistic background, of which he made a most critically intelligent use: he attended Oxford (1906–8), and taught at Strasbourg and Brussels. He translated Jammes (q.v.), Péguy (q.v.) and Charles-Louis Philippe and seems to have been as aware of what was going on in literature in this turbulent period as anyone in Europe. 'His', wrote Flake, 'was a European approach based on mutual comparisons and understanding.' It is most appropriate to discuss the complex phenomenon of German expressionism in the context of his work for, although he never had time to entirely find himself as a poet, the transition between his only two collections of poetry (*Präludien*, 1905, and *Der Aufbruch*, 1914, *Starting-Point*) is crucial, and in it we may most clearly and fully detect the fundamental changes in literary procedure that characterized the first decade of the century. Stadler's early poems were influenced by George (q.v.) and Hofmannsthal and were only proto-expressionist in the sense that these poets were: the procedures are conventional, traditional form is not challenged. But in later poems he had to find himself as a twentieth-century man and he turns to Whitman (for use of a very long line–though he often retains rhyme–which he might later have rejected as inadequate or inappropriate to his needs) in order to establish a procedure entirely new in German poetry. What happens–or what, sometimes, he is trying to make happen–in his later, unquestionably expressionist, poetry helps us to understand the essence of expressionism–and explains its historical necessity. This is seen more radically in the few poems of van Hoddis (q.v.) and Lichtenstein, but there it is more exaggerated, more purely a matter of presentation: the content is slight. Stadler was slower, more cautious, more substantial in content. However, they, like Heym (q.v.), do exemplify more clearly than Stadler one feature of early German expressionist poetry: its tight forms. But he, with more to say, is moving, with poetic majesty, in their direction. In their grotesque and deliberately distorted poems the loud, shrieking element in German expressionism is more obvious, but they have less intellectual scope and less imagination. There is thus more of the conventional in Stadler's late work than is sometimes admitted, but he would have been *the* major German expressionist poet had he survived. Expressionism at rock-bottom implies a literary procedure in which the *external* features of a work are predominantly *expressions* of *internal* states of mind: the old external disciplines by which people had lived were finally breaking up, and were therefore questionable. To this basic attitude that lies at the heart of expressionism there are all kinds of corollaries and possibilities. It is necessary to dwell upon the irrational because, as distinct from the 'reason' that governed the old external disciplines, the released mind is not 'reasonable'. Authority is challenged and even, by some expressionists (not Stadler) 'shrieked' at (hence the importance to the early expressionists of Edvard Munch's famous, vivid 'The Shriek'). Neo-romanticism is seen as far too pretty: adjectives are to be 'nounal' in impact, rather than decorative, but the verb is the dominant part of speech, because it represents the *action* of the internal state of anguish or protest (or whatever) against the old substantive solidity represented by the noun—and still clung to by the bourgeois, rightly seen as ignorant, unaware of change, helpless (or evil) builders of a 'reality' now exposed as false; even the adjective-noun combination is given the force of a verb by the process of constructing a syntax that will release its hitherto latent and mysterious energy. A landscape will no longer be seen as 'beautiful', but as a (probably) sinister and disturbing state of mind; in any case it is likely to be an urban landscape—here the expressionists were influenced by Verhaeren's (q.v.) *Les Villes tentaculaires,* a fact which demonstrates how the good poets of all 'schools' are related, how in fact every movement, seen in terms of its best practitioners, shades almost imperceptibly into its successor, how real poetry remains real poetry despite the efforts of some literary historians to dispense altogether with both imaginative and individual achievement. (Stadler's 'Kleine Stadt', 'Small Town', should be studied in relation to Verhaeren's *Les Villes tentaculaires:* it is a later, procedurally more expressionist and less vehement version of the Belgian's earlier vision.) The specifically German school of expressionism was succeeded by dada (*see* Ball) and then by surrealism (*see* Breton). But all the poetry of industrialized or 'civilized' countries will have to become expressionistic in the *general*—though not of course in the specifically German—sense outlined above if poetry is to remain viable: hence the poverty of contemporary British poetry. Hence it is necessary to point out that this kind of poetry requires as much effort, integrity and discipline (though not in the old sense) as that of the past. The *German* expressionist movement disintegrated: the 'shriek', the urban obsession, the freneticism–these led the surviving expressionists to become mad (van Hoddis, q.v.), hard-line communists (Becher and others) or fascists (Bronnen, Johst, Rehberg) or quasi-Nazis (Jünger, q.v.)–and some of course, if not entirely broken by enforced exile, went on to make individual achievements that transcended the movement (Döblin, q.v. and others). Stadler's actual achievement is, in any case, considerable in itself (his own most substantial expressionist poem is 'Fahrt über die Kölner Rheinbrücke bei Nacht', 'Journey over the Rhein Bridge at Cologne by Night'), and his promise massive. The complete poems, *Dichtungen,* appeared in 1954.

Stafford, Jean (1915) American fiction writer. Her novels are slight but delicate evocations of childhood and loneliness. *The Mountain Lion* (1947) is the best. The short-story form (*Collected Stories,* 1969) is well suited to her gifts of psychological exactitude. But perhaps the best of all her books is the non-fiction *A Mother in History* (1966), a portrait of Lee Harvey Oswald's mother, and a masterpiece of restraint.

Stead, Christina (1902) Expatriate Australian novelist and (after Richardson, q.v., and White, q.v.) her nation's most gifted. She is versatile, with undoctrinaire 'left-wing' sympathies, a streak of the bizarre, an intelligently and firmly controlled felinity (cf. Patricia Highsmith, q.v.; but Stead puts the gift to subtler and infinitely wider use), a mastery of dialogue and the unemotional, inspiredly selective depiction of marital tensions. Much influenced by Louis Guilloux, the Brothers Grimm, Virginia Woolf (q.v.), her early background (Sydney, studies in psychology, teaching backward children) and naturalism, her methods are nevertheless inimitable and original. For long a 'writer's writer', she emerged into some light only in the sixties in America, when her *The Man Who Loved Children* (1940), a scarifying study of an unhappy marriage and of its children's strategies for survival, was republished with an introduction by Jarrell (q.v.). Also notable are *Seven Poor Men of Sydney* (1934), and *For Love Alone* (1944), both of which (though the latter only in the first part) have Australian settings. *The Salzburg Tales* (1934) reflects the fantastic aspect, and may have been influenced by Karen Blixen (q.v.). *Cotters' England* (1966) looks at another difficult marriage. *The Puzzleheaded Girl* (1967) contains four memorable novellas. Her neglect by critics (she is missing from, patronized or perfunctorily dismissed in all but one of the standard reference books in English) is a strong reason to feel dismay about the practice of letters in our times.

Stein, Gertrude (1874–1946) American writer. She studied medicine, and psychology under William James (q.v.), but from 1903 she made her home in Paris. She was rich and able to patronize painters, including Picasso (the genius for selecting the best of such then unknowns was, however, that of her brother Leo). In time she became an American Queen in Paris, to whom nearly all the expatriates and visitors in the twenties paid homage. She was a strange mixture: she retained a folksy Americanism (it comes out in e.g., *Brewsie and Willie*, 1946, a sentimental account of GIS in Paris), and yet her experiments—rooted in her work in psychology under James and her intuitions of the procedures of the painters she patronized—were original and important, though hardly intrinsically so. She could write popular 'straight' books, such as *The Autobiography of Alice B. Toklas* (1933)—Alice B. Toklas was her Lesbian or crypto-Lesbian secretary-companion, and survived her—which brought her popularity. Her influence was fortuitous in the sense that those who benefited from it (e.g. Hemingway, q.v.) did not understand the reasons for her experimentalism. The death of Gertrude Stein as a writer of substance (as distinct from one of homely appeal, of experimental importance or of unreadable meanderings—e.g. *The Making of Americans*, 1925, abridged 1934; 1966) was announced in the third of the three stories, 'Melanctha', in her first book, *Three Lives* (1909). Here she projects herself into the figure of a negress who, once she has taught a young doctor to love her, loses interest in him—and dies, defeated, of consumption. This, written in 1905, is a regretful farewell by an essentially nineteenth-century figure to the nineteenth century, and a farewell to a heterosexuality which she felt, probably rightly, that she could not manage. Henceforth she devoted herself to abstractionism, to the construction of a language that would exist simply as sound (or 'music'), and not as sense. The project was only partially cubist (*see* Reverdy); but her fierce desire to deny 'meaning' is explained by her deliberate emptying of herself of imaginative energy, which must derive from painful as well as joyful experience. She put her energy instead into her showmanship and conventional reminiscence. Her attempts to give 'meaning' to her abstract texts were spurious: *The Making of Americans* tells us nothing about the making of Americans. Both James (q.v.) and Bergson (q.v.) had solved, in their different ways, the 'Zeno paradox' (*see* Svevo) by positing an intuitive and *non*-cinematographic process (Bergson's *la durée,* a continuous flux); Gertrude Stein was, ironically, non-modernist—despite appearances—in employing a repetitious technique based on the notion of cinematographic frames: each one changes ever so slightly, giving the illusion of continuity. She wrote, 'it [her method] was like a cinema picture made up of succession and each movement having its own emphasis that it is its own difference. . . .' Now the most viable kind of truly expressionist stream-of-consciousness (*see* Bergson) would reflect Bergson's *la durée;* but Gertrude Stein did of course capture, indeed emphasize, in a peculiarly old-fashioned way, the 'spatializing' and non-intuitive manner of experiencing time—which Bergson never suggested was not an inevitable process. She is thus in this sense a modernist anti-modernist. The men she influenced were in any case not expressionists. Hemingway at his best is a transformer of newspaper-reportage technique into literature; his main catalyst was Gertrude Stein. Anderson is a special case and anyway he appreciated her work (a 'writer's writer') more than he used it. Gertrude Stein was very prolific and much of her work has been posthumously published: *Unpublished Work* (1951–8). *Tender Buttons* (1911)—the title of this collection of abstractionist pieces means that you can no longer unbutton Miss Stein, because her buttons are too tender; *Composition as Explanation* (1926)—the classic exposition of her method; *Picasso* (1938); *Paris France* (1939)—homely reminiscence; *Selected Writings 1909–44* (1946); *Operas and Plays 1913–30* (1932); *Look at Me Now and Here I am: Writings and Lectures 1911–45* (1967—contains the novel *Ida,* 1946). There is much other work.

Steinbeck, John (1902–68) American (Californian) fiction writer. Nobel Prize 1962. Steinbeck has the virtue that he cannot be classified but his imagination was feeble and for most of the time he has to work too hard to make it look strong. If he has any 'position', then it can only be defined as a kind of latter-day unanimism (*see* Romains), derived from his interests in marine biology, which he studied at Stanford. His first novel *Cup of Gold* (1929) was a romantic melodrama: though he developed, he never could rid himself of the notion that fiction ought to have such elements in it, and most of his own is vitiated by this. *Tortilla Flat* (1935) has its virtues as a description, often humorous, of the lives of Monterey *paisanos* but Steinbeck injects a pseudo-optimistic note which his artistic conscience could destroy only by resort to final 'tragic' melodrama. *The Grapes of Wrath* (1939) is a finely documented account of a family's migration from Oklahoma to California in search of work, but Steinbeck's radicalism is never properly integrated with his naive and unworked-out view of men as creatures-in-movement. He would have done better to abandon thought and concentrate on regionalism. *Of Mice and Men* (1937) has its moments of pathos, but its misogyny is uncontrolled. Later work is notably inferior, and culminates in the allegorical pretentiousness of *East of Eden* (1952). His admiration for the ideas of the mystical charlatan and biologist Edward F. Ricketts, who sometimes appears in his fiction (notably as 'Doc' in *Cannery Row*, 1945), is indicative of his intellectual stature. In Steinbeck an enthusiastic unanimist type of thinking can happily co-exist with a contemptuous view of masses of men as a 'big beast'. He wrote *Sea of Cortez* (1941) with Ricketts. His best book is the short story collection *The Lost Valley* (1938), which contains the famous four-part 'Red Pony', in which Steinbeck's descriptive powers are seen at their best; but even here a certain confused pseudo-mysticism intrudes into the texture. *The Portable Steinbeck* (1946); *The Steinbeck Omnibus* (1951); *Short Novels* (1953).

Stevens, Wallace (1879–1955) American poet, critic. He is unusual in that he was an executive of an insurance company (he worked for them as a lawyer). As his *Letters* (1967)–a selection edited by his daughter–reveal, he in many ways posed as a politically naive man. Yet as a poet he is one of the most sophisticated of this century. And he can be moving. One does not feel impelled to take him to task for even the nastiest of his political feelings: he was quite clearly not a 'fascist' or an authoritarian, nor was he cruel; it is unfortunate that he ever chose to express himself on political or allied subjects at all. None of his colleagues knew, until relatively late, that he was a poet at all; one exclaimed, on hearing of the matter: 'What, Wally a poet!' What is his poetry like? How shall we explain and categorize him? A good deal has been written about him as 'poet-as-philosopher'; but his best is poetry, not philosophy. His immediate American ancestors were various decadent poetasters, such as the suicide Donald Evans (1884–1921), the quasi-imagist minor, Alfred Kreymborg (1883–1969), and what may be called the frustrated-modernist school of American poetry–represented by such gifted but poetically impotent men as Moody and Stickney. Clearly, too, the crass materialism of the commerce he chose to practise pushed him towards aestheticism (though he would never have admitted this). His first viable source, though, was French poetry–and in particular that of Fargue (q.v.). He wrote of Fargue that he was not 'first rate' because he 'substituted Paris for the imagination' (an unfair comment); but he used him none the less and it should be added that he himself, as super-bourgeois, substituted insurance for authenticity–a graver and no less unfair charge if one is to make such charges. He began to write his mature poetry late: after publishing poems in Harriet Monroe's *Poetry Chicago,* his *Harmonium* did not appear until 1923, when he was forty-four. His poetry (*Collected Poems,* 1954; *Opus Posthumous,* 1957) consists of some true poems and much barren, dull and yet occasionally fascinating philosophizing. The prime example of the latter is the title-piece of *The Man With the Blue Guitar* (1937), in whose very procedures, however admirably literary they may be, one may detect an aestheticism gone wild. Yet he continued to produce good poems until his death. One way in which he got at, and pulled out of himself, his good poetry was undoubtedly by a gift of 'substantializing' the finical nature of some French and over-*précieux* American poetry. Another way was that his political position, however ridiculous, was in a sense pure: he was no populist, but simply, as it has been put, a 'Taft Republican'. He saved his subtleties for art–'life', he may have felt at bottom, isn't worth subtlety. Just as he stuck to his business, he also obstinately stuck to his 1909–13 political position. It was a hedonist strategy, and Stevens was a hedonist; but out of hedonism, willy nilly, conscience flows. Hence Stevens's sudden and surprisingly warm humanity. Poetry was for him, in part, a secret bohemian adventure, an unrespectable life: this most European of all American poets never needed to leave America and never did. He is at his best in such poems as 'Sunday Morning', 'The Emperor of Ice Cream' ('I scream'), 'Le Monocle de Mon Oncle'. The first is, by general consent, one of the great modern poems about death. The second is supposed to tease on the surface, but a tragic and exact meaning–a 'story'–lies behind it, so that when we return to it, having discovered that meaning, the words are after all moving and even terrible. The third is an autobiography of the spirit, witty, casual, even absurd—but eventually tragic because, like other of his poems, it embodies a pessimistic vision of the good vainly trying to survive the bad. Stevens is called an abstract poet, and so at his worst he is. But he is in fact an ironic anti-abstractionist using aesthetic masks and impressionistic devices in order to distract his own and his readers' attention from his poetic purposes. In the good poems he is telling the truth about himself in society, and he is at least (here) melancholy: in poetry, anyway, insurance can be a potent metaphor for original sin. Not that Stevens wrote about insurance. His only sustained attempt to write about 'politics', the reactionary 'Owl Clover' (in *Opus Posthumous,* 1957), is an utter failure and he left it out of his *Collected Poems* (1954). He wasn't easy, deep in his mind, on the subject of his simplistic notions. Since one side of Stevens was so 'American', in the vulgar sense, he constructed his unvulgar poetry out of French preciosity and decadence (e.g. Toulet, Lafourgue, Baudelaire—the poet as dandy, and above all Mallarmé, whom he often echoes). But he never wanted to see France and was a very American poet. He seems to be an abstract and philosophical one—and so indeed he often tries to be—exploring and speculating upon the nature of reality. Frank Kermode, in an excellent study (1960) which takes a view of him almost exactly contrary to the one expressed here, thinks that he *is* an abstract poet and admires his longer poems. He clearly thinks it 'vulgar' and irrelevant to mention the oddity of his having been an insurance lawyer. But that is to ignore something that is in the poetry, something that helps to explain it. Stevens was a private and lonely poet and the body of his poetry that will really live—perhaps fifty poems, and none of them longer than 'Le Monocle de Mon Oncle' or 'Sunday Morning'—is not about the nature of reality but about finding a style for decent survival. That is why it is often so perturbing, delicate and unexpectedly moving: he split himself—the poet was, paradoxically, at a great distance from the man. Thus, when in old age and more than ever interested in his poetic activity, he desperately hung on to his job: that distance had to be maintained. In the collection of aphorisms called *Adagio* (*Opus Posthumous*) he wrote: 'One cannot spend one's time in being modern when there are so many more important things to be.' He was, of course, modernist but his modernism is a subtle extension of nineteenth-century proto-modernism, a robust drawing out of the *symboliste*-decadent line, a strategy—as I have implied—for survival.

And so Kermode is in a limited sense right: there was no 'wrong turning' taken by Stevens in going into commerce. It was a deliberate split, requiring poetic honesty. Too many of his poems are about the 'supreme fiction', the point at which reality and the imagination meet; they are excessively phenomenological, tracing, with a cool purged preciosity, the exact meanderings of a poetic mind. But they were a necessary foundation for the really moving ones: as he wrote of himself in one of his last poems, 'A Quiet Normal Life': '. . . his actual candle blazed with artifice'. *The Necessary Angel* (1951), essays, contains observations on poetry. *Wallace Stevens, Mattino Domenicale ed Altre Poesie* (1954) contains some translations into Italian by Renato Poggioli and is important for some of Stevens's own notes; it was published by Einaudi. A good general introduction to this difficult poet, apart from that of Kermode, is by William York Tindall (1961).

Stoppard, Tom (1937) English playwright, novelist. Stoppard came into prominence with *Rosencrantz and Guildenstern Are Dead* (1968), followed by various other successes. Currently fashionable, Stoppard's plays reveal good ideas theatrically well developed but intellectually unexplored (reflecting a lack of grasp of his material), a clever ear for merging his predecessors' (e.g. Beckett, q.v., Ionesco, q.v.) effects, and a frothy, infectious, vacuous excitement.

Strachey, Lytton (1880–1932) English biographer, essayist, critic. He is generally thought of as one of those at the centre of the 'Bloomsbury Group' (*see* Forster). He was the inheritor of the set of inferior and feeble critical standards (a paradigmatic example is Stopford A. Brooke) that characterized the late Victorian and Edwardian age; upon these he markedly improved, not by better scholarship but by adding a new psychological dimension: his acerbity, wit and astringency were the result of his own critical attitude to the literary tradition into which he had been born. *Landmarks in French Literature* (1912) displays his wide reading and has the inestimable virtue of creating enthusiasm. *Eminent Victorians* (1918), his best book, debunks the Victorian myths of Thomas Arnold, Florence Nightingale, General Gordon and Cardinal Manning. Its estimations (except in the case of the really hideous Manning) now require considerable revision but it retains validity because its exposure of the falseness of the specifically *Victorian* estimations is correct, and because it retains flashes of genuine insight. *Queen Victoria* (1921), however, overestimates a stupid personality. *Elizabeth and Essex* (1928), historically inaccurate, is the weakest of all his books. *Portraits in Miniature* (1931) contains more excellent essays. Strachey was a conscientious objector and a highly neurotic man, as Michael Holroyd's possibly over-exhaustive biography (1967–8) makes clear. His *Letters* to his friend Virginia Woolf (q.v.) were published in 1956.

Strindberg, August (1849–1912) Swedish playwright, fiction writer, poet, polemicist, satirist, critic. Although Strindberg survived, like Ibsen, into this century, he was essentially a nineteenth-century writer. But he is mentioned here (while Ibsen hardly need be) because he is an important and influential proto-modernist in a number of ways: he is frenetic, neurotic and 'morbid' (as well as, in some aspects, perfectly clear-headed and rational) in a way with which we have now grown familiar; the line of 'decadence' which he practically initiated, though it has developed, has persisted; his influence as a dramatist is ubiquitous; he anticipated expressionism; he prepared the Swedish language for modernism; he defied convention. It must be added that, outside Scandinavia, his literary production as a whole is practically unknown—he is regarded as a dramatist—but he was as great a novelist, short-story writer and autobiographer as he was a playwright. Strindberg's straining and breaking of the conventions of the stage of his time had incalculable influence: his psychological dramas of the man-woman struggle, though nominally realist, prepared the way for the serious melodrama and the violence of the German expressionist drama; he also helped to usher in both the oneiric and the 'psychoanalytical' play; he has affected the course of the symbolic, the pageant, the 'intimate' and the historical drama. Most of his work has been translated.

Styron, William (1925) American (Virginian) novelist. *Lie Down in Darkness* (1951) is his initial (very long) analysis of the South: it traces the motivations for the breakdown and suicide of the daughter of a rich Virginian couple. It has some passages of sustained grandeur but is frequently over-rhetorical and melodramatic. To correct this tendency Styron then wrote the brief *The Long March* (1952), a demonstration of semi-psychotic southern ferocity (in the form of a colonel of Marines) and the tragic collapse of liberal decency in direct confrontation with it. This is his best work. *Set This House on Fire* (1960), extremely readable and intelligent, is again very long. Eventually it fails to cohere: it is over-ambitious in trying to portray, in three characters respectively, the essence of American evil, the torments of the artist, and a less fully imagined and more intellectually contrived authorial 'point of view'. However, Styron had the courage to try to build up a novel of Dostoievskian dimensions, and his attempt is by no means feeble. *The Confessions of Nat Turner* (1967), based on the facts of the Negro Nat Turner's 1831 rebellion, is markedly weaker: like Malamud's (q.v.) *The Fixer*, it is far too self-conscious an attempt to solve an enormous problem—that of the plight of the past (and, by implication, present) southern Negro.

Supervielle, Jules (1884–1960) French poet, fiction writer, playwright. His parents, who died in his infancy, were Basque; he was born in Uruguay and spent half his life (until after the Second World War) in South America, to whose poetic tradition he in one sense belongs. Though he reached seventy-six he for long lived with a serious heart ailment; a sense of impending death permeates his poetry. He is one of the most original poets of his generation in any language. He was going to be a diplomat (in the Latin-American tradition), but instead married and became a poet. His extreme personal modesty emerges in his poetry as a substantial, reassuring quality. Though (the ubiquitous) fear of death is one of the staple elements of his mature poetry, he overcomes this by an almost Rilkean (q.v.) tremulous serenity. He preserved the purity of his sympathy with nature (usually seen in terms of South American landscape and fauna and flora), but his approach is *sentimentalisch* and frequently paradoxical. He has no system of salvation, and he can on occasions be more gloomy than critics as a whole suggest; yet, while his eyes can discern 'no footprints of God', and he suffers from vertigo in the search, this dizziness—if with difficulty—'heals into a distant scar'. His fiction, for adults and children, is delicate and allegorical or fantastical (e.g. *Le Voleur d'enfants*, 1926; tr. *The Colonel's Children*, 1950); his plays are charming and slight. There is as yet no collected edition, but *Choix de poèmes* (1947) is a good representation. Two important collections are in the Poésie/Gallimard series: *Le Forçat innocent* (1930) and *Les Amis inconnus* (1934). The powerful *Poèmes de la France malheureuse* (1941) show that he was not immune to suffering. In English: *L'Enfant de la haute mer* (1931; tr. *Souls of the Soulless,* 1933)–excellent stories–and a bilingual *Selected Writings* (1967).

Svevo, Italo (ps. Ettore Schmitz) (1861–1928) Italian novelist. A Trieste Jew of mixed Italian-Austrian parentage–his pseudonym means 'Italo the Swabian'–Svevo is a strange case; he is also a major European novelist. Only his last and most famous novel, *La coscienza di Zeno* (1923; tr. *Confessions of Zeno,* 1962), was successful, and then not until three years after its publication. Not long after this Svevo died in a car crash. Trieste was then Austrian, and Svevo, a businessman, spoke both German and Italian, but neither perfectly; his prose style is undistinguished, but then his characters feel, above all, undistinguished. His first two novels, *Una Vita* (1892; tr. *A Life,* 1963) and *Senilità* (1898; tr. *As a Man Grows Older,* 1932), fell flat. They deal with the subject-matter of his masterpiece of 1923–namely, a certain kind of *abulia* arising from what existentialists call 'bad faith' and psychoanalysts 'rationalization'. The early novels are good but no one hailed them: not only because Italy was totally unprepared for fiction deliberately written without stylistic distinction–in businessman's Italian–but also because Svevo's ironic treatment of his material was unfamiliar. The Austro-Hungarian Trieste was cosmopolitan; Italy was provincial and has always been embarrassed by Svevo. He owed his international fame to a piece of luck: he went in 1906 to a teacher of English then living in Trieste, James Joyce (q.v.) and was encouraged in his fiction; when *Zeno* came out Joyce had become influential and was able to press its merits on to his friend Larbaud, who, with Benjamin Crémieux, praised it enthusiastically. *Zeno* is a complex work, a novel within a novel, a comic examination of an age-old problem first posed by Zeno of Elea: how can an arrow reach its destination? How therefore can life be lived, how does the present travel forwards? Christians had solved this problem–psychologically very real, though philosophically trite–by assuming the existence of a divine purpose. Bergson (q.v.) solved it by advocating an intuitive rather than a 'cinematographic' approach. But Svevo's Zeno, whose isolated 'moments' are symbolized by his chain-smoking of cigarettes, each one of which is to be the 'last', is rooted in intellect: ultimately it is a relentlessly alyrical and urban examination of man's intellectual alienation of himself from the world's reality. The practitioners of the *nouveau roman* use parodic literary forms to destroy literature because it is sentimentally anthropomorphic; Svevo reached this point long before them but, more aware, less didactic, did not try to throw away the mystery of his humanity.

Synge, John Millington (1871–1909) Irish (his father was a Protestant Dublin barrister) dramatist, poet. With Pirandello (q.v.), Brecht (q.v.), and O'Neill (q.v.) he forms the great quadrumvirate of twentieth-century dramatists. Synge studied music, travelled, engaged in journalism and then met, in Paris, Yeats (q.v.), whose influence on him was decisive. Synge's art was partly the result of the yearning of a man of very frail health (he was tubercular, and died young of cancer) for brutality and coarseness. Yeats, as Moore (q.v.) implied, tried to 'invent' him, but his visits to the Aran Islands, recommended by Yeats, produced a rather different artist from the one Yeats had contemplated. In Aran he found the coarseness and brutality he sought but this was infused with a beauty of intonation and a simplicity that fired him to poetry and drama. Of the great quadrumvirate, he is the master of poetic language and of idiom. He was, as St John Ervine remarked with an unusual percipience, 'the sick man in literature'—personally he was morbidly shy, an isolate, looking as he was: a man seeking out the darkness in himself. Poetry, he asserted, must be brutal before it can be human. His own poems are underrated: deceptively simple, certainly death-haunted—and prophetically so in more ways than one—often beautifully made. They are the least literary of all 'literary' folk poems. He wrote several dramatic masterpieces—and the unfinished verse-drama *Deirdre of the Sorrows* might have been one more. *Riders to the Sea* (1905), a one-act tragedy on what would have been in most hands an unpromising and even sentimental theme—a widow's loss of all her sons by drowning—is technically flawless and owes its greatness to Synge's ear for the vernacular, which he had studied (like Pirandello) intensively. *The Playboy of the Western World* (1907), Synge's only full-length play, is his greatest: comic in form, it both savages the patronizing Irish bourgeois myth about their peasants (its first audience, as readers of Yeats's poetry will know, were deeply affronted and made an uproar) and simultaneously creates its own ambiguous, vital, tragic world. The hero, like the heroes of so many twentieth-century masterpieces, is among other things a surrogate for the figure of the artist. Already, in *The Shadow of the Glen* (1905), his first play, Synge had found himself and his capacity to adapt Irish speech rhythms to his needs. An *Autobiography* has been reconstructed (1965). At the time of his tragically early death Synge was engaged to the actress who played the leading lady in the Abbey Theatre's production of *Playboy*, Maire O'Neill. *Collected Works* (1962–8).

T

Tagore, Rabindranath (1861–1941) Bengali poet, novelist, playwright (born in Calcutta) who was popular amongst English readers in the earlier part of the century, and who still has many admirers. Nobel Prize 1913. Yeats (q.v.) and Jiménez (q.v.) were devoted to his lyrics. There is now some controversy about his qualities because few people know Bengali and because his own English adaptations of his works are banal. But Pound (q.v.) too admired his work in the early years of this century. It was the poems of *Gitanjali* (1909; tr. 1912), *Handful of Songs*, introduced by Yeats, that gained him the Nobel Prize; but those of *Balaka* (1914), *A Flight of Wild Cranes*, are superior. Rabindranath was a notable educator and fighter for Indian freedom (though he was one of Gandhi's opponents); he also made important innovations in painting and music. In 1916 he published *Gharer baire* (tr. *The Home and the World*, 1919), a novel in which he substituted colloquial Bengali for the ponderous literary kind favoured by academics. The novel *Gora* (1908) was translated by him in 1924. Although called the 'Bengal Shelley'–he was immensely prolific–and regarded as a sage, Rabindranath never posed as one. He is obviously over-fluent and his fiction and other miscellaneous prose is probably superior to his poetry. But even in his own English versions a good deal may be seen to be going on beneath the lushness or the inept lyricism (the English *Gitanjali* are in prose), and he is more humorous and less mystical than most of his earlier admirers believed. *Collected Poems and Plays* (1936; 1961); *A Tagore Reader* (1961).

Tanizaki Junichiro (1886–1965) Japanese fiction writer, dramatist. Japan's greatest modern prose writer, and one of international stature. He has been much translated into English, French and German. Tanizaki, a fundamentally 'decadent' (the word here deserves its quotation marks, which it does not always) writer, preoccupied with sex in the specifically Japanese manner (which, in the hands of writers, is often distinctly Freudian, q.v., in its detached, analytical intensity), possesses a consummate control over his material. In his first phase, typified by 'Shisei' (1909; tr. 'The Tattooer' in *Seven Japanese Tales,* 1963), he brings out the murderous beauty of the ugly, terrifying and morbid; few writers have so brilliantly caught the hidden motivations of sexual fascination. *Otsuyagorishi* (1914; tr. *A Springtime Case,* 1927) is sensationalist, and is again concerned with the demonic nature of lust. But from the beginning Tanizaki attributes the lust-horror to the male: in most of his fiction the women function, ironically, as ciphers—manipulatees—of the males. *Akuma* (1912), *The Demon,* is a peculiarly early example of a study in sexual fetishism (a man licks his girl's handkerchief). *Chijin no ai* (1924–5), *A Fool's Love,* adapts Maugham's (q.v.) *Of Human Bondage* theme to a Japanese setting, and acutely examines the author's own ambivalent attitude towards the West. *Tade kuu muhi* (1928; tr. *Some Prefer Nettles,* 1955), which brought Tanizaki into prominence in English-speaking countries when it appeared in translation, is less 'morbid' and more straightforwardly autobiographical. Again it touches on Tanizaki's divided feelings towards the old and the new Japan, and again it transfers them to an erotic plane. When Japan became militarized Tanizaki's position was a difficult one. After writing some novels illustrating his exquisite feeling for women (e.g. *Ashikari,* 1932, *Shunkinsho,* 1933, tr. *Ashikari and the Story of Shunkin,* 1936) he was forced to concentrate on an adaptation of the classic eleventh-century *Tale of Genji.* With *Sasameyuki* (1943–8; tr. *The Makioka Sisters,* 1957), the publication of which was delayed by the authorities, he turned to a much less sensational type of fiction, rather more in the spirit of Toson (q.v.); this plotless saga is one of the most exact pieces of realism ever attempted. *Shosho Shigemoto no hana* (1950), *Captain Shigemoto's Mother,* is a historical novel set in the ninth century. *Kagi* (1960; tr. *The Key,* 1961) returns to the sexual theme, this time describing the sexual difficulties of an elderly couple. It shocked a number of readers, and is an excellent study. *Futen rojin nikki* (1962; tr. *Diary of a Mad Old Man,* 1965), viciously reviewed in Great Britain, describes in minute clinical detail the illness, and sexual infatuation, of a very old man, and is almost certainly in part autobiographical. Tanizaki's three plays, dating from the early twenties, have been translated into French. He is never a sordid writer, for he does not gratuitously invent sordid experience; but the genteel will never enjoy his decent truthfulness.

Tate, Allen (1899) American critic, poet, novelist, teacher. Tate has helped many poets younger than himself (e.g. Lowell, q.v., Berryman, q.v.) and criticism of his creative achievement has often led to fierce counter-attacks. Yet this achievement is not, as a whole, easy to praise highly. This is not necessarily to comment in any way on Tate's virtues as teacher or man. Born in Kentucky, he graduated from Vanderbilt (1923) and became a leading member of the Fugitive group and of the 'southern agrarians'. He also knew Crane (q.v.) and most of the other poets of his generation. Tate is a complex, over-involute man whose best work probably comes out in his criticism; but his novel *The Fathers* (1938; 1960) has its qualities, as, if usually through a heavy veil of intellectualism, do a few of his poems (not, in an age of trivia, low praise). In poetry he took much from Ransom (q.v.), Crane (q.v.) and the Eliot (q.v.) of *The Waste Land;* but his manner is finally his own. He invariably uses very tight forms, but is never mellifluous; the effect is crabbed, tortured, harsh, packed, immensely cerebral. He has to suppress immediate feeling–an intended strategy–to gain 'tension' (his essay 'Tension in Poetry' is famous, and is really a defence of his practice): in his special sense, tension is the clash produced in a poem by the literal and the metaphorical, the concrete and the abstract. Unfortunately in his own poetry the element of spontaneity has too often been crushed out. In his most famous poem, 'Ode to the Confederate Dead', which took him years to write, the process does almost succeed, and in later poems, written since his divorce from Caroline Gordon, re-marriage, and subsequent further changes, there is a new relaxation–the best of all is 'The Swimmers', which gives the title to a selection of 1970. Unfortunately such of 'The Seasons of the Soul', a long autobiographical poem, as have been published are cliché-ridden and bathetically neo-metaphysical. Tate's novel *The Fathers* is correctly regarded as a remarkable psychological and symbolic study–its central subject is the one that obsesses Tate, the Civil War, which is seen retrospectively from 1911–but it isn't able to deal satisfactorily with the problem of what was wrong with the South itself. Implicit in 'The Swimmers' is, so to say, some realization of this defeat. As essayist Tate is at his most brilliant when writing of individual authors (e.g. Emily Dickinson, Hardy, q.v., Crane, q.v.). As a theorist he is stimulating. As a critic of society he has much that is valid to say. *Poems* (1960); *Collected Essays* (1959); *Essays of Four Decades* (1969).

Tennant, Emma (1937) English novelist whose first novel, *The Colour of Rain* (1963), was published under the pseudonym of Catherine Ady. *The Time of the Crack* (1973) was followed by the ingenious and intelligent *The Last of the Country House of Murders* (1975), at once a powerful dystopia and a cunning parody of the vogue for novels written in the style of the 'old' detective story and a clever use of this form.

Thomas, Dylan (1914–53) Welsh poet, fiction writer, occasional critic, scriptwriter, broadcaster, poetry-reader, radio-playwright. The events of Thomas's life have become confused with his work. He drank excessively, engaged in bohemian exploits (even before alcohol got its hold on him he would speak, to audiences of polite ladies, about 'reaching up the underclothes of words'), and died young and dramatically (while on a tour of America) as a result. He has been the object of a cult in Great Britain, America and Europe. In Britain he became both famous and notorious while very young, partly because he was 'taken up' by Edith Sitwell (q.v.), who then had some influence; his thirties audience believed him to be more original than he was, confusing his dynamic power with a capacity for poetic thought; his later poetry (*Deaths and Entrances*, 1946), which is more apparently lucid, has meant a great deal to very young readers. Certain American critics (e.g. Elder Olson) have eruditely taken him up as a profound metaphysical poet (which he is not). In Europe–especially in Hungary–he is regarded as a great modern English poet, and has been influential. His radio play *Under Milk Wood* (1954) has reached a wide audience. There is controversy as to whether he had an inspired or bad ear. His early poetry (*Eighteen Poems*, 1934; *Twenty-Five Poems*, 1936; *The Map of Love*, 1939–this also contains stories) is inchoate and ill-accomplished, but bright and forceful. It looks surrealist, but in fact draws mainly on five non-surrealistic sources: Hopkins (q.v.), Joyce (q.v.), the Bible, Welsh demagoguery (cf. Lloyd George)–and on his own resources and obsessions. The 'surrealist' element consists of careless obscurity indulging itself in a whirl of words. He had little real technical skill and no intellect to speak of but his 'nerve', or Welsh effrontery, concealed this. However, what were his resources and obsessions? His resources were unhappiness and confusion and a powerful pressure to resolve his state of mind in poetic form. He had great rhetorical ability and some originality in this field. Too soon he took refuge in rhetoric—it is complex as rhetoric but not at all complex as poetry. His best poems and passages are minor, simple and lucid (e.g. 'The Hand that Signed the Paper'), but even these are often marred by undisciplined adjectival self-indulgence. His obsession was with masturbation and the inability to avoid it in sexual intercourse. It is surprising, reading through his works (*The Poems,* 1971), how ineptly, in the prewar poetry, he dealt with his despair, and how in so many of his poems he is simply failing to say something entirely prosaic. Thomas's supposedly recondite, puzzling effects are the result of laziness: they are either slick verbalisms or insubstantial efforts to express truisms. The proportion of successes is very low. The later poems are different. He worked for the BBC in the war and learned to take time off from drinking and socializing by going down to his home in Wales (he had married, and had children) and working—with more effort than he had hitherto displayed—at his craft. The necessity of producing acceptable scripts for the BBC, with its wide public, doubtless helped him in this. Most of these later poems, including the (comparatively) long 'A Winter's Tale' and 'Fern Hill', are better accomplished than his earlier work, but they are none the less a development of his rhetorical rather than of his poetic gift. 'A Winter's Tale' is probably the nearest he ever got to a sustained poetic attempt; but, under keen analysis, even this cleverly wrought poem proves to be, at its centre, romantically lush and commonplace and even ingratiating; the surface encrusting it, however, approaches the dexterity of some of the comic prose accounts of Welsh life (included in, e.g., *Quite Early One Morning,* 1954, or the two *Miscellanies,* 1963, 1970) and of the revealingly crass *Under Milk Wood.* Thomas became a highly skilled entertainer and popular poet, the affirmations of whose later poetry were as spurious as his rhetoric. At heart he is a sentimentalist, although his comic prose—at its best when performed either by himself or the actor-writer Emlyn Williams—is mostly unpretentious and has a genuine vitality. His stories (*A Prospect of the Sea,* 1955, collects the thirties ones from *The Map of Love* and adds later work; *Portrait of the Artist as a Young Dog,* 1940; *Adventures in the Skin Trade,* 1955) draw very heavily, like *Under Milk Wood,* on T. F. Powys (q.v.), and have debts to Caradoc Evans (q.v.) and others superior to Thomas. The early ones add nothing to Powys but a morbid sickness and ineptitude. The later ones are better written but never engage in real self-examination. *Adventures in the Skin Trade* is derived from Beckett's (q.v.) *Murphy*, of which Thomas had written a hostile review. There are of course more positive views of Thomas and the best and most moderate expositor of such views is G. S. Fraser in his general study (1957, reprinted in his *Vision and Rhetoric*, 1959). But one is hard put to it to ascribe any quality of maturity to a famous poem by Thomas—one of his last—that is admired by all his devotees: 'Do Not Go Gentle Into That Good Night'. This is, in its way, neatly made; Thomas obviously worked at it. But its content is trivial and even, perhaps, puerile. Thomas, for all that he once seemed so original and 'modern', is a curiously old fashioned and childish figure; a criticism that can continue to accord him major status is weak. The *Life* (1965) and the *Selected Letters* (1966), by the autolatric Irishman Constantine Fitzgibbon are poor. *Early Prose Writings* (1972).

Thomas, Edward (1878–1917) Welsh (born in London) poet, novelist, critic, miscellaneous prose writer. He was killed at Arras but is never classified simply as one of the 'war poets'—rather he was a poet killed in the war, which is not one of his main subjects. He was educated at Oxford and then became a sad literary journalist. He was a solitary man: a quiet rambler in search of the sources of his own melancholy (e.g. the extraordinary and complex 'The Other'). He had written poetry as a boy (and there is one pseudonymous poem, 'Eluned', in a 1905 illustrated book about Wales whose text he wrote), but his mature work all belongs to the last five years of his life. He married Helen Noble in 1899; her accounts of life with this difficult and lonely man, whom she none the less loved, have almost classic status: *As It Was* (1926), *World Without End* (1931). At his weakest Thomas could appear Georgian (*see* Brooke), but attempts to classify him as such are pointless. His editorial work (e.g. on Marlowe) is not less slovenly than that of his generation and some of his nature anthologies (e.g. *The Book of the Open Air*, 1907–8) are excellent, as are such studies as *Richard Jeffries* (1909) and *George Borrow* (1912). *Four and Twenty Blackbirds* (1915; 1965; in USA as *Complete Fairy Tales*, 1966) reflect his poetic genius, which developed late but surely. There is merit, and interest, too, in his semi-autobiographical novel *The Happy-Go-Lucky Morgans* (1913), and in *The South Country* (1909; 1932) which he knew so well. Frost (q.v.) encouraged him to write poetry; but his own influence on Frost is as considerable. His poems in his lifetime (*Six Poems*, 1916; *An Annual of New Poetry*–containing fourteen new poems) were published under the pseudonym of Edward Eastaway. *Collected Poems* (1920 rev. 1928 rev. 1949), with a foreword by Walter de la Mare (q.v.), firmly established him as a popular poet and has remained in print ever since. But, popular though he is, Thomas has never received completely adequate critical treatment: the critical study by H. Coombes (1956) and the critical biography by W. Cooke (1970) are useful, but neither does justice to Thomas's profundity. The very excellence of the consolations offered by the surface of his poetry have perhaps obscured its depths; in fact he is a major poet and one may see his sad life as a hack writer as an existential apprenticeship for the poetry of his last years. There is more in this poetry than has been suspected: its subject-matter is not nature–though he evokes nature finely–but the menacing and tormenting web of eroticism, beauty (as felt in nature) and solipsist experience. It is all the more remarkable that Thomas, living in the Georgian era, with only very tenuous personal connections with the proto-modernist imagists (*see* Pound), should have been able to produce a poetry that is ultimately nearer to Rilke (q.v.)–if only in its implications–than to Frost; and that he should be able to exercise so exquisite a lyrical gift ('Harry, you know at night/The larks in Castle Alley/Sing from the attic's height/As if the electric light/Were the true sun above a summer valley:/Whistle, don't knock, tonight . . .'). We must not be put off by some of his archaisms; rather we must look at his marvellous and almost unheeded rhythmical breakthroughs, and grasp his originality. Only C. H. Sisson (q.v.) has given him his full due: in his *English Poetry 1900–1950*, he accords him his place as one of the 'most profound poets of the century'.

Thomas, R. S. (1913) Welsh poet. He is a clergyman (in the minority, and disestablished, Church of Wales) who ministers to a rural flock of hill-farmers about whose nature he suffers no illusions, but with whose difficulties he persistently identifies. Although he writes in English, he took the trouble to learn Welsh and his work has distinctly 'Welsh Nationalist' overtones–though he is not strident on any subject. He is a dour, reticent poet; a stubborn regionalist severely critical of his region–though his attitude towards his parishioners has notably relaxed in recent years. Although influenced in attitude by Welsh-language writers such as Saunders Lewis, it is Frost (q.v.) who has influenced Thomas most clearly in his procedures: he is a stolid, doggedly clear (if not pellucid) writer, committed to traditionalist presentation but equally committed to the avoidance of sentimentality. He seldom sounds an ostensibly personal note and his poetry is minor because—though sometimes concerned with his isolation from his flock—it is in part a strategy of defence against impulses towards self-examination. The element of linguistic excitement is totally absent. But, with those (rather strict) reservations in mind, Thomas is an honest and straightforward, though unsympathetic and conceited poet: his work is such that, if he could put more of himself into it (however he chose to accomplish this), it might be revelatory. He has written, not very helpfully, of his own approach in *Words and the Poet* (1964). *Not That He Brought Flowers* (1968), *H'm* (1972), *Selected Poems 1946–1968*, 1974. (Nothing in *H'm* is represented in the selection.)

Thurber, James (1894–1961) American humorist and maker of drawings. He represents the very best produced by the *New Yorker*, with which he was closely associated from 1927 (*The Years with Ross*, 1959, is a useful account of his friendship with Harold Ross, its editor from 1925 until 1957). Thurber could be attacked for slick gentility but he would prove immune. What makes him immune is his absolute innocence (of his virtues as of his faults). He could not draw, and did not try to: his line is absolutely innocent. He can make fun of the over-sophisticated modern world because he has this innocence of it. He is not in the least profound but he does have an innate sense of moral responsibility. Consequently his good-natured send-ups of sexology (*Is Sex Necessary?*, 1929, with E. B. White) and psychoanalysis (*Let Your Mind Alone*, 1937) have a certain gentle relevance. His most serious work, though a comedy, was the play *The Male Animal* (1940, with Eliot Nugent). *The Thurber Carnival* (1945); *The Thurber Album* (1952).

Tolkien, J. R. R. (1892–1974) English fantasist and Oxford academic (philologist and expert on Norse and allied subjects). Tolkien's Hobbit stories (*The Hobbit*, 1937; *The Lord of the Rings*, 1954–5) became the subject of a cult, but, as Edmund Wilson (q.v.) demonstrated, their basic appeal is to readers with a 'lifelong appetite for juvenile trash'. Tolkien himself called them (disingenuously) an unserious game. The earlier *The Hobbit,* though the foundation of the later overrated edifice, is a pleasant tale. Tolkien wrote some useful criticism (e.g. *Beowulf, The Monsters and the Critics,* 1936).

Toller, Ernst (1893–1939) German expressionist (*see* Stadler) dramatist, prose writer, poet. He fought in the war, spent five years in prison for his involvement in the formation of the abortive Bavarian Republic, left Germany in 1932, and committed suicide in New York. Much of his drama is over-strident and characterless, and has dated, but *Die Maschinenstürmer* (1922; tr. *The Machine Wreckers,* 1923), on the Luddites, and *Hinkemann* (tr. 1923) are exceptions. *Eine Jugend in Deutschland* (1933; tr. *I Was a German,* 1934) is a revealing autobiography. *Ausgewählte Schriften* (1959) and *Prosa, Briefe, Dramen, Gedichte* (1961) collect most of his plays, prose, letters and poetry.

Tomlinson, Charles (1927) English poet, academic, critic. Tomlinson is an odd and complex case. He has very considerable abilities but in his clever poetry his excellent perceptions are at odds with his old-fashioned romantic-decadent temperament. He is anti-existential: something is therefore lacking, something between humour and humanity. There are two more important and of course related factors: he is a frustrated painter, and (in contrast to his immense sophistication) he is enormously ambitious in an, again, old-fashioned, 'heroic' romantic manner. The contorted and so easily analysable literary character of the Tomlinson of today is something of a loss to English letters but this condition is not irremediable, as the collection *The Way In* (1975) implies. He began, a frustrated schoolmaster, by attempting a neo-Blakean epic with illustrations by himself, which failed to bring him immediate fame. He seems to have thenceforward renounced experience as a poetic source but he is too intelligent not to at least intuit that this is an act fatal to a poet. All his evasions–some of them, like his introduction to Bottrall's (q.v.) *Collected Poems,* highly suggestive–unhappily point towards the necessity of experience. His achievement one might call both hidden and involuntary (enthusiastic appreciations of his poetry have been somewhat wooden inasmuch as they begin with the premise that he is perfect). As a critic Tomlinson is acute but exasperated and prissy. None of his English contemporaries has shown more awareness of non-English poetries. But the criticism—including appreciation of Vallejo (q.v.), Machado (q.v.) and many other major poets—offers invaluable clues as to what is going on in Tomlinson's poetry: it mutes, in the interests of such concepts as 'tact', the vivid humanity of those it puts forward as excellent. In the poetry we have a high level of sophistication combined with an unnecessarily immature emotionality. Tomlinson claims to create a 'moral landscape' through 'images' of a 'certain mental climate'; but this cannot explain away the actual climate, in his poetry, of fear of expression, of lack of attack or vigour. His fascination with decay, compounded of adolescent-Gothic, nostalgia, and anguish at his lack of graphic genius, has never been resolved; but the super-modernist veil he has drawn over this is exceedingly perceptive. He claims to be a phenomenological poet but the only phenomenology in Tomlinson is brilliantly procedural. And, suffusing the whole *oeuvre,* is the glum spectre of his friend and admirer Davie's (q.v.) ultimately anti-poetic concept of poem-as-artifact. But, if we can ignore his pomposity and furiously repressed critical authoritarianism, we can discover intelligence, discernment and a certain excellent and even original capacity to translate the products of his visual imagination—one suspects these to be less aesthetically exquisite than he would like them to be: after all, they are the 'great' paintings he cannot execute—into a carefully modulated verse. For there is real feeling in his technique of evoking mental climate by description of landscape; it is simply that he must recognize the vulgarity in himself, put away his flattering, demi-dehumanized portrait of himself—and become a truly phenomenological poet. *Seeing is Believing* (1960); *Poems: A Selection* (1964); *The Way of a World* (1969); and other collections.

Torga, Miguel (ps. Adolfo Coelho Da Rocha) (1907) Portuguese novelist, poet, playwright, diarist. He is a physician by profession. He has tended to try too many styles, finally emerging as a self-styled 'rebel Orpheus' (not a too happy solution); but he has achieved enough to deserve his position as Portugal's leading living writer. One has to bear in mind the political pressures with which he (and others) have had, and certainly still have, to contend. His poetry is one of despair, recalling the attitudes of Camus (q.v.), but without his hope, and Pessoa (q.v.) in his self-effacing, nihilistic mood; but it is lyrically expressive and often moving. His best prose is in the vivid and harrowing novel *Vindima* (1945), *Grape-harvest,* and, especially, *Bichos* (1940), *Worms,* humorous animal fables. His *Diário* (1941–), *Diary*, which appears at regular intervals, is an intelligent, revealing and fascinating record.

Toson Shimazaki (ps. Shimazaki Haruki) (1872–1943) Japanese novelist and poet. One of the world's major modern novelists and an excellent poet, he remains virtually untranslated (there are a few of his innovatory early poems and some extracts scattered in anthologies). All Toson's novels but the first, *Hakai* (1906), *Broken Commandment*—about a member of an outcast group, the *eta,* who breaks his father's commandment not to reveal this—are autobiographical. Autobiographical fiction is an accepted form in Japan and its inevitably 'confessional' elements are not as shocking to intelligent readers. *Haru* (1908), *Spring,* is about his early connections with a literary group; *Ie* (1911), *The Destiny of Two Households,* is a meticulous account of his married life; *Shinsei* (1919), *A New Life,* his masterpiece, describes his incestuous relationship with his niece in astonishingly exact detail; *Yoakemae* (1935), *Before the Dawn,* is about the tragic life of his idealistic father. Toson's combination of objectivity and lyricism—it is first seen in his laconic poetry—is quite extraordinary; it might (it should) influence Western writing if it were available in translation instead of only in the summaries contained in K. B. Shinokai's *Introduction to Classic Japanese Literature.*

Toynbee, Philip (1916) English novelist, critic, memoirist, journalist. He is the son of the historian Arnold Toynbee. *Friends Apart* (1954), about his early experiences as a leftist rebel (he ran away from school) and about two of his friends, is beautifully and sensitively written, and leads one to wish that he had written further such accounts of his sometimes difficult life. His first three novels are prentice work and give little sign of the genuine experimentalism that was to come in *Tea With Mrs Goodman* (1947) and *The Garden to the Sea* (1953). These anticipated, in their form and deliberate use of depth-psychology (the influence of Jung, q.v., was evident), the more ubiquitous and now almost fashionable experimentalism (often a pseudo-experimentalism) of the seventies. Whatever verdict the critic may finally arrive at, the quality and seriousness of the books makes it evident that he is obliged to study them with attention. They have been wrongly neglected in recent years. In 1961 Toynbee began to use verse as a form: his *Pantaloon; or the Valediction,* the first in an as yet unfinished series

(*Two Brothers*, 1964, &c.). These are certainly readable, and it may well be that they carry more weight than reviewers—at least—have generally allowed. They bear re-reading carefully. It has been implied that Toynbee is not a poet and that therefore his *roman fleuve* is bound to fail. Against this view, it must be pointed out that his use of the verse form can viably be interpreted as an experimental use of prose. The latter opinion is perhaps the more cogent one; the completion of the work may well accord Toynbee the critical attention he deserves.

Trakl, Georg (1887–1914) Austrian poet. Although he had expressionist (*see* Stadler) connections, Trakl cannot be described as a part of the German expressionist movement. Yet he is a paradigmatic poet of expressionism used in its wider sense. To describe his poetry as 'surrealist-type' is seriously to mislead; the resemblance between it and any of the later surrealist (*see* Breton) poetry is superficial. The point is that the coherence he achieved is irrational; it effortlessly and non-polemically broke with the tradition by ignoring a quasi-logical framework. Just as R. Walser (q.v.) was at the same time in prose expressing the real by completely ignoring its conventional structure, the more acutely disturbed and disturbing Trakl was doing the same thing in poetry. He became addicted to drugs and alcohol at a very early age and probably his pharmaceutical training helped him to keep supplied. As a member of the Medical Corps he witnessed a mass execution of deserters and then the casualties of the battle of Grodek; these experiences unhinged him and in November, in a military hospital, he died of an overdose of drugs. Trakl's visionary poetry requires a relaxation of logical expectation; he juxtaposes aspects of the external world—decay, colour, rural landscape (most vividly evoked), the key figure of the declining youth Elis, both dead and yet unborn, seen in sombre natural surroundings—to express his inner unease, terror and joy. One can usefully trace and classify the clusters of images, symbols and *motifs* in Trakl's poetry; but complete response can ultimately come only from surrender to a poetic integrity so absolute that it approaches Buber's (q.v.) ideal of an 'I' that is speaking to a 'Thou' and not to an 'It'. This is a new language whose 'hermeticism' (*see* Ungaretti) conceals a profound and agonized sense of human brotherhood. It contains both joy and black despair and, while one may reject 'glimpses of Christian faith' in Trakl, there can be no doubt that his poetry is religious at the most mysterious level of that universal manifestation: to read him is to investigate the true meaning of the 'religious' in human beings. His work is collected in *Gesammelte Werke* (1948–51) and *Dichtungen, historische-kritische Gesamtausgabe* (1969). In English: *20 Poems of Georg Trakl* (1961); *Selected Poems* (1968).

Traven, Ben or **Bruno** (ps.? Berick Traven Torsvan) (1890–1969) Novelist and mystery man who probably posed as his own spokesman. It is most likely that he was born in Chicago of Norwegian-American parents and died in Mexico City. He was an active communist in Germany in 1918–19 and went in 1923 to South America where he did almost every kind of work. He wrote in German. Among his fiction the outstanding titles are *Das Totenschiff* (1926; tr. *The Death Ship,* 1934), *Der Schatz der Sierra Madre* (1927; tr. *The Treasure of Sierra Madre,* 1956), made famous by John Huston's movie, and the stories in *Der Banditendoktor* (1954). Despite his early communist activities, Traven as a writer combined effective adventure narrative with a social protest that is anarchic (sometimes, as it emerges in his brilliant use of dialogue of a near Célineesque, q.v., or Hašekian, q.v., sort). He is uneven, and his narrative line might be described as crude. But he is not unsubtle, the excitement he generates is never of the bourgeois-manipulative variety (he contrasts here with, e.g., Hammond Innes), and he is a profound and moving critic of the horrors of bureaucracy: his masterpiece, *Das Totenschiff,* is about a hell-ship, but it is also a refuge for men without papers, without legal status: the victims of bureaucrats. There is a selection of stories in English: *The Night Visitor* (1967).

Trilling, Lionel (1905–75) American critic, teacher (Columbia), fiction writer. Trilling stands outside the new criticism (*see* Brooks) because he is a radical humanist who has never taken the view that a text is simply a text: he judges it, ultimately, on its contribution to culture; and, a rationalist, he regards culture as necessary to human survival. He has been widely influential as teacher, essayist, and as an adviser to both the *Kenyon* and the *Partisan* reviews. He stems directly from the tradition of Matthew Arnold, on whom he wrote a standard book (*Matthew Arnold,* 1939). He has tried to understand post-liberal attitudes–one may broadly define these as 'existentialist'–but, despite his fine intelligence, has not shown real ability to do so. As a critic (*The Liberal Imagination,* 1950, and further collections) he is always worth reading but he is weak on such writers as Dreiser (q.v.) or Anderson (q.v.) because he resents both their appeal and the non-academic nature of their work. His novel *The Middle of the Journey* (1947) is an intelligent examination of the radical temperament in the style of Henry James (q.v.), but Trilling's best work of fiction is the story 'Of this Time, of that Place', in which he makes his one serious attempt to study his own predicament as academic liberal-humanist professor in a non-academic context. There is a savage and in some ways justified attack on him in Louis Simpson's (q.v.) *Air for an Armed Mission* (1972).

Twain, Mark (ps. S. L. Clemens) (1835–1910) American writer. Twain is a nineteenth-century figure who need be mentioned here only to draw attention to his importance to modern literature. He could write at a very low level indeed but his prophetic insight into the hypocritical nature of the new technology was occasionally expressed in great works, chiefly in *The Adventures of Huckleberry Finn* (1885), which also deals with the 'American dream', with the loss of childhood, and with most other seminally American themes. His very complexity and unevenness make him into an important figure. In some way or other almost all the American literature produced since his death may be significantly related to his predicament and his achievement.

Tzara, Tristan (ps. Sami Rosenstock) (1896–1963) Rumanian poet and literary activist who left his native country at nineteen and nearly all of whose work is in French (he died in Paris). He was one of the founders of the dada movement (*see* Ball) in Zurich, and was, from 1929 until 1934, a prominent surrealist (*see* Breton). In 1934 he evolved an attitude of a kind of quasi-political revolt which was not Marxist but which was not to the liking of Breton. His only substantial poem is *L'Homme approximatif* (1931), which foreshadows his later desperate and frustrated efforts to achieve a valid being: a creation of that 'consciousness'—in humane terms, capable of relationships with events—which in his youth he had totally repudiated. The repentance is similar to that of Ball (q.v.), but came later and more slowly. Tzara had simply wanted to 'abolish' the rational (one can sympathize with him: the war was 'rational'); but he lacked Arp's (q.v.) genius, and by the mid-twenties, exhausted by his efforts (which included automatic writing) to evade it, he was an intellectually if not an emotionally sick man. It was he who 'found' the word dada in *Larousse:* that it meant 'horse', or 'fad', is neither here nor there—but what an appropriate cry, supposed to be 'meaningless', from despairing young men: 'Daddy, Daddy!'. Tzara did not possess the poetic genius to conquer his original nihilism. But *L'Homme approximatif* is a fascinating and at times poetically possessed account of the attempt of a man who has rejected reality to regain a sense of it. His non-achievement—a remarkable one—is essentially that of the non-totalitarian expressionist (*see* Stadler), and is one of the most instructive and impressive of our time: for here is a central artistic predicament. There is a sense in which he is 'bigger' than Breton. Even in the later poetry there is always substantial evidence of the struggle—and this is paralleled by his courageous Resistance work in Southern France in the war. Tzara's creative energy was spent, first, in trying to smash 'bourgeois' language, then in trying (*L'Homme approximatif*) to reconstitute it according to its proper, irrationalist, principles; he failed in both enterprises, and only a few passages in the later poetry (there is a selection of this in *De la Coupe aux lèvres,* 1962, *Twixt the Cup and the Lip*) possess power. There is no collected edition of his works, but R. Lacôte's study (1952) contains a selection. See also *Morceaux choisis* (1947).

U

Unamuno, Miguel De (1864–1936) Spanish (Basque) thinker, novelist, dramatist, poet, critic, classicist, polemicist, academic. Unamuno is one of the most fascinating figures of modern literature, as original as Nietzsche but not (yet) as directly influential. He is as proto-existentialist (*see* Sartre) as Nietzsche, but he read Kierkegaard (in Danish: he knew fifteen languages well), whereas Nietzsche heard of him only a few months before he went mad and did not know his works. Ortega (q.v.), who argued with Unamuno, could not have existed without him. Unamuno fought throughout his life to bring Spain to life, and Unamuno will certainly still have his part to play. Those who influenced him represent an encyclopedia of the most important European thinkers; they include Herbert Spencer, Bergson (q.v.), Ibsen and Hegel, whom he translated. He was a man within whom conflicts raged; his attempted resolution of these was, naturally, a failure–but it was one of the most remarkable of the century. His novels and poetry have been consistently underrated, even patronized, outside Spain. For Spain, as Unamuno was the first to realize, is peculiarly isolated from Europe, even though it is a part of it. Almost all of his works deal with Spain but they transcend its particular problems by posing the universal ones of what man is to do about his loss of faith, his (selfish and yet unselfish) love of his country, his terror of extinction and, above all, his anxiety. Usually Unamuno's non-fiction books are taken as his masterpieces and these are assuredly vital; but he did his greatest work in the novel. Nor is his poetry, obstinately independent of fashion, nearly as negligible as non-hispanic criticism suggests. With Ortega, Unamuno still expresses, for those who are interested, the paradoxical spirit of Spain: love of enjoyment, belief in *ennui;* cultivation of sweet hatred; 'amor amargo' (acrid love)–as a critic has put it. However, as Demetrios Basdekis has stated in his invaluable (and properly enthusiastic, though wry) short introductory study to Unamuno (1969), the 'central themes which . . . pervade [his] complete works are reducible to the human biped, God, and Spain and the world, perhaps in that order of importance'. The general extra-hispanic notion of Unamuno (that he could not bear the idea of extinction and was a failed creative writer) is a barbaric one: in the understanding of him, provided we allow for his fierce idiosyncracies, we may discover the essential themes of most, if not all, of the vital fictions of this century. Not only did he pose the Nietzschean problem in a humane manner, but he anticipated every kind of novelistic experimentalism except those concerned with the manipulation of language (i.e. wrenched or 'smashed' syntax, neologisms, the blend of the archaic and the colloquial). Unamuno was one of the leading spirits of the 'Generation of 1898' (Azorin's term), which really means little more than that at about this time Spanish literature underwent a renewal: it absorbed (and reacted against) Darío's (q.v.) *modernismo,* it went to Europe (particularly to German philosophy) for ideas, it was urgent—above all it *questioned* the values (or non-values) of the moribund literature. Unamuno's most famous book is *Del sentimiento trágico de la vida* (1913; tr. *The Tragic Sense of Life,* 1958). This exhorts people to base their 'faith' in 'doubt', which alone gives life meaning—even if there is oblivion at death, man can exist authentically only by resisting the absurdity and the injustice of such a fact. This amounts to a fiercely constructive scepticism: draw strength, drama, 'glory', from uncertainty. History he preferred to see as *intrahistoria:* the history that is lived down the ages by the folk—not the 'facts' in the books. This *intrahistoria* is not a 'glorious' conception: it can be noble or the opposite of noble, but it cannot be ignored. In the novel *Niebla* (1914; tr. *Mist,* 1928) Augusto doubts his own existence because, of course, he is Unamuno's creation; Unamuno enters the novel and tells him that he cannot allow him to commit suicide because he has no will of his own (being his, the novelist's, creature)—but Augusto suggests to him that he, the novelist, may, after all, only be an instrument, also without will, for the perpetuation of characters. . . . Critics who dislike this dislike the destruction of their illusions about the nature of fictions—and, indeed, of their certainties about their own identities. It is in fact a great novel. *Abel Sánchez* (1917; tr., with other stories, 1956) is, as its title suggests, a variation on the Cain-Abel myth, though Joaquín is Abel's brother only in a metaphorical sense. This, again complexly constructed, consists mainly of Joaquín's confessions, to be read by his daughter after his death, and is a study of envy. *Tres novelas ejemplares* (1920; tr. *Three Exemplary Novels*, 1930), with an important prologue, contains his most 'realistic' characters–which is to say that he (ironically?) gives them an impact. *San Manuel Bueno, mártir* (1931; tr. *Saint Manuel the Good, Martyr*, 1957, in a bilingual edition) springs partly from *La agonia del Cristianismo* (1924; tr. *The Agony of Christianity*, 1928; 1960)–which takes a hispanicized Nietzschean view of Christianity having become the tragic and ironic opposite of itself–and is about a priest who does not believe in God but who dedicates himself to his flock. As a poet Unamuno was prolific, independent, crabbed, uneven, excessively metrical, and influential (on, e.g. Darío, q.v., whose *modernismo* he rejected). His long poem *El Cristo de Vélazquez* (1920; tr. 1951) is deeply interesting but fails through its extreme unevenness. He is at his best in shorter forms. His plays are failures. Much more remains to be said of Unamuno and much more will be said. His *Obras completas*, containing most of his work (but not some of the journalism), was published in 1958. Also in English translation: *Essays and Soliloquies* (a sel. tr. 1925); *Vida de Don Quijote y Sancho* (1905; tr. *The Life of Don Quixote*, 1927; *Our Lord Don Quixote*–with more sel. essays–1967). The early and excellent realistic novel *Paz en la guerra* (1897), *Peace in War*, is untranslated.

Ungaretti, Giuseppe (1888–1970) Italian poet, translator, essayist. Born in Egypt of Lucchese parents, Ungaretti first visited Italy only in his twenty-sixth year; soon afterwards he joined the army and fought on the Austrian front. Between 1912 and 1914 he lived in Paris, writing sometimes in French, and becoming friendly with Apollinaire (q.v.), Breton (q.v.) and others. His first collection, *Il porto sepolto* (1916), *The Buried Harbour*, carried a preface by Mussolini (who had just been expelled from the socialist party); it ranks, with poetry by Rebora and Jahier (q.v.), as the best Italian poetry to be produced by the war. Of the five indisputably great Italian poets of this century–Campana (q.v.), Saba (q.v.), Montale (q.v.), Quasimodo (q.v.)–Ungaretti presents the most immediate difficulties, and behind his work indeed lies a recondite and controversial 'poetic'. By 1947 Ungaretti's work, entitled *Vita d'un uomo* (1966; part tr. *Life of a Man*, 1958), in which the expanse of white on the page represents silence and desert, is essentially an attempt to recapture the original, pristine significance of each word: the project is thus a religious and social one, for the poet never abandons his faith in meaning (the 'absurd' does not exist in Ungaretti except as an illusion) and he regards the modern chaos—first seen in the trenches—as the result of verbal corruption. Ungaretti begins in total subjectivity, solipsism, and he uses technique in an almost primitive way to express this—the image is 'born from the sound'. But the initial solipsism, the persistent accent of honest desperation, is, in Sanguineti's words, a 'search for reasons of hope in the heart of history itself'. The earliest war poems are, as it happens, perfect examples of expressionism: the poet internalizes and verbalizes the agonies going on around him: this subjectivity is the opposite of selfish, for it is a man taking upon himself the burden of a pain that most would consider unnecessary. As he puts it in a very early epigram, 'Eternal', written in Milan before Italy's entry into the war, 'Between the plucked flower and the one given/the unutterable void'. It was this void that he doggedly set out to fill, taking his example from the Mallarmé of *Coup de dès* but his chief inspiration, perhaps, came from the naked despair of Leopardi. Thus: 'A whole night/flung close/to a comrade/slain/his teeth bared/in a grin/head twisted towards full moon/with the plethora/of his hands/piercing/my silence/I have written letters ripe with love//have never been/so/near to life.' The critic and poet Francesco Flora first used the word 'hermetic' of Ungaretti's poetry in 1936, and then pejoratively; but the movement, which was never a school or a program, had been in existence for almost twenty years. 'Hermeticism', in Montale and Quasimodo as in Ungaretti, was a form of 'inner resistance' to fascism: one could not speak out under Mussolini and so one could either join the fascists, or keep silent—or retreat into oneself and simultaneously keep faith with human values by purifying speech. Ungaretti, though influenced by literatures and painters not Italian (but we must not forget his tap-root in Leopardi), undoubtedly pioneered hermeticism both by his moral example and his achievement. His development is predictable. Beginning with short poems and single word lines, he then goes on to develop more complex and elaborate procedures: to create a baroque poetry that, as he said of the baroque, is 'born of the horror of emptiness . . . a void that has to be filled at all costs'. The poetry of this period, from the mid-twenties to the middle of the Second World War (he was teaching in Brazil from 1936 until 1942) is highly cerebral and yet strangely visual in impact—certainly in part 'cubist' in inspiration, and harking back to his friendships with Apollinaire (and with the macabre expressionist Anglo-Belgian painter James Ensor). With the volume *Il dolore* (1947), *Grief*, some of it consisting of meditations on the loss of his little son in Brazil, Ungaretti entered his final and most deliberate phase: consciously going back to the Italian tradition, more purely 'literary', more rhetorical (though not seeming so), originating less in spontaneity—or what he would have called inspiration. Certainly Ungaretti wrote less as he grew older, and certainly his last poetry is his most artificial. For his imagery Ungaretti often drew on the Egypt where he was born, a desert whose presence in his mind he treats visually—even when apparently most 'metaphysical'—in terms of cubist and surrealist painting. He also wrote much of rivers. Reading him one must try to follow him visually, keeping in sight not only the modern painters he knew but also the canals of Rembrandt's Amsterdam which distort, destroy and then recreate the old houses in their waters—and the light of Caravaggio which 'shatters things . . . releases a tragedy and establishes a structure'. He made distinguished translations from Gongora, Mallarmé, Blake, Racine and Shakespeare's sonnets. More than any modern major European poet he defies translation; but he is worth learning Italian for.

Updike, John (1932) American novelist, poet. He is a product of the *New Yorker* school; in a sense this is below his level and it has tended to pull him down into an over-concentration on sophistication and polish at the expense of the excellent characterization of which he is clearly capable. His over-manneredness does not go well with his high intelligence. *The Poorhouse Fair* (1959) is spoiled by a deliberate grotesqueness which clashes with the author's intention, which is to express pity for old people without patronizing them or evading the issues. *Rabbit, Run* (1960) and *Rabbit Redux* (1971) are brilliant—but, like his stories, too much so; *Beck: A Book* (1970) tries to deal with the difficulties of the writer, but is too slick and enforcedly casual. Updike's poetry is at the level of sophisticated light verse.

V

Valéry, Paul (1871–1945) French poet, poetic dramatist, prose writer, critic, letter-writer and diarist. Indubitably one of France's and the century's greatest poets and thinkers, who combines in himself ironic establishmentarianism, severe classicism, scorn of literature, enjoyment of fame, high sophistication—and a glowing romantic lyricism. Valéry, like Rilke (q.v.), whom he otherwise does not at all resemble, is one of the rare ones whose passion is not crippled by thought. He is the paradigmatic major twentieth-century poet: the reconciler of feeling and intellect. It is therefore unsurprising that his poetry came to him only in relatively short bursts. Valéry's influence on French and European letters is second only in importance to his work, which includes *Monsieur Teste* (complete edition 1946), the *Cahiers* (1957–61), *Notebooks*, correspondence and miscellaneous items as well as the poetry: though ultimately romantic, he is in a critically anti-romantic current, since he opposes as much as possible of the rational to the irrational. But his great achievement, in the poetry and the *Cahiers*, is to effect the reconciliation between science and imagination that both yearn for. His hubristic inclinations ('A man who has never attempted to make himself like the gods, is less than a man', he wrote) led him into postures of coldness and ungenerousness; but this is more than compensated for when he is at his strongest and most humble: writing in his diaries in the early morning, and, above all, heroically resisting but never suppressing his passion, sensuality and wildness in his two greatest poems—'La Jeune Parque', 'The Young Fate', 'Le Cimetière marin', 'The Cemetery by the Sea'. Born in Sète, on the Mediterranean coast of France, Valéry had strong southern elements in his blood: his father was of Corsican descent, his mother of Venetian. His first interests were in painting, music and architecture, and his first enthusiasms were for Hugo, Rimbaud, Poe and Huysmans (q.v.), but Mallarmé soon became his idol and he was able to meet him through Pierre Louÿs (q.v.), with whom he had become friendly, in 1891. Mallarmé, whose 'L'Après-midi d'un faune', 'Afternoon of a Fawn', was now Valéry's ideal, encouraged him and praised his poems. Thus he entered into the *artistic* rather than the *magic* stream of symbolist poetry that had divided from the source of Baudelaire; he also, twenty-five years later, brought it to a greater perfection than his master, though he could not have done this without him. At this time he became friendly with Gide (q.v.) and began to publish his poems–alongside Swinburne's, Mallarmé's, and many others–in Louÿs's magazine *La Conque, The Conch,* and elsewhere. Because Louÿs was undoubtedly a second- or even third-rate writer, though not unimportant, his personal influence on Valéry may have been underestimated: an aesthete and a lush sensualist struggled in him and the detached Valéry may well have looked critically at his achievement–in the decadent atmosphere of the nineties–and been helped towards his own sudden decision to abandon poetry. And many of his early poems (collected 1920, *Album des vers anciens, Album of Old Verse*) are relatively poor: lush, tinselly, mannered, derivative–as well as highly talented and brilliant in technique. There is one exception: 'Narcisse parle', 'Narcissus Speaks'. This simultaneously adumbrates his obsession with the subject (natural to one who wished to be, as Mallarmé said of Poe, 'magnificent, complete and solitary'), his abandonment of poetry–and his then unconscious determination to take it up again, to in effect bring it into more contact with life than even Mallarmé was able to, when he was prepared. His distrust of poetry had been, in fact, shattered by Mallarmé, who seemed to Valéry just then to have gone as far with it as was possible; but in his heart he believed he could take it further. After a crisis of spirit which he chose, with typical artistry, to represent as having occurred during a stormy night spent in Genoa in the autumn of 1892, he decided to dedicate himself to knowledge and self-understanding: in the succeeding years he studied Leonardo da Vinci, physics, mathematics, history and (significantly) literature. The solitary he now became found its objective correlative in the creation of *Monsieur Teste* (1896). Earlier he had written an introduction to Leonardo (1895); but this was less an examination of the man than a discourse on the potentialities of the isolated human mind. Teste is entirely his own creation, 'superior' to the real Leonardo: an anonymous entity whose name puns on 'tête', 'tester' (test) and perhaps, ironically, 'testicule', testicle. For even this 'intellectual *animal*' (my italics), as Valéry describes him, has to live. Teste rejects fame, personality, the necessity of writing or even of possessing books; yet he transcends genius, he is not even to be called 'great' because he is self-sufficient. For Teste, as for Coleridge, there is 'something inherently mean in action'. However, he is forced to live by speculating on the Bourse (the details, to Valéry, sound like poetry), and he suffers from illness. He is, in part, a tragi-comic creation: much later Valéry called him a 'monster', and wryly invented a wife for him in *Lettre de Madame Emilie Teste* (1924), whose greatest pleasure is in not understanding him. In 1900 Valéry married and soon afterwards obtained what amounted to a sinecure: he became a private secretary to a wealthy businessman, a partner in a large news agency. He devoted his time to further study until, in 1912, Gide suggested he publish his early poems as a volume. He agreed, and started to round them off with a final poem: this became 'La Jeune Parque'. This is a great poem, but Valéry himself on its subject becomes tiresome. How much was his tongue in his cheek? Certainly he was a humorous and warm man, as his correspondence with Gide (in particular) reveals. He spoke of it as an exercise, an attempt to 'break in the animal *Language* and . . . lead it where it is not accustomed to go'. For him it may certainly have been an exercise in pure intellect (not spirit); but in consciously making its classical versification its subject, he was in fact making it clear that it was magic—that he himself did not know what it meant. He came closest to the truth when he wrote, in a private letter to Gide, that it was 'an artificial construction that came . . . to develop naturally'. He was dealing here, as he later admitted, with a region of the mind from which he had fled. The poem has been interpreted very variously: as the essence of the feminine; the monologue of a young Fate torn between immortality and sensual mortality; the struggles of a mind trying to free itself from the flesh, or of a writer thrusting himself richly against a complex scheme of versification. . . . But it is all these, and more—and, above all, it is the conjuring of concrete images to reflect an inner state. 'La Jeune Parque' is 'beautiful' in the Racinian, Gallic sense, but it is not so earnest as it appears (just as life is not). After publishing it in 1917, he wrote 'Le Cimetière marin', which appeared in 1920, and other important poems such as 'La Pythie', 'The Pythoness', which is among other things a kind of acknowledgement, even celebration, of the quality of 'inspiration', the most explicit Valéry ever wrote. After *Odes* (1920) and *Charmes* (1922) Valéry wrote little more verse and this not of a high order. His patron died but he was able to earn his living as a man of letters with irony, elegance and grace. His correspondence with Gide (selection translated into English, 1966) reveals much of both men. His *Collected Works* in (uneven) English translation are in progress; and other translations are available. *Valéry*, by A. W. Thomson, is a useful introduction.

Valle-Inclán, Ramón del (ps. Ramón del Valle Y Peña) (1866–1936) Spanish novelist, dramatist, poet, critic. Valle-Inclán is still underrated, though he was a famous figure in his day—black-bearded, Bohemian, one-armed (he lost his arm in a dawn encounter with a journalist later to become a fascist), the subject of many fantastic tales (some invented by himself). In 1929 the shoddy dictator Primo de Rivera had him thrown into gaol. He is usually dismissed as a showman and a sensationalist but he was an early expressionist (*see* Stadler) who profoundly influenced the course of Spanish literature. He began as a decadent and stylistic perfectionist under French influences, but he soon turned his decadence into an awareness of the twentieth century. His own public personality was a subtle invention, a fiction. His four *Sonatas* (1902–5) explore this projection of himself as the Marqués de Bradomín. Later he invented a form of drama which he called *esperpento* ('fun-house distorting mirror'): mocking, distorting, Spanish-expressionist. Outstanding is *Los cuernos de Don Frislera* (novel 1921, play 1925), *The Horns of Don Frislera. Tirano Banderas* (1926) is an 'esperpentic' treatment of a Mexican dictator. The complete works appeared in 1945.

Vallejo, César (1892–1938) Peruvian poet, novelist, playwright. He was of Indian blood (both his father and his mother were bastards of Indians by priests, which explains much in his work). His childhood was poor but happy. *Los heraldos negros* (1918), *The Dark Messengers,* is perhaps the most astonishing first book of poetry ever to appear. It was followed (1922) by *Trilce* (*Dulche* and *Triste*), in which traditional form is wrenched to its utmost limits. Vallejo, having had some education at the universities of Trujillo and San Marcos, had in the meantime been in prison on a false charge. He had grown up in a Tungsten mining area where the ordinary people were viciously exploited and though he had sympathies with the poor he was at this time an anti-Marxist. In 1923 Vallejo went to Paris, where he died in 1938. He had in the meantime committed himself to communism, visited Spain and Russia, and written the *Poemas humanas* (1939; tr. *Human Poems*, 1969–strange versions which have not met with universal approval, and which his widow has condemned) and the anguished responses to the Spanish Civil War *España, aparta de mé este cáliz* (1940), *Spain, Take Thou This Cup From Me*–some of these, with other poems, are translated in the best English selection: *Neruda* [q.v.] *and Vallejo* (1971). Vallejo was no conventional Catholic or communist but the Catholicism of his childhood had a deep influence on him, and in the twenties and thirties that part of him which did not write poetry found Soviet communism the only alternative to the Europe of Hitler, Franco, Baldwin and their kind. No modern 'Marxist' would find comfort in Vallejo's poetry, which breaks every rule of socialist realism (*see* Gorky), though his poor novel (*El tungsteno*, 1931) and his plays might not offend. Much of his work, chiefly journalism, has not been collected and his poetry has never been properly edited (there are two 'complete' editions, *Poesîas completas*, 1965; *Obra poética completa*, 1968); but he left enough to make it clear that he is probably the century's greatest poet in any language. His poetry is not definable–except as the nakedly honest verbal response of a man of nearly unbearable sensibility and sensitivity to human suffering. 'It is vital to stink like a psychotic postulating/ how hot snow is, how fast the tortoise/ how easy the *how*/ how deadly the *when!*'

Vargas Llosa, Mario (1936) Peruvian fiction writer. He has travelled widely but his fiction is set in Peru, whose sociological and political problems he explores with humour, intelligence and a technique much influenced by European modernist procedures (e.g. the use of 'phenomenological' time from various points of view). His later novels are more ambitious than his first, *La ciudad y los perros* (1958; tr. *The City and the Dogs*, 1967), and not perhaps as uniformly successful. *La ciudad y los perros* (the 'dogs' are cadets at a Lima army school) is a searing study of the corrupt and brutal life of military cadets. *La casa verde* (1966; tr. *The Green House*, 1969) contrasts the urban and the remote rural worlds of Peru, and demonstrates the strange relationship between them. Vargas Llosa continues to attempt to put Peru's dilemma into perspective and is one of the most intelligent (he is often very funny) of the younger Latin American novelists. His main strength lies in his ability to see the priceless advantages of the past–

and, at the same time, its disadvantages. He affirms; but is never idealistic.

Veblen, Thorstein (1857–1929) American (of Norwegian stock) 'institutionalist' economist, sociologist, influential critic of the middle classes and of business 'ethics'. Veblen's contortedly ironic style ('desperately accurate circumlocutions' wrote his admirer Mumford) could lead one to claim him as having belonged to any number of 'schools'. In fact he was very much his own man; he is discussed here mainly because of his influence. He was the chief theoretical castigator of the bourgeois materialism with which almost every American writer of his time was concerned. He gave American creative and imaginative protest an intellectual backbone and was worthy of the role. He was wildly eccentric and was perhaps more admired than liked by his personal friends. Of his many books two of the most important are the crucial *The Theory of the Leisure Class* (1899) and *The Instinct of Workmanship* (1914). The best introduction is David Riesman's *Thorstein Veblen* (1953).

Verga, Giovanni (1840–1922) Italian (Sicilian) novelist, short-story writer, playwright. The pioneer of *verismo* (a largely meridional movement), the Italian version of naturalism–which, as might be expected, lays more emphasis on the primitive, the inescapably sensual; but Verga was much more than a mere theorist. His early fiction, urban in setting, is skilful but sentimental; the turning point came with the short story 'Nedda' (1874), in which he treated Sicilian peasant life. He planned a whole cycle of novels (*I vinti, The Vanquished*) in which he proposed to present this with absolute realism, relying on objective techniques which included extensive dialogue, the attempted 'disappearance' of the author by means of impersonal, non-moralistic narrative, and a 'choral' or 'polyphonic' approach by which all the characters tell the story; only two of these (and a few pages of a third) actually got written: *I Malavoglia* (1881; tr. *The House by the Medlar Tree,* 1950), about the destruction of a family of fishermen, and *Mastro-don Gesualdo* (1888; tr. 1928), about a builder whose lust for material possessions brings him wealth but which cuts him off from others, including his family. He wrote many brilliant stories (some tr., *Little Novels of Sicily,* 1925) and some successful plays, of which the most famous formed the basis for Mascagni's opera *Cavalleria rusticana* (this was first, 1880, a story, then, 1884, recast as a play). Verga is important in Italian literature for a number of reasons: his Sicilian realism was and is needed; his attempts at objectivity introduced a new kind of 'detached' technique; his use of the standard language to represent the dialect was brilliant (cf. Reymont, q.v.). He was brought to silence because he found that his methods were inadequate to deal with the more sophisticated levels of society and perhaps because he discovered that the author cannot in fact be absent from his production—he must show himself not only in every invention but also in every choice. His earlier novels were very popular; his best fiction was received coldly and in his last years of silence he became almost forgotten by the general reader. But he is one of the most important of European novelists. *Opere* (1955). *Tutte le novelle* (1968), *Collected Short Fiction.*

Verhaeren, Émile (1855–1916) Flemish poet, art critic and playwright who wrote in French; Belgium's greatest poet, but now misunderstood and largely neglected. Verhaeren is popularly represented as having simply moved from naturalism through Parnassianism and introspective decadence to socialistic, materialistic optimism. These are certainly phases he passed through as a man, aspects of his character; but thus to characterize his poetry is superficial. It transcends its influences and the last poetry is richly ambiguous. He was a passionately good, honest man, gloomy, noble, nerve-wracked, lovable, of enormous linguistic vitality and power; a radiantly happy marriage (1891) not only rescued him from nihilism and despair but also reinforced his characteristically Flemish preoccupation with the capacity of art (as use of colour) magically to transmute a flat and sombre landscape, so to say, into its own soul. The early poems, *Les Flamandes* (1883), *The Flemish,* are as near to paintings as poems can get and Barrès's description of them as 'glorious brutalities' is brilliantly accurate. His influence, especially in *Les Villes tentaculaires* (1895), *The Tentacular Cities,* became immense. On the one hand the city became for him a substitute for God, a place of hope; on the other technology filled him with terror—of increasing anomie, ruination of the country, destruction of domestic privacy. He died in an accident at Rouen railway station crying out 'Ma patrie . . . ma femme!' His art criticism (e.g. *Ensor,* 1909) is profound; his plays fail at the stage level, but read well. He is rescued from his faults—over-prolificity, lack of regard for structure in the later poems, refusal to compress—by his vigour. There are a number of English translations, notably by F. S. Flint.

Vesaas, Tarjei (1897–1970) Norwegian fiction writer, dramatist, critic, poet. Vesaas is the leading Norwegian writer in *Landsmål* (now usually referred to as *Nynorsk*). All the Scandinavian languages are mutually understandable but the 'country speech', *Landsmål*, differs considerably from the *Riksmål* or *Bokmål*, which was the Dano-Norwegian 'state' language of Norway while it was under Danish domination and in which most Norwegian writers still write–though there is a tendency to combine the two into *Samnorsk*, a 'combined Norwegian'. Vesaas, a difficult, mostly unfulfilled but important writer, tried (it may be said) to assimilate the best of Hamsun (q.v.), including what he anticipated, and to spit out the rest. His *Landsmål* style is a great and enduring achievement but his later work, though regionally based, fails because it is over-intellectually oriented towards a modernism that is undigested because (ironically) Vesaas insisted on being a farmer and staying close to his sources. *Det store spelet* (1934; tr. *The Great Cycle*, 1967), and its untranslated sequel, are powerful but inexorably confused accounts of peasant life. His greatest achievement came with the transitional novel *Kimen* (1940; tr. *The Seed*, 1964), in which he almost resolves–in the face of the catastrophe he clearly foresaw–the conflict between his subtle bucolicism and his pessimistic sense of commitment. He was sensitive and sophisticated, and he displayed a fine understanding of the 'simple' (whether children or adult). But from 1945 onwards his procedures became self-consciously modernistic: neither *Fuglane* (1957; tr. *The Birds*, 1968) nor *Isslottet* (1963; tr. *The Ice Palace*, 1966) is successful. His verse and drama are minor byproducts, though often excellent and lucid. His greatest contribution lies in his thirties novels and in his style. *Vårnatt* (1954; tr. *Spring Night*, 1964); *Båten om kvelden* (1968; tr. *The Boat in the Evening*, 1971).

Vestdijk, Simon (1898–1971) Dutch fiction writer, poet, essayist, miscellaneous writer, translator. From the end of the war until his death this astonishingly prolific author (over one hundred books) was regarded by many Dutchmen as Holland's leading Nobel Prize contender and some critics still refer to him as 'Holland's greatest writer of this century'. He was associated with the Dutch expressionist movement in the thirties and he wrote a book of poetry in collaboration with Adriaan Holst. He had studied medicine, psychiatry, music and psychology and this is evident in his fiction, which is an odd mixture of clinicism and violence. His poetry is neither here nor there—competent, energetic, diffuse. His essays, highly controversial, deal with writers and with such subjects as astrology. Vestdijk's versatility was quite remarkable, even if he usually seems in somewhat too much of a hurry. Although he was influenced by everything, Vestdijk had especial debts to Proust (q.v.), Freud (q.v.) and Dostoievski. His most famous work is the partly autobiographical eight-novel sequence *Anton Wachter* (1934–50), an exploration of childhood, and especially of the son-mother relationship (which gives both points of view), in a frenetic tapestry of recollection. This impressive cycle was developed and elaborated from *Kind tussen vier vrouman* (1972), *Child Between Four Women,* written in 1933. For all their weaknesses—a tendency to abstraction, a conflict between objectivity of treatment and the wild vitalism of the material—the sequence tells us something about childhood, especially about the way in which dissimulation is developed, that no other European fiction does. Vestdijk was a very good psychologist. His many historical novels are not as good (e.g. *Rumeiland,* 1940; tr. *Rum Island,* 1963); but some of his modern novels are remarkable: in *Meneer Visser's hellevaart* (1936), *Mr Visser's Descent Into Hell,* a 'little man' sets out to emulate the Marquis de Sade; *De Koperen tuin* (1950; tr. *The Garden Where the Brass Band Played,* 1965) is a tragic love-story set in the first decade of the century, powerfully evoking small town stiflingness; *De kellner en de levenden* (1949; French tr. *Les Voyageurs,* 1966), *The Waiter and the Living,* incorporates a nightmarish and sinister eschatological vision, ironically counterpointed with banal descriptions—this may be Vestdijk's greatest novel. His final view of love, an affirmative one, may be found in *De doktor en het lichte meisje* (1951), *The Doctor and the Whore.* It is surprising that only two of Vestdijk's novels—he wrote more than thirty—should have been translated into English.

Vian, Boris (1920–59) French playwright, fiction writer, poet. Vian was a bohemian polymath—actor, trumpeter, science-fictionist, jazz expert, engineer, anarchist, translator, pornographer, writer of popular 'tough' novels, singer, inventor—whose refusal to take much heed of his serious heart ailment killed him early. He wrote his popular fiction (e.g. *J'irai cracher sur vos tombes,* 1946, *I Will Spit on Your Tombs*) under the name of Vernon Sullivan; he was watching a preview of Michel Gast's film (1959) of *J'irai cracher sur vos tombes* when he died. He was a leading 'pataphysician' (*see* Jarry). The best of his many writings are the novels *L'Écume des jours* (1947; tr. *Froth on the Daydream*, 1967) and *L'Arrache-coeur* (1953; tr. *Heartsnatcher*, 1968), and the play *Les Bâtisseurs d'empire* (1959; tr. *The Empire Builders*, 1962). The first, a love story, is his most restrained book; the second is a near classic study of stifling mother-love, which bears comparison with Mauriac's (q.v.) very different *Genetrix*. The play, although in surrealist music-hall style, is a truly terrifying study of death and introduces the strange bandaged figure of the *Schmürz*, an ambiguous and battered emblem of human pain who stands for the author himself as well as for his heart-pains. Vian is a remarkable tragi-comic writer: one of the few whose doomed condition and self-destructive way of life found full expression outside bars and the rooms of drunken or drugged friends. *Théâtre* (1965). There is an excellent introductory study by David Noakes (1964).

Vidal, Gore (1925) American novelist, playwright, essayist, ex-politician (he ran for Congress in 1960), urbane or bizarre publicist for disgust at political corruption (the best of his accounts of the moral miasma that is Washington is in the novel *Washington D.C.*, 1967). Vidal is intelligent and aware; the contrast between the lines taken by him and Mailer (q.v.) is interesting. Vidal remains sophisticated and polished; Mailer is deliberately rough, desperate and 'naked'. His decent bitterness remains perfectly apparent, though in the comic sex-change extravaganza *Myra Breckinridge* (1968) the message tends to be lost, since it plays rather too easily into the hands of the enemy. Previous novels were superior. The first, *Williwaw* (1946)—later, like other earlier work, rewritten—is a tense, promising, 'straight' war novel. *The City and the Pillar* (1948) was not the first novel to deal with the homosexual world but it was the first to gain a wide public. The best of all, *Julian* (1964), deals expertly with one of the most fascinating personalities in history, Julian the Apostate. Excellent essays are collected in *Rocking the Boat* (1962) and *Reflections upon a Sinking Ship* (1969). Plays are in *Visit to a Small Planet* (1956). Vidal's entertaining detective-stories of the fifties were issued under the name of Edgar Box.

Vittorini, Elio (1908–66) Italian (Sicilian) novelist, critic, translator (Poe, Faulkner, Steinbeck). Vittorini was an important and influential writer—perhaps the most influential in post-war Italy—who educated himself in face of great obstacles. Yet the consensus is correct: his only wholly successful novel is *Conversazione in Sicilia* (1941; tr. *Conversation in Sicily*, 1948), which the fascists disliked and half-banned by preventing booksellers from stocking it. Like his brother-in-law Quasimodo (q.v.), Vittorini is both puzzled and obsessed by the opposition between Sicily and northern Italy (particularly Milan). As a critic and as founder-editor of the important review *Il Politecnico* (1945–7) he has been one of the most profound critics of 'socialist realism' (*see* Gorky) and, at the same time, explorer of the notion of 'commitment'. He felt (again like Quasimodo, but earlier) that literature must concern itself with social ethics, with justice. *Conversazione in Sicilia* is, ironically, his best book because the existence of the fascist censorship forced him on to a metaphorical, and more personal, plane. Not that his other novels do not contain superb passages—and some early short stories are also good. He is uneven, at his best when moved to lyricism and away from his important but creatively crippling conscious concerns. Some of his criticism is unequalled in insight and brilliance. He and Pavese (q.v.) helped to make Italy aware of the American novel. He encouraged and helped many younger writers. He was a writer of major gifts, an intuitive with a deeply poetic mind and a penetrating intelligence. Several of his other novels have been translated.

Vonnegut, Kurt (1922) American fiction writer. Vonnegut's concerns stem from his studies in biochemistry and anthropology, and his traumatic war experiences. He can be classed as a science-fiction writer but the scope of his intentions enlarges this genre to the point where one may reasonably assert that he merely makes use of it. His position, a kind of watered-down combination of pragmatism (*see* Dewey) and Vaihinger's 'As If', is made most clear in *Cat's Cradle* (1963). His despair at the human condition is genuine but black pessimism, guiltily convoluted irony and black humour tend to rob his work of lucidity. *Slaughterhouse-Five* (1969), which gave him an international reputation, fails to carry the weight of its modernist procedures, and, paradoxically, lacks the very humanity that Vonnegut would like to be able to believe is an ingredient of our existence. His more modest short stories (*Welcome to the Monkey House*, 1968) are superbly good at their level. *Player Piano* (1952); *The Sirens of Titan* (1959); *Mother Night* (1961).

Voznesensky, Andrei (1933) Russian poet. He is so far a minor poet, but more original than his contemporary Evtushenko (q.v.). He learned at the elbow of Pasternak (q.v.), and is more complex, intellectual and subtle. Yet he has even more energy than Evtushenko and his sense of horror at the world around him is considerably more deeply felt. He is emphatically not a 'civic' poet, as Evtushenko, following the tradition of Nekrasov (1821–77), tries to be; and his poetry looks westwards, as Mandelstam's (q.v.) did. He is playful and verbally dextrous (especially in *Treogolnaya grusha,* 1962, *Triangular Pear*) and sometimes this runs away with him; but at his best he is moving, lucid and exact, as in 'First Frost': 'A girl is freezing in a phone-box,/hiding in her thin coat/her face covered/in lipstick and tears.//She breathes on lean hands./Her fingers freeze. Her lobes wear glass.//She has to get back home alone/down the frozen street.//First frost. Beginning of losses./The first frost of telephone obsequies//Winter tears shine on her cheeks:/the first frost of being hurt'. *Vzgliad* (1972), *Glance* (or *Look,* or *Opinion,* or *View,* or all four) was a disappointing, almost frivolous collection. In translation: *Selected Poems* (1964); *Antiworlds* (1966 rev. 1973).

Wain, John (1925) English novelist, critic, poet, dramatist. Born Stoke-on-Trent. Elected Professor of Poetry at Oxford 1973. Author of some sensitive short stories, a few sharp (early) poems and sensible though seldom really penetrative criticism, Wain has not fully realized his talents except as a vigorous journalist and publicist. None of his novels is better than the first, *Hurry on Down* (1953), full of picaresque verve but in literary and stylistic terms a frenetically ill-judged performance. Sensitivity, craftsmanship, sensibility, cleverness—all are abundantly present, but Wain seems to be unable, not to take thought, but to stop and take it. His biography of Samuel Johnson (1975) is excellent.

Wallace, Edgar (1875–1932) English thriller writer, journalist. He was an actress's bastard put out to foster-parents. Margaret Lane gives a useful account of him in her biography (1938 rev. 1964). His prolific output of thriller-detective stories and West African romances (e.g. the phenomenally successful *Sanders of the River*, 1911) appears at first sight to be merely popular trash, and he does not, indeed, possess a good style or a good mind, but he is an interesting writer. *The Fellowship of the Frog* (1925), for example, is in fact a superb—if illiterate—surrealist novel; it is magnificently imagined and, if only in a socio-anthropological sense, critical of society. Wallace began (in South Africa) as an imitator of Kipling (q.v.), with *The Mission that Failed!* (1898), about the Jameson raid. It was *The Four Just Men* (1905), a novel founded on an essentially subversive and anti-establishment concept, that made him famous. Wallace is certainly not a literary phenomenon but he is an intensely fascinating one. He wrote almost 200 books.

Wallant, Edward Lewis (1926–62) American Jewish novelist whose premature death was a major loss to literature. He wrote four novels:

The Human Season (1960), *The Pawnbroker* (1961), *The Tenants of Moonbloom* (1963) and *The Children at the Gate* (1964). Wallant's theme is always to demonstrate how a reconciliation between internal anguish and bitterness and a difficult external environment *can* be effected; it is the brilliant psychology and the compassion with which he describes the process that make him into a major novelist.

Walpole, Hugh (1884–1941) English (born in New Zealand: his father was a clergyman) novelist, critic. Rupert Hart-Davis's biography (1952) is a sympathetic and valuable account but it fails to discuss his homosexual sadism. He wrote one good novel: *Mr Perrin and Mr Traill* (1911). Thereafter he wrote highly competent fiction, which, smooth and moderately intelligent, lacks psychological penetration of power. In the posthumous *The Killer and the Slain* (1942) he came nearest to self-examination and his more macabre books (e.g. *Portrait of a Man with Red Hair,* 1925) are on the whole his best. He is very readable and informed and should be treated as a potentially excellent novelist who sacrificed his art to his facility. *Works* (1934–40).

Walser, Robert (1878–1956) Swiss (German language) fiction writer, prose-poet, poet; a major author now in process of rediscovery. He struggled with mental ill-health throughout his life. He is still best known for having influenced Kafka (q.v.). Two of his best books have been translated: *Der Spaziergang* (1917; tr. *The Walk,* 1957), sketches, and the novel *Jakob von Gunten* (1909; tr. 1970). His two other novels are *Die Geschwister Tanner* (1907), *The Tanner Family,* and *Der Gehülfe* (1908), *The Assistant,* which contains two classic characters: the indeterminate Joseph Marti and his employer, Tobler. The poetry is collected in two volumes (1909 and 1958); most of his writings are in the uncompleted *Gesamtausgabe* (1953–62) and *Das Gesamtwerk* (1906–8). It is odd that, despite the praise of Morgenstern (who first 'discovered' his genius, in 1907), Hofmannsthal, Kafka, (q.v.), Musil (q.v.), Hesse (q.v.)—'the silent works of this magician'—and Walter Benjamin, and the devotion of his friend, executor and editor Carl Seelig, Walser should only just lately have become recognized as a major writer. Much is due to the pioneer efforts of Christopher Middleton, his English translator: see his useful article in *Texas Quarterly,* VII (1964). Walser produced his best work (he began to write in 1898) over a period of about twenty years (1904–25)—some, including three novels, was destroyed. The lucidity of his stories and sketches conveys a sense of what can only be described as the world-as-lyrical-nightmare. Walser is light, always playful; but, as Musil (q.v.) wrote in 1914: 'it is no mere literary playfulness, but something fundamentally human, with much softness, musing and freedom and the moral richness of one of those apparently useless, lazy days when our firmest convictions relax into comfortable indifference.' *Der Gehülfe* may well have influenced Musil's *Der Mann ohne Eigenschaften*. Walser is a lovely and haunting writer, about whom much remains to be said.

Warner, Sylvia Townsend (1893) English fiction writer, poet, biographer. Her work was admired by T. F. Powys (q.v.), with whom she has affinities but her control of her impulses towards the grotesque is surer. Her poetry (*Opus 7*, 1931, *Rainbow*, 1931; *Whether a Dove or a Seagull*, 1933–with her lifelong, now deceased, female companion Valantine Ackland) has not received the attention it deserves, and should be reissued: it is conventional in form, but sharply original. Her best novels are *Lolly Willowes* (1926), about a witch, *Mr Fortune's Maggot* (1927) and *The Corner That Held Them* (1948), an extraordinary *tour de force* set in medieval England. She is an expert on Tudor music and on parapsychology. Her stories (e.g. *A Moral Ending*, 1931, *A Stranger with a Bag*, 1966) have, quite scandalously, not been collected. Beyond pointing out that her fiction belongs to the same category as that of 'Saki' (q.v.), Garnett, Powys (q.v.) and (to a certain extent) Richard Hughes (q.v.), one can only recommend her for her uncanny capacity to avoid fantasy entirely in the process of working on fantastic material. She is dry, ironic, compassionate, a joker, a scholar. For years she worked at a biography of T. F. Powys, but the project apparently defeated her (as well it might). Her biography of T. H. White (q.v., 1967) is excellent. In the thirties she was active against Franco. *Summer Will Show* (1936) and *A Spirit Rises* (1962) are novels; more stories are in *The Museum of Cheats* (1947).

Warren, Robert Penn (1905) American novelist, poet, critic. 'Red' (because of his hair, not his politics) Warren was one of the youngest members of the Fugitives (*see* Ransom), and one of the most conservatively inclined contributors to the southern agrarian symposium 'I'll Take My Stand'. Like Tate (q.v.), he was born in Kentucky. He has changed his views since his youth, when he seems to have felt that southern Negroes were best off as they then were; and not only events have changed them—as one may see from *Segregation* (1956) and *Who Speaks for the Negro?* (1965). Polemics and politics are clearly not subjects with which he would wish to be involved. His poetry is as neo-metaphysical as his prose is neo-Jacobean-dramatic. Except in *Promises* (1957), containing many relaxed personal poems written under the influence of the presence of the children produced by his second marriage (1952), it tends to be over-convoluted: the author of the highly academic new-critical text books *Understanding Poetry* (1938; 1951, with Cleanth Brooks, q.v.) and *Understanding Fiction* (1943; 1960, with C. Brooks) subdues his rawly violent, intractable material by an over-vigorous cerebralism. Nor can Warren succeed in throwing off his fatal habit of rhetoric. The narrative *Brother to Dragons* (1953), centred around Jefferson, is bursting with exciting ideas, but in it Warren can never resolve his interests in personalities and public issues. The poems of *Incarnations* (1968) are more direct and much more moving and effective; 'Keep That Morphine Moving, Cap' shows us a Warren prepared to abandon his elaborate complexities in favour of straightforward statement. He protests ('Where Purples Now the Fig'), begging his flesh to keep his bones covered, and not to depart leaving 'me . . . exposed, like Truth'; but he is convinced of what he means. These are less literary poems. The earlier ones may be found in *Selected Poems 1923–1968* (1968). As novelist Warren has found a wide audience; his intention may be summed up as an attempt to probe the problems of the South, of the South as humanity, in neo-Jacobean terms. What wrecks them is, in Walter Allen's words, an 'unbearable pretentiousness', seen most clearly in the figure of Jack Burden in *All the King's Men* (1946). Except in the first novel, *Night Rider* (1939), Warren is guilty of misuse of rhetoric and of a kind of concealed sensationalism. The worst, *World Enough and Time* (1950), is an almost intolerable (though ingenious) attempt to reify Jacobean melodrama in a modern version of an early nineteenth-century Southern romantic *cause célèbre*. *The Cave* (1959) is not much more than a competent performance. But *Circus in the Attic* (1948), stories, is excellent. As critic (e.g. *Selected Essays,* 1958) Warren is intelligent, stimulating, over-literary. Essentially and with exceptions (the most powerful is 'The Ballad of Billie Potts'), he is a man whose creative powers have been somewhat stifled by his over-sophistication.

Waugh, Evelyn (1903–66) English novelist, essayist, biographer. He is the younger brother of Alec Waugh (1898), a competent middlebrow novelist. Waugh certainly had genius but in the main he misused it and he must be accounted a failure. After a period spent sowing wild oats, he became a Roman Catholic (1930) and began a career as a writer. He had written a long poem, privately printed, in 1916, but his first publications were a bad biography of Rossetti and a novel, *Decline and Fall* (both 1928). The latter is a rumbustious Dickensian satire, of tremendous energy, on the preparatory school industry (he had himself been sacked from one for drinking). *Decline and Fall* and its hilarious successors are minor work; they draw very heavily on Dickens and on surrealism and they anticipate 'black humour'. They are brilliant but cruel in an unnecessary way. One may go so far as to say that their brilliance is almost cancelled out by their moral unpleasantness. But Waugh was never, perhaps, for long mentally well: he was oppressed by fears the nature of which his work can never define. His defence against his torment took the form of bad taste and a reactionary, 'stage Tory' aggression. Possibly it has not been sufficiently emphasized that Waugh was not a very intelligent man—or that, at least, he was prevented by illness from exercising his full intelligence and sense of decency. He was not devoid of the latter, but in almost all his work it is frustrated. The four thirties novels (e.g. *Vile Bodies,* 1930 rev. 1965, *Scoop,* 1938 rev. 1964) are funny, and they do amount to social criticism, though this is formless and incidental; but only in *A Handful of Dust* (1934 rev. 1964) do we find a note of real tragedy: only here is the black, heartless farceur 'extended'. His travel books of this period are not distinguished. Soon after taking part in the war (and finding time to write during it) he published *The Loved One* (1948 rev. 1965), an excellent satire on the American undertaking racket. In *The Ordeal of Gilbert Pinfold* (1958), a self-study of a bout of madness, he wrote his finest novel, and most clearly revealed the full nature of the sickness that prevented full expression of his genius (he treated his manic-depressive illness with paraldehyde, which in itself would induce hallucinations). Significantly this is by far the least distorted of Waugh's books—even though its subject is that of how reality becomes distorted in the mind of a writer—and the best and most clearly written. The ambitious *Brideshead Revisited* (1945 rev. 1960), a frankly religious novel, has been praised by some critics but, after an interesting beginning, it lapses into an incoherence that demonstrates Waugh's inability to cope with his theme. The trilogy *Sword of Honour* (1965: this is the author's recension of the trilogy *Men at Arms, Officers and Gentlemen, Unconditional Surrender,* 1952–61) is an attempt by Waugh to do justice to his sense of decency and of balance. It is based on Ford's (q.v.) war-tetralogy, and it too deals with a sensitive man whose life is interrupted by war. In part it succeeds; but where Waugh needs to be moving—is, in fact, himself moved—he is (or so it seems to me, though other critics have disagreed) banal; his verve has gone; now that he wants at last to treat the material in a moral manner, it becomes merely commonplace. To the last Waugh shrank from the horrors that tormented him. *The World of Waugh* (1958) is a selection.

Wedekind, Frank (1864–1918) German dramatist, fiction writer, cabaret-entertainer, actor, poet. Wedekind is still popular and played on the stage (sometimes in disgraceful adaptations); his most famous play is the relatively immature *Spring's Awakening* (1891; tr. in *Five Tragedies of Sex,* 1952), an uncharacteristically lyrical *exposé* of bourgeois 'education'. He disturbs some critics, perhaps because they mistake his sardonic audience-manipulation for 'nihilism': the point is that, although his techniques are proto-expressionistic (*see* Stadler) and have been widely influential, his range is less wide than may be immediately apparent: he is an intense satirist. His character of Lulu—famous through Berg's opera, and protagonist of *Der Erdgeist* (1895; tr. *Earth Spirit, Five Tragedies of Sex*)—is created less in a spirit of 'ambiguous eroticism' than in one of satirical frenzy and anti-bourgeois glee. More creatively ambitious are the neglected—and splendidly offensive—stories of *Feuerwerk* (1905), *Fireworks.* A very distinguished minor writer.

Weil, Simone (1909–43) French writer, thinker and, according to some, saint. Simone Weil wrote no novels or poetry, but her remarkable life and thought are correctly seen as tragically seminal. She has certain affinities with Nietzsche: her thinking is contradictory and/or paradoxical, she is a genuine visionary, she sacrificed everything in pursuit of truth. Born of Jewish but free-thinking parents, she was consistent throughout her life in her refusal to enjoy more comfort than those who were suffering elsewhere: thus as a small child she refused to eat sugar because the French soldiers at the front did not get any, and would not wear socks because workers' children could not. She would not, in the thirties, eat more than unemployed workers could obtain;

though the then most brilliant pupil of the philosopher Alain (*see* Maurois), she ruined her fragile health by working, under atrocious conditions, in the Renault car factory. She shared the agonies of the loyalists in Spain and was badly burned. In England in her last year she could not get permission to be parachuted into France to join the Resistance and she died of 'voluntary starvation' when, a persistent sufferer (like Nietzsche) from racking migraines, she once again refused to eat more than her oppressed compatriots were getting from the Nazis. She never joined any organization, but moved from a quasi-socialist to a quasi-Christian activism. She published articles and finished *L'Enracinement* (1949; tr. *The Need for Roots,* 1955); the rest of her voluminous work consists of posthumously edited notes and letters: the most important source is *Cahiers* (1951–6; tr. *Notebooks,* 1956). Her relevance to modern literature? She lucidly (and in her lifetime almost entirely privately) explored the confusions of the modern world: orthodox Christianity had poisoned the world by its exclusiveness, its heresy of progress and its failure to absorb the Greek experience (her arch-villain, as for Buber, q.v., was the hysterico-astralist Paul); she penetratingly abhorred bureaucracy and all forms (left and right) of totalitarianism; Rome itself, paradoxically, inhibited her tendency towards Catholicism; an anti-anti-Semite, she abhorred certain aspects of Judaism in rather the same spirit as the anti-anti-Semite Nietzsche did (cf. Hannah Arendt); she was continuously and 'existentially' impelled towards nakedly absolute, activist rejection of the evil inherent in her situation; like Vallejo, she died through the total anguish she suffered because injustice existed and triumphed. Many works have been translated; two helpful, objective introductions are by J. Cabaud (1964) and Orwell's friend the late Sir Richard Rees (1965). She touches our most intense concerns at almost every point except those of the surrealist (*see* Breton) and the comic.

Welty, Eudora (1909) American (born in Mississippi, but not of Southern parentage) short-story writer, novelist. Eudora Welty, admired by Ford (q.v.), Warren (q.v.), Katherine Anne Porter (q.v.) and many others, has chosen to be a 'Southern' writer; but she is not a victim (as one may put it) of the Southern heritage. Rather she finds the South she knows so well a perfect setting for her stories. Her main subject is the loneliness of individuals, and her grotesques—far more than those of McCullers (q.v.) or O'Connor (q.v.)—are cruel parodies of 'normality': they show us, either semi-surrealistically or 'Gothically', and seldom sympathetically, the insides of ourselves. As she has developed she has written more stories of people's entry into a humanity whose enigmatic nature, however, she chooses to emphasize. If she wants to end on a positive note, then hope is symbolized by natural mystery. The lush Mississippi landscape suits her odd genius perfectly –as the title of her first collection, *A Curtain of Green* (1941), implies. But it is a slender genius, as the over-experimental stories in *The Bride of the Innisfallen* (1954)–where she tries to get away from herself by use of mythological symbols–makes clear. The short novel of the same year, *The Ponder Heart,* is, however, successful because the author has let loose her humour on her predilections; indeed, her strategy has always been, in one way or another, to by-pass or eliminate the over-morbidity of these. Her novels, with the exception of *The Ponder Heart* (hardly, in any case, a novel) do not contain her best work, and the ambitious and lengthy *Losing Battle* (1970) is obviously not the direction in which she should travel: this is more conventional, and even sentimental. *Selected Stories* (1954).

Weidmann, Jerome (1913) American Jewish novelist and playwright. His early novels *I Can Get it For You Wholesale* (1937) and *What's In It For Me* (1938) have hardly had their due. They both concern the ruthless behaviour of an ambitious Jew in the rag-trade in New York. Later novels exploring similar types are as funny but are badly flawed by sentimentality and hurried writing. His best stories are in *The Horse that Could Whistle Dixie* (1939).

Wen-I-To (1889–1946) The greatest Chinese poet of the century. He early came to know the poetry of the English romantics, who deeply influenced him. He became involved in some radical activities, but concentrated mostly on his poetry and on the difficulties of employing the vernacular–in which style he was ultimately to triumph. Although deeply humanitarian, Wen believed in an art free of politics and from 1925 he fought for this; he was the co-founder of the Crescent Society, and was attacked for being over-aesthetic. None the less, his second and last book (his collected works appeared in Shanghai in 1948), *Ssu-shui* (1928), *The Dead Water,* is one of the best volumes to appear in the twenties anywhere. His first book *Hungchu* (1923), *Red Candle,* was mostly written while he was studying in America

(1922–5); this was somewhat over-romantic and lush, but it already showed his promise. *The Dead Water* is an intensely depressed and yet lyrical collection; the poems are in the vernacular, but Wen reacts against free verse by introducing his own often tight forms. He was closely associated in his aesthetic programme with the only other modern Chinese poet to come near to him in achievement Hsü Chih-Mo (1895–1931), whom many incorrectly believe to be his equal. After *The Dead Water* Wen wrote little more poetry, but devoted himself to criticism, to teaching, to studies of the T'ang and Sung dynasties and other researches into Chinese classical literature. With the outbreak of the Sino-Japanese War (1937), however, Wen felt that he must take some kind of action: he eventually joined the Democratic League, spoke out against the devilish megalomaniac Chiang Kai-chek, who had him murdered by one of his terror squads. He was never a communist. He is an elegiac, elegant, synaesthetic poet.

Wells, H. G. (1866–1946) English fiction writer, historian, popularizer of science, social reformer, polemicist, thinker. The astonishingly versatile Wells, a small man with a squeaky voice who pulled himself up out of genteel poverty (he graduated in science in 1890, after studying biology with T. H. Huxley), has been underrated and misunderstood. Probably he holds the twentieth-century record for the most mistresses possessed in a lifetime by a public man; he was exceedingly decent to them. He was twice married and his comparatively long liaison with Rebecca West (q.v.) is well known and has been fairly fully documented. He had a more poetic–which is to say, among other things, an ambivalent–mind than his critics have allowed. He did indeed write (bad) poetry as a young man. His temperament was violently pessimistic, but he stuck for as long as he could to faith in socialism and in the enlightenment he hoped (he knew the hope was vain) that scientific discovery might bring. He was not a simple positivist, though he got into moods when he could write as though he were. His personality was what may fairly be called manic-depressive and the work of his last fifteen years, which has been critically neglected, represents a heroic and imaginative control of his mental state. In fact some of Wells's greatest work was done as he fought his way through this ordeal, which was complicated by other illnesses. His first important stories (*The Time Machine, The Stolen Bacillus and other Incidents*) appeared in 1895. They were scientific-poetic romances, full of invention (Wells's odd gift of prophecy, often wrong in detail but correct in direction, has been confirmed again and again), curiosity and blackly subversive feeling. The novel *The Invisible Man* (1897) is, as everyone agrees, a *tour de force*; it is also Wells's portrait of himself as poet-scientist-prophet. This novel has not been treated as seriously as it deserves and Wells, the perhaps too public man, the Fabian and so-called Utopian, has too easily been pushed into the category of 'great entertainer'. In fact he was a major, and probably a great, imaginative writer. His *Complete Stories* (1966) omits only three published short stories. Here, again, his versatility may be seen (e.g. 'The Cone'). Wells wrote fewer 'scientific romances' after the turn of the century; he had already done enough to put himself into a major category–if only as chief pioneer of science fiction, in which genre he has never been surpassed–and one might have concluded that, to all imaginative intents and purposes, he was finished. But he now began to write a different sort of fiction, which attracted the sincere admiration of Henry James (q.v.): this dealt with 'little men' against the shabby-genteel background of his early years–his father a professional cricketer and then failed shopkeeper, his mother 'in service', himself once apprentice to a pharmacist and a draper's assistant. . . . The first of these novels was *Love and Mr Lewisham* (1900); the finest are *Kipps* (1905), *Tono-Bungay* (1908), *The History of Mr Polly* (1910) and–but this is contentious–sections of *The Bulpington of Blup* (1932), partly based on the character of his friend Ford (q.v.). All of the novels of this type are eminently readable and intelligent, but in general the best are those in which he draws upon his own experience. His massive *Outline of History* (1919–20, and many later rev. editions) is a failure, but it did more good than harm and is clearly the work of a remarkable mind. He attached himself to many causes (world peace, a socialist future, and so on): the products of this side of his activity are not important except as part of the history of the 'ideas' of the epoch. In such books as *A Modern Utopia* (1905) he was indulging himself in hope; but, as text, we may read it as ironic parody. It is the fashion to denigrate Wells. But *Mr. Blettsworthy on Rampole Island* (1928) is a dystopia that is far superior to Huxley's (q.v.) *Brave New World* and it anticipates Orwell's (q.v.) 'double think'; why it is now forgotten is inexplicable. *Mind at the End of Its Tether* (1945) is his last despairing cry; *The Fate of Homo Sapiens* (1939) is justifiably and intelligently pessimistic. Wells had seen what was going to happen (unlike Shaw, q.v., and others, he was not taken in by Stalin: *Stalin-Wells Talk*, 1934), and he tried to prevent it—all the time feeling assured that this would be in vain. He wrote much else of interest and originality: *The World of William Clissold* (1926), *Experiment in Autobiography* (1934; 1966), and some of the last novels (e.g. *Apropos of Dolores*, 1938). *Works* (1924–7); *Works* (1926–7); *The Scientific Romances* (1933); *A Quartette of Comedies* (1928: *Love and Mr Lewisham, Kipps, Mr Polly, Bealby*).

Wesker, Arnold (1932) English dramatist and writer. He was born and brought up in London's East End and pulled himself up by his bootstraps. He has genuine dramatic talent (*Chicken Soup with Barley*, 1958; *Roots*, 1959; *The Kitchen*, 1961): his dialogue is often excellent and he has a sense of structure. It is a pity that his passionate idealism has so badly interfered with his creative work, which, since *Chips With Everything* (1962)—a routine but brilliantly executed portrait of service life—has badly deteriorated. *Plays* (1971).

West, Nathanael (ps. Nathan Wallenstein Weinstein) (1903–40) American novelist, scriptwriter. He was killed, with his wife, when he (unfortunately characteristically) failed to observe a stop signal. He was one of the supreme American Jewish writers of his time and is hardly surpassed even by the great Henry Roth (q.v.). His first work, *The Dream Life of Balso Snell* (1931), was immature and derivative, a young man's Paris début; the second, *Miss Lonelyhearts* (1933) was a masterpiece; the third, *A Cool Million* (1934), a satire on materialism of sometimes Swiftian proportions that has possibly been underrated; the last, *The Day of the Locust* (1939), is West's greatest book, at once terrifying and prophetic. 'Pep' West at one time ran a magazine with W. C. Williams (q.v.); at another he mismanaged a hotel where indigent writers could be sure of free bed if not board; he ended by working in Hollywood. His range of acquaintance was surprisingly wide, his intelligence acute, his cheerfulness infectious, his sadness and integrity known to his sensitive friends. West is the original modern 'black humorist' (he learned much from Melville), and his work above all makes the more recent American vogue for this genre look as tawdry as it generally is. *Miss Lonelyhearts* is the name given to a newspaper columnist who deals with the 'problem' letters, most of them ridiculous and 'funny', sent to his paper; he becomes involved with this unaesthetic, unintelligent, scarcely articulate anguish, and is destroyed. *A Cool Million* reverses the Alger myth: the hero loses everything, including his limbs, is exploited by everyone, and then becomes a hero. The style here is deceptively brilliant. *The Day of the Locust* is an imaginative, frightened (but never paranoid) indictment of modern show business: of its violence, its emptiness, its absurdity. It gains its strength from the steady assurance of its own writing: we feel from this alone that human values exist. It is odd that certain critics have called West 'detached', 'unconcerned': this is of course his strategy for dealing with his terrifying material. He faced issues that such critics prefer to ignore: the real horror of the technological world, the grotesque and crippled nature of much true suffering.

West, Rebecca (ps. C. I. Fairfield, later Andrews) (1892) Irish (but resident in England after an adolescence in Scotland) novelist, critic, miscellaneous writer. She was for some time the mistress of H. G. Wells (q.v.), by whom she had children; she married another man in 1930. Her fiction, though always evincing respect, has not had its due. The earlier novels (e.g. *The Return of the Soldier*, 1918; *The Judge*, 1922; *The Thinking Reed*, 1936) are influenced by Freudianism (q.v.) and 'feminism', but contain originality of psychological insight and are structurally ingenious. Her *St Augustine* (1933), despite its lack of profound theological and historical knowledge, remains the most instructive study: it is a shrewd and revealing work. *Black Lamb and Grey Falcon* (1941), about a journey through Yugoslavia in 1937, is great journalism if journalism can be great. With *The Meaning of Treason* (1947 rev. 1964 rev. 1965), on Joyce and other traitors and their trials, a less pleasant note crept into her work. This is a series of brilliant studies but it shows signs of a hardening of the artistic arteries —the author's sense of shock, revulsion, pity, are slightly ingratiating: her experience of her traitors has not been fully felt through. The novels *The Fountain Overflows* (1957) and *The Birds Fall Down* (1966) come from a different and more self-explorative side of Rebecca West and, like her earlier fiction, they demand attention beyond that of frightened reviewers. They remind one that her first book was on *Henry James* (q.v., 1916) and they intelligently and imaginatively encompass a long-pondered-upon experience of this century. *The Harsh Voice* (1935) contains four short novels; *The Court and the Castle* (1957) contains essays on a level with the fine study of St Augustine.

Wharton, Edith (1862–1937) American novelist, story writer, critic, essayist. Edith Wharton is among the most effective of all the post-Jamesian woman writers (cf. Elizabeth Bowen, q.v., Rosamund Lehmann, q.v., Hortense Callisher, and others of a much younger generation). She knew James well from early in her life and he encouraged her generously and usefully. She began as a member and critic of New York high society; later, when her difficult marriage (1885) to an older and neurotic man had finally broken up, she settled in Paris (1907). She is an eclectic and accomplished novelist who is still very seriously underestimated. She wrote forty-seven books, including two of poetry. Her viewpoint is Jamesian in that it is firmly based in character and in individual reactions to corrupt social values or (as in many of her stories) to the sense of evil. The first important novel is *The House of Mirth* (1905), a relentless, ironic study of a girl's attempt to penetrate high society. Her most uncharacteristic novel, the bitter *Ethan Frome* (1911), which in part reflects the psychological aspects of her unhappy marriage, deals brilliantly with primitive, rural people. She became desperately concerned with the war, and with America's over-delayed entry into it; her books about it are distorted by direct passionate indignation. But *The Age of Innocence* (1920) and *The Children* (1928), to mention two of the twenties novels, show a return to previous form and her powers of satire are sharpened, her despair is deeper. She may lack Henry Handel Richardson's epic sweep and her positively (George) Eliotian range, but she is a most important novelist, many of whose books provide reading that is not only pleasurable but profound in its insights. Her stories, especially of the supernatural, are generally superb (*Collected Short Stories,* 1968); her autobiography *A Backwards Glance* (1934) indispensable; her *The Writing of Fiction* (1925) invaluable as guide and criticism. Several of her books are currently in print; others are worth searching for.

White, Patrick (1912) Australian novelist, playwright. Nobel Prize 1973. Australia's greatest writer since Richardson (q.v.) and greater in range and depth than she. Born in London, he grew up in Sydney, worked as a farmer, went to Cambridge, served in the war and finally settled in Australia. Just as in Thomas Mann (q.v.), with whom he is worthy to be ranked, there is an element of pretentiousness in White; but instead of seeing himself as confidence-man he has settled down to an examination of his convulsed and learned decadence that is at the same time a brilliant exploitation. The extreme complexity and sophistication of our century involve a kind of pretentiousness: an evasion of or inability to achieve simplicity. This is the problem White has dealt with in his series of novels, which are heavily charged with symbolism but at the same time lyrical and despairingly affirmative. Human entropy, deadness, absurdity: these obsess him, and yet he turns towards the upwards thrust of life in all its richness with a violent excitement modified only by his rational uncertainty. He began with poetry (*The Ploughman,* 1935) but soon discovered that its disciplines constrained him. Loving the world for its beauty and strangeness, White seeks to heal the Nietzschean wound—that made by the 'death of God'—between himself and it. But White understands that the terrible Nietzchean message is not simply atheistic, but says, rather, that 'God is dead' because 'we have killed him', yet the 'tremendous event . . . has not yet reached the ears of man' (Nietzsche's words). White, possibly the greatest of living novelists, and certainly one of them, has made it his business to try to bring that message to 'the ears of man', and further, to add something more to it. No wonder he has sometimes floundered and has been attacked for his pessimism and bleakness and impenetrability and obsession with mad people and freaks. To be as good as White is at his best is to have to be bad (cf. Faulkner, q.v., Mann, q.v.), and White's badness is astonishingly small in extent. He is a visionary who is also a realist; his controlling intelligence is very great; he is admired but not often more than half-understood; he is a near-recluse —and he has kept clear of the literary world. Just as Latin-American writers use the wonderful and mysterious interior of their continent as a metaphor for the secret depths of the human mind, so White uses Australia—not just its interior (as in *Voss,* 1957), but also its hateful suburbia and their outskirts. He has become Australia's completest historian and his bleakness is always illuminated by the light of a passionate though often contorted curiosity. His first major book is *The Aunt's Story* (1948), the paradoxical study of the life of a 'plain' woman which ends in madness and yet in the achievement of a personal authenticity; White uses a mixture of stream-of-consciousness (of the phenomenological rather than ultra-realist type), distorted flashback and lucid realism. This is a book of despair; its flaws lie in its patches of reconditeness and in its too self-conscious introduction of mystical characters. *The Tree of Life* (1955) deals, in an on the whole more generally coherent manner, with inarticulate farmers. *Voss* improves on both of these novels. In *The Aunt's Story* White had probed at the problem of his loneliness, projecting it into an account of the 'feminine' (in the Freudian sense) side of his nature. *The Tree of Life* dealt with his feelings for the life of the earth, explored the nature of the human relationship to this, and had shuddered at the odious encroachments of the city. That novel established him internationally and he now found an objective correlative for himself in the form of the contradictory figure of the German explorer Voss–charlatan, holy man, seer, genius and fool. This is a magnificent achievement, whose very pretentiousness is inevitably part of its own theme. One should use the word 'massive' sparingly; but this is truly massive and it is difficult to think of anything outside Latin America that can match it in this respect. *Riders in the Chariot* (1961) goes right into urban Australia: of the citizens of the sprawling and hateful suburb of Sarsparilla only four freaks and cripples have an affirming vision; this contains White's most ferocious criticism of Australian gentility and ugliness. *The Solid Mandala* (1966) is again set in Sarsparilla and contrasts a 'madman' with his 'sane' twin. In *The Vivisector* (1970) and *The Eye of the Storm* (1973)–which was on the whole not well received by British reviewers, who failed to comprehend it–he has kept up his high standards, although neither is as profound as *The Solid Mandala.* White has written short stories (*The Burnt Ones,* 1964) and *Four Plays* (1965), of which *The Ham Funeral,* a tragic farce set in Sarsparilla, is the most effective.

Wilbur, Richard (1921) American poet, critic, translator. Wilbur has resisted both the Whitmanesque-pragmatic American tradition, and has generally eschewed the free-form 'deep image' poetics of such as Bly (q.v.). He prefers formal elegance and exactitude. But he is no 'tight' 'new-critical' poet and has the general respect of all schools except the 'way-out' or Black Mountain (*see* Dewey, Olson, Creeley), who regard him, quite incorrectly, with scorn. His achievement is exquisite. It is none the less slight: Wilbur's obstinate faith in the power of perfected texts (and he has a pure and fine sense of the quality of the best poetry of the past), of grace, elegance, courteous restraint, is not adequate in an age that is not only over-sophisticated but also raw. His very procedures defeat his intelligent purposes. He was born in 1921, not 1895. Wilbur wants to elevate aesthetics, subtle beautifications, against a chaos, corruption and horror of which he is keenly aware; but for all his critical shrewdness, for all the pleasure he gives, for all his excellent technique, he is at heart an escapist: his 'message' that a suitably restrained and sensitive 'high poetry' *can* contain answers is invalid. He is an excellent light poet, and a magnificent translator (e.g. of Molière). Unhappily Fielder's (q.v.) reluctant accusation is ultimately unanswerable: '. . . there is no personal voice anywhere.'

Wilder, Thornton (1897–1975) American novelist, playwright from Wisconsin. Wilder, a very popular, intelligent and clever writer, with the capacity to exploit such modernist techniques as those of Gertrude Stein (q.v.) in comparatively commercial interests, has been the subject of considerable controversy. He has written only two indisputably good works, both novels, *The Cabala* (1926) and *Heaven's My Destination* (1934). His streak of vulgarity and pseudo-profundity early emerged in *The Bridge of San Luis Rey* (1927), a pretentious pseudo-modernist novel that reached its big-readership target with distressingly unerring ease. *The Eighth Day* (1967), another novel, reveals quite clearly the triumph of the ingratiating and phoney optimism that has tended to vitiate almost all his writings. His many plays (the most famous are *Our Town*, 1938, and *The Skin of Our Teeth*, 1942) are good theatre but they are empty of real thought. *The Cabala*, a promising first novel, did not attract attention; Wilder gained his readership in the following year. *Heaven's My Destination*, while it is a novel to be dealt with in its own right as a study of an American 'holy fool', is also Wilder's (only) exploration of his own predicament. George Brush is a naively good man: a Fundamentalist (Wilder's father was a Congregationalist) who, while he pursues his job of selling school textbooks, infuriates everyone by his absolutely innocent but ridiculous fairness, devotion to his beliefs and mad integrity. The novel is good in its own right because the background detail, of small towns and their inhabitants, is finely rendered and because Brush comes convincingly to life as a genuinely tragi-comic figure in an authentically created realistic context.

Williams, Tennessee (ps. Thomas Lanier Williams) (1911–not 1914 as usually given) American playwright, fiction writer, poetaster. Williams became, with Miller (q.v.), America's leading playwright of the forties and fifties; only Albee (q.v.) since then has come anywhere near to reaching their popular esteem. He was born in Mississippi but spent his adolescence in St Louis. Williams's plays, which are almost always theatrically viable to a high degree, may be interpreted in a number of ways. First, they are an attempt to solve the problem that O'Neill (q.v.) saw clearly much earlier: to put it briefly, that today we can't write like Shakespeare (i.e. for the time being the poetry-drama isn't possible). Secondly they are quite obviously self-therapeutic (though to label them as merely that is grossly unfair to Williams): through them the author is resolving a grossly histrionic, complex neurosis—one that has relevance to a definitely 'Southern' situation, with all the 'Gothic', here thoroughly sexualized, that this implies. Thirdly, they are violent and desperate expressions of a lonely man's sense of tenderness and search for love—for a *subjective* correlative that could express the meaning of that always abused word. This last rescues Williams from the publicity that so often erupts about his person. His pain is very real; his achievement is touching enough partly to redeem its tendency to fade in the mind: we remember the initial impact of his anguish, though we forget (usually) the details. Williams fails to create an effective poetic language but his rhetoric can have a cumulatively convincing effect: the tensions of people squashed into a common situation are built up into a moving, even tragic, demonstration of the fact that this hideous situation is of their own making. Williams's stock figure in his best plays (*The Glass Menagerie*, 1947; *A Streetcar Named Desire*, 1947) is an anguishedly receptive woman, savaged by neurosis, who lives in a fantasy world. Into this Williams can inject moments of superb tenderness in which the terribleness of individual vulnerability is in this memorably highlighted. He has little to offer in the way of motivation; little, really, to explain how his situations have come into being. His themes are loneliness, hysteria and the ripple-effect they create through the lives of those who may, from ignorance or selfishness or both, have helped intensify those conditions. Intelligence is not much present; control is a matter of effective presentation rather than an effort of mind. The later and more experimental plays are generally less effective, since they only exploit the vein that was so successful in *The Glass Menagerie* and *Streetcar*. But they are always interesting studies in hysterical behaviour and the author's integrity, despite his extreme and increasing limitations, is sound. *Cat on a Hot Tin Roof* (1955) is the best of the fifties plays, but *Orpheus Descending* (1958), a revision of an earlier play, is a fascinating investigation of decadent-homosexual impulses. With *Sweet Bird of Youth* (1959) and *The Night of the Iguana* (1962) Williams began to 'think': to work out a post-naturalist (*see*

Zola) system of man-as-victim-of-nature. The result has been poor and feeble. His fiction (e.g. the novel *The Roman Spring of Mrs Stone,* 1950) is negligible.

Williams, William Carlos (1883–1963) American poet, fiction writer, critic, autobiographer, physician. He was pure English on his father's side; Jewish-French-Spanish on his mother's. Of the immensity of Williams's influence on American poetry there can be no dispute. But the degree of his own achievement is difficult to assess. Williams the poet, very determinedly *Dr* Williams of Rutherford (his birthplace), New Jersey, is the first decisively pragmatic (*see* Dewey) poet of America, though his pragmatism is not of the subtle kind. No American poet, from Lowell to Olson or Wilbur, can afford not to come to terms with him. He is in opposition to all the accepted positions. If Williams's poetics could be dignified by the term 'philosophical'–but they rather nobly cannot, being exceedingly simple–then, curiously, this aggressively regional, concrete ('no ideas but in things') poet could be described as a 'philosophical' one. For his poetry was, from his maturity, dominated–indeed limited–by his theory. While studying medicine at university he met Pound (q.v.) and HD (q.v.), and he has acknowledged the important influence of the former. His first model was Keats; his second was Whitman, most of whose poetry, however, he disliked. One has to understand that Williams, as a poet, is not complex–though he may be accused of trying to be in *Paterson.* Though his lifelong friend Pound influenced him initially, he deliberately avoided his culturally allusive manner; Eliot (q.v.) he deplored as a literary traitor to America–a traitor, that is to say, to the soil, the place, the environment, which had produced him. He married 'Flossie', so important in his poems, in 1912. What are the bases of Williams's poetics? He is a super-regionalist in the sense that he 'knows' he is *American;* he will write only of what he sees, touches, is certain of. He is absolutely against anything that (to him) smacks of generalization from his own quotidian particulars (coming in late, doing his rounds, watching his wife do chores, parking the car, looking at a wheelbarrow or at flowers or birds). Nothing is 'symbolic'. He is the leading twentieth-century exponent of the philistine-didactic tradition that is continued in Olson and Creeley–and when one considers the nature of the academic tradition one sees the reason and even the need for this. From *The Tempers* (1913) until *Pictures from Brueghel*

(1962)—which collects *The Desert Music* (1954) and *Journey to Love* (1955)—there is not much change: Brueghel fascinates him because he paints great canvases crowded with *everyday* detail (it is a limited view of Brueghel. . . . .), which Williams loves: that *is* life, there isn't anything more than what is happening *now,* what is going through my *mind* now. Between object and subject there is the poem, the 'glimpse', of which Burke (q.v.) called Williams the master. As for 'prosody': Williams was determined to write as Americans *spoke:* he therefore claimed to have done away with metre and rhyme (too 'English'; sonnets were actually 'fascistic') and to have invented a 'measure'. Thus (his own illustration) in the three staggered lines 'The smell of the heat is boxwood/ when rousing us/ a movement of the air . . .' we must 'count a beat to each [line] . . . that is the way I count the line'. The 'beat' is only in Williams's mind, since in the first line there are three stresses and in the second one and in the third two. Such a theory is quite useless except to its progenitor. Further, Williams continually confused duration with accent, a dangerous error. Williams's involvement with 'objectivism' is important. Objectivism was cubist in only one sense: it believed in the poem-as-thing-in-itself, done for its own sake. Williams believed that reality was not created except by words, so did the objectivists. He, like them, was heavily influenced by paintings (by the French, and also by the American 'Ash Can' school, and above all by the superb Edward Hopper). The objectivists, who first called their press TO, and only later the 'Objectivists' press, consisted of Williams (q.v.), Zukofsky (q.v.), Reznikoff (q.v.), Oppen and Carl Rakosi (ps. Callman Rawley, 1903), a Berlin-born psychologist, social worker and later (1955) psychotherapist whose *Selected Poems* appeared in 1941 (in 1957 he published *Amulet*). The Press issued an objectivist anthology (with poems by Pound, q.v., Eliot, q.v., McAlmon, Bunting, q.v., Rexroth, q.v.) and Williams's *Collected Poems 1921–1931* (1934). Their aims were to restore to imagistic (*see* Pound) 'free verse' 'a measure of some sort'; to see the poem as 'an object that in itself formally presents its case and its meaning by the very form it assumes'; to invent poem-objects 'consonant with [the] day': an 'antidote to the bare image haphazardly presented in loose verse' (these are Williams's comments). Despite his quintessential Americanness, Williams's poetry is mostly minor—and it does not usually have the impact on non-Americans that it has on Americans. It is, as Stevens (q.v.) charged, too 'casual'. It is local, the poetry of a good man and a dedicated doctor; it is sometimes tinnily exquisite (e.g. 'This is Just to Say'). But it lacks concentration or tension and its pragmatism (this must not be confused with that of W. James, q.v.) is over-dogmatic. The poet *nags* away at these little things that he notes, setting a whole school in motion (most of them 'meagrely talented iconoclasts', as John Malcolm Brinnin, q.v., justly comments), and he sacrifices everything for this by no means Blakean simplicity. He is obstinately Pelagian and he could not really express the notion of love that obsessed him—ironically, it does operate as something of a 'generalization', since Williams regards even thinking itself as 'abstract', and relies somewhat disingenuously on the notion of 'perception'. There are of course certain exceptions: the superb fury in the Sacco-Vanzetti poem 'Prelude: The Suckers', the famous, late 'Asphodel, That Greeny Flower', flows with an utterly authentic personal sweetness—and exhibits his idiosyncratic technique at its most effective. But towards the end of his life the pressures of thinking (a part, after all, of life) forced him into the project of creating an epic. This is *Paterson* (1946–58), in five books (Williams, crippled by a series of strokes, was unable to write a sixth), of which the fifth is a sort of postscript. In this poem, despite fine passages, two intentions cancel each other out: the old 'pragmatist' poetics and a new attempt to create an ultimately coherent personal myth out of chaos—a contradiction of his life's work. Paterson is a city on the Passiac river; it has a history; and 'Dr Paterson' is a man. The first book (1946) is the most spontaneous and the best: the least planned. But as a whole the poem, much of which consists of prose collage of a historical or personal nature, falls to pieces. The conception, as Brinnin points out, is not really part of Williams's natural poetic process. There is here, at last and distressingly, a pretentiousness: for beyond pressing home the point that all a poet can honestly do is to record his own perceptions at the time he experiences them, Williams has nothing at all to say. And in *Paterson* Williams fails to 'prove' that his own notion of art is the only true one: how could he succeed when he tries to do it by applying procedures that deny this very notion? (There is a good and extremely intelligent, as yet uncollected, essay by Eric Mottram putting the case for the defence.) In the last analysis Williams's poetic achievement is a minor one: he never succeeds, even in *Paterson,* in really saying anything about the subject that obsessed him most of all: the nature of woman. We feel his awareness—that of a good man—and his fascination, but he is ultimately inarticulate. Williams's stories (collected in *The Farmers' Daughters*, 1961), often drawing on his medical experiences, are at their best excellent *tranches de vie;* the novel trilogy *White Mule* (1937), *In the Money* (1940) and *The Build-Up* (1952), about his wife's past, fails as a whole but contains many brilliant passages. Experimental plays are in *Many Loves* (1961). *In the American Grain* (1925), criticism, is essential for anyone who wishes to begin to understand American literature and Williams: it is his most lucid definition of 'Americanness', and contains invaluable insights into American writers. The *Autobiography* (1951) is another essential book; one of its virtues is that Williams never tries to conceal himself. The poems are in *Collected Earlier Poems* (1951), *Collected Later Poems* (1960) and *Pictures from Brueghel* (1962). An earlier *Collected Poems* had appeared in 1938. *Selected Poems* (1963). *The William Carlos Williams Reader* (1966) is excellent. *Selected Essays* (1954); *Selected Letters* (1957).

Wilson, Angus (1913) English novelist, critic, playwright, and now part-time academic (at the University of East Anglia). He is a versatile writer, capable of employing both nineteenth- and twentieth-century techniques. His heroic attempt to revive the 'old-fashioned' nineteenth-century novel (*Anglo-Saxon Attitudes*, 1956) is an important and intelligent failure. *Hemlock and After* (1952), a novel, is a compassionate and moving study of a married man who has for too long repressed his homosexual tendencies–even though its technical seams show a little too obtrusively and it sometimes lapses into sentimentality. His early stories in *The Wrong Set* (1949) and *Such Darling Dodos* (1950) display a fine ear for the false and an unsnobbish one for the vulgar; they often expose the sad ridiculousness of the (then) 'underground' world of homosexuals. *Anglo-Saxon Attitudes* is an advance on *Hemlock and After;* it fails only in that its network of complex relationships is not entirely convincing in a twentieth-century context. The treatment of the central figure, a man who wants to be useful in society, is excellent, and is one of the best fictional accounts of the cost (in Freudian terms) of renunciation and of an intelligent man's difficult attempt at self-adjustment. In *The Middle Age of Mrs Eliot* (1958) Wilson succeeded in solving his technical problems: his scene is not over-cluttered, and the presentation of Mrs Eliot in psychological depth is a triumph (though Walter Allen, q.v., finds her only a 'literary conception'). Since then Wilson has produced a series of more obviously experimental novels, including the political satire *The Old Men at the Zoo* (1961) and the excellent *Late Call* (1964). He is a continuously interesting writer, who has advanced his powers of psychological penetration and tempered his (not disagreeable) tendency to confuse compassion with sentimentality. He is no longer taken as critically seriously as he should be. His criticism (e.g. *Émile Zola,* q.v., 1952) is sensible, lucid, stimulating, good-humored and eclectic. His writing is in itself better than critics have allowed. The play *The Mulberry Bush* (1956), despite a degree of technical maladroitness, is successful. *A Bit Off the Map* (1957) collects mature stories; the best of the later novels, often extremely funny as well as full of acute social observation (it deals with the between-wars period) is *No Laughing Matter* (1967).

Wilson, Edmund (1895–1972) American critic, journalist, editor, man-of-letters, fiction writer, poet, playwright, historian, miscellaneous writer, polymath. He knew most of the prominent members of his literary generation, especially Fitzgerald (q.v.) and Edna St Vincent Millay. Wilson's creative work (e.g. the novel *I Thought of Daisy,* 1929, the short stories of *Memoirs of Hecate County,* 1946 rev. 1969, the verse and prose collected in *Notebooks of Night,* 1942, and the plays in *Five Plays,* 1954) is slight but distinguished enough to give his criticism the edge that almost all academic criticism lacks: an understanding of the act of creation. As a critic he was, essentially, a Freudian (q.v.) pragmatist: fairly weak on larger cultural issues but strong on psychology (though his essay on Ben Jonson's 'anal sadism' is a masterpiece of Freudian misapplication). He was almost oblivious to poetic quality but penetrative and stimulating on fiction. The charge that he 'tacitly accepted the principle of the separability of form and content' has weight. On the other hand, he was the best reviewer of his generation (reviews are included in *Classics and Commercials,* 1950, and *The Shores of Light,* 1952): informative, quirky, provocative, witty. He was always prepared to go out on a limb, and if this sometimes led him into wrong judgements (e.g. Dreiser, q.v.), it also enabled him to point to the real nature of generally ignored achievements (that of, e.g., John Peale Bishop). He remained a consistently non-communist radical critic of the capitalist system; his personal note is always an independent one. *Axel's Castle* (1931), a study of (mostly French) Symbolism, has been overrated, but did help to explain the difficulties of Joyce (q.v.) and Valéry (q.v.). *The Scrolls from the Dead Sea* (1955), for which he learned Hebrew, is a contentious but certainly illuminating guide to a complex subject. *Apologies to the Iroquois* (1960) is an important and informative study. There are many other books, always readable and revealing (e.g. *To the Finland Station,* 1940, on the origins of the Bolshevist Revolution). Wilson's limitation is, to state it briefly, that he is a positivist, and insensitive to the facts of non-positivist experience; but he is eminently sane, and the word most appropriate to him is 'permanently useful'—no mean achievement.

Wilson, Ethel (1890) Canadian novelist—born in South Africa—who did not publish her first novel until she was fifty-seven. She is acute, intelligent and does not mind making technical innovations if her intentions demand them. She usually writes of love, or rather of what people think they mean by it. *Hetty Dorval* (1947) studies female promiscuity; *Mrs Golightly* (1961) collects brilliant short stories. Ethel Wilson is a subtle and humorous writer of very high calibre whose work should have an international reputation; she exposes Murdoch (q.v.), Spark (q.v.), Sagan (q.v.) and other such widely known woman novelists as merely trivial exponents.

Wimsatt, W. K. (1907) American critic, scholar. Wimsatt has written on Johnson and Shakespeare, but is best known for the hyper-philosophical 'theory of poetry' embodied in the essays collected in *The Verbal Icon* (1954). With Cleanth Brooks (q.v.) he wrote *Literary Criticism: A Short History* (1957), a useful though unnecessarily dense work. Wimsatt's style is often pompous, but his overconfidently stated position is clear. He is first and foremost and by deliberate intention, a super-academic 'moulder of taste'. He is a literary behaviourist, concerned with the 'public art of evaluating poems'. He (and Monroe K. Beardsley) have in their two famous 'affective' and 'intentional' 'fallacy' essays (in *The Verbal Icon*) striven to free criticism, first, from considerations of the effect that a poem may have on the reader, and, secondly, from the author's intention. Wimsatt himself has gone on to try to build up an ambitious *schema* in which a literary criticism might have an important function within a moral (Christian) system. He has, with great ingenuity, slashed out the poet himself, psychology, and feeling. . . . What is left is the 'verbal icon': 'an interpretation of reality in its metaphoric and symbolic dimensions'. Wimsatt is never silly (though his exegeses of actual poems are feeble, since they dissociate the textual material from experience, which is life-stuff), but his system depends on a series of totalitarian instructions to ignore certain realities. He eschews all depth-psychology and desires to turn criticism into science (thus, though he would not admit it, destroying poetry by destroying the mysteries from which it arises). Wimsatt would not be caught being excited by poetry—not even in order to recollect his excitement in tranquillity. But Wimsatt does raise vital questions, since he is in effect an enemy of romanticism, of what he calls the 'psychologistic', of, indeed, poetry itself as it is thought of by poets (most of whom know very well that they produce 'neutral' texts and that their conscious intentions are mere strategies). *Hateful Contraries* (1965) contains further essays.

Winters, Yvor (1900–68) American critic, versifier. Winters, who was married to the novelist Janet Lewis, and who bred dogs, taught for most of his life at Stanford University. He has been quite influential (on Gunn, q.v., Cunningham, Bowers, and other American poets), and has gained more respect than he deserves. He is the most rigidly anti-romantic critic of the age and has a most unfortunate, often enraged, style; he lacks humour or flexibility, and almost all his criticism is vitiated by over-didacticism and extremism. His preferences (e.g. Very over Emerson, Bridges over Hopkins, Edith Wharton over James) are exceedingly odd. But, as a classical extremist, some of his best essays have value: his strictures on Hopkins (q.v.) and Yeats (q.v.) have point and require answering. Winters is at his best when he is good tempered, which he often is not; then he challenges fashionable views (of Yeats, Hopkins, Crane, q.v. and many others) with some cogency. He is anti-expressionist (*see* Stadler) and his chief faults lie in his failure to understand that poets have always had little choice but to experiment in the face of a changing environment and in his stubborn refusal to try to understand modernism. His own earliest poems (*Collected Poems,* 1963) were ineptly modernistic and trite. He turned to a false classicism, to which his own (really disastrously bad, stilted) poetry is the true key: this work is metrical without being in any sense rhythmical; its themes are, quite literally, most frequently lucubratedly 'public' —'moral' in the purely bourgeois sense. But *In Defence of Reason* (1947)—collecting the contents of three books—and *Uncollected Essays* (1973) should be read. From his detailed criticism (of, e.g. Poe, Emily Dickinson, Williams, Crane) we can select immediately useful and stimulating criticism. The trick of reading him is usually to ignore his framework and discover his actual thought. He is, inevitably, a minor critic, but not one to ignore: he can be a useful antidote to expressionistic excess and he can accidentally stumble on serious faults in modernist poetry. *The Function of Criticism* (1957); *Yvor Winters on Modern Poets* (1959).

Wodehouse, P. G. (1881–1975) English humorous novelist, playwright. Wodehouse began as a writer of traditional school stories, but then, soon after the turn of the century, moved to the type of fiction that made his name a household word. His most famous works concern the idle Bertie Wooster and his man, Jeeves (e.g. *My Man Jeeves*, 1919, *The Code of the Woosters*, 1938). There were also other characters such as the people at Blandings Castle, Mr Mulliner, Psmith. His world, upper-class and essentially Edwardian (even though he later moved it into the post-First-World-War period), is wholly escapist: nothing serious ever happens in it. He is highly professional, and can spin a trivial plot out of nothing. He was very industrious; his work, which repeated itself continuously, fell off soon after the Second World War. He is an excellent entertainer and has given relaxation and laughter to millions. But he is not a serious writer and the critics who try to pretend that he is are as silly as he deliberately made his silliest character, the drone Bertie Wooster. He wrote over a hundred books. *Autograph Edition* (1956–). *The World of Jeeves* (1957).

Wolfe, Thomas (1900–38) American novelist from North Carolina. Wolfe began his career abortively, as a playwright. In 1925 he began an affair (finally broken off in 1930) with a woman seventeen years his senior, Mrs Aline Bernstein. She was, for him, a maternal figure as well as a lover, and it is likely that he owed her a large debt in the composition of *Look Homeward, Angel* (1929), his first and best novel. She is the 'Esther Jack' of the two last, posthumous novels. In his first novel (his plays are negligible) Wolfe wrote a sprawling, rhapsodic, sometimes powerful and vivid account of his own early years in 'Altamont', the Asheville of his birth. This is certainly autobiography-as-fiction–the citizens of Asheville did not forgive him until he was famous, so we know that he captured much of their true selves–but, despite the faults of rhetoric and the complete lack of organizational capacity, Wolfe's possession of genius is perfectly evident. What did he do with his genius? The answer is that it was largely wasted, as most of his critics agree—but that it was, however, rather less wasted than the general (academic) view allows. Wolfe appears in his first two novels as Eugene Gant; in the second, posthumous two, as George Webber. Since his primary drive was as compulsive, egoistic, egotistic autobiographer it may seem paradoxical that his greatest failure is in his presentation of himself. But it is not paradoxical: obsessed with *justifying* himself, he continuously got himself off-target. Maxwell Perkins of Scribner's had published the first book; he not only published the second, *Of Time and the River* (1935), in which Gant's career is followed through university (escape from family), Europe and New York, but he shaped its final form, drastically cutting it down. There has been much debate about the effectiveness of Perkins' editing and of his influence, but the responsibility must in any case lie with Wolfe, who allowed it to be done. A fiercely and angrily independent man, he was never able effectually to separate himself from his estranged parents—from his self-assertive father, a stonecutter, and his mother, who lived apart from him and ran a boarding-house in the same town. Mrs Bernstein provided the intellect that his mother lacked; onto the unfortunate Perkins he projected the paternal authoritarianism which, of course, he could never accept. Wolfe finally felt that he had to leave Perkins and for his last two novels he went to Harper, where his editor was Edward C. Aswell. Of the Webber books, *The Web and the Rock* (1939) is probably much as he intended; *You Can't Go Home Again* (1940) was cobbled together by Aswell from the enormous mass of material Wolfe left behind him. In 1938 he had contracted pneumonia and this led to a tubercular infection of the brain from which, after surgery, he died. The best of Wolfe is to be found in *From Death to Morning* (1935), stories; this includes 'The Web of Earth', in which he made intelligent use of Joycean (q.v.) techniques. Wolfe was over-ambitious in his intentions: he wanted to present the 'whole of experience'. Yet it is wrong to assert that he had no capacity for structure: *From Death to Morning* disproves this. He could be intolerably verbose and feebly rhetorical but he could also be powerful, and he could render portraits of people and of their environments of immense vividness and conviction. 'Genius is not enough,' declared a hostile critic. There is much in this remark as applied to Wolfe, for his project—to render experience directly in art—was naive. But we do still read him and we respond to much that is vital in his work. *The Face of a Nation: Poetical* [sic] *Passages from Wolfe* (1939). *Letters* (1956). *The Portable Thomas Wolfe* (1946).

Wolfe, Tom (1931) American reporter, journalist, pop-critic. Wolfe has cleverness and acuity but lacks judgement; his style meretriciously mixes the patter of a hopped-up, nagging disc-jockey with sharp reportage; he is essentially superficial, but none the less informative. *The Kandy-Colored Tangerine-Flake Streamline Baby* (1965); *The Electric Kool-Aid Acid Test* (1968) is on Kesey (q.v.) and the Mad Pranksters.

Wolkers, Jan (1925) Dutch novelist, dramatist, sculptor. For a while it seemed as if Wolkers might throw off his sensationalism and turn into a major writer but he has chosen the path of self-indulgence in sick neo-decadence. He is not nearly as serious or substantial as Boon (q.v.). Three of his novels appear in English: *Een roos van vlees* (1964; tr. *The Rose of Flesh,* 1967), *Horrible Tango* (1964; tr. 1970) and *Turks fruit* (1969; tr. *Turkish Delight,* 1974). This last was compared by the English publisher to Eric Segal's disgusting *Love Story*—and with unwitting appropriateness. Previously Wolkers had shown some originality in his black humour, but he has now decided, it seems, to offer no more than a best-selling, sentimental, modish unpleasantness.

Woolf, Virginia (1882–1941) English novelist, critic, miscellaneous writer. She was the daughter of the Victorian critic Leslie Stephen, and the sister of Vanessa Bell (wife of Clive Bell). She was at the centre of the 'Bloomsbury Group' (*see* Forster) and her friends included Forster, Roger Fry—an art critic and translator—Lytton Strachey (q.v.) and Leonard Woolf, whom she married in 1912. He has written of her in his long series of biographies. She suffered, rather severely, from a form of manic-depressive illness and it was he above all who helped her overcome this—until, depressed by war and a sense of creative failure, and, above all, terrified of a recurrence of her illness, she drowned herself in the Ouse near her home at Rodwell (outside Lewes in Sussex). She and her husband founded the important Hogarth Press, which published, among others, Eliot (q.v.), Freud (q.v.) and Virginia's novels. She was unquestionably a master of technical method (her most notable failure is her most extreme book, *The Waves,* 1931), and a true novelist. She is also important in the history of the development of the English novel which (almost but not quite) stopped with her. But she should not be overrated: she does lack robustness. Her first two novels, *The Voyage Out* (1915) and *Night and Day* (1919), are competent, traditional books, intelligent and clearly though in no way obtrusively influenced by Henry James (q.v.). They are distinguished for their insight into female psychology; the men in them, as in almost all Virginia Woolf's fiction, are rather shadowy. But at this time she was finding the fiction of such as Wells (q.v.) and Bennett (q.v.) unsatisfactory; later she would attack them somewhat unfairly, failing to discern that their methods had virtues and that she was confusing what she still considered to be her own shortcomings with theirs—and that she envied (as is understandable) their access to substantial experience. Still, she was not unfair when she wrote (1924) that Edwardian novelists 'established conventions which do their business; and that business is not our business'. After producing a series of impressionistic sketches—they suffer from the tendency to lapse into the 'poetical' and the 'purple passage', as does all Virginia Woolf's fiction—collected in *Monday or Tuesday* (1921), she wrote the novel *Jacob's Room* (1922). It was here that she began to experiment with stream-of-consciousness (*see* Bergson) —and she did this because, as a novelist, her desire was to record life in its *minutiae*: 'Let us record the atoms as they fall upon the mind. . . .' She was more successful, in *Mrs Dalloway* (1925) and *To The Lighthouse* (1927), than Dorothy Richardson: she does not simply extend realism, but records images. The most familiar complaint against her is that she neglected Bergson's 'spatial' reality (which he acknowledged as inevitable) for her phenomenological investigations. This hardly applies in the case of these two novels, since they both deal, explicitly, with characters 'trapped' in reverie. She could not have treated the material of *The Voyage Out* in this manner, and that is one of her limitations. She had humour (when in exalted states she would often indulge in elaborate practical jokes), and she was no prude; but she manipulated life to suit her technique (as Joyce, q.v., who influenced her, had not); she tried desperately to be sympathetic to the poor or vulgar, to drop her snobbery—but, as Forster pointed out in his long obituary essay (1942), she could not do it. One must, however, point out that she showed what sensitivity she could—and it was great—to the inevitability of the collapse of the nineteenth-century fictional technique. There is some very fine writing in these two novels, her best, but there is also more precious and weak writing than it is usual to acknowledge. Virginia Woolf, for all her courage, sometimes hid her lack of substance behind a false aestheticism. *The Waves* is an attempt to write poetry in prose, and is boring: it is very ambitious to try to 'give the moment whole', and it is not surprising that the book fails. *Orlando* (1928) explores, in an often over-whimsical fantasy influenced by Freud, her own ambisexuality; but it turns into rationalization, in so far as it is tolerable. *The Years* (1937) is an attempt—one sees how conscious of her limitations Virginia Woolf was—to treat 'solid' material in her peculiar expressionistic way, but it does not cohere. Many good critics see the posthumous *Between the Acts* (1941) as Virginia Woolf's masterpiece (many are satisfied, too, by *The Waves*), and it must be conceded that it is her most honest book (not that she was ever dishonest; but at this very high level there are degrees of honesty): she treats a 'robust' situation from the aesthetic point of view that she could never abandon. But it seems to me to be a curiously old-fashioned book: it has a too obvious 'message', and that message is that art can unify life. Something like that might be true; but *Between the Acts,* a very self-conscious mixture of symbolism and unsuccessful poesy, oversimplifies it to a point that makes it positively *fin de siècle* in nature. Virginia Woolf was undoubtedly (as Forster, again, remarked) an utterly dedicated writer and, though one cannot allow one's judgement of her texts to be influenced by this, she was forced into using writing as therapy. In the light of this, at least, her achievement is a remarkable one. I think, however (one must be tentative about this), that her importance as an innovator will diminish. *Collected Works* (1929–55) is a uniform edition. *Collected Essays* (1966–7).

Wright, James (1927) American poet, born in Ohio. Much of his poetry reflects his urban-midwestern upbringing. He is one of the best American poets of his generation; significantly, he has learned a good deal from foreign poetry and has moved from the fairly formal type of poety of *The Green Wall* (1957) to a potent expressionism. His forms are now free but carefully controlled: this is not 'free verse'. He understands the qualities of good poets who have been somewhat neglected by critics (e.g. Robinson, q.v., Hardy, q.v.), and his early poems reflect their influence. He is not a 'political' poet inasmuch as he is not partisan; but he has written some of the sharpest satire of the age, as in the justly praised poem about Eisenhower's meeting with Franco. More recently, Wright has come under the influence of Trakl and of Chinese poetry. This has led him into some irritatingly 'miniaturist' poetry but also to some remarkable lyrical successes: '. . . Suddenly I realize/ That if I stepped out of my body I would break/ Into blossom.' It is not easy for a man of humour to bring off a passionate and lyrical poem ('The Blessing') of this kind. But this, in its context, is not unintentionally comic; it is beautiful. *Collected Poems* (1971).

Wright, Judith (1915) Doyenne of Australia's woman poets, but less acute and distinctive than Rosemary Dobson (q.v.) or Gwen Harwood (q.v.). She is, however, a serious poet and an excellent historical novelist (of her own ancestors: *Generations of Men*, 1959), short-story writer, and a useful critic. The comparison with Dobson and Harwood has been made only to correct a popular misconception. She succeeds when she writes of the Australian landscape and its flora and fauna, but fails at what she is most famous for: the expression of the feminine viewpoint. Here she is too self-conscious and, in the Flaubertian rather than the Marxist sense of the word, bourgeois; for all the intelligence and sincerity of effort, something cloys and clogs. But she has been a good influence in Australian poetry and her criticism is often perceptive and finely angled. *Five Senses* (1963); *The Other Half* (1966).

Wright, Richard (1908–60) American novelist, short-story writer, critic. A poor Negro from Mississippi, Wright had a traumatic childhood —his father deserted his mother when he was five and a few years afterwards his mother became incapacitated by a series of strokes. Like Baldwin (q.v.), Wright was badly treated by his relatives, got no proper schooling, and was early exposed to fanatical religion (Seventh Day Adventism); this turned him into a fierce if pessimistic humanist. He is America's Negro naturalist (*see* Zola); but he is also an existentialist and in his later years in Paris he came to know Sartre (q.v.) and others well. His best works are *Black Boy* (1945), the scarifying tale of his childhood, and the short story 'The Man Who Lived Underground' (1942 rev. 1944; in *Eight Men*, 1961); *Native Son* (1940), which made him famous, has been overrated, but it is in its earlier parts excellent. The case of Wright is a complicated one. Always independent and rebellious, he violently rejected his own people's acceptance of their role. He wrongly judged Negro culture to be debilitated. He feared the human void into which Mississippi whites cast the Negroes, and which the latter seemed to accept. There was a good deal of self-hate in him, and later Negro critics were to attack him for his misjudgements of the value and potentiality of his own people. *Black Boy*, however, shows pure genius: it is never spoiled by didacticism, and its language reflects its story. Already here Wright is existentialist in the sense that he is describing a condition of nausea and a search for an identity. After a first book of stories (1938) Wright produced *Native Son*, a long novel about Bigger Thomas, a Chicago Negro youth who murders a young white woman and is electrocuted for it. This owes much to Dreiser's (q.v.) *American Tragedy*, something to Dostoievski; it is spoiled by its communist thesis, which distorts Wright's own imaginative processes. Wright had come to Chicago in 1927. He did many menial jobs, and relentlessly educated himself, especially in sociology. In 1932 he joined the communist party, from which he was expelled in 1944. He described his disillusion in the symposium *The God that Failed* (1950). *Native Son*, partly based on a 1938 case (of a Negro called, oddly enough, Nixon), is a mixture of very fine descriptive and psychological writing, and ideology. Wright, who draws especial attention in *Black Boy* to the small crimes he himself committed in order to run away from home at seventeen, felt closely identified with Bigger Thomas (whom he played in a disastrous film of *Native Son* made in Argentina in 1951)–but Bigger also represented to him just what he had managed to avoid: illiteracy, cruelty, murder. The successful parts of the novel deal with Bigger himself, a personality largely stunted by his environment but also with deficiencies of character. The shorter 'The Man Who Lived Underground', which makes some use of surrealistic techniques, is more successful, and is Wright's masterpiece. It anticipates Ellison's (q.v.) *Invisible Man*, and is not less effective as an account of a man alienated from himself and from society. Wright's later books, written when he was living in Paris (1946–60), are vastly inferior. He had become a celebrity and, increasingly separated from his imagination, was above all concerned to justify his position *vis-à-vis* the Negro problem. *The Outsider* (1953) tries to explore his own predicament, but is didactic and too obviously written under the influence of the existentialist movement. Its language is wholly inappropriate. He travelled and wrote a number of socio-political travel books, the best of which is *Pagan Spain* (1957). He died of a heart attack. *12 Million Black Voices* (1941) is a 'folk history of the Negro in the United States' illustrated with photographs.

Yeats, W. B. (1865–1939) Irish poet, playwright, occultist, autobiographer and critic. Nobel Prize 1923. Yeats is generally regarded as being the greatest English-language poet of the century; this is by no means a foolish assessment, but critical work on him has usually been over-deferential which has not helped in the elucidation of his poetry. His father was a lawyer, his brother a painter; as an Irish senator (1922–8) he represented Protestant landed interests without political distinction, though he was not illiberal on non-political issues. His early work is influenced by the Pre-Raphaelites (most of whom he knew in his years in London: he founded the Rhymers' Club with Lionel Johnson and Ernest Dowson), Irish folksong and theosophy. In it one may already discern a true poet's ear for natural melody (e.g. 'Down by the Sally Gardens'). His is a very complex case indeed: an acute and shrewd intelligence co-exists with a credulous naivety; pretentiousness is matched by genuine passion, self-indulgent rhetoric by lucidity; the 'system of thought' from which his work cannot be divorced, and on which it was self-supposedly based, is vulgar gobbledegook hardly worthy of a suburban spiritualist; he cared desperately about humanity and yet he was almost as cruelly insensitive and simple-minded as Eliot (q.v.) about contemporary injustices—he could seriously advance an intellectually absurd crypto-fascist, neo-feudalist program *and* write 'The Second Coming', which is hardly an unintellectual poem. . . . The earlier poetry is ornamental, sometimes decadent, self-consciously symbolist. An important influence was Blake, an edition of whose works he published (with E. J. Ellis) in 1893; the introduction to, and notes in, his own selection of Blake's poetry (1893; 1905; 1969) is a helpful guide to his theoretical attitudes in this period. The earlier poetry is also influenced by his unrequited love for the revolutionary actress Maud Gonne; it would otherwise have been less concerned with Irish nationalism, which was not really as important to him as the so-called Celtic Revival, of which he was a leader. Before the beginning of the century he had begun to take an active interest in the Irish theatre, and in 1899 he founded, with others, the Irish Literary Theatre which (1904) moved into the Abbey Theatre in Dublin. But (in this context at least) his importance as a playwright, which is considerable, must be considered separately from his development as a poet. Perhaps as a reaction to the hopelessness and the ultra-romanticism of his love for Maud Gonne–reinforced by his desperate struggle to employ the Abbey as a theatre for poetic rather than realist drama–Yeats sharpened his poetic style in the first decade of the century: *Responsibilities* (1914) displays the 'decadent' romantic criticizing himself by the use of a harder, more concrete diction. The poems about the tragedy of the Anglo-Irish conflict (in particular the famous 'Easter, 1916'), collected in *The Wild Swans at Coole* (1917 enlarged 1919), display him at his most intellectually lucid, independent, sharp. Interest in the occult has to some extent given way to social awareness–or so it seems. He has perfected his technique with immense intelligence and, dreamer, he has come to terms with the real world. For some, such poems as 'Easter, 1916' remain his best because they are the most balanced and poised between the reality of dream and the reality of the world. But the later poems have such power–whatever other virtues and/or defects they may possess–that they cannot be ignored. In 1917 Yeats married a younger woman and (clearly) manipulated her into a female-authority figure (this does not mean that their relationship did not have other aspects). His own policy at the Abbey had failed (the uproar over Synge's, q.v., *Playboy of the Western World*, 1907, had filled him with a wholly understandable bitterness); his romantic love-project had failed; he had been traumatized, as were all other intelligent Irishmen, by the ferocious events of 1916: though tempered, purged of lushness and excess, he needed to turn again to the dream. The post-war poetry is successful in direct proportion to Yeats's success in his own self-critical examination of his predicament, but this success is not easy to measure, for his self-appraisal was oblique. The guiding intelligence, partially external to the imaginative performance, of the 'middle period' had vanished; a rationalizing (to use Freudian terminology) faculty has taken its place. But Yeats also moved into an area of pure intuition, which led to greater richness. To what extent was his intuition corrupted by his (Freudian) rationalization? We can forget *A Vision* (1925 rev. 1937 corrected 1962), his 'system'. We can forget his obedience to his wife's 'Unknown Instructors'. We can even forget the influence upon him of Japanese No drama (originally introduced to him by Pound, q.v., in 1913). His mind was now a machine that transformed all data into what he required by way of 'confirmation'. But how dynamic was the poet? As he self-consciously transformed himself into a beautiful-looking old chaser after young women, even undergoing a phoney 'rejuvenation' operation, how did the man suffer because of his falsities? Any answer, let alone a short one, will be contentious. Yeats is not of the calibre of, say, Rilke (q.v.), Vallejo (q.v.), Machado (q.v.), Pessoa (q.v.): the 'hard' 'middle period' poetry cuts out too much that concerned him and the later is too theatrical, too contrived. The poems of *The Tower* (1928) and *The Winding Stair* (1929), considered by most to be his greatest, are on the whole less good than the last ones, published in *New Poems* (1938) and *Last Poems and Two Plays* (1939): here, almost past the ability to taste pleasure or its idea, he may well, as O'Brien has suggested, have begun, if only intuitively, to understand and refine the tragically prophetic implications of the 'aristocratic' view of poetry he had adopted during the period of the war —and have begun to transcend the immature components of the mask of lover-ruined-by-age that he had so dramatically donned. The 'Byzantium' poems, and others from the favoured period, are certainly majestic in their rhetoric, but there is some disturbingly simplistic element in them that robs them of anything like total conviction. As a playwright Yeats moved from lush poetry (but *The Countess Cathleen*, 1892, written for Maud Gonne, is the finest verse play of its decade) to, at his best, spare prose: *The Words Upon the Window Pane* (1934). Curiously, his achievement in this sphere has hardly had its due—perhaps because he wrote so many slight, over-poetical, programmatic plays for the Abbey during the time of his faith in its capacity to rid the Irish stage of realism. That poet whose later career is so often, and rightly associated with coldness, Wordsworth, once remarked that one had to love a poet to understand him. Perhaps one can never love and therefore never wholly understand Yeats; but he presents a formidable and fascinating puzzle. G. S. Fraser's study (1954 rev. 1962 rev. 1965 rev. 1968), which contains a useful bibliography, gives a more sympathetic and a very persuasive picture. *Collected Poems* (1949); *Variorum Edition of the Poems* (1957); *Collected Plays* (1952); *Variorum Edition of the Plays* (1966); *Letters* (1954) could now be supplemented.

Yevtushenko, Yevgeny *see* **Evtushenko, Evgeny.**

Young, Andrew (1885–1971) Scottish poet, playwright and writer on flowers and rural subjects. He was a minister of the United Free Church of Scotland but later (1938) became a Church of England clergyman. He was Vicar of Stonegate, a tiny village in Sussex (1941–59); he spent his last years in Chichester, of whose Cathedral he had been a Canon since 1948. He published his first small volume in 1910 and this was followed by nine others before the first *Collected Poems* of 1936; but Young attracted little attention until 1950, with the *Collected Poems* of that year (a revised selection). Even now he has had little critical attention, and none of this has risen above the level of the mediocre. But he has been much read and loved by good poets and since his death his work has attracted younger writers. He worked within traditional forms and was of the Georgian (*see* Brooke) generation; but there is nothing Georgian about his work, which is cunningly innocent and thewed. He was somehow canny enough to know his limitations and he never wrote outside them—a most rare accomplishment. He is a 'nature poet' but hardly one in the tradition of Clare (the most acutely observant of all nature poets): his observations, never sentimental, are always precise; but, though he did not fully know it, they are beautifully appropriate metaphors for states of existential (frequently erotic) disturbance. This is not to say that his real subject is not the natural (as distinct from the urban) world: he sees through this to his inner states and calms his Calvinistic conscience in so doing. His fear of being guilty is dealt with by a thoroughly honest transference of guilt to nature, the 'earth', upon which he 'trespasses': When ('The Fear') he turns to face 'the beast' that chases him he therefore sees only a wind-shaken bough or a bird raking leaves. The honesty lies in the conscientious vividness. His verse-play *Nicodemus* (1937) is surprisingly readable; the music for it is by Imogen Holst. His two final poems, experimental for him, collected under the title of *Out of the World and Back* (1958: this contains a revision of *Into Hades*, 1952, and *A Traveller in Time*), are lengthy meditations on his own death. They are very well done, but because they reflect certainties the poet in him never felt, they lack the compact power of the earlier work. His books on flowers (*A Prospect of Flowers*, 1945; *A Retrospect of Flowers*, 1950) are pleasant, learned and precise; *A Prospect of Britain* (1956) is topographical. *Collected Poems* (1960).

Z

Zamyatin, Yevgeny (1884–1937) Russian fiction writer, critic. He took part in the 1905 revolution and was exiled for a time. A naval engineer, he spent eighteen months in Glasgow and the north of England supervising the construction of Russian icebreakers (1916–17). He supported the Bolsheviks (though he left the party in 1917) and became the leading member of the 'fellow-travelling' Serapion Brothers, who advocated autonomy in art, though they did not challenge political Leninism. But his novel *My* (written in 1920, tr. *We*, 1924; 1970; in Russian, 1952, in New York; never published, though circulated amongst a few in typescript, in Russia) was translated in a Czech magazine in 1927, and this gave Stalin's henchmen the chance to move against him and his anti-socialist-realist ideas. It was only through Gorky (q.v.) that he and his wife were able to get to France (1931). Zamyatin has been described by the Nabokov (q.v.) -inspired Andrew Field as 'not really an artist'; however, Zamyatin is an immeasurably better artist and critic than Nabokov. The contents of *The Dragon* (1972), selected stories in English translation, make this abundantly and immediately clear. As a critic Zamyatin would be great without his context; within his context he is heroic. Furthermore, his mature fiction springs directly from his critical convictions. His earlier work, sharply satirical accounts of provincial life, was influenced by Gogol, Leskov and Remizov (q.v.), it includes *Uyezdnoye* (1911), *District Tales,* and *Na kulichkakh* (1914), *At the World's End. Ostrovityane* (1918), *The Islanders,* a shrewd satire on English life (although he affected English manners, and was known as 'the Englishman'), confirmed his reputation. Zamyatin is still the best critic of Wells (q.v.), who influenced the dystopia *We,* which not only prophesies Stalinism and the failure of the revolution to be revolutionary, but also exemplifies his theories about literature. Zamyatin, who began by attacking Bely (q.v.) and ended by accepting him as one of his mentors, called himself a neo-realist. But his neo-realism involves an expressionist distortion of what is usually taken to be reality. His art rejects entropy, seeking 'crucifixion', a 'tormentingly endless movement'. His 'impressionism' involved 'incomplete phrases, false denials and assertions, omitted associations, allusions and reminiscences': a 'joint creative effort' of author and reader in which 'every word must be supercharged'. Most of Zamyatin's best stories are in *The Dragon.* His plays, a few of which were performed, remain untranslated, as does his last unfinished novel about Atila, *Bich Bozhiy* (1938), *Scourge of God. A Soviet Heretic* (1970) collects his most important critical essays. *We* has exercised a world-wide influence; Zamyatin's fiction and his teaching (in the early twenties) were decisive for many Soviet writers.

Zola, Émile (1840–1902) French novelist. Zola is a nineteenth-century novelist, but is important as the early and chief representative of naturalism, a development and narrowing down of the earlier realism. It is important to realize that he did not actually believe in the claims he made for the naturalistic approach in *Le Roman experimental* (1880), *The Experimental Novel.* But the theoretical framework, never of course realized in any novel, is important. Briefly, naturalism set out to make fiction into a 'science': it would demonstrate that heredity and environment absolutely determined the life of individuals—and it would change society! Zola himself (whose actual works need not be discussed here), like most other naturalists, was not actually a positivist at all. No creative writer can be positivist—he can only be influenced by positivist doctrine. Zola was a romantic decadent (his novels are increasingly symbolic), devoted to truth and justice, who wanted to portray the 'lower depths' of society, to draw attention to the *effects* of heredity and environment, and—at a deeper level—to 'heal' the body-mind split so often and inaccurately called Cartesian. Naturalism owes much to scientific or pseudo-scientific concepts (*see* Dreiser), but the good naturalists are frustrated poets and their novels can easily be linked to the decadence that developed in the second half of the nineteenth century: they are gloomy and they, like their books, have a deterministic tone; but they relish the horrors of the sordid and the psychopathology of their characters. In their obsession with the urban, and with the neurotic or psychotic, they foreshadow expressionism (*see* Stadler); impressionism, a more ostensibly romantic blurring of realism, does so less thoroughly. The full-blown naturalist novels of Zola are proto-expressionistic in that they reflect at least an internal desperation—and they deliberately distort at least the bourgeois view of reality. Accounts of naturalism often over-emphasize the pessimistic, deterministic aspect of it: this is more or less programmatic (Beckett, q.v., on this view, is more 'naturalistic' than Zola; accounts confuse conscious authorial intention with the nature of the texts). There are many 'choices' taken in the course of Zola's massive fiction and these choices are by no means all 'inevitable'. Literary journalists, particularly those who hurriedly describe their impressions of theatrical performances, confuse naturalism with realism. This is a misleading error. Certainly, then, there was a naturalist program, and this was influential; but what came out of it contradicted it.

Zoshchenko, Mikhail (1895–1958) Russian fiction writer, dramatist, autobiographer: the greatest humorist of the Soviet period. A 'Serapion Brother' (*see* Zamyatin), he had fought for the Bolsheviks but recognized very early that their rule would not work. Like many humorists, he was an exceedingly depressed man—the perpetual attacks on him, culminating in his expulsion from the Union of Soviet Writers in 1946, depressed him still further. The form he usually chooses is the *skaz* (*see* Remizov) sketch or *feuilleton;* the narrator is often an idiot caught up in ideological cliché and ignorance. Zoshchenko's attitude is ambivalent: he is sorry for his victims, yet he also despises them. But in the thirties he was forced to take a more ostensibly serious approach, and even to write wretched tales of Lenin for children. *Vozvrashchonnaya molodost* (1933), *Youth Restored,* is a hilarious novel satirizing the very essence of Marxist-Leninism (that human nature will be changed by a new socio-economic structure). His most fascinating book is the autobiographical *Pered voskhodom solutsa* (1943), *Before the Sunrise,* which was suppressed after two instalments had appeared. This, a part of which was published in English in *Partisan Review* (3 and 4, 1961) is a truly serious confessional piece, in which Zoshchenko examines his depressive hypochondria and neuroticism by resorting to Freudian (q.v.) concepts—hated in Soviet Russia. His later work is poor. There are a number of collections in English: *Russia Laughs* (1935), *The Woman Who Could Not Read* (1940), *The Wonderful Dog* (1942), *Scenes from the Bathhouse* (1961).

Zuckmayer, Carl (1896) German dramatist, poet, novelist, prose writer. He fought in the First World War, was associated with Brecht (q.v.), and eventually went into exile. After a false (expressionist) start, he wrote a sparkling rustic comedy, *Der Fröliche Weinberg* (1925), and then the anti-militaristic, Hašekian, Hauptmannesque *Der Hauptmann von Köpenik* (1931; tr. *The Captain of Köpenik*, 1932). His most famous play, about an inactive anti-Nazi quartermaster-general in the Luftwaffe and his actively anti-Nazi chief engineer, is *Des Teufels General* (1946); this is an entirely successful 'well-made play'. He had written the masterly script of the Dietrich-Jannings movie, *Der blaue Engel* (*Blue Angel*), based on H. Mann's (q.v.) *Professor Unrat*. The later plays are more contrived and conservative and are less successful. His fiction and poetry are neglected: the best novels are *Salvàre* (1936; tr. *The Moons Ride Over*, 1937) and *Die Fastnachtsbeichte* (1959; tr. *Carnival Confession*, 1961); the finely direct, lyrical minor poetry, very seriously underrated, is collected in *Gedichte* (1960). *A Part of Myself* (1970) is an undeclaredly abridged version of the superb autobiography *Als wär's ein Stück von mir* (1966). Much of his production is in *Gesammelte Werke* (1947–60).

Zukofsky, Louis (1904) American poet, critic, fiction writer. Zukofsky, the leading theorist of the objectivists (*see* Williams) and lifelong friend of Pound (q.v.), is this century's most indefatigable experimenter. He is a Manhattan Jew whose domestic life is at the centre of his poetry, much of which is based on ideas about meaning being a necessarily significant development from an approach based, Stein (q.v.) -like, on sound. He is a hero of Black Mountain poets such as Creeley (q.v.) because of his emphasis on sound, his rejection of metaphor, and his war against the literary. His son Paul is a distinguished violinist. Zukofsky himself is as near to being a musician as it is possible for a poet to be: his words are, in fact, often too like musical notes. He will not acknowledge that some poems are 'better' than others, and relentlessly and courageously presents his work as one whole: *All: The Collected Short Poems 1923–1958* (1965), *All: The Collected Short Poems 1956–1964* (1966), the as yet unfinished autobiographical poem *A* (1–12, 1959; 13–21, 1969), and prose works such as the collected essays of *Prepositions* (1967), the impenetrable Shakespearean criticism of *Bottom: on Shakespeare* (1963) and the translations from *Catullus* (with his wife Celia Zukofsky, 1969). Some of his experimental poems are admired because of the theories from which they spring; but others, and parts of *A*—which is a kind of domestic *Cantos*, much influenced by Pound—have a lucid sweetness and a true melody. The effect of the whole is impressive, even though it is poetically diffuse. The tribute to a happy marriage in a bad age is Zukofsky's purest and most enduring achievement. *Ferdinand/It Was* (1968) is fiction.

INDEX